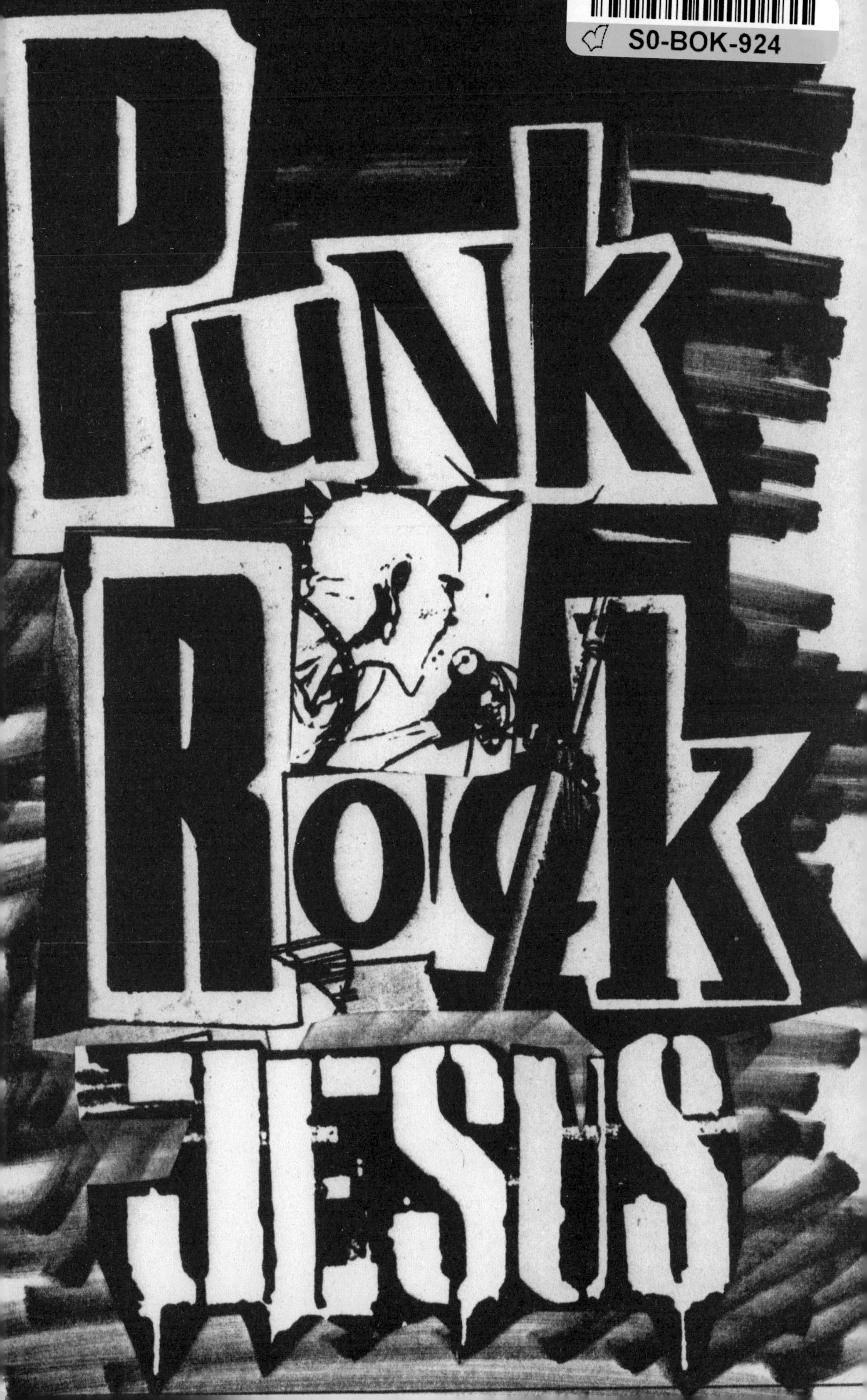
Punk
Rock
Jesus

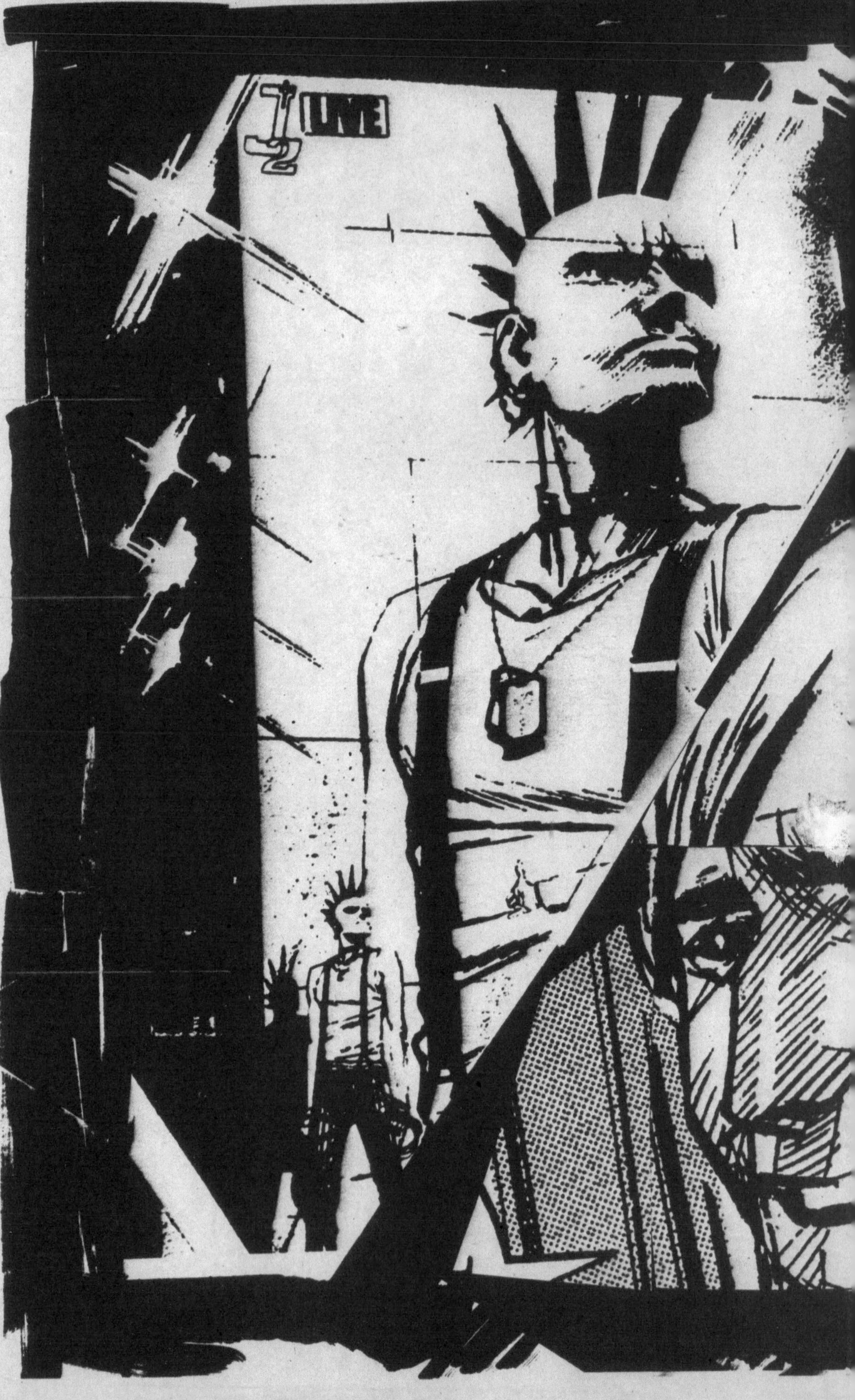
LIVE

THANK YOU
THANKS A
EVERYO[...]

PUNK ROCK

Sean Murphy
Story and art

Todd Klein | letterer

Punk Rock Jesus created by | Sean Murphy

Special thanks to Rob Paolucci for layout assists on chapter six

JESUS

Karen Berger Senior VP – Executive Editor, VERTIGO and Editor – Original Series
Joe Hughes, Gregory Lockard Assistant Editors – Original Series
Peter Hamboussi Editor
Robbin Brosterman Design Director – Books
Louis Prandi Publication Design

Bob Harras VP – Editor-in-Chief

Diane Nelson President
Dan DiDio and Jim Lee Co-Publishers
Geoff Johns Chief Creative Officer
John Rood Executive VP – Sales, Marketing and Business Development
Amy Genkins Senior VP – Business and Legal Affairs
Nairi Gardiner Senior VP – Finance
Jeff Boison VP – Publishing Operations
Mark Chiarello VP – Art Direction and Design
John Cunningham VP – Marketing
Terri Cunningham VP – Talent Relations and Services
Alison Gill Senior VP – Manufacturing and Operations
Hank Kanalz Senior VP – Digital
Jay Kogan VP – Business and Legal Affairs, Publishing
Jack Mahan VP – Business Affairs, Talent
Nick Napolitano VP – Manufacturing Administration
Sue Pohja VP – Book Sales
Courtney Simmons Senior VP – Publicity
Bob Wayne Senior VP – Sales

DC Comics, 1700 Broadway, New York, NY 10019
A Warner Bros. Entertainment Company.
Printed in the USA. First Printing.
ISBN: 978-1-4012-3768-4

Library of Congress Cataloging-in-Publication Data

Murphy, Sean Gordon, 1980-
  Punk Rock Jesus / Sean Murphy.
    pages cm
  "Originally published in single magazine form in Punk Rock Jesus 1-6."
  ISBN 978-1-4012-3768-4
  1. Graphic novels. I. Title.
  PN6727.M783P86 2013
  741.5'973--dc23
                          2012048651

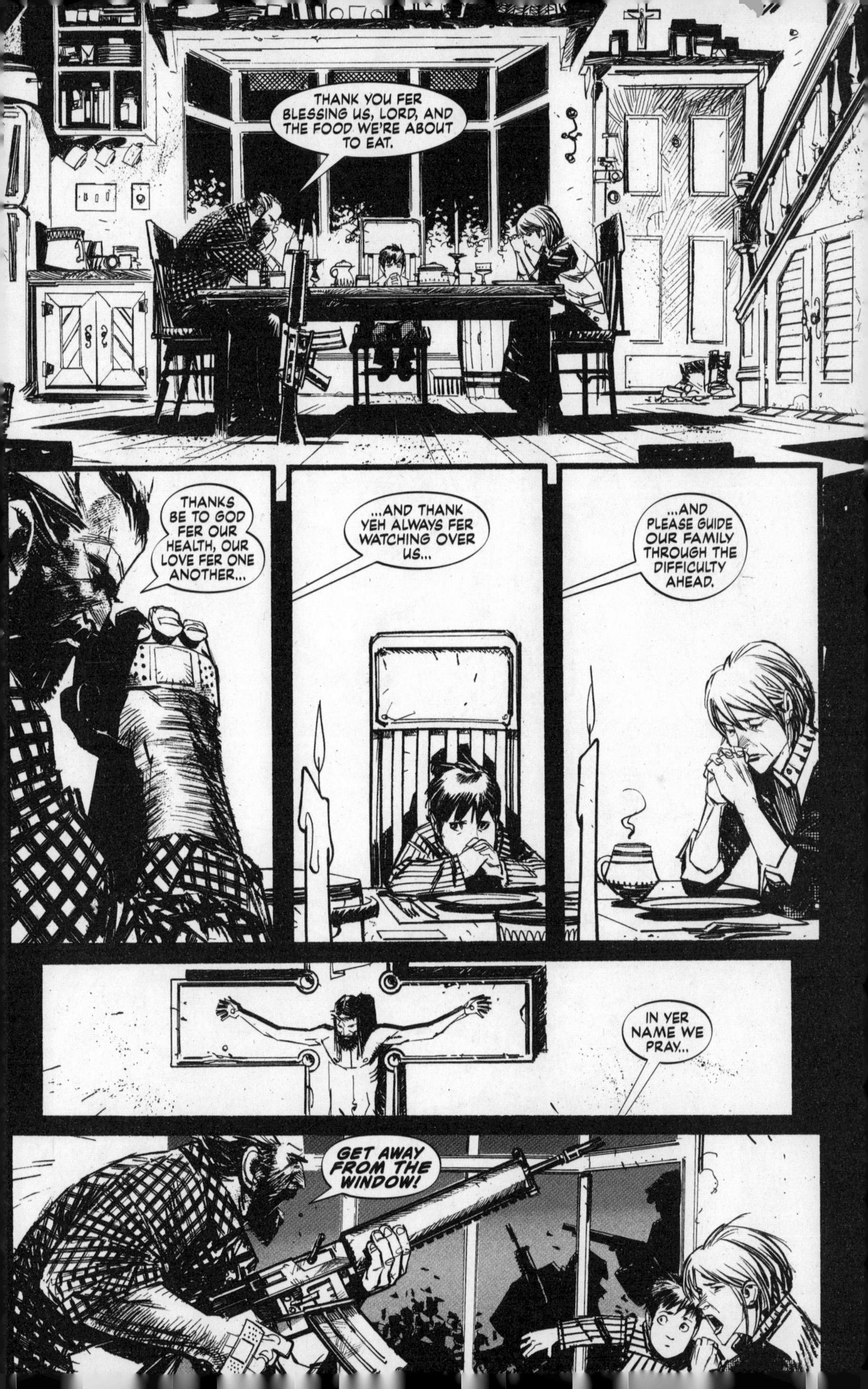
THANK YOU FER BLESSING US, LORD, AND THE FOOD WE'RE ABOUT TO EAT.
THANKS BE TO GOD FER OUR HEALTH, OUR LOVE FER ONE ANOTHER...
...AND THANK YEH ALWAYS FER WATCHING OVER US...
...AND PLEASE GUIDE OUR FAMILY THROUGH THE DIFFICULTY AHEAD.
IN YER NAME WE PRAY...
GET AWAY FROM THE WINDOW!

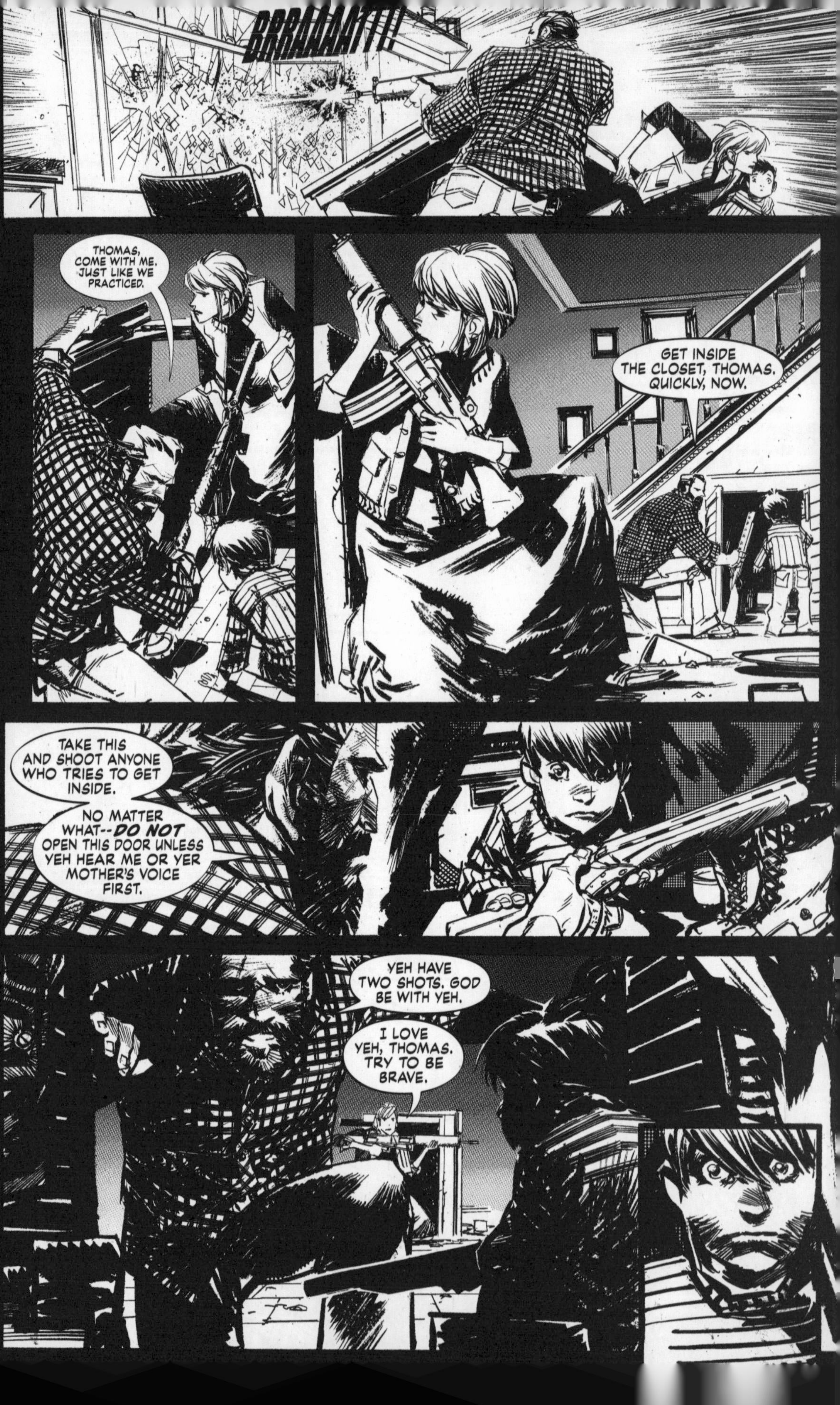
BRRAAAAPTT!!
THOMAS, COME WITH ME. JUST LIKE WE PRACTICED.
GET INSIDE THE CLOSET, THOMAS. QUICKLY, NOW.
TAKE THIS AND SHOOT ANYONE WHO TRIES TO GET INSIDE.
NO MATTER WHAT--DO NOT OPEN THIS DOOR UNLESS YEH HEAR ME OR YER MOTHER'S VOICE FIRST.
YEH HAVE TWO SHOTS. GOD BE WITH YEH.
I LOVE YEH, THOMAS. TRY TO BE BRAVE.

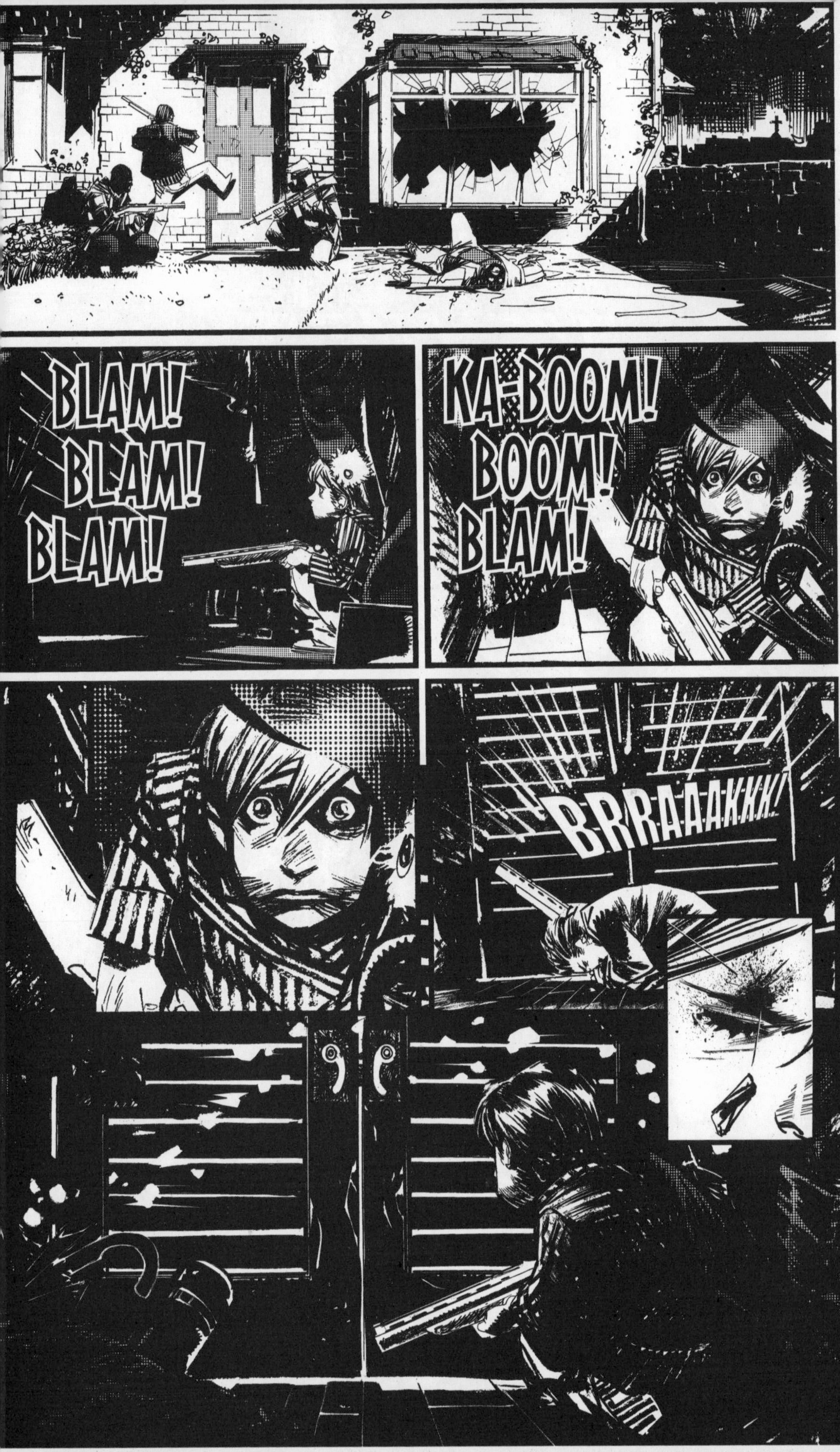

BLAM! BLAM! BLAM!
KA-BOOM! BOOM! BLAM!
BRRAAAKKK!

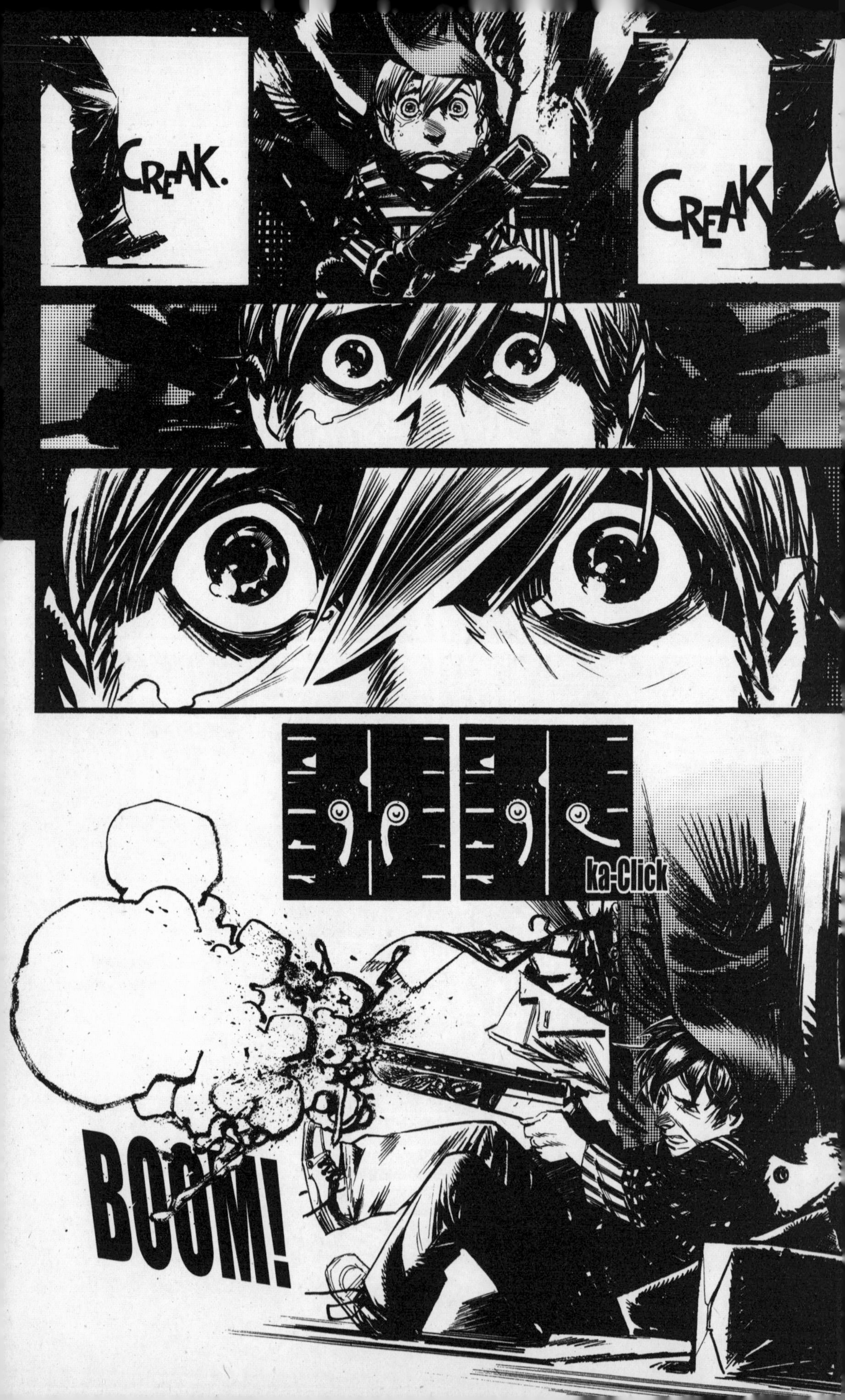
CREAK.
CREAK
ka-Click
BOOM!

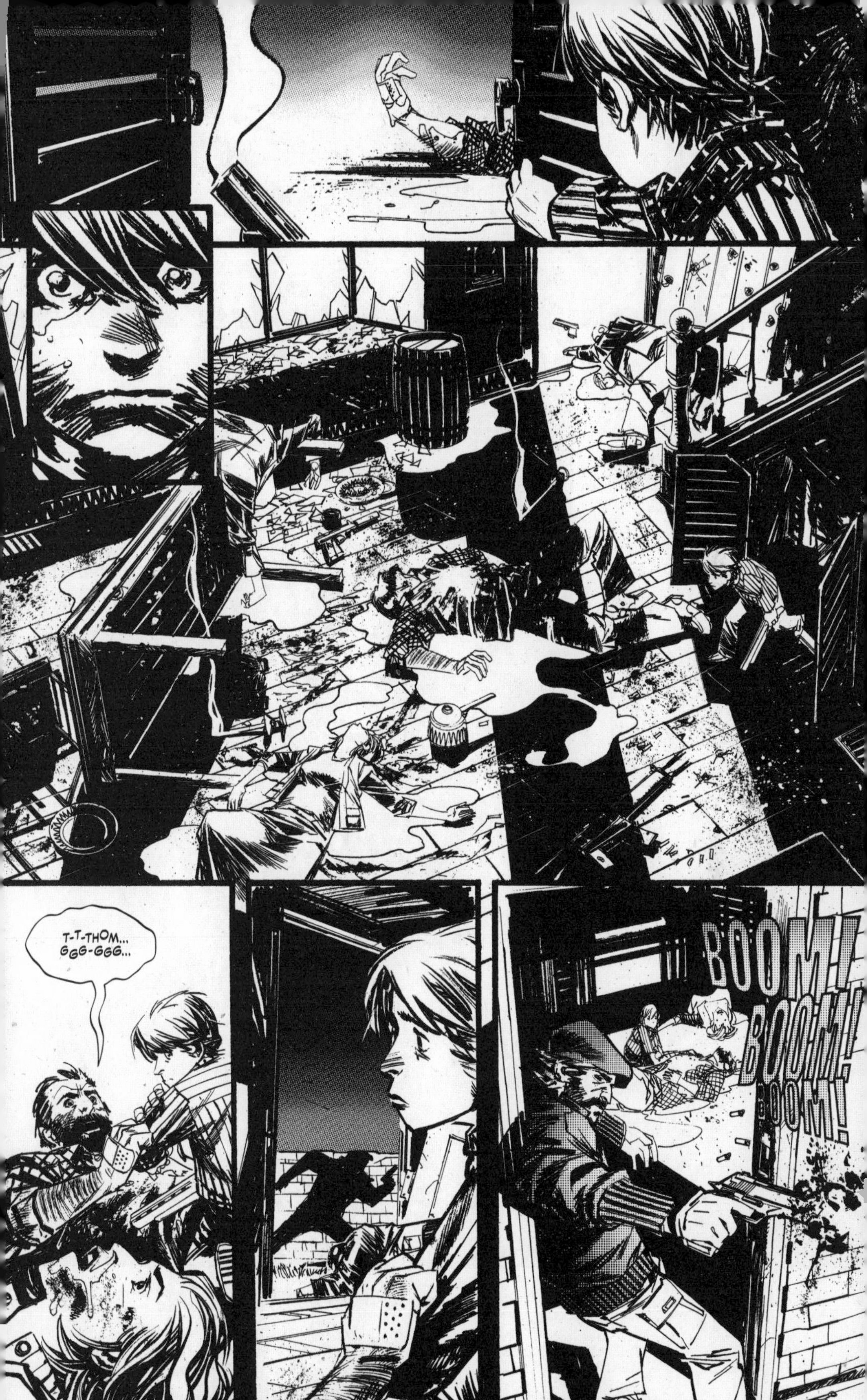
T-T-THOM... GGG-GGG...
BOOM!
BOOM!
BOOM!

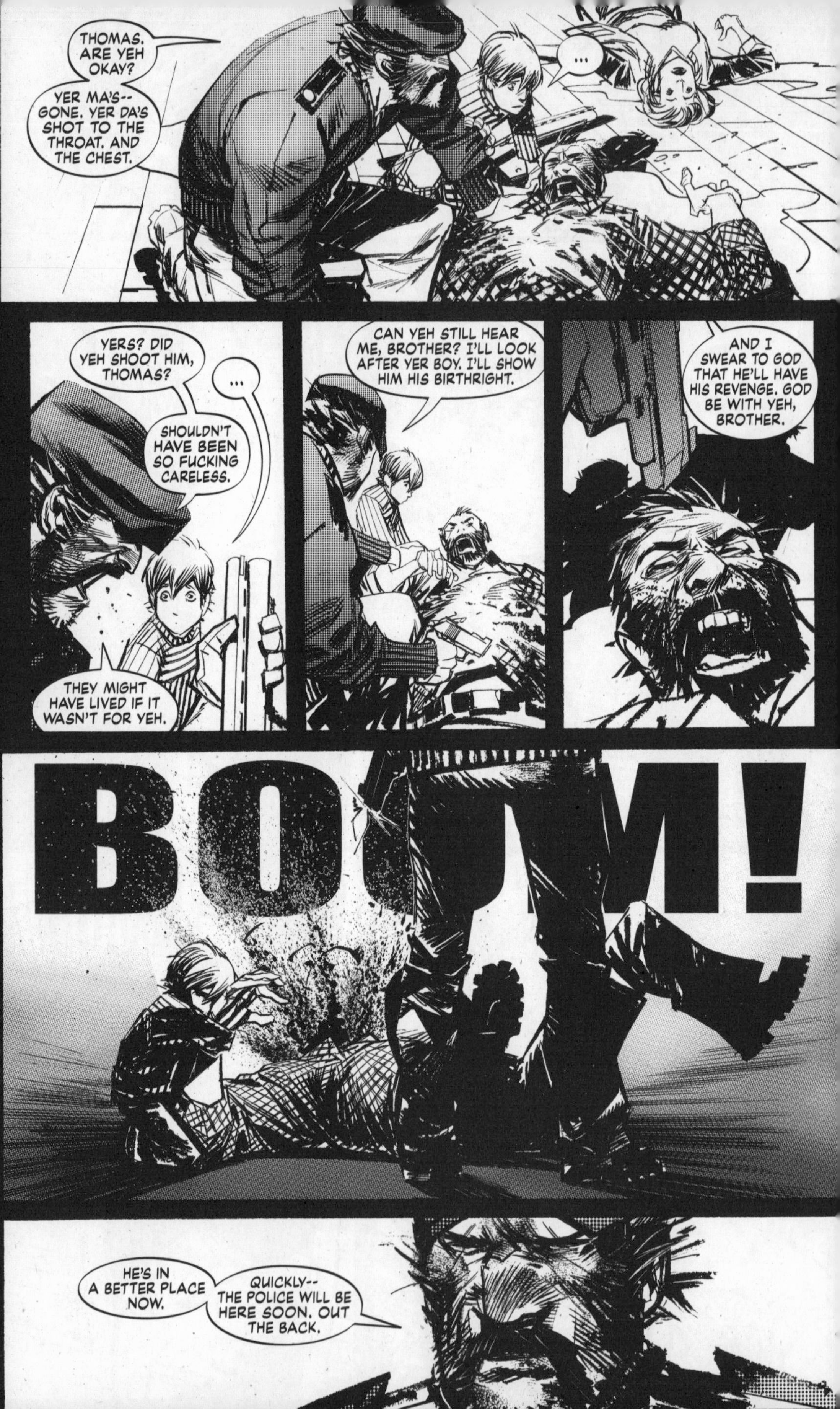
THOMAS. ARE YEH OKAY?
YER MA'S-- GONE. YER DA'S SHOT TO THE THROAT. AND THE CHEST.
...
YERS? DID YEH SHOOT HIM, THOMAS?
...
SHOULDN'T HAVE BEEN SO FUCKING CARELESS.
THEY MIGHT HAVE LIVED IF IT WASN'T FOR YEH.
CAN YEH STILL HEAR ME, BROTHER? I'LL LOOK AFTER YER BOY. I'LL SHOW HIM HIS BIRTHRIGHT.
AND I SWEAR TO GOD THAT HE'LL HAVE HIS REVENGE. GOD BE WITH YEH, BROTHER.
BOOM!
HE'S IN A BETTER PLACE NOW.
QUICKLY-- THE POLICE WILL BE HERE SOON. OUT THE BACK.

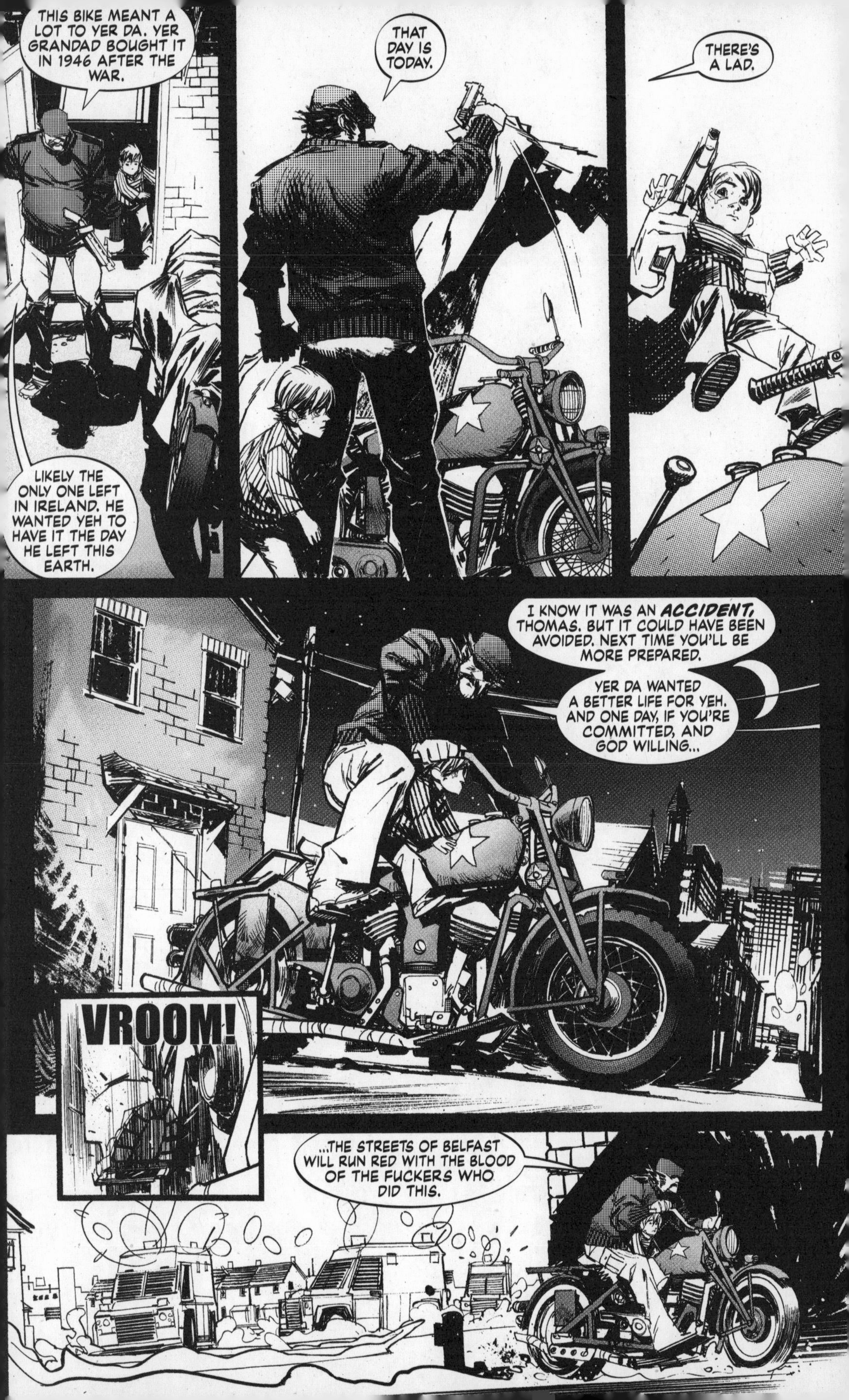
THIS BIKE MEANT A LOT TO YER DA. YER GRANDAD BOUGHT IT IN 1946 AFTER THE WAR.
LIKELY THE ONLY ONE LEFT IN IRELAND. HE WANTED YEH TO HAVE IT THE DAY HE LEFT THIS EARTH.
THAT DAY IS TODAY.
THERE'S A LAD.
I KNOW IT WAS AN ACCIDENT, THOMAS. BUT IT COULD HAVE BEEN AVOIDED. NEXT TIME YOU'LL BE MORE PREPARED.
YER DA WANTED A BETTER LIFE FOR YEH. AND ONE DAY, IF YOU'RE COMMITTED, AND GOD WILLING...
VROOM!
...THE STREETS OF BELFAST WILL RUN RED WITH THE BLOOD OF THE FUCKERS WHO DID THIS.

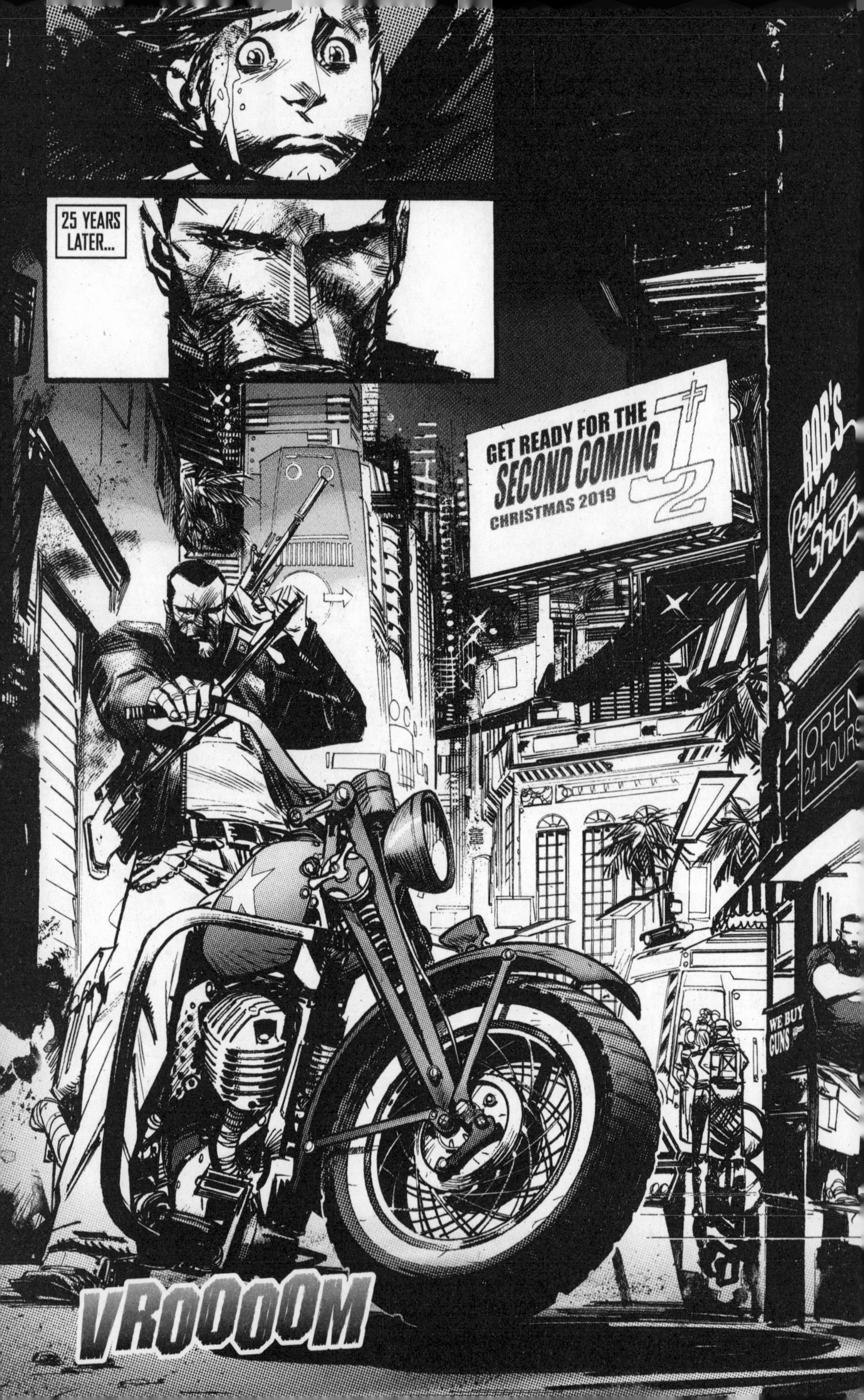
25 YEARS LATER...
GET READY FOR THE
SECOND COMING
J2
CHRISTMAS 2019
ROB'S
Pawn Shop
OPEN
24 HOURS
WE BUY GUNS
VROOOOOM

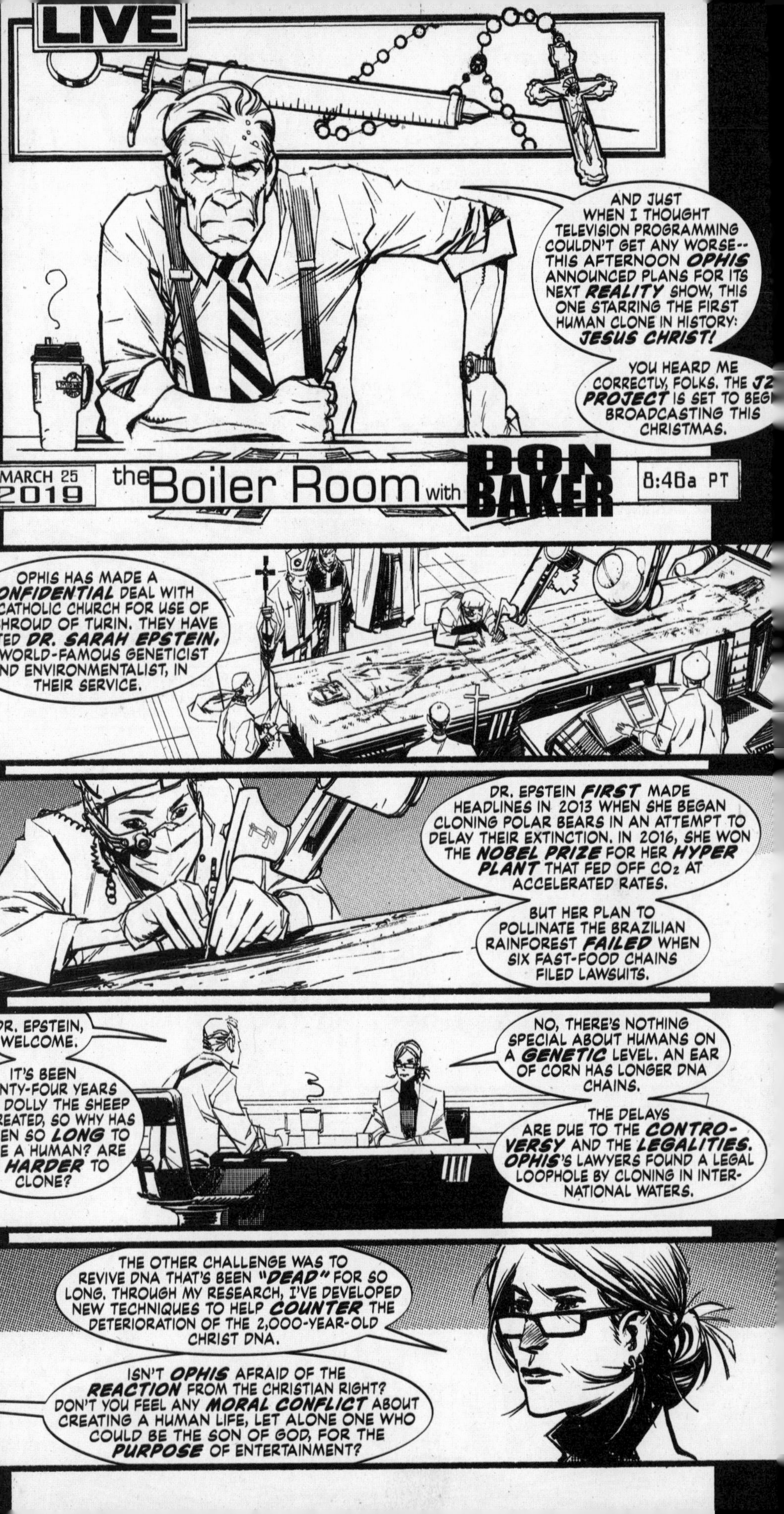
LIVE
AND JUST WHEN I THOUGHT TELEVISION PROGRAMMING COULDN'T GET ANY WORSE-- THIS AFTERNOON OPHIS ANNOUNCED PLANS FOR ITS NEXT REALITY SHOW, THIS ONE STARRING THE FIRST HUMAN CLONE IN HISTORY: JESUS CHRIST!
YOU HEARD ME CORRECTLY, FOLKS. THE J2 PROJECT IS SET TO BEGI BROADCASTING THIS CHRISTMAS.
MARCH 25 2019
the Boiler Room with RON BAKER
8:46a PT
OPHIS HAS MADE A CONFIDENTIAL DEAL WITH THE CATHOLIC CHURCH FOR USE OF THE SHROUD OF TURIN. THEY HAVE ENLISTED DR. SARAH EPSTEIN, THE WORLD-FAMOUS GENETICIST AND ENVIRONMENTALIST, IN THEIR SERVICE.
DR. EPSTEIN FIRST MADE HEADLINES IN 2013 WHEN SHE BEGAN CLONING POLAR BEARS IN AN ATTEMPT TO DELAY THEIR EXTINCTION. IN 2016, SHE WON THE NOBEL PRIZE FOR HER HYPER PLANT THAT FED OFF CO_2 AT ACCELERATED RATES.
BUT HER PLAN TO POLLINATE THE BRAZILIAN RAINFOREST FAILED WHEN SIX FAST-FOOD CHAINS FILED LAWSUITS.
DR. EPSTEIN, WELCOME.
IT'S BEEN TWENTY-FOUR YEARS SINCE DOLLY THE SHEEP WAS CREATED, SO WHY HAS IT TAKEN SO LONG TO CLONE A HUMAN? ARE WE HARDER TO CLONE?
NO, THERE'S NOTHING SPECIAL ABOUT HUMANS ON A GENETIC LEVEL. AN EAR OF CORN HAS LONGER DNA CHAINS.
THE DELAYS ARE DUE TO THE CONTROVERSY AND THE LEGALITIES. OPHIS'S LAWYERS FOUND A LEGAL LOOPHOLE BY CLONING IN INTERNATIONAL WATERS.
THE OTHER CHALLENGE WAS TO REVIVE DNA THAT'S BEEN "DEAD" FOR SO LONG. THROUGH MY RESEARCH, I'VE DEVELOPED NEW TECHNIQUES TO HELP COUNTER THE DETERIORATION OF THE 2,000-YEAR-OLD CHRIST DNA.
ISN'T OPHIS AFRAID OF THE REACTION FROM THE CHRISTIAN RIGHT? DON'T YOU FEEL ANY MORAL CONFLICT ABOUT CREATING A HUMAN LIFE, LET ALONE ONE WHO COULD BE THE SON OF GOD, FOR THE PURPOSE OF ENTERTAINMENT?

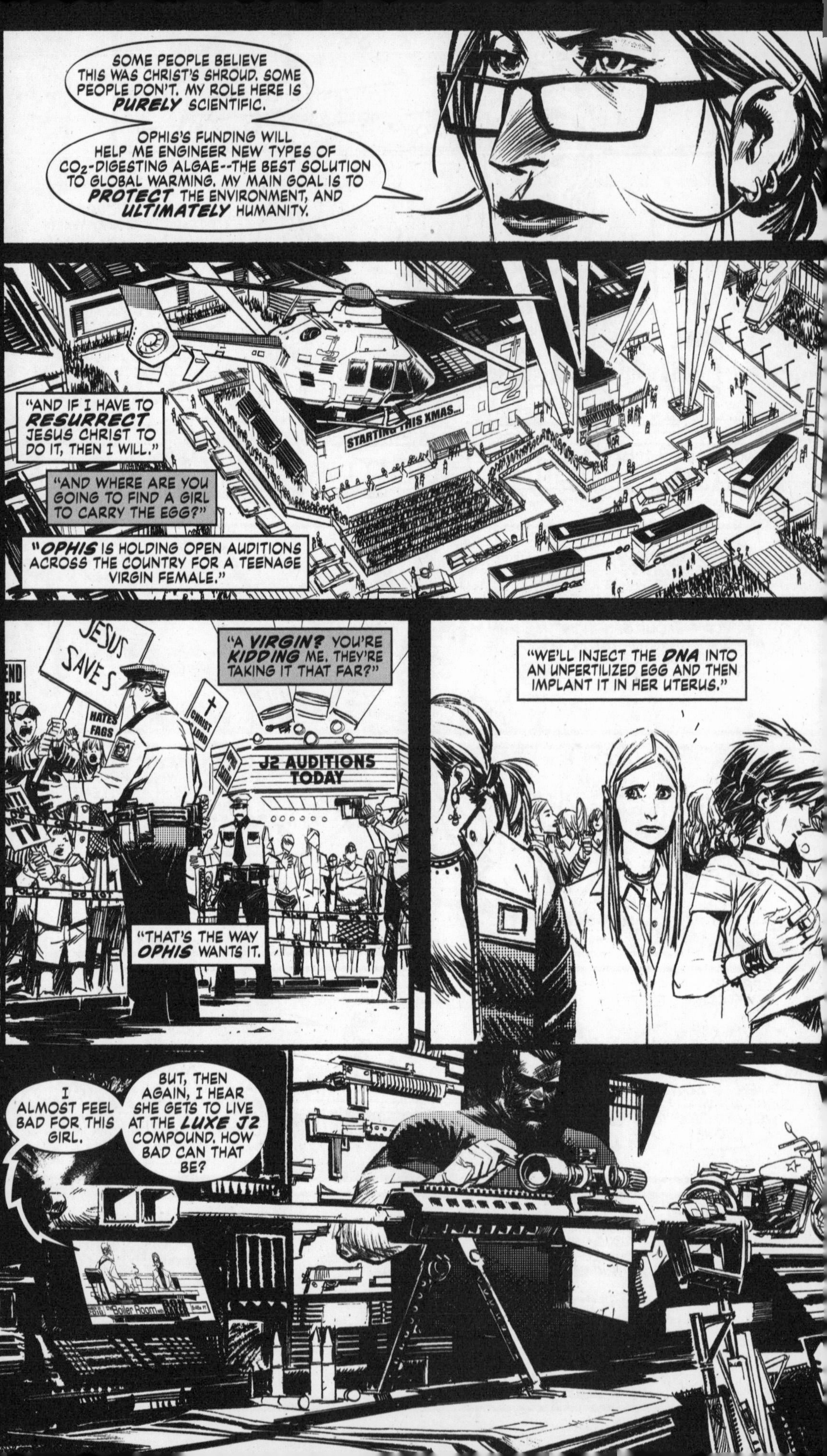

SOME PEOPLE BELIEVE THIS WAS CHRIST'S SHROUD. SOME PEOPLE DON'T. MY ROLE HERE IS PURELY SCIENTIFIC.
OPHIS'S FUNDING WILL HELP ME ENGINEER NEW TYPES OF CO_2-DIGESTING ALGAE--THE BEST SOLUTION TO GLOBAL WARMING. MY MAIN GOAL IS TO PROTECT THE ENVIRONMENT, AND ULTIMATELY HUMANITY.
STARTING THIS XMAS...
AUDITIONS
"AND IF I HAVE TO RESURRECT JESUS CHRIST TO DO IT, THEN I WILL."
"AND WHERE ARE YOU GOING TO FIND A GIRL TO CARRY THE EGG?"
"OPHIS IS HOLDING OPEN AUDITIONS ACROSS THE COUNTRY FOR A TEENAGE VIRGIN FEMALE."
JESUS SAVES
HATES FAGS
CHRIST IS LORD
TV
J2 AUDITIONS TODAY
"A VIRGIN? YOU'RE KIDDING ME. THEY'RE TAKING IT THAT FAR?"
"THAT'S THE WAY OPHIS WANTS IT.
"WE'LL INJECT THE DNA INTO AN UNFERTILIZED EGG AND THEN IMPLANT IT IN HER UTERUS."
I ALMOST FEEL BAD FOR THIS GIRL.
BUT, THEN AGAIN, I HEAR SHE GETS TO LIVE AT THE LUXE J2 COMPOUND. HOW BAD CAN THAT BE?
Boiler Room

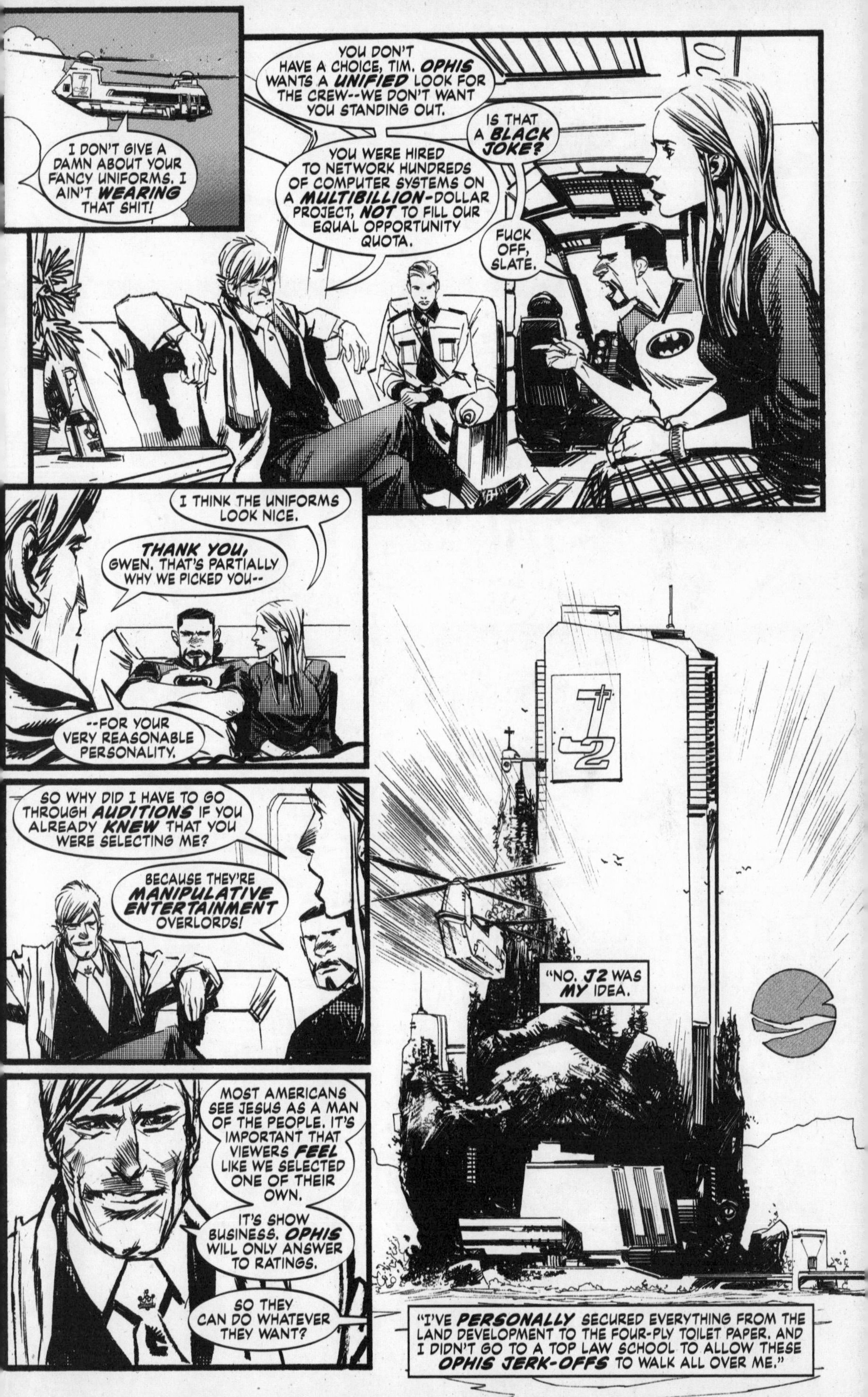
I DON'T GIVE A DAMN ABOUT YOUR FANCY UNIFORMS. I AIN'T WEARING THAT SHIT!
YOU DON'T HAVE A CHOICE, TIM. OPHIS WANTS A UNIFIED LOOK FOR THE CREW--WE DON'T WANT YOU STANDING OUT.
YOU WERE HIRED TO NETWORK HUNDREDS OF COMPUTER SYSTEMS ON A MULTIBILLION-DOLLAR PROJECT, NOT TO FILL OUR EQUAL OPPORTUNITY QUOTA.
IS THAT A BLACK JOKE?
FUCK OFF, SLATE.
I THINK THE UNIFORMS LOOK NICE.
THANK YOU, GWEN. THAT'S PARTIALLY WHY WE PICKED YOU--
--FOR YOUR VERY REASONABLE PERSONALITY.
SO WHY DID I HAVE TO GO THROUGH AUDITIONS IF YOU ALREADY KNEW THAT YOU WERE SELECTING ME?
BECAUSE THEY'RE MANIPULATIVE ENTERTAINMENT OVERLORDS!
MOST AMERICANS SEE JESUS AS A MAN OF THE PEOPLE. IT'S IMPORTANT THAT VIEWERS FEEL LIKE WE SELECTED ONE OF THEIR OWN.
IT'S SHOW BUSINESS. OPHIS WILL ONLY ANSWER TO RATINGS.
SO THEY CAN DO WHATEVER THEY WANT?
"NO. J2 WAS MY IDEA.
"I'VE PERSONALLY SECURED EVERYTHING FROM THE LAND DEVELOPMENT TO THE FOUR-PLY TOILET PAPER. AND I DIDN'T GO TO A TOP LAW SCHOOL TO ALLOW THESE OPHIS JERK-OFFS TO WALK ALL OVER ME."

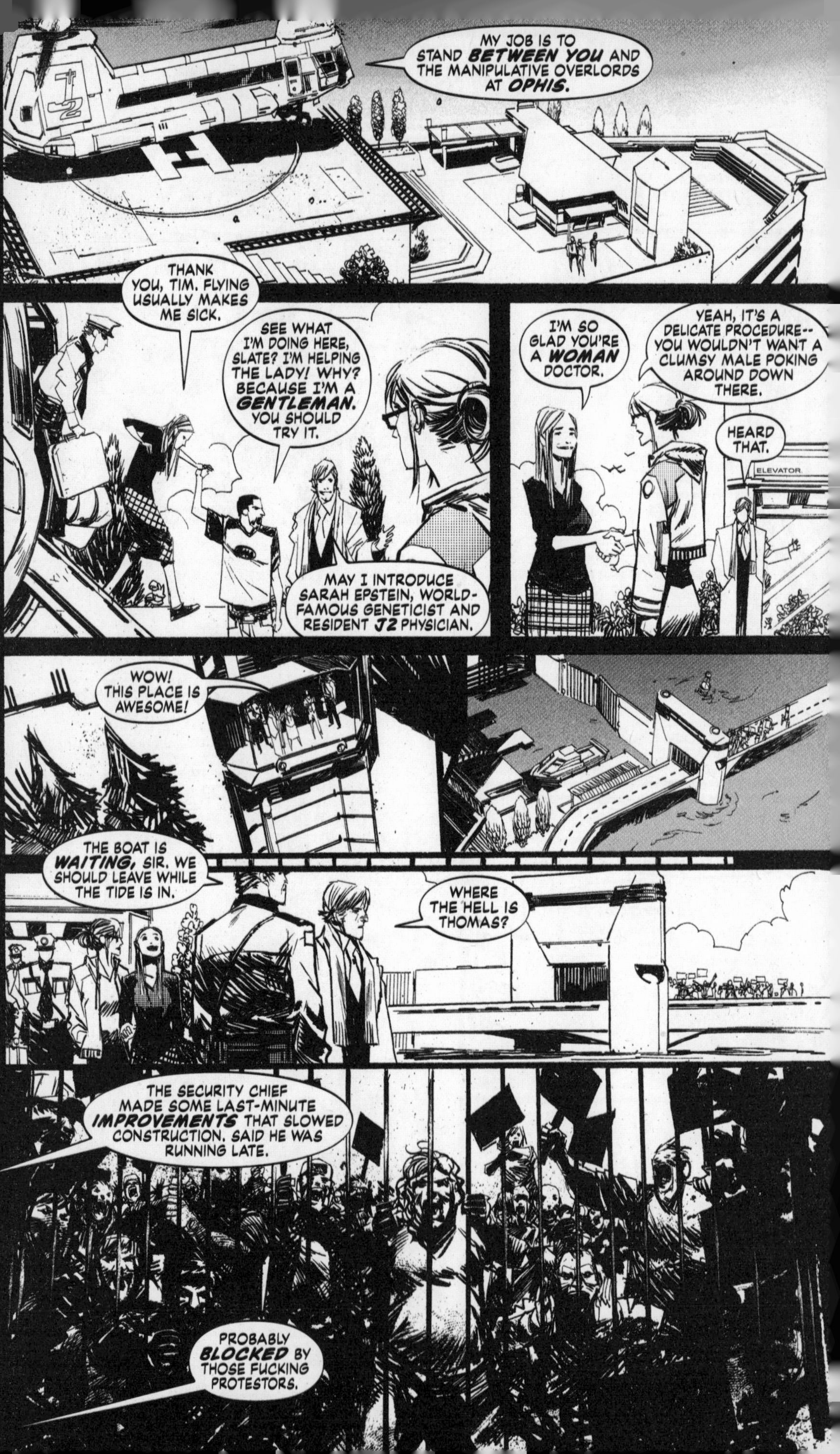
MY JOB IS TO STAND BETWEEN YOU AND THE MANIPULATIVE OVERLORDS AT OPHIS.
J2
THANK YOU, TIM. FLYING USUALLY MAKES ME SICK.
SEE WHAT I'M DOING HERE, SLATE? I'M HELPING THE LADY! WHY? BECAUSE I'M A GENTLEMAN. YOU SHOULD TRY IT.
MAY I INTRODUCE SARAH EPSTEIN, WORLD-FAMOUS GENETICIST AND RESIDENT J2 PHYSICIAN.
I'M SO GLAD YOU'RE A WOMAN DOCTOR.
YEAH, IT'S A DELICATE PROCEDURE--YOU WOULDN'T WANT A CLUMSY MALE POKING AROUND DOWN THERE.
HEARD THAT.
ELEVATOR
WOW! THIS PLACE IS AWESOME!
THE BOAT IS WAITING, SIR. WE SHOULD LEAVE WHILE THE TIDE IS IN.
WHERE THE HELL IS THOMAS?
THE SECURITY CHIEF MADE SOME LAST-MINUTE IMPROVEMENTS THAT SLOWED CONSTRUCTION. SAID HE WAS RUNNING LATE.
PROBABLY BLOCKED BY THOSE FUCKING PROTESTORS.

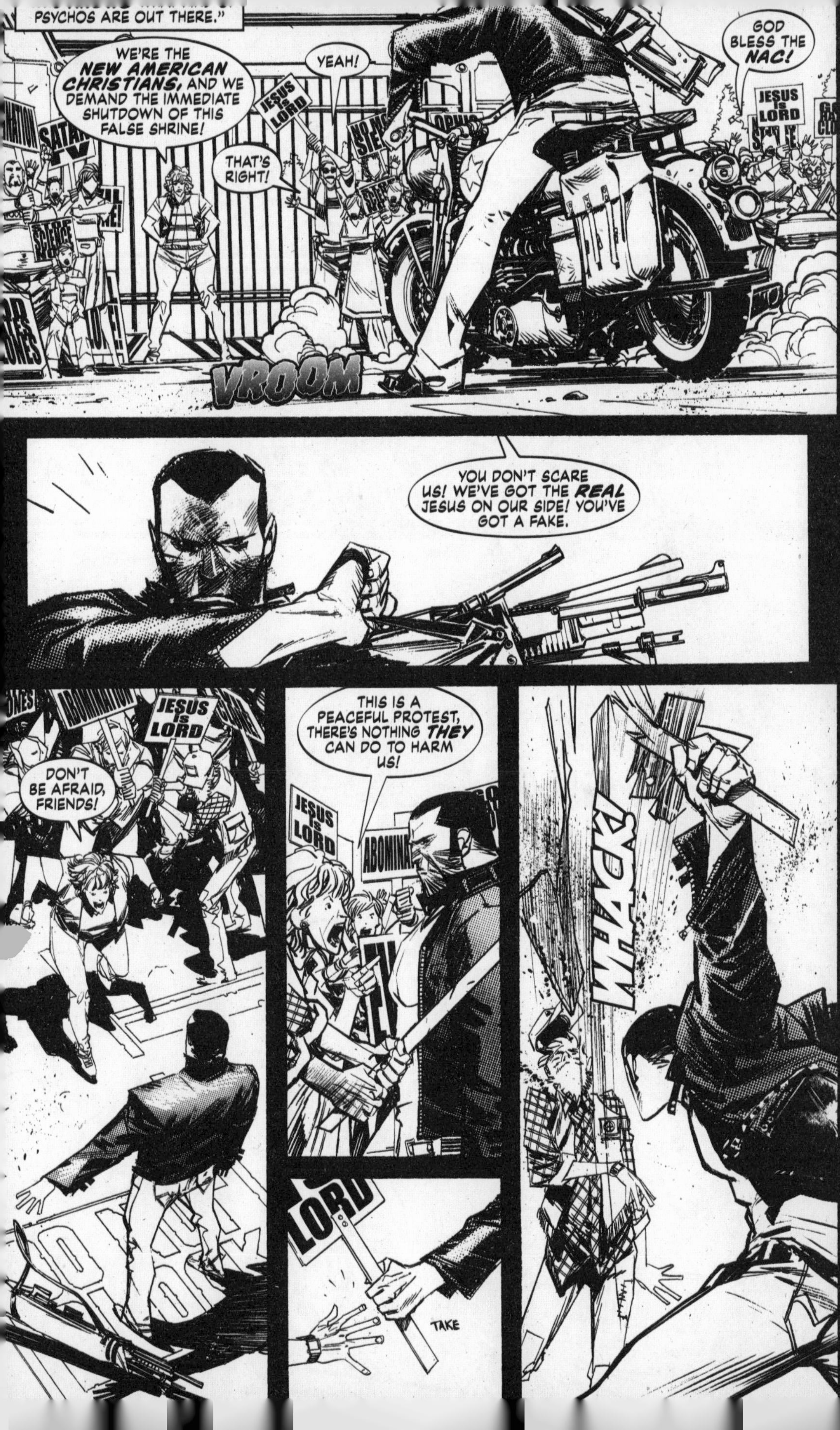

PSYCHOS ARE OUT THERE."
WE'RE THE NEW AMERICAN CHRISTIANS, AND WE DEMAND THE IMMEDIATE SHUTDOWN OF THIS FALSE SHRINE!
YEAH!
THAT'S RIGHT!
GOD BLESS THE NAC!
JESUS IS LORD
JESUS IS LORD
VROOM
YOU DON'T SCARE US! WE'VE GOT THE REAL JESUS ON OUR SIDE! YOU'VE GOT A FAKE.
ABOMINATION
JESUS IS LORD
DON'T BE AFRAID, FRIENDS!
THIS IS A PEACEFUL PROTEST, THERE'S NOTHING THEY CAN DO TO HARM US!
JESUS IS LORD
LORD
TAKE
WHACK!

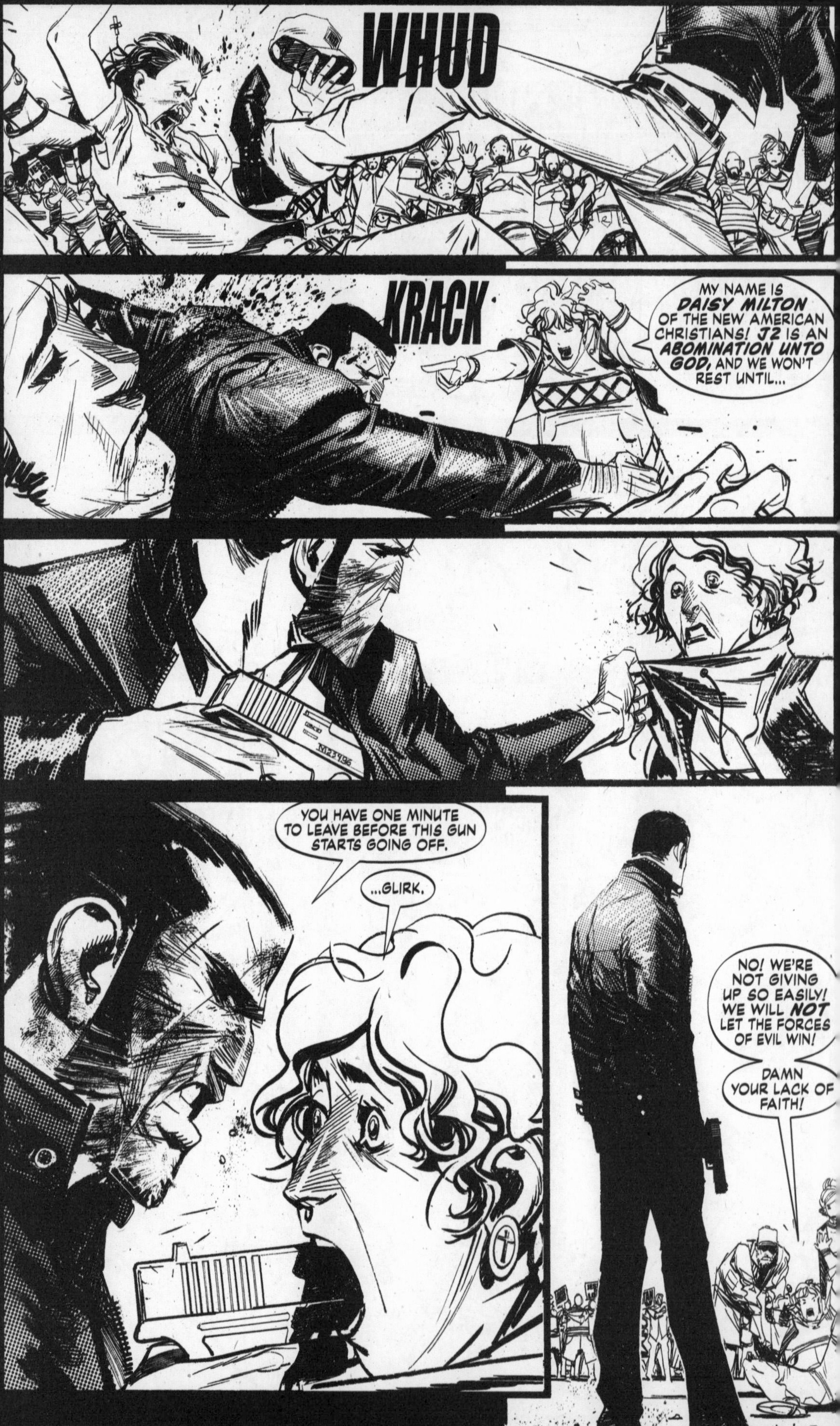
WHUD
KRACK
MY NAME IS DAISY MILTON OF THE NEW AMERICAN CHRISTIANS! J2 IS AN ABOMINATION UNTO GOD, AND WE WON'T REST UNTIL...
YOU HAVE ONE MINUTE TO LEAVE BEFORE THIS GUN STARTS GOING OFF.
...GLIRK.
NO! WE'RE NOT GIVING UP SO EASILY! WE WILL NOT LET THE FORCES OF EVIL WIN!
DAMN YOUR LACK OF FAITH!

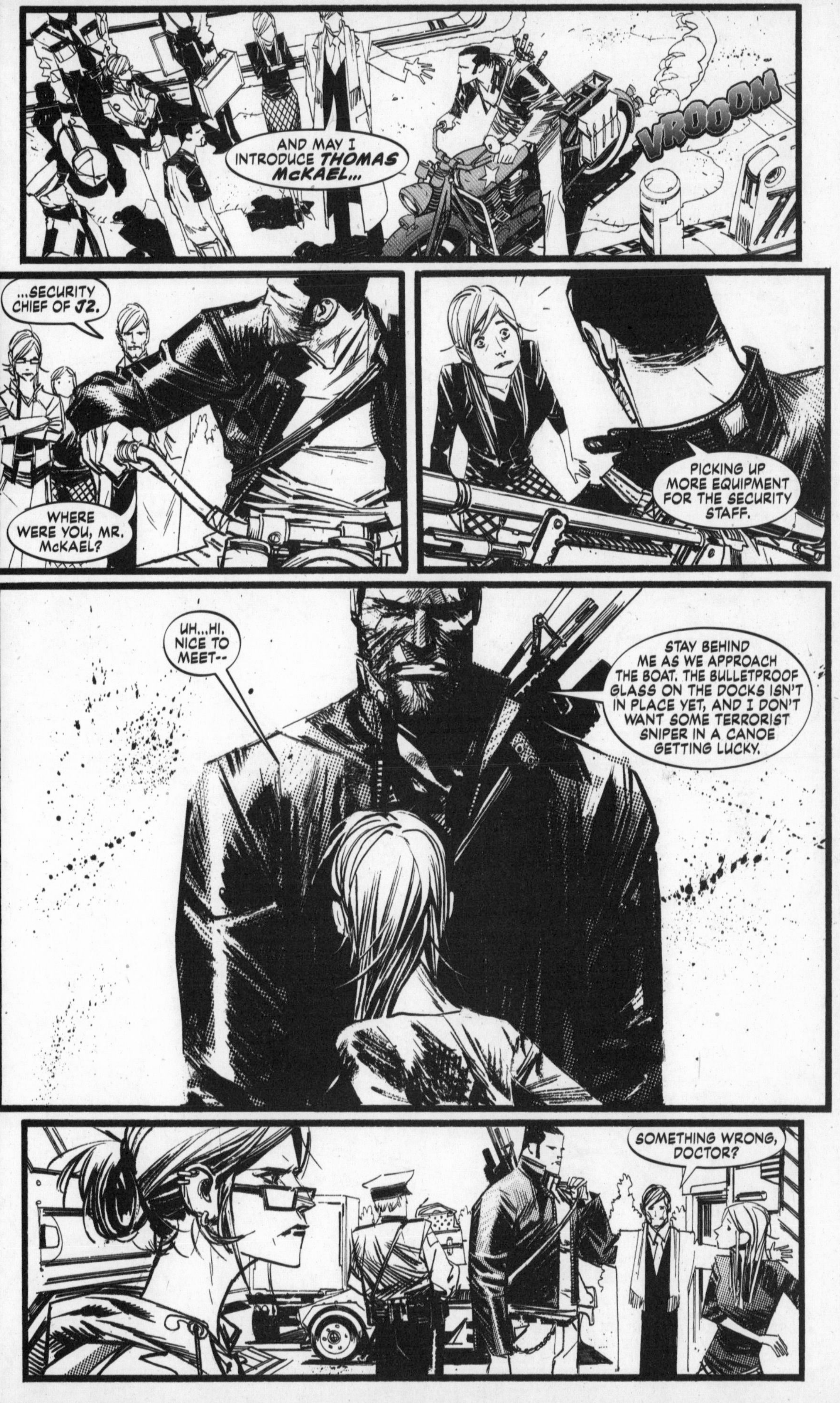

AND MAY I INTRODUCE THOMAS McKAEL...
VROOOM
...SECURITY CHIEF OF J2.
WHERE WERE YOU, MR. McKAEL?
PICKING UP MORE EQUIPMENT FOR THE SECURITY STAFF.
UH...HI. NICE TO MEET--
STAY BEHIND ME AS WE APPROACH THE BOAT. THE BULLETPROOF GLASS ON THE DOCKS ISN'T IN PLACE YET, AND I DON'T WANT SOME TERRORIST SNIPER IN A CANOE GETTING LUCKY.
SOMETHING WRONG, DOCTOR?

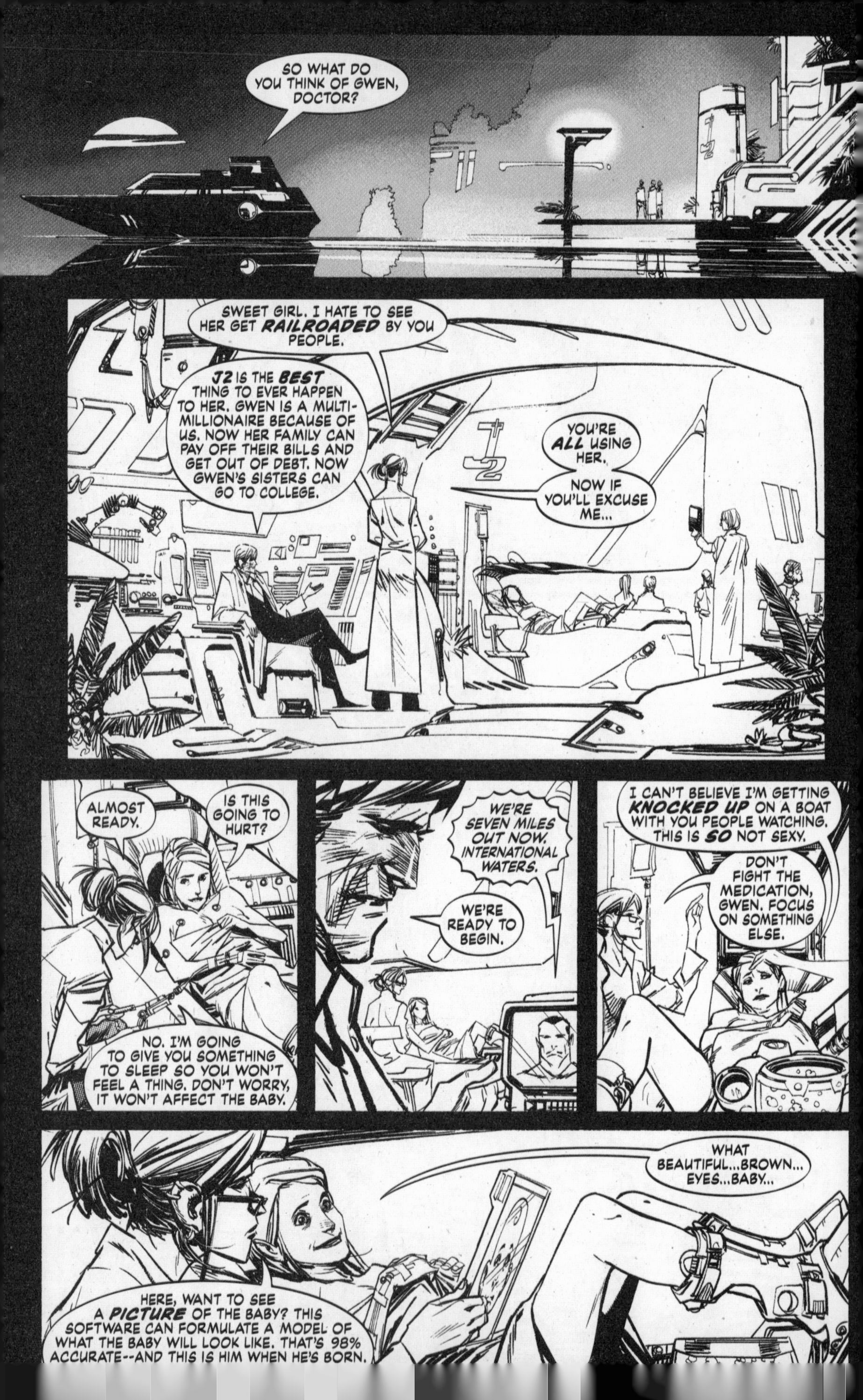
SO WHAT DO YOU THINK OF GWEN, DOCTOR?
SWEET GIRL. I HATE TO SEE HER GET RAILROADED BY YOU PEOPLE.
J2 IS THE BEST THING TO EVER HAPPEN TO HER. GWEN IS A MULTI-MILLIONAIRE BECAUSE OF US. NOW HER FAMILY CAN PAY OFF THEIR BILLS AND GET OUT OF DEBT. NOW GWEN'S SISTERS CAN GO TO COLLEGE.
YOU'RE ALL USING HER.
NOW IF YOU'LL EXCUSE ME...
ALMOST READY.
IS THIS GOING TO HURT?
NO. I'M GOING TO GIVE YOU SOMETHING TO SLEEP SO YOU WON'T FEEL A THING. DON'T WORRY, IT WON'T AFFECT THE BABY.
WE'RE SEVEN MILES OUT NOW. INTERNATIONAL WATERS.
WE'RE READY TO BEGIN.
I CAN'T BELIEVE I'M GETTING KNOCKED UP ON A BOAT WITH YOU PEOPLE WATCHING. THIS IS SO NOT SEXY.
DON'T FIGHT THE MEDICATION, GWEN. FOCUS ON SOMETHING ELSE.
HERE, WANT TO SEE A PICTURE OF THE BABY? THIS SOFTWARE CAN FORMULATE A MODEL OF WHAT THE BABY WILL LOOK LIKE. THAT'S 98% ACCURATE--AND THIS IS HIM WHEN HE'S BORN.
WHAT BEAUTIFUL...BROWN... EYES...BABY...

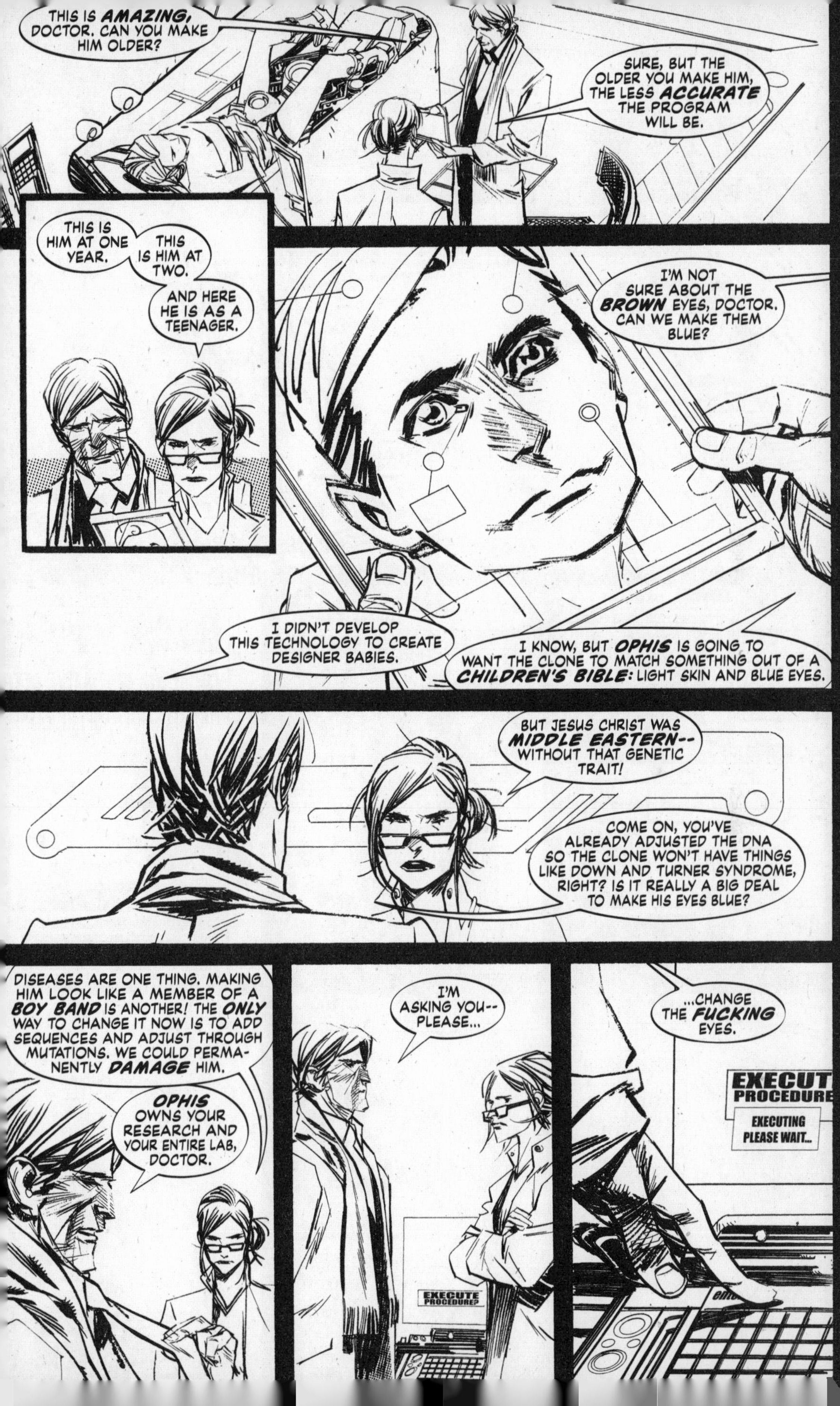
THIS IS AMAZING, DOCTOR. CAN YOU MAKE HIM OLDER?
SURE, BUT THE OLDER YOU MAKE HIM, THE LESS ACCURATE THE PROGRAM WILL BE.
THIS IS HIM AT ONE YEAR.
THIS IS HIM AT TWO.
AND HERE HE IS AS A TEENAGER.
I'M NOT SURE ABOUT THE BROWN EYES, DOCTOR. CAN WE MAKE THEM BLUE?
I DIDN'T DEVELOP THIS TECHNOLOGY TO CREATE DESIGNER BABIES.
I KNOW, BUT OPHIS IS GOING TO WANT THE CLONE TO MATCH SOMETHING OUT OF A CHILDREN'S BIBLE: LIGHT SKIN AND BLUE EYES.
BUT JESUS CHRIST WAS MIDDLE EASTERN--WITHOUT THAT GENETIC TRAIT!
COME ON, YOU'VE ALREADY ADJUSTED THE DNA SO THE CLONE WON'T HAVE THINGS LIKE DOWN AND TURNER SYNDROME, RIGHT? IS IT REALLY A BIG DEAL TO MAKE HIS EYES BLUE?
DISEASES ARE ONE THING. MAKING HIM LOOK LIKE A MEMBER OF A BOY BAND IS ANOTHER! THE ONLY WAY TO CHANGE IT NOW IS TO ADD SEQUENCES AND ADJUST THROUGH MUTATIONS. WE COULD PERMANENTLY DAMAGE HIM.
OPHIS OWNS YOUR RESEARCH AND YOUR ENTIRE LAB, DOCTOR.
I'M ASKING YOU--PLEASE...
EXECUTE PROCEDURE?
...CHANGE THE FUCKING EYES.
EXECUT PROCEDURE
EXECUTING PLEASE WAIT...

DAY 105

NEW SEARCH...

Thomas McKael

theguardian

October 19, 2007

3 POLICE, 1 CHILD KILLED IN CARBOMB

Thomas McKael
ARRESTED ON SITE

THE TIM

IRA SUSPECT DETAINE

McKAEL
MISSING
SINCE 1987

June 4, 2009 The Belfast Telegra

LOCAL IRA OPERATIVE DETA

IRA MAN GOES SUPERGRASS
TESTIFIES AGAINST HIS OWN BRIGADE
IN EXCHANGE FOR SHORTENED SENTENCE

4 ARRESTED DURING PROTESTANT PROTEST

Telegraph

November 6, 1987

BOY GOES MISSING AFTER PARENTS FOUND SLAIN

THOMAS MCKAEL, AGE 7

SUSPECTED IRA INVOLVEMENT

mrph....

THINK I
SHOULD?

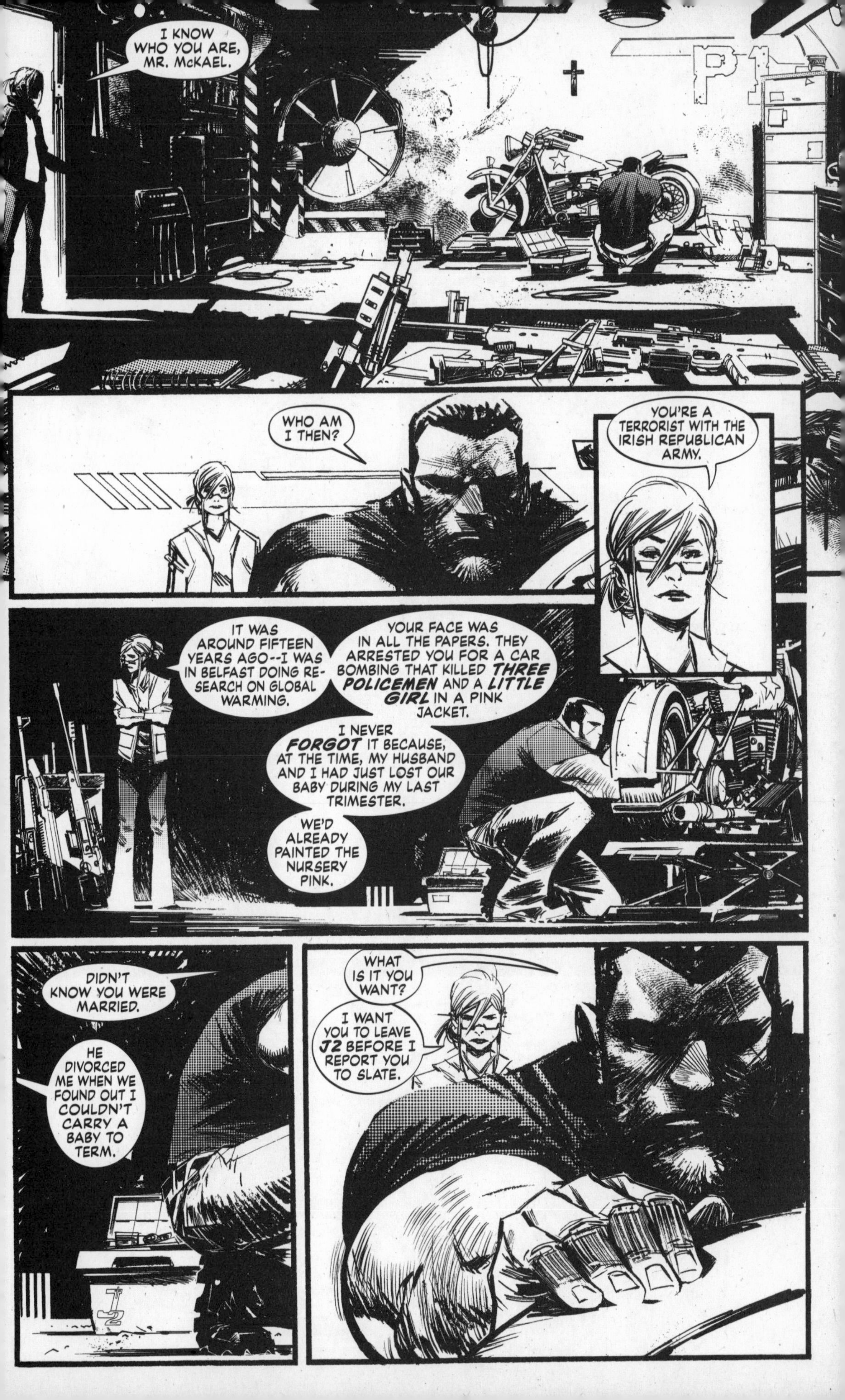
I KNOW WHO YOU ARE, MR. McKAEL.
WHO AM I THEN?
YOU'RE A TERRORIST WITH THE IRISH REPUBLICAN ARMY.
IT WAS AROUND FIFTEEN YEARS AGO--I WAS IN BELFAST DOING RE-SEARCH ON GLOBAL WARMING.
YOUR FACE WAS IN ALL THE PAPERS. THEY ARRESTED YOU FOR A CAR BOMBING THAT KILLED THREE POLICEMEN AND A LITTLE GIRL IN A PINK JACKET.
I NEVER FORGOT IT BECAUSE, AT THE TIME, MY HUSBAND AND I HAD JUST LOST OUR BABY DURING MY LAST TRIMESTER.
WE'D ALREADY PAINTED THE NURSERY PINK.
DIDN'T KNOW YOU WERE MARRIED.
HE DIVORCED ME WHEN WE FOUND OUT I COULDN'T CARRY A BABY TO TERM.
WHAT IS IT YOU WANT?
I WANT YOU TO LEAVE J2 BEFORE I REPORT YOU TO SLATE.

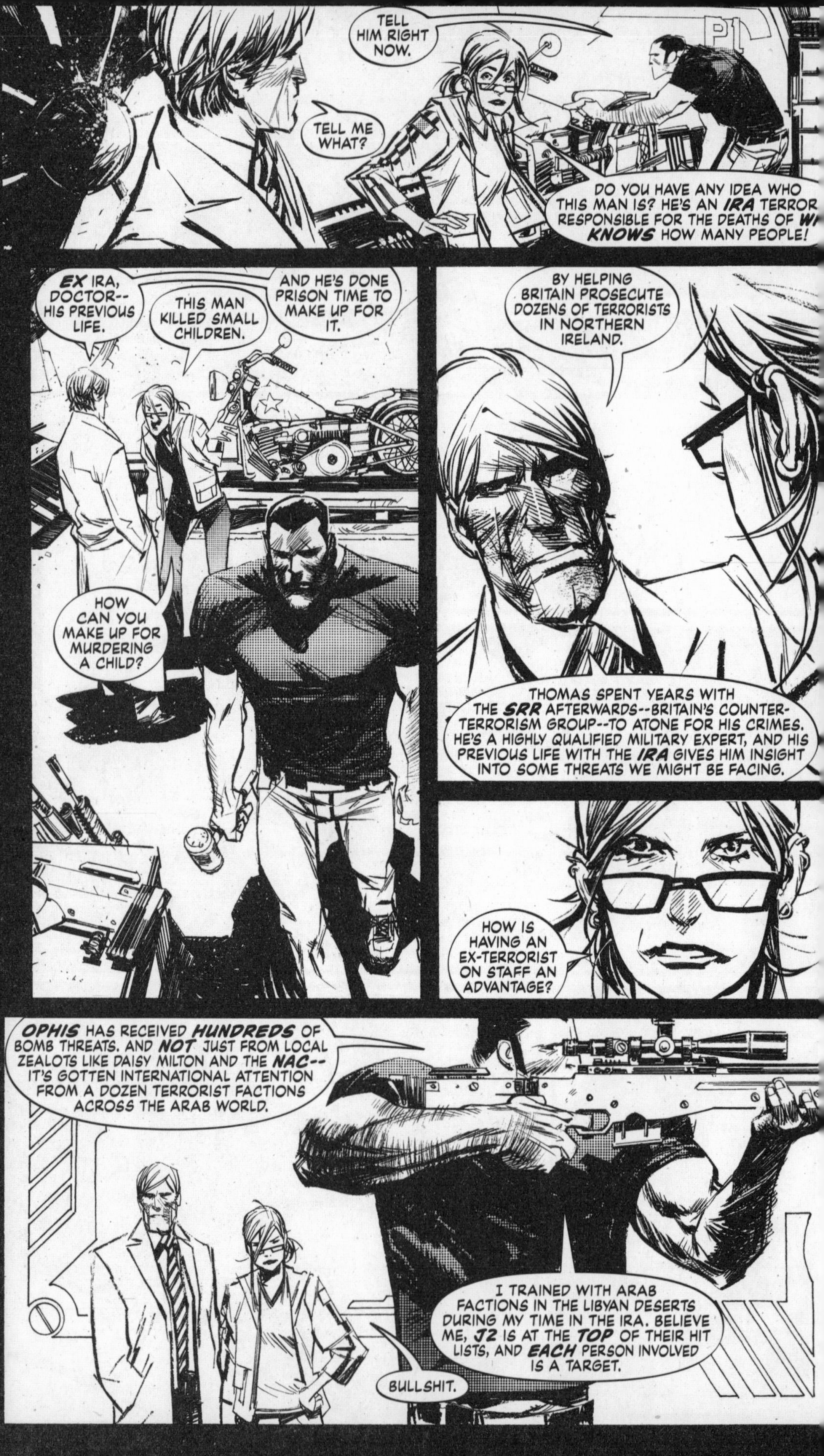
TELL HIM RIGHT NOW.
TELL ME WHAT?
DO YOU HAVE ANY IDEA WHO THIS MAN IS? HE'S AN IRA TERROR RESPONSIBLE FOR THE DEATHS OF WH KNOWS HOW MANY PEOPLE!
EX IRA, DOCTOR-- HIS PREVIOUS LIFE.
THIS MAN KILLED SMALL CHILDREN.
AND HE'S DONE PRISON TIME TO MAKE UP FOR IT.
HOW CAN YOU MAKE UP FOR MURDERING A CHILD?
BY HELPING BRITAIN PROSECUTE DOZENS OF TERRORISTS IN NORTHERN IRELAND.
THOMAS SPENT YEARS WITH THE SRR AFTERWARDS--BRITAIN'S COUNTER-TERRORISM GROUP--TO ATONE FOR HIS CRIMES. HE'S A HIGHLY QUALIFIED MILITARY EXPERT, AND HIS PREVIOUS LIFE WITH THE IRA GIVES HIM INSIGHT INTO SOME THREATS WE MIGHT BE FACING.
HOW IS HAVING AN EX-TERRORIST ON STAFF AN ADVANTAGE?
OPHIS HAS RECEIVED HUNDREDS OF BOMB THREATS. AND NOT JUST FROM LOCAL ZEALOTS LIKE DAISY MILTON AND THE NAC-- IT'S GOTTEN INTERNATIONAL ATTENTION FROM A DOZEN TERRORIST FACTIONS ACROSS THE ARAB WORLD.
I TRAINED WITH ARAB FACTIONS IN THE LIBYAN DESERTS DURING MY TIME IN THE IRA. BELIEVE ME, J2 IS AT THE TOP OF THEIR HIT LISTS, AND EACH PERSON INVOLVED IS A TARGET.
BULLSHIT.

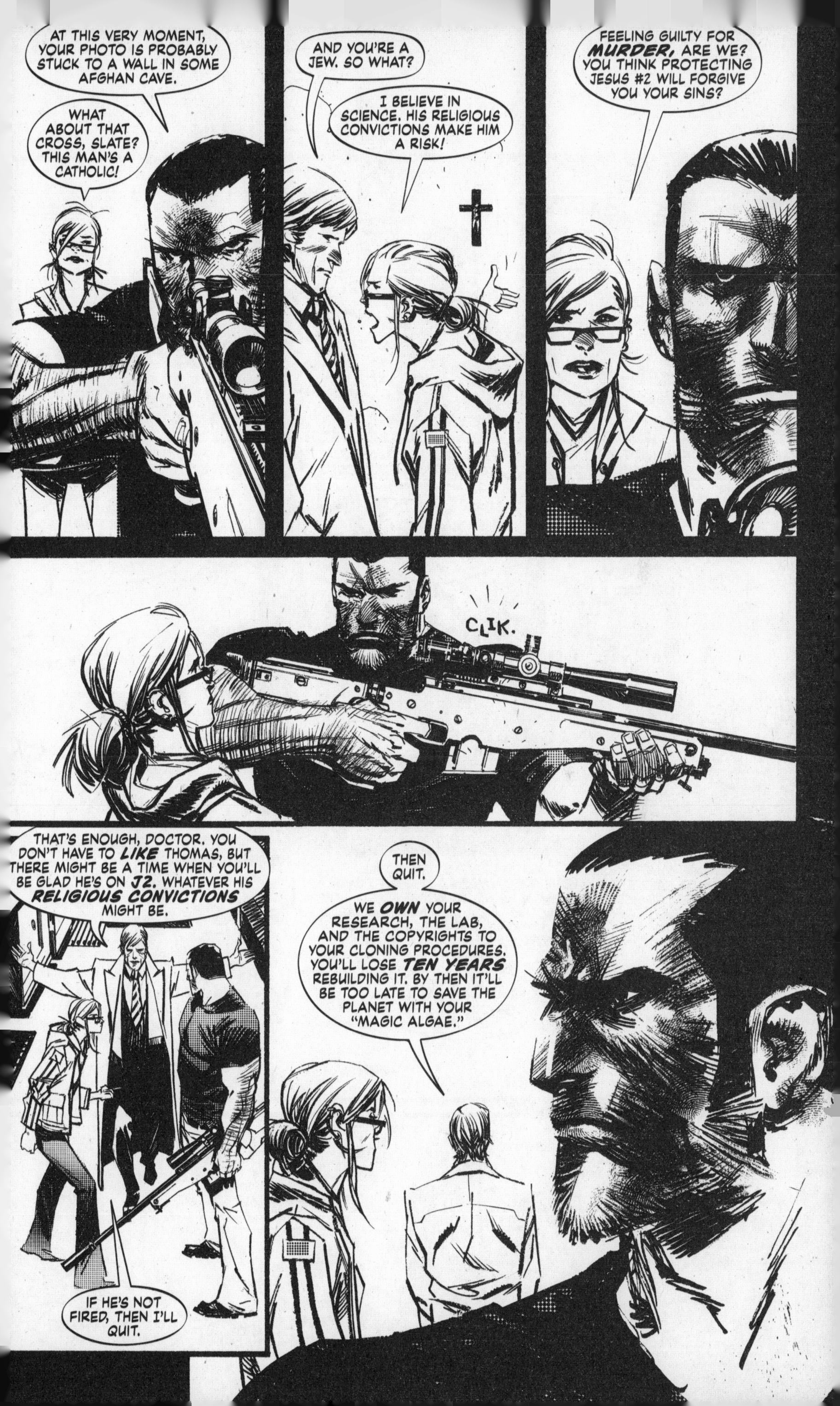

AT THIS VERY MOMENT, YOUR PHOTO IS PROBABLY STUCK TO A WALL IN SOME AFGHAN CAVE.
WHAT ABOUT THAT CROSS, SLATE? THIS MAN'S A CATHOLIC!
AND YOU'RE A JEW. SO WHAT?
I BELIEVE IN SCIENCE. HIS RELIGIOUS CONVICTIONS MAKE HIM A RISK!
FEELING GUILTY FOR MURDER, ARE WE? YOU THINK PROTECTING JESUS #2 WILL FORGIVE YOU YOUR SINS?
CLIK.
THAT'S ENOUGH, DOCTOR. YOU DON'T HAVE TO LIKE THOMAS, BUT THERE MIGHT BE A TIME WHEN YOU'LL BE GLAD HE'S ON J2. WHATEVER HIS RELIGIOUS CONVICTIONS MIGHT BE.
IF HE'S NOT FIRED, THEN I'LL QUIT.
THEN QUIT.
WE OWN YOUR RESEARCH, THE LAB, AND THE COPYRIGHTS TO YOUR CLONING PROCEDURES. YOU'LL LOSE TEN YEARS REBUILDING IT. BY THEN IT'LL BE TOO LATE TO SAVE THE PLANET WITH YOUR "MAGIC ALGAE."

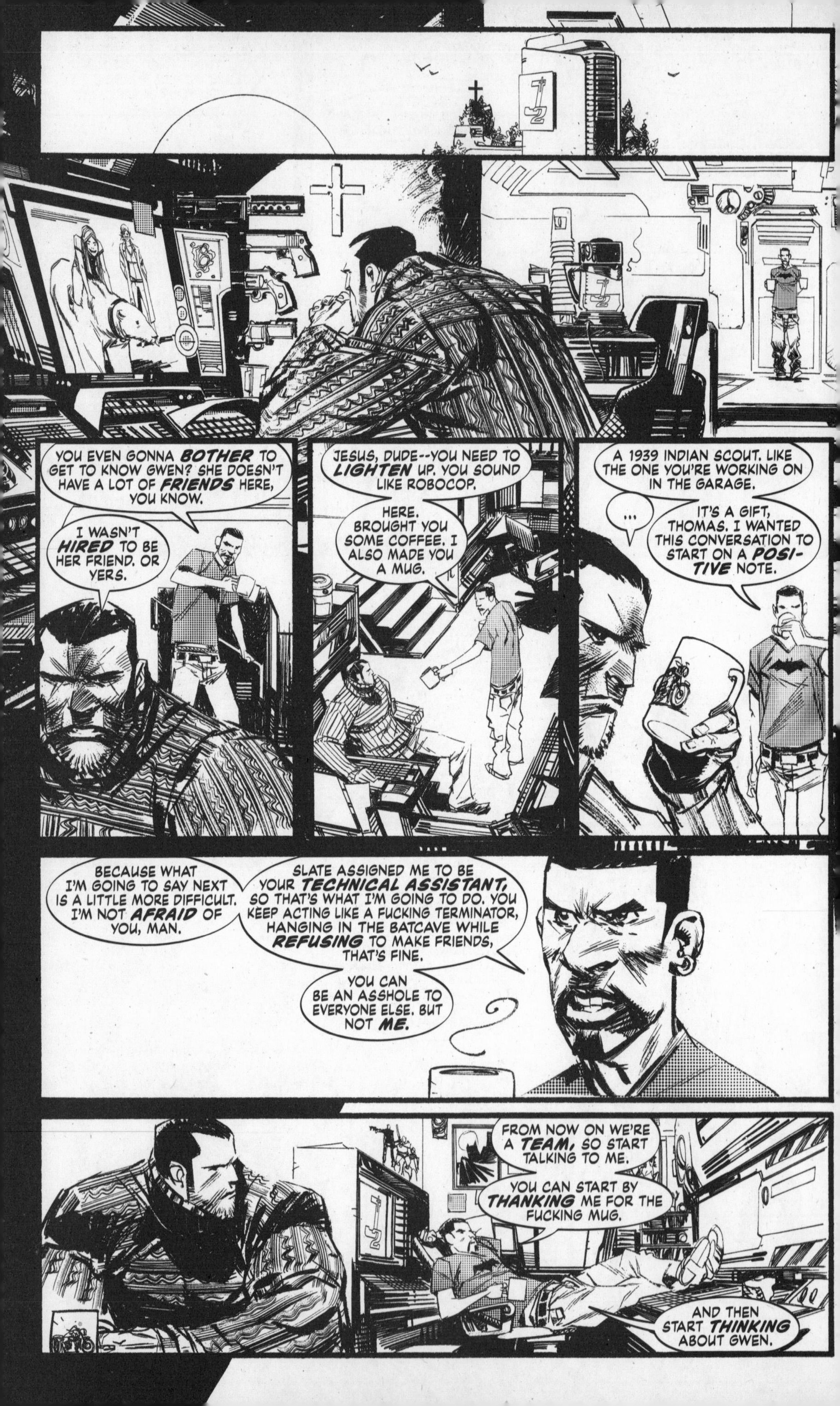
YOU EVEN GONNA BOTHER TO GET TO KNOW GWEN? SHE DOESN'T HAVE A LOT OF FRIENDS HERE, YOU KNOW.
I WASN'T HIRED TO BE HER FRIEND. OR YERS.
JESUS, DUDE--YOU NEED TO LIGHTEN UP. YOU SOUND LIKE ROBOCOP.
HERE. BROUGHT YOU SOME COFFEE. I ALSO MADE YOU A MUG.
A 1939 INDIAN SCOUT. LIKE THE ONE YOU'RE WORKING ON IN THE GARAGE.
...
IT'S A GIFT, THOMAS. I WANTED THIS CONVERSATION TO START ON A POSI-TIVE NOTE.
BECAUSE WHAT I'M GOING TO SAY NEXT IS A LITTLE MORE DIFFICULT. I'M NOT AFRAID OF YOU, MAN.
SLATE ASSIGNED ME TO BE YOUR TECHNICAL ASSISTANT, SO THAT'S WHAT I'M GOING TO DO. YOU KEEP ACTING LIKE A FUCKING TERMINATOR, HANGING IN THE BATCAVE WHILE REFUSING TO MAKE FRIENDS, THAT'S FINE.
YOU CAN BE AN ASSHOLE TO EVERYONE ELSE. BUT NOT ME.
FROM NOW ON WE'RE A TEAM, SO START TALKING TO ME.
YOU CAN START BY THANKING ME FOR THE FUCKING MUG.
AND THEN START THINKING ABOUT GWEN.

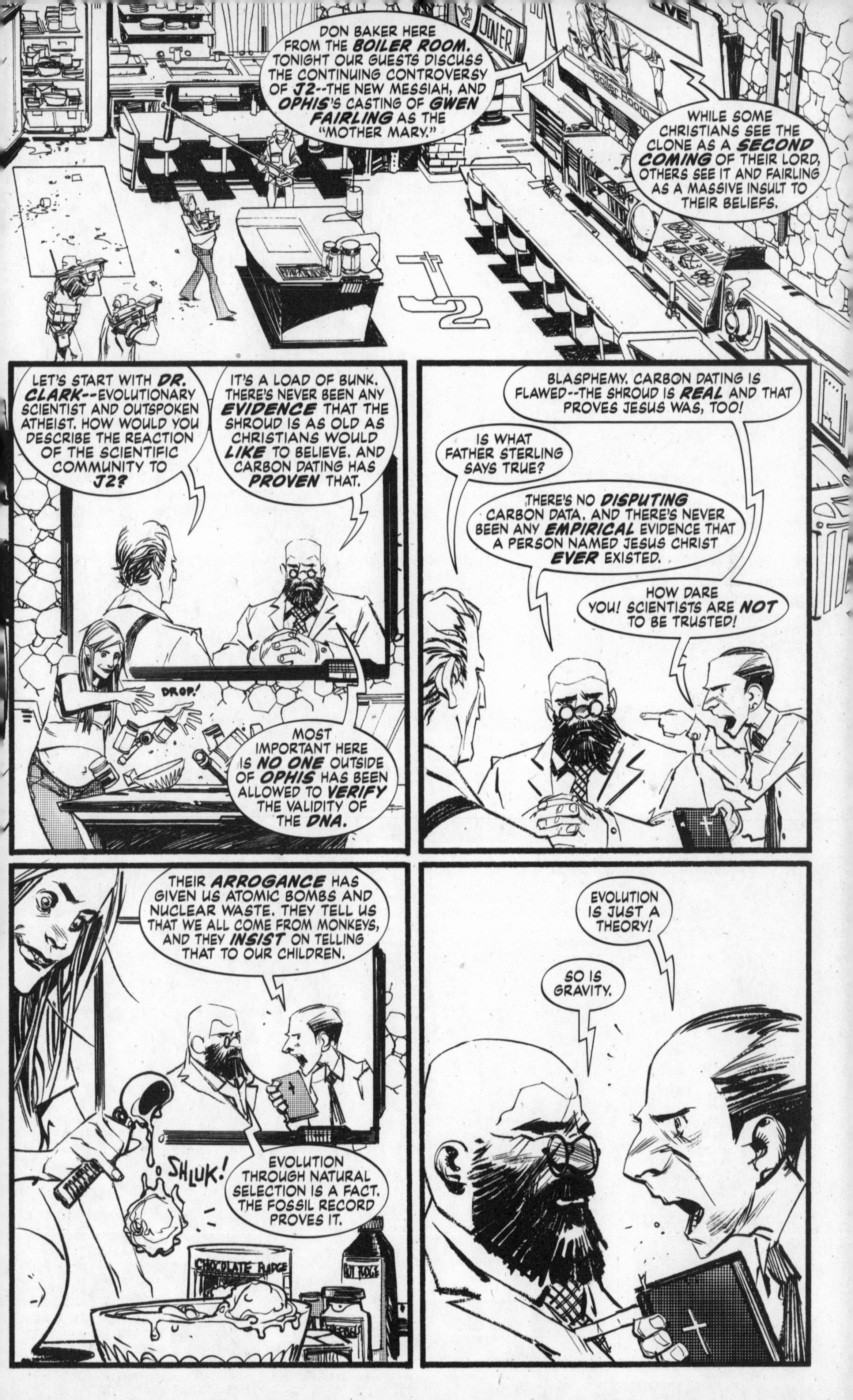

DON BAKER HERE FROM THE BOILER ROOM. TONIGHT OUR GUESTS DISCUSS THE CONTINUING CONTROVERSY OF J2--THE NEW MESSIAH, AND OPHIS'S CASTING OF GWEN FAIRLING AS THE "MOTHER MARY."
WHILE SOME CHRISTIANS SEE THE CLONE AS A SECOND COMING OF THEIR LORD, OTHERS SEE IT AND FAIRLING AS A MASSIVE INSULT TO THEIR BELIEFS.
DINER
J2
LET'S START WITH DR. CLARK--EVOLUTIONARY SCIENTIST AND OUTSPOKEN ATHEIST. HOW WOULD YOU DESCRIBE THE REACTION OF THE SCIENTIFIC COMMUNITY TO J2?
IT'S A LOAD OF BUNK. THERE'S NEVER BEEN ANY EVIDENCE THAT THE SHROUD IS AS OLD AS CHRISTIANS WOULD LIKE TO BELIEVE. AND CARBON DATING HAS PROVEN THAT.
DROP!
MOST IMPORTANT HERE IS NO ONE OUTSIDE OF OPHIS HAS BEEN ALLOWED TO VERIFY THE VALIDITY OF THE DNA.
BLASPHEMY. CARBON DATING IS FLAWED--THE SHROUD IS REAL AND THAT PROVES JESUS WAS, TOO!
IS WHAT FATHER STERLING SAYS TRUE?
THERE'S NO DISPUTING CARBON DATA. AND THERE'S NEVER BEEN ANY EMPIRICAL EVIDENCE THAT A PERSON NAMED JESUS CHRIST EVER EXISTED.
HOW DARE YOU! SCIENTISTS ARE NOT TO BE TRUSTED!
THEIR ARROGANCE HAS GIVEN US ATOMIC BOMBS AND NUCLEAR WASTE. THEY TELL US THAT WE ALL COME FROM MONKEYS, AND THEY INSIST ON TELLING THAT TO OUR CHILDREN.
SHLUK!
EVOLUTION THROUGH NATURAL SELECTION IS A FACT. THE FOSSIL RECORD PROVES IT.
CHOCOLATE FUDGE
HOT FUDGE
EVOLUTION IS JUST A THEORY!
SO IS GRAVITY.

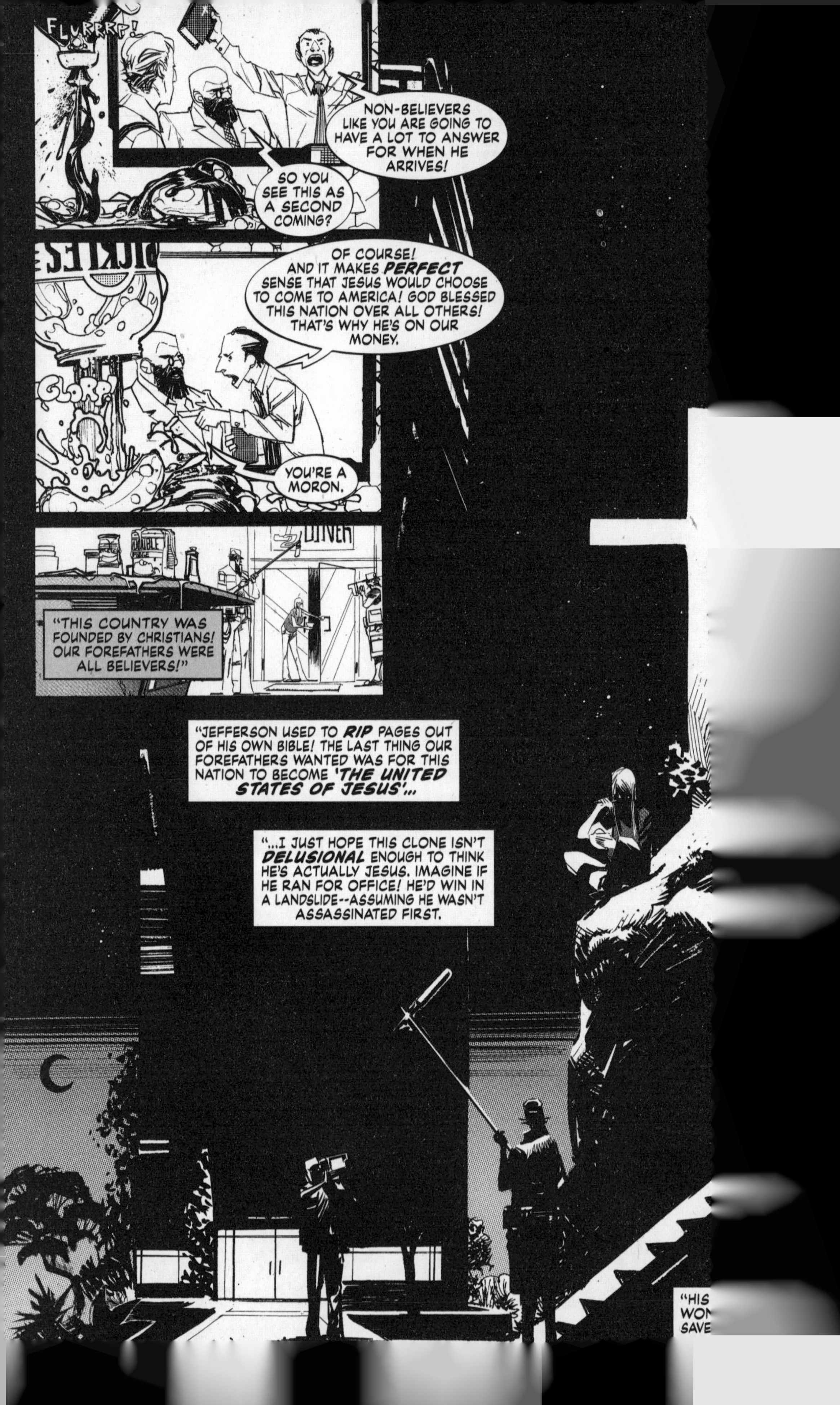
FLURRRP!
NON-BELIEVERS LIKE YOU ARE GOING TO HAVE A LOT TO ANSWER FOR WHEN HE ARRIVES!
SO YOU SEE THIS AS A SECOND COMING?
OF COURSE! AND IT MAKES PERFECT SENSE THAT JESUS WOULD CHOOSE TO COME TO AMERICA! GOD BLESSED THIS NATION OVER ALL OTHERS! THAT'S WHY HE'S ON OUR MONEY.
GLORP
YOU'RE A MORON.
DINER
"THIS COUNTRY WAS FOUNDED BY CHRISTIANS! OUR FOREFATHERS WERE ALL BELIEVERS!"
"JEFFERSON USED TO RIP PAGES OUT OF HIS OWN BIBLE! THE LAST THING OUR FOREFATHERS WANTED WAS FOR THIS NATION TO BECOME 'THE UNITED STATES OF JESUS'...
"...I JUST HOPE THIS CLONE ISN'T DELUSIONAL ENOUGH TO THINK HE'S ACTUALLY JESUS. IMAGINE IF HE RAN FOR OFFICE! HE'D WIN IN A LANDSLIDE--ASSUMING HE WASN'T ASSASSINATED FIRST.
"HIS
WON
SAVE

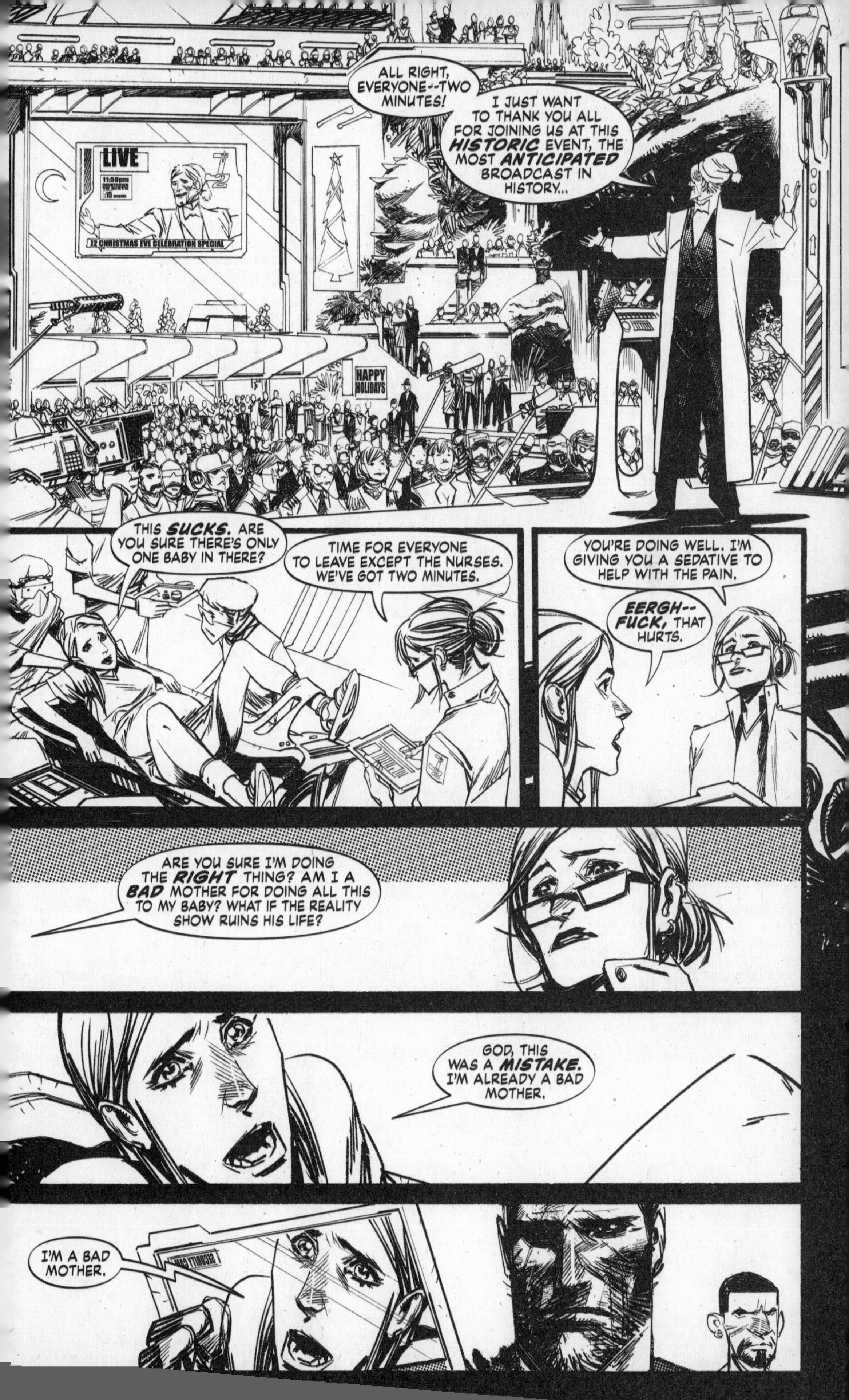

LIVE
J2 CHRISTMAS EVE CELEBRATION SPECIAL
HAPPY HOLIDAYS
ALL RIGHT, EVERYONE--TWO MINUTES!
I JUST WANT TO THANK YOU ALL FOR JOINING US AT THIS HISTORIC EVENT, THE MOST ANTICIPATED BROADCAST IN HISTORY...
THIS SUCKS. ARE YOU SURE THERE'S ONLY ONE BABY IN THERE?
TIME FOR EVERYONE TO LEAVE EXCEPT THE NURSES. WE'VE GOT TWO MINUTES.
YOU'RE DOING WELL. I'M GIVING YOU A SEDATIVE TO HELP WITH THE PAIN.
EERGH-- FUCK, THAT HURTS.
ARE YOU SURE I'M DOING THE RIGHT THING? AM I A BAD MOTHER FOR DOING ALL THIS TO MY BABY? WHAT IF THE REALITY SHOW RUINS HIS LIFE?
GOD, THIS WAS A MISTAKE. I'M ALREADY A BAD MOTHER.
I'M A BAD MOTHER.

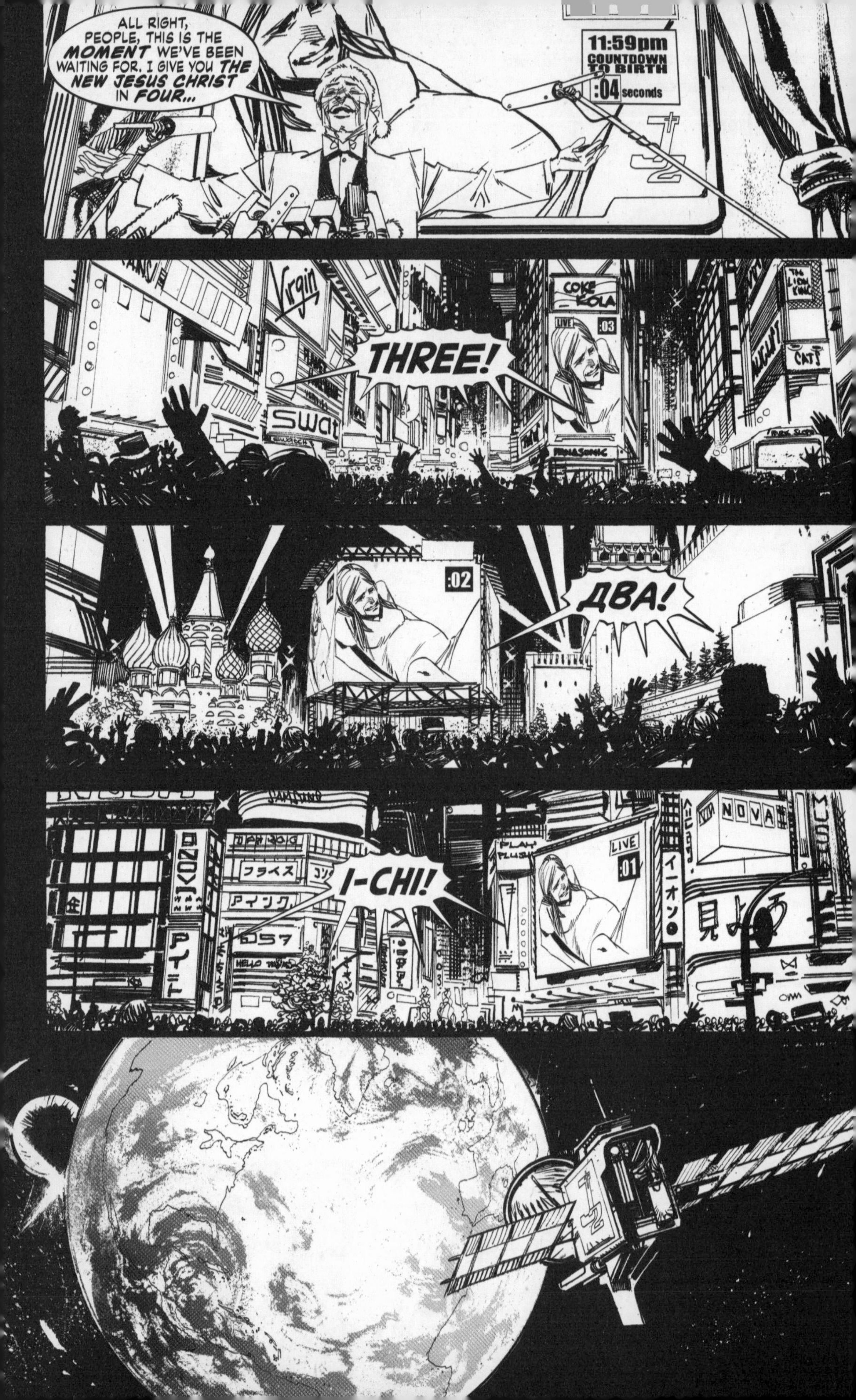

ALL RIGHT, PEOPLE, THIS IS THE MOMENT WE'VE BEEN WAITING FOR. I GIVE YOU THE NEW JESUS CHRIST IN FOUR...
11:59pm
COUNTDOWN TO BIRTH
:04 seconds
Virgin
COKE KOLA
LIVE :03
THREE!
SWAT
PANASONIC
THE LION KING
CATS
:02
ДВА!
NOVA
LIVE :01
I-CHI!
イーオン

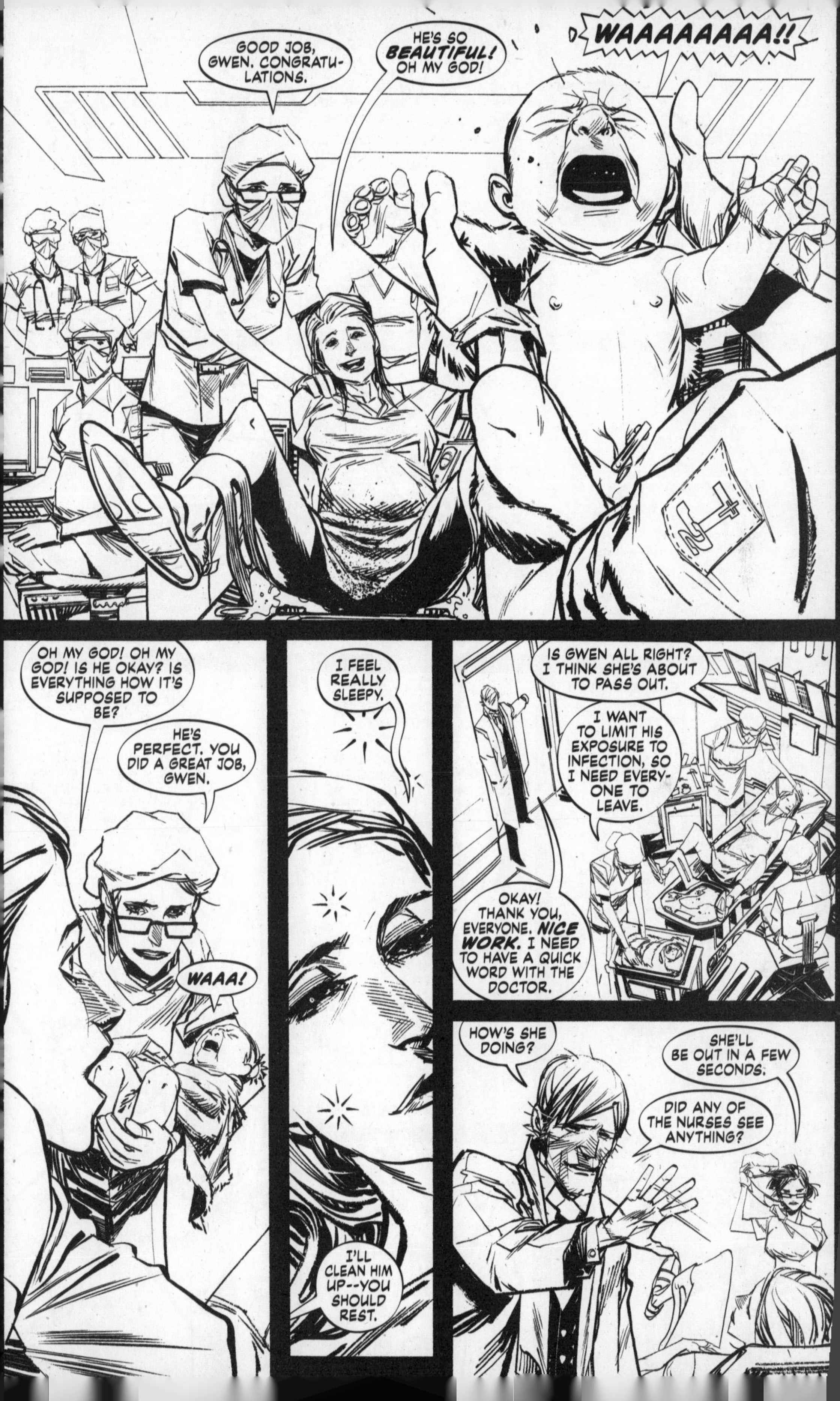
GOOD JOB, GWEN. CONGRATU-LATIONS.
HE'S SO BEAUTIFUL! OH MY GOD!
WAAAAAAAA!!
OH MY GOD! OH MY GOD! IS HE OKAY? IS EVERYTHING HOW IT'S SUPPOSED TO BE?
HE'S PERFECT. YOU DID A GREAT JOB, GWEN.
WAAA!
I FEEL REALLY SLEEPY.
I'LL CLEAN HIM UP--YOU SHOULD REST.
IS GWEN ALL RIGHT? I THINK SHE'S ABOUT TO PASS OUT.
I WANT TO LIMIT HIS EXPOSURE TO INFECTION, SO I NEED EVERY-ONE TO LEAVE.
OKAY! THANK YOU, EVERYONE. NICE WORK. I NEED TO HAVE A QUICK WORD WITH THE DOCTOR.
HOW'S SHE DOING?
SHE'LL BE OUT IN A FEW SECONDS.
DID ANY OF THE NURSES SEE ANYTHING?

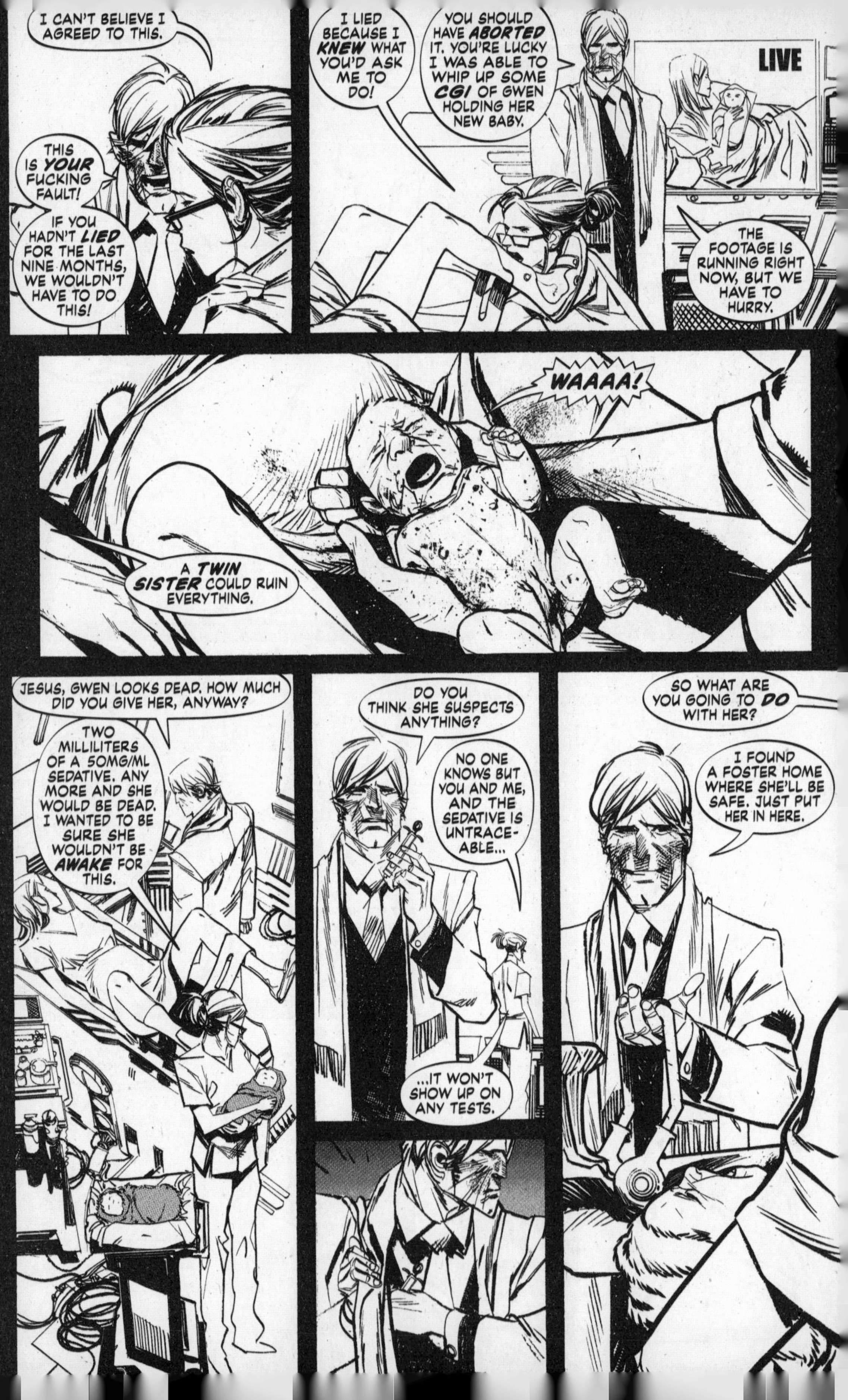
I CAN'T BELIEVE I AGREED TO THIS.
THIS IS YOUR FUCKING FAULT!
IF YOU HADN'T LIED FOR THE LAST NINE MONTHS, WE WOULDN'T HAVE TO DO THIS!
I LIED BECAUSE I KNEW WHAT YOU'D ASK ME TO DO!
YOU SHOULD HAVE ABORTED IT. YOU'RE LUCKY I WAS ABLE TO WHIP UP SOME CGI OF GWEN HOLDING HER NEW BABY.
LIVE
THE FOOTAGE IS RUNNING RIGHT NOW, BUT WE HAVE TO HURRY.
WAAAA!
A TWIN SISTER COULD RUIN EVERYTHING.
JESUS, GWEN LOOKS DEAD. HOW MUCH DID YOU GIVE HER, ANYWAY?
TWO MILLILITERS OF A 50MG/ML SEDATIVE. ANY MORE AND SHE WOULD BE DEAD. I WANTED TO BE SURE SHE WOULDN'T BE AWAKE FOR THIS.
DO YOU THINK SHE SUSPECTS ANYTHING?
NO ONE KNOWS BUT YOU AND ME, AND THE SEDATIVE IS UNTRACE-ABLE...
...IT WON'T SHOW UP ON ANY TESTS.
SO WHAT ARE YOU GOING TO DO WITH HER?
I FOUND A FOSTER HOME WHERE SHE'LL BE SAFE. JUST PUT HER IN HERE.

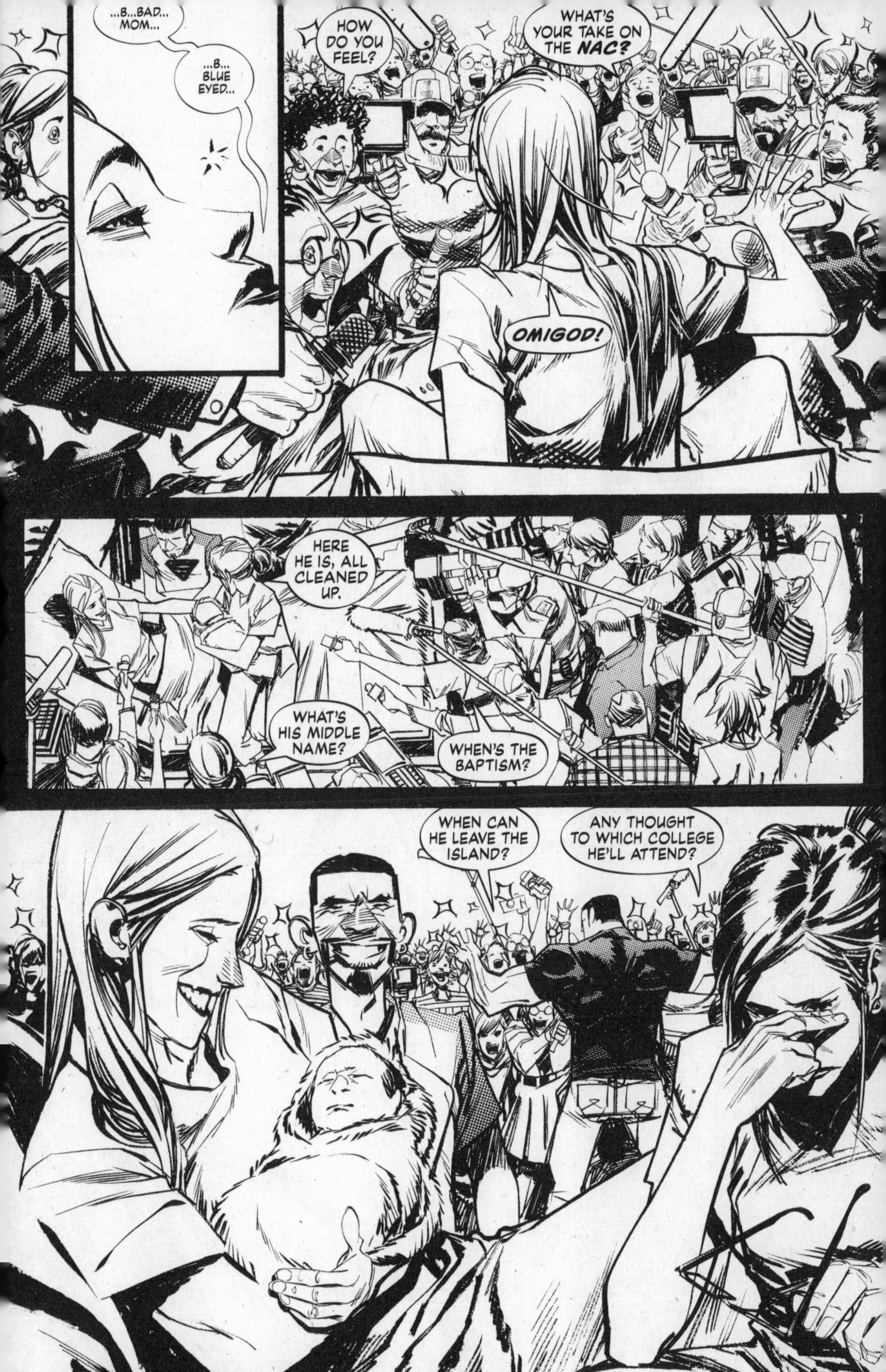
...B...BAD... MOM...
...B... BLUE EYED...
HOW DO YOU FEEL?
WHAT'S YOUR TAKE ON THE NAC?
OMIGOD!
HERE HE IS, ALL CLEANED UP.
WHAT'S HIS MIDDLE NAME?
WHEN'S THE BAPTISM?
WHEN CAN HE LEAVE THE ISLAND?
ANY THOUGHT TO WHICH COLLEGE HE'LL ATTEND?

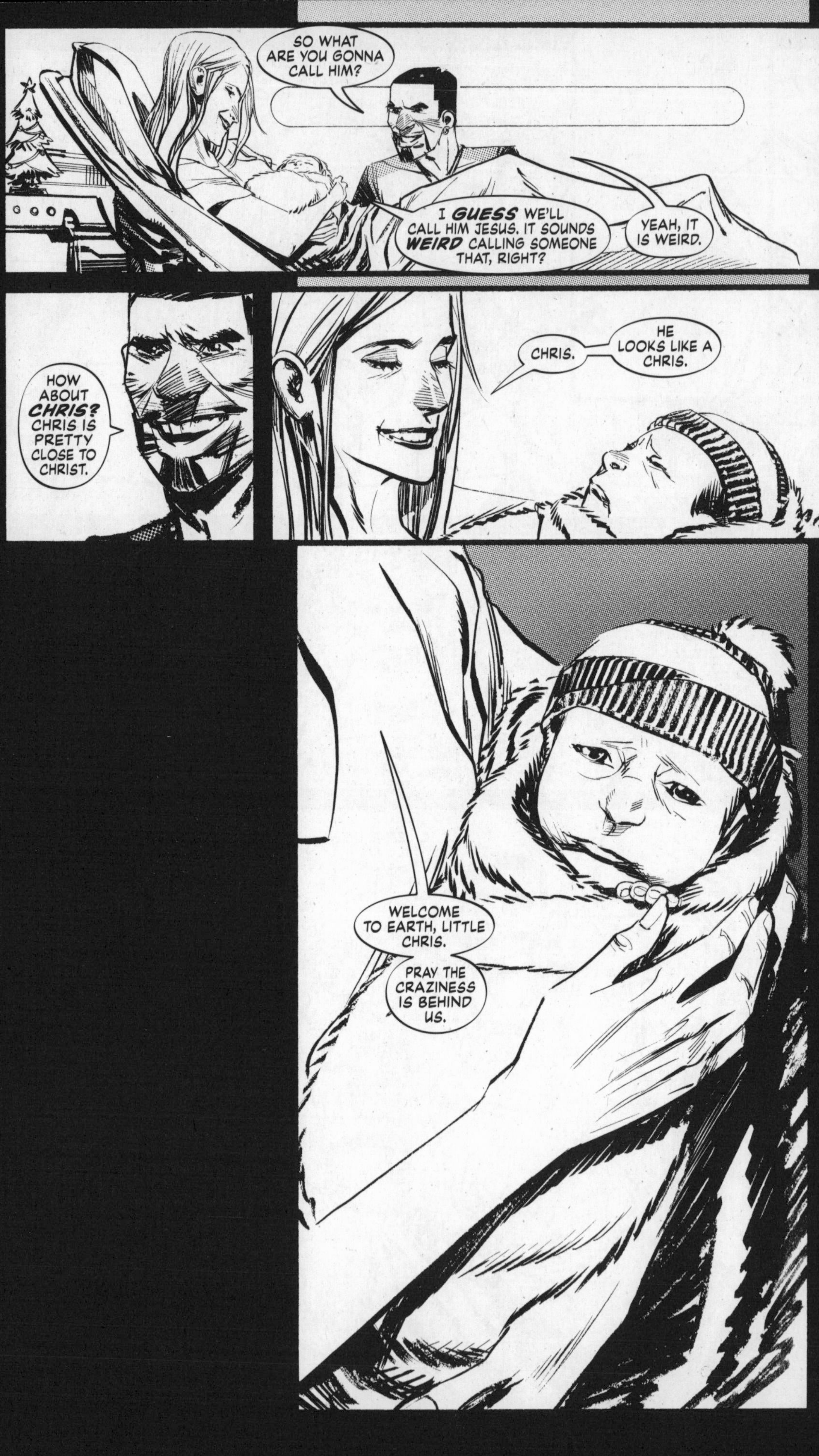
SO WHAT ARE YOU GONNA CALL HIM?
I GUESS WE'LL CALL HIM JESUS. IT SOUNDS WEIRD CALLING SOMEONE THAT, RIGHT?
YEAH, IT IS WEIRD.
HOW ABOUT CHRIS? CHRIS IS PRETTY CLOSE TO CHRIST.
CHRIS.
HE LOOKS LIKE A CHRIS.
WELCOME TO EARTH, LITTLE CHRIS.
PRAY THE CRAZINESS IS BEHIND US.

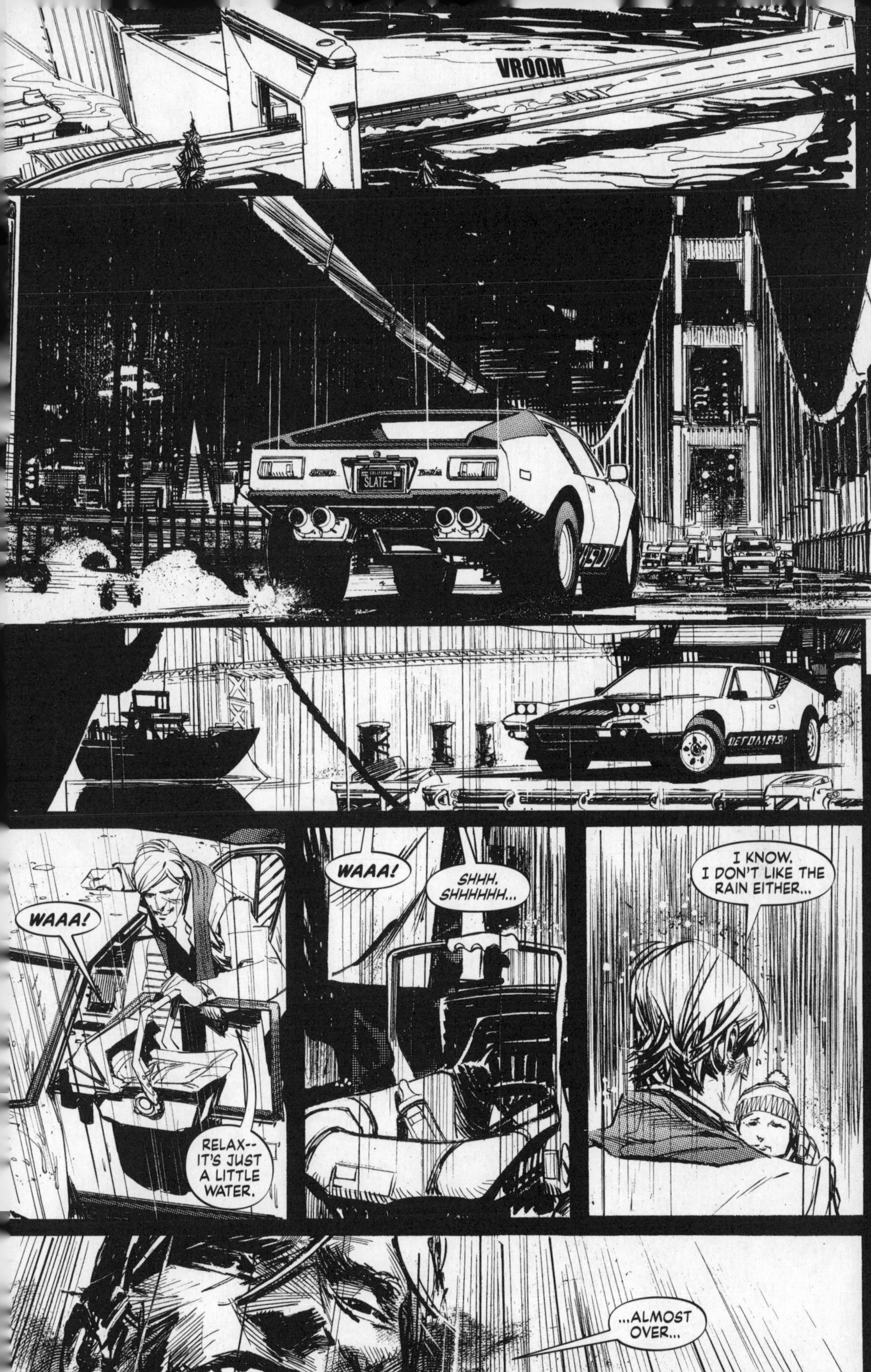
VROOM
CALIFORNIA
SLATE-T
WAAA!
RELAX-- IT'S JUST A LITTLE WATER.
WAAA!
SHHH. SHHHHHH...
I KNOW. I DON'T LIKE THE RAIN EITHER...
...ALMOST OVER...

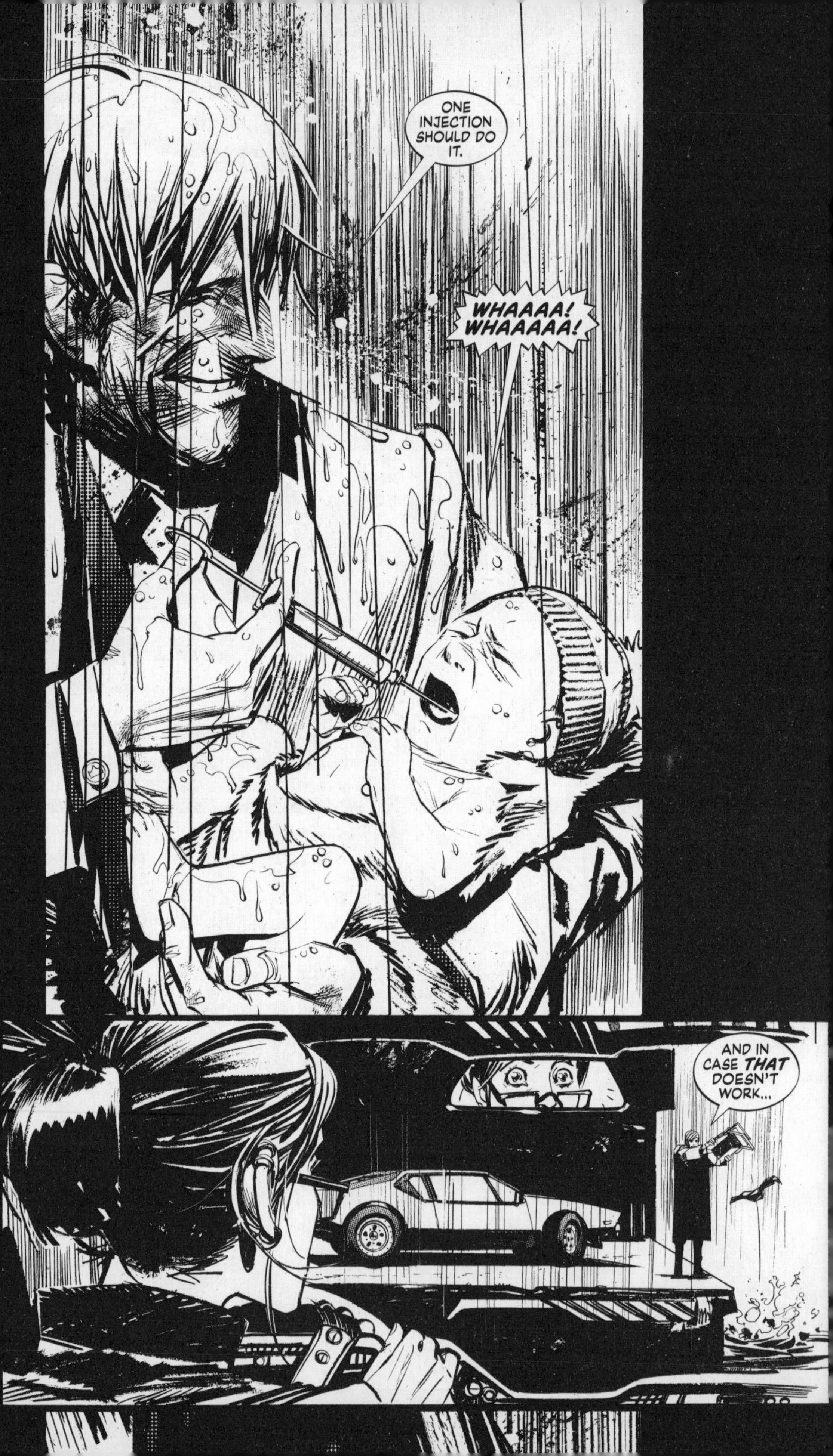
ONE INJECTION SHOULD DO IT.
WHAAAA! WHAAAAA!
AND IN CASE THAT DOESN'T WORK...

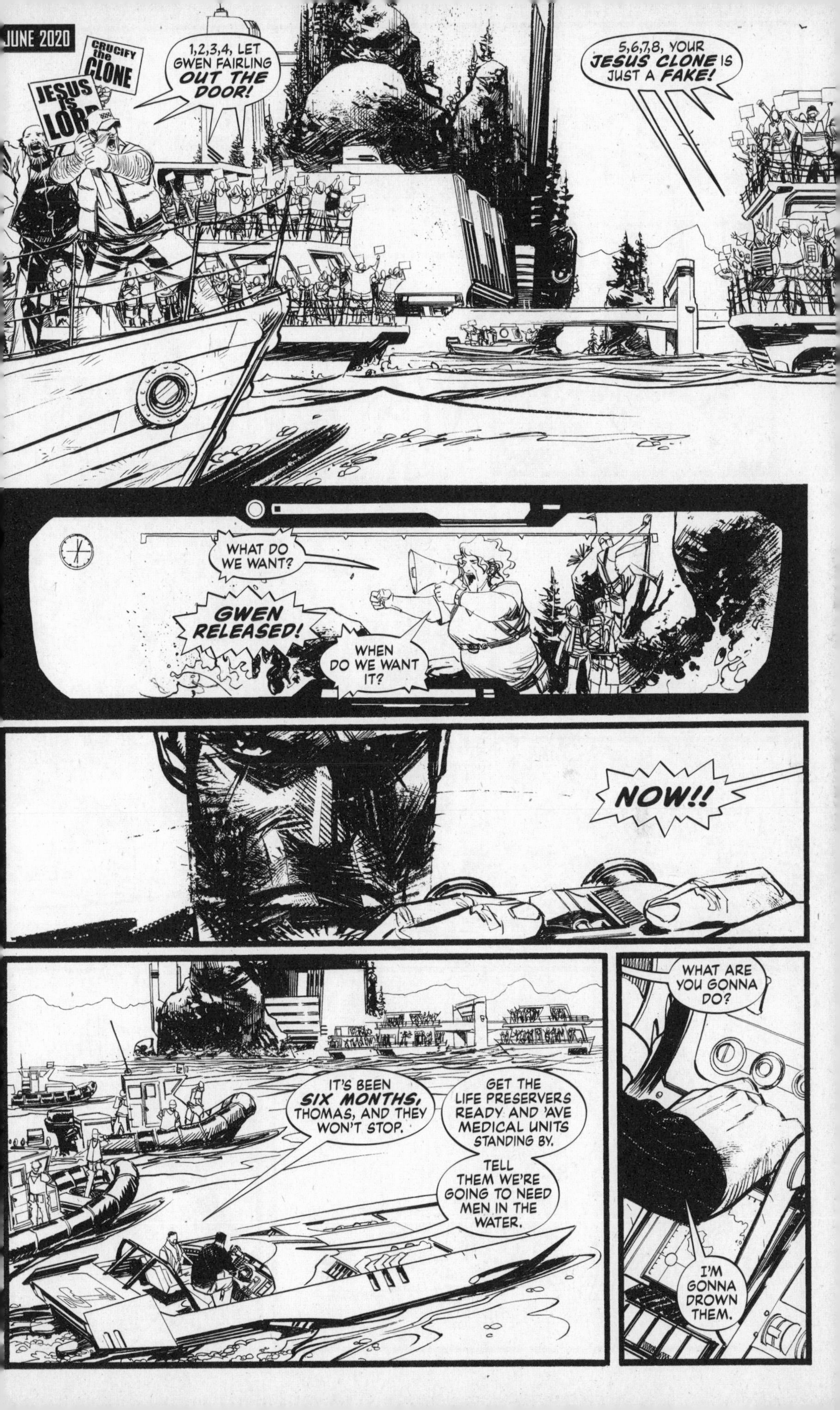
JUNE 2020
CRUCIFY the CLONE
JESUS IS LORD
1,2,3,4, LET GWEN FAIRLING OUT THE DOOR!
5,6,7,8, YOUR JESUS CLONE IS JUST A FAKE!
WHAT DO WE WANT?
GWEN RELEASED!
WHEN DO WE WANT IT?
NOW!!
IT'S BEEN SIX MONTHS, THOMAS, AND THEY WON'T STOP.
GET THE LIFE PRESERVERS READY AND 'AVE MEDICAL UNITS STANDING BY.
TELL THEM WE'RE GOING TO NEED MEN IN THE WATER.
WHAT ARE YOU GONNA DO?
I'M GONNA DROWN THEM.

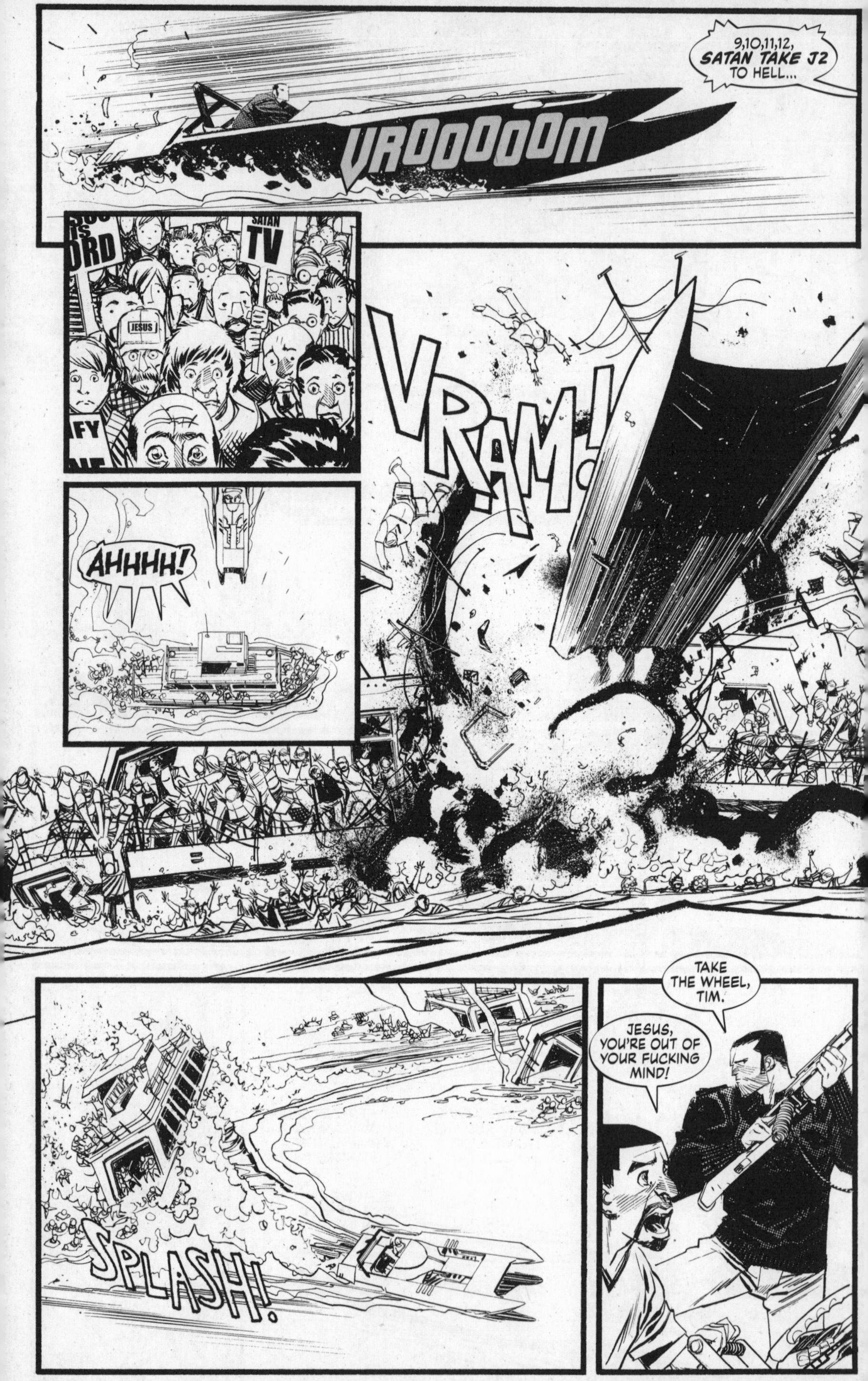
9,10,11,12,
SATAN TAKE J2
TO HELL...
VROOOOOOM
SATAN
TV
JESUS
AHHHH!
VRAM!
SPLASH!
TAKE
THE WHEEL,
TIM.
JESUS,
YOU'RE OUT OF
YOUR FUCKING
MIND!

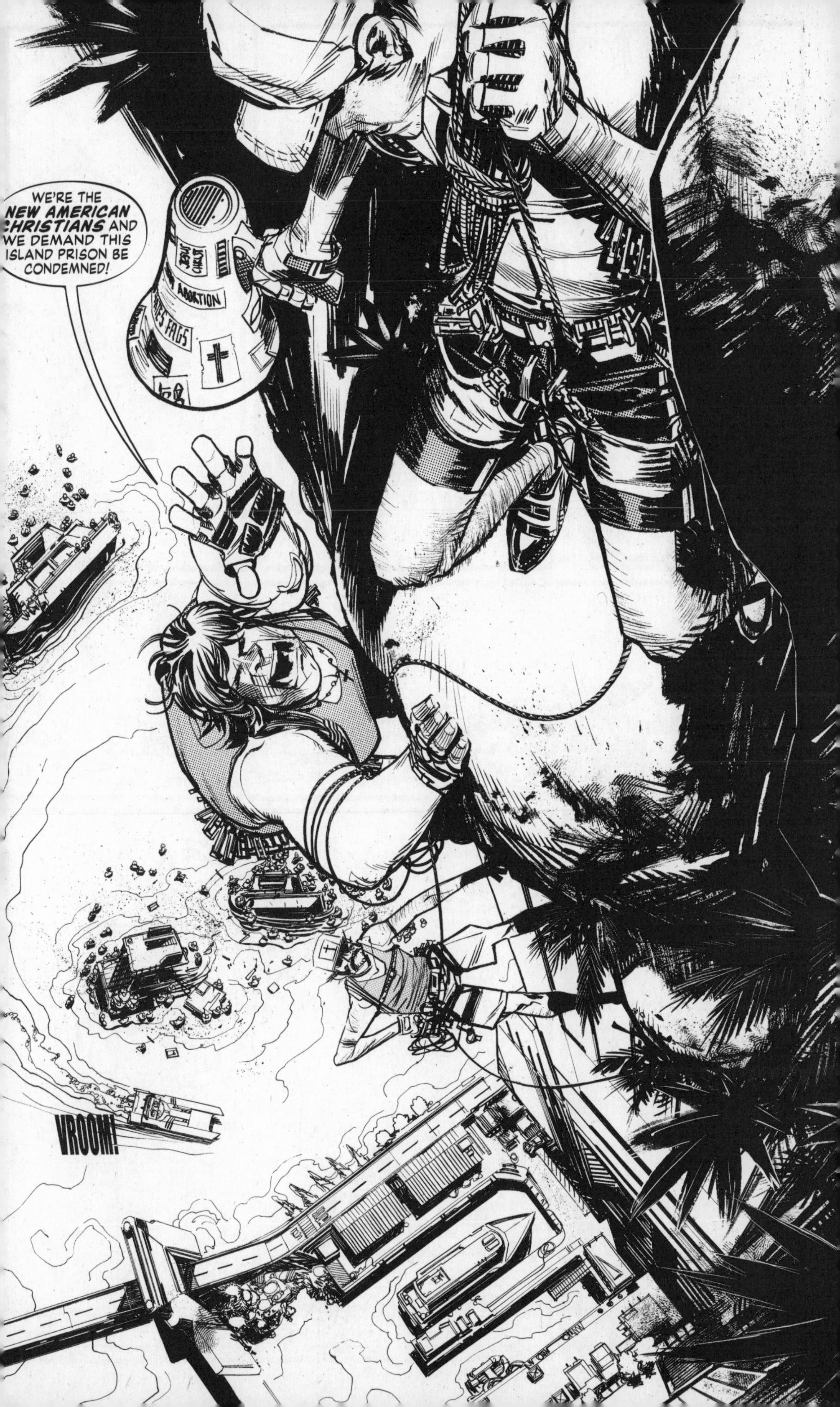
WE'RE THE NEW AMERICAN CHRISTIANS AND WE DEMAND THIS ISLAND PRISON BE CONDEMNED!
VROOM!

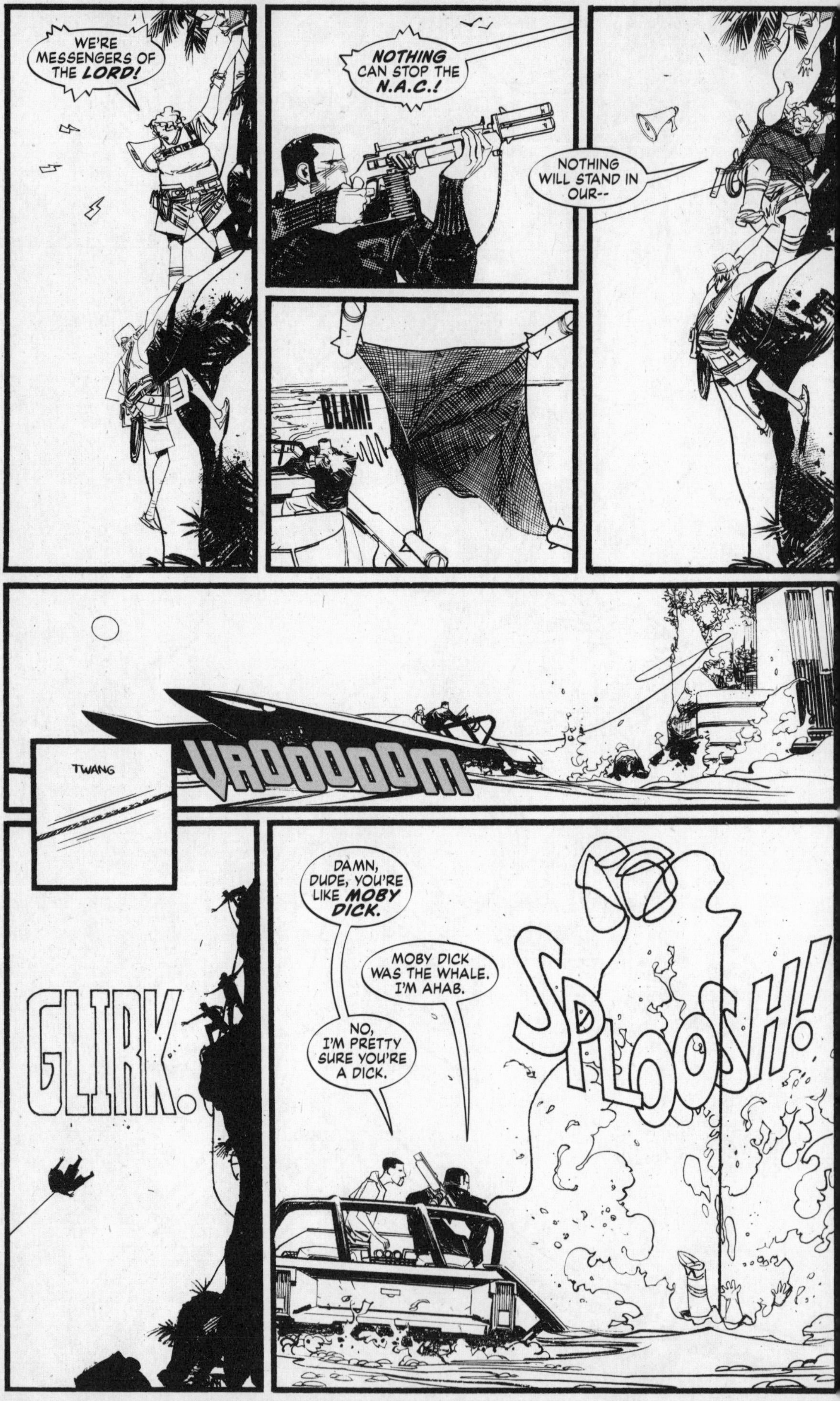

WE'RE MESSENGERS OF THE LORD!
NOTHING CAN STOP THE N.A.C.!
BLAM!
NOTHING WILL STAND IN OUR--
VROOOOOOM
TWANG
GLIRK.
DAMN, DUDE, YOU'RE LIKE MOBY DICK.
MOBY DICK WAS THE WHALE. I'M AHAB.
NO, I'M PRETTY SURE YOU'RE A DICK.
SPLOOSH!

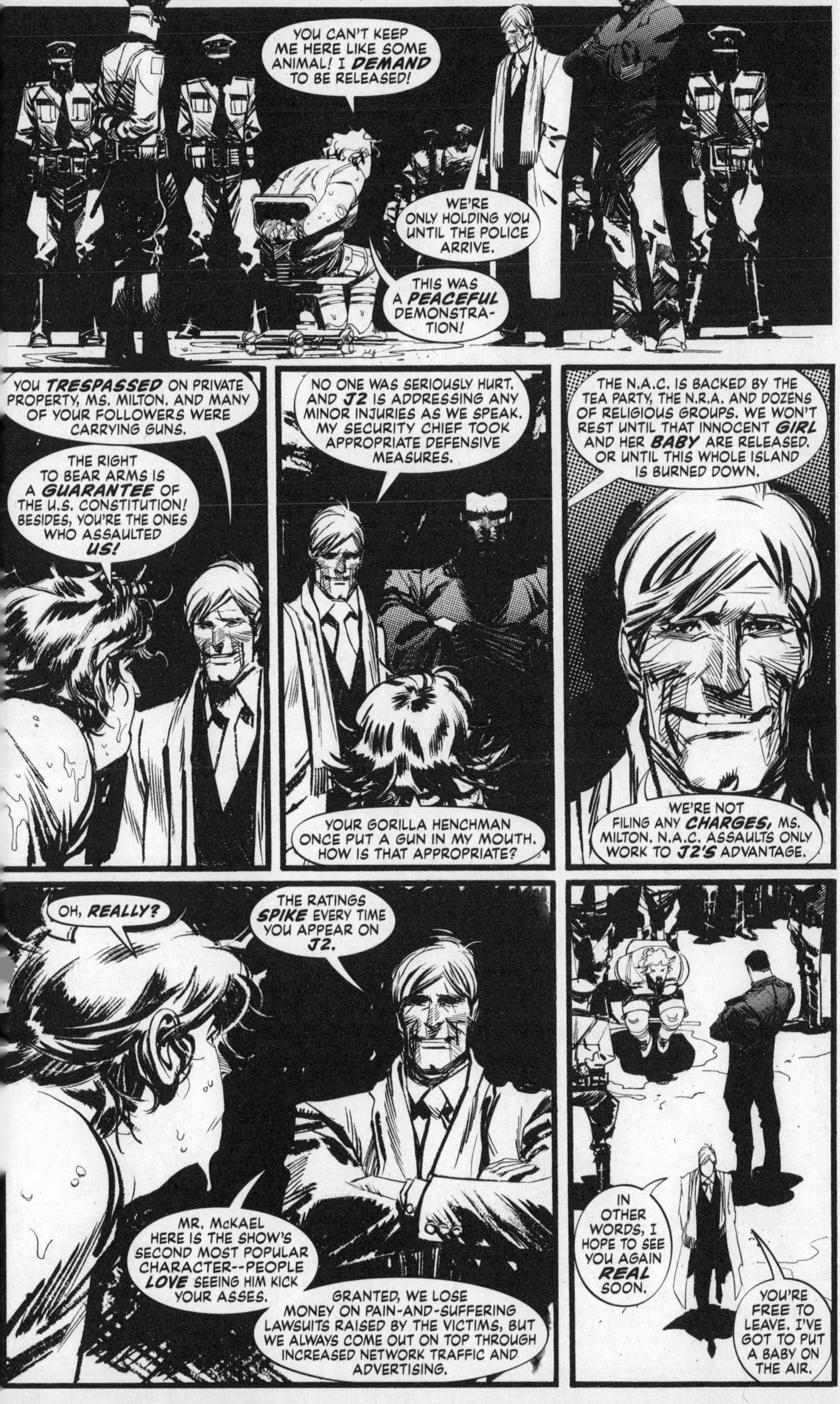

YOU CAN'T KEEP ME HERE LIKE SOME ANIMAL! I DEMAND TO BE RELEASED!
WE'RE ONLY HOLDING YOU UNTIL THE POLICE ARRIVE.
THIS WAS A PEACEFUL DEMONSTRATION!
YOU TRESPASSED ON PRIVATE PROPERTY, MS. MILTON. AND MANY OF YOUR FOLLOWERS WERE CARRYING GUNS.
THE RIGHT TO BEAR ARMS IS A GUARANTEE OF THE U.S. CONSTITUTION! BESIDES, YOU'RE THE ONES WHO ASSAULTED US!
NO ONE WAS SERIOUSLY HURT. AND J2 IS ADDRESSING ANY MINOR INJURIES AS WE SPEAK. MY SECURITY CHIEF TOOK APPROPRIATE DEFENSIVE MEASURES.
YOUR GORILLA HENCHMAN ONCE PUT A GUN IN MY MOUTH. HOW IS THAT APPROPRIATE?
THE N.A.C. IS BACKED BY THE TEA PARTY, THE N.R.A. AND DOZENS OF RELIGIOUS GROUPS. WE WON'T REST UNTIL THAT INNOCENT GIRL AND HER BABY ARE RELEASED. OR UNTIL THIS WHOLE ISLAND IS BURNED DOWN.
WE'RE NOT FILING ANY CHARGES, MS. MILTON. N.A.C. ASSAULTS ONLY WORK TO J2'S ADVANTAGE.
OH, REALLY?
THE RATINGS SPIKE EVERY TIME YOU APPEAR ON J2.
MR. McKAEL HERE IS THE SHOW'S SECOND MOST POPULAR CHARACTER--PEOPLE LOVE SEEING HIM KICK YOUR ASSES.
GRANTED, WE LOSE MONEY ON PAIN-AND-SUFFERING LAWSUITS RAISED BY THE VICTIMS, BUT WE ALWAYS COME OUT ON TOP THROUGH INCREASED NETWORK TRAFFIC AND ADVERTISING.
IN OTHER WORDS, I HOPE TO SEE YOU AGAIN REAL SOON.
YOU'RE FREE TO LEAVE. I'VE GOT TO PUT A BABY ON THE AIR.

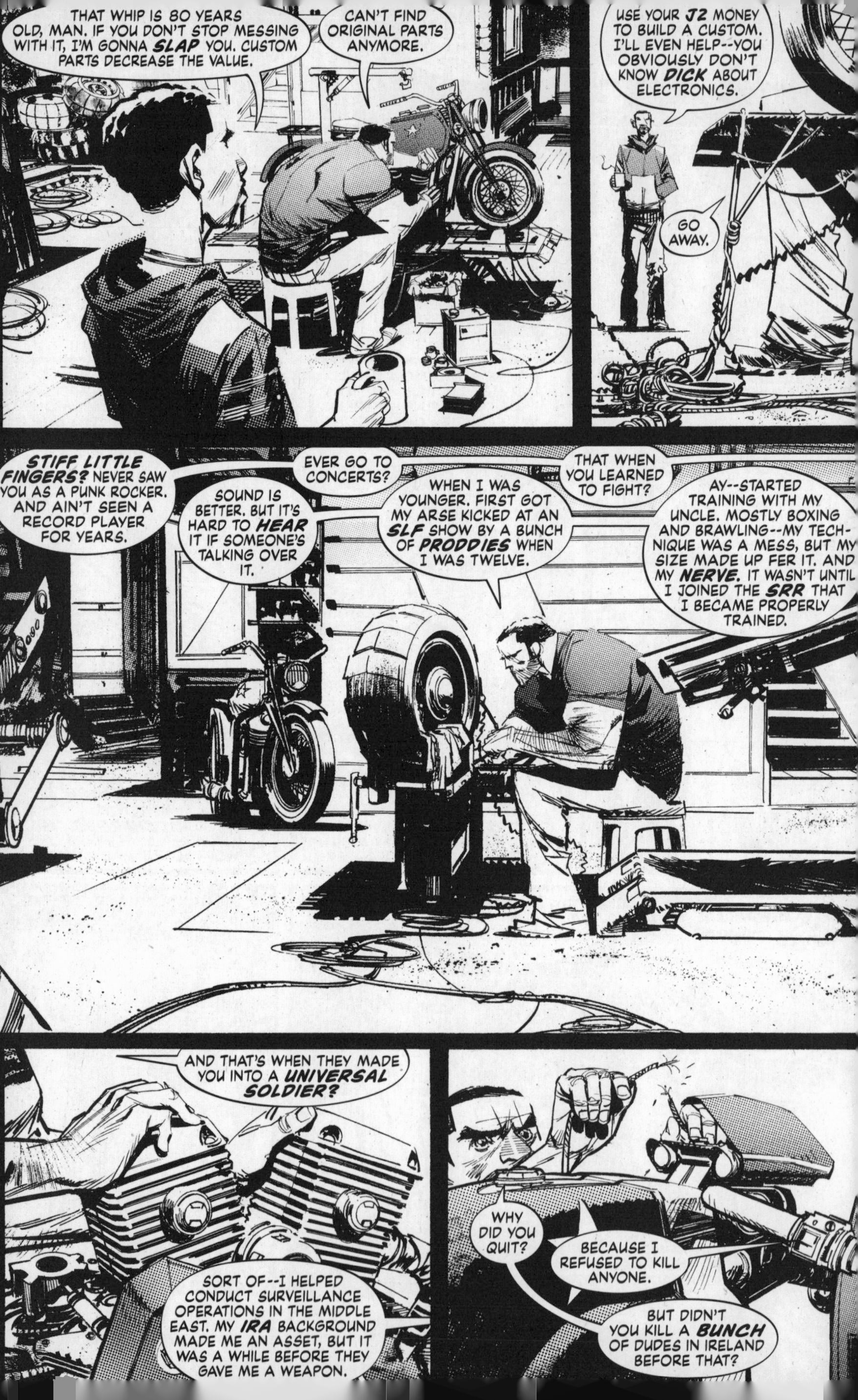

THAT WHIP IS 80 YEARS OLD, MAN. IF YOU DON'T STOP MESSING WITH IT, I'M GONNA SLAP YOU. CUSTOM PARTS DECREASE THE VALUE.
CAN'T FIND ORIGINAL PARTS ANYMORE.
USE YOUR J2 MONEY TO BUILD A CUSTOM. I'LL EVEN HELP--YOU OBVIOUSLY DON'T KNOW DICK ABOUT ELECTRONICS.
GO AWAY.
STIFF LITTLE FINGERS? NEVER SAW YOU AS A PUNK ROCKER. AND AIN'T SEEN A RECORD PLAYER FOR YEARS.
SOUND IS BETTER. BUT IT'S HARD TO HEAR IT IF SOMEONE'S TALKING OVER IT.
EVER GO TO CONCERTS?
WHEN I WAS YOUNGER. FIRST GOT MY ARSE KICKED AT AN SLF SHOW BY A BUNCH OF PRODDIES WHEN I WAS TWELVE.
THAT WHEN YOU LEARNED TO FIGHT?
AY--STARTED TRAINING WITH MY UNCLE. MOSTLY BOXING AND BRAWLING--MY TECHNIQUE WAS A MESS, BUT MY SIZE MADE UP FER IT. AND MY NERVE. IT WASN'T UNTIL I JOINED THE SRR THAT I BECAME PROPERLY TRAINED.
AND THAT'S WHEN THEY MADE YOU INTO A UNIVERSAL SOLDIER?
SORT OF--I HELPED CONDUCT SURVEILLANCE OPERATIONS IN THE MIDDLE EAST. MY IRA BACKGROUND MADE ME AN ASSET, BUT IT WAS A WHILE BEFORE THEY GAVE ME A WEAPON.
WHY DID YOU QUIT?
BECAUSE I REFUSED TO KILL ANYONE.
BUT DIDN'T YOU KILL A BUNCH OF DUDES IN IRELAND BEFORE THAT?

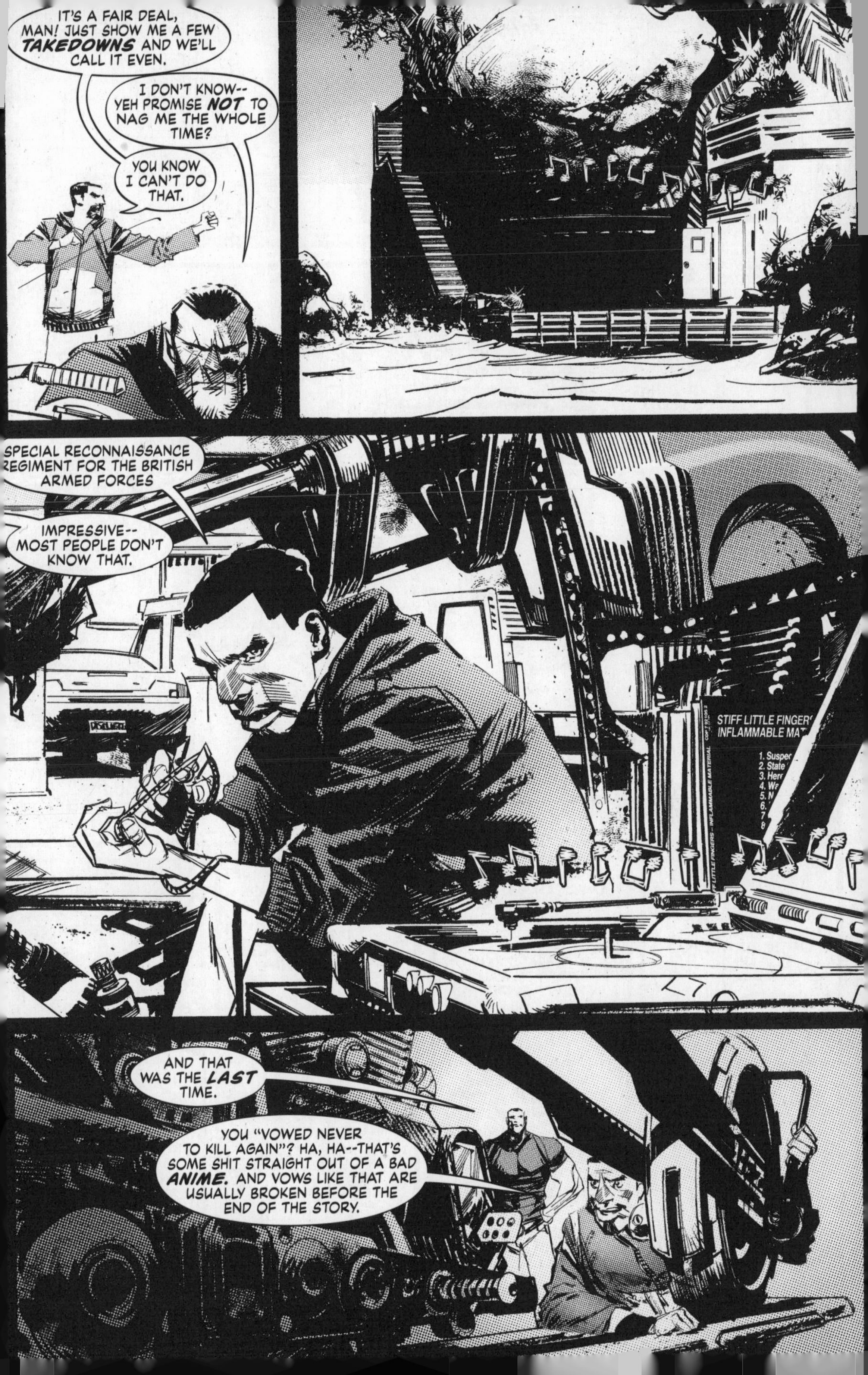
IT'S A FAIR DEAL, MAN! JUST SHOW ME A FEW TAKEDOWNS AND WE'LL CALL IT EVEN.
I DON'T KNOW-- YEH PROMISE NOT TO NAG ME THE WHOLE TIME?
YOU KNOW I CAN'T DO THAT.
SPECIAL RECONNAISSANCE REGIMENT FOR THE BRITISH ARMED FORCES
IMPRESSIVE-- MOST PEOPLE DON'T KNOW THAT.
AND THAT WAS THE LAST TIME.
YOU "VOWED NEVER TO KILL AGAIN"? HA, HA--THAT'S SOME SHIT STRAIGHT OUT OF A BAD ANIME. AND VOWS LIKE THAT ARE USUALLY BROKEN BEFORE THE END OF THE STORY.

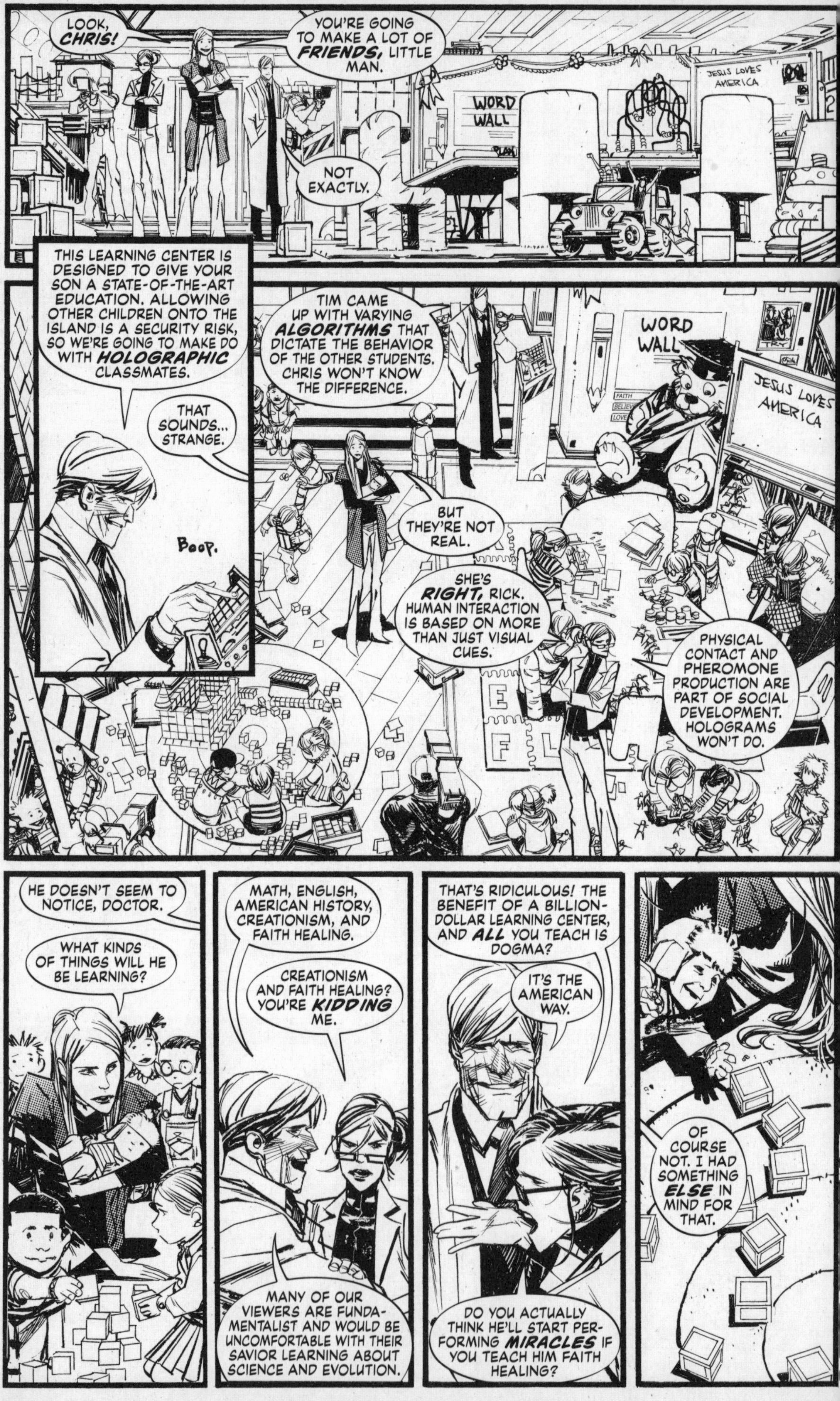
LOOK, CHRIS!
YOU'RE GOING TO MAKE A LOT OF FRIENDS, LITTLE MAN.
NOT EXACTLY.
WORD WALL
JESUS LOVES AMERICA
THIS LEARNING CENTER IS DESIGNED TO GIVE YOUR SON A STATE-OF-THE-ART EDUCATION. ALLOWING OTHER CHILDREN ONTO THE ISLAND IS A SECURITY RISK, SO WE'RE GOING TO MAKE DO WITH HOLOGRAPHIC CLASSMATES.
TIM CAME UP WITH VARYING ALGORITHMS THAT DICTATE THE BEHAVIOR OF THE OTHER STUDENTS. CHRIS WON'T KNOW THE DIFFERENCE.
THAT SOUNDS... STRANGE.
BOOP.
WORD WALL
JESUS LOVES AMERICA
BUT THEY'RE NOT REAL.
SHE'S RIGHT, RICK. HUMAN INTERACTION IS BASED ON MORE THAN JUST VISUAL CUES.
PHYSICAL CONTACT AND PHEROMONE PRODUCTION ARE PART OF SOCIAL DEVELOPMENT. HOLOGRAMS WON'T DO.
HE DOESN'T SEEM TO NOTICE, DOCTOR.
WHAT KINDS OF THINGS WILL HE BE LEARNING?
MATH, ENGLISH, AMERICAN HISTORY, CREATIONISM, AND FAITH HEALING.
CREATIONISM AND FAITH HEALING? YOU'RE KIDDING ME.
MANY OF OUR VIEWERS ARE FUNDA-MENTALIST AND WOULD BE UNCOMFORTABLE WITH THEIR SAVIOR LEARNING ABOUT SCIENCE AND EVOLUTION.
THAT'S RIDICULOUS! THE BENEFIT OF A BILLION-DOLLAR LEARNING CENTER, AND ALL YOU TEACH IS DOGMA?
IT'S THE AMERICAN WAY.
DO YOU ACTUALLY THINK HE'LL START PER-FORMING MIRACLES IF YOU TEACH HIM FAITH HEALING?
OF COURSE NOT. I HAD SOMETHING ELSE IN MIND FOR THAT.

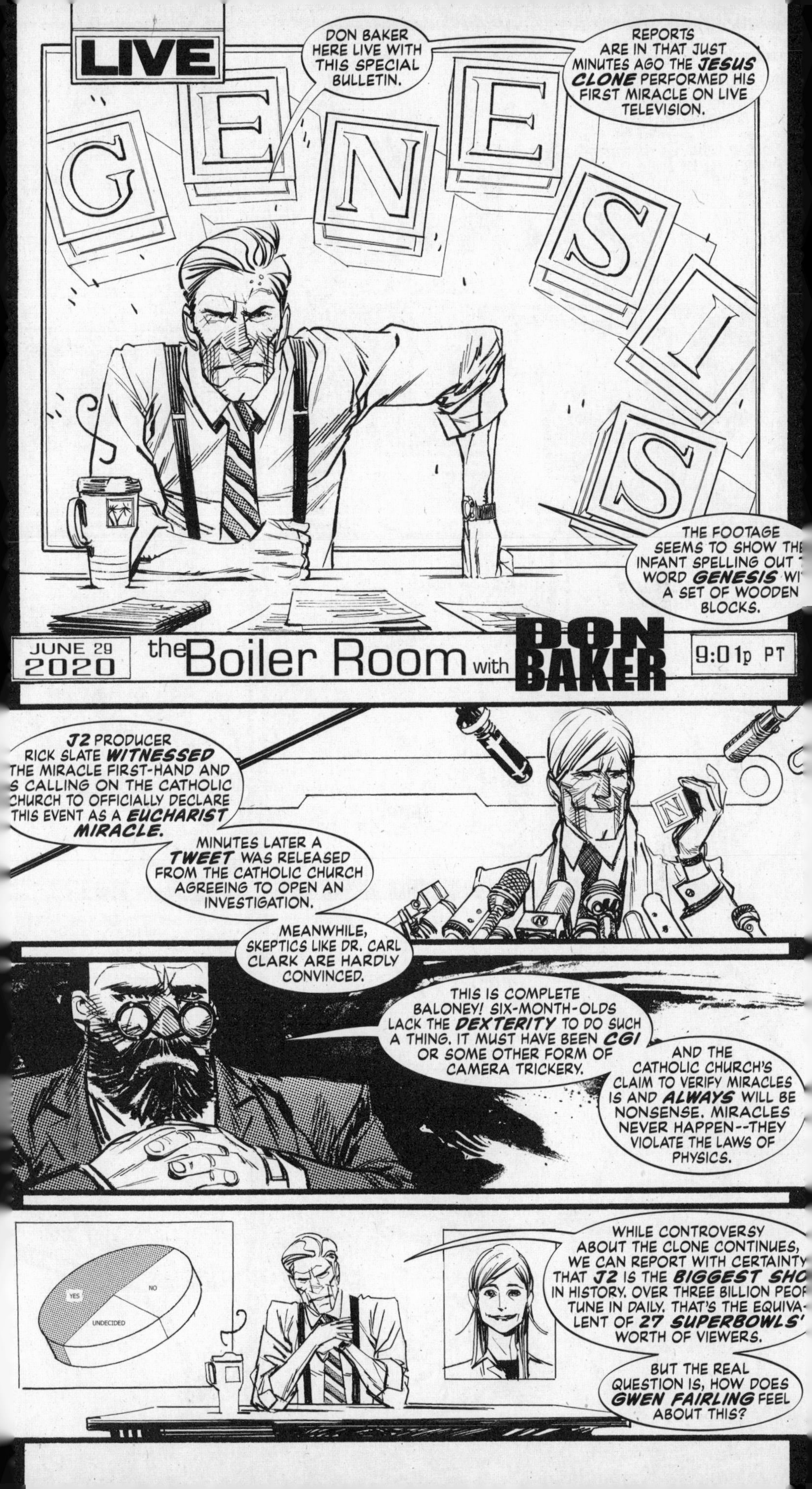
LIVE
DON BAKER HERE LIVE WITH THIS SPECIAL BULLETIN.
REPORTS ARE IN THAT JUST MINUTES AGO THE JESUS CLONE PERFORMED HIS FIRST MIRACLE ON LIVE TELEVISION.
GENESIS
THE FOOTAGE SEEMS TO SHOW THE INFANT SPELLING OUT THE WORD GENESIS WITH A SET OF WOODEN BLOCKS.
JUNE 29 2020
the Boiler Room with DON BAKER
9:01p PT
J2 PRODUCER RICK SLATE WITNESSED THE MIRACLE FIRST-HAND AND IS CALLING ON THE CATHOLIC CHURCH TO OFFICIALLY DECLARE THIS EVENT AS A EUCHARIST MIRACLE.
MINUTES LATER A TWEET WAS RELEASED FROM THE CATHOLIC CHURCH AGREEING TO OPEN AN INVESTIGATION.
MEANWHILE, SKEPTICS LIKE DR. CARL CLARK ARE HARDLY CONVINCED.
THIS IS COMPLETE BALONEY! SIX-MONTH-OLDS LACK THE DEXTERITY TO DO SUCH A THING. IT MUST HAVE BEEN CGI OR SOME OTHER FORM OF CAMERA TRICKERY.
AND THE CATHOLIC CHURCH'S CLAIM TO VERIFY MIRACLES IS AND ALWAYS WILL BE NONSENSE. MIRACLES NEVER HAPPEN--THEY VIOLATE THE LAWS OF PHYSICS.
YES
NO
UNDECIDED
WHILE CONTROVERSY ABOUT THE CLONE CONTINUES, WE CAN REPORT WITH CERTAINTY THAT J2 IS THE BIGGEST SHOW IN HISTORY. OVER THREE BILLION PEOPLE TUNE IN DAILY. THAT'S THE EQUIVALENT OF 27 SUPERBOWLS' WORTH OF VIEWERS.
BUT THE REAL QUESTION IS, HOW DOES GWEN FAIRLING FEEL ABOUT THIS?

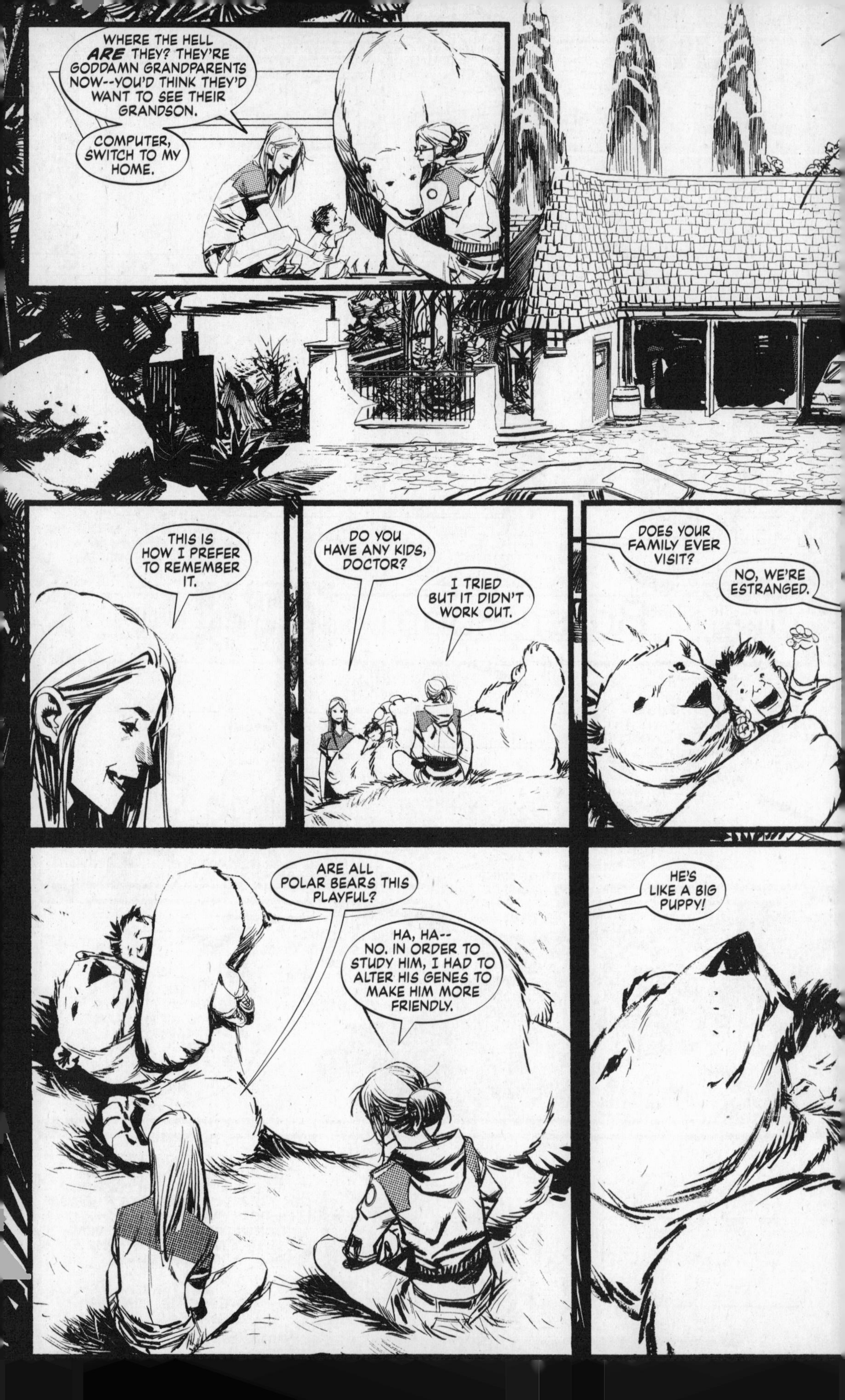
WHERE THE HELL *ARE* THEY? THEY'RE GODDAMN GRANDPARENTS NOW--YOU'D THINK THEY'D WANT TO SEE THEIR GRANDSON.
COMPUTER, SWITCH TO MY HOME.
THIS IS HOW I PREFER TO REMEMBER IT.
DO YOU HAVE ANY KIDS, DOCTOR?
I TRIED BUT IT DIDN'T WORK OUT.
DOES YOUR FAMILY EVER VISIT?
NO, WE'RE ESTRANGED.
ARE ALL POLAR BEARS THIS PLAYFUL?
HA, HA-- NO. IN ORDER TO STUDY HIM, I HAD TO ALTER HIS GENES TO MAKE HIM MORE FRIENDLY.
HE'S LIKE A BIG PUPPY!

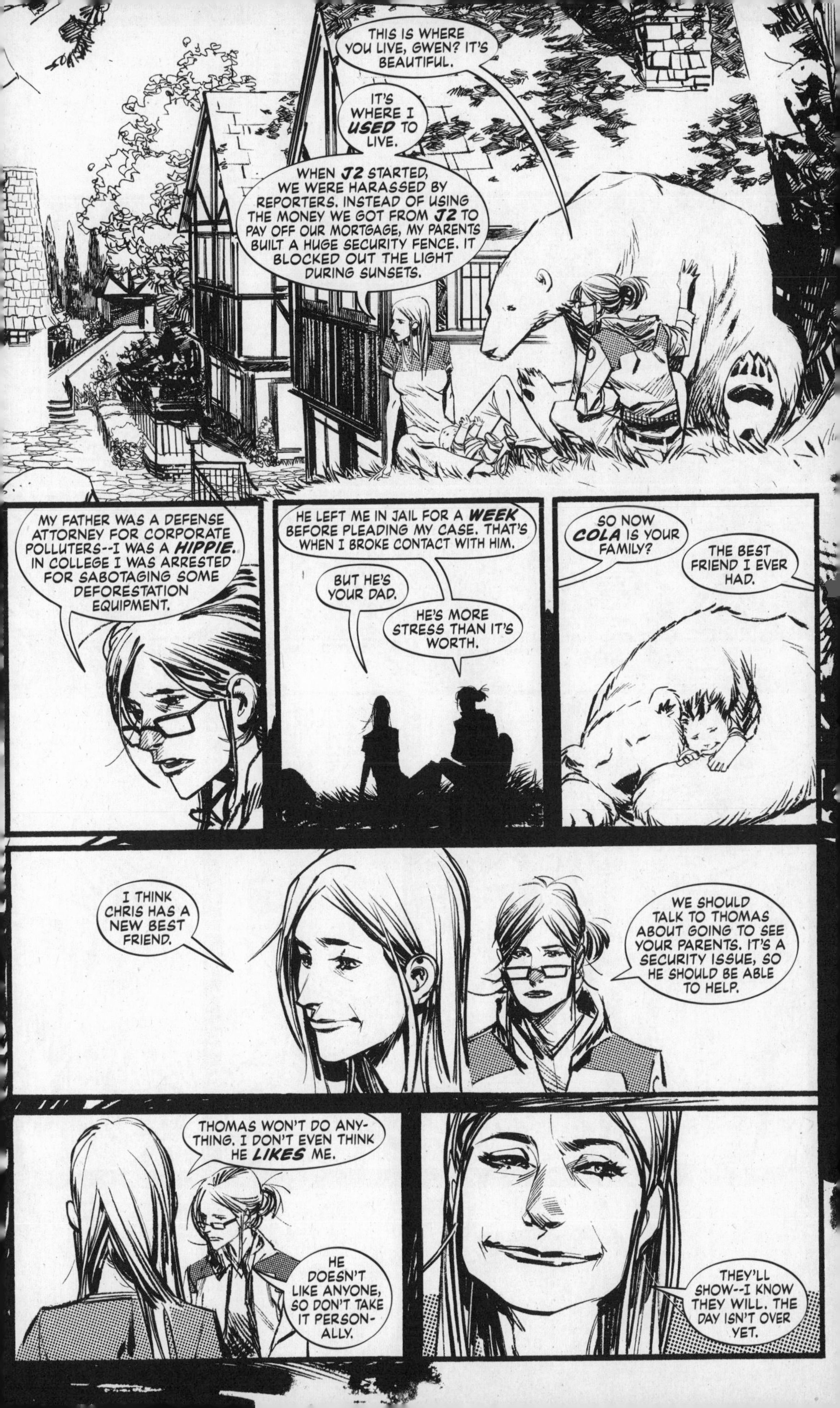
THIS IS WHERE YOU LIVE, GWEN? IT'S BEAUTIFUL.
IT'S WHERE I USED TO LIVE.
WHEN J2 STARTED, WE WERE HARASSED BY REPORTERS. INSTEAD OF USING THE MONEY WE GOT FROM J2 TO PAY OFF OUR MORTGAGE, MY PARENTS BUILT A HUGE SECURITY FENCE. IT BLOCKED OUT THE LIGHT DURING SUNSETS.
MY FATHER WAS A DEFENSE ATTORNEY FOR CORPORATE POLLUTERS--I WAS A HIPPIE. IN COLLEGE I WAS ARRESTED FOR SABOTAGING SOME DEFORESTATION EQUIPMENT.
HE LEFT ME IN JAIL FOR A WEEK BEFORE PLEADING MY CASE. THAT'S WHEN I BROKE CONTACT WITH HIM.
BUT HE'S YOUR DAD.
HE'S MORE STRESS THAN IT'S WORTH.
SO NOW COLA IS YOUR FAMILY?
THE BEST FRIEND I EVER HAD.
I THINK CHRIS HAS A NEW BEST FRIEND.
WE SHOULD TALK TO THOMAS ABOUT GOING TO SEE YOUR PARENTS. IT'S A SECURITY ISSUE, SO HE SHOULD BE ABLE TO HELP.
THOMAS WON'T DO ANYTHING. I DON'T EVEN THINK HE LIKES ME.
HE DOESN'T LIKE ANYONE, SO DON'T TAKE IT PERSONALLY.
THEY'LL SHOW--I KNOW THEY WILL. THE DAY ISN'T OVER YET.

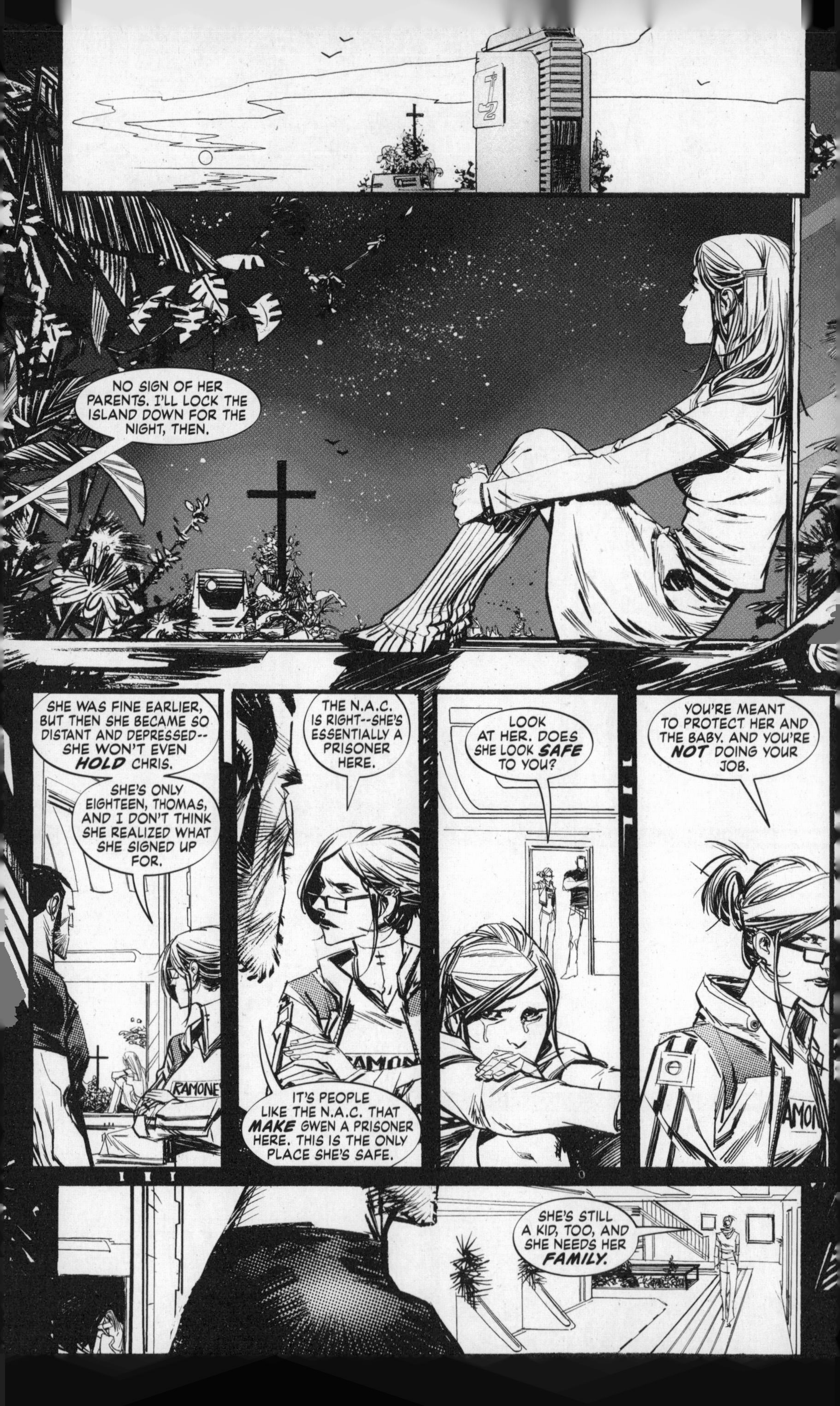
NO SIGN OF HER PARENTS. I'LL LOCK THE ISLAND DOWN FOR THE NIGHT, THEN.
SHE WAS FINE EARLIER, BUT THEN SHE BECAME SO DISTANT AND DEPRESSED-- SHE WON'T EVEN HOLD CHRIS.
SHE'S ONLY EIGHTEEN, THOMAS, AND I DON'T THINK SHE REALIZED WHAT SHE SIGNED UP FOR.
THE N.A.C. IS RIGHT--SHE'S ESSENTIALLY A PRISONER HERE.
IT'S PEOPLE LIKE THE N.A.C. THAT MAKE GWEN A PRISONER HERE. THIS IS THE ONLY PLACE SHE'S SAFE.
LOOK AT HER. DOES SHE LOOK SAFE TO YOU?
YOU'RE MEANT TO PROTECT HER AND THE BABY. AND YOU'RE NOT DOING YOUR JOB.
SHE'S STILL A KID, TOO, AND SHE NEEDS HER FAMILY.

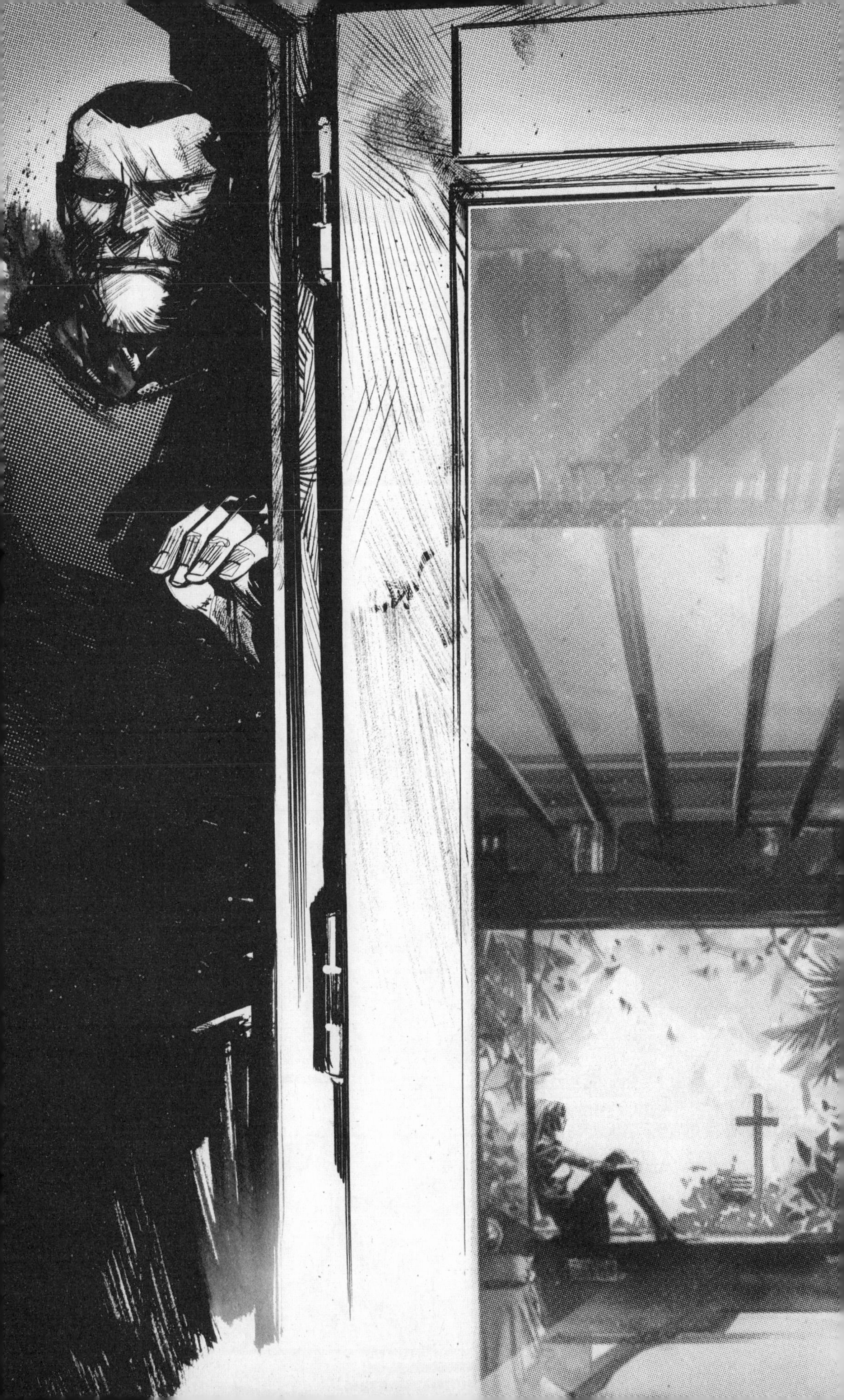

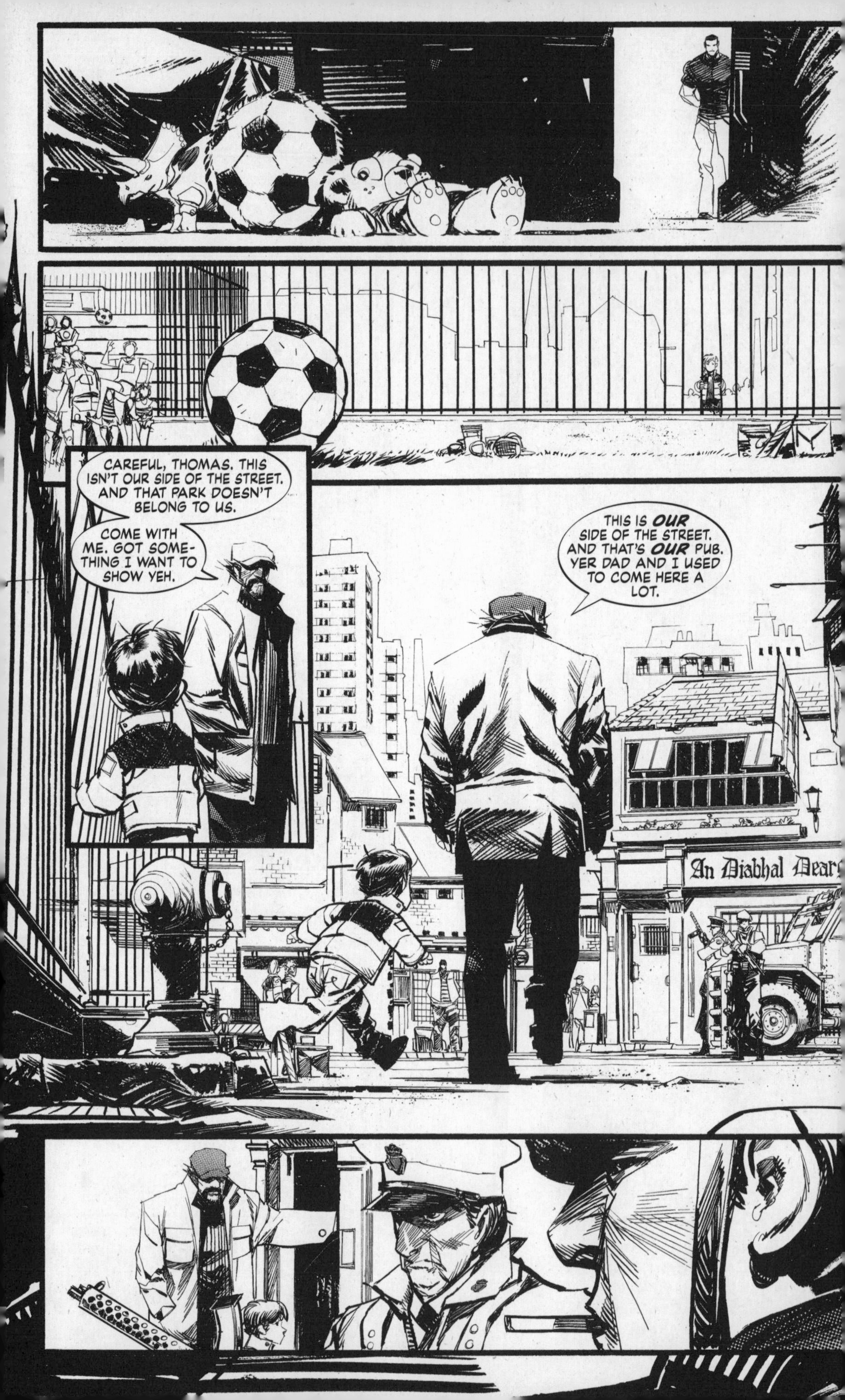

CAREFUL, THOMAS. THIS ISN'T OUR SIDE OF THE STREET. AND THAT PARK DOESN'T BELONG TO US.
COME WITH ME. GOT SOME-THING I WANT TO SHOW YEH.
THIS IS OUR SIDE OF THE STREET. AND THAT'S OUR PUB. YER DAD AND I USED TO COME HERE A LOT.
An Diabhal Dear

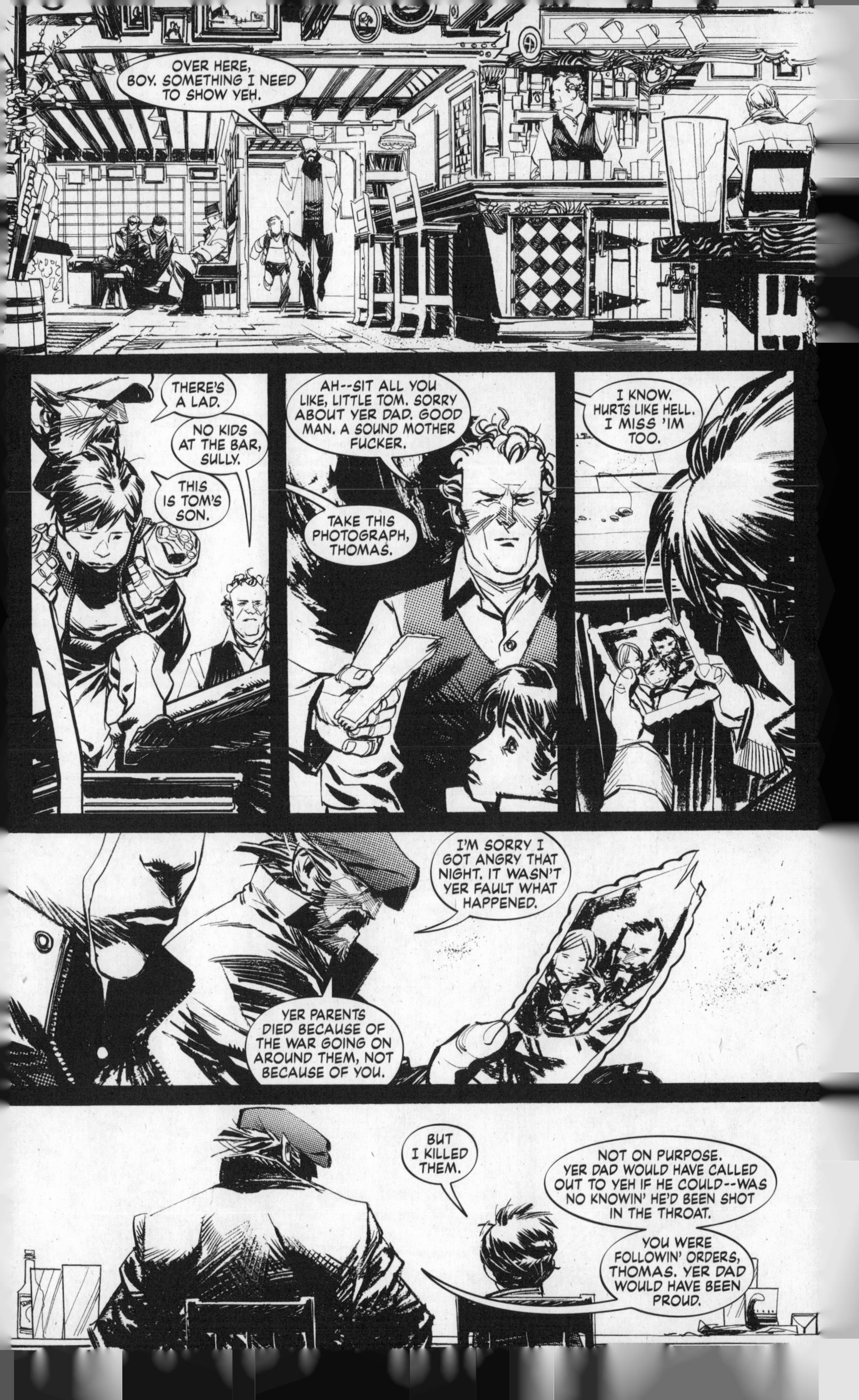
OVER HERE, BOY. SOMETHING I NEED TO SHOW YEH.
THERE'S A LAD.
NO KIDS AT THE BAR, SULLY.
THIS IS TOM'S SON.
AH--SIT ALL YOU LIKE, LITTLE TOM. SORRY ABOUT YER DAD. GOOD MAN. A SOUND MOTHER FUCKER.
TAKE THIS PHOTOGRAPH, THOMAS.
I KNOW. HURTS LIKE HELL. I MISS 'IM TOO.
I'M SORRY I GOT ANGRY THAT NIGHT. IT WASN'T YER FAULT WHAT HAPPENED.
YER PARENTS DIED BECAUSE OF THE WAR GOING ON AROUND THEM, NOT BECAUSE OF YOU.
BUT I KILLED THEM.
NOT ON PURPOSE. YER DAD WOULD HAVE CALLED OUT TO YEH IF HE COULD--WAS NO KNOWIN' HE'D BEEN SHOT IN THE THROAT.
YOU WERE FOLLOWIN' ORDERS, THOMAS. YER DAD WOULD HAVE BEEN PROUD.

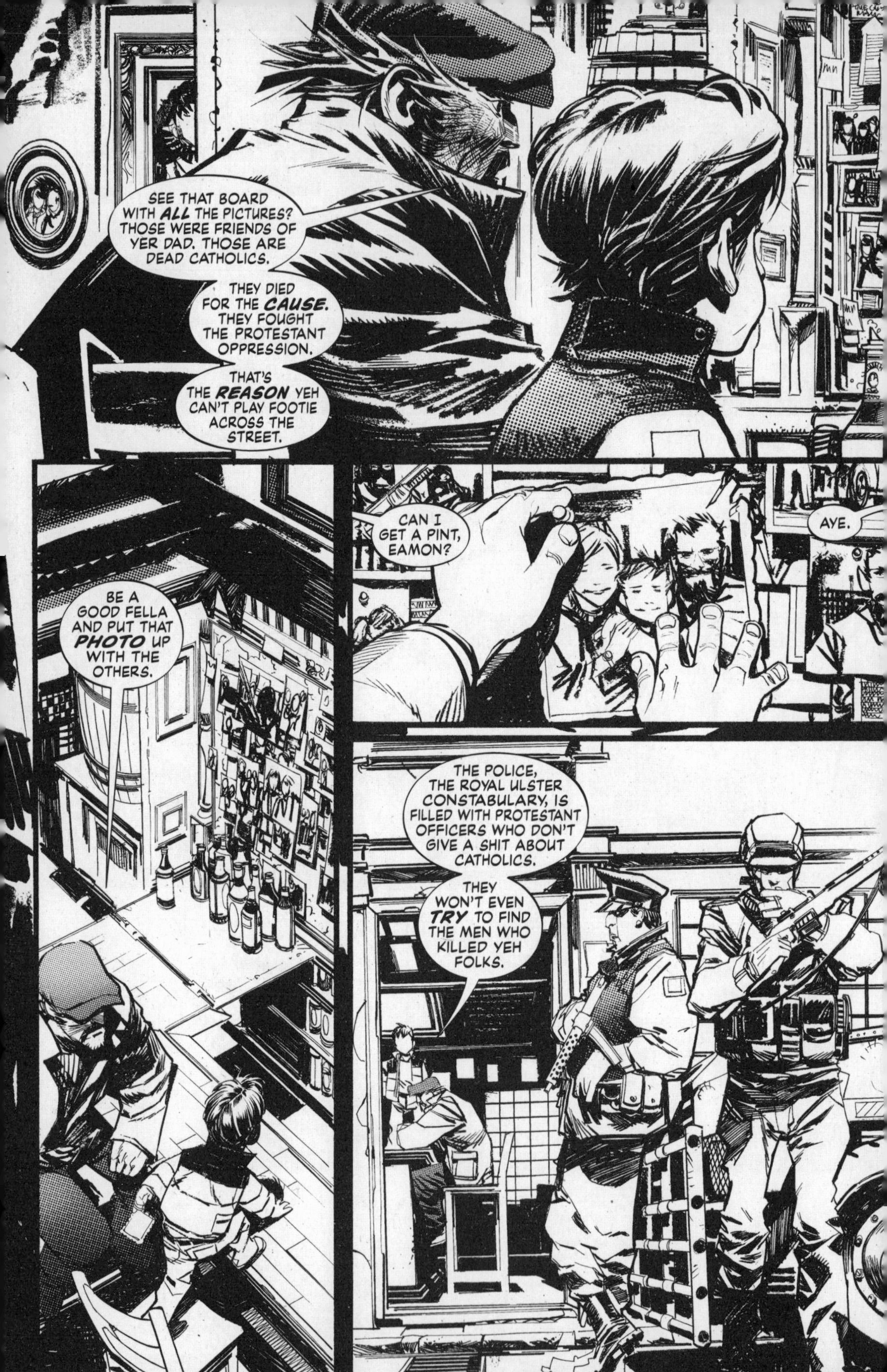

SEE THAT BOARD WITH ALL THE PICTURES? THOSE WERE FRIENDS OF YER DAD. THOSE ARE DEAD CATHOLICS.
THEY DIED FOR THE CAUSE. THEY FOUGHT THE PROTESTANT OPPRESSION.
THAT'S THE REASON YEH CAN'T PLAY FOOTIE ACROSS THE STREET.
BE A GOOD FELLA AND PUT THAT PHOTO UP WITH THE OTHERS.
CAN I GET A PINT, EAMON?
AYE.
THE POLICE, THE ROYAL ULSTER CONSTABULARY, IS FILLED WITH PROTESTANT OFFICERS WHO DON'T GIVE A SHIT ABOUT CATHOLICS.
THEY WON'T EVEN TRY TO FIND THE MEN WHO KILLED YEH FOLKS.

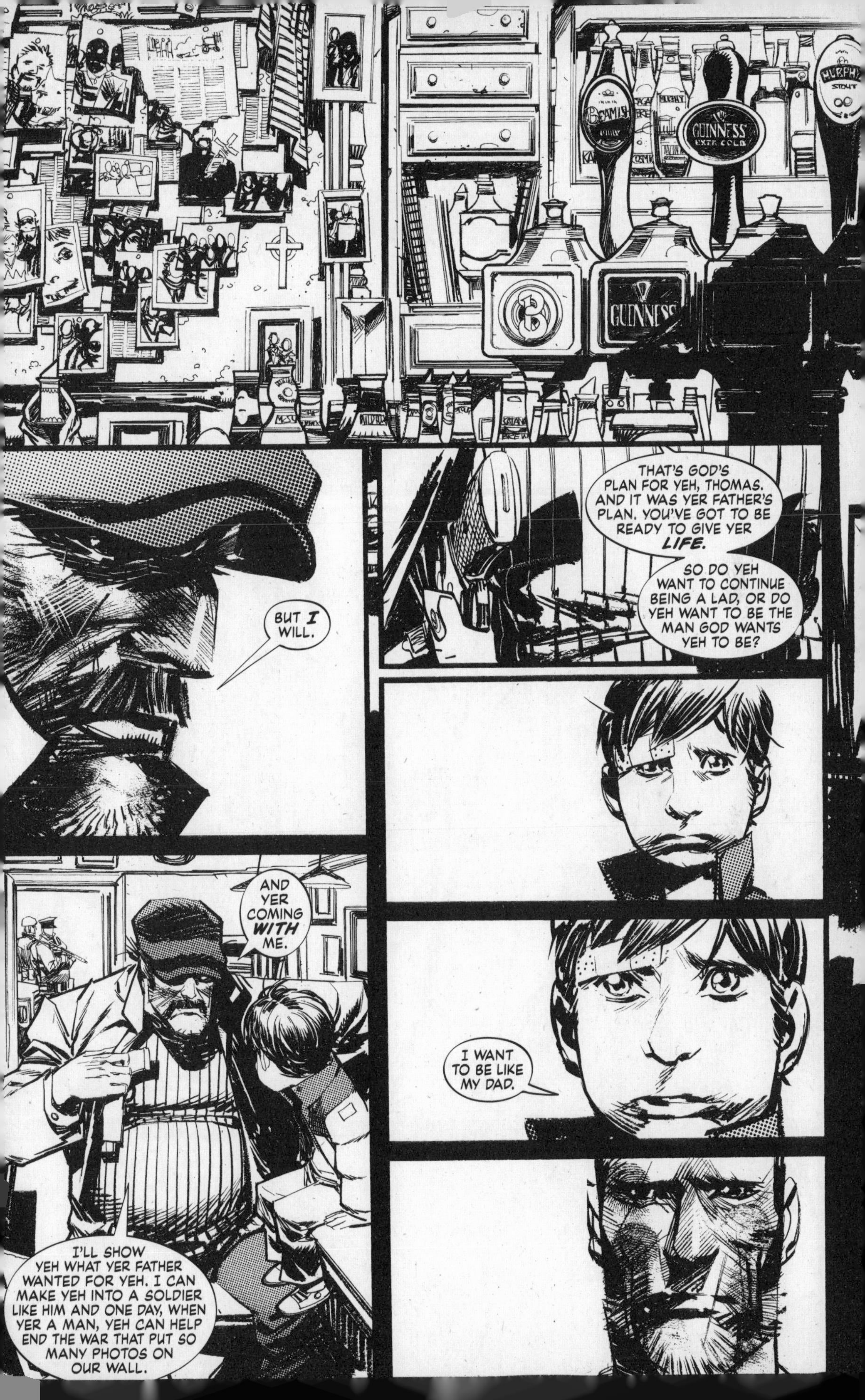
BEAMISH
GUINNESS EXTRA COLD
MURPHY'S STOUT
GUINNESS
BUT I WILL.
THAT'S GOD'S PLAN FOR YEH, THOMAS. AND IT WAS YER FATHER'S PLAN. YOU'VE GOT TO BE READY TO GIVE YER LIFE.
SO DO YEH WANT TO CONTINUE BEING A LAD, OR DO YEH WANT TO BE THE MAN GOD WANTS YEH TO BE?
I WANT TO BE LIKE MY DAD.
AND YER COMING WITH ME.
I'LL SHOW YEH WHAT YER FATHER WANTED FOR YEH. I CAN MAKE YEH INTO A SOLDIER LIKE HIM AND ONE DAY, WHEN YER A MAN, YEH CAN HELP END THE WAR THAT PUT SO MANY PHOTOS ON OUR WALL.

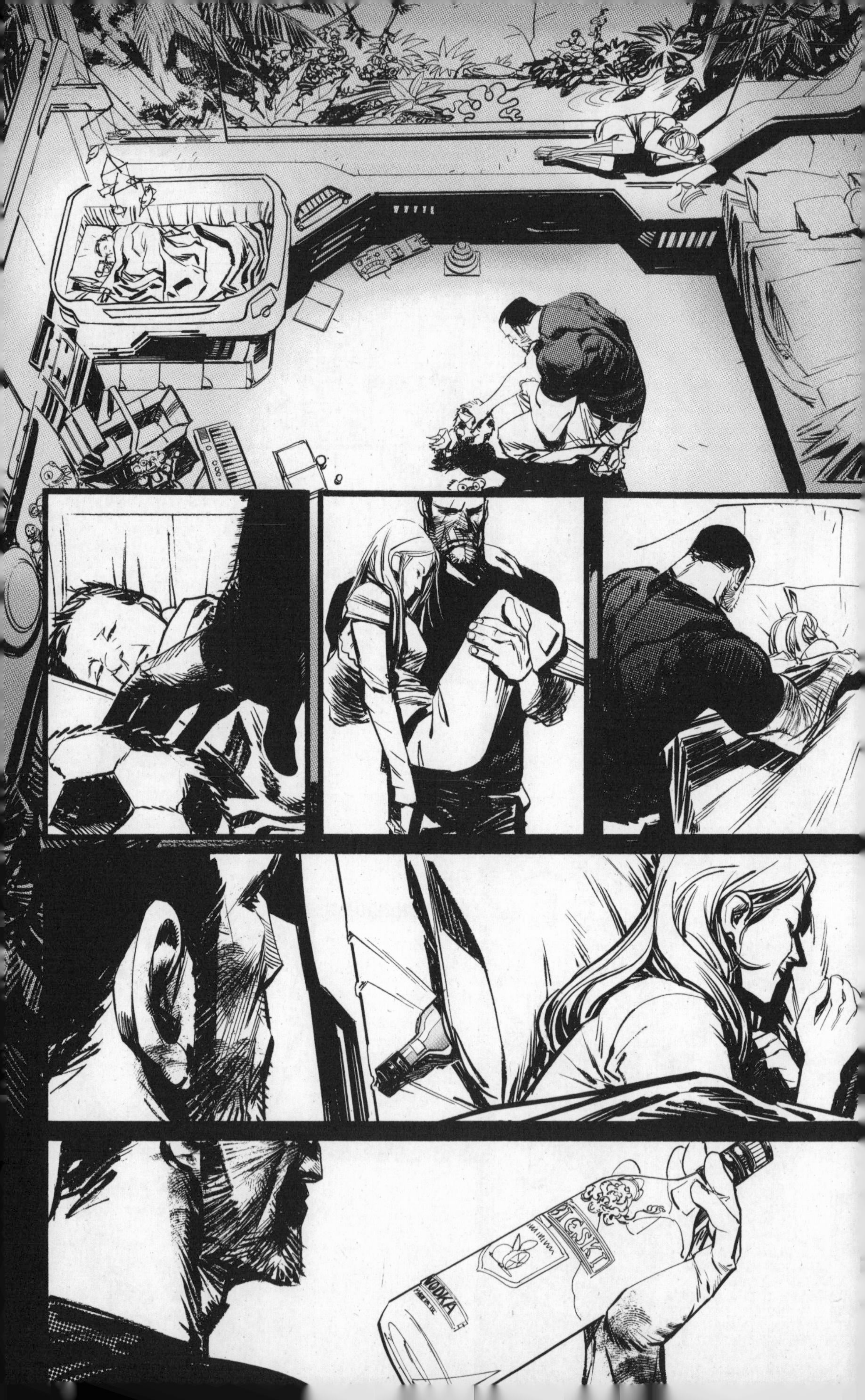
BIESKI
VODKA

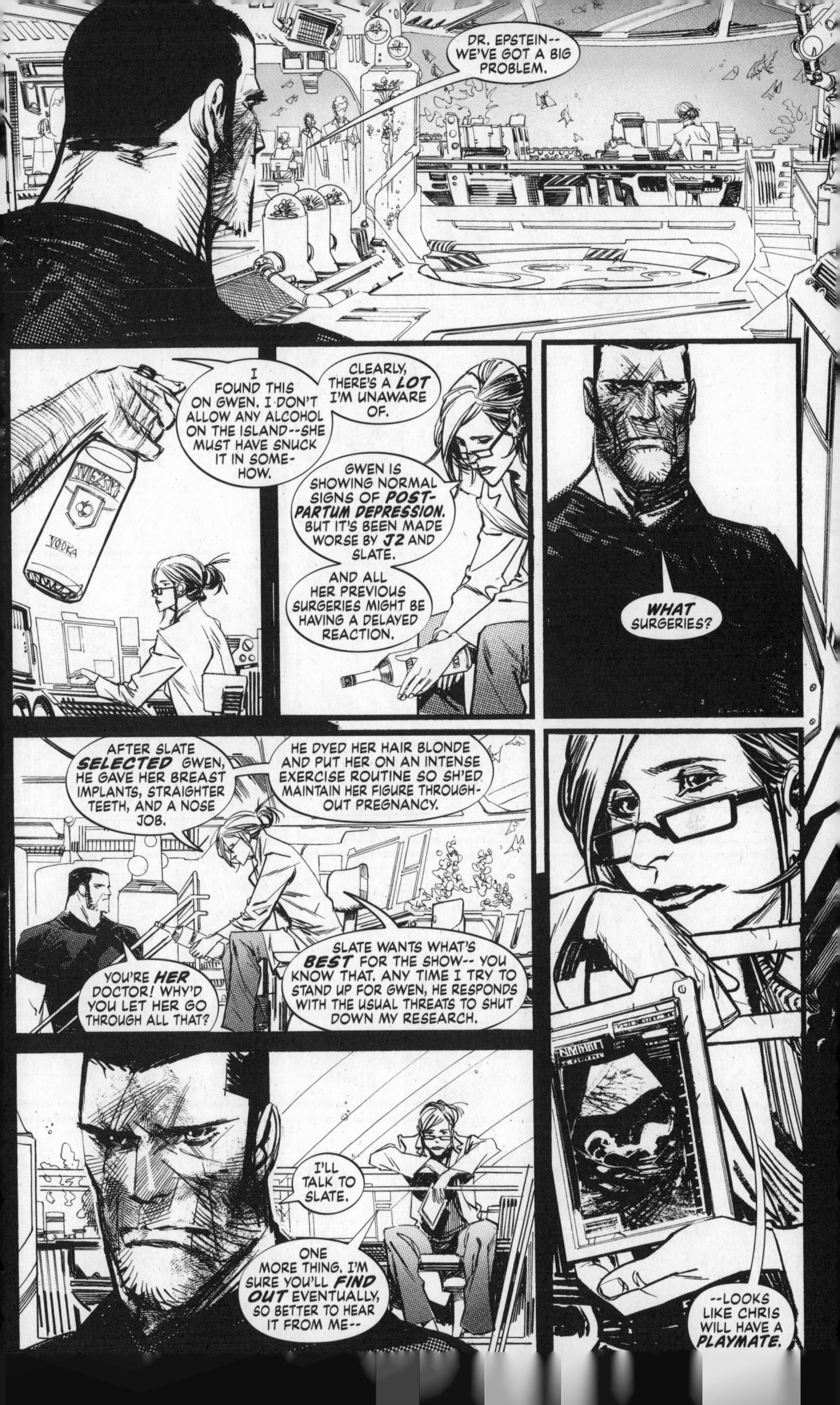
DR. EPSTEIN--
WE'VE GOT A BIG PROBLEM.
I FOUND THIS ON GWEN. I DON'T ALLOW ANY ALCOHOL ON THE ISLAND--SHE MUST HAVE SNUCK IT IN SOME-HOW.
VODKA
CLEARLY, THERE'S A LOT I'M UNAWARE OF.
GWEN IS SHOWING NORMAL SIGNS OF POST-PARTUM DEPRESSION. BUT IT'S BEEN MADE WORSE BY J2 AND SLATE.
AND ALL HER PREVIOUS SURGERIES MIGHT BE HAVING A DELAYED REACTION.
WHAT SURGERIES?
AFTER SLATE SELECTED GWEN, HE GAVE HER BREAST IMPLANTS, STRAIGHTER TEETH, AND A NOSE JOB.
HE DYED HER HAIR BLONDE AND PUT HER ON AN INTENSE EXERCISE ROUTINE SO SH'ED MAINTAIN HER FIGURE THROUGH-OUT PREGNANCY.
YOU'RE HER DOCTOR! WHY'D YOU LET HER GO THROUGH ALL THAT?
SLATE WANTS WHAT'S BEST FOR THE SHOW-- YOU KNOW THAT. ANY TIME I TRY TO STAND UP FOR GWEN, HE RESPONDS WITH THE USUAL THREATS TO SHUT DOWN MY RESEARCH.
I'LL TALK TO SLATE.
ONE MORE THING. I'M SURE YOU'LL FIND OUT EVENTUALLY, SO BETTER TO HEAR IT FROM ME--
--LOOKS LIKE CHRIS WILL HAVE A PLAYMATE.

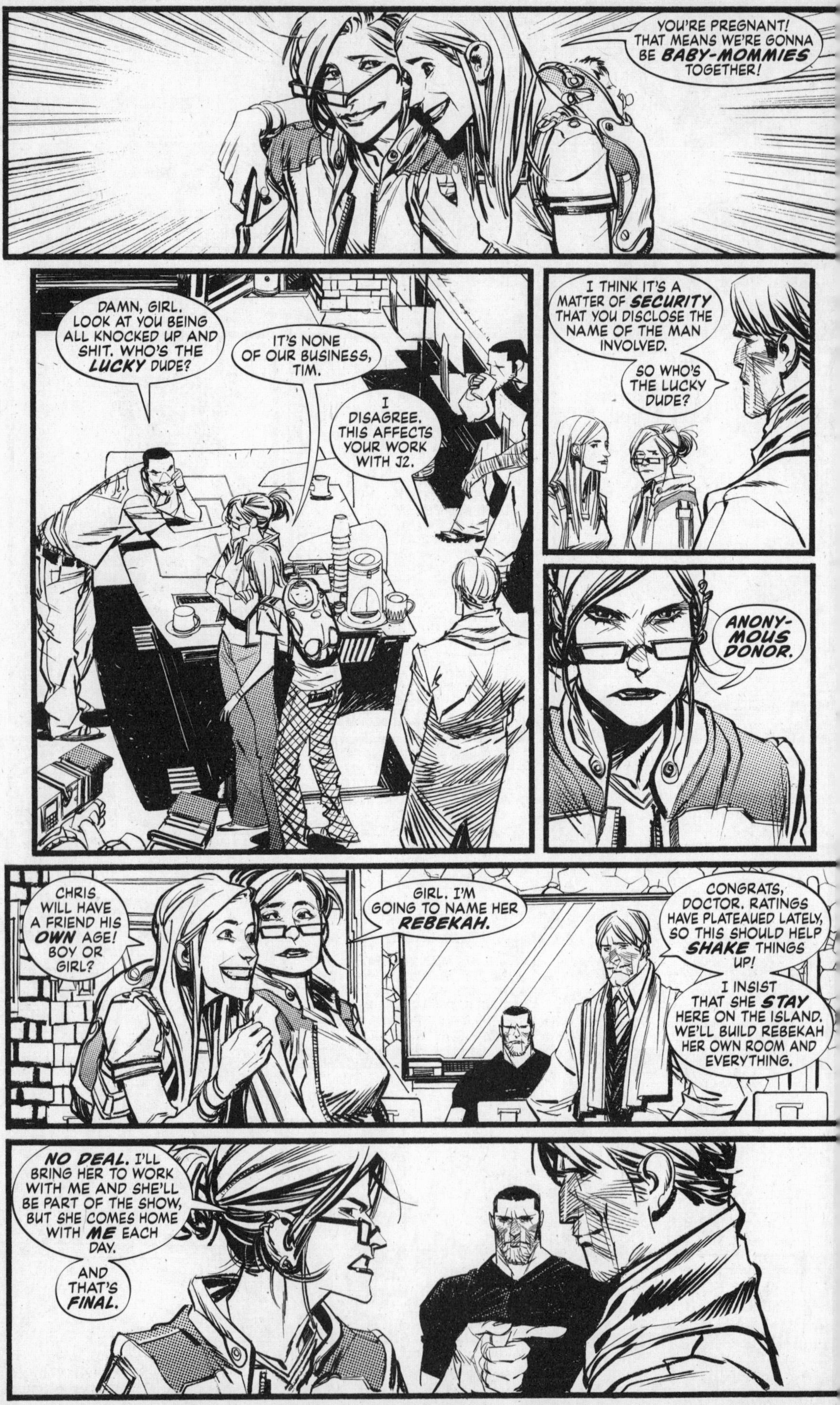
YOU'RE PREGNANT! THAT MEANS WE'RE GONNA BE BABY-MOMMIES TOGETHER!
DAMN, GIRL. LOOK AT YOU BEING ALL KNOCKED UP AND SHIT. WHO'S THE LUCKY DUDE?
IT'S NONE OF OUR BUSINESS, TIM.
I DISAGREE. THIS AFFECTS YOUR WORK WITH J2.
I THINK IT'S A MATTER OF SECURITY THAT YOU DISCLOSE THE NAME OF THE MAN INVOLVED.
SO WHO'S THE LUCKY DUDE?
ANONY-MOUS DONOR.
CHRIS WILL HAVE A FRIEND HIS OWN AGE! BOY OR GIRL?
GIRL. I'M GOING TO NAME HER REBEKAH.
CONGRATS, DOCTOR. RATINGS HAVE PLATEAUED LATELY, SO THIS SHOULD HELP SHAKE THINGS UP!
I INSIST THAT SHE STAY HERE ON THE ISLAND. WE'LL BUILD REBEKAH HER OWN ROOM AND EVERYTHING.
NO DEAL. I'LL BRING HER TO WORK WITH ME AND SHE'LL BE PART OF THE SHOW, BUT SHE COMES HOME WITH ME EACH DAY.
AND THAT'S FINAL.

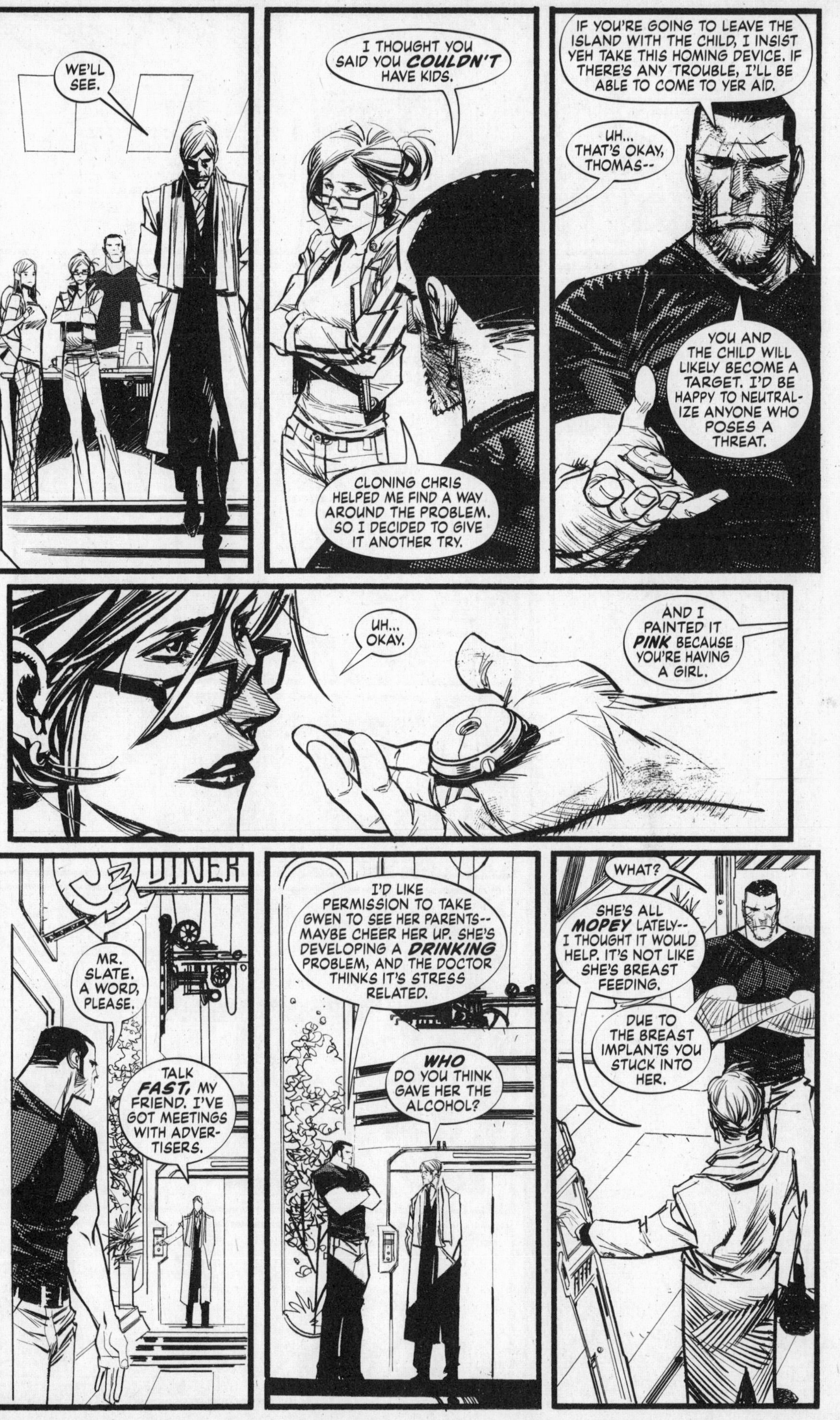

WE'LL SEE.
I THOUGHT YOU SAID YOU COULDN'T HAVE KIDS.
CLONING CHRIS HELPED ME FIND A WAY AROUND THE PROBLEM. SO I DECIDED TO GIVE IT ANOTHER TRY.
IF YOU'RE GOING TO LEAVE THE ISLAND WITH THE CHILD, I INSIST YEH TAKE THIS HOMING DEVICE. IF THERE'S ANY TROUBLE, I'LL BE ABLE TO COME TO YER AID.
UH... THAT'S OKAY, THOMAS--
YOU AND THE CHILD WILL LIKELY BECOME A TARGET. I'D BE HAPPY TO NEUTRAL-IZE ANYONE WHO POSES A THREAT.
UH... OKAY.
AND I PAINTED IT PINK BECAUSE YOU'RE HAVING A GIRL.
DINER
MR. SLATE. A WORD, PLEASE.
TALK FAST, MY FRIEND. I'VE GOT MEETINGS WITH ADVER-TISERS.
I'D LIKE PERMISSION TO TAKE GWEN TO SEE HER PARENTS-- MAYBE CHEER HER UP. SHE'S DEVELOPING A DRINKING PROBLEM, AND THE DOCTOR THINKS IT'S STRESS RELATED.
WHO DO YOU THINK GAVE HER THE ALCOHOL?
WHAT?
SHE'S ALL MOPEY LATELY-- I THOUGHT IT WOULD HELP. IT'S NOT LIKE SHE'S BREAST FEEDING.
DUE TO THE BREAST IMPLANTS YOU STUCK INTO HER.

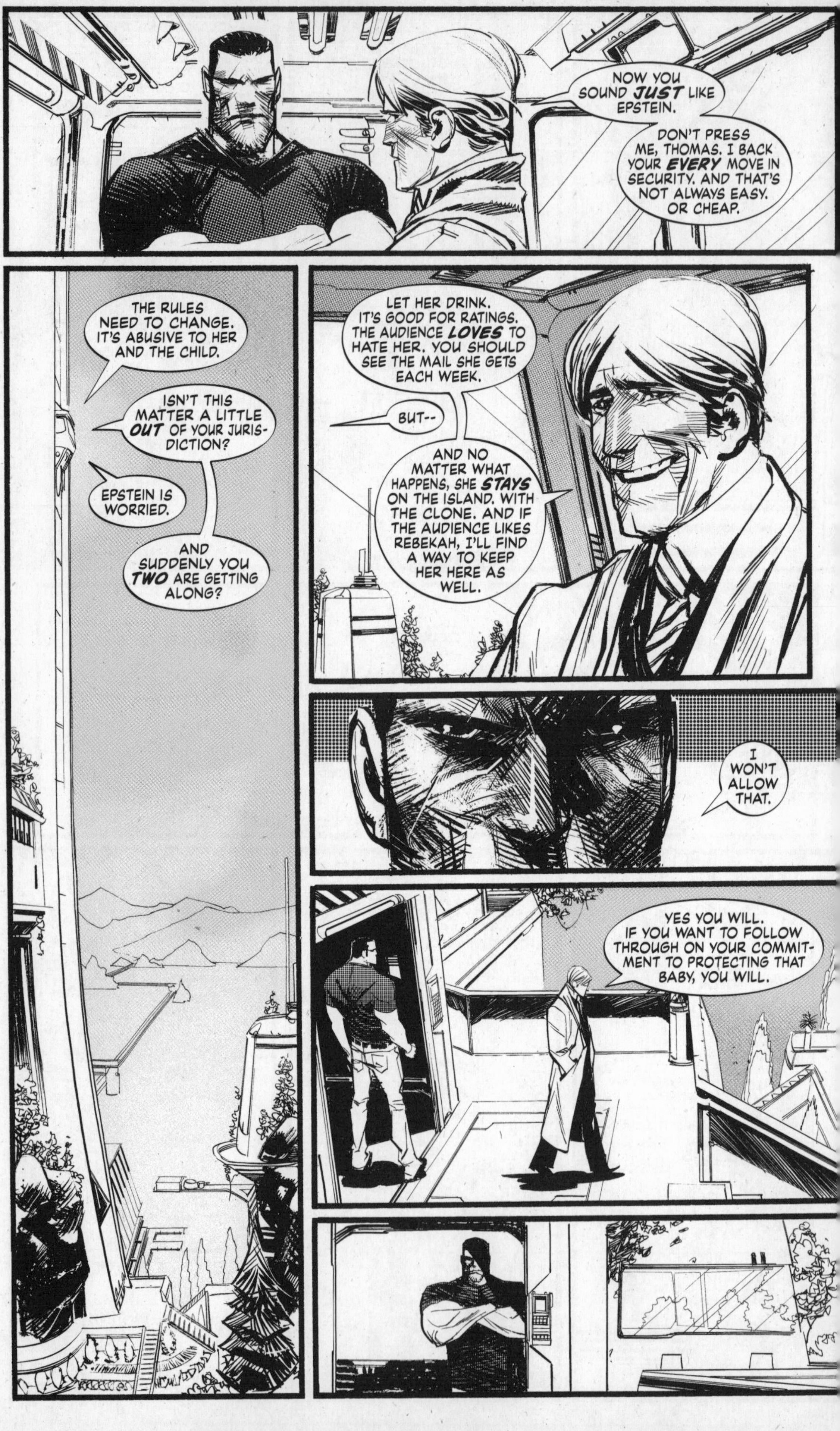
NOW YOU SOUND JUST LIKE EPSTEIN.
DON'T PRESS ME, THOMAS. I BACK YOUR EVERY MOVE IN SECURITY. AND THAT'S NOT ALWAYS EASY. OR CHEAP.
THE RULES NEED TO CHANGE. IT'S ABUSIVE TO HER AND THE CHILD.
ISN'T THIS MATTER A LITTLE OUT OF YOUR JURIS-DICTION?
EPSTEIN IS WORRIED.
AND SUDDENLY YOU TWO ARE GETTING ALONG?
LET HER DRINK. IT'S GOOD FOR RATINGS. THE AUDIENCE LOVES TO HATE HER. YOU SHOULD SEE THE MAIL SHE GETS EACH WEEK.
BUT--
AND NO MATTER WHAT HAPPENS, SHE STAYS ON THE ISLAND. WITH THE CLONE. AND IF THE AUDIENCE LIKES REBEKAH, I'LL FIND A WAY TO KEEP HER HERE AS WELL.
I WON'T ALLOW THAT.
YES YOU WILL. IF YOU WANT TO FOLLOW THROUGH ON YOUR COMMIT-MENT TO PROTECTING THAT BABY, YOU WILL.

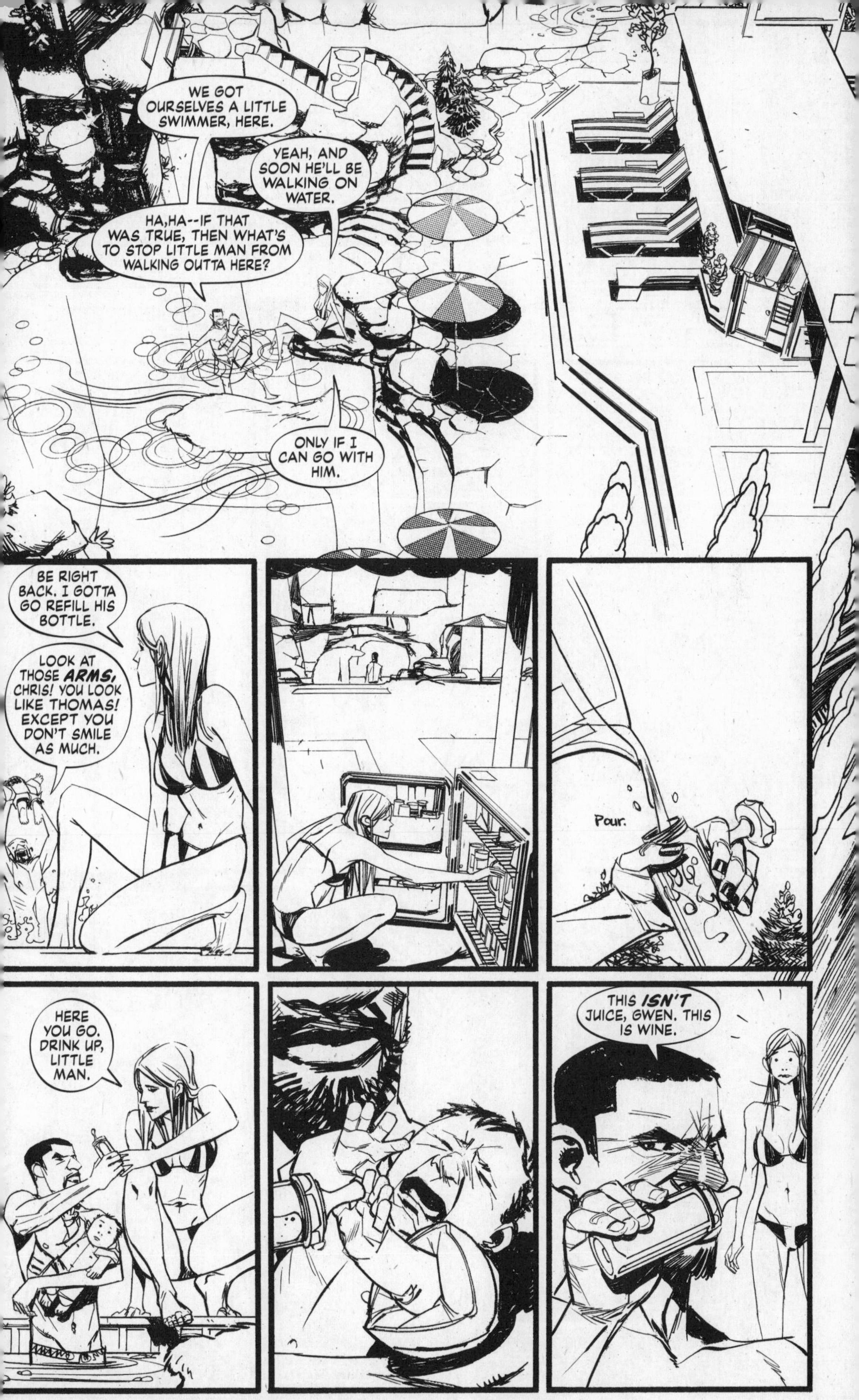
WE GOT OURSELVES A LITTLE SWIMMER, HERE.
YEAH, AND SOON HE'LL BE WALKING ON WATER.
HA,HA--IF THAT WAS TRUE, THEN WHAT'S TO STOP LITTLE MAN FROM WALKING OUTTA HERE?
ONLY IF I CAN GO WITH HIM.
BE RIGHT BACK. I GOTTA GO REFILL HIS BOTTLE.
LOOK AT THOSE ARMS, CHRIS! YOU LOOK LIKE THOMAS! EXCEPT YOU DON'T SMILE AS MUCH.
Pour.
HERE YOU GO. DRINK UP, LITTLE MAN.
THIS ISN'T JUICE, GWEN. THIS IS WINE.

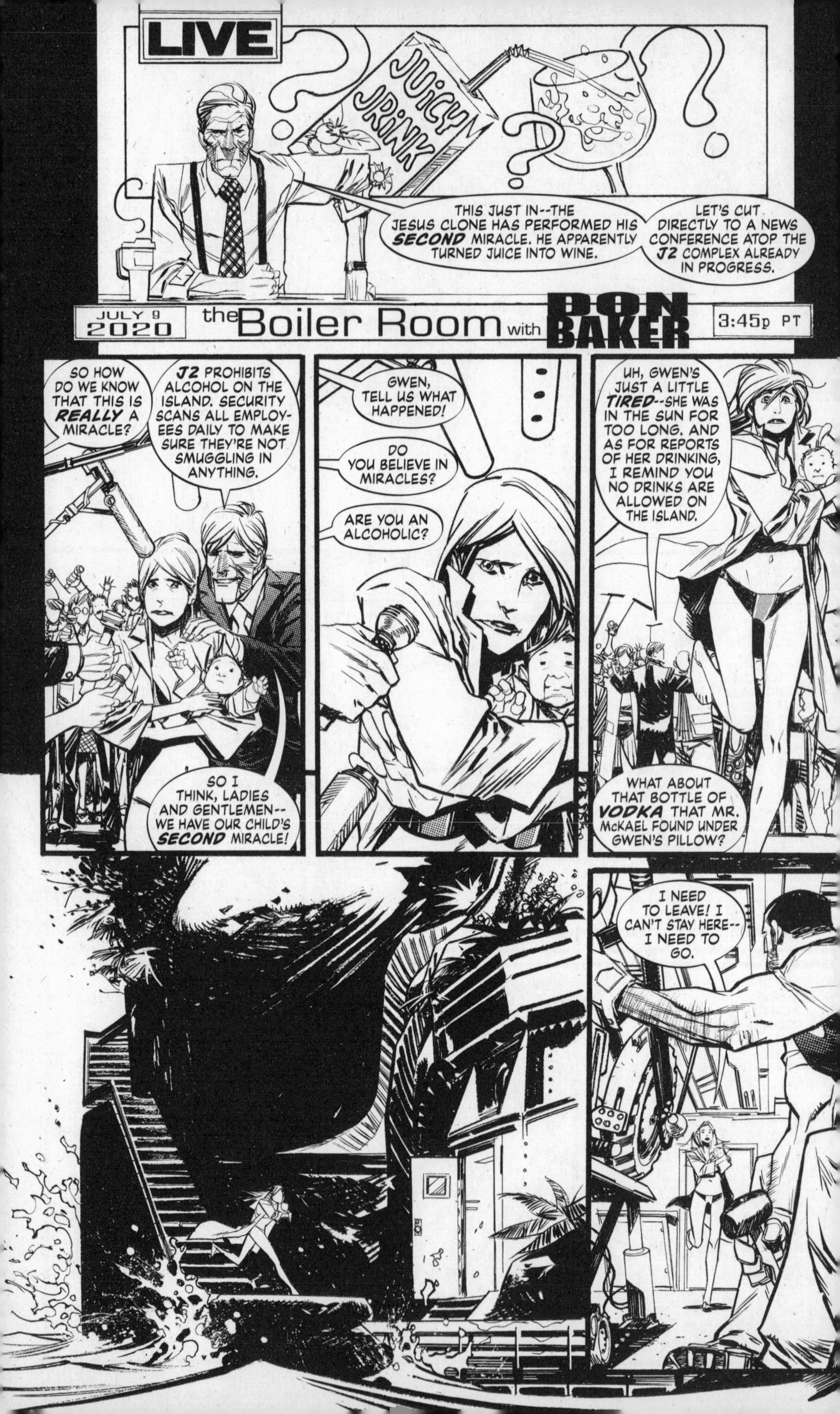
LIVE
JUICY DRINK
THIS JUST IN--THE JESUS CLONE HAS PERFORMED HIS SECOND MIRACLE. HE APPARENTLY TURNED JUICE INTO WINE.
LET'S CUT DIRECTLY TO A NEWS CONFERENCE ATOP THE J2 COMPLEX ALREADY IN PROGRESS.
JULY 9 2020
the Boiler Room with DON BAKER
3:45p PT
SO HOW DO WE KNOW THAT THIS IS REALLY A MIRACLE?
J2 PROHIBITS ALCOHOL ON THE ISLAND. SECURITY SCANS ALL EMPLOYEES DAILY TO MAKE SURE THEY'RE NOT SMUGGLING IN ANYTHING.
SO I THINK, LADIES AND GENTLEMEN--WE HAVE OUR CHILD'S SECOND MIRACLE!
GWEN, TELL US WHAT HAPPENED!
DO YOU BELIEVE IN MIRACLES?
ARE YOU AN ALCOHOLIC?
UH, GWEN'S JUST A LITTLE TIRED--SHE WAS IN THE SUN FOR TOO LONG. AND AS FOR REPORTS OF HER DRINKING, I REMIND YOU NO DRINKS ARE ALLOWED ON THE ISLAND.
WHAT ABOUT THAT BOTTLE OF VODKA THAT MR. McKAEL FOUND UNDER GWEN'S PILLOW?
I NEED TO LEAVE! I CAN'T STAY HERE--I NEED TO GO.

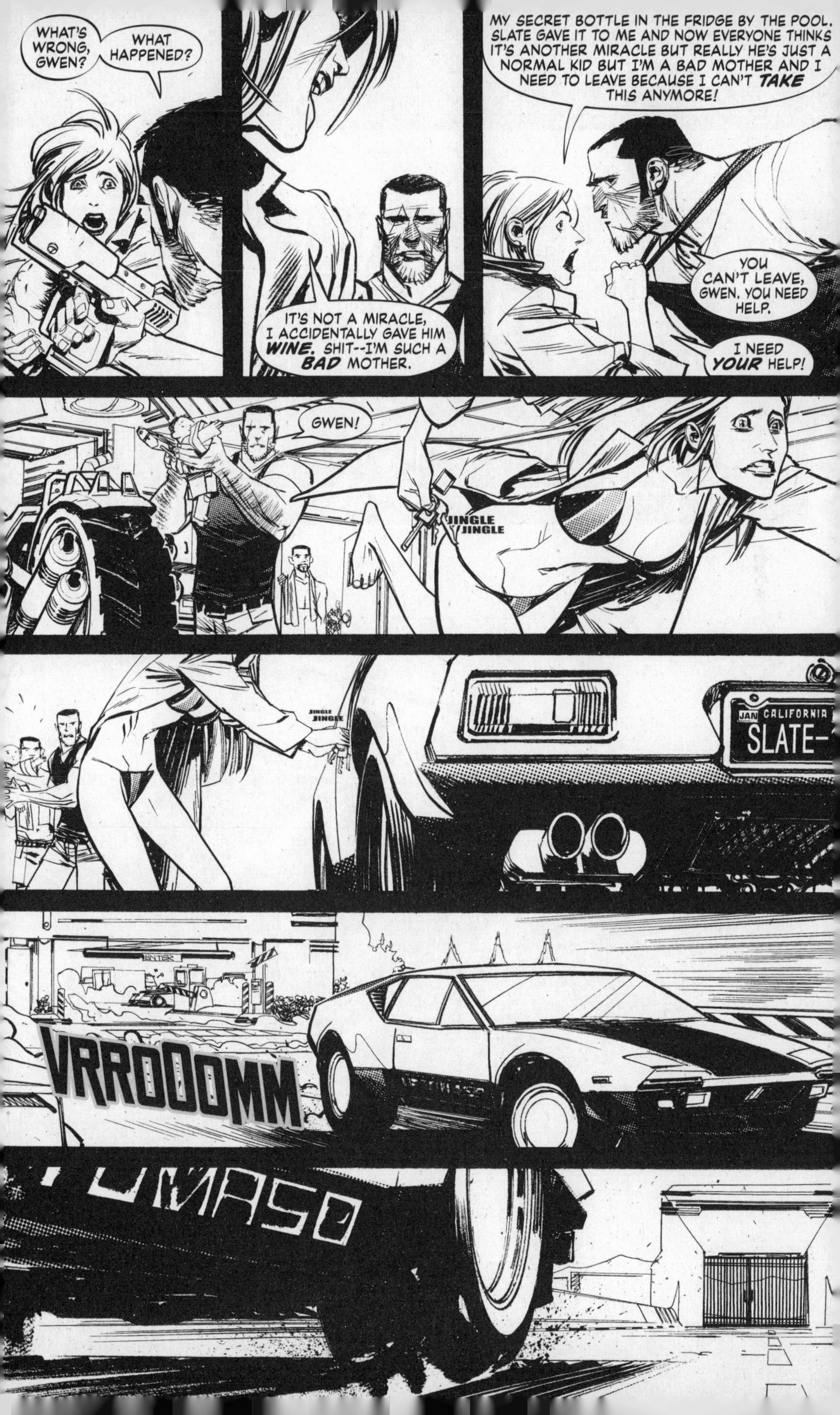

WHAT'S WRONG, GWEN?
WHAT HAPPENED?
IT'S NOT A MIRACLE, I ACCIDENTALLY GAVE HIM WINE. SHIT--I'M SUCH A BAD MOTHER.
MY SECRET BOTTLE IN THE FRIDGE BY THE POOL. SLATE GAVE IT TO ME AND NOW EVERYONE THINKS IT'S ANOTHER MIRACLE BUT REALLY HE'S JUST A NORMAL KID BUT I'M A BAD MOTHER AND I NEED TO LEAVE BECAUSE I CAN'T TAKE THIS ANYMORE!
YOU CAN'T LEAVE, GWEN. YOU NEED HELP.
I NEED YOUR HELP!
GWEN!
JINGLE JINGLE
JINGLE JINGLE
CALIFORNIA
SLATE-
VRROOOMM

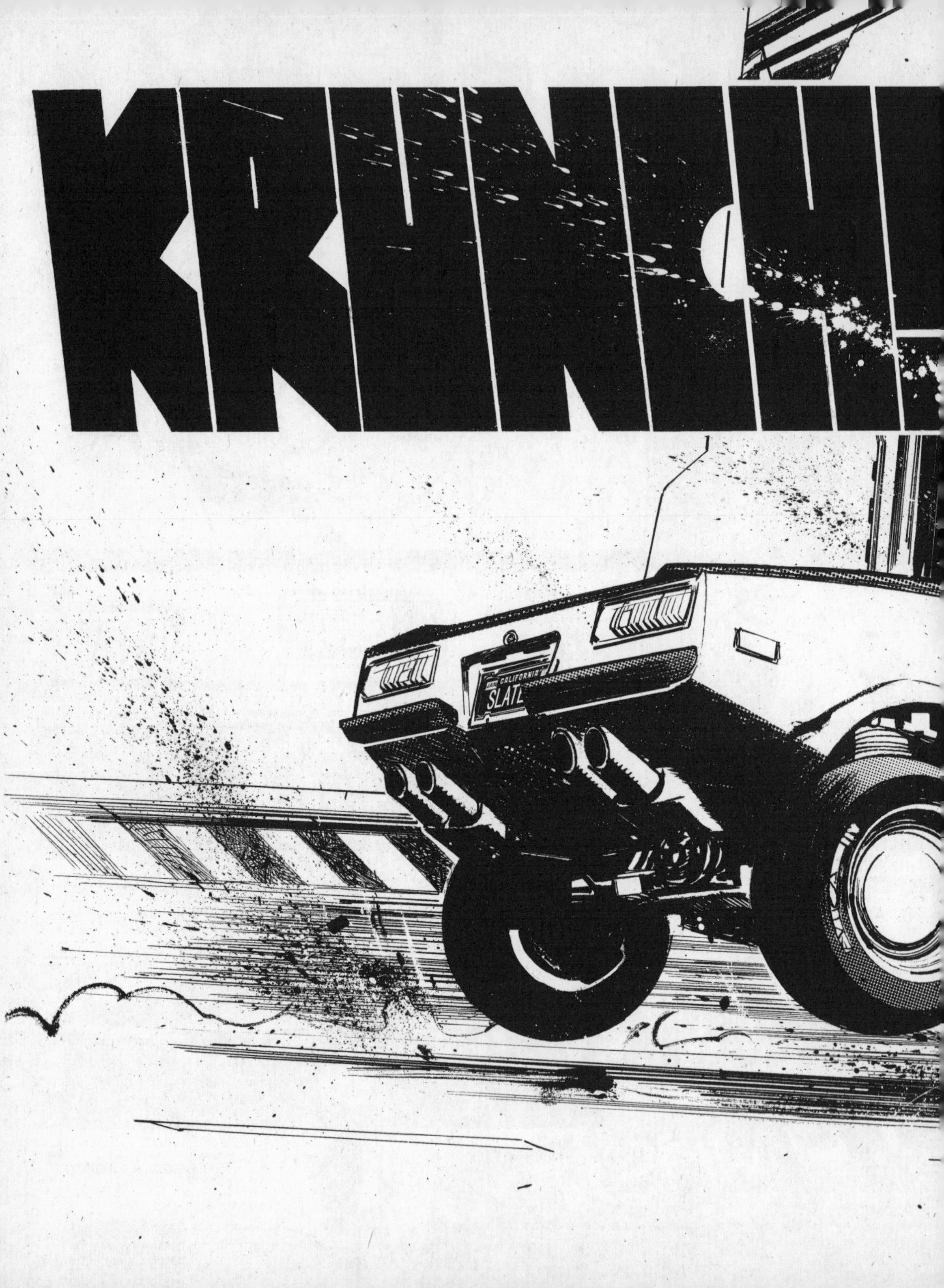

KRUNCH
CALIFORNIA

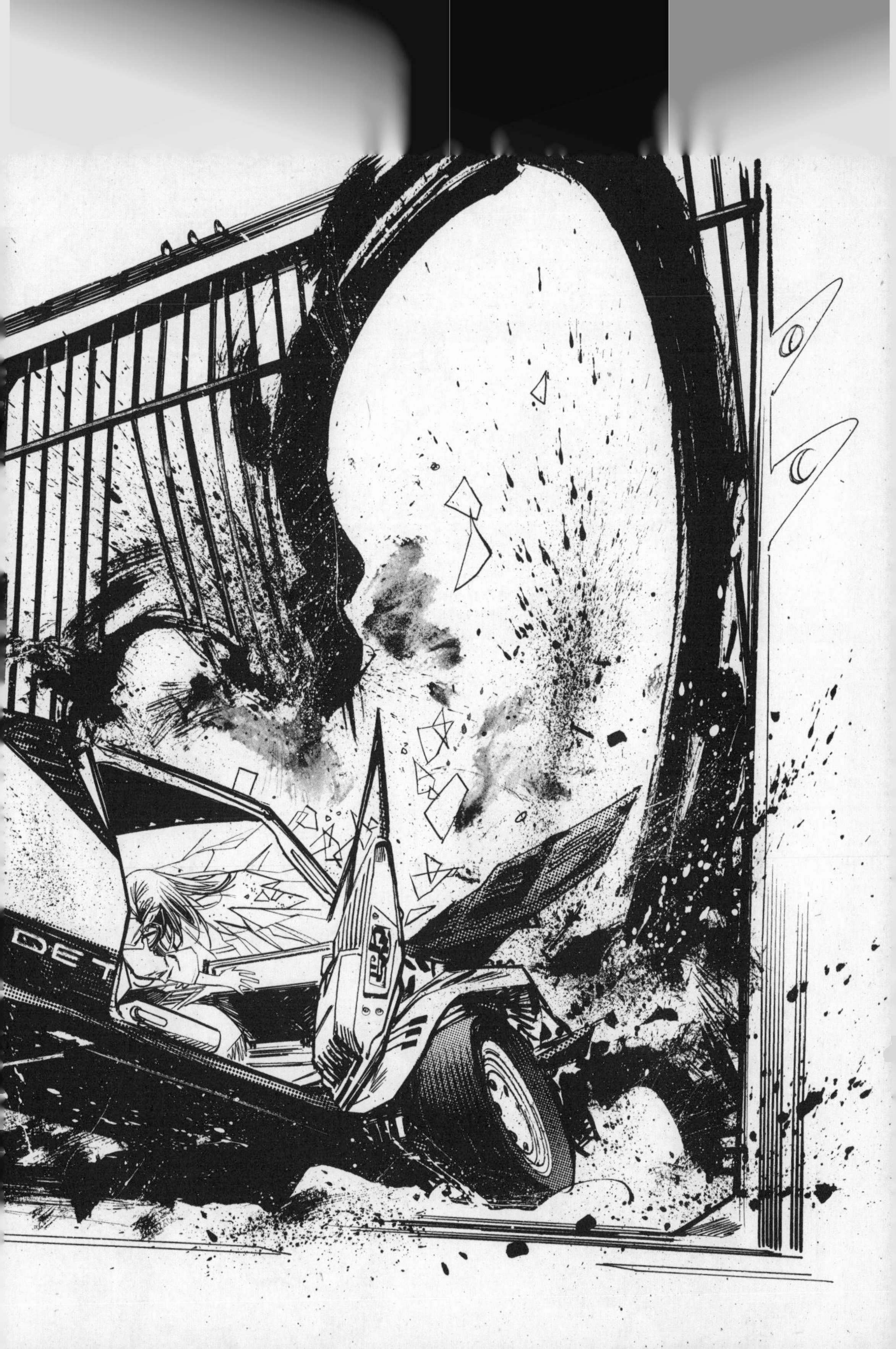

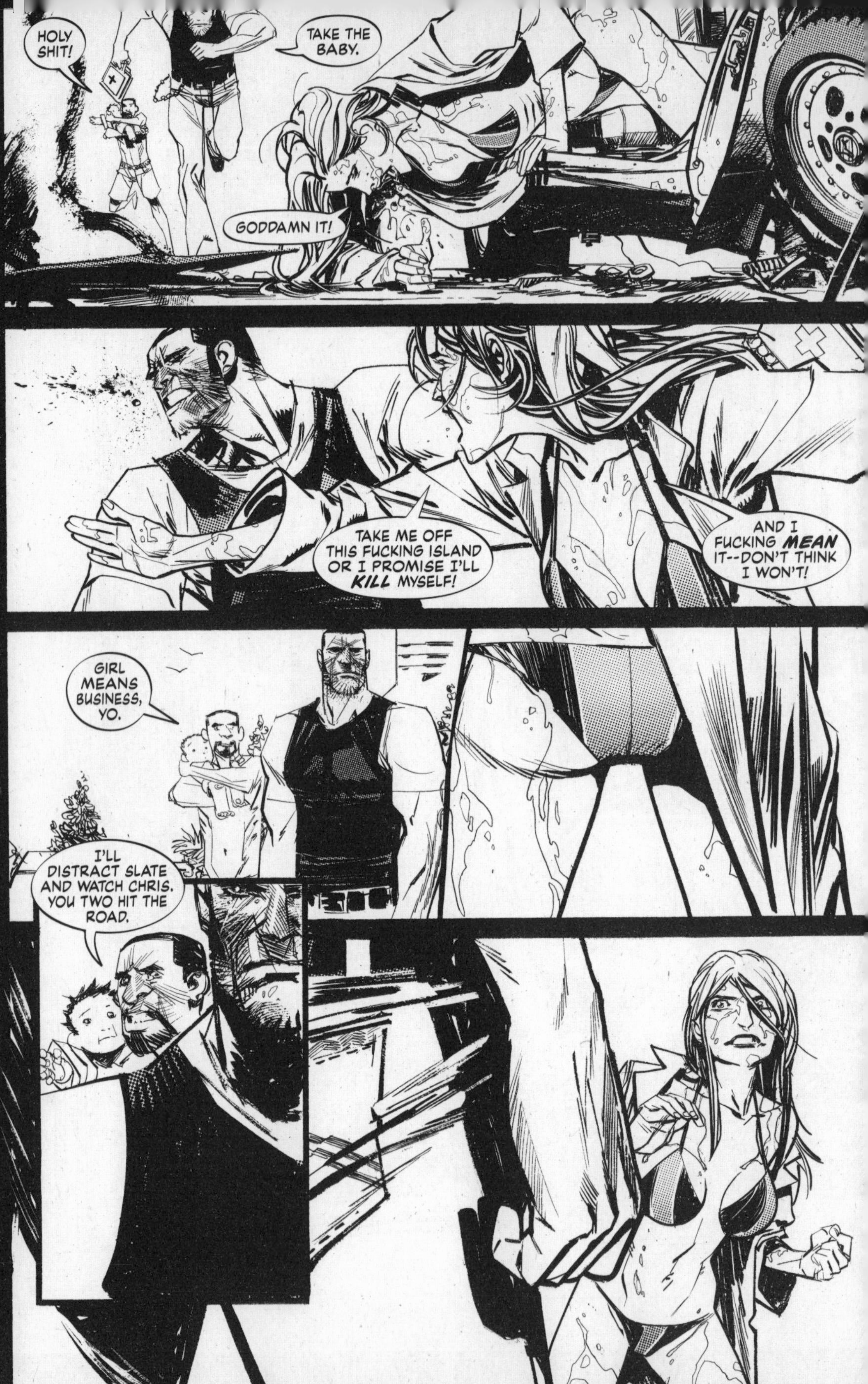
HOLY SHIT!
TAKE THE BABY.
GODDAMN IT!
TAKE ME OFF THIS FUCKING ISLAND OR I PROMISE I'LL KILL MYSELF!
AND I FUCKING MEAN IT--DON'T THINK I WON'T!
GIRL MEANS BUSINESS, YO.
I'LL DISTRACT SLATE AND WATCH CHRIS. YOU TWO HIT THE ROAD.

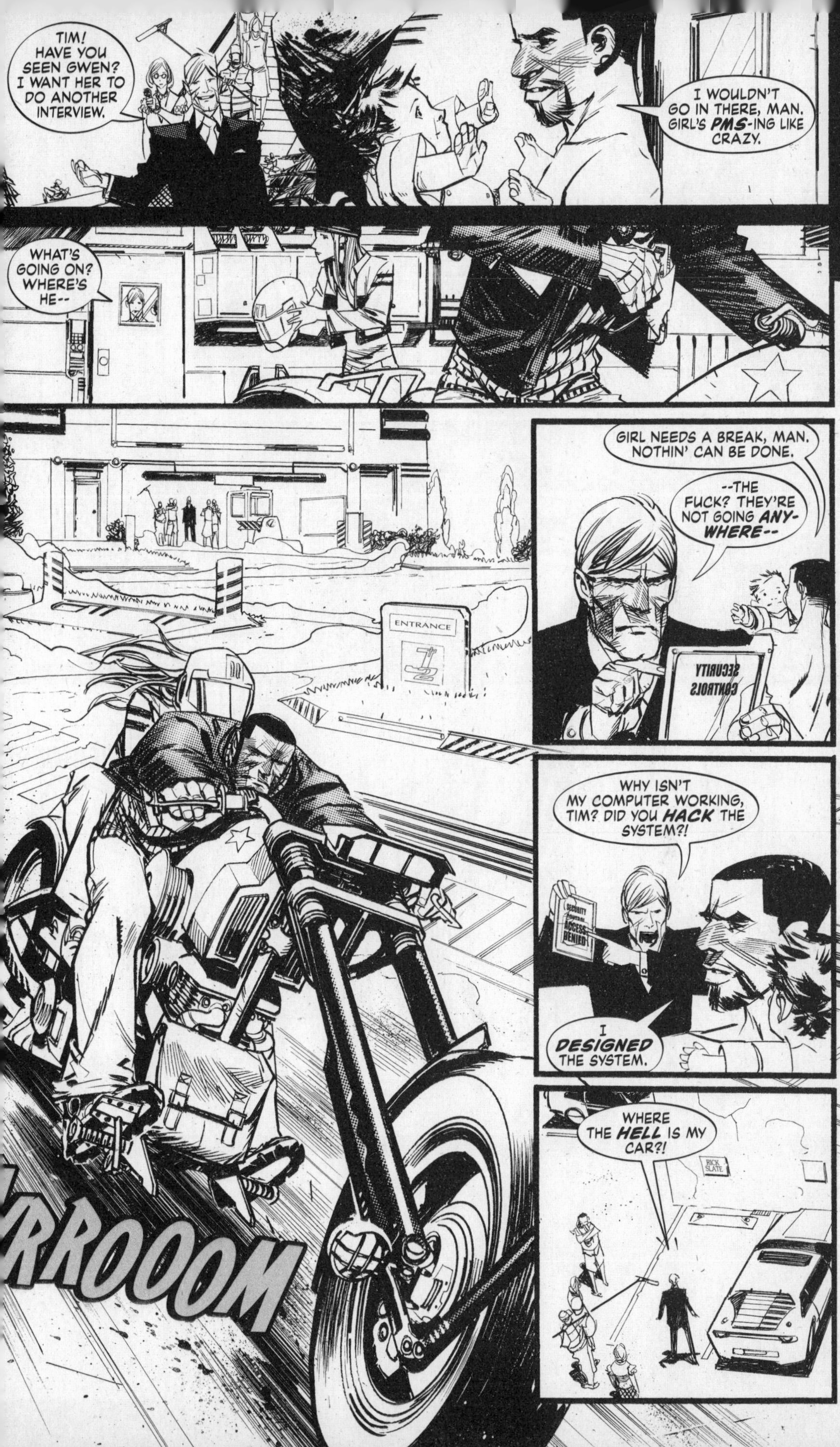
TIM! HAVE YOU SEEN GWEN? I WANT HER TO DO ANOTHER INTERVIEW.
I WOULDN'T GO IN THERE, MAN. GIRL'S PMS-ING LIKE CRAZY.
WHAT'S GOING ON? WHERE'S HE--
ENTRANCE
GIRL NEEDS A BREAK, MAN. NOTHIN' CAN BE DONE.
--THE FUCK? THEY'RE NOT GOING ANYWHERE--
SECURITY CONTROLS
VRROOOM
WHY ISN'T MY COMPUTER WORKING, TIM? DID YOU HACK THE SYSTEM?!
ACCESS DENIED
I DESIGNED THE SYSTEM.
WHERE THE HELL IS MY CAR?!
RICK SLATE

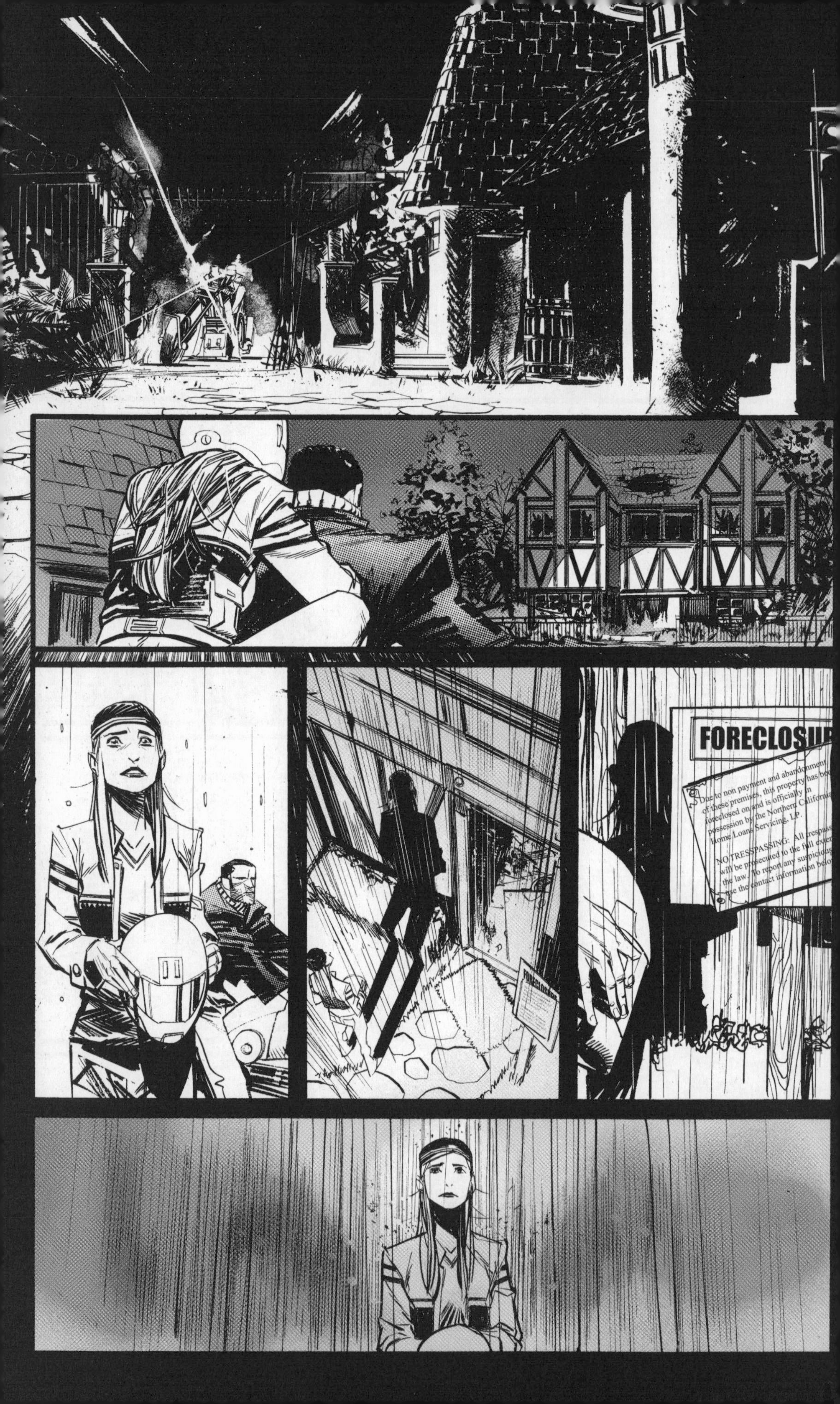
FORECLOSUR
Due to non payment and abandonment of these premises, this property has bee foreclosed on and is officially in possession by the Northern California Home Loans Servicing, LP.
NO TRESSPASSING: All trespass will be prosecuted to the full exten the law. To report any suspicious use the contact information belo

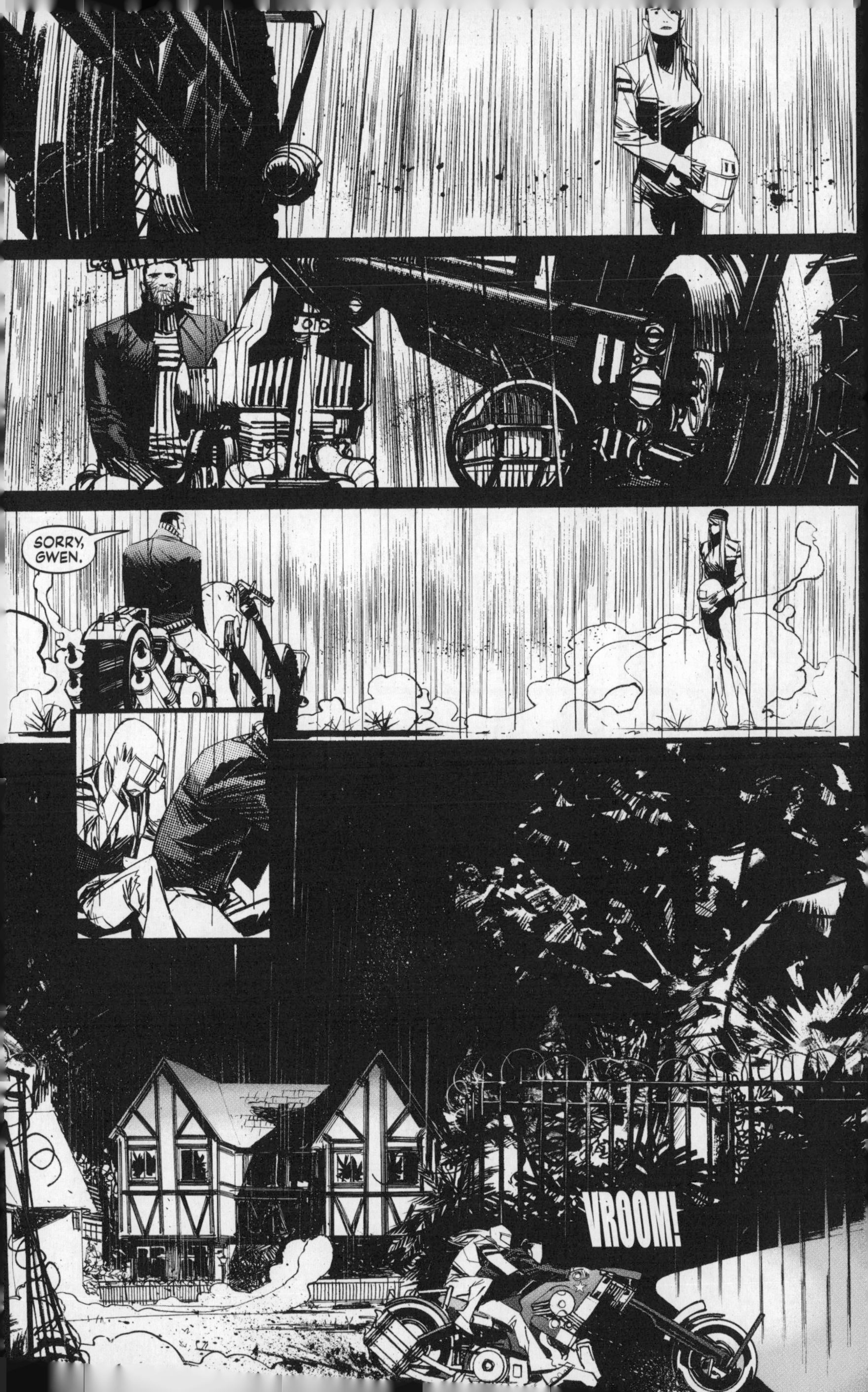
SORRY, GWEN.
VROOM!

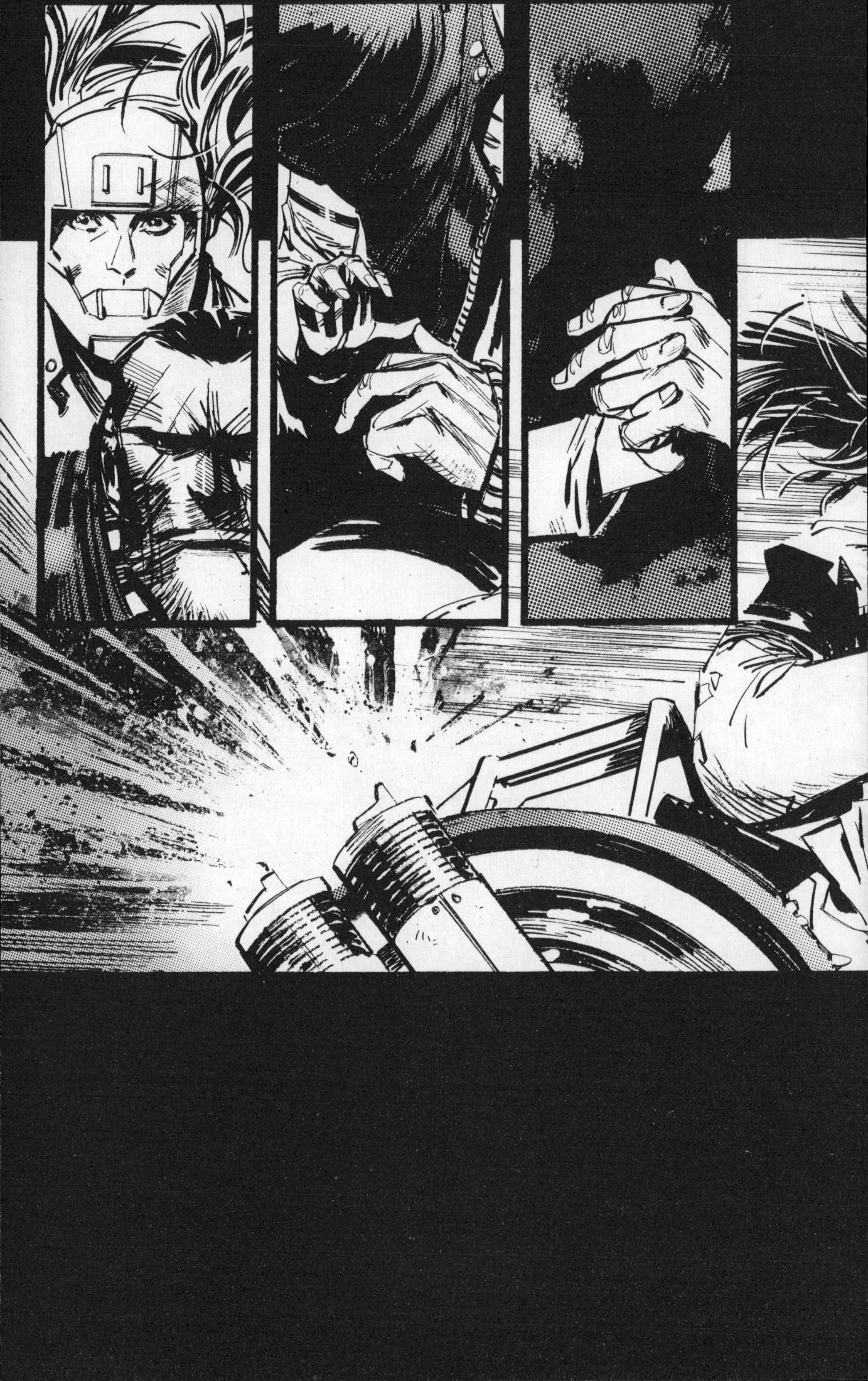

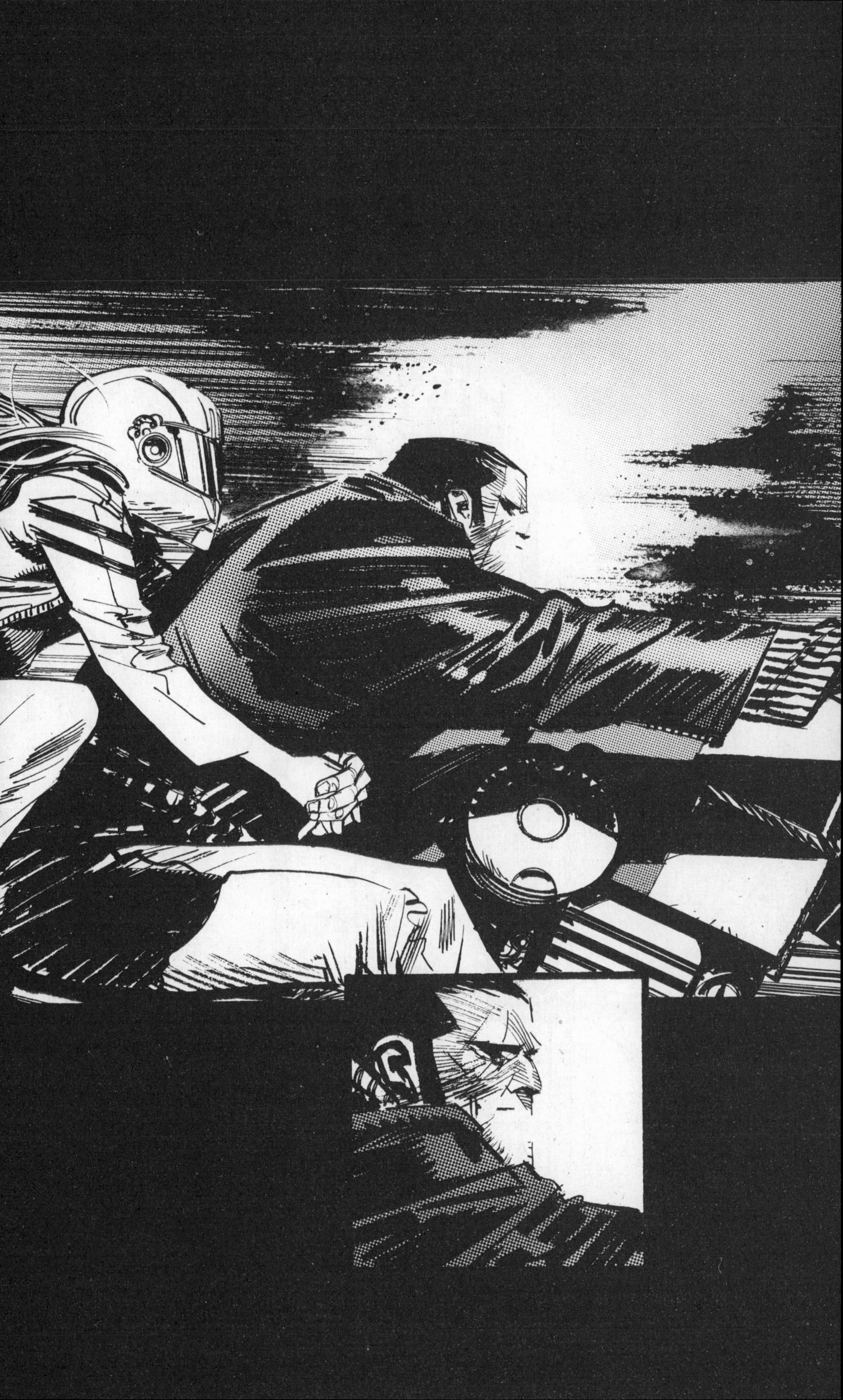

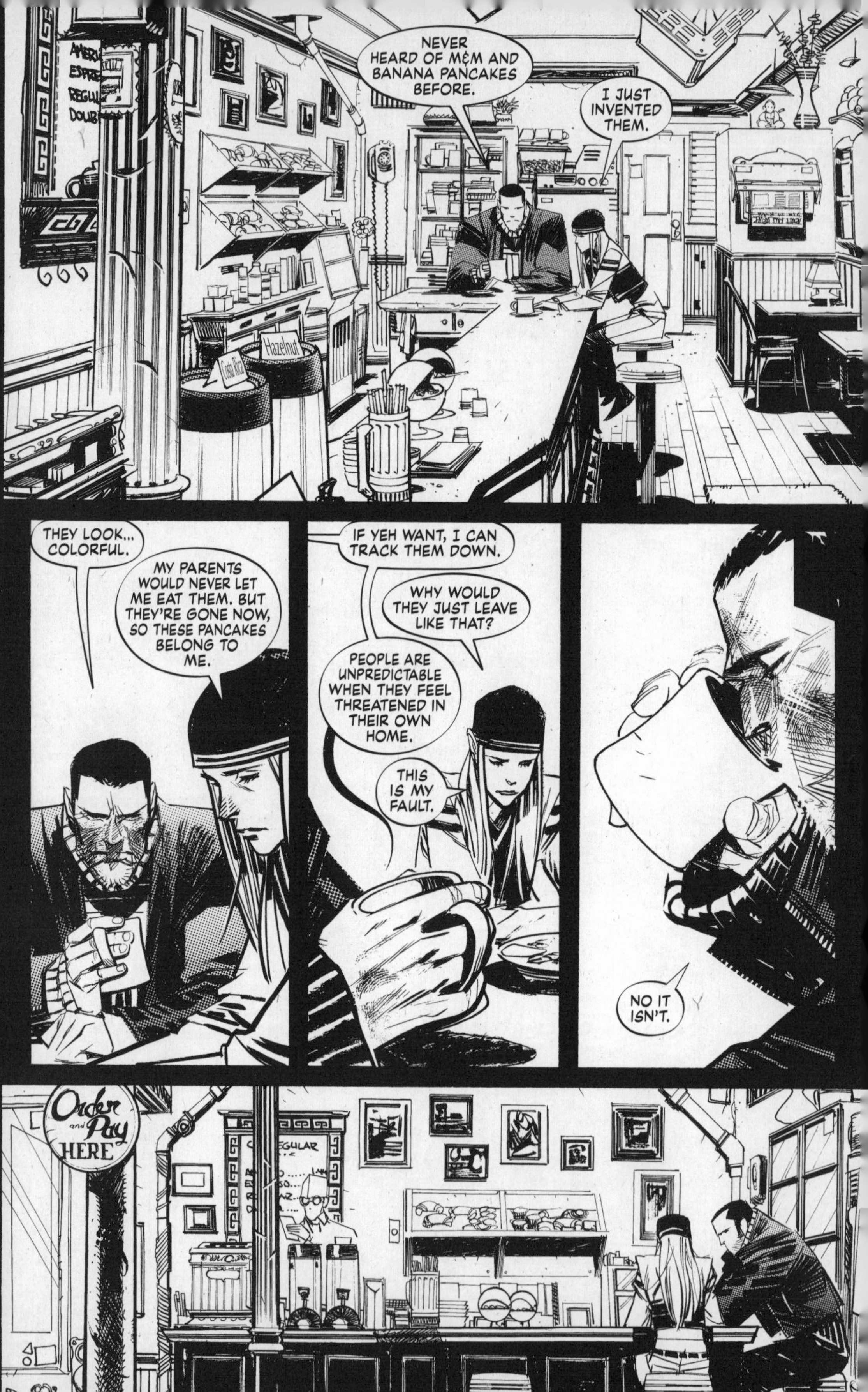
NEVER HEARD OF M&M AND BANANA PANCAKES BEFORE.
I JUST INVENTED THEM.
Hazelnut
Costa Rica
THEY LOOK... COLORFUL.
MY PARENTS WOULD NEVER LET ME EAT THEM. BUT THEY'RE GONE NOW, SO THESE PANCAKES BELONG TO ME.
IF YEH WANT, I CAN TRACK THEM DOWN.
WHY WOULD THEY JUST LEAVE LIKE THAT?
PEOPLE ARE UNPREDICTABLE WHEN THEY FEEL THREATENED IN THEIR OWN HOME.
THIS IS MY FAULT.
NO IT ISN'T.
Order and Pay HERE

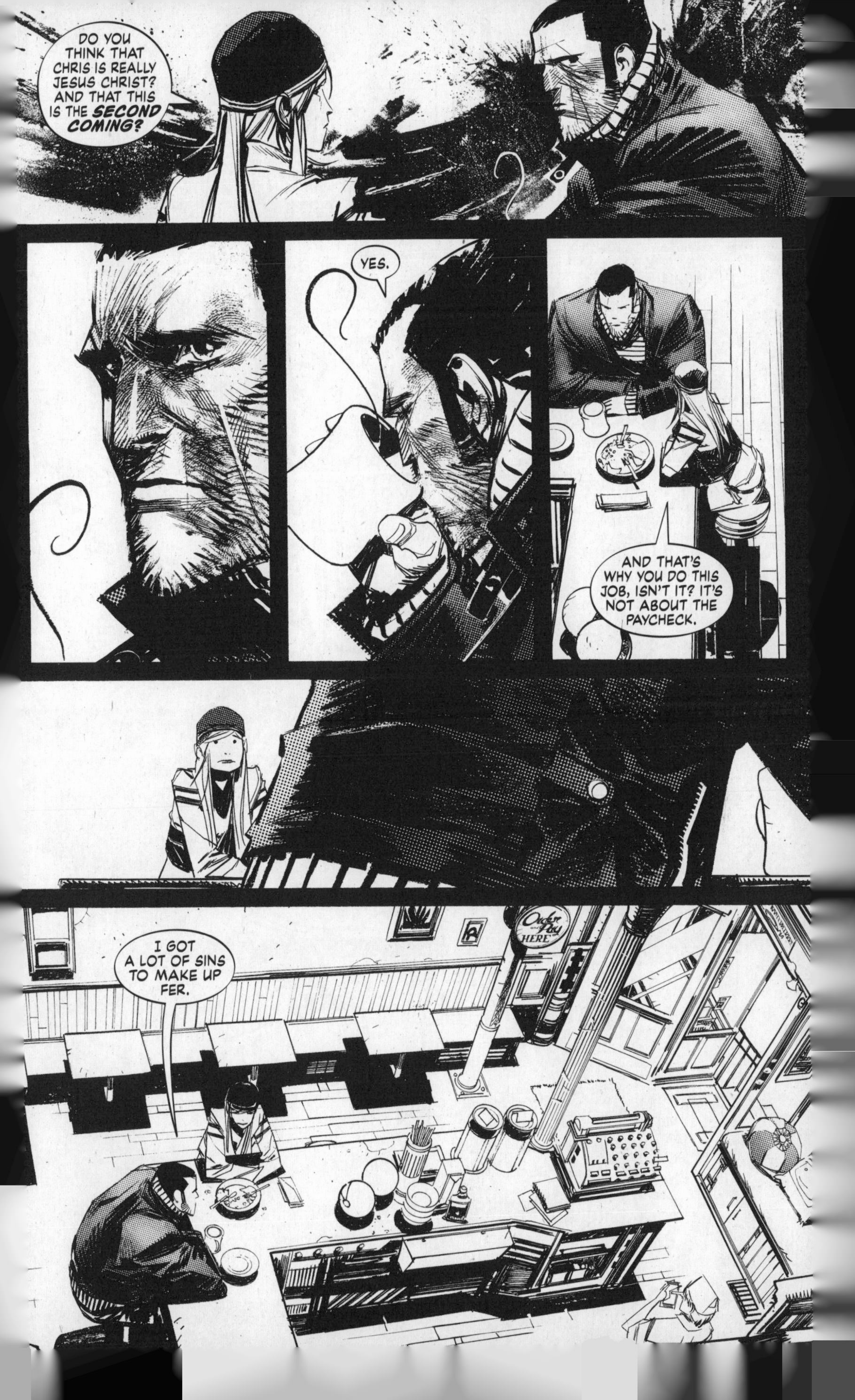
DO YOU THINK THAT CHRIS IS REALLY JESUS CHRIST? AND THAT THIS IS THE SECOND COMING?
YES.
AND THAT'S WHY YOU DO THIS JOB, ISN'T IT? IT'S NOT ABOUT THE PAYCHECK.
I GOT A LOT OF SINS TO MAKE UP FER.
Order and Pay HERE

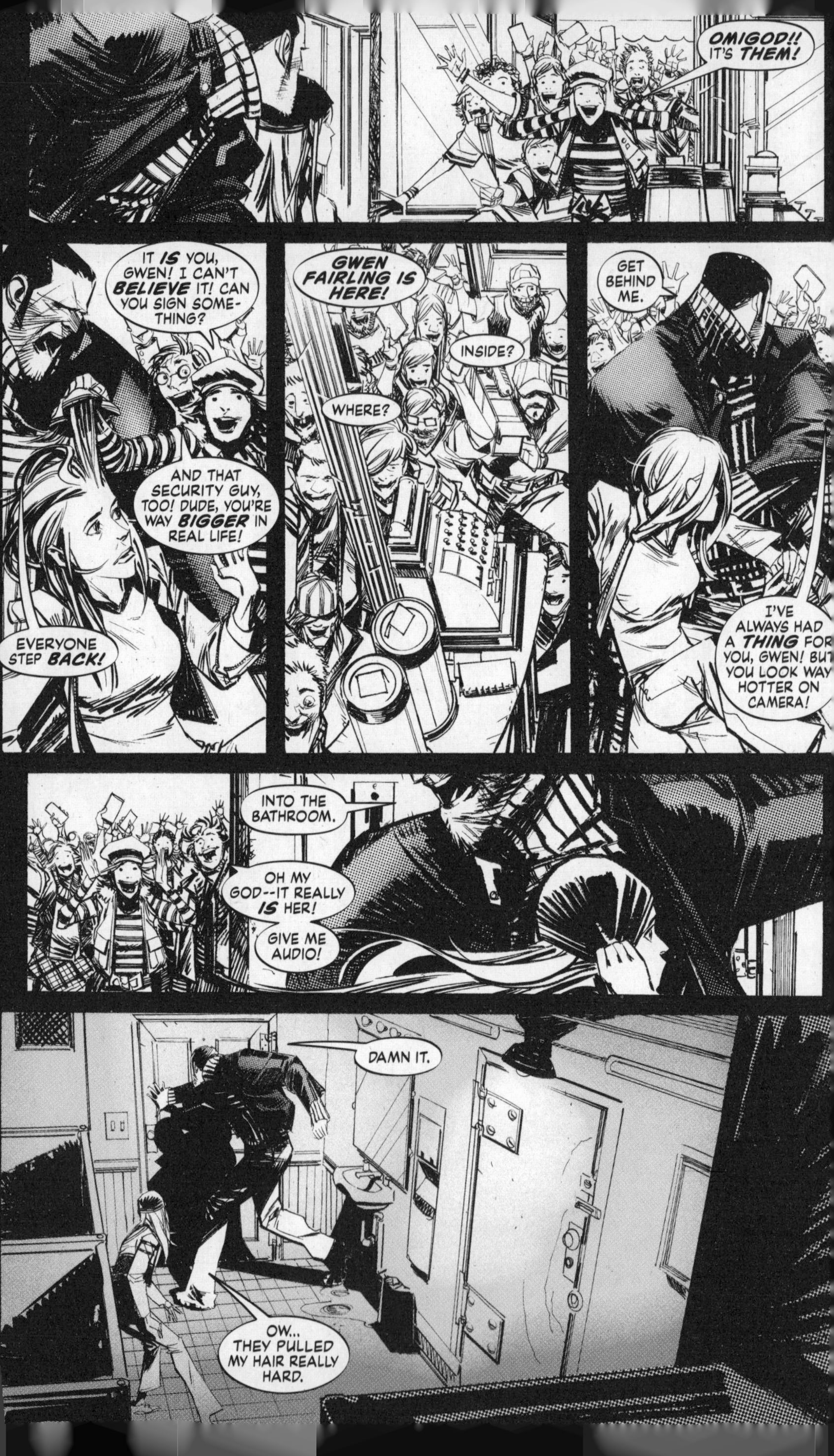

OMIGOD!! IT'S THEM!
IT IS YOU, GWEN! I CAN'T BELIEVE IT! CAN YOU SIGN SOMETHING?
AND THAT SECURITY GUY, TOO! DUDE, YOU'RE WAY BIGGER IN REAL LIFE!
EVERYONE STEP BACK!
GWEN FAIRLING IS HERE!
INSIDE?
WHERE?
GET BEHIND ME.
I'VE ALWAYS HAD A THING FOR YOU, GWEN! BUT YOU LOOK WAY HOTTER ON CAMERA!
INTO THE BATHROOM.
OH MY GOD--IT REALLY IS HER!
GIVE ME AUDIO!
DAMN IT.
OW... THEY PULLED MY HAIR REALLY HARD.

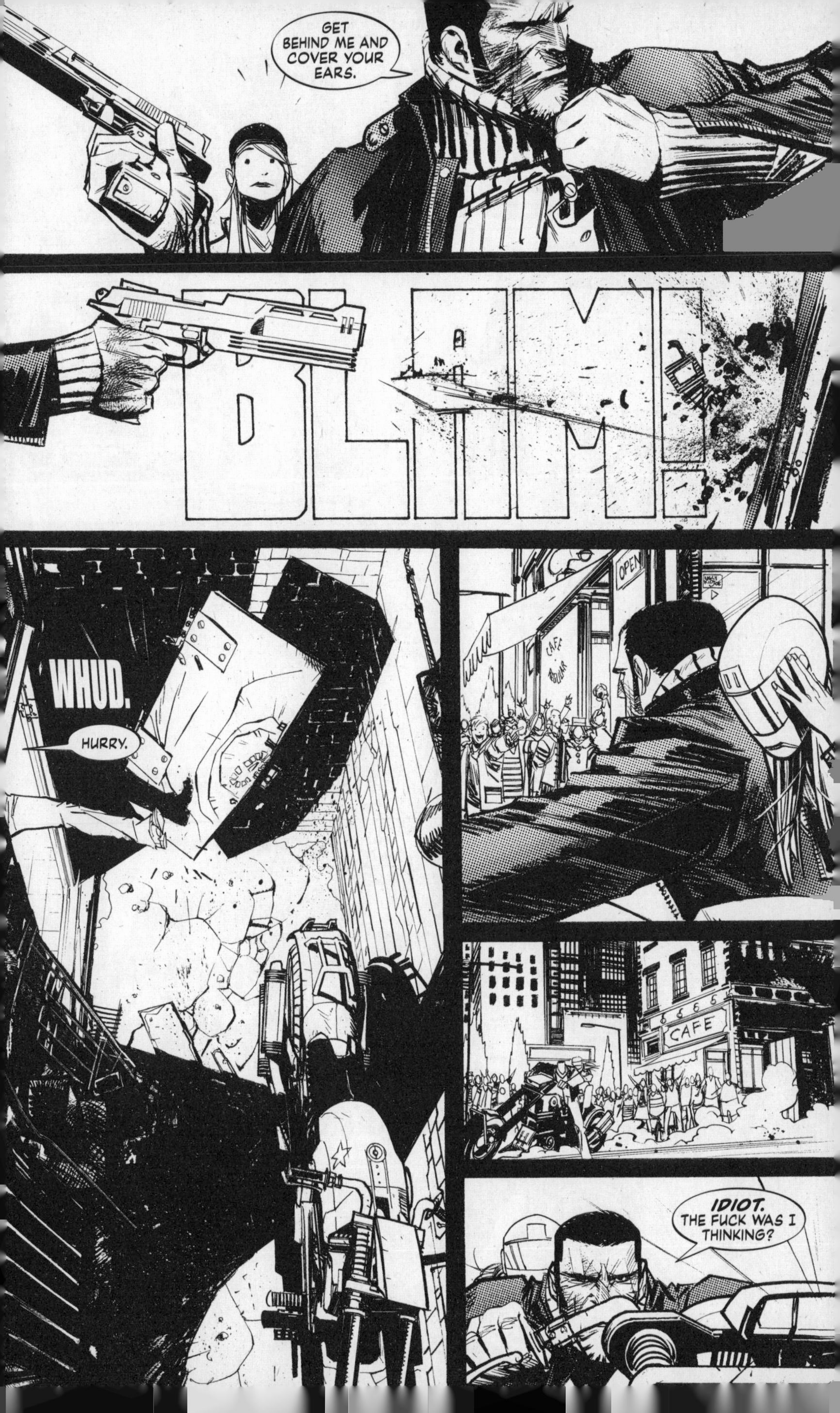
GET BEHIND ME AND COVER YOUR EARS.
BLAM!
WHUD.
HURRY.
OPEN
CAFE
CAFE
IDIOT. THE FUCK WAS I THINKING?

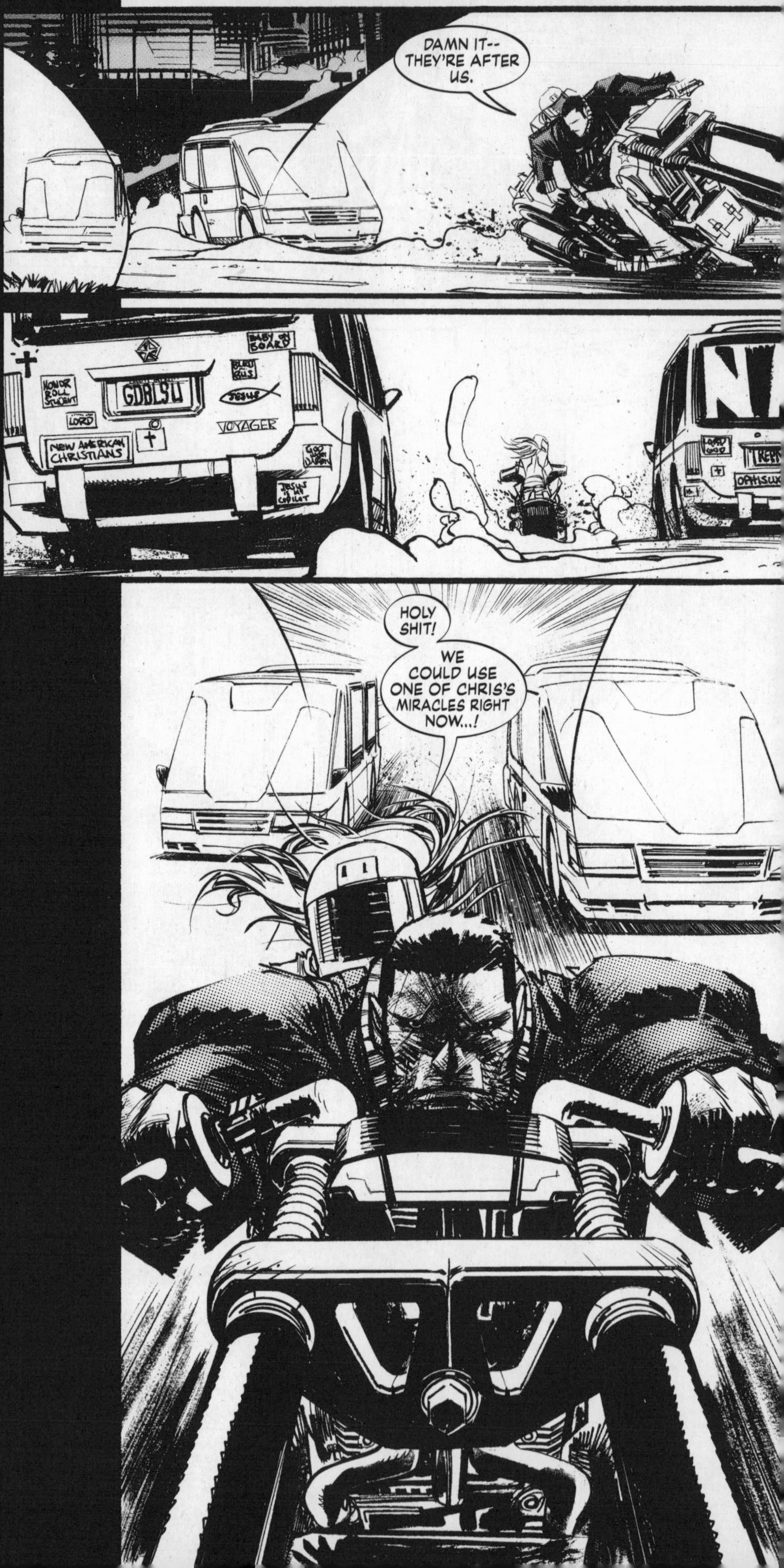
DAMN IT-- THEY'RE AFTER US.
BABY ON BOARD
HONOR ROLL STUDENT
GDBLSU
JESUS
LORD
VOYAGER
NEW AMERICAN CHRISTIANS
JESUS IS MY COPILOT
HOLY SHIT!
WE COULD USE ONE OF CHRIS'S MIRACLES RIGHT NOW...!

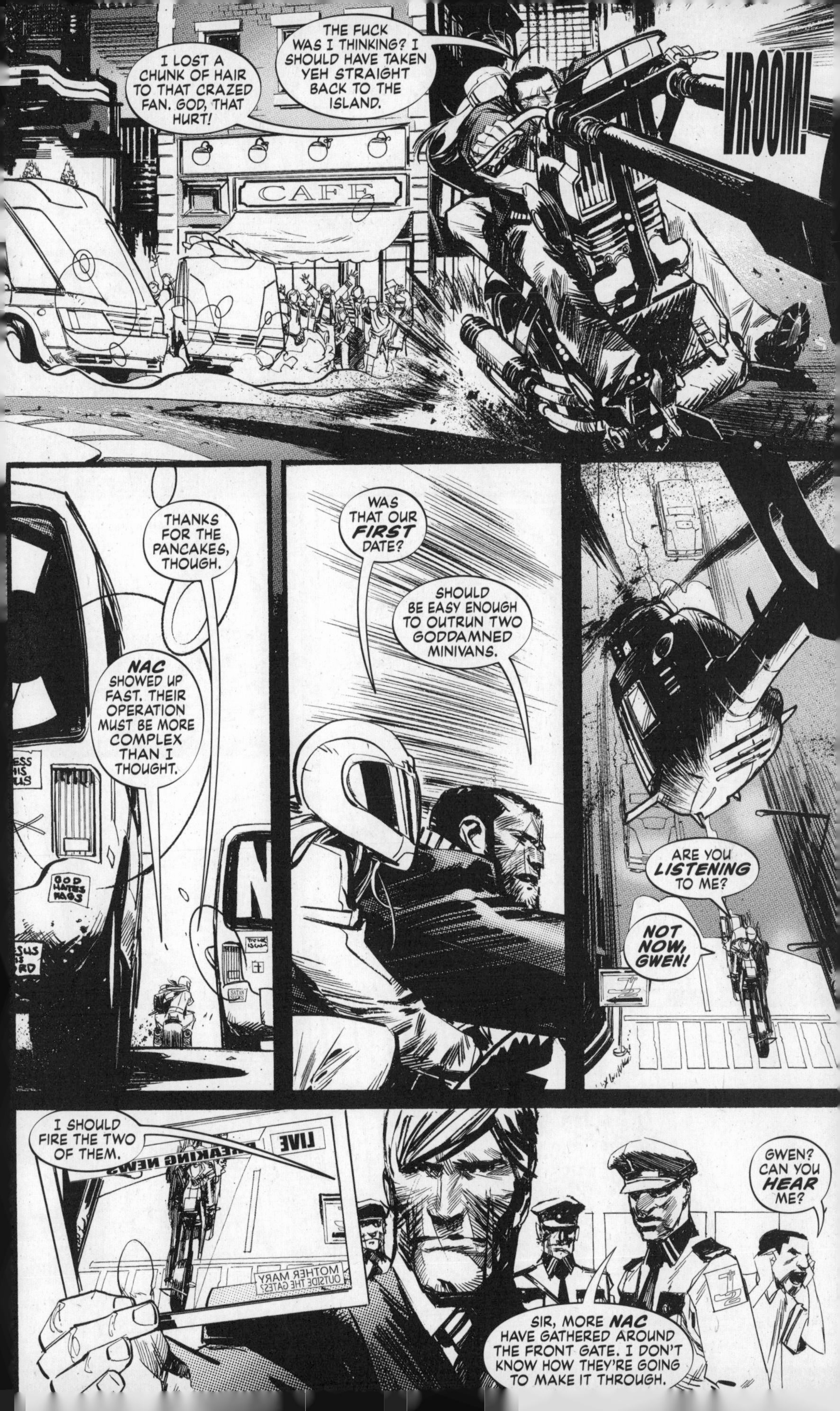
I LOST A CHUNK OF HAIR TO THAT CRAZED FAN. GOD, THAT HURT!
THE FUCK WAS I THINKING? I SHOULD HAVE TAKEN YEH STRAIGHT BACK TO THE ISLAND.
VROOM!
CAFE
THANKS FOR THE PANCAKES, THOUGH.
NAC SHOWED UP FAST. THEIR OPERATION MUST BE MORE COMPLEX THAN I THOUGHT.
WAS THAT OUR FIRST DATE?
SHOULD BE EASY ENOUGH TO OUTRUN TWO GODDAMNED MINIVANS.
ARE YOU LISTENING TO ME?
NOT NOW, GWEN!
I SHOULD FIRE THE TWO OF THEM.
GWEN? CAN YOU HEAR ME?
SIR, MORE NAC HAVE GATHERED AROUND THE FRONT GATE. I DON'T KNOW HOW THEY'RE GOING TO MAKE IT THROUGH.

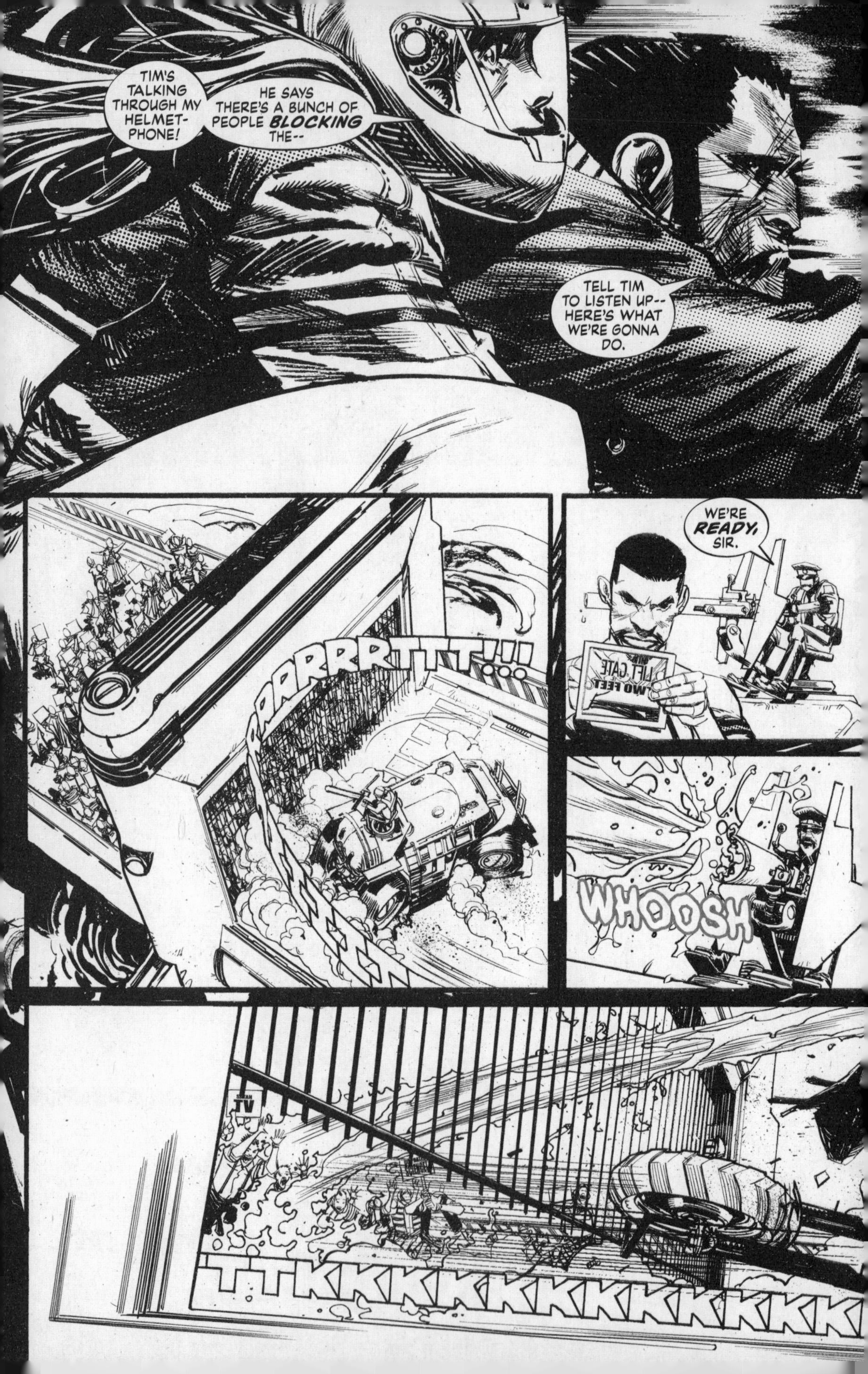
TIM'S TALKING THROUGH MY HELMET-PHONE!
HE SAYS THERE'S A BUNCH OF PEOPLE BLOCKING THE--
TELL TIM TO LISTEN UP-- HERE'S WHAT WE'RE GONNA DO.
RRRTTTT!!!
WE'RE READY, SIR.
WHOOSH
TTKKKKKKKKKKKKK

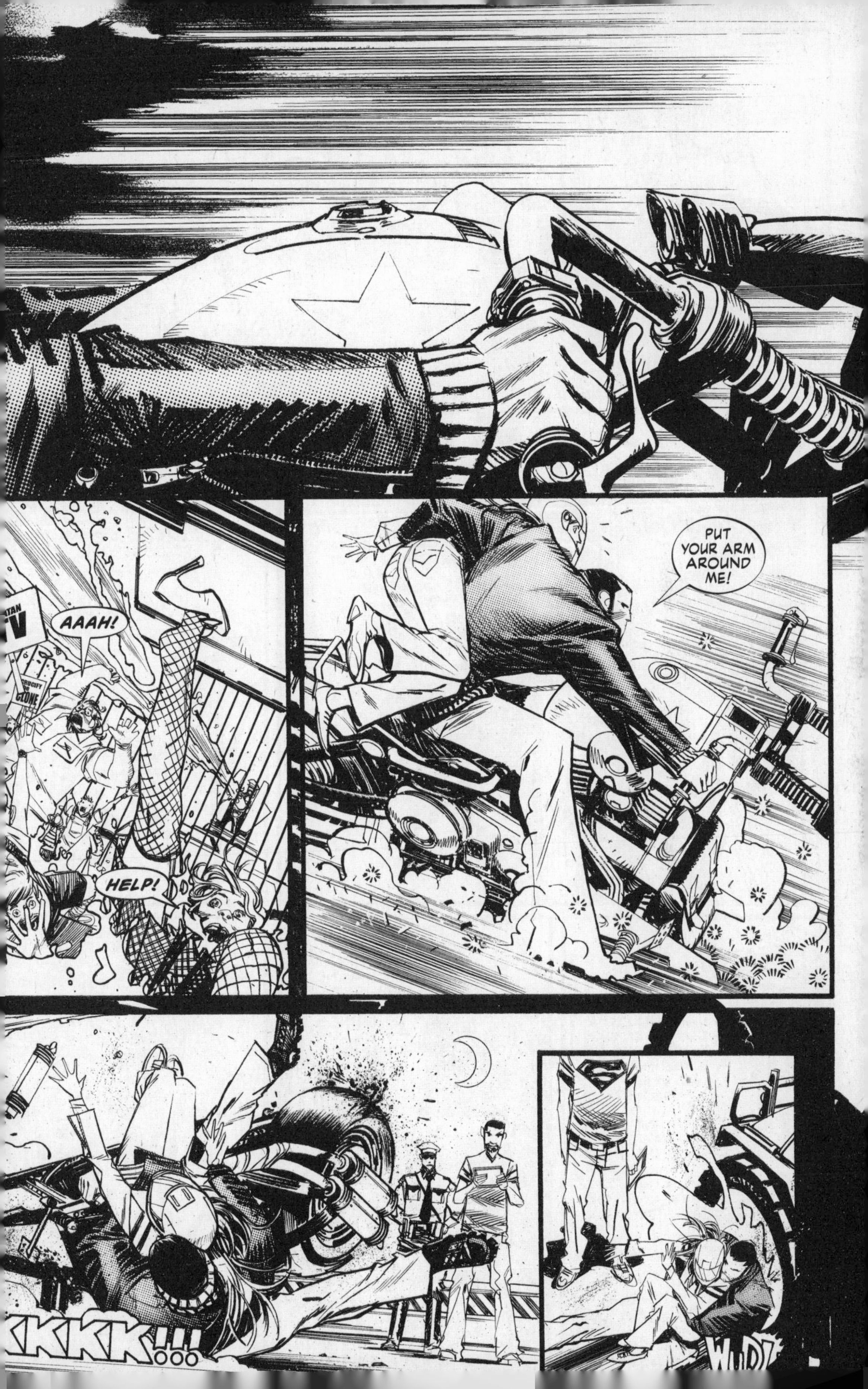

AAAH!
HELP!
PUT YOUR ARM AROUND ME!
KKKK!!!

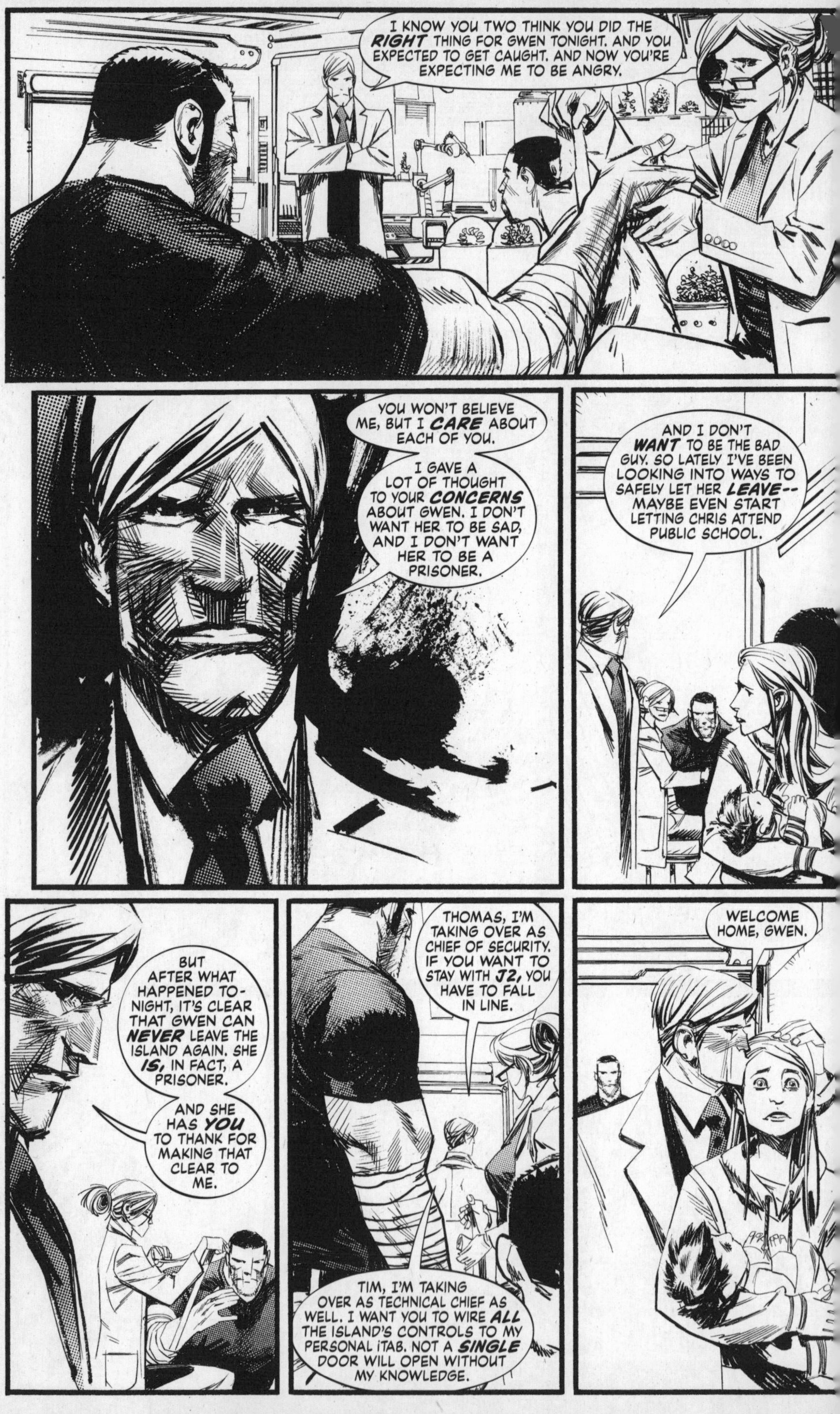
I KNOW YOU TWO THINK YOU DID THE RIGHT THING FOR GWEN TONIGHT. AND YOU EXPECTED TO GET CAUGHT. AND NOW YOU'RE EXPECTING ME TO BE ANGRY.
YOU WON'T BELIEVE ME, BUT I CARE ABOUT EACH OF YOU.
I GAVE A LOT OF THOUGHT TO YOUR CONCERNS ABOUT GWEN. I DON'T WANT HER TO BE SAD, AND I DON'T WANT HER TO BE A PRISONER.
AND I DON'T WANT TO BE THE BAD GUY. SO LATELY I'VE BEEN LOOKING INTO WAYS TO SAFELY LET HER LEAVE-- MAYBE EVEN START LETTING CHRIS ATTEND PUBLIC SCHOOL.
BUT AFTER WHAT HAPPENED TO-NIGHT, IT'S CLEAR THAT GWEN CAN NEVER LEAVE THE ISLAND AGAIN. SHE IS, IN FACT, A PRISONER.
AND SHE HAS YOU TO THANK FOR MAKING THAT CLEAR TO ME.
THOMAS, I'M TAKING OVER AS CHIEF OF SECURITY. IF YOU WANT TO STAY WITH J2, YOU HAVE TO FALL IN LINE.
TIM, I'M TAKING OVER AS TECHNICAL CHIEF AS WELL. I WANT YOU TO WIRE ALL THE ISLAND'S CONTROLS TO MY PERSONAL iTAB. NOT A SINGLE DOOR WILL OPEN WITHOUT MY KNOWLEDGE.
WELCOME HOME, GWEN.

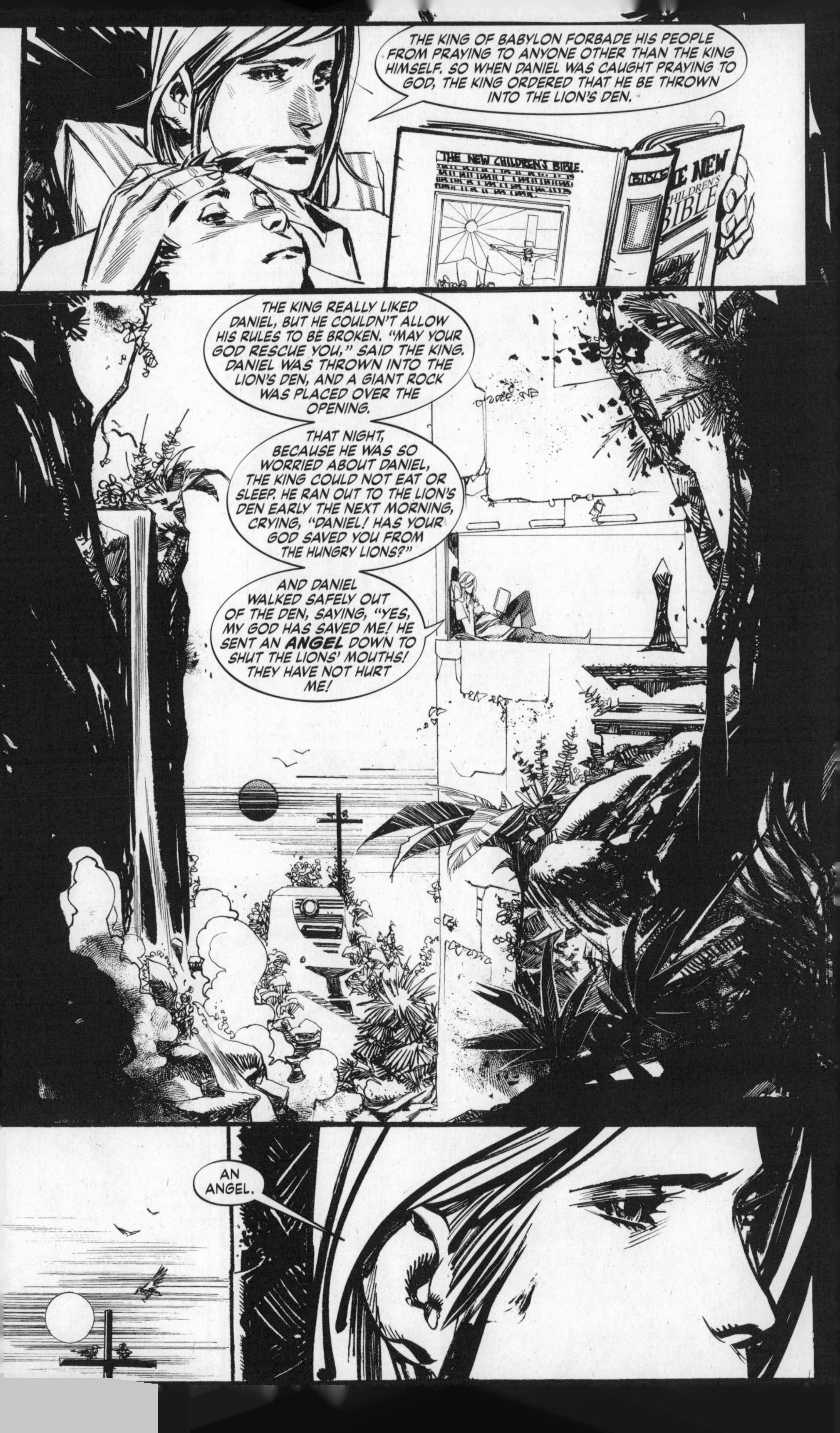
THE KING OF BABYLON FORBADE HIS PEOPLE FROM PRAYING TO ANYONE OTHER THAN THE KING HIMSELF. SO WHEN DANIEL WAS CAUGHT PRAYING TO GOD, THE KING ORDERED THAT HE BE THROWN INTO THE LION'S DEN.
THE NEW CHILDREN'S BIBLE
THE KING REALLY LIKED DANIEL, BUT HE COULDN'T ALLOW HIS RULES TO BE BROKEN. "MAY YOUR GOD RESCUE YOU," SAID THE KING. DANIEL WAS THROWN INTO THE LION'S DEN, AND A GIANT ROCK WAS PLACED OVER THE OPENING.
THAT NIGHT, BECAUSE HE WAS SO WORRIED ABOUT DANIEL, THE KING COULD NOT EAT OR SLEEP. HE RAN OUT TO THE LION'S DEN EARLY THE NEXT MORNING, CRYING, "DANIEL! HAS YOUR GOD SAVED YOU FROM THE HUNGRY LIONS?"
AND DANIEL WALKED SAFELY OUT OF THE DEN, SAYING, "YES, MY GOD HAS SAVED ME! HE SENT AN ANGEL DOWN TO SHUT THE LIONS' MOUTHS! THEY HAVE NOT HURT ME!
AN ANGEL.

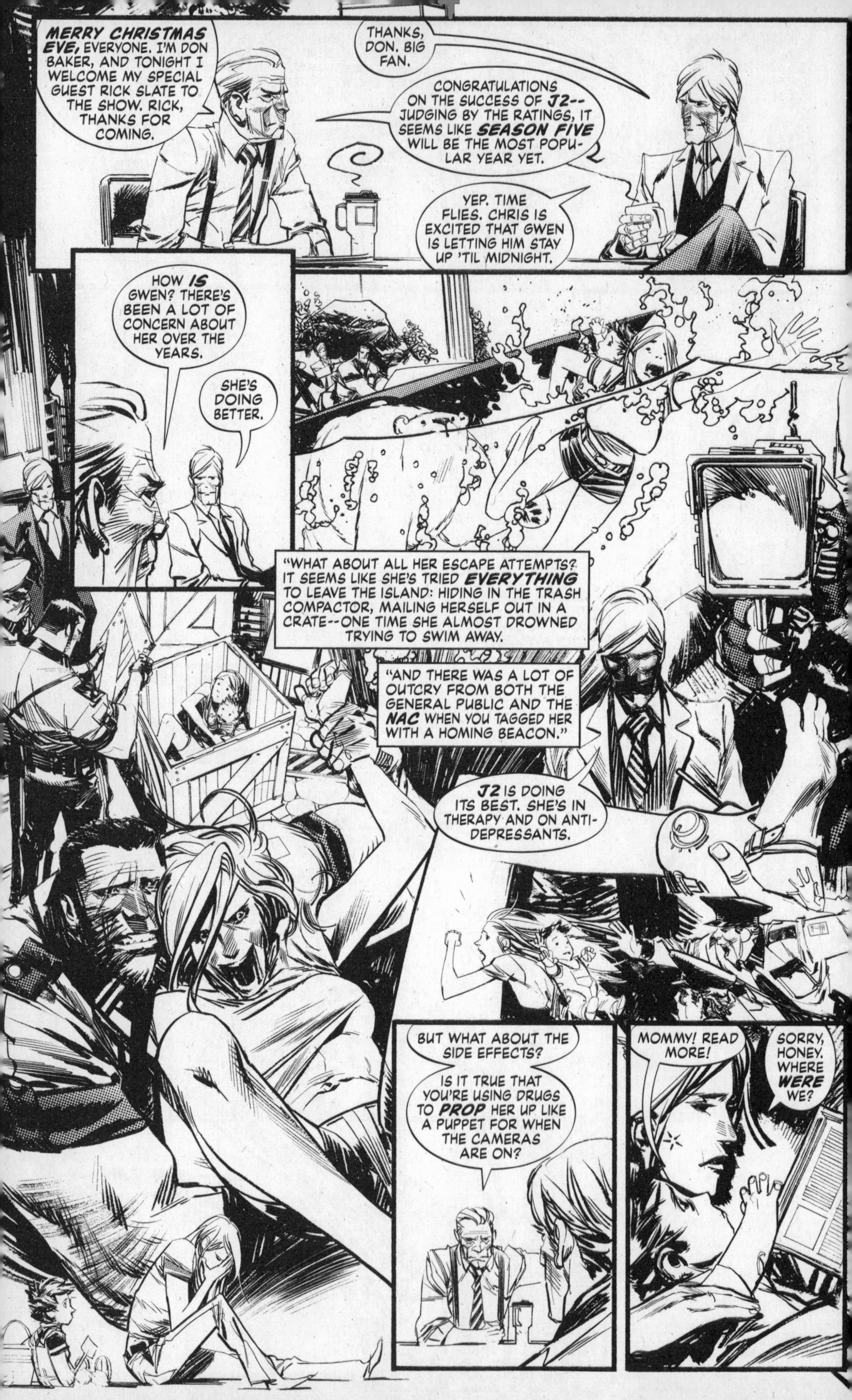
MERRY CHRISTMAS EVE, EVERYONE. I'M DON BAKER, AND TONIGHT I WELCOME MY SPECIAL GUEST RICK SLATE TO THE SHOW. RICK, THANKS FOR COMING.
THANKS, DON. BIG FAN.
CONGRATULATIONS ON THE SUCCESS OF J2--JUDGING BY THE RATINGS, IT SEEMS LIKE SEASON FIVE WILL BE THE MOST POPULAR YEAR YET.
YEP. TIME FLIES. CHRIS IS EXCITED THAT GWEN IS LETTING HIM STAY UP 'TIL MIDNIGHT.
HOW IS GWEN? THERE'S BEEN A LOT OF CONCERN ABOUT HER OVER THE YEARS.
SHE'S DOING BETTER.
"WHAT ABOUT ALL HER ESCAPE ATTEMPTS? IT SEEMS LIKE SHE'S TRIED EVERYTHING TO LEAVE THE ISLAND: HIDING IN THE TRASH COMPACTOR, MAILING HERSELF OUT IN A CRATE--ONE TIME SHE ALMOST DROWNED TRYING TO SWIM AWAY.
"AND THERE WAS A LOT OF OUTCRY FROM BOTH THE GENERAL PUBLIC AND THE NAC WHEN YOU TAGGED HER WITH A HOMING BEACON."
J2 IS DOING ITS BEST. SHE'S IN THERAPY AND ON ANTI-DEPRESSANTS.
BUT WHAT ABOUT THE SIDE EFFECTS?
IS IT TRUE THAT YOU'RE USING DRUGS TO PROP HER UP LIKE A PUPPET FOR WHEN THE CAMERAS ARE ON?
MOMMY! READ MORE!
SORRY, HONEY. WHERE WERE WE?

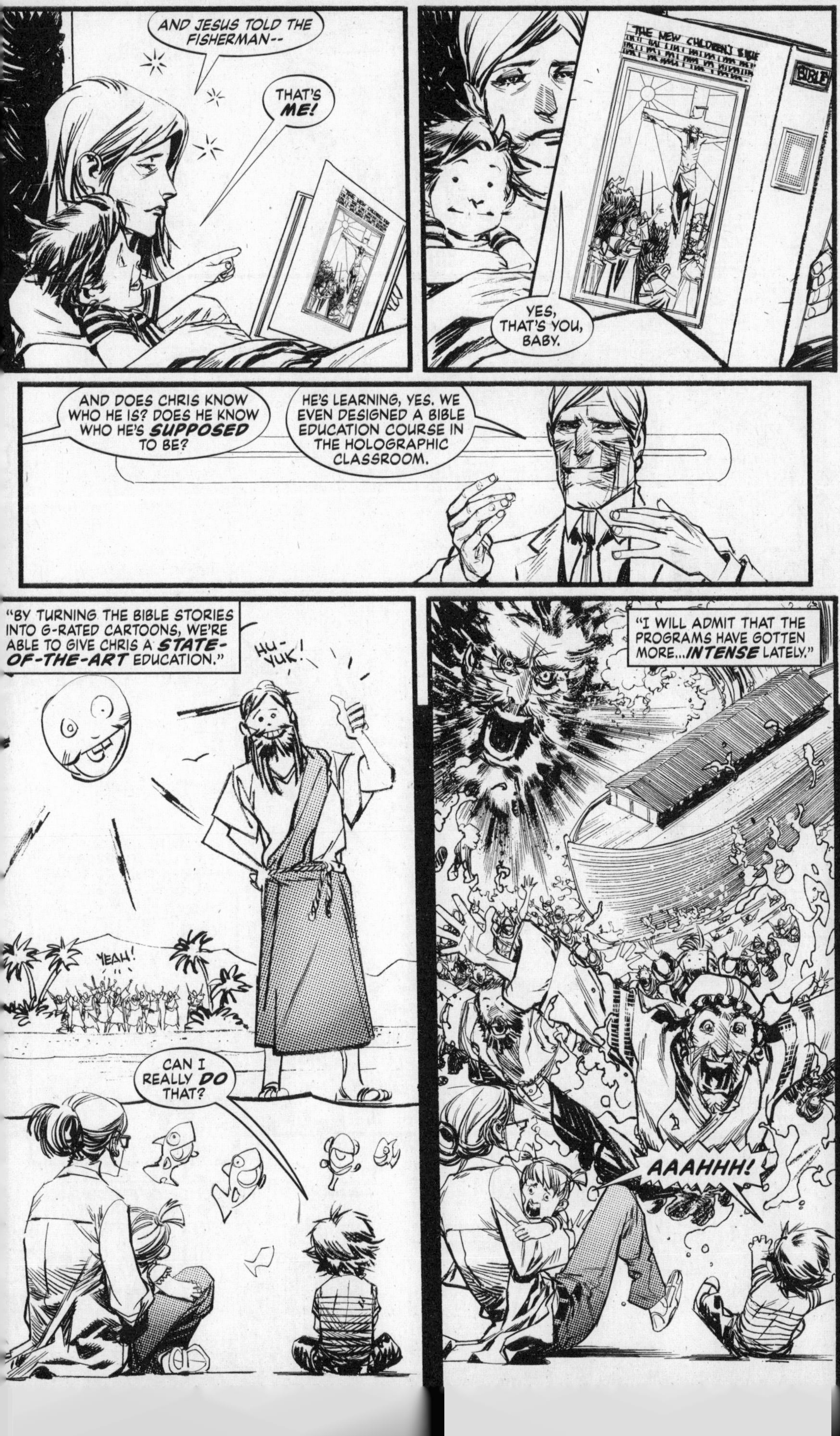
AND JESUS TOLD THE FISHERMAN--
THAT'S ME!
THE NEW CHILDREN'S BIBLE
BIBLE
YES, THAT'S YOU, BABY.
AND DOES CHRIS KNOW WHO HE IS? DOES HE KNOW WHO HE'S SUPPOSED TO BE?
HE'S LEARNING, YES. WE EVEN DESIGNED A BIBLE EDUCATION COURSE IN THE HOLOGRAPHIC CLASSROOM.
"BY TURNING THE BIBLE STORIES INTO G-RATED CARTOONS, WE'RE ABLE TO GIVE CHRIS A STATE-OF-THE-ART EDUCATION."
HU-YUK!
YEAH!
CAN I REALLY DO THAT?
"I WILL ADMIT THAT THE PROGRAMS HAVE GOTTEN MORE...INTENSE LATELY."
AAAHHH!

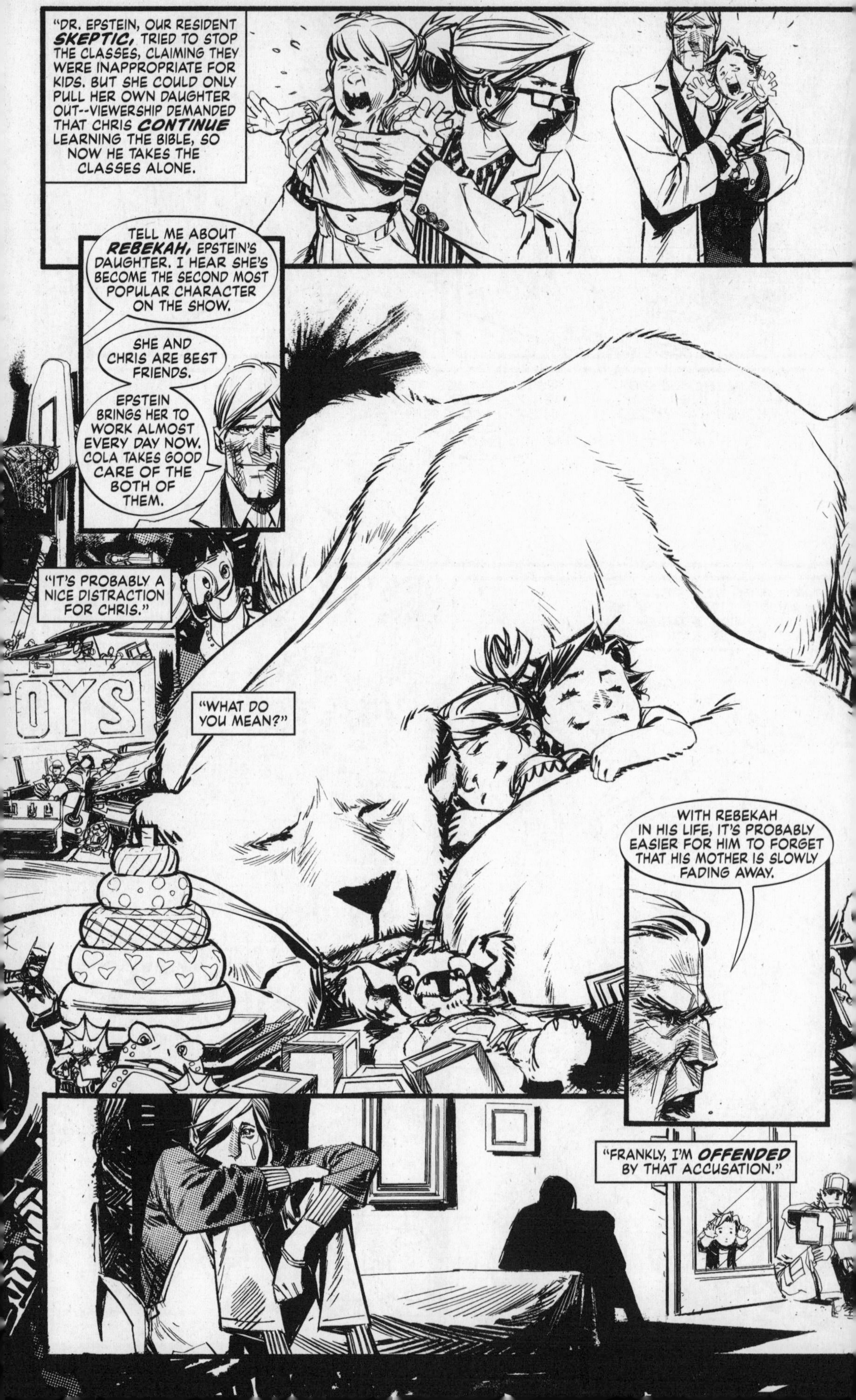
"DR. EPSTEIN, OUR RESIDENT SKEPTIC, TRIED TO STOP THE CLASSES, CLAIMING THEY WERE INAPPROPRIATE FOR KIDS. BUT SHE COULD ONLY PULL HER OWN DAUGHTER OUT--VIEWERSHIP DEMANDED THAT CHRIS CONTINUE LEARNING THE BIBLE, SO NOW HE TAKES THE CLASSES ALONE.
TELL ME ABOUT REBEKAH, EPSTEIN'S DAUGHTER. I HEAR SHE'S BECOME THE SECOND MOST POPULAR CHARACTER ON THE SHOW.
SHE AND CHRIS ARE BEST FRIENDS.
EPSTEIN BRINGS HER TO WORK ALMOST EVERY DAY NOW. COLA TAKES GOOD CARE OF THE BOTH OF THEM.
"IT'S PROBABLY A NICE DISTRACTION FOR CHRIS."
TOYS
"WHAT DO YOU MEAN?"
WITH REBEKAH IN HIS LIFE, IT'S PROBABLY EASIER FOR HIM TO FORGET THAT HIS MOTHER IS SLOWLY FADING AWAY.
"FRANKLY, I'M OFFENDED BY THAT ACCUSATION."

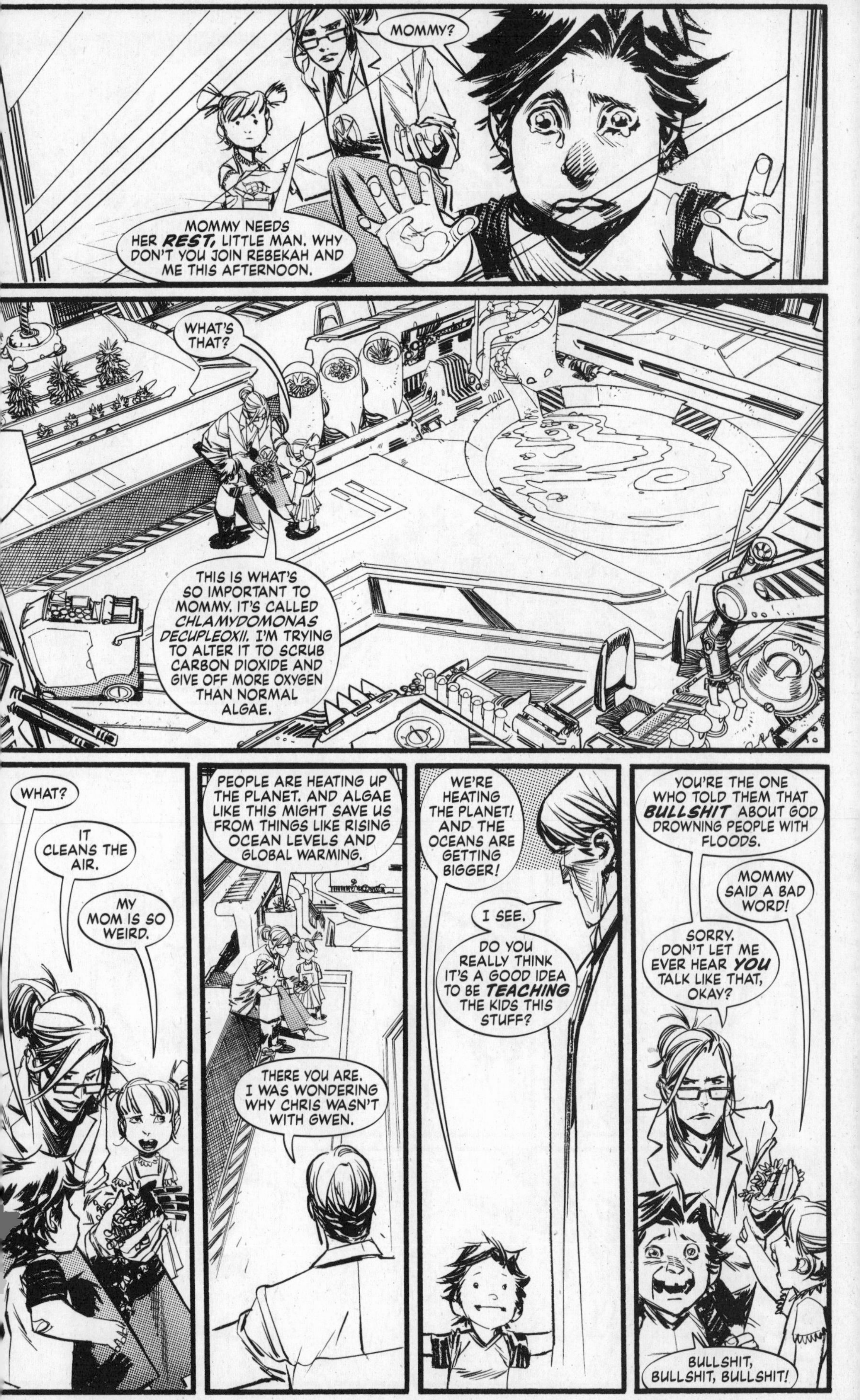
MOMMY?
MOMMY NEEDS HER REST, LITTLE MAN. WHY DON'T YOU JOIN REBEKAH AND ME THIS AFTERNOON.
WHAT'S THAT?
THIS IS WHAT'S SO IMPORTANT TO MOMMY. IT'S CALLED CHLAMYDOMONAS DECUPLEOXII. I'M TRYING TO ALTER IT TO SCRUB CARBON DIOXIDE AND GIVE OFF MORE OXYGEN THAN NORMAL ALGAE.
WHAT?
IT CLEANS THE AIR.
MY MOM IS SO WEIRD.
PEOPLE ARE HEATING UP THE PLANET. AND ALGAE LIKE THIS MIGHT SAVE US FROM THINGS LIKE RISING OCEAN LEVELS AND GLOBAL WARMING.
THERE YOU ARE. I WAS WONDERING WHY CHRIS WASN'T WITH GWEN.
WE'RE HEATING THE PLANET! AND THE OCEANS ARE GETTING BIGGER!
I SEE.
DO YOU REALLY THINK IT'S A GOOD IDEA TO BE TEACHING THE KIDS THIS STUFF?
YOU'RE THE ONE WHO TOLD THEM THAT BULLSHIT ABOUT GOD DROWNING PEOPLE WITH FLOODS.
MOMMY SAID A BAD WORD!
SORRY. DON'T LET ME EVER HEAR YOU TALK LIKE THAT, OKAY?
BULLSHIT, BULLSHIT, BULLSHIT!

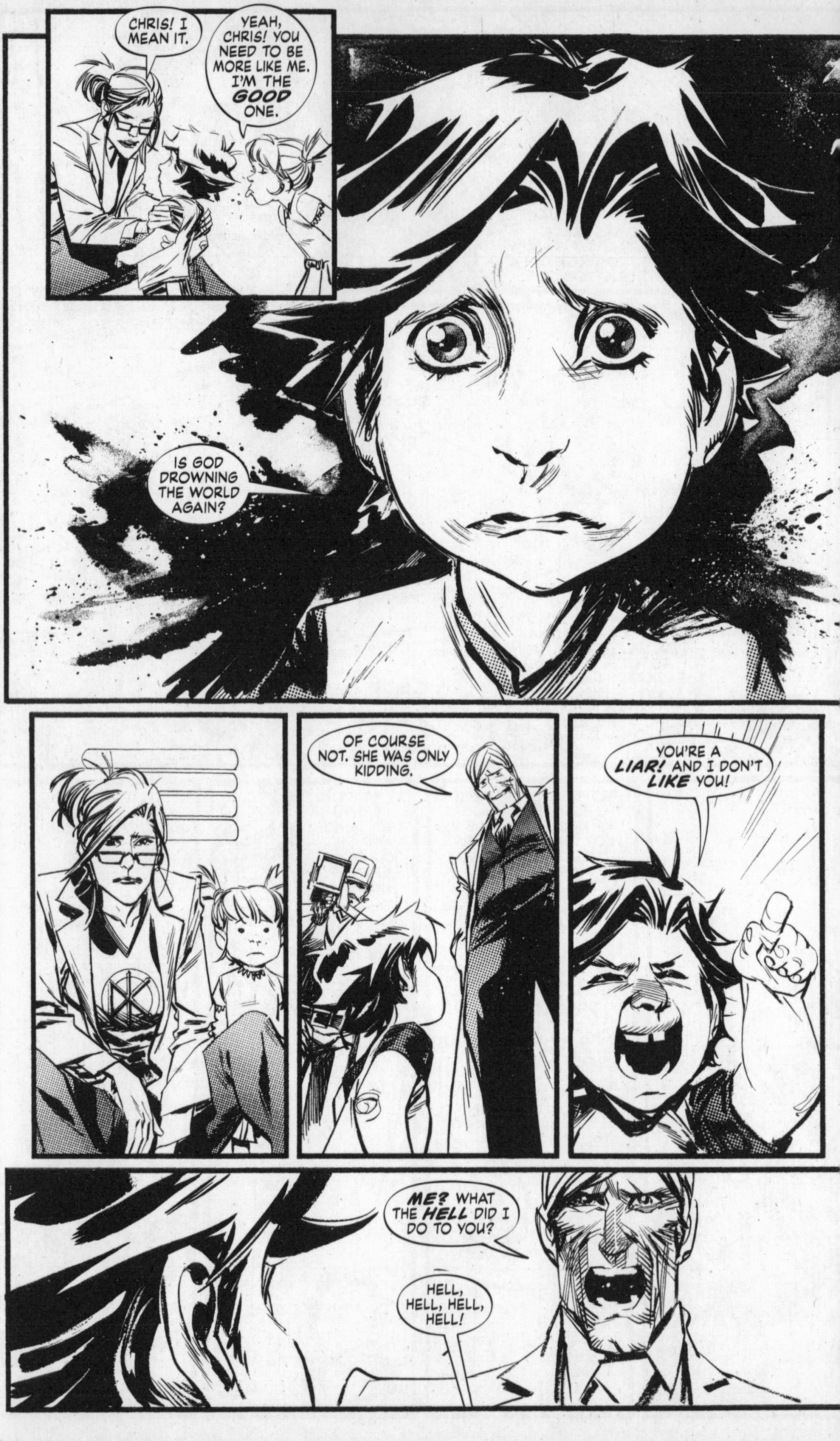
CHRIS! I MEAN IT.
YEAH, CHRIS! YOU NEED TO BE MORE LIKE ME. I'M THE GOOD ONE.
IS GOD DROWNING THE WORLD AGAIN?
OF COURSE NOT. SHE WAS ONLY KIDDING.
YOU'RE A LIAR! AND I DON'T LIKE YOU!
ME? WHAT THE HELL DID I DO TO YOU?
HELL, HELL, HELL, HELL!

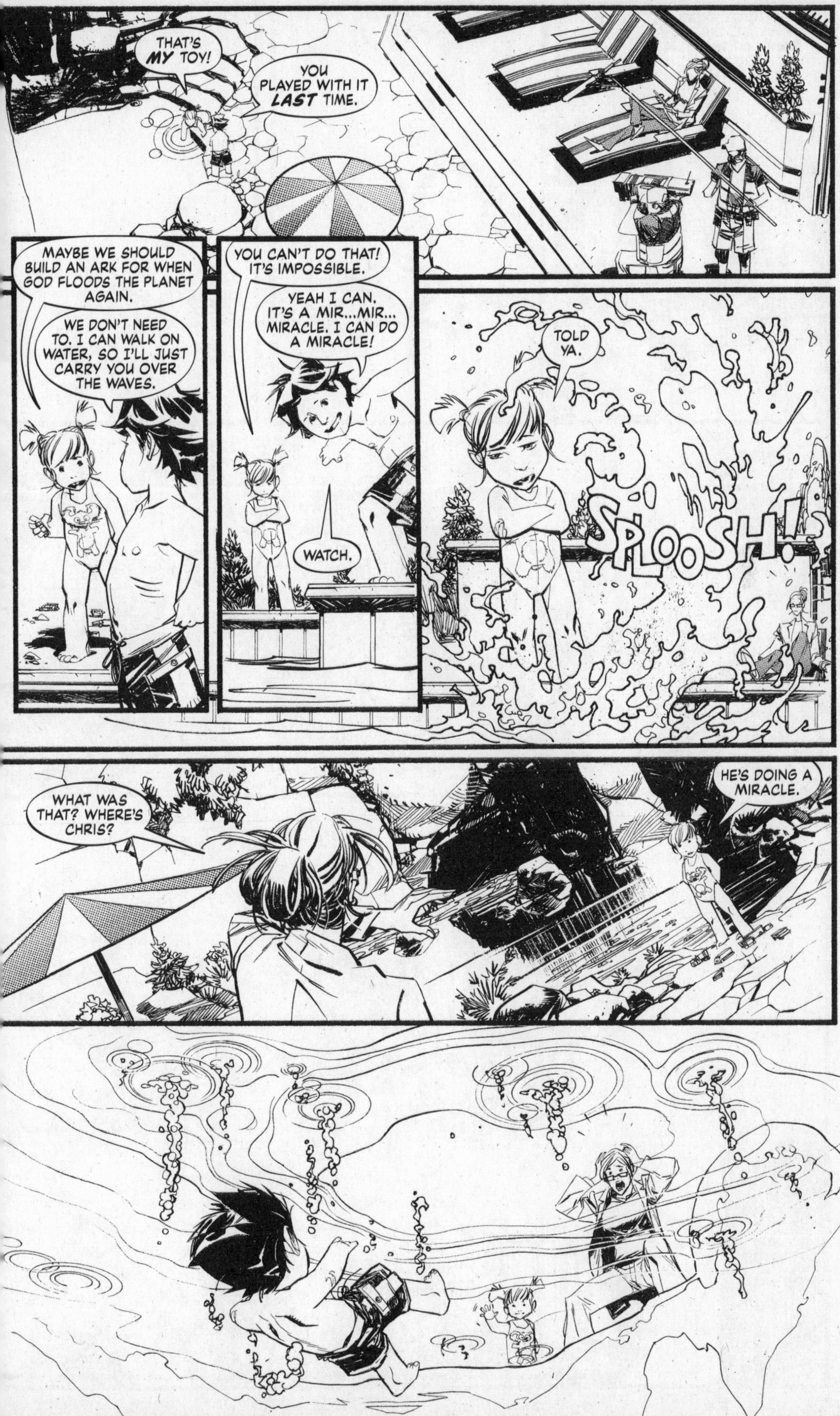
THAT'S *MY* TOY!
YOU PLAYED WITH IT *LAST* TIME.
MAYBE WE SHOULD BUILD AN ARK FOR WHEN GOD FLOODS THE PLANET AGAIN.
WE DON'T NEED TO. I CAN WALK ON WATER, SO I'LL JUST CARRY YOU OVER THE WAVES.
YOU CAN'T DO THAT! IT'S IMPOSSIBLE.
YEAH I CAN. IT'S A MIR...MIR... MIRACLE. I CAN DO A MIRACLE!
WATCH.
TOLD YA.
SPLOOSH!
WHAT WAS THAT? WHERE'S CHRIS?
HE'S DOING A MIRACLE.

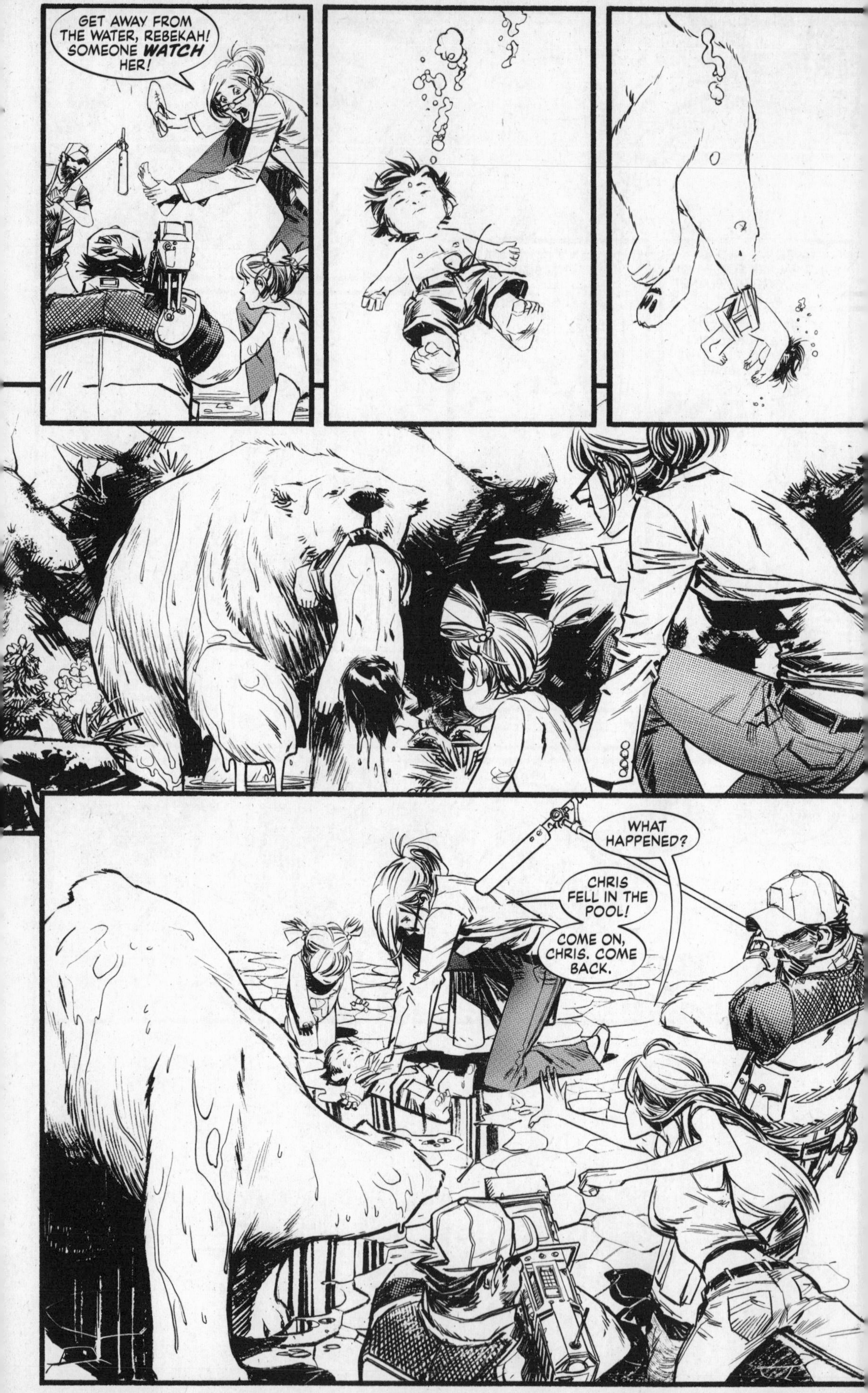

GET AWAY FROM THE WATER, REBEKAH! SOMEONE WATCH HER!
WHAT HAPPENED?
CHRIS FELL IN THE POOL!
COME ON, CHRIS. COME BACK.

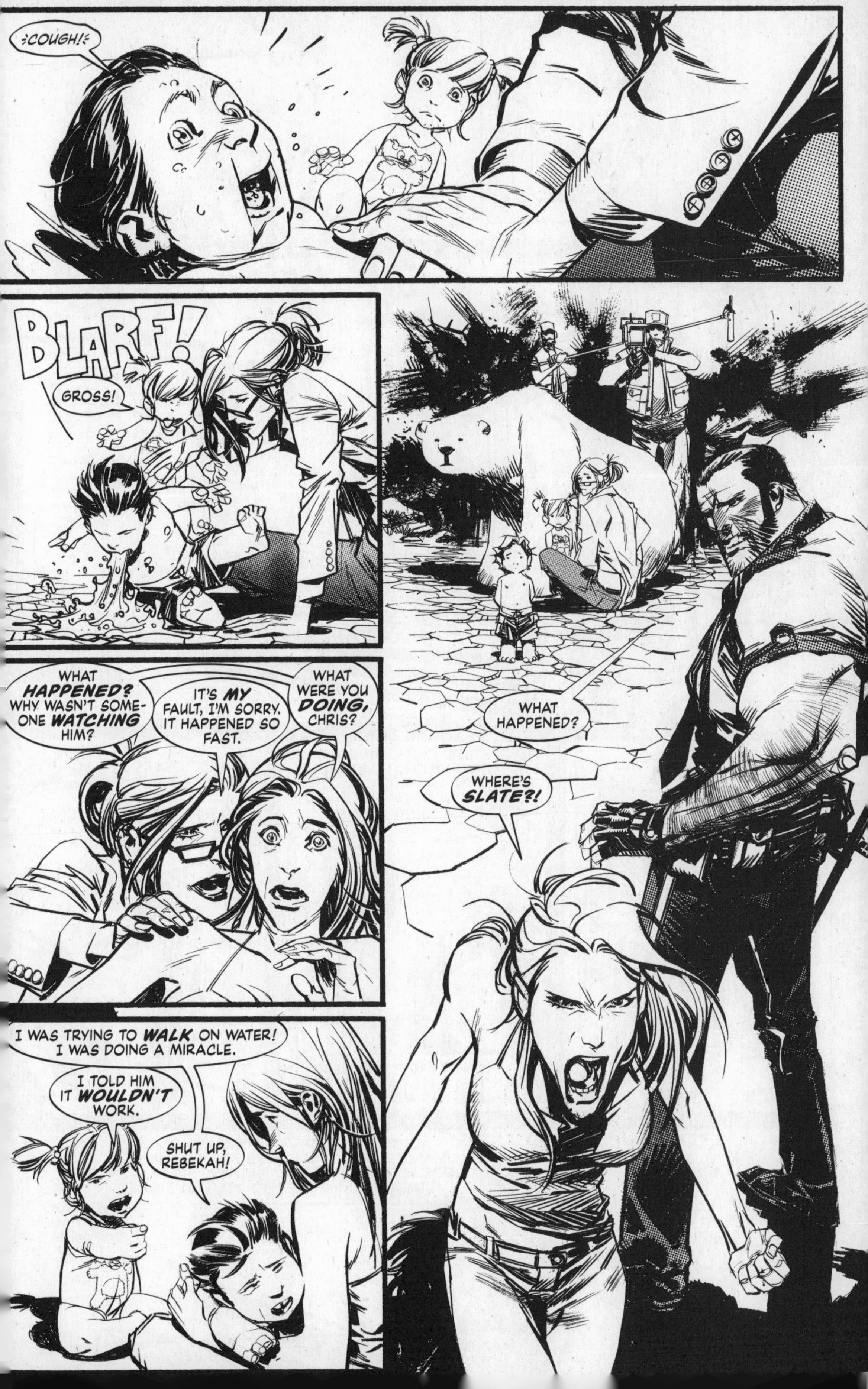

COUGH!
BLARF!
GROSS!
WHAT HAPPENED? WHY WASN'T SOMEONE WATCHING HIM?
IT'S MY FAULT, I'M SORRY. IT HAPPENED SO FAST.
WHAT WERE YOU DOING, CHRIS?
I WAS TRYING TO WALK ON WATER! I WAS DOING A MIRACLE.
I TOLD HIM IT WOULDN'T WORK.
SHUT UP, REBEKAH!
WHAT HAPPENED?
WHERE'S SLATE?!

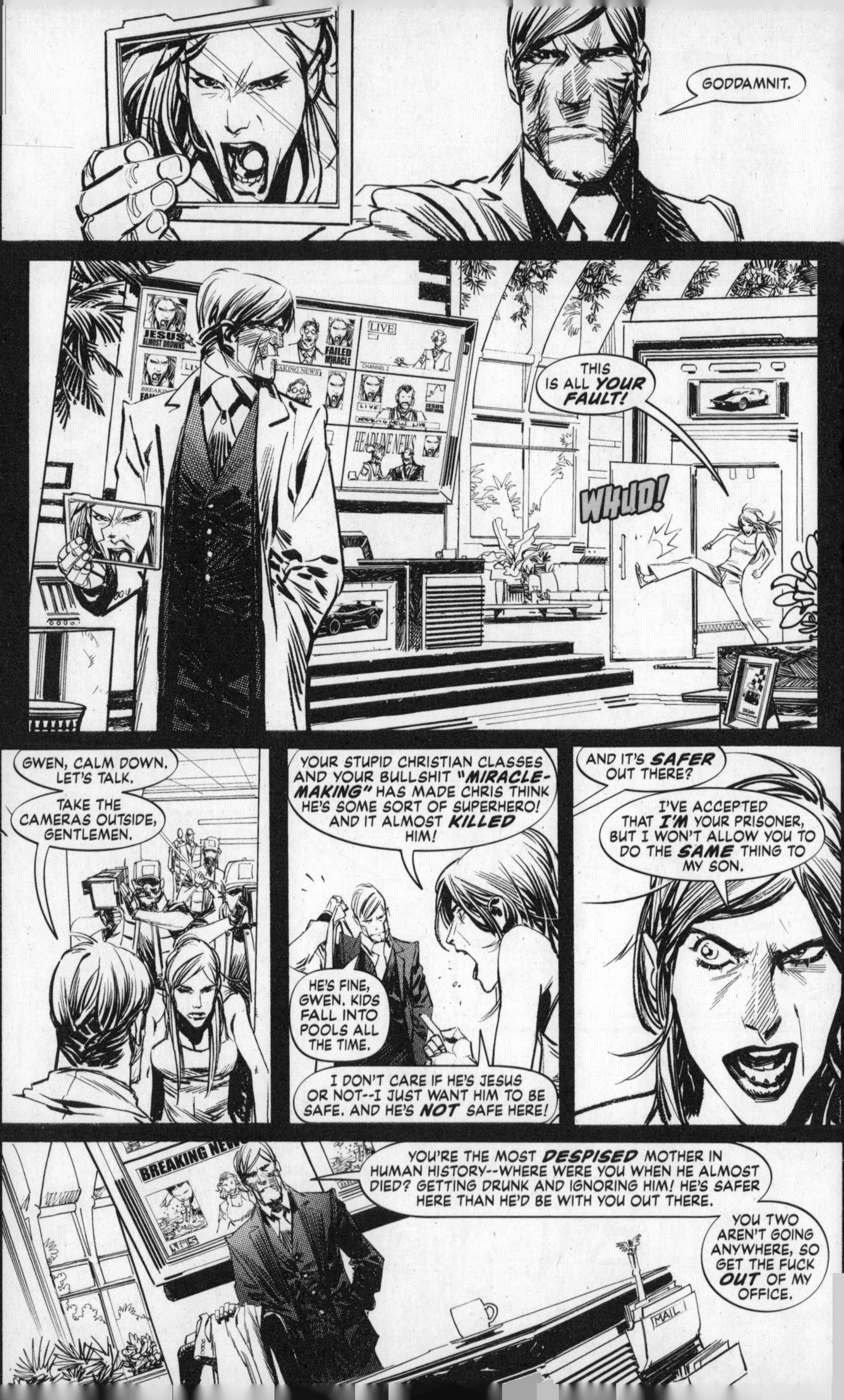

GODDAMNIT.
JESUS ALMOST DROWNS
FAILED MIRACLE
LIVE
CHANNEL 2
HEADLINE NEWS
THIS IS ALL *YOUR FAULT!*
WHUD!
GWEN, CALM DOWN. LET'S TALK.
TAKE THE CAMERAS OUTSIDE, GENTLEMEN.
YOUR STUPID CHRISTIAN CLASSES AND YOUR BULLSHIT *"MIRACLE-MAKING"* HAS MADE CHRIS THINK HE'S SOME SORT OF SUPERHERO! AND IT ALMOST *KILLED* HIM!
HE'S FINE, GWEN. KIDS FALL INTO POOLS ALL THE TIME.
I DON'T CARE IF HE'S JESUS OR NOT--I JUST WANT HIM TO BE SAFE. AND HE'S *NOT* SAFE HERE!
AND IT'S *SAFER* OUT THERE?
I'VE ACCEPTED THAT *I'M* YOUR PRISONER, BUT I WON'T ALLOW YOU TO DO THE *SAME* THING TO MY SON.
YOU'RE THE MOST *DESPISED* MOTHER IN HUMAN HISTORY--WHERE WERE YOU WHEN HE ALMOST DIED? GETTING DRUNK AND IGNORING HIM! HE'S SAFER HERE THAN HE'D BE WITH YOU OUT THERE.
YOU TWO AREN'T GOING ANYWHERE, SO GET THE FUCK *OUT* OF MY OFFICE.
MAIL

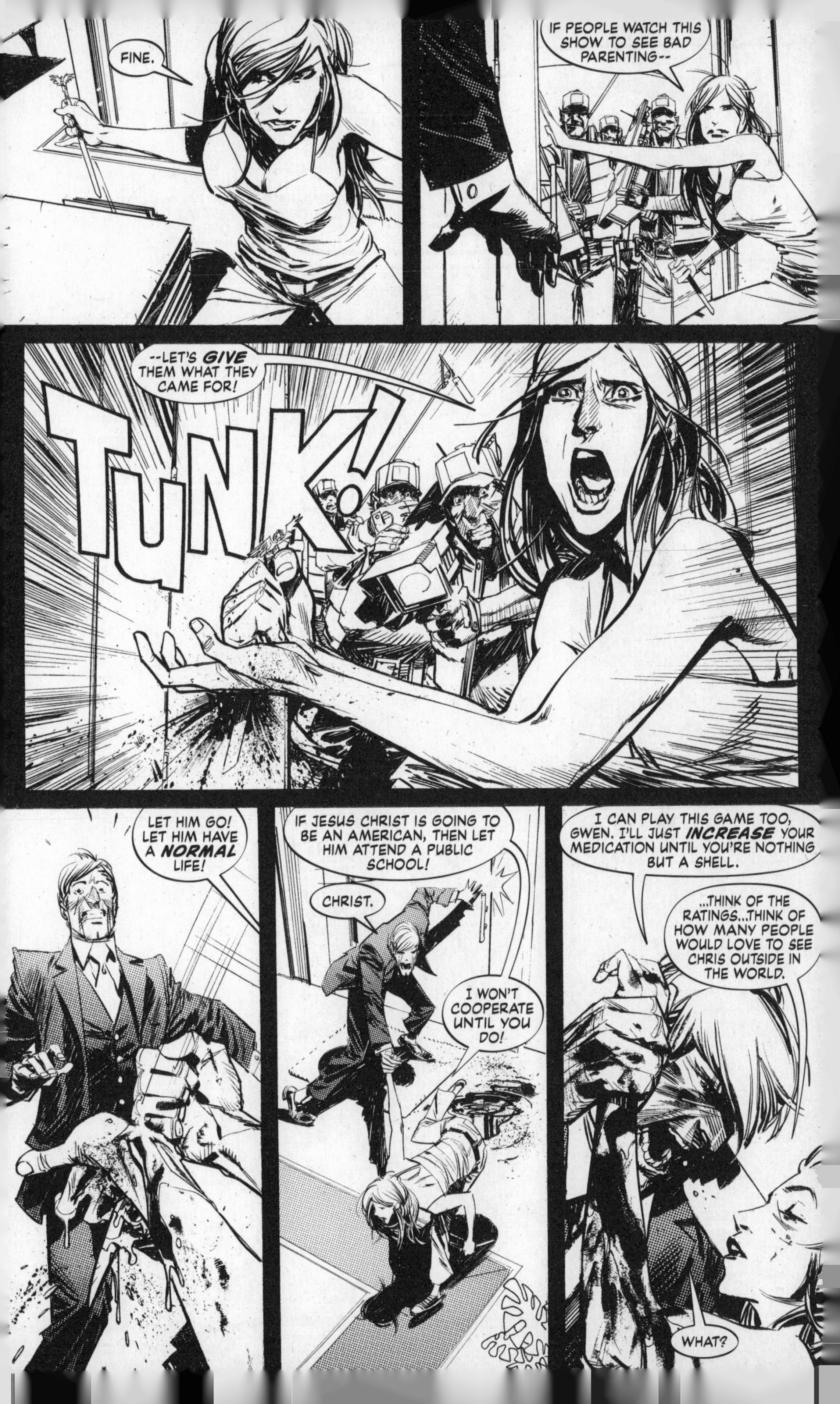
FINE.
IF PEOPLE WATCH THIS SHOW TO SEE BAD PARENTING--
--LET'S GIVE THEM WHAT THEY CAME FOR!
TUNK!
LET HIM GO! LET HIM HAVE A NORMAL LIFE!
IF JESUS CHRIST IS GOING TO BE AN AMERICAN, THEN LET HIM ATTEND A PUBLIC SCHOOL!
CHRIST.
I WON'T COOPERATE UNTIL YOU DO!
I CAN PLAY THIS GAME TOO, GWEN. I'LL JUST INCREASE YOUR MEDICATION UNTIL YOU'RE NOTHING BUT A SHELL.
...THINK OF THE RATINGS...THINK OF HOW MANY PEOPLE WOULD LOVE TO SEE CHRIS OUTSIDE IN THE WORLD.
WHAT?

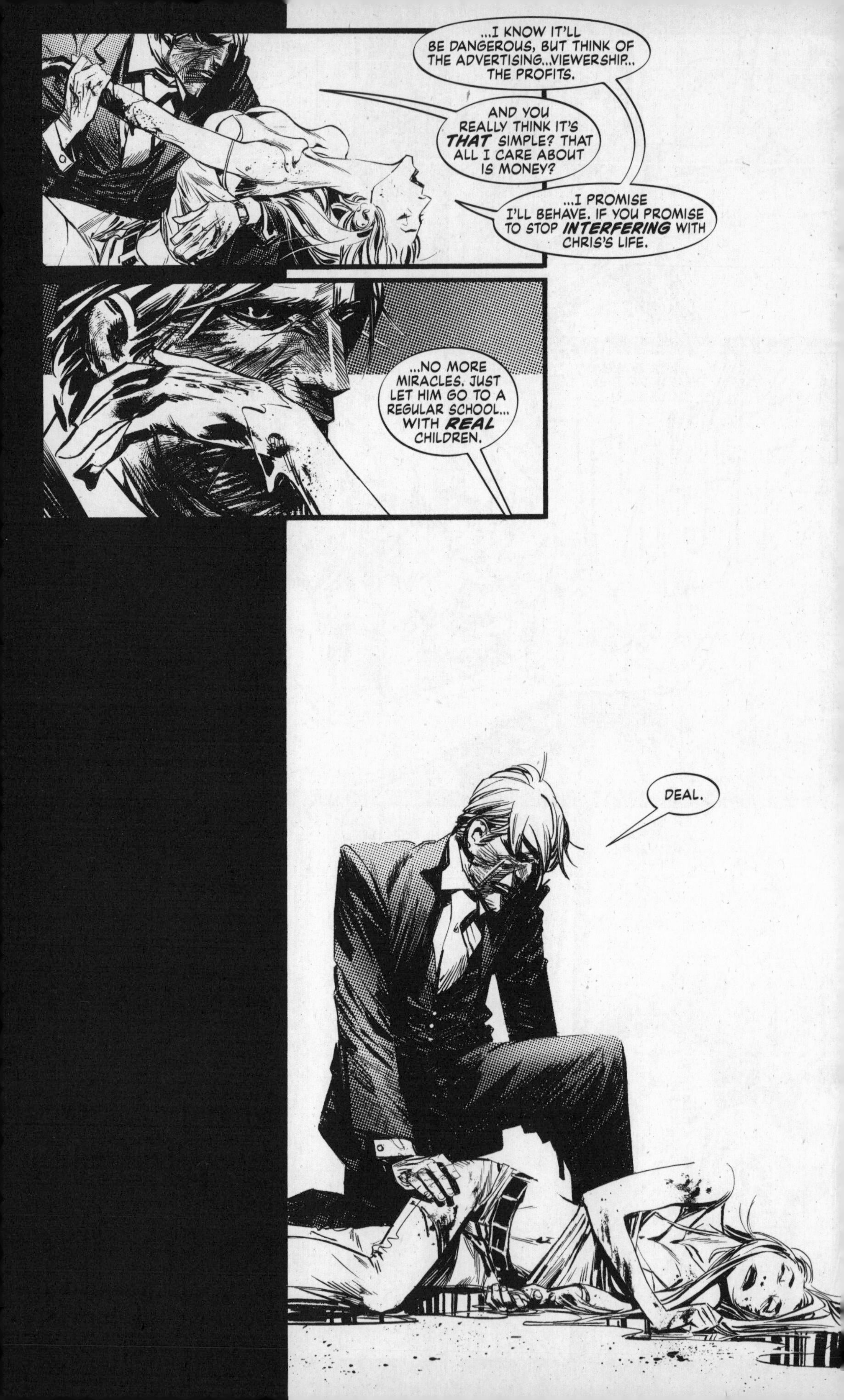
...I KNOW IT'LL BE DANGEROUS, BUT THINK OF THE ADVERTISING...VIEWERSHIP... THE PROFITS.
AND YOU REALLY THINK IT'S **THAT** SIMPLE? THAT ALL I CARE ABOUT IS MONEY?
...I PROMISE I'LL BEHAVE. IF YOU PROMISE TO STOP **INTERFERING** WITH CHRIS'S LIFE.
...NO MORE MIRACLES. JUST LET HIM GO TO A REGULAR SCHOOL... WITH **REAL** CHILDREN.
DEAL.

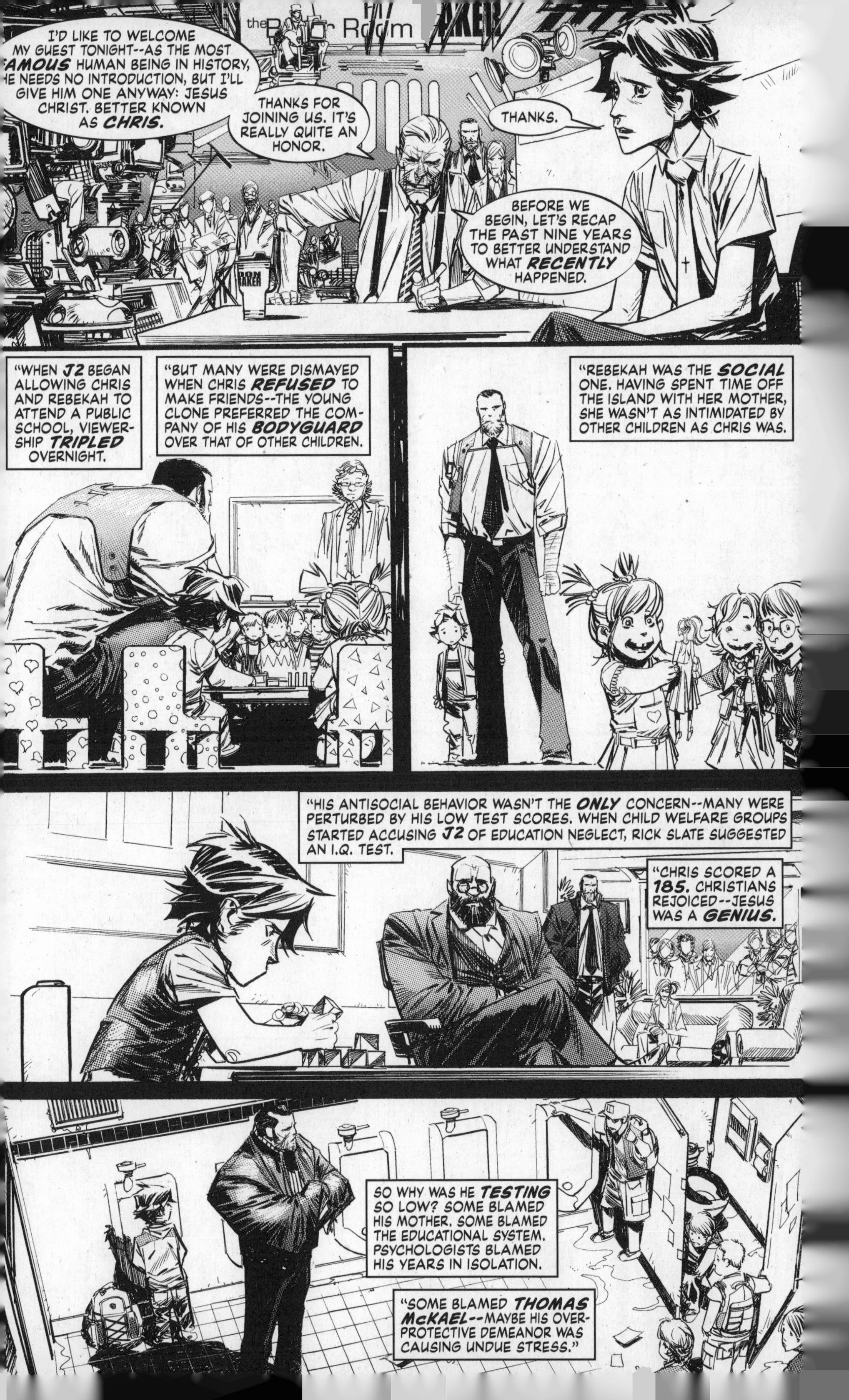
the B... Room
I'D LIKE TO WELCOME MY GUEST TONIGHT--AS THE MOST FAMOUS HUMAN BEING IN HISTORY, HE NEEDS NO INTRODUCTION, BUT I'LL GIVE HIM ONE ANYWAY: JESUS CHRIST. BETTER KNOWN AS CHRIS.
THANKS FOR JOINING US. IT'S REALLY QUITE AN HONOR.
THANKS.
BEFORE WE BEGIN, LET'S RECAP THE PAST NINE YEARS TO BETTER UNDERSTAND WHAT RECENTLY HAPPENED.
"WHEN J2 BEGAN ALLOWING CHRIS AND REBEKAH TO ATTEND A PUBLIC SCHOOL, VIEWERSHIP TRIPLED OVERNIGHT.
"BUT MANY WERE DISMAYED WHEN CHRIS REFUSED TO MAKE FRIENDS--THE YOUNG CLONE PREFERRED THE COMPANY OF HIS BODYGUARD OVER THAT OF OTHER CHILDREN.
"REBEKAH WAS THE SOCIAL ONE. HAVING SPENT TIME OFF THE ISLAND WITH HER MOTHER, SHE WASN'T AS INTIMIDATED BY OTHER CHILDREN AS CHRIS WAS.
"HIS ANTISOCIAL BEHAVIOR WASN'T THE ONLY CONCERN--MANY WERE PERTURBED BY HIS LOW TEST SCORES. WHEN CHILD WELFARE GROUPS STARTED ACCUSING J2 OF EDUCATION NEGLECT, RICK SLATE SUGGESTED AN I.Q. TEST.
"CHRIS SCORED A 185. CHRISTIANS REJOICED--JESUS WAS A GENIUS.
SO WHY WAS HE TESTING SO LOW? SOME BLAMED HIS MOTHER. SOME BLAMED THE EDUCATIONAL SYSTEM. PSYCHOLOGISTS BLAMED HIS YEARS IN ISOLATION.
"SOME BLAMED THOMAS McKAEL--MAYBE HIS OVERPROTECTIVE DEMEANOR WAS CAUSING UNDUE STRESS."

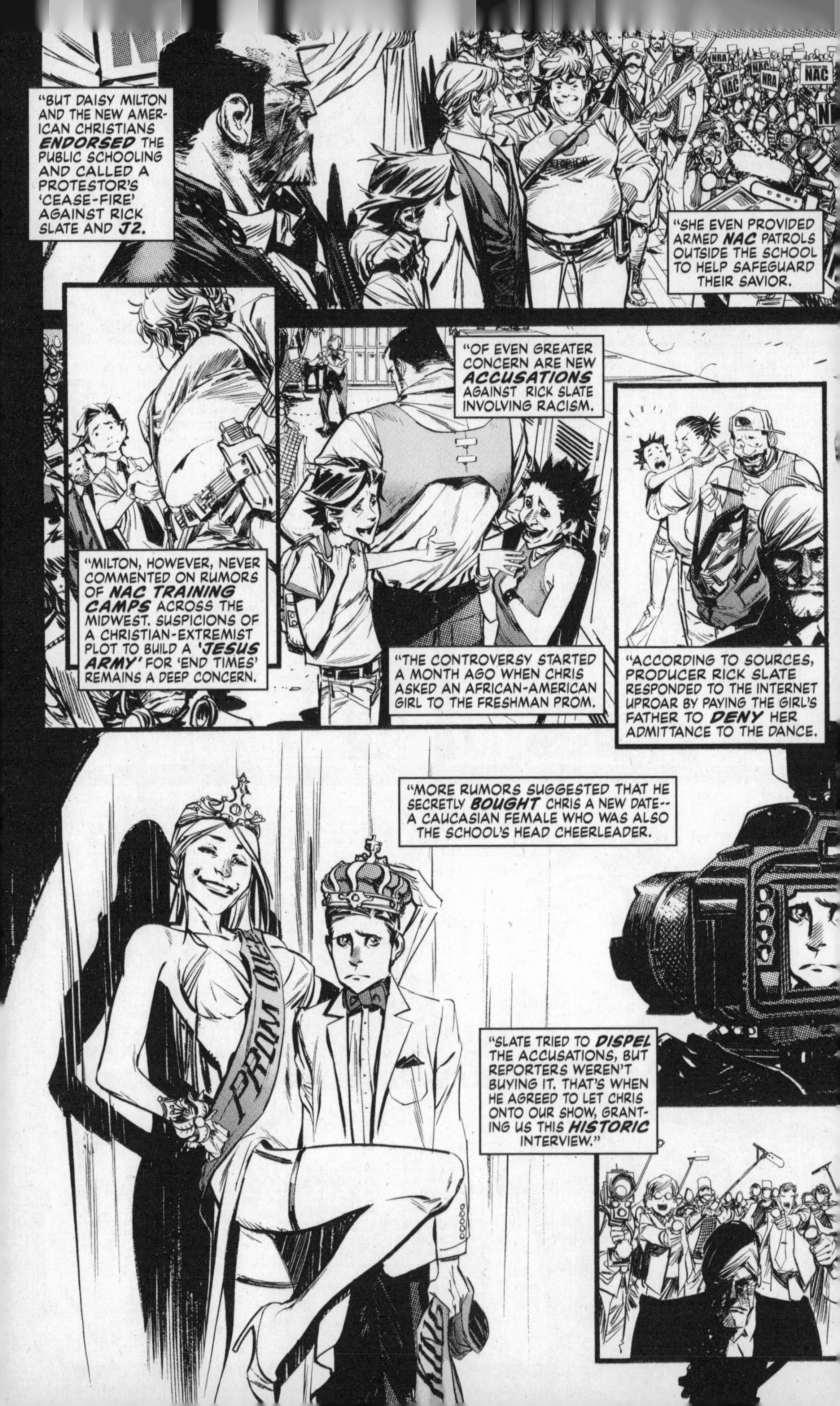
"BUT DAISY MILTON AND THE NEW AMERICAN CHRISTIANS ENDORSED THE PUBLIC SCHOOLING AND CALLED A PROTESTOR'S 'CEASE-FIRE' AGAINST RICK SLATE AND J2.
NRA
NAC
"SHE EVEN PROVIDED ARMED NAC PATROLS OUTSIDE THE SCHOOL TO HELP SAFEGUARD THEIR SAVIOR.
"MILTON, HOWEVER, NEVER COMMENTED ON RUMORS OF NAC TRAINING CAMPS ACROSS THE MIDWEST. SUSPICIONS OF A CHRISTIAN-EXTREMIST PLOT TO BUILD A 'JESUS ARMY' FOR 'END TIMES' REMAINS A DEEP CONCERN.
"OF EVEN GREATER CONCERN ARE NEW ACCUSATIONS AGAINST RICK SLATE INVOLVING RACISM.
"THE CONTROVERSY STARTED A MONTH AGO WHEN CHRIS ASKED AN AFRICAN-AMERICAN GIRL TO THE FRESHMAN PROM.
"ACCORDING TO SOURCES, PRODUCER RICK SLATE RESPONDED TO THE INTERNET UPROAR BY PAYING THE GIRL'S FATHER TO DENY HER ADMITTANCE TO THE DANCE.
"MORE RUMORS SUGGESTED THAT HE SECRETLY BOUGHT CHRIS A NEW DATE-- A CAUCASIAN FEMALE WHO WAS ALSO THE SCHOOL'S HEAD CHEERLEADER.
PROM QUEEN
"SLATE TRIED TO DISPEL THE ACCUSATIONS, BUT REPORTERS WEREN'T BUYING IT. THAT'S WHEN HE AGREED TO LET CHRIS ONTO OUR SHOW, GRANTING US THIS HISTORIC INTERVIEW."

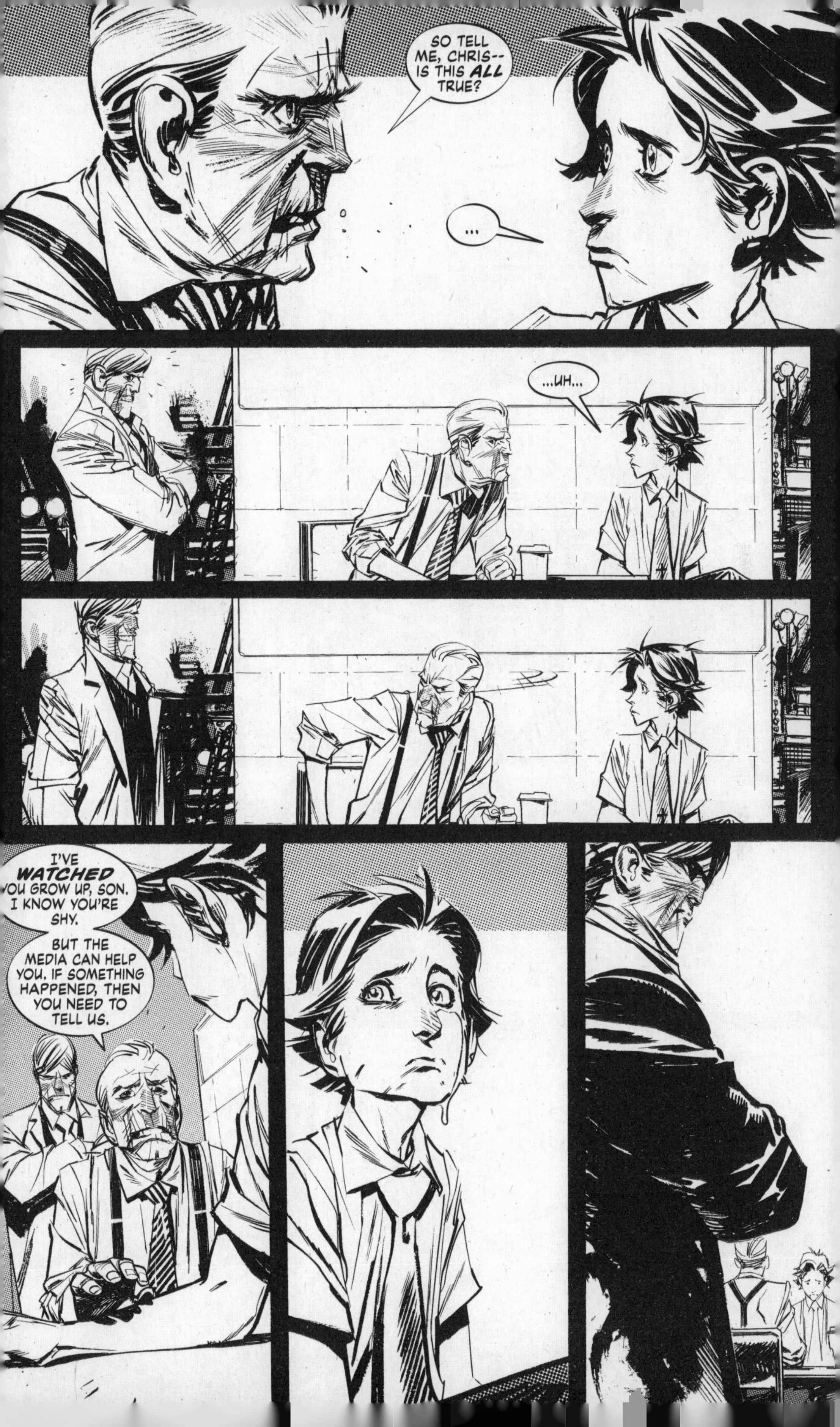
SO TELL ME, CHRIS-- IS THIS ALL TRUE?
...
...UH...
I'VE WATCHED YOU GROW UP, SON. I KNOW YOU'RE SHY.
BUT THE MEDIA CAN HELP YOU. IF SOMETHING HAPPENED, THEN YOU NEED TO TELL US.

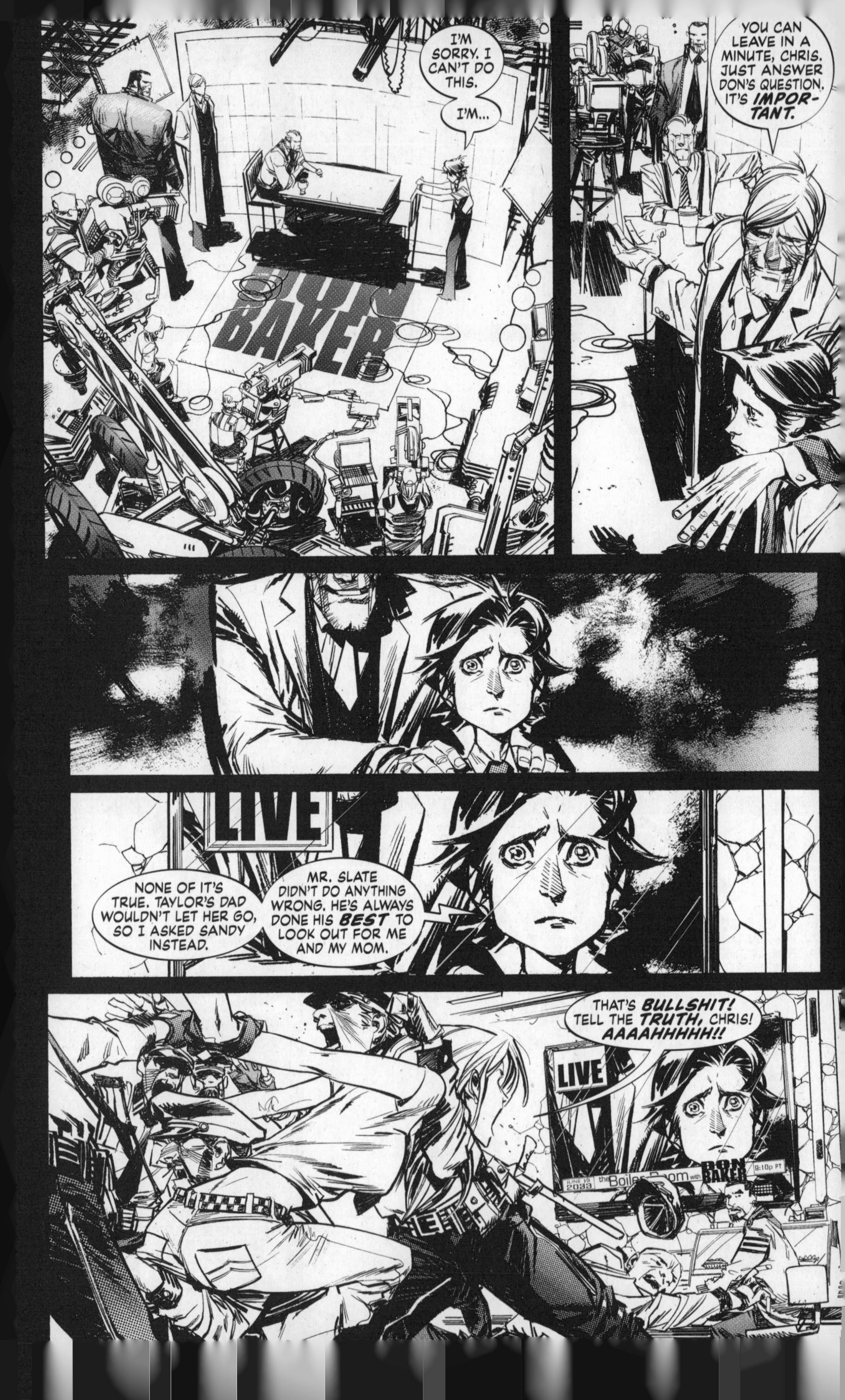
DON BAKER
I'M SORRY. I CAN'T DO THIS.
I'M...
YOU CAN LEAVE IN A MINUTE, CHRIS. JUST ANSWER DON'S QUESTION. IT'S IMPORTANT.
LIVE
NONE OF IT'S TRUE. TAYLOR'S DAD WOULDN'T LET HER GO, SO I ASKED SANDY INSTEAD.
MR. SLATE DIDN'T DO ANYTHING WRONG. HE'S ALWAYS DONE HIS BEST TO LOOK OUT FOR ME AND MY MOM.
THAT'S BULLSHIT! TELL THE TRUTH, CHRIS! AAAAHHHHH!!
LIVE
DON BAKER

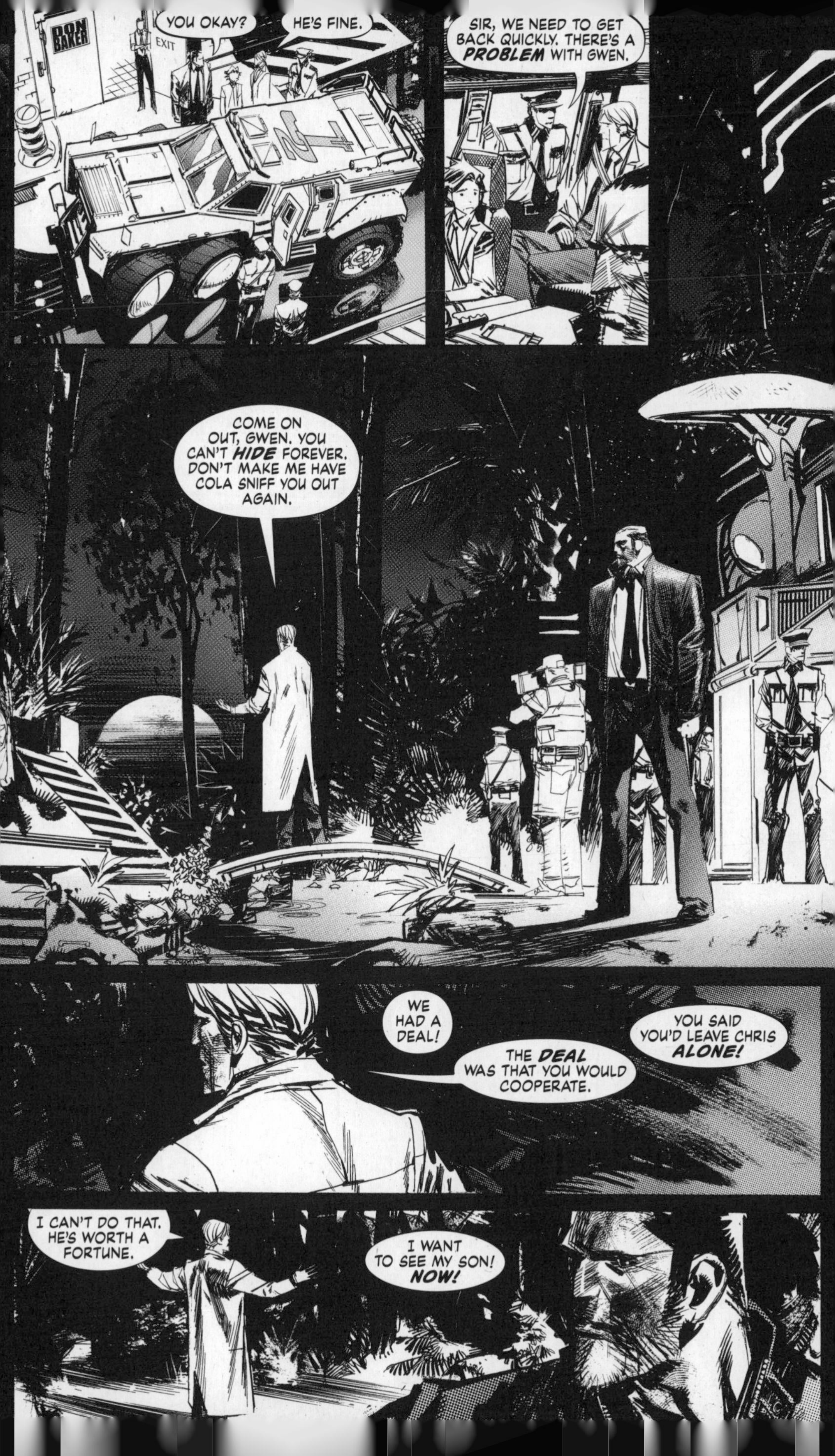
DON BAKER
EXIT
YOU OKAY?
HE'S FINE.
SIR, WE NEED TO GET BACK QUICKLY. THERE'S A PROBLEM WITH GWEN.
COME ON OUT, GWEN. YOU CAN'T HIDE FOREVER. DON'T MAKE ME HAVE COLA SNIFF YOU OUT AGAIN.
WE HAD A DEAL!
YOU SAID YOU'D LEAVE CHRIS ALONE!
THE DEAL WAS THAT YOU WOULD COOPERATE.
I CAN'T DO THAT. HE'S WORTH A FORTUNE.
I WANT TO SEE MY SON! NOW!

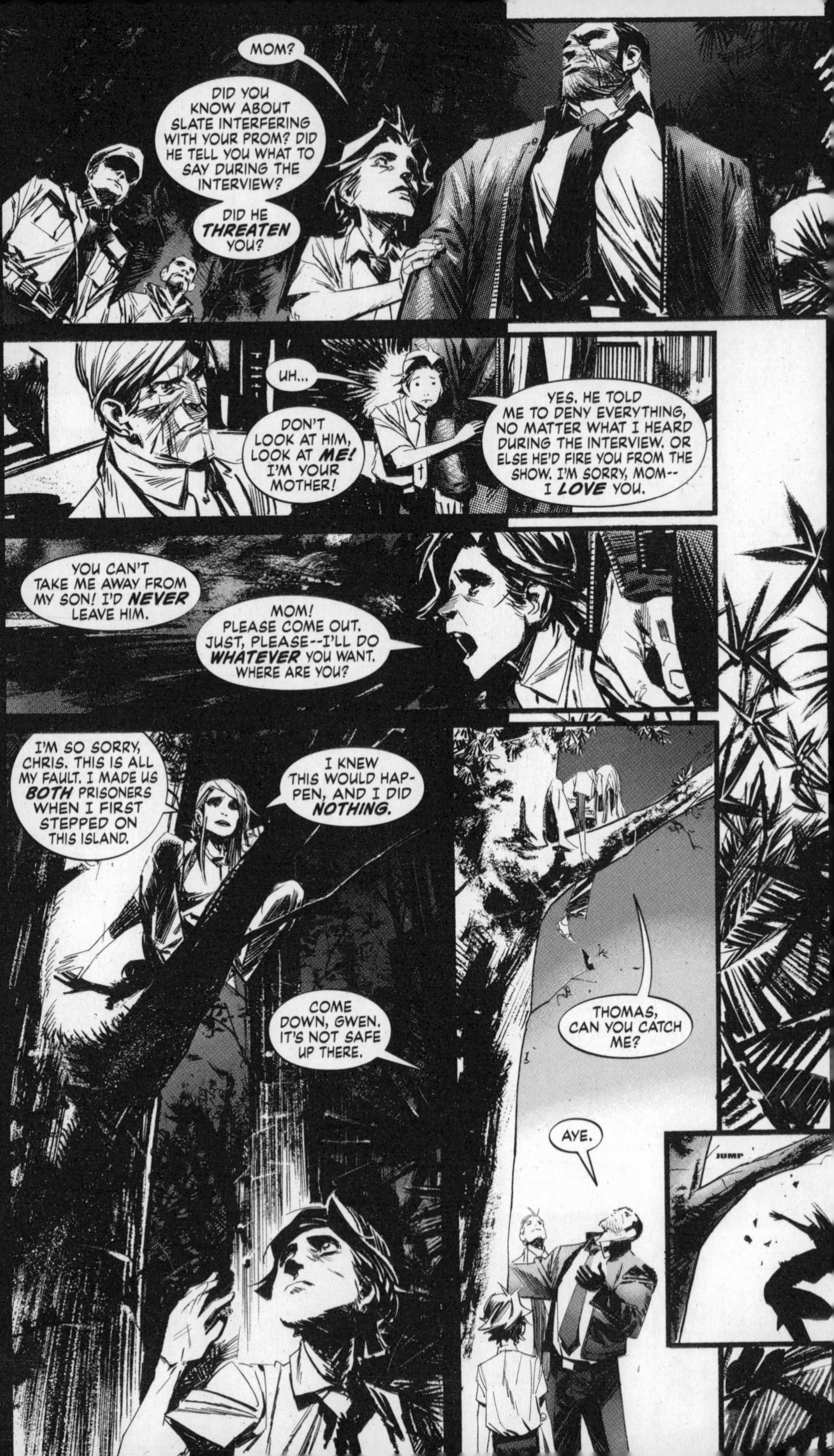
MOM?
DID YOU KNOW ABOUT SLATE INTERFERING WITH YOUR PROM? DID HE TELL YOU WHAT TO SAY DURING THE INTERVIEW?
DID HE THREATEN YOU?
UH...
DON'T LOOK AT HIM, LOOK AT ME! I'M YOUR MOTHER!
YES. HE TOLD ME TO DENY EVERYTHING, NO MATTER WHAT I HEARD DURING THE INTERVIEW. OR ELSE HE'D FIRE YOU FROM THE SHOW. I'M SORRY, MOM-- I LOVE YOU.
YOU CAN'T TAKE ME AWAY FROM MY SON! I'D NEVER LEAVE HIM.
MOM! PLEASE COME OUT. JUST, PLEASE--I'LL DO WHATEVER YOU WANT. WHERE ARE YOU?
I'M SO SORRY, CHRIS. THIS IS ALL MY FAULT. I MADE US BOTH PRISONERS WHEN I FIRST STEPPED ON THIS ISLAND.
I KNEW THIS WOULD HAP-PEN, AND I DID NOTHING.
COME DOWN, GWEN. IT'S NOT SAFE UP THERE.
THOMAS, CAN YOU CATCH ME?
AYE.
JUMP

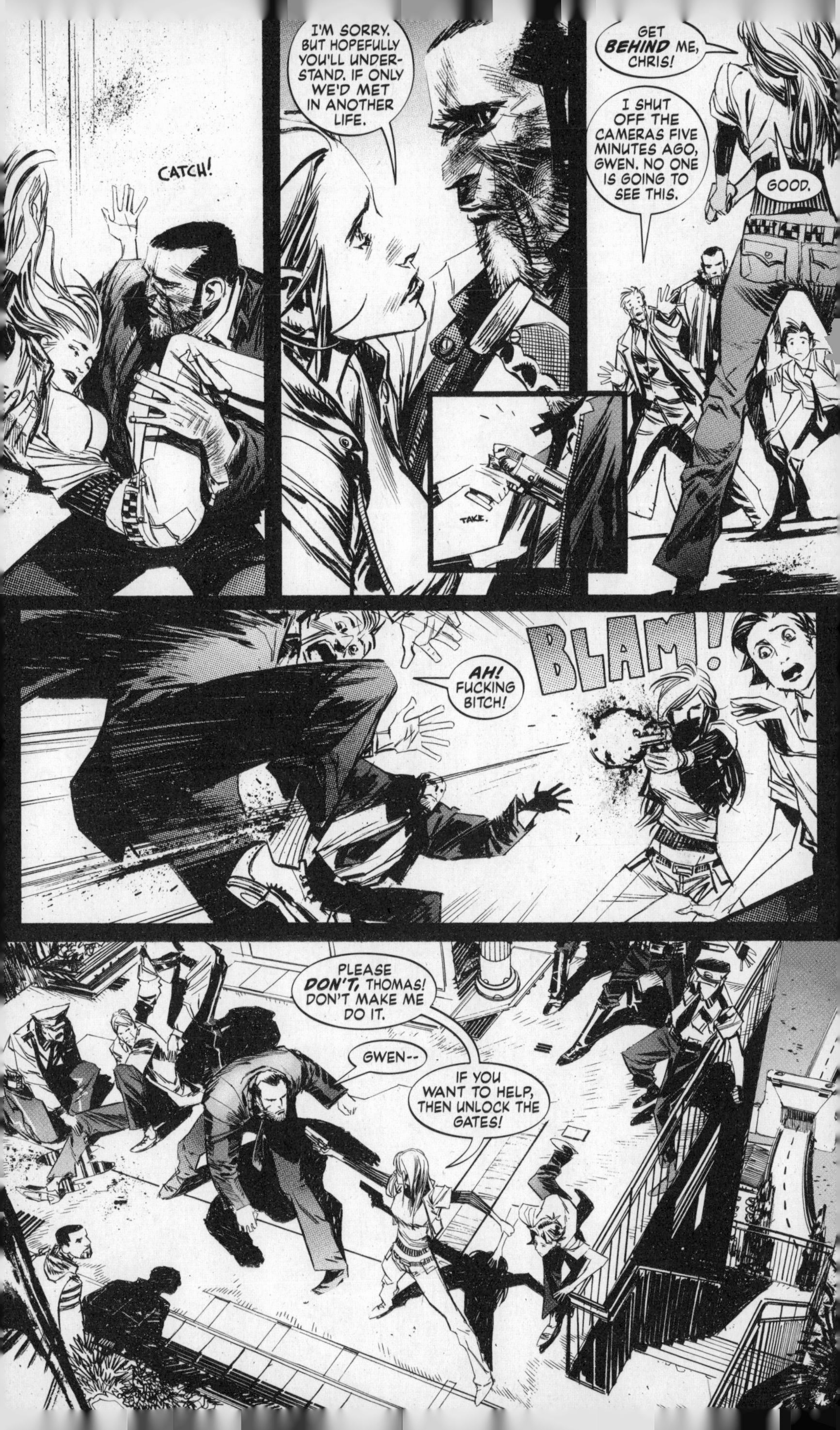
CATCH!
I'M SORRY. BUT HOPEFULLY YOU'LL UNDERSTAND. IF ONLY WE'D MET IN ANOTHER LIFE.
TAKE.
GET BEHIND ME, CHRIS!
I SHUT OFF THE CAMERAS FIVE MINUTES AGO, GWEN. NO ONE IS GOING TO SEE THIS.
GOOD.
AH! FUCKING BITCH!
BLAM!
PLEASE DON'T, THOMAS! DON'T MAKE ME DO IT.
GWEN--
IF YOU WANT TO HELP, THEN UNLOCK THE GATES!

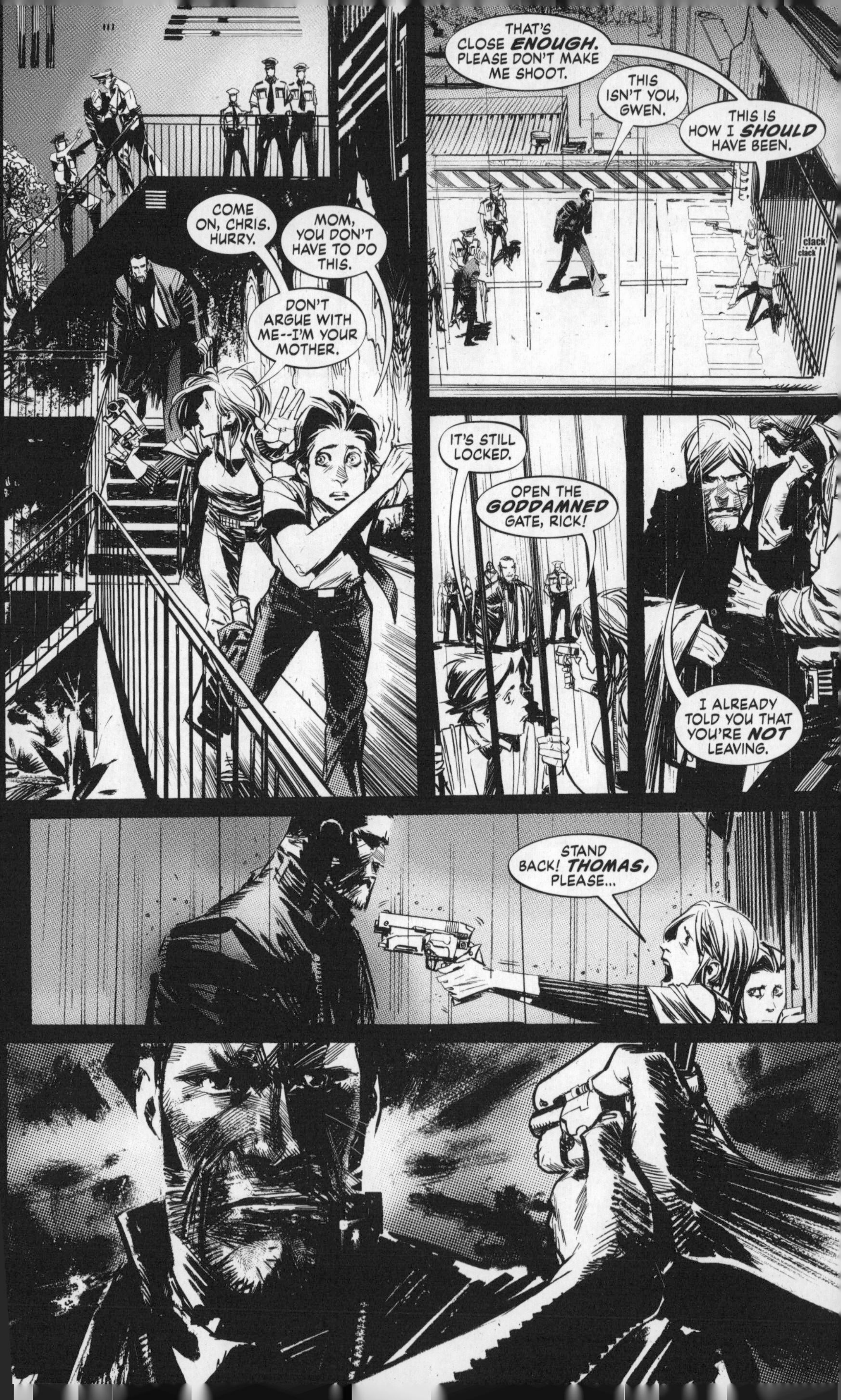
COME ON, CHRIS. HURRY.
MOM, YOU DON'T HAVE TO DO THIS.
DON'T ARGUE WITH ME--I'M YOUR MOTHER.
THAT'S CLOSE ENOUGH. PLEASE DON'T MAKE ME SHOOT.
THIS ISN'T YOU, GWEN.
THIS IS HOW I SHOULD HAVE BEEN.
clack
clack
IT'S STILL LOCKED.
OPEN THE GODDAMNED GATE, RICK!
I ALREADY TOLD YOU THAT YOU'RE NOT LEAVING.
STAND BACK! THOMAS, PLEASE...

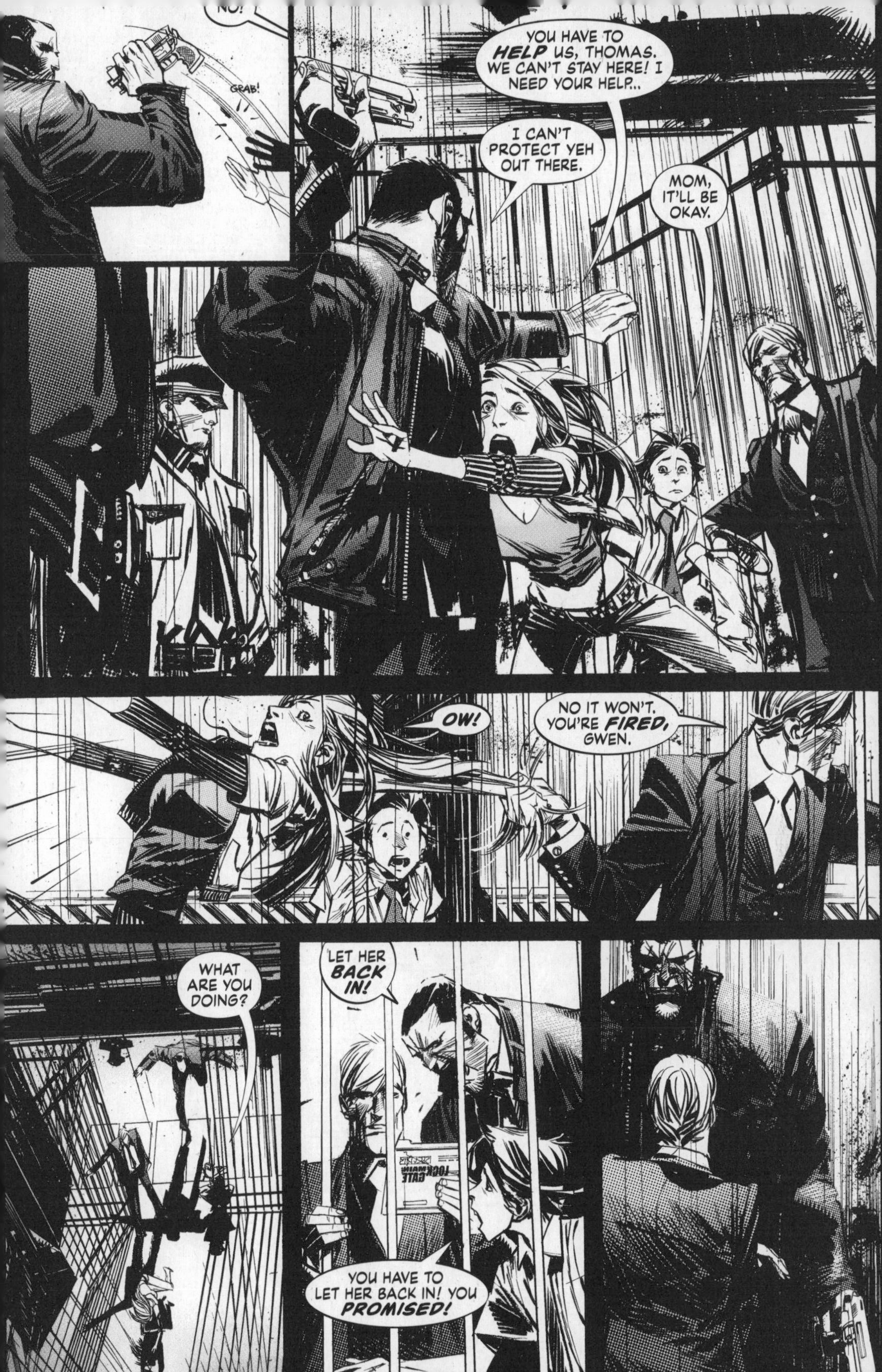
NO!
GRAB!
YOU HAVE TO HELP US, THOMAS. WE CAN'T STAY HERE! I NEED YOUR HELP...
I CAN'T PROTECT YEH OUT THERE.
MOM, IT'LL BE OKAY.
OW!
NO IT WON'T. YOU'RE FIRED, GWEN.
WHAT ARE YOU DOING?
LET HER BACK IN!
YOU HAVE TO LET HER BACK IN! YOU PROMISED!

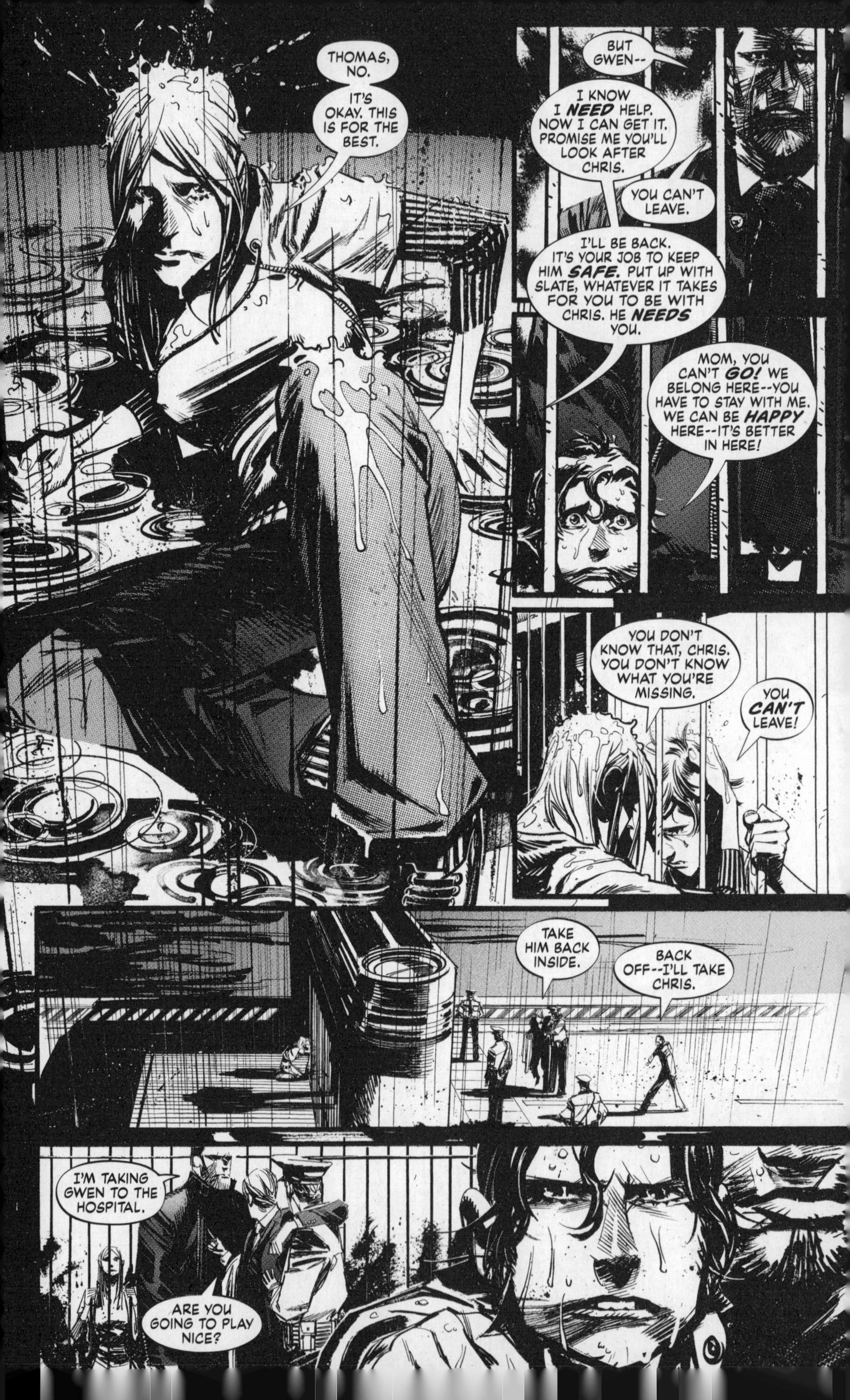

THOMAS, NO.
IT'S OKAY. THIS IS FOR THE BEST.
BUT GWEN--
I KNOW I NEED HELP. NOW I CAN GET IT. PROMISE ME YOU'LL LOOK AFTER CHRIS.
YOU CAN'T LEAVE.
I'LL BE BACK. IT'S YOUR JOB TO KEEP HIM SAFE. PUT UP WITH SLATE, WHATEVER IT TAKES FOR YOU TO BE WITH CHRIS. HE NEEDS YOU.
MOM, YOU CAN'T GO! WE BELONG HERE--YOU HAVE TO STAY WITH ME. WE CAN BE HAPPY HERE--IT'S BETTER IN HERE!
YOU DON'T KNOW THAT, CHRIS. YOU DON'T KNOW WHAT YOU'RE MISSING.
YOU CAN'T LEAVE!
TAKE HIM BACK INSIDE.
BACK OFF--I'LL TAKE CHRIS.
I'M TAKING GWEN TO THE HOSPITAL.
ARE YOU GOING TO PLAY NICE?

AAAAHH!

CRASH!

PEOPLE OF THE WORLD, I'M A PRISONER HERE! THEY SENT MY MOTHER *AWAY*, AND NOW THEY'RE HOLDING ME HOSTAGE!

I REFUSE TO COOPERATE UNTIL THEY LET ME *GO*!

SO UNTIL I GET MY *MOTHER* BACK...

TSSSSS!

TSSSSS!

...THE SHOW'S *OVER*!

TTTSISSSSSSSSSSSSSSS

SSSSSSSSSSSSS!!

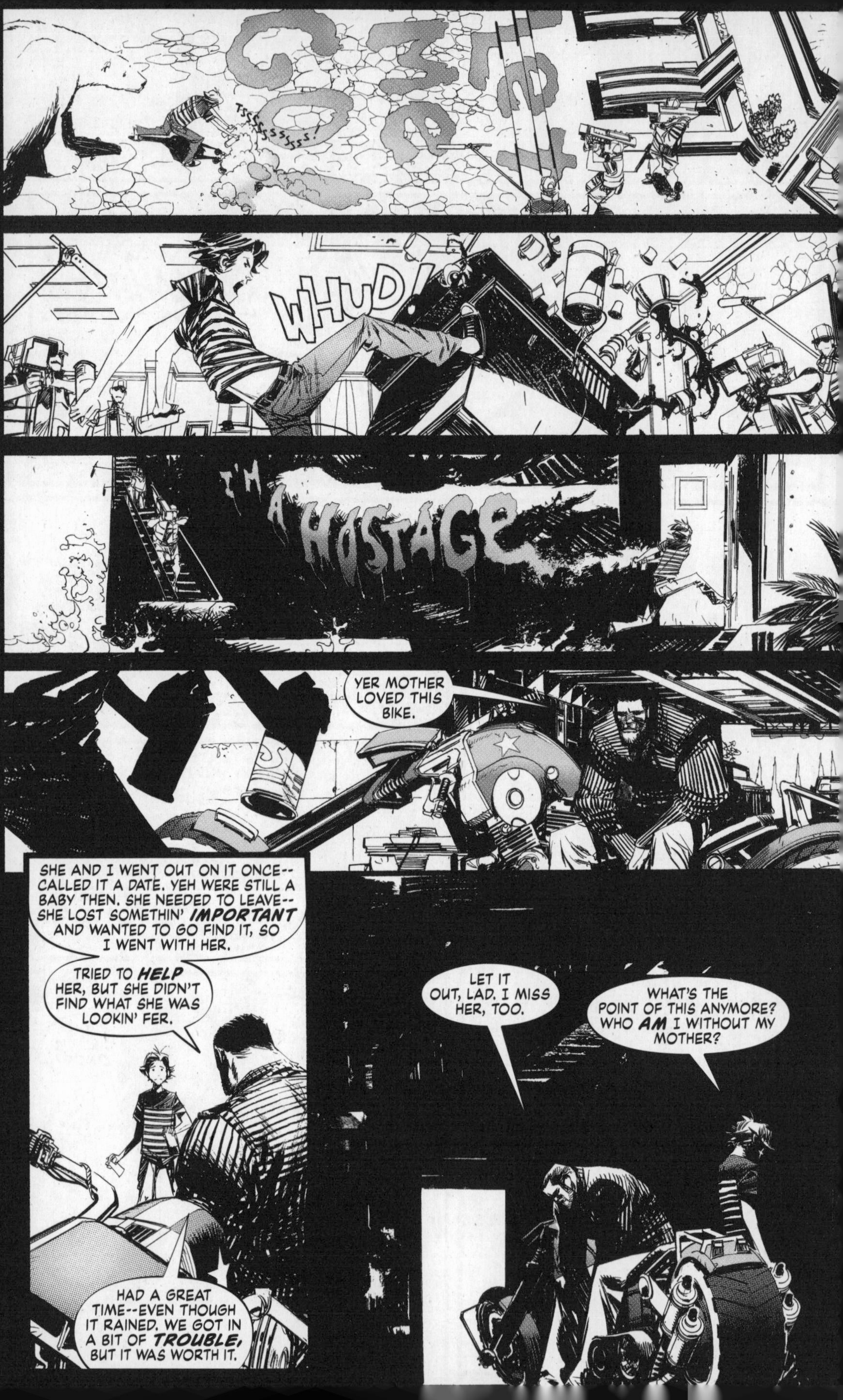
TSSSSSSSSSS!
WHUD!
I'M A HOSTAGE
YER MOTHER LOVED THIS BIKE.
SHE AND I WENT OUT ON IT ONCE--CALLED IT A DATE. YEH WERE STILL A BABY THEN. SHE NEEDED TO LEAVE--SHE LOST SOMETHIN' IMPORTANT AND WANTED TO GO FIND IT, SO I WENT WITH HER.
TRIED TO HELP HER, BUT SHE DIDN'T FIND WHAT SHE WAS LOOKIN' FER.
HAD A GREAT TIME--EVEN THOUGH IT RAINED. WE GOT IN A BIT OF TROUBLE, BUT IT WAS WORTH IT.
LET IT OUT, LAD. I MISS HER, TOO.
WHAT'S THE POINT OF THIS ANYMORE? WHO AM I WITHOUT MY MOTHER?

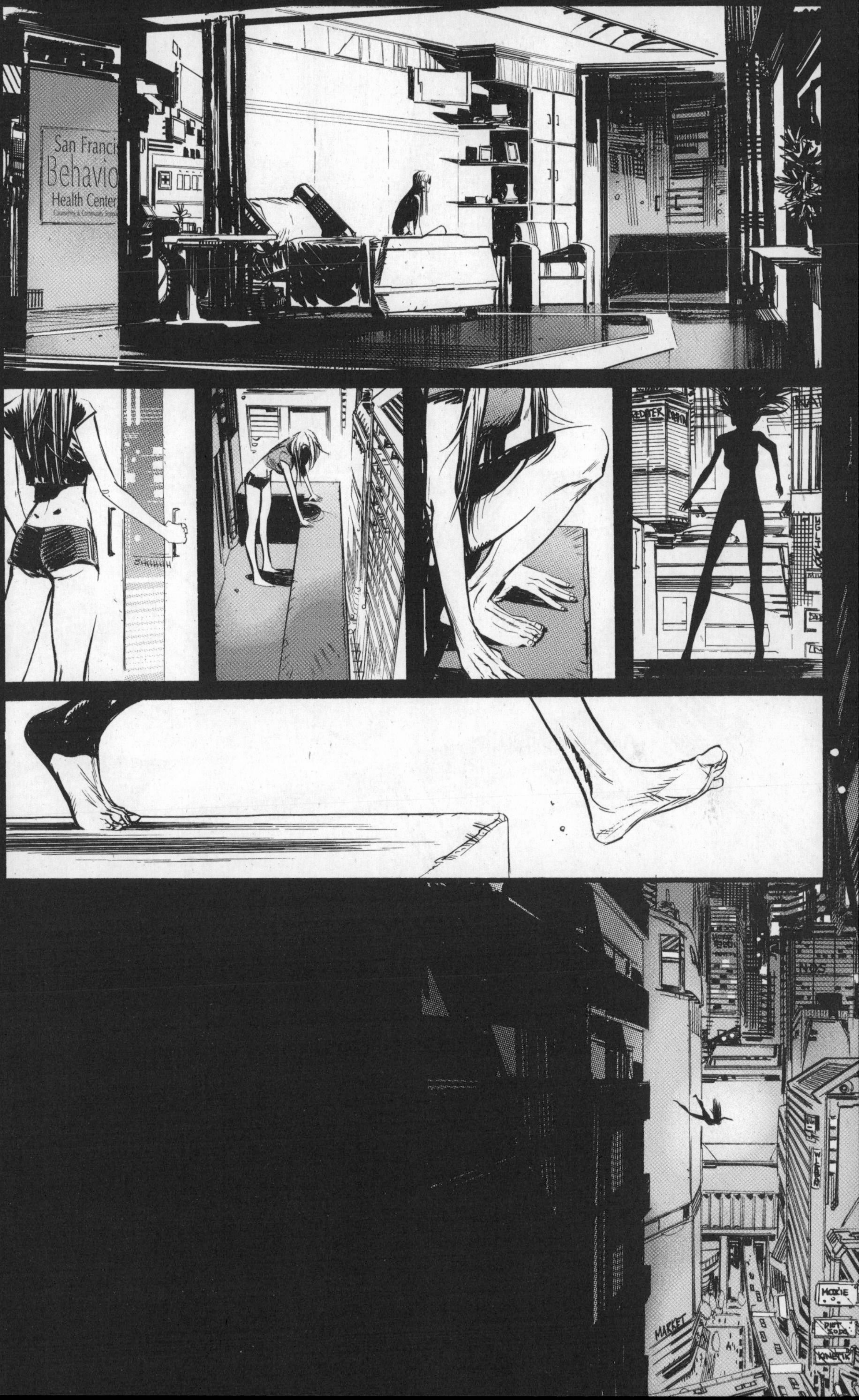
San Francis
Behavio
Health Center
SHHHHH
MARKET
MOXIE
DIET SODA
KINETIK

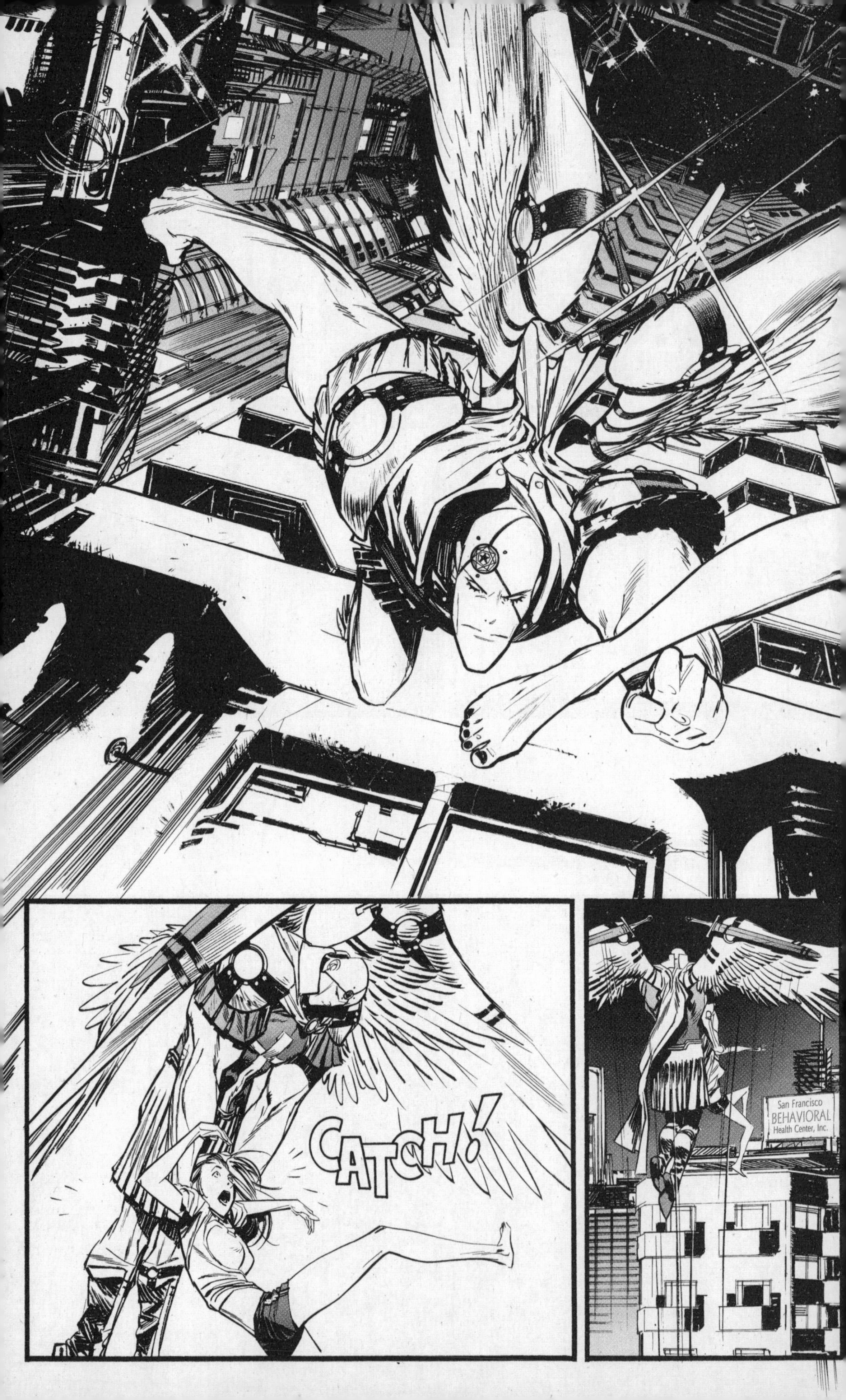
CATCH!
San Francisco BEHAVIORAL Health Center, Inc.

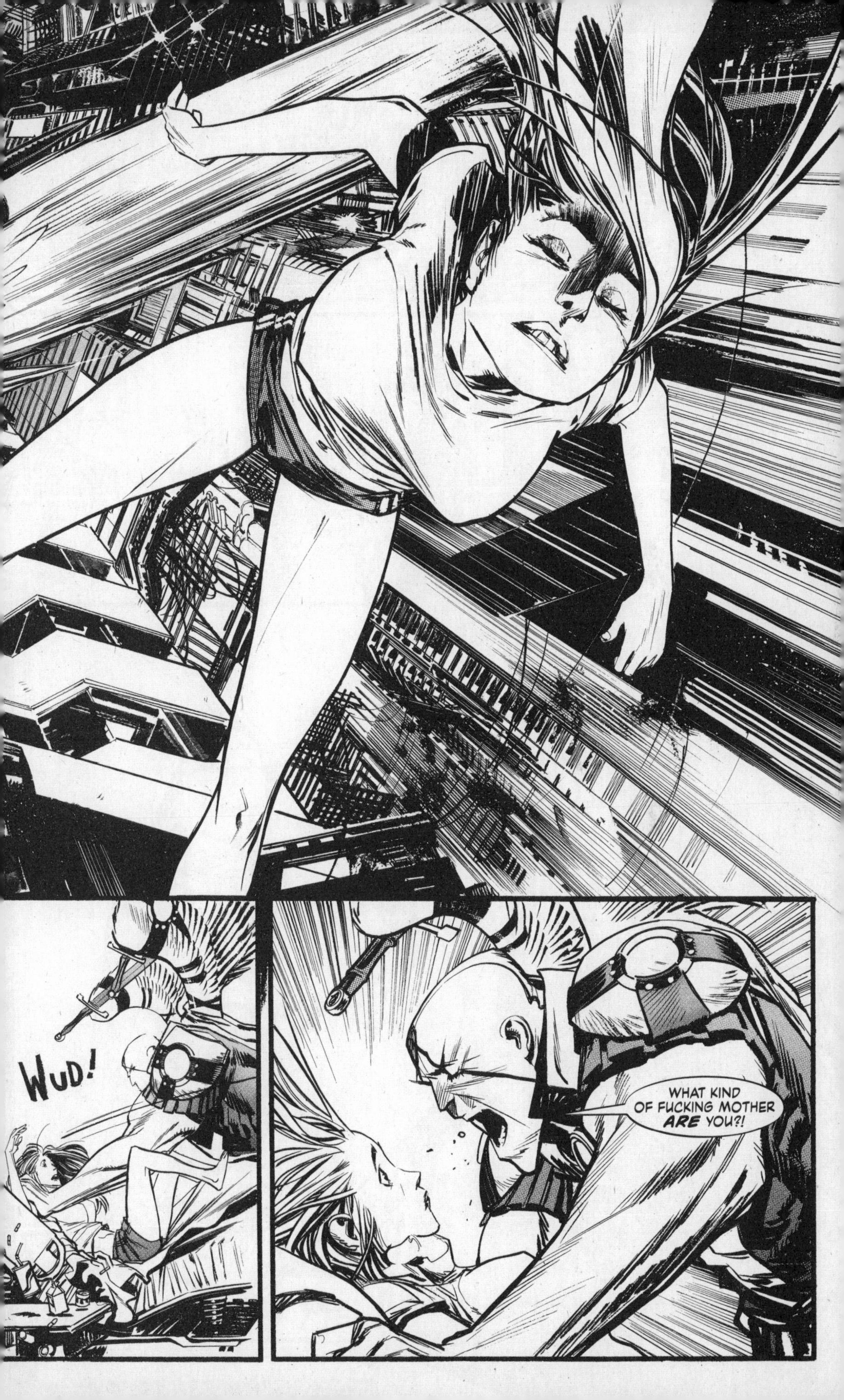
WUD!
WHAT KIND OF FUCKING MOTHER ARE YOU?!

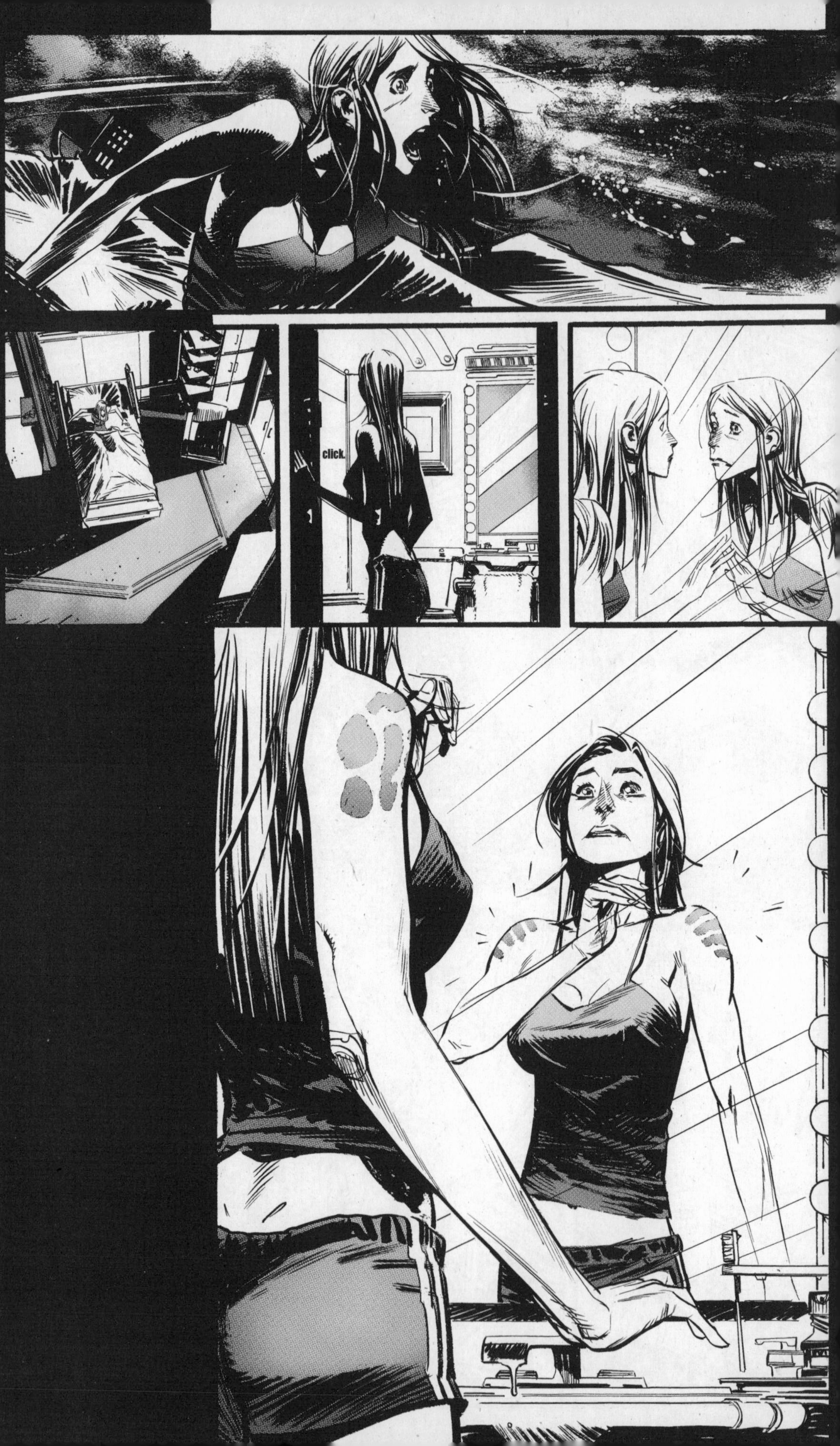
click.

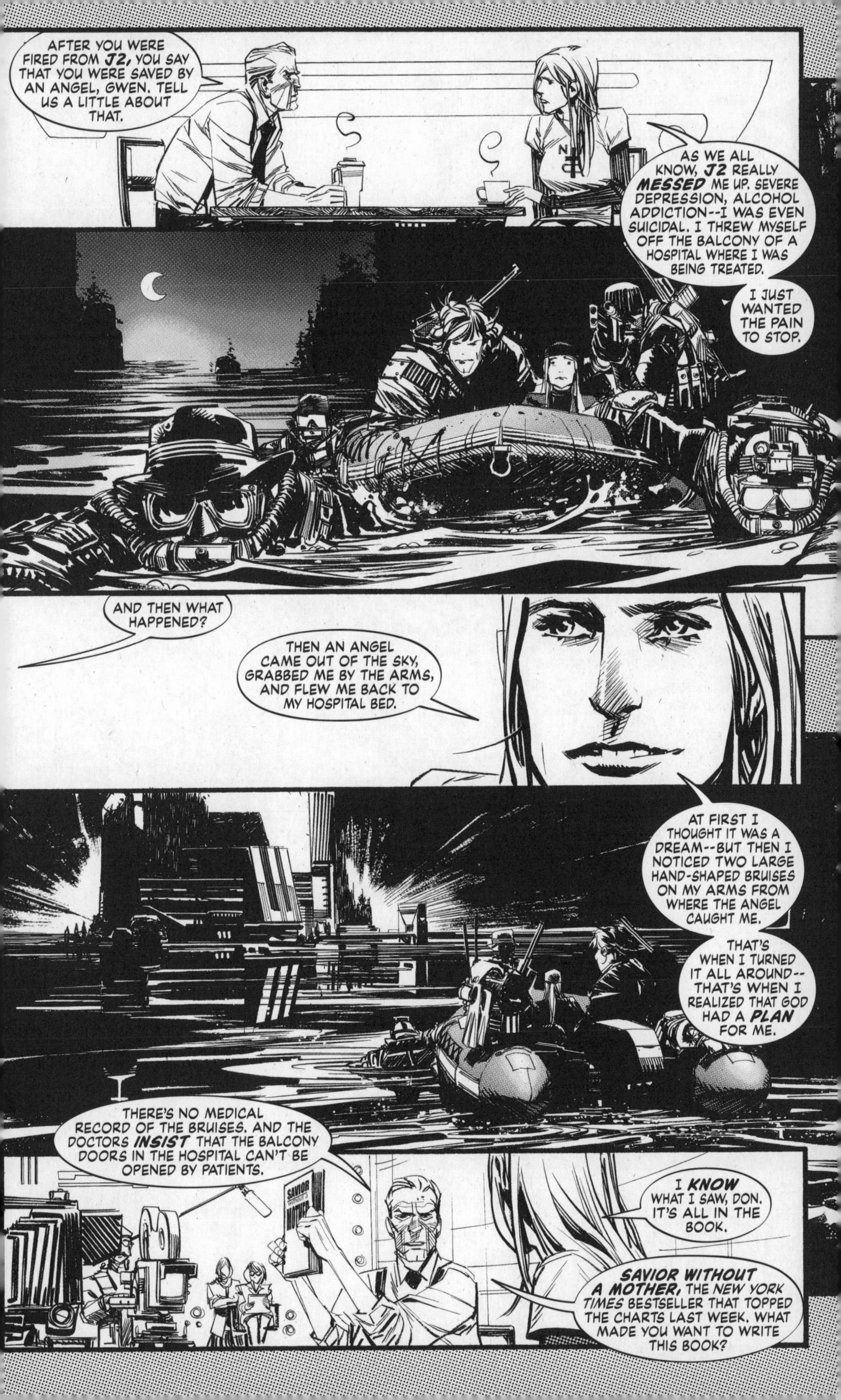
AFTER YOU WERE FIRED FROM J2, YOU SAY THAT YOU WERE SAVED BY AN ANGEL, GWEN. TELL US A LITTLE ABOUT THAT.
AS WE ALL KNOW, J2 REALLY MESSED ME UP. SEVERE DEPRESSION, ALCOHOL ADDICTION--I WAS EVEN SUICIDAL. I THREW MYSELF OFF THE BALCONY OF A HOSPITAL WHERE I WAS BEING TREATED.
I JUST WANTED THE PAIN TO STOP.
AND THEN WHAT HAPPENED?
THEN AN ANGEL CAME OUT OF THE SKY, GRABBED ME BY THE ARMS, AND FLEW ME BACK TO MY HOSPITAL BED.
AT FIRST I THOUGHT IT WAS A DREAM--BUT THEN I NOTICED TWO LARGE HAND-SHAPED BRUISES ON MY ARMS FROM WHERE THE ANGEL CAUGHT ME.
THAT'S WHEN I TURNED IT ALL AROUND--THAT'S WHEN I REALIZED THAT GOD HAD A PLAN FOR ME.
THERE'S NO MEDICAL RECORD OF THE BRUISES. AND THE DOCTORS INSIST THAT THE BALCONY DOORS IN THE HOSPITAL CAN'T BE OPENED BY PATIENTS.
I KNOW WHAT I SAW, DON. IT'S ALL IN THE BOOK.
SAVIOR WITHOUT A MOTHER, THE NEW YORK TIMES BESTSELLER THAT TOPPED THE CHARTS LAST WEEK. WHAT MADE YOU WANT TO WRITE THIS BOOK?

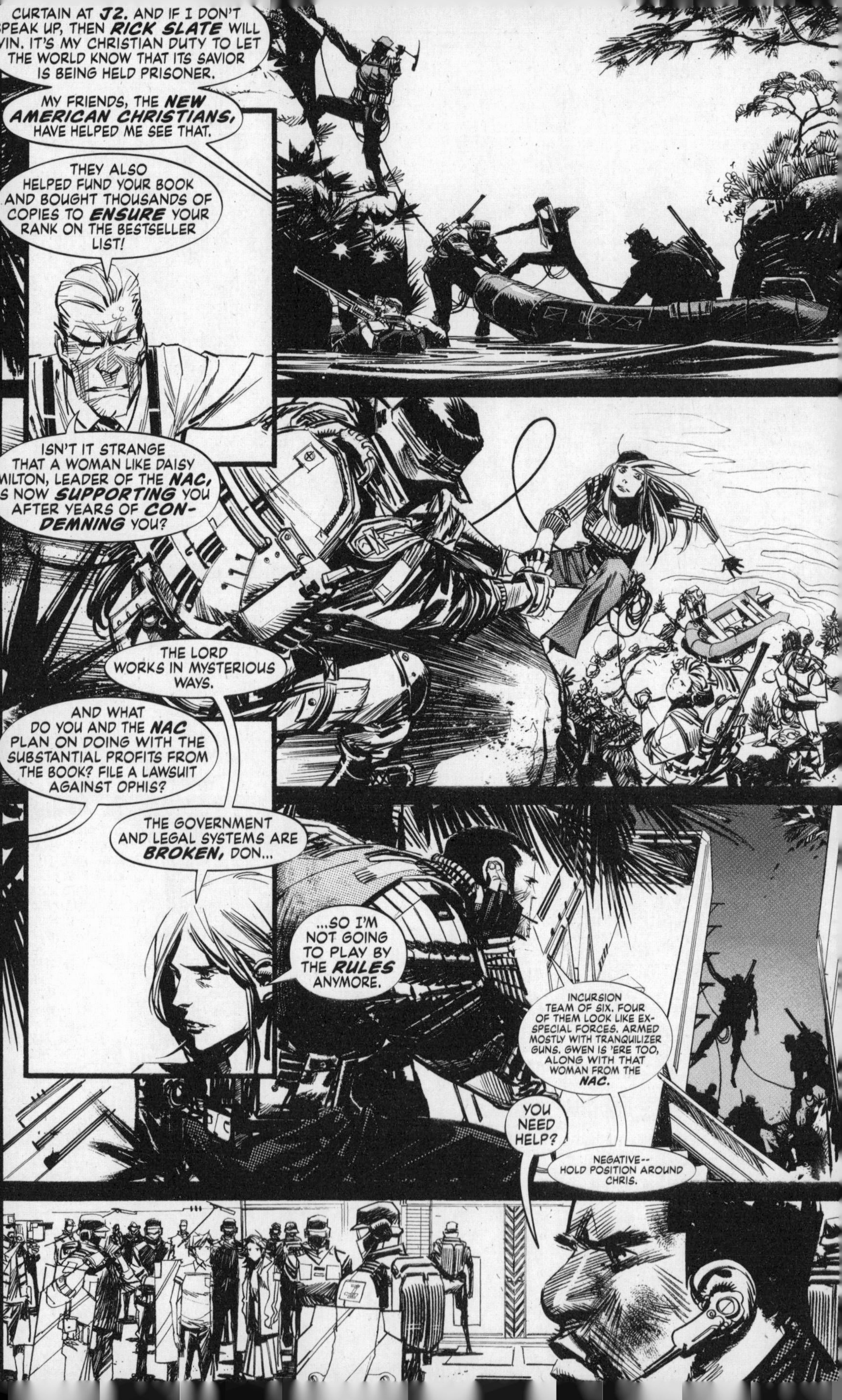

CURTAIN AT J2. AND IF I DON'T SPEAK UP, THEN RICK SLATE WILL WIN. IT'S MY CHRISTIAN DUTY TO LET THE WORLD KNOW THAT ITS SAVIOR IS BEING HELD PRISONER.
MY FRIENDS, THE NEW AMERICAN CHRISTIANS, HAVE HELPED ME SEE THAT.
THEY ALSO HELPED FUND YOUR BOOK AND BOUGHT THOUSANDS OF COPIES TO ENSURE YOUR RANK ON THE BESTSELLER LIST!
ISN'T IT STRANGE THAT A WOMAN LIKE DAISY MILTON, LEADER OF THE NAC, IS NOW SUPPORTING YOU AFTER YEARS OF CON-DEMNING YOU?
THE LORD WORKS IN MYSTERIOUS WAYS.
AND WHAT DO YOU AND THE NAC PLAN ON DOING WITH THE SUBSTANTIAL PROFITS FROM THE BOOK? FILE A LAWSUIT AGAINST OPHIS?
THE GOVERNMENT AND LEGAL SYSTEMS ARE BROKEN, DON...
...SO I'M NOT GOING TO PLAY BY THE RULES ANYMORE.
INCURSION TEAM OF SIX. FOUR OF THEM LOOK LIKE EX-SPECIAL FORCES, ARMED MOSTLY WITH TRANQUILIZER GUNS. GWEN IS 'ERE TOO, ALONG WITH THAT WOMAN FROM THE NAC.
YOU NEED HELP?
NEGATIVE-- HOLD POSITION AROUND CHRIS.

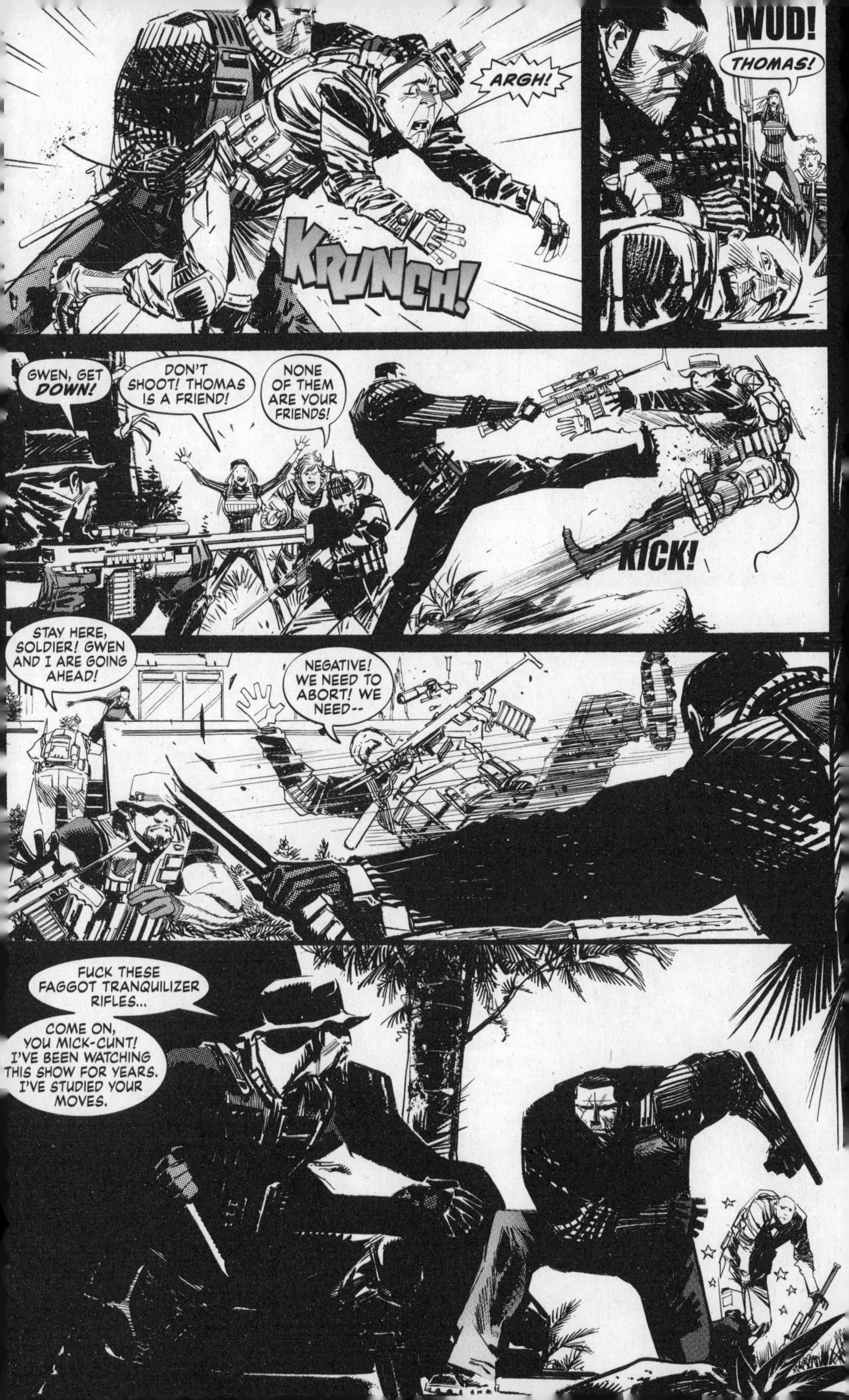

ARGH!
KRUNCH!
WUD!
THOMAS!
GWEN, GET DOWN!
DON'T SHOOT! THOMAS IS A FRIEND!
NONE OF THEM ARE YOUR FRIENDS!
KICK!
STAY HERE, SOLDIER! GWEN AND I ARE GOING AHEAD!
NEGATIVE! WE NEED TO ABORT! WE NEED--
FUCK THESE FAGGOT TRANQUILIZER RIFLES...
COME ON, YOU MICK-CUNT! I'VE BEEN WATCHING THIS SHOW FOR YEARS. I'VE STUDIED YOUR MOVES.

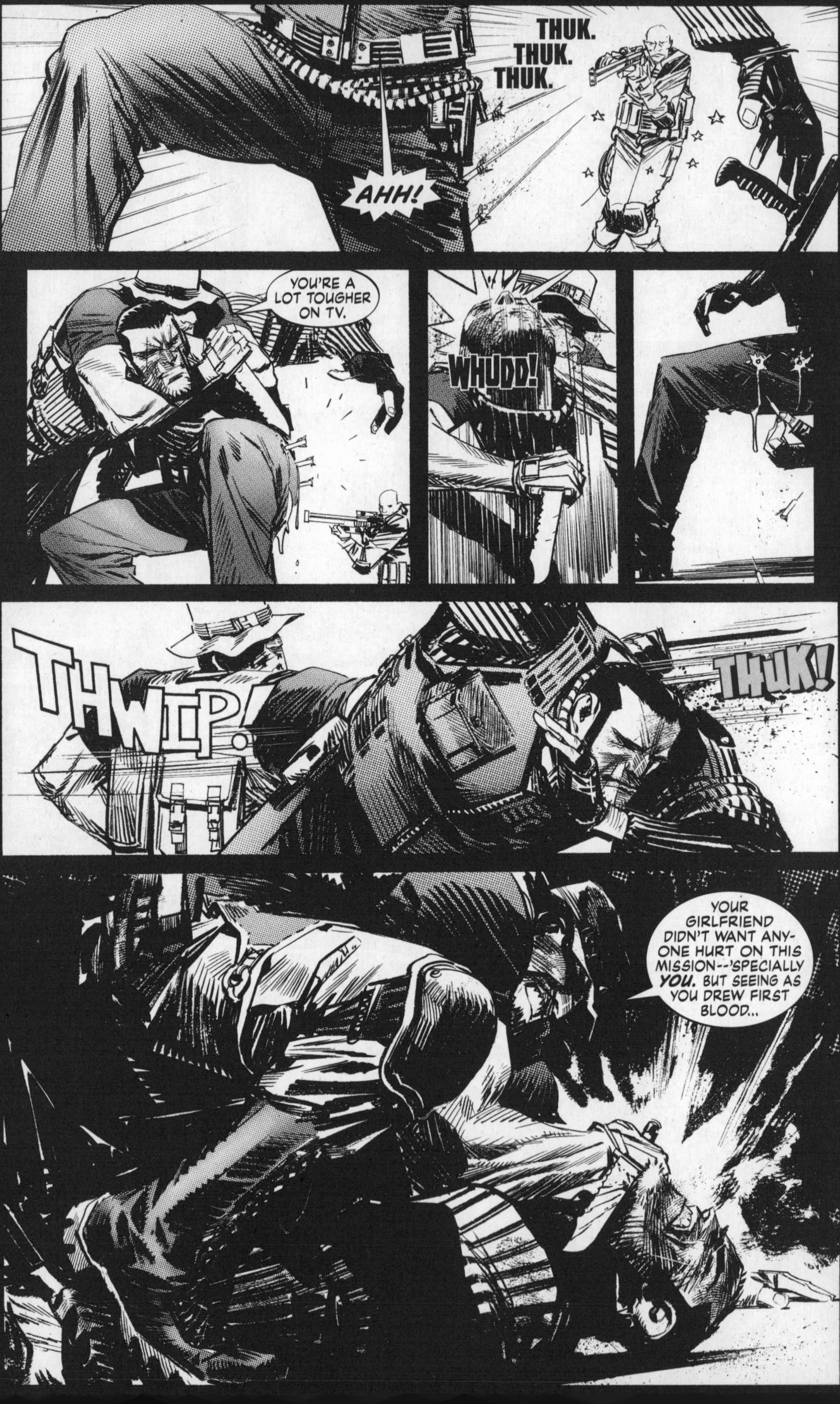
THUK.
THUK.
THUK.
AHH!
YOU'RE A LOT TOUGHER ON TV.
WHUDD!
THWIP!
THUK!
YOUR GIRLFRIEND DIDN'T WANT ANY-ONE HURT ON THIS MISSION--'SPECIALLY YOU. BUT SEEING AS YOU DREW FIRST BLOOD...

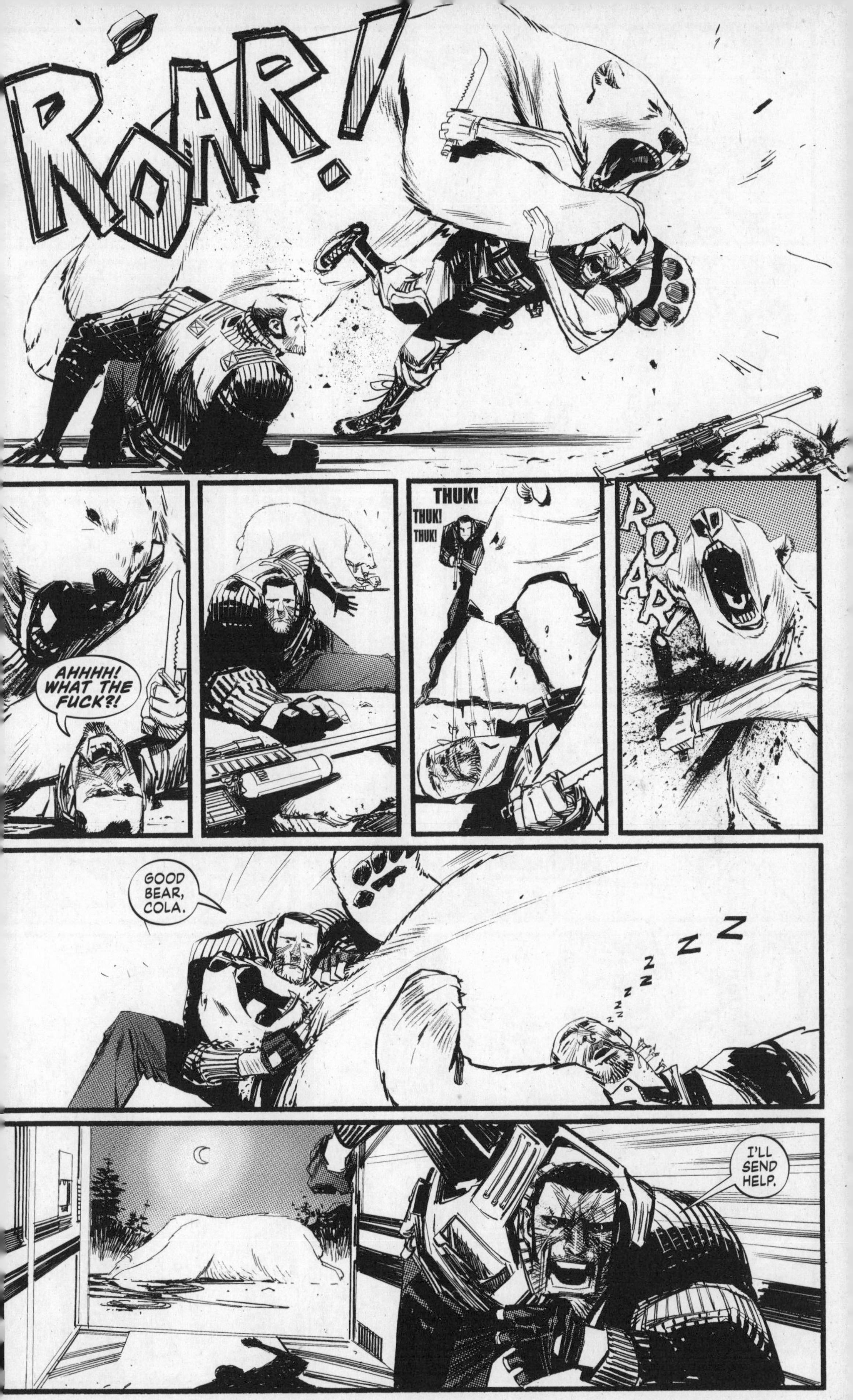
ROAR!
AHHHH! WHAT THE FUCK?!
THUK!
THUK!
THUK!
ROAR!
GOOD BEAR, COLA.
Z Z Z Z Z Z Z
I'LL SEND HELP.

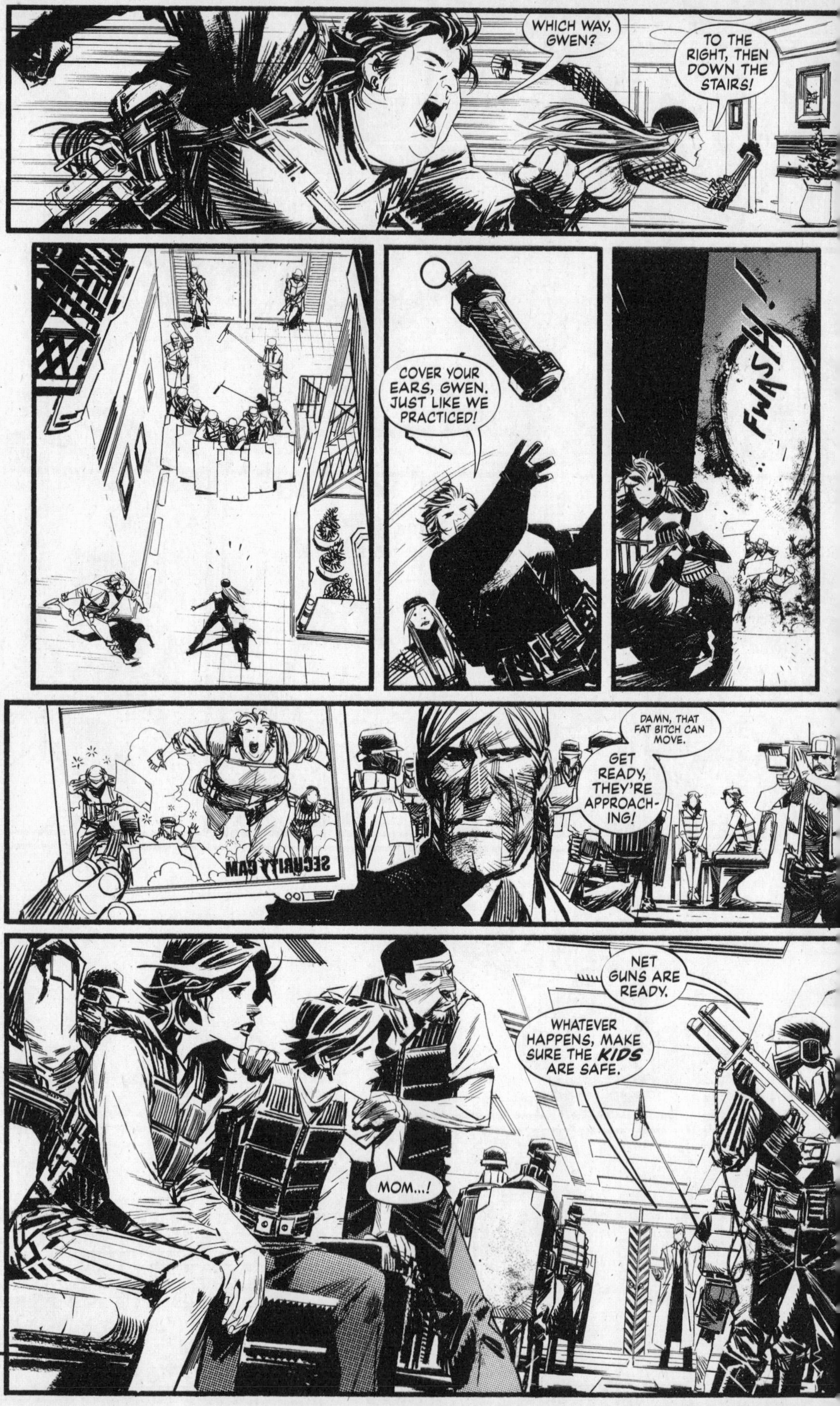
WHICH WAY, GWEN?
TO THE RIGHT, THEN DOWN THE STAIRS!
COVER YOUR EARS, GWEN. JUST LIKE WE PRACTICED!
FWASH!!
SECURITY CAM
DAMN, THAT FAT BITCH CAN MOVE.
GET READY, THEY'RE APPROACHING!
NET GUNS ARE READY.
WHATEVER HAPPENS, MAKE SURE THE *KIDS* ARE SAFE.
MOM...!

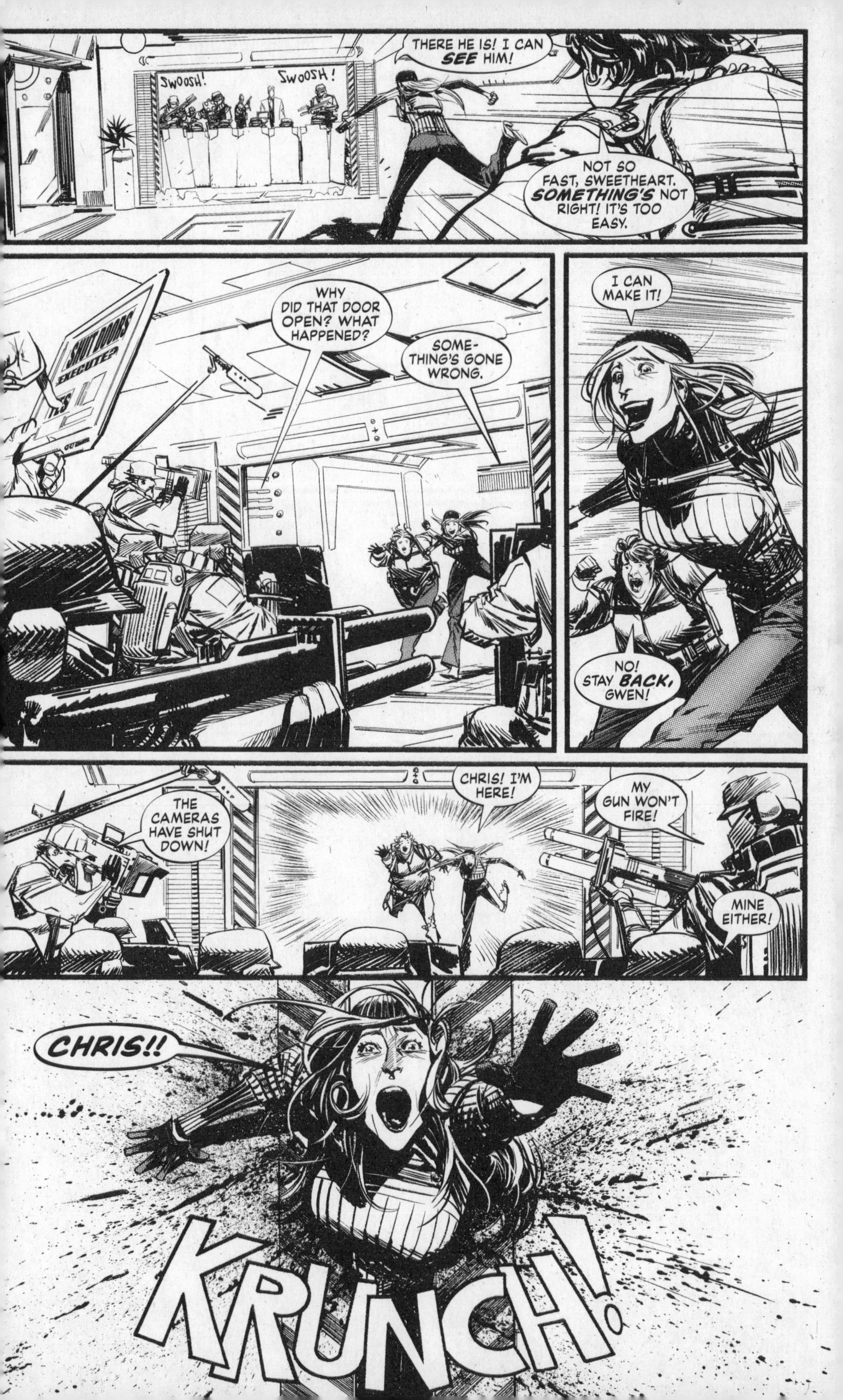
SWOOSH!
SWOOSH!
THERE HE IS! I CAN SEE HIM!
NOT SO FAST, SWEETHEART. SOMETHING'S NOT RIGHT! IT'S TOO EASY.
SHUT DOORS
EXECUTE?
WHY DID THAT DOOR OPEN? WHAT HAPPENED?
SOME-THING'S GONE WRONG.
I CAN MAKE IT!
NO! STAY BACK, GWEN!
THE CAMERAS HAVE SHUT DOWN!
CHRIS! I'M HERE!
MY GUN WON'T FIRE!
MINE EITHER!
CHRIS!!
KRUNCH!

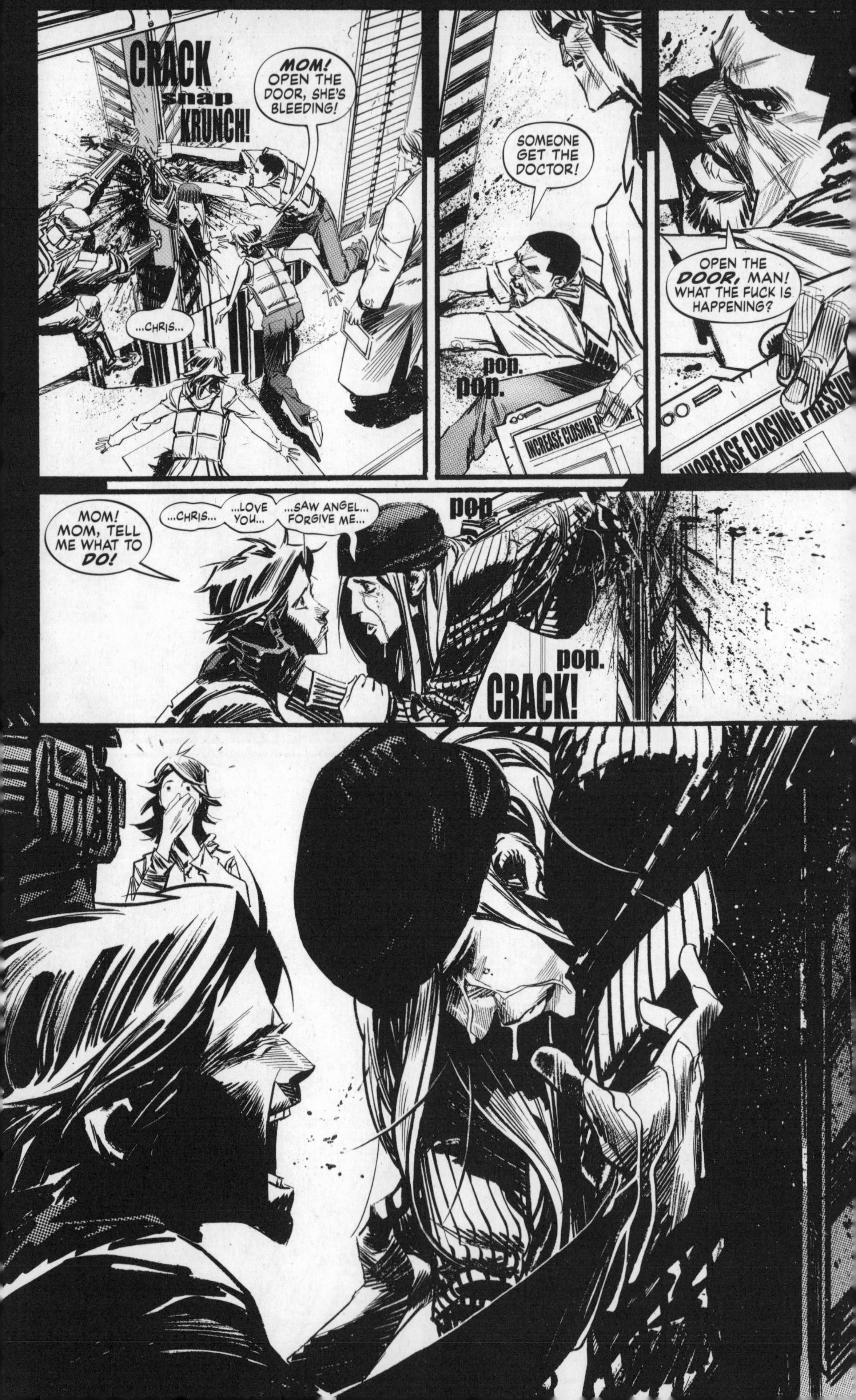
CRACK
snap
KRUNCH!
MOM! OPEN THE DOOR, SHE'S BLEEDING!
...CHRIS...
SOMEONE GET THE DOCTOR!
pop.
pop.
INCREASE CLOSING
OPEN THE DOOR, MAN! WHAT THE FUCK IS HAPPENING?
INCREASE CLOSING PRESSU
MOM! MOM, TELL ME WHAT TO DO!
...CHRIS...
...LOVE YOU...
...SAW ANGEL... FORGIVE ME...
pop.
pop.
CRACK!

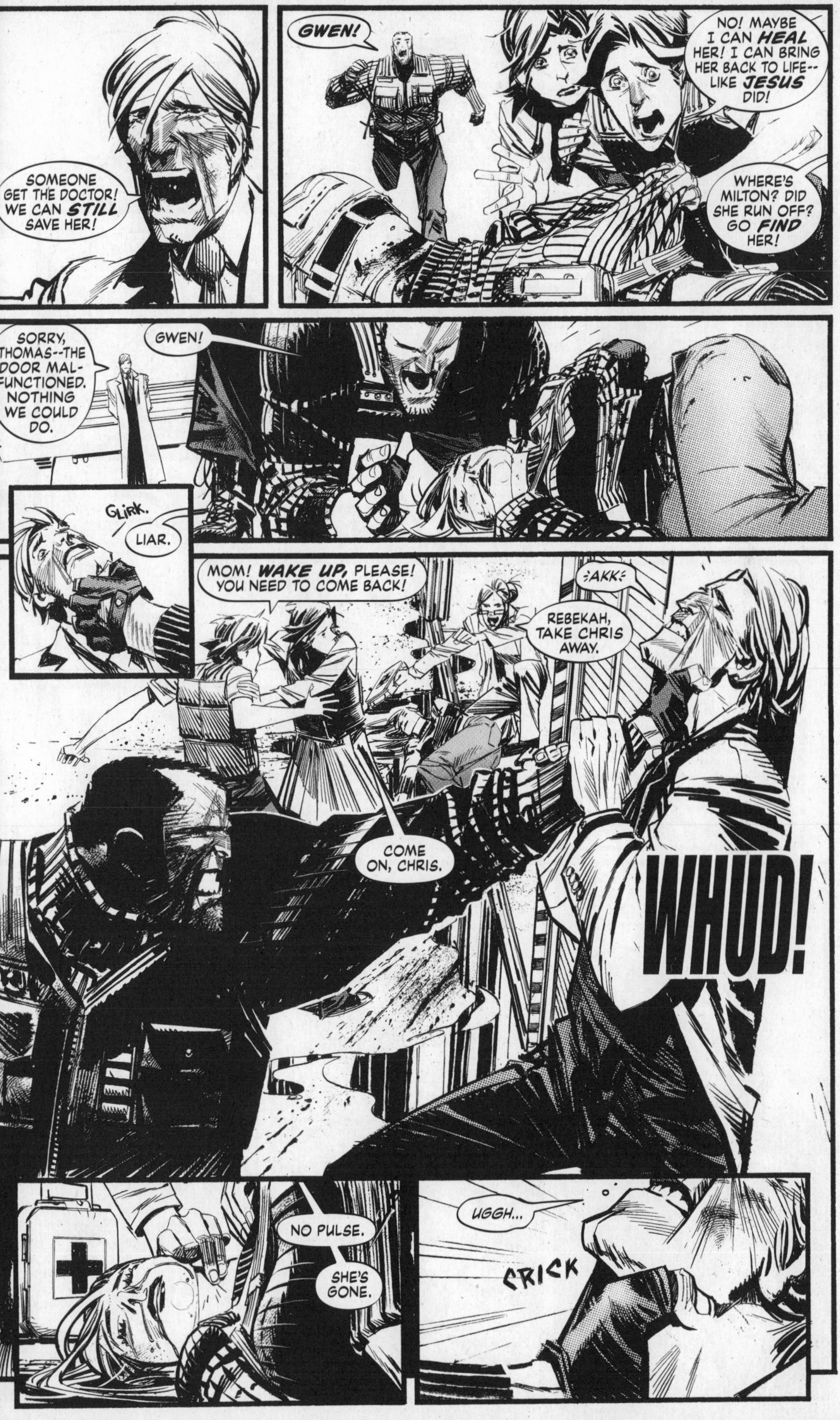
SOMEONE GET THE DOCTOR! WE CAN STILL SAVE HER!
GWEN!
NO! MAYBE I CAN HEAL HER! I CAN BRING HER BACK TO LIFE-- LIKE JESUS DID!
WHERE'S MILTON? DID SHE RUN OFF? GO FIND HER!
SORRY, THOMAS--THE DOOR MAL-FUNCTIONED. NOTHING WE COULD DO.
GWEN!
GLIRK.
LIAR.
MOM! WAKE UP, PLEASE! YOU NEED TO COME BACK!
AKK
REBEKAH, TAKE CHRIS AWAY.
COME ON, CHRIS.
WHUD!
NO PULSE.
SHE'S GONE.
UGGH...
CRICK

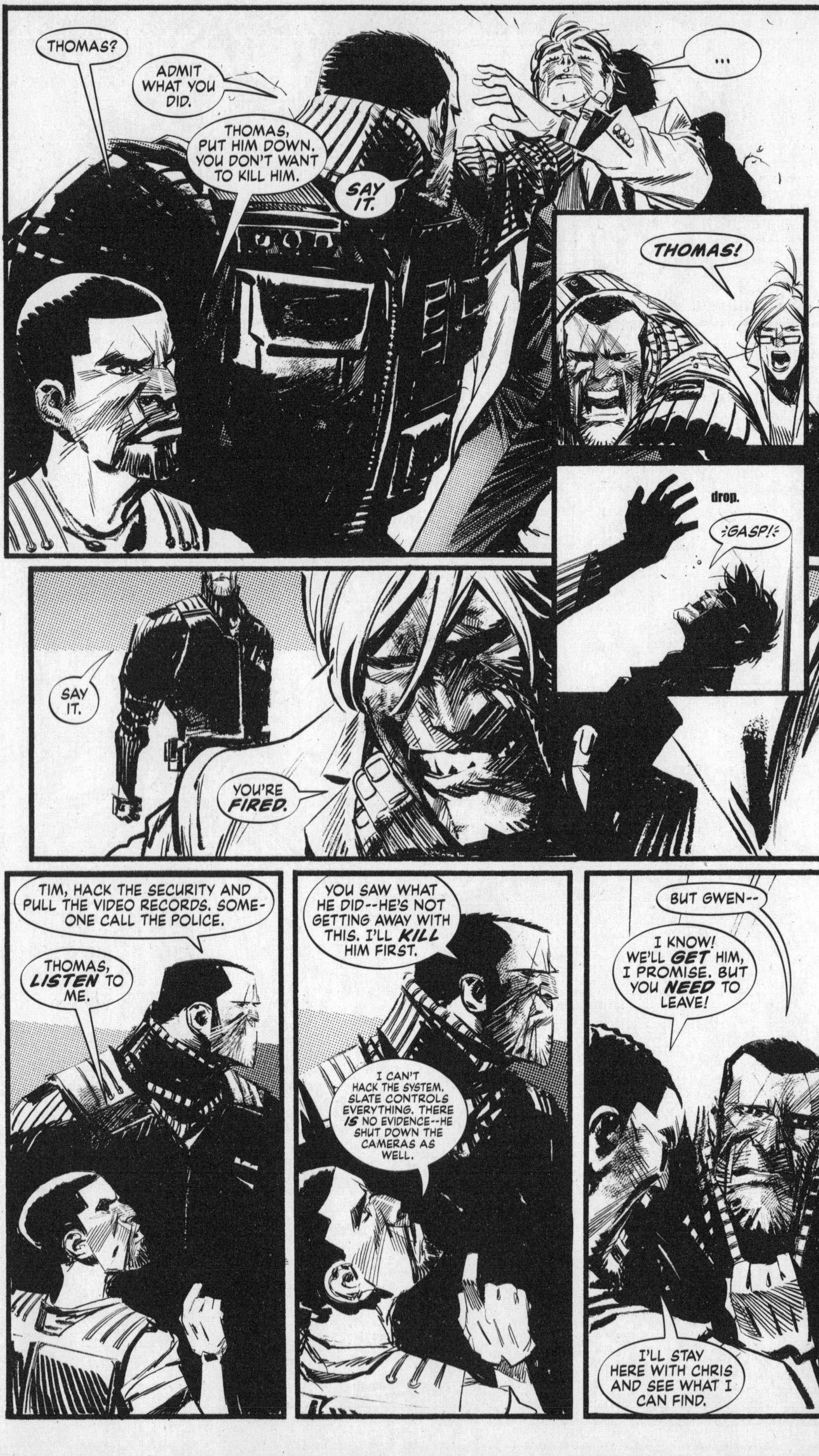
THOMAS?
ADMIT WHAT YOU DID.
THOMAS, PUT HIM DOWN. YOU DON'T WANT TO KILL HIM.
SAY IT.
...
THOMAS!
drop.
GASP!
SAY IT.
YOU'RE FIRED.
TIM, HACK THE SECURITY AND PULL THE VIDEO RECORDS. SOMEONE CALL THE POLICE.
THOMAS, LISTEN TO ME.
YOU SAW WHAT HE DID--HE'S NOT GETTING AWAY WITH THIS. I'LL KILL HIM FIRST.
I CAN'T HACK THE SYSTEM. SLATE CONTROLS EVERYTHING. THERE IS NO EVIDENCE--HE SHUT DOWN THE CAMERAS AS WELL.
BUT GWEN--
I KNOW! WE'LL GET HIM, I PROMISE. BUT YOU NEED TO LEAVE!
I'LL STAY HERE WITH CHRIS AND SEE WHAT I CAN FIND.

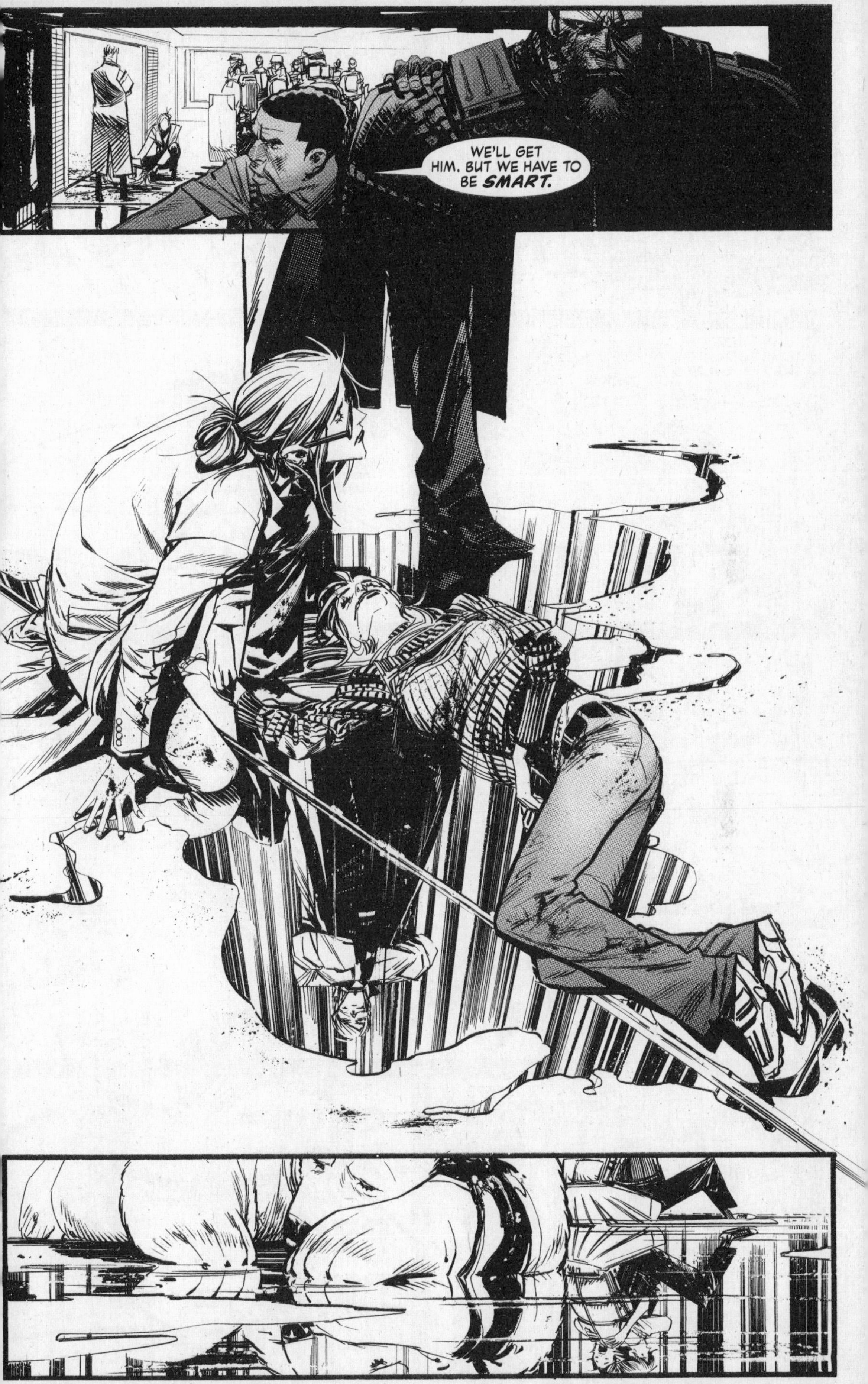
WE'LL GET HIM. BUT WE HAVE TO BE SMART.

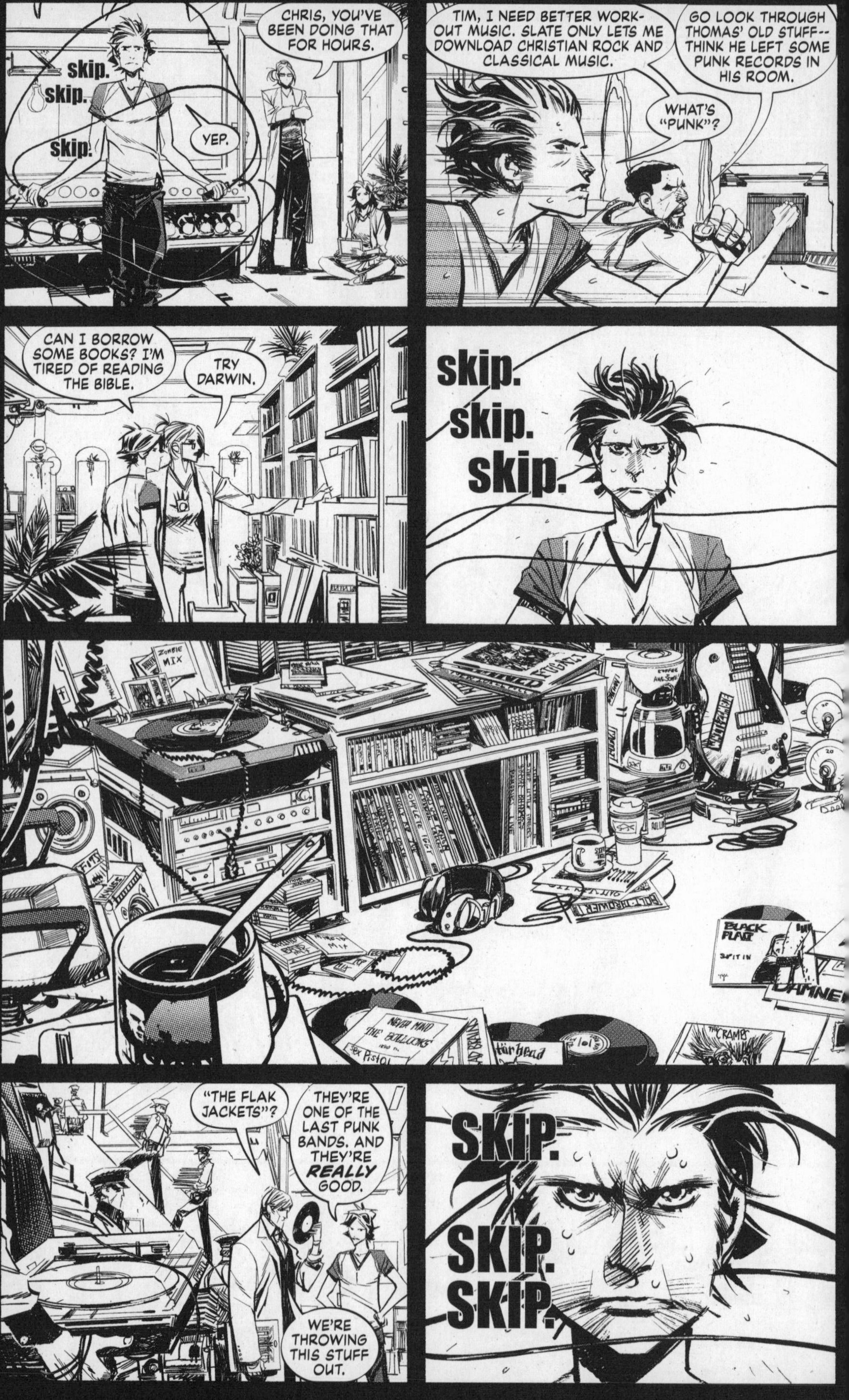
skip.
skip.
skip.
CHRIS, YOU'VE BEEN DOING THAT FOR HOURS.
YEP.
TIM, I NEED BETTER WORK-OUT MUSIC. SLATE ONLY LETS ME DOWNLOAD CHRISTIAN ROCK AND CLASSICAL MUSIC.
GO LOOK THROUGH THOMAS' OLD STUFF-- THINK HE LEFT SOME PUNK RECORDS IN HIS ROOM.
WHAT'S "PUNK"?
CAN I BORROW SOME BOOKS? I'M TIRED OF READING THE BIBLE.
TRY DARWIN.
skip.
skip.
skip.
ZOMBIE MIX
BLACK FLAG
NEVER MIND THE BOLLOCKS
THE CRAMPS
"THE FLAK JACKETS"?
THEY'RE ONE OF THE LAST PUNK BANDS. AND THEY'RE *REALLY* GOOD.
WE'RE THROWING THIS STUFF OUT.
SKIP.
SKIP.
SKIP.

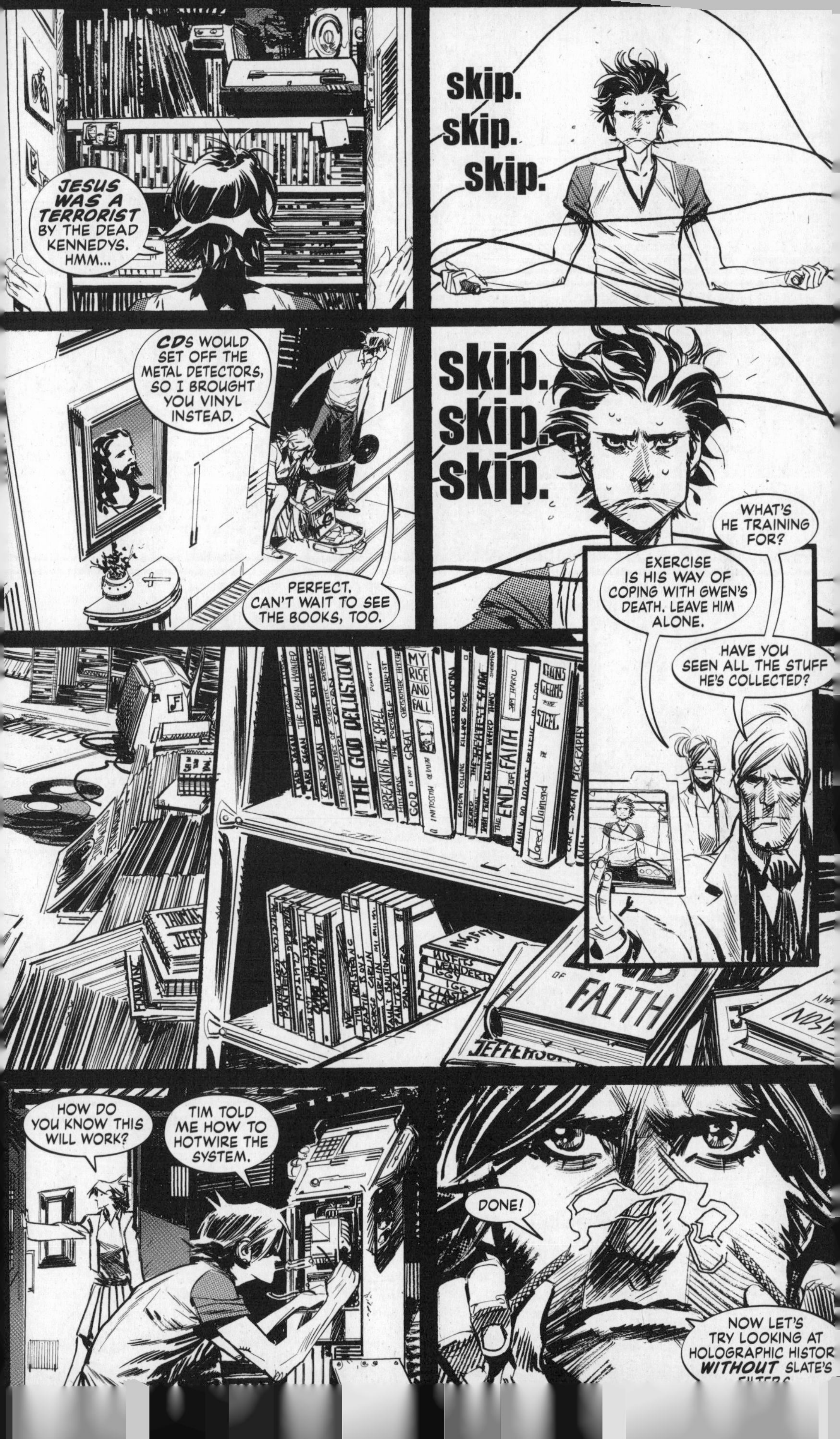

JESUS WAS A TERRORIST BY THE DEAD KENNEDYS. HMM...
skip. skip. skip.
CDs WOULD SET OFF THE METAL DETECTORS, SO I BROUGHT YOU VINYL INSTEAD.
PERFECT. CAN'T WAIT TO SEE THE BOOKS, TOO.
skip. skip. skip.
WHAT'S HE TRAINING FOR?
EXERCISE IS HIS WAY OF COPING WITH GWEN'S DEATH. LEAVE HIM ALONE.
HAVE YOU SEEN ALL THE STUFF HE'S COLLECTED?
HOW DO YOU KNOW THIS WILL WORK?
TIM TOLD ME HOW TO HOTWIRE THE SYSTEM.
DONE!
NOW LET'S TRY LOOKING AT HOLOGRAPHIC HISTOR WITHOUT SLATE'S

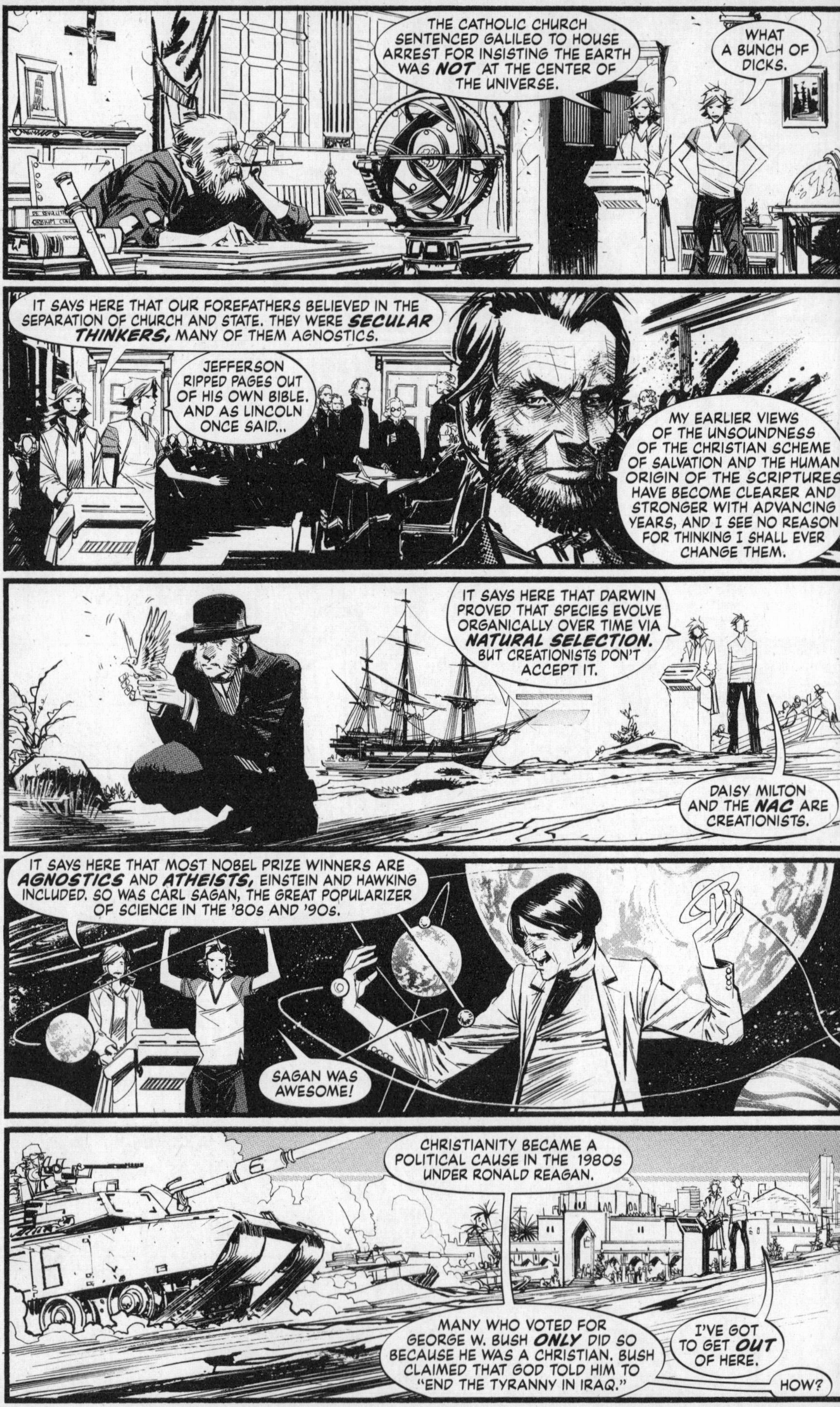
THE CATHOLIC CHURCH SENTENCED GALILEO TO HOUSE ARREST FOR INSISTING THE EARTH WAS NOT AT THE CENTER OF THE UNIVERSE.
WHAT A BUNCH OF DICKS.
IT SAYS HERE THAT OUR FOREFATHERS BELIEVED IN THE SEPARATION OF CHURCH AND STATE. THEY WERE SECULAR THINKERS, MANY OF THEM AGNOSTICS.
JEFFERSON RIPPED PAGES OUT OF HIS OWN BIBLE. AND AS LINCOLN ONCE SAID...
MY EARLIER VIEWS OF THE UNSOUNDNESS OF THE CHRISTIAN SCHEME OF SALVATION AND THE HUMAN ORIGIN OF THE SCRIPTURES HAVE BECOME CLEARER AND STRONGER WITH ADVANCING YEARS, AND I SEE NO REASON FOR THINKING I SHALL EVER CHANGE THEM.
IT SAYS HERE THAT DARWIN PROVED THAT SPECIES EVOLVE ORGANICALLY OVER TIME VIA NATURAL SELECTION. BUT CREATIONISTS DON'T ACCEPT IT.
DAISY MILTON AND THE NAC ARE CREATIONISTS.
IT SAYS HERE THAT MOST NOBEL PRIZE WINNERS ARE AGNOSTICS AND ATHEISTS, EINSTEIN AND HAWKING INCLUDED. SO WAS CARL SAGAN, THE GREAT POPULARIZER OF SCIENCE IN THE '80s AND '90s.
SAGAN WAS AWESOME!
CHRISTIANITY BECAME A POLITICAL CAUSE IN THE 1980s UNDER RONALD REAGAN.
MANY WHO VOTED FOR GEORGE W. BUSH ONLY DID SO BECAUSE HE WAS A CHRISTIAN. BUSH CLAIMED THAT GOD TOLD HIM TO "END THE TYRANNY IN IRAQ."
I'VE GOT TO GET OUT OF HERE.
HOW?

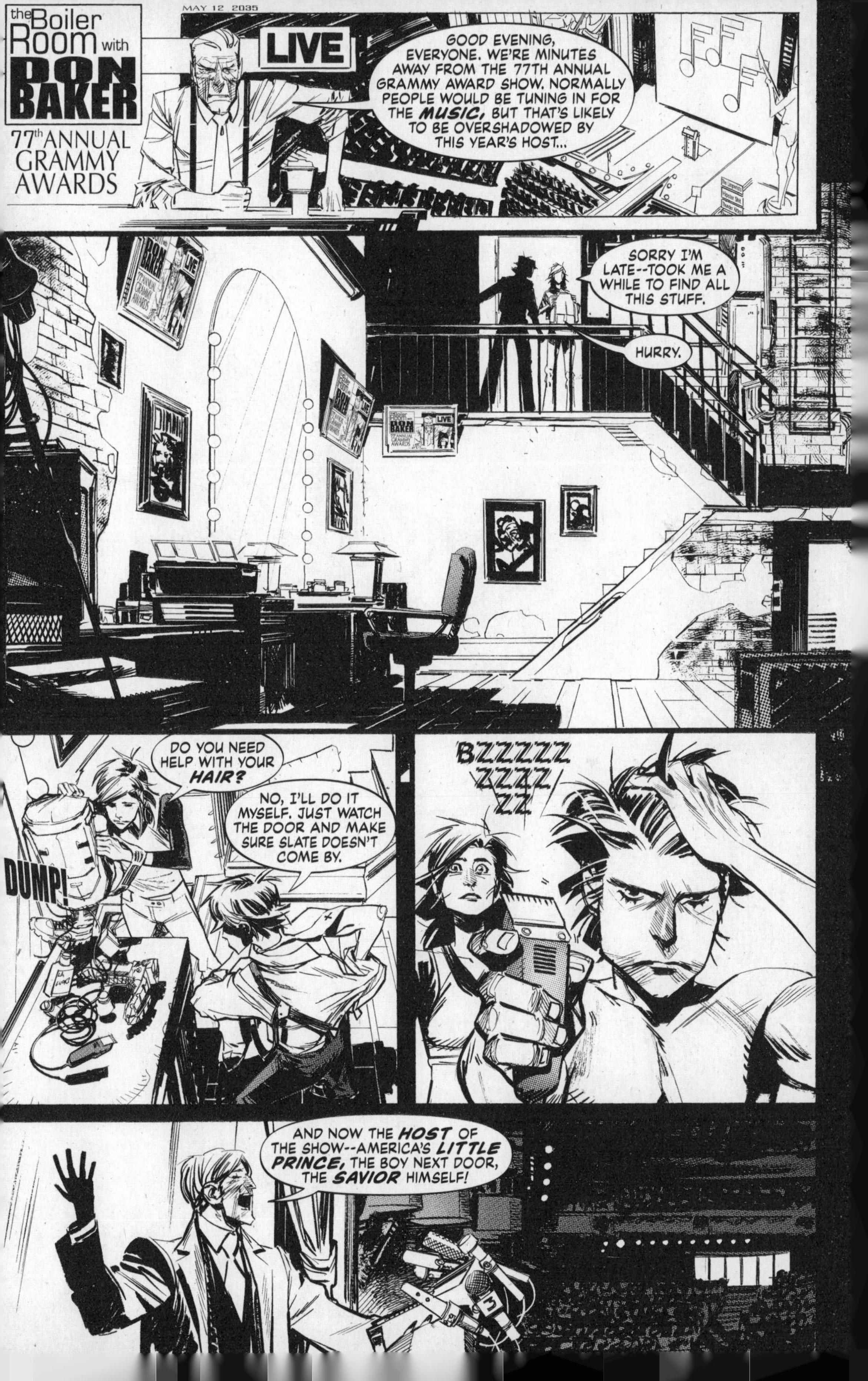

the Boiler Room with DON BAKER
77th ANNUAL GRAMMY AWARDS
MAY 12 2035
LIVE
GOOD EVENING, EVERYONE. WE'RE MINUTES AWAY FROM THE 77TH ANNUAL GRAMMY AWARD SHOW. NORMALLY PEOPLE WOULD BE TUNING IN FOR THE MUSIC, BUT THAT'S LIKELY TO BE OVERSHADOWED BY THIS YEAR'S HOST...
SORRY I'M LATE--TOOK ME A WHILE TO FIND ALL THIS STUFF.
HURRY.
DO YOU NEED HELP WITH YOUR HAIR?
NO, I'LL DO IT MYSELF. JUST WATCH THE DOOR AND MAKE SURE SLATE DOESN'T COME BY.
DUMP!
BZZZZZ ZZZZ ZZ
AND NOW THE HOST OF THE SHOW--AMERICA'S LITTLE PRINCE, THE BOY NEXT DOOR, THE SAVIOR HIMSELF!

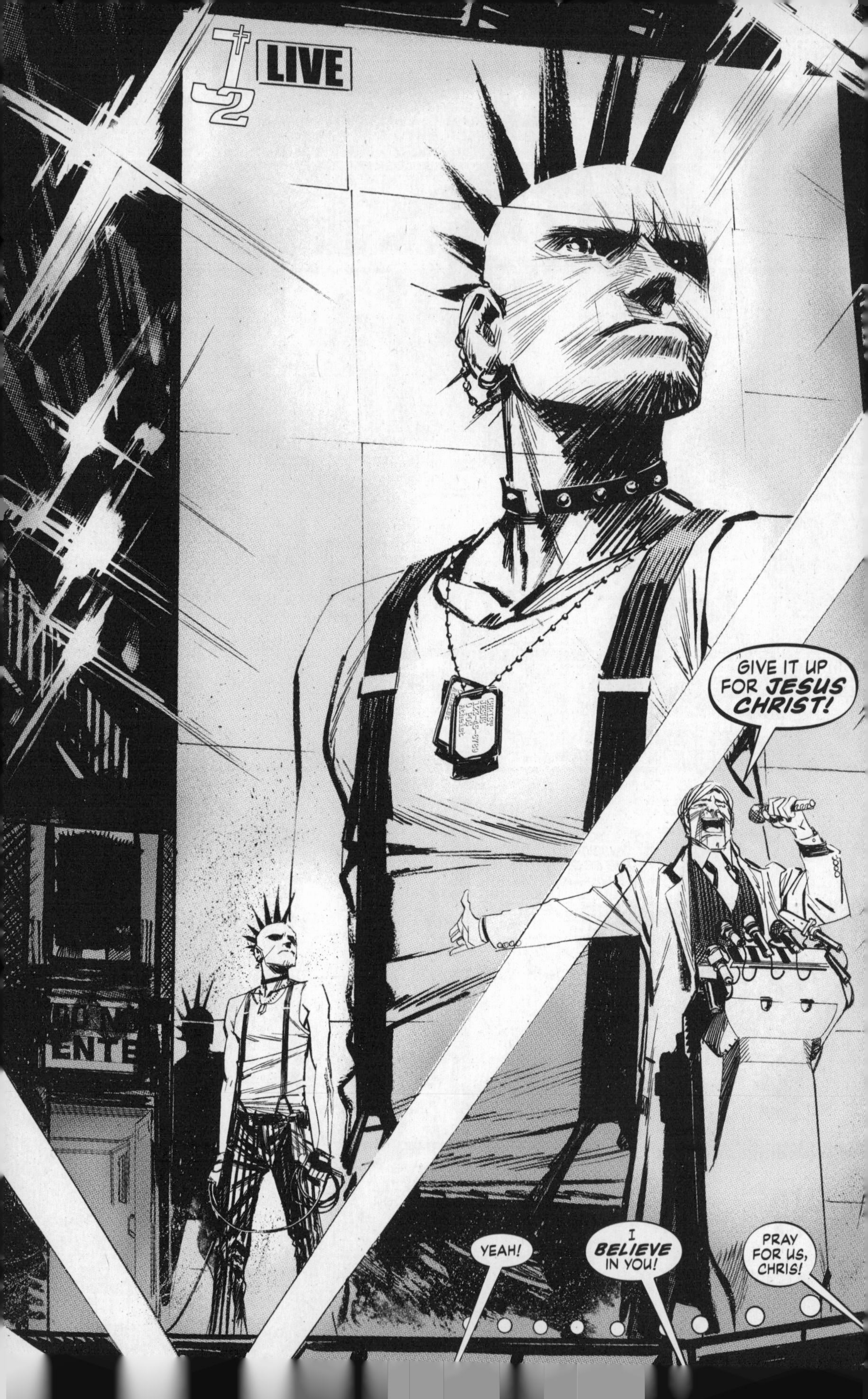
LIVE
GIVE IT UP FOR *JESUS CHRIST!*
YEAH!
I *BELIEVE* IN YOU!
PRAY FOR US, CHRIS!

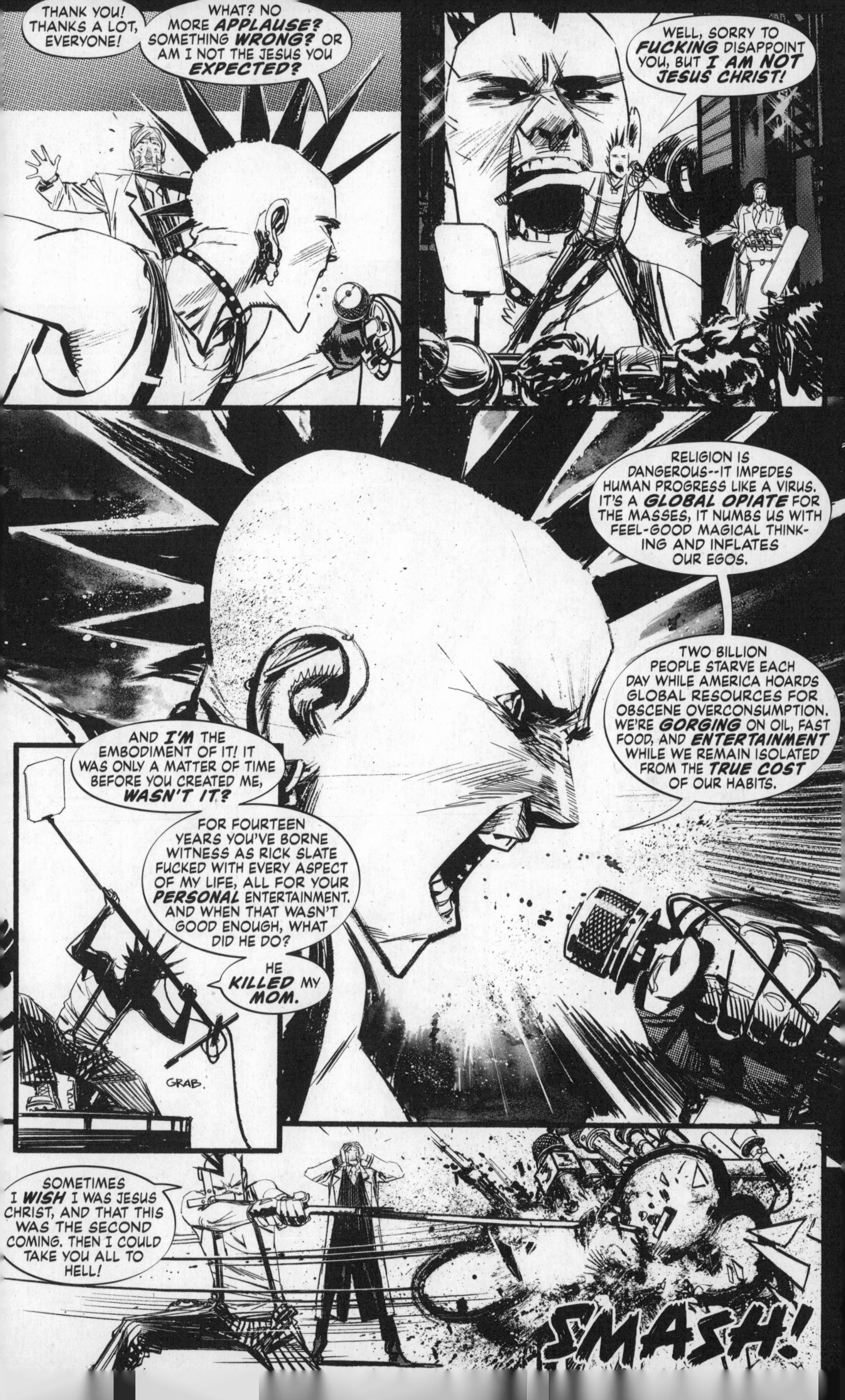
THANK YOU! THANKS A LOT, EVERYONE!
WHAT? NO MORE APPLAUSE? SOMETHING WRONG? OR AM I NOT THE JESUS YOU EXPECTED?
WELL, SORRY TO FUCKING DISAPPOINT YOU, BUT I AM NOT JESUS CHRIST!
RELIGION IS DANGEROUS--IT IMPEDES HUMAN PROGRESS LIKE A VIRUS. IT'S A GLOBAL OPIATE FOR THE MASSES, IT NUMBS US WITH FEEL-GOOD MAGICAL THINKING AND INFLATES OUR EGOS.
TWO BILLION PEOPLE STARVE EACH DAY WHILE AMERICA HOARDS GLOBAL RESOURCES FOR OBSCENE OVERCONSUMPTION. WE'RE GORGING ON OIL, FAST FOOD, AND ENTERTAINMENT WHILE WE REMAIN ISOLATED FROM THE TRUE COST OF OUR HABITS.
AND I'M THE EMBODIMENT OF IT! IT WAS ONLY A MATTER OF TIME BEFORE YOU CREATED ME, WASN'T IT?
FOR FOURTEEN YEARS YOU'VE BORNE WITNESS AS RICK SLATE FUCKED WITH EVERY ASPECT OF MY LIFE, ALL FOR YOUR PERSONAL ENTERTAINMENT. AND WHEN THAT WASN'T GOOD ENOUGH, WHAT DID HE DO?
HE KILLED MY MOM.
GRAB.
SOMETIMES I WISH I WAS JESUS CHRIST, AND THAT THIS WAS THE SECOND COMING. THEN I COULD TAKE YOU ALL TO HELL!
SMASH!

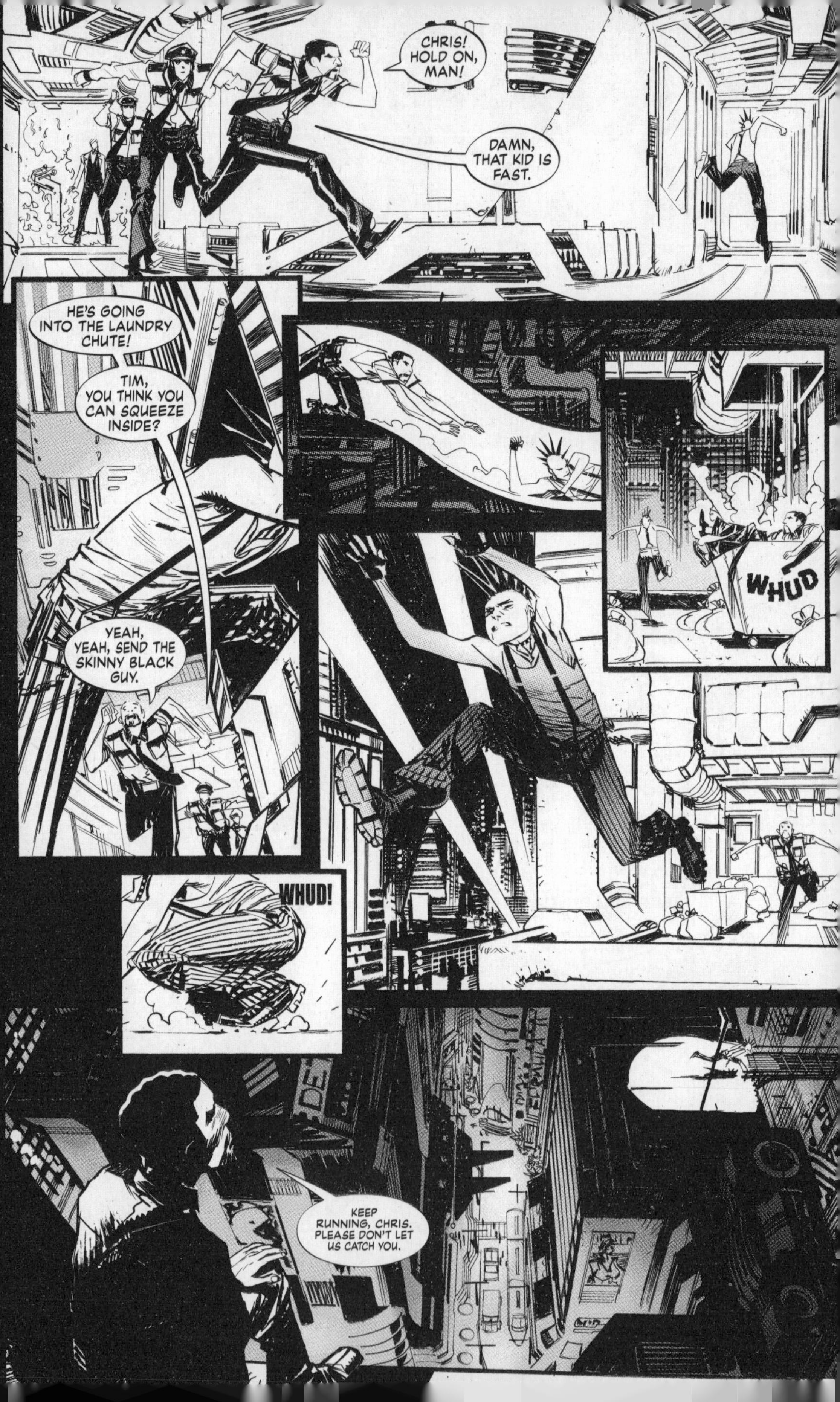
CHRIS! HOLD ON, MAN!
DAMN, THAT KID IS FAST.
HE'S GOING INTO THE LAUNDRY CHUTE!
TIM, YOU THINK YOU CAN SQUEEZE INSIDE?
YEAH, YEAH, SEND THE SKINNY BLACK GUY.
WHUD
WHUD!
KEEP RUNNING, CHRIS. PLEASE DON'T LET US CATCH YOU.

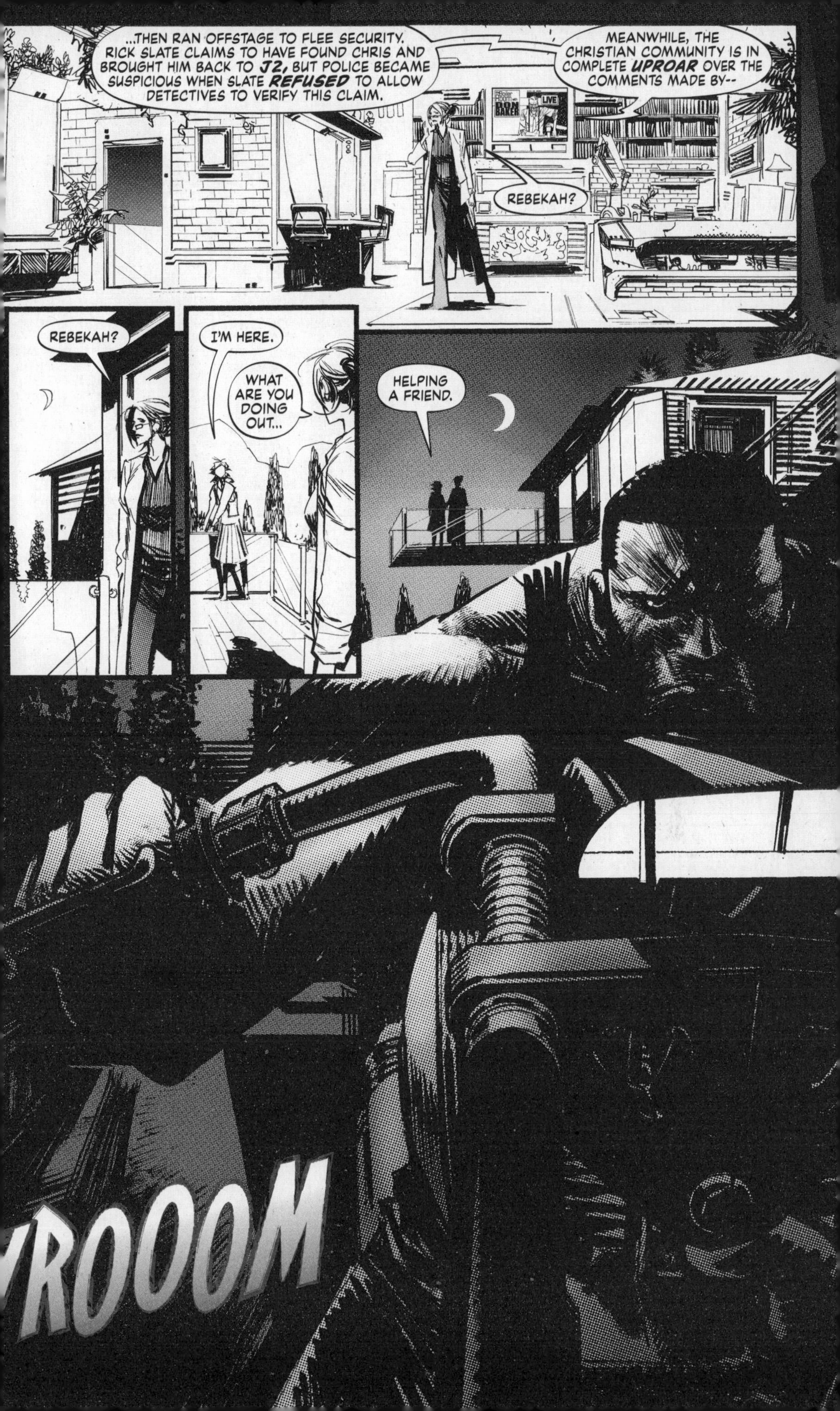
...THEN RAN OFFSTAGE TO FLEE SECURITY. RICK SLATE CLAIMS TO HAVE FOUND CHRIS AND BROUGHT HIM BACK TO J2, BUT POLICE BECAME SUSPICIOUS WHEN SLATE REFUSED TO ALLOW DETECTIVES TO VERIFY THIS CLAIM.
MEANWHILE, THE CHRISTIAN COMMUNITY IS IN COMPLETE UPROAR OVER THE COMMENTS MADE BY--
Boiler Room with DON BAKER
LIVE
REBEKAH?
REBEKAH?
I'M HERE.
WHAT ARE YOU DOING OUT...
HELPING A FRIEND.
VROOOM

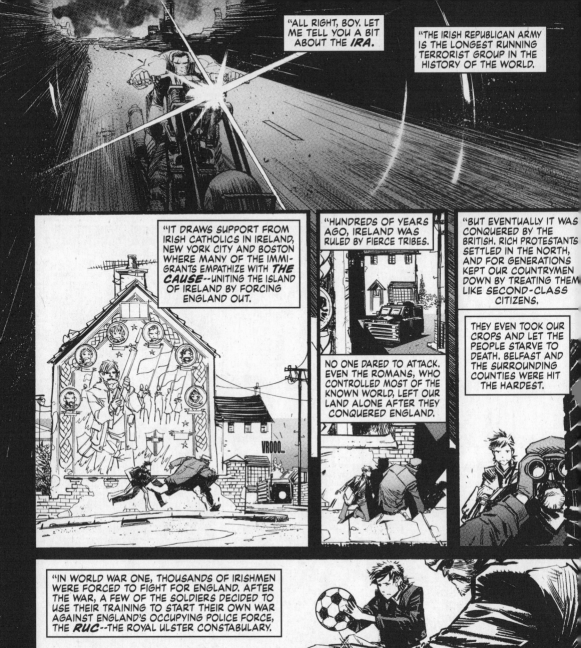

"ALL RIGHT, BOY. LET ME TELL YOU A BIT ABOUT THE *IRA*.

"THE IRISH REPUBLICAN ARMY IS THE LONGEST RUNNING TERRORIST GROUP IN THE HISTORY OF THE WORLD.

"IT DRAWS SUPPORT FROM IRISH CATHOLICS IN IRELAND, NEW YORK CITY AND BOSTON WHERE MANY OF THE IMMIGRANTS EMPATHIZE WITH *THE CAUSE*--UNITING THE ISLAND OF IRELAND BY FORCING ENGLAND OUT.

"HUNDREDS OF YEARS AGO, IRELAND WAS RULED BY FIERCE TRIBES.

NO ONE DARED TO ATTACK. EVEN THE ROMANS, WHO CONTROLLED MOST OF THE KNOWN WORLD, LEFT OUR LAND ALONE AFTER THEY CONQUERED ENGLAND.

"BUT EVENTUALLY IT WAS CONQUERED BY THE BRITISH. RICH PROTESTANTS SETTLED IN THE NORTH, AND FOR GENERATIONS KEPT OUR COUNTRYMEN DOWN BY TREATING THEM LIKE SECOND-CLASS CITIZENS.

THEY EVEN TOOK OUR CROPS AND LET THE PEOPLE STARVE TO DEATH. BELFAST AND THE SURROUNDING COUNTIES WERE HIT THE HARDEST.

VROOO...

"IN WORLD WAR ONE, THOUSANDS OF IRISHMEN WERE FORCED TO FIGHT FOR ENGLAND. AFTER THE WAR, A FEW OF THE SOLDIERS DECIDED TO USE THEIR TRAINING TO START THEIR OWN WAR AGAINST ENGLAND'S OCCUPYING POLICE FORCE, THE *RUC*--THE ROYAL ULSTER CONSTABULARY.

"EVENTUALLY THEY FORCED THE BRITISH TO ALLOW SOUTHERN IRELAND TO BECOME AN INDEPENDENT STATE. BUT IN ULSTER, THE NINE NORTHERN COUNTIES OF IRELAND, THE WAR GOES ON.

BOUNCE
BOUNCE
BOUNCE

"THIS IS *YOUR* WAR, THOMAS."

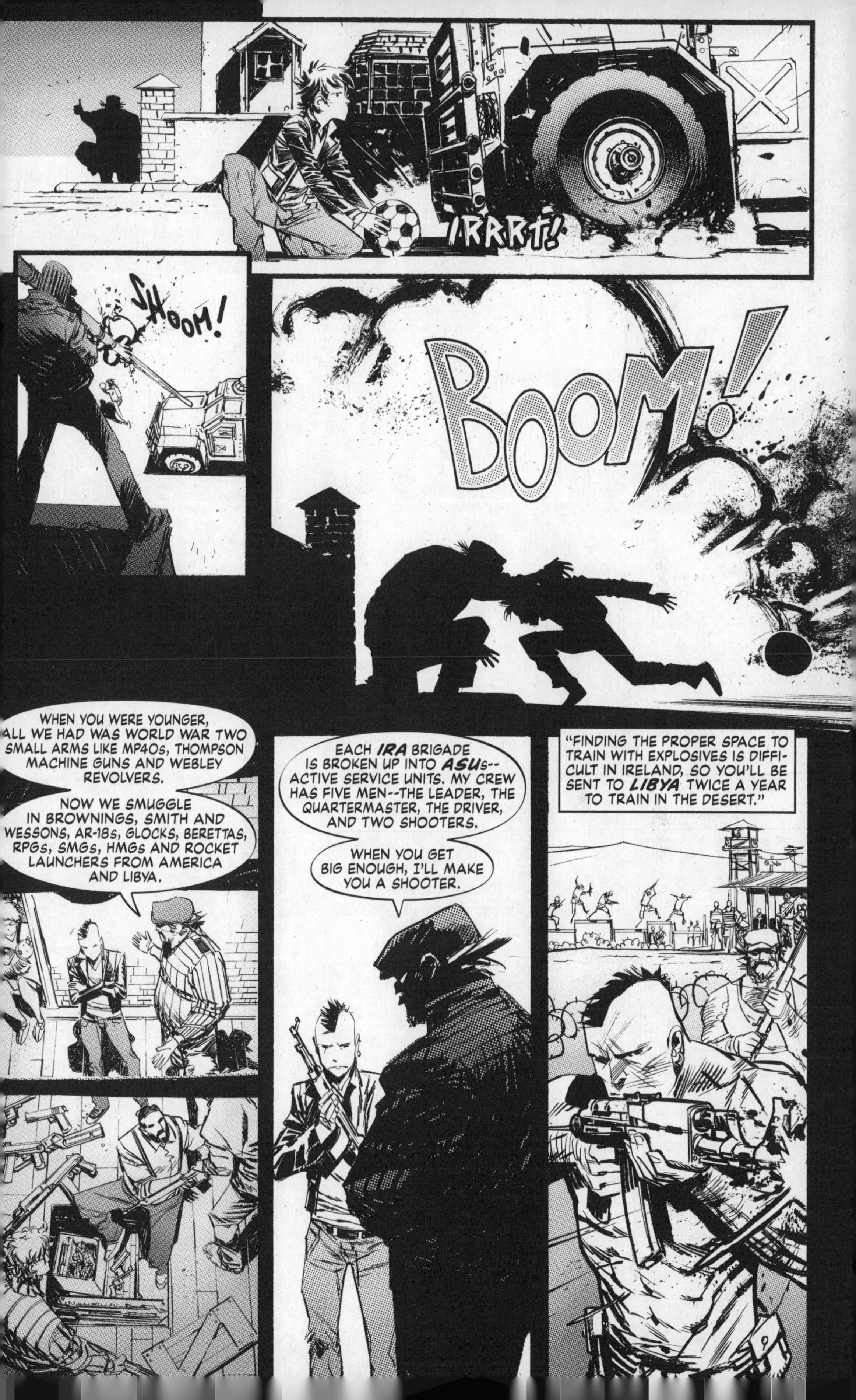

IRRRT!
SHOOM!
BOOM!
WHEN YOU WERE YOUNGER, ALL WE HAD WAS WORLD WAR TWO SMALL ARMS LIKE MP40s, THOMPSON MACHINE GUNS AND WEBLEY REVOLVERS.
NOW WE SMUGGLE IN BROWNINGS, SMITH AND WESSONS, AR-18s, GLOCKS, BERETTAS, RPGs, SMGs, HMGs AND ROCKET LAUNCHERS FROM AMERICA AND LIBYA.
EACH IRA BRIGADE IS BROKEN UP INTO ASUs--ACTIVE SERVICE UNITS. MY CREW HAS FIVE MEN--THE LEADER, THE QUARTERMASTER, THE DRIVER, AND TWO SHOOTERS.
WHEN YOU GET BIG ENOUGH, I'LL MAKE YOU A SHOOTER.
"FINDING THE PROPER SPACE TO TRAIN WITH EXPLOSIVES IS DIFFICULT IN IRELAND, SO YOU'LL BE SENT TO LIBYA TWICE A YEAR TO TRAIN IN THE DESERT."

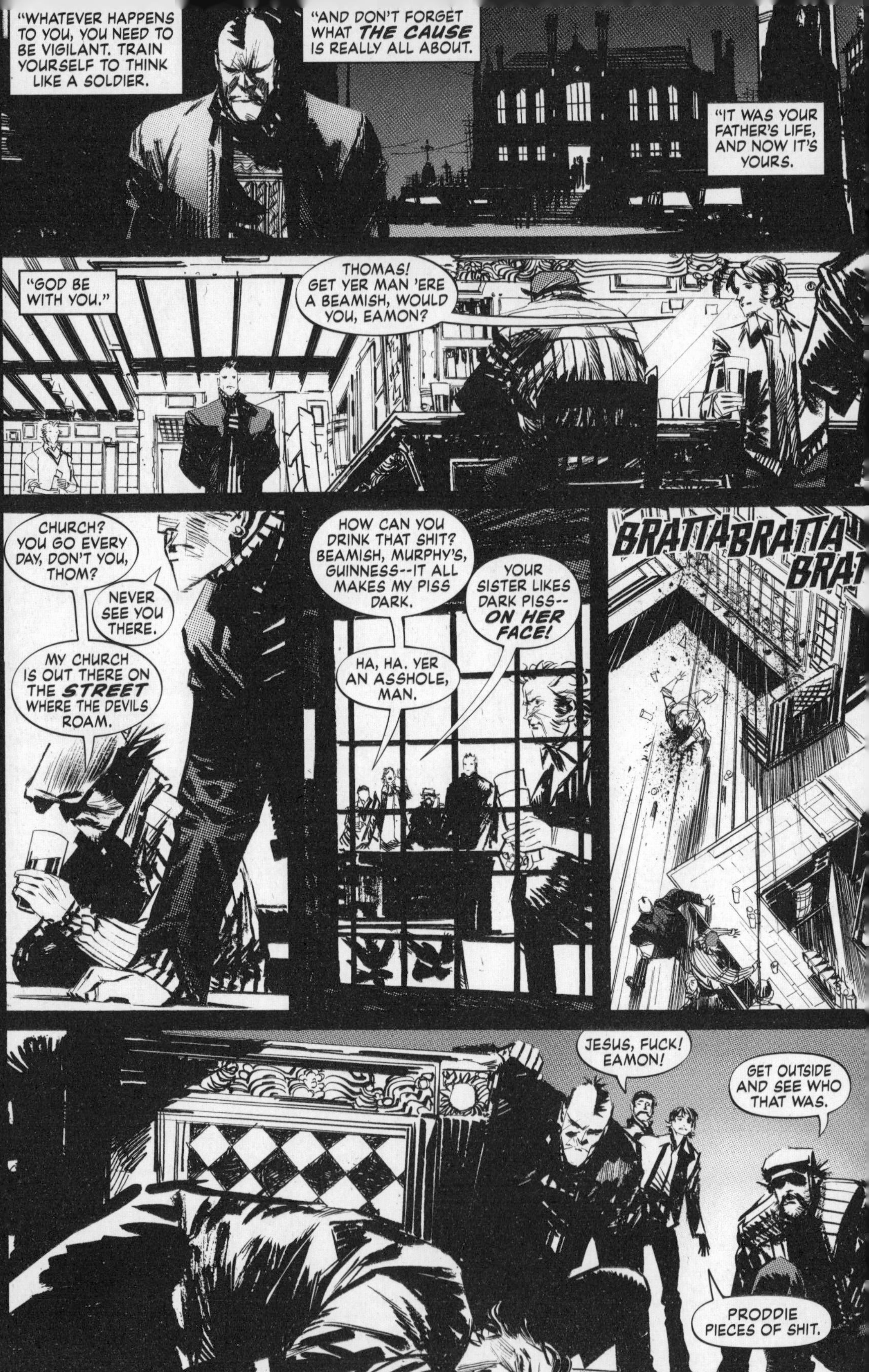
"WHATEVER HAPPENS TO YOU, YOU NEED TO BE VIGILANT. TRAIN YOURSELF TO THINK LIKE A SOLDIER.
"AND DON'T FORGET WHAT THE CAUSE IS REALLY ALL ABOUT.
"IT WAS YOUR FATHER'S LIFE, AND NOW IT'S YOURS.
"GOD BE WITH YOU."
THOMAS! GET YER MAN 'ERE A BEAMISH, WOULD YOU, EAMON?
CHURCH? YOU GO EVERY DAY, DON'T YOU, THOM?
NEVER SEE YOU THERE.
MY CHURCH IS OUT THERE ON THE STREET WHERE THE DEVILS ROAM.
HOW CAN YOU DRINK THAT SHIT? BEAMISH, MURPHY'S, GUINNESS--IT ALL MAKES MY PISS DARK.
YOUR SISTER LIKES DARK PISS-- ON HER FACE!
HA, HA. YER AN ASSHOLE, MAN.
BRATTABRATTA BRAT
JESUS, FUCK! EAMON!
GET OUTSIDE AND SEE WHO THAT WAS.
PRODDIE PIECES OF SHIT.

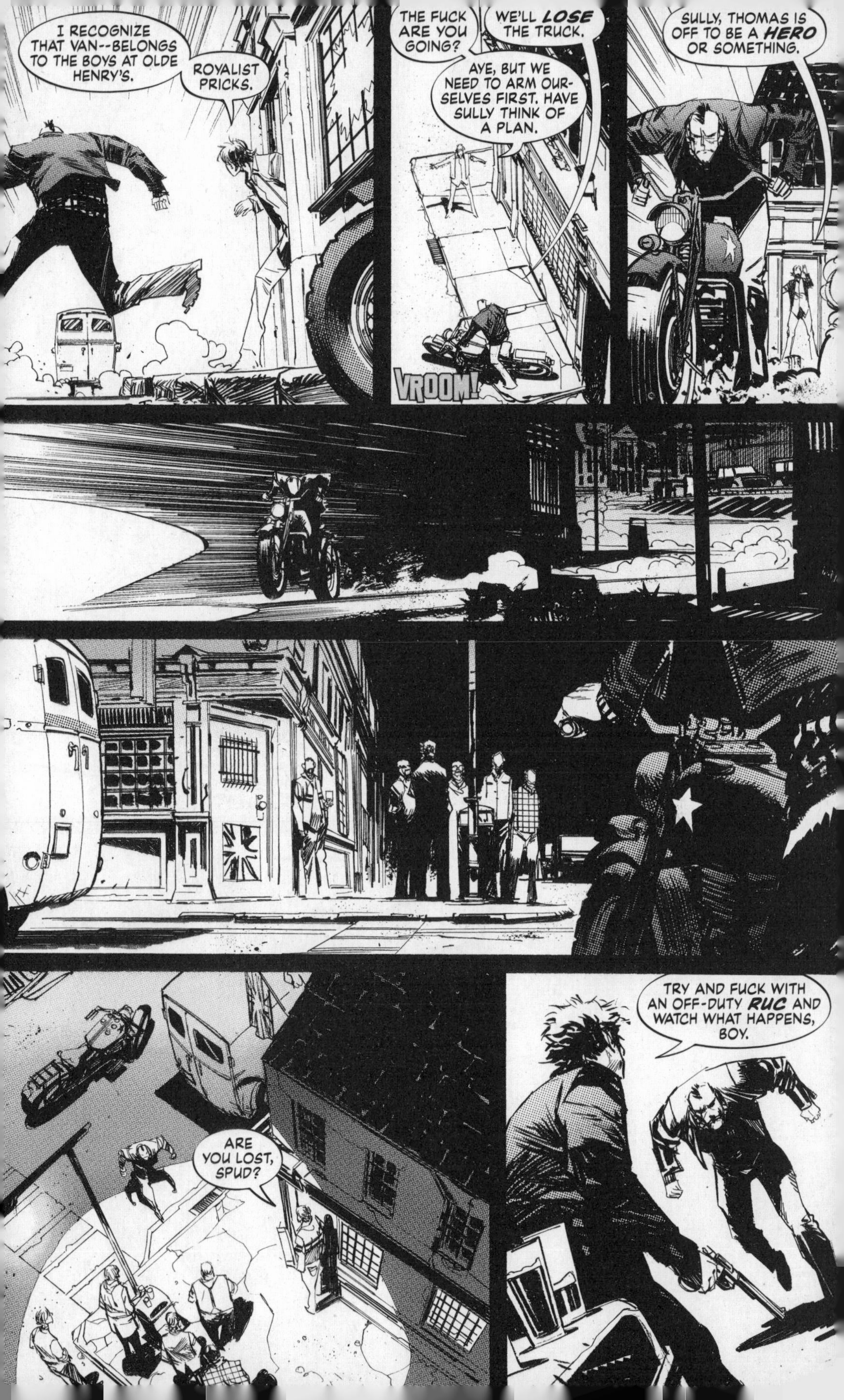
I RECOGNIZE THAT VAN--BELONGS TO THE BOYS AT OLDE HENRY'S.
ROYALIST PRICKS.
THE FUCK ARE YOU GOING?
WE'LL LOSE THE TRUCK.
AYE, BUT WE NEED TO ARM OURSELVES FIRST. HAVE SULLY THINK OF A PLAN.
VROOM!
SULLY, THOMAS IS OFF TO BE A HERO OR SOMETHING.
ARE YOU LOST, SPUD?
TRY AND FUCK WITH AN OFF-DUTY RUC AND WATCH WHAT HAPPENS, BOY.

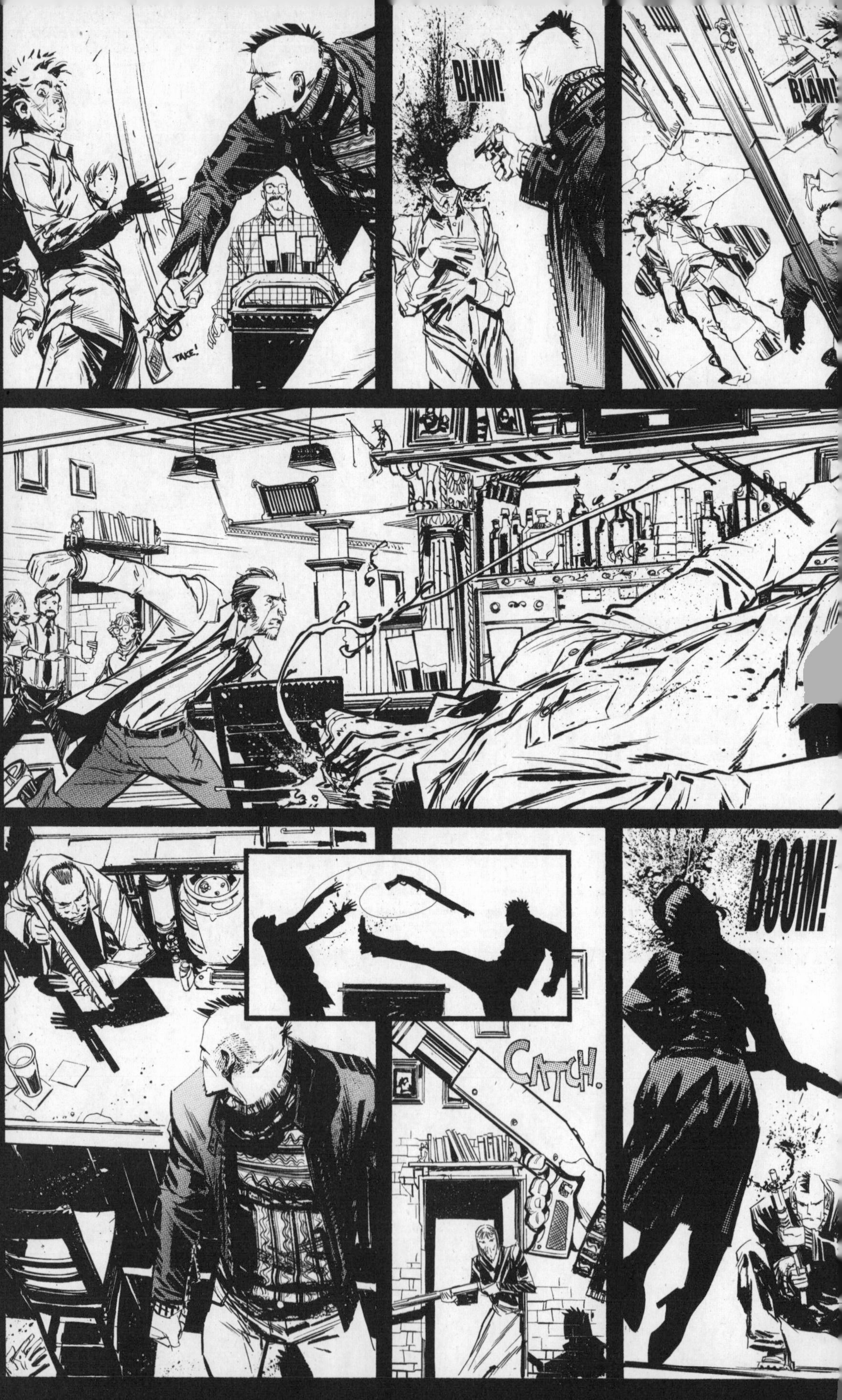
TAKE!
BLAM!
BLAM!
CATCH.
BOOM!

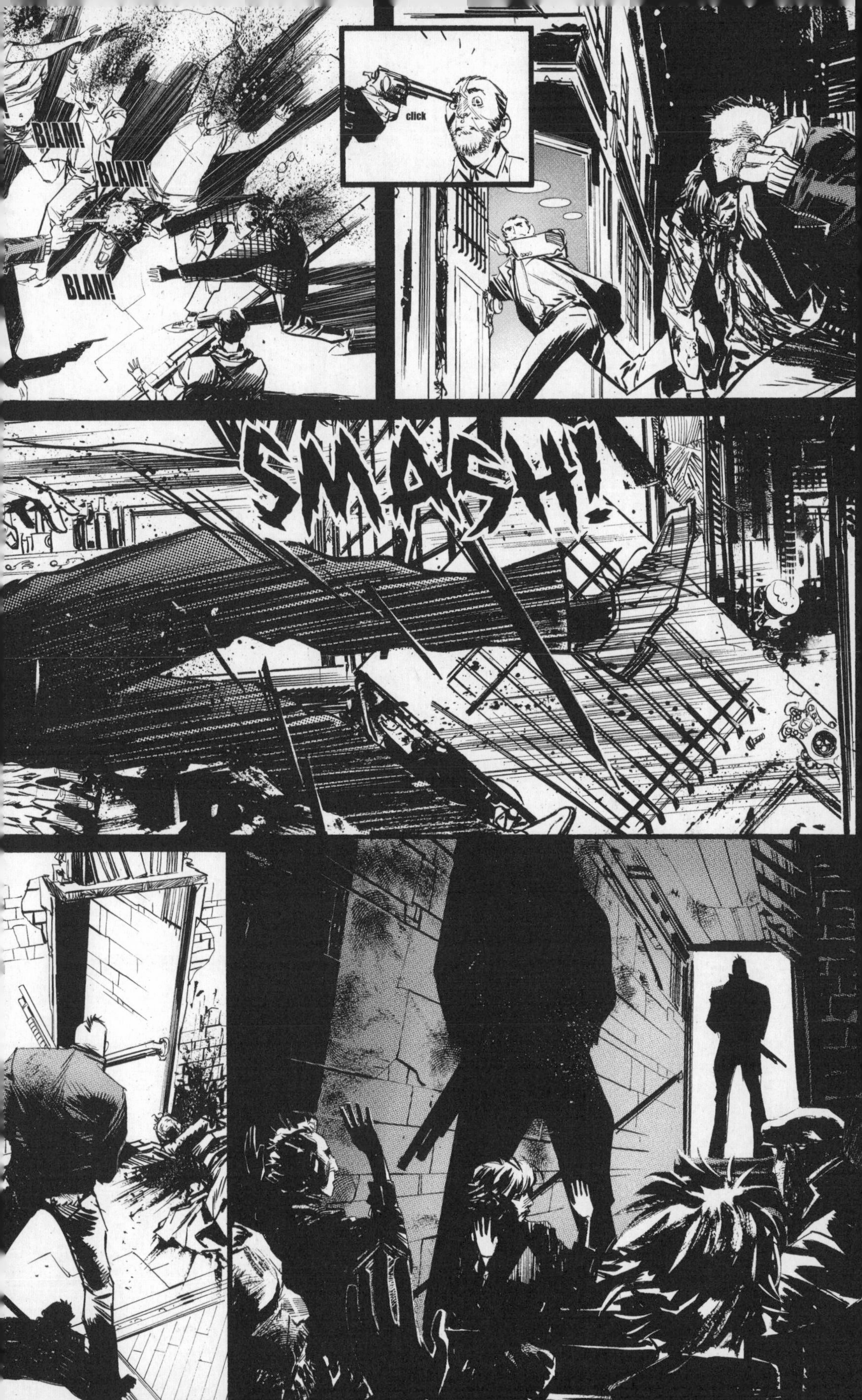
BLAM!
BLAM!
BLAM!
click
SMASH!

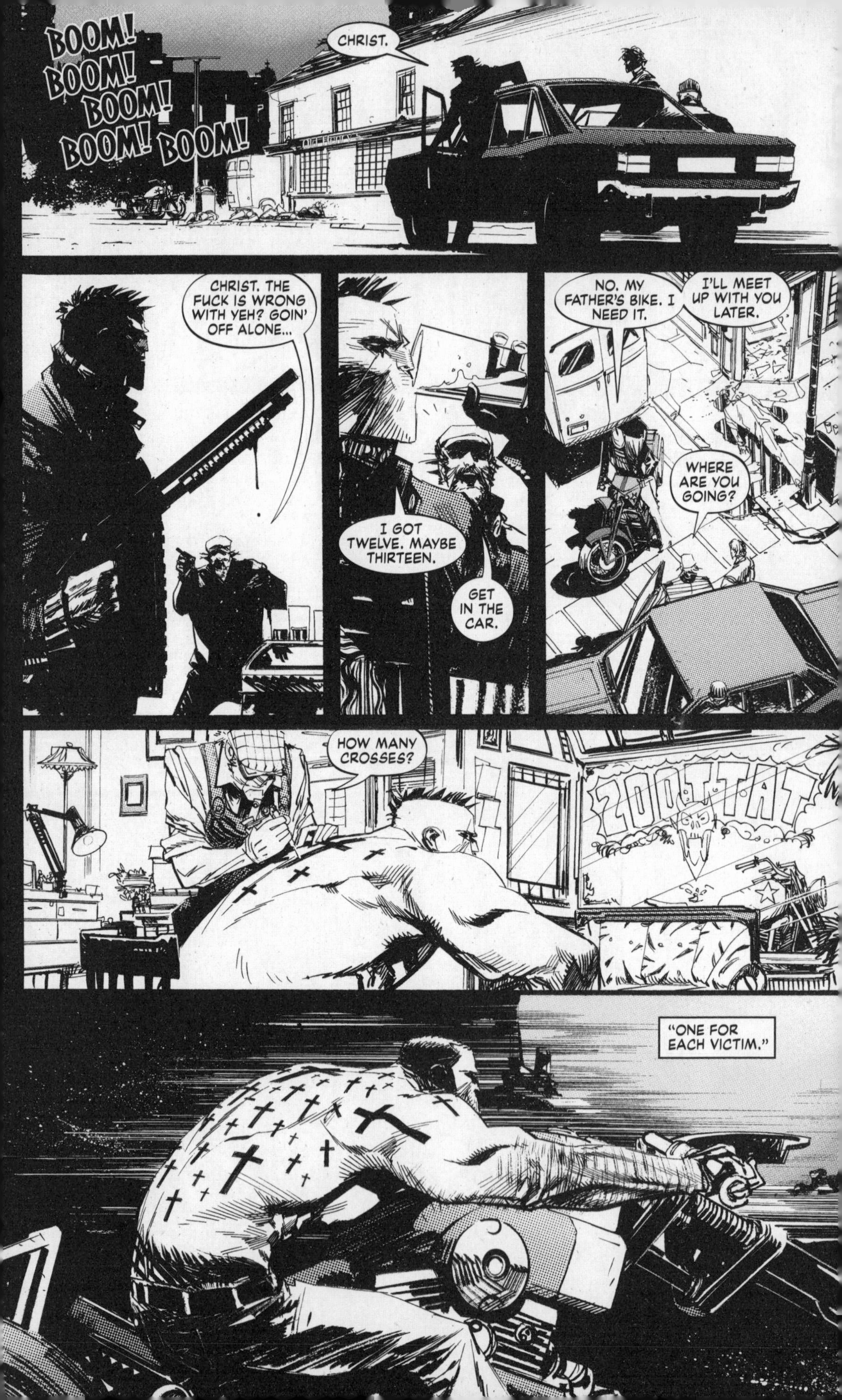
BOOM! BOOM! BOOM! BOOM! BOOM!
CHRIST.
CHRIST. THE FUCK IS WRONG WITH YEH? GOIN' OFF ALONE...
I GOT TWELVE. MAYBE THIRTEEN.
GET IN THE CAR.
NO. MY FATHER'S BIKE. I NEED IT.
I'LL MEET UP WITH YOU LATER.
WHERE ARE YOU GOING?
HOW MANY CROSSES?
"ONE FOR EACH VICTIM."

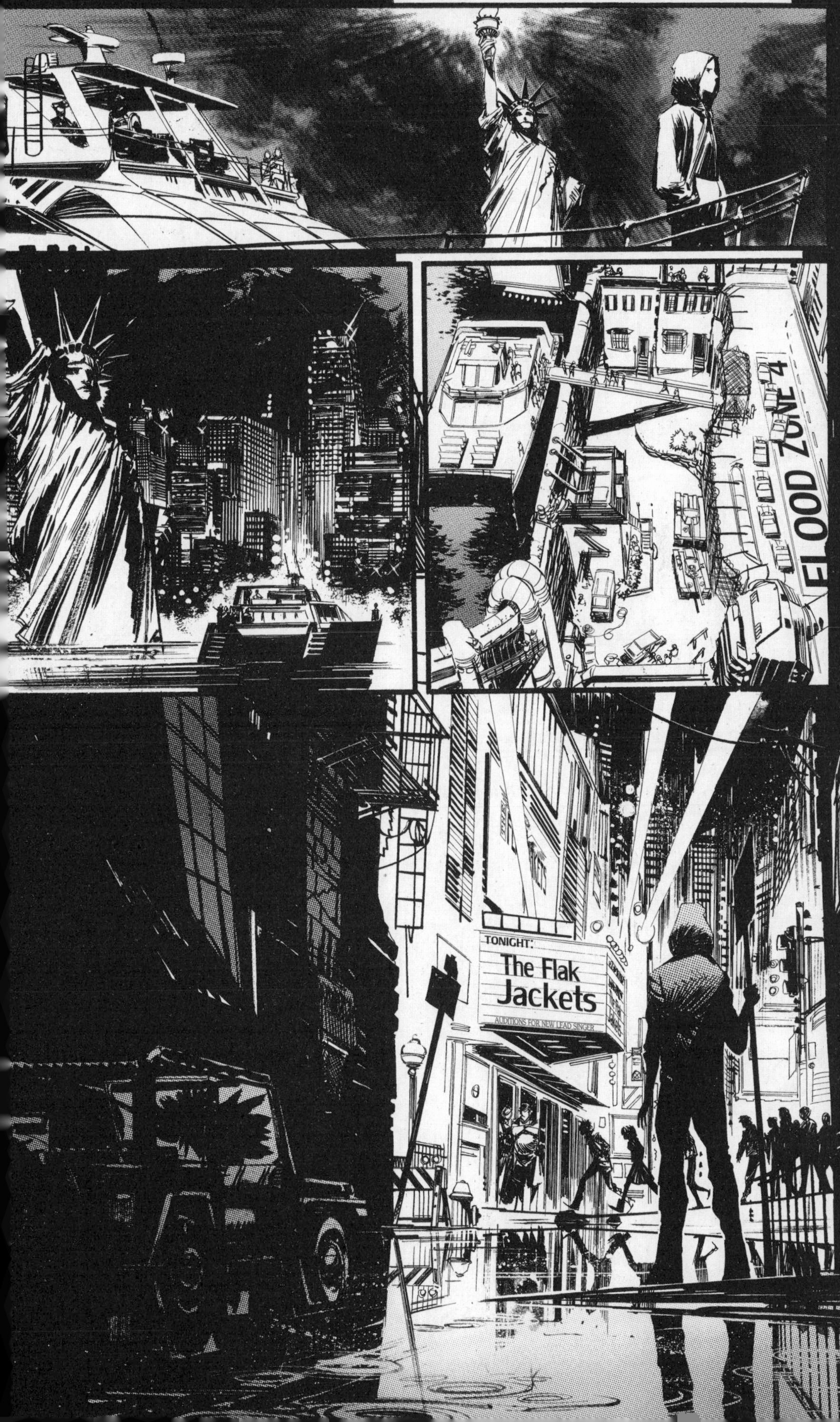
FLOOD ZONE 4
TONIGHT:
The Flak Jackets
AUDITIONS FOR NEW LEAD SINGER

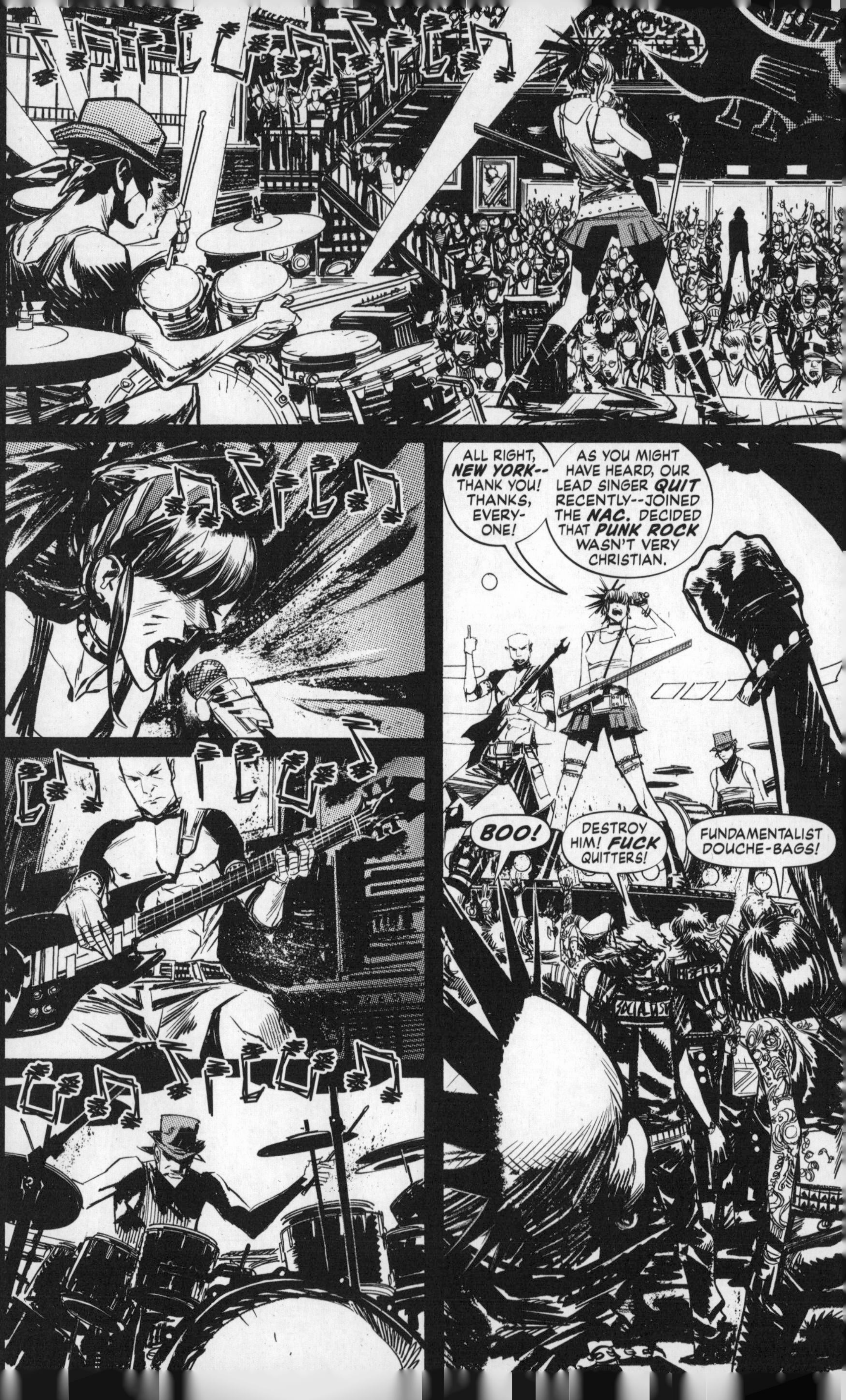
ALL RIGHT, NEW YORK-- THANK YOU! THANKS, EVERY-ONE!
AS YOU MIGHT HAVE HEARD, OUR LEAD SINGER QUIT RECENTLY--JOINED THE NAC. DECIDED THAT PUNK ROCK WASN'T VERY CHRISTIAN.
BOO!
DESTROY HIM! FUCK QUITTERS!
FUNDAMENTALIST DOUCHE-BAGS!

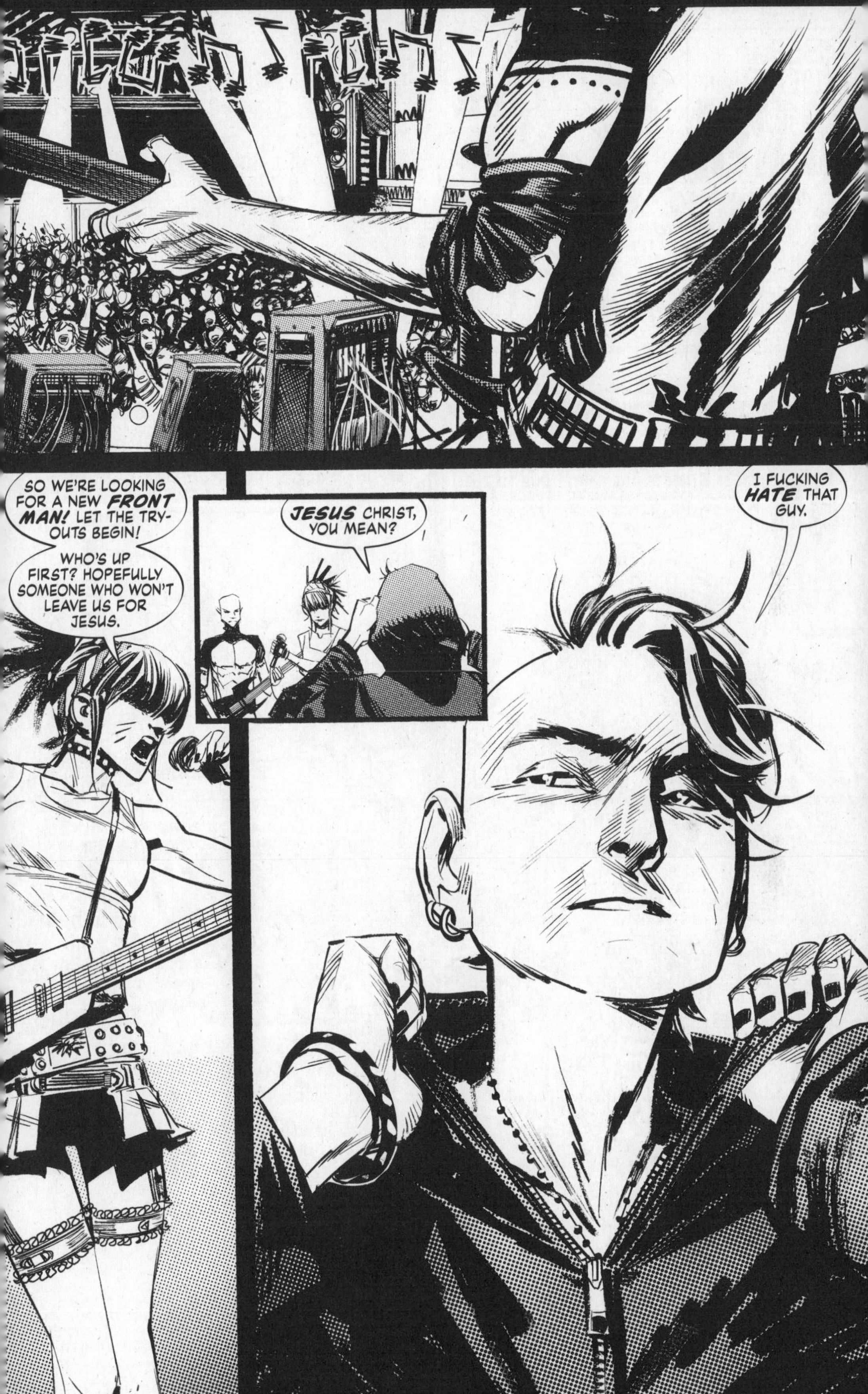
SO WE'RE LOOKING FOR A NEW FRONT MAN! LET THE TRY-OUTS BEGIN!
WHO'S UP FIRST? HOPEFULLY SOMEONE WHO WON'T LEAVE US FOR JESUS.
JESUS CHRIST, YOU MEAN?
I FUCKING HATE THAT GUY.

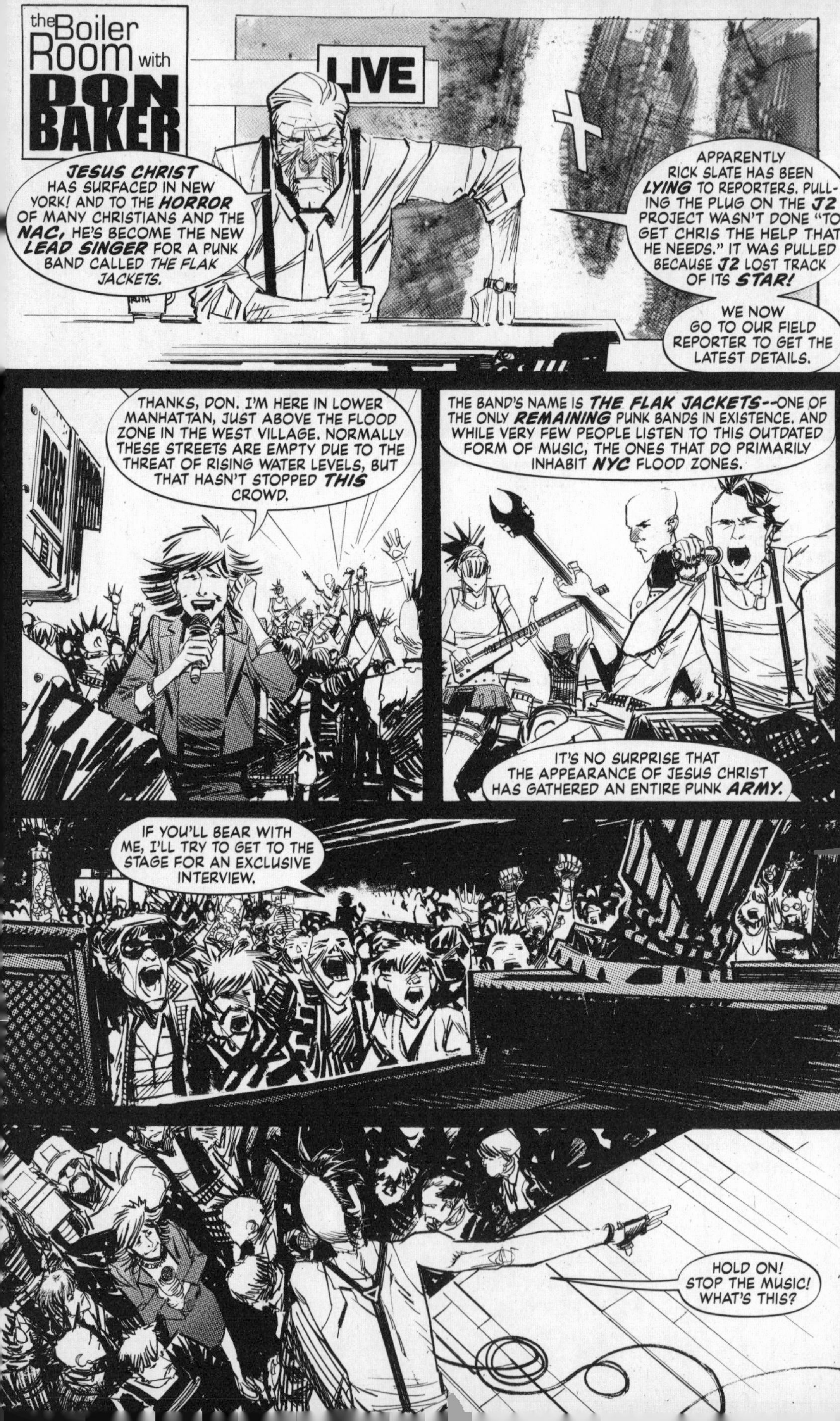
the Boiler Room with DON BAKER
LIVE
JESUS CHRIST HAS SURFACED IN NEW YORK! AND TO THE HORROR OF MANY CHRISTIANS AND THE NAC, HE'S BECOME THE NEW LEAD SINGER FOR A PUNK BAND CALLED THE FLAK JACKETS.
APPARENTLY RICK SLATE HAS BEEN LYING TO REPORTERS. PULLING THE PLUG ON THE J2 PROJECT WASN'T DONE "TO GET CHRIS THE HELP THAT HE NEEDS." IT WAS PULLED BECAUSE J2 LOST TRACK OF ITS STAR!
WE NOW GO TO OUR FIELD REPORTER TO GET THE LATEST DETAILS.
THANKS, DON. I'M HERE IN LOWER MANHATTAN, JUST ABOVE THE FLOOD ZONE IN THE WEST VILLAGE. NORMALLY THESE STREETS ARE EMPTY DUE TO THE THREAT OF RISING WATER LEVELS, BUT THAT HASN'T STOPPED THIS CROWD.
THE BAND'S NAME IS THE FLAK JACKETS--ONE OF THE ONLY REMAINING PUNK BANDS IN EXISTENCE. AND WHILE VERY FEW PEOPLE LISTEN TO THIS OUTDATED FORM OF MUSIC, THE ONES THAT DO PRIMARILY INHABIT NYC FLOOD ZONES.
IT'S NO SURPRISE THAT THE APPEARANCE OF JESUS CHRIST HAS GATHERED AN ENTIRE PUNK ARMY.
IF YOU'LL BEAR WITH ME, I'LL TRY TO GET TO THE STAGE FOR AN EXCLUSIVE INTERVIEW.
HOLD ON! STOP THE MUSIC! WHAT'S THIS?

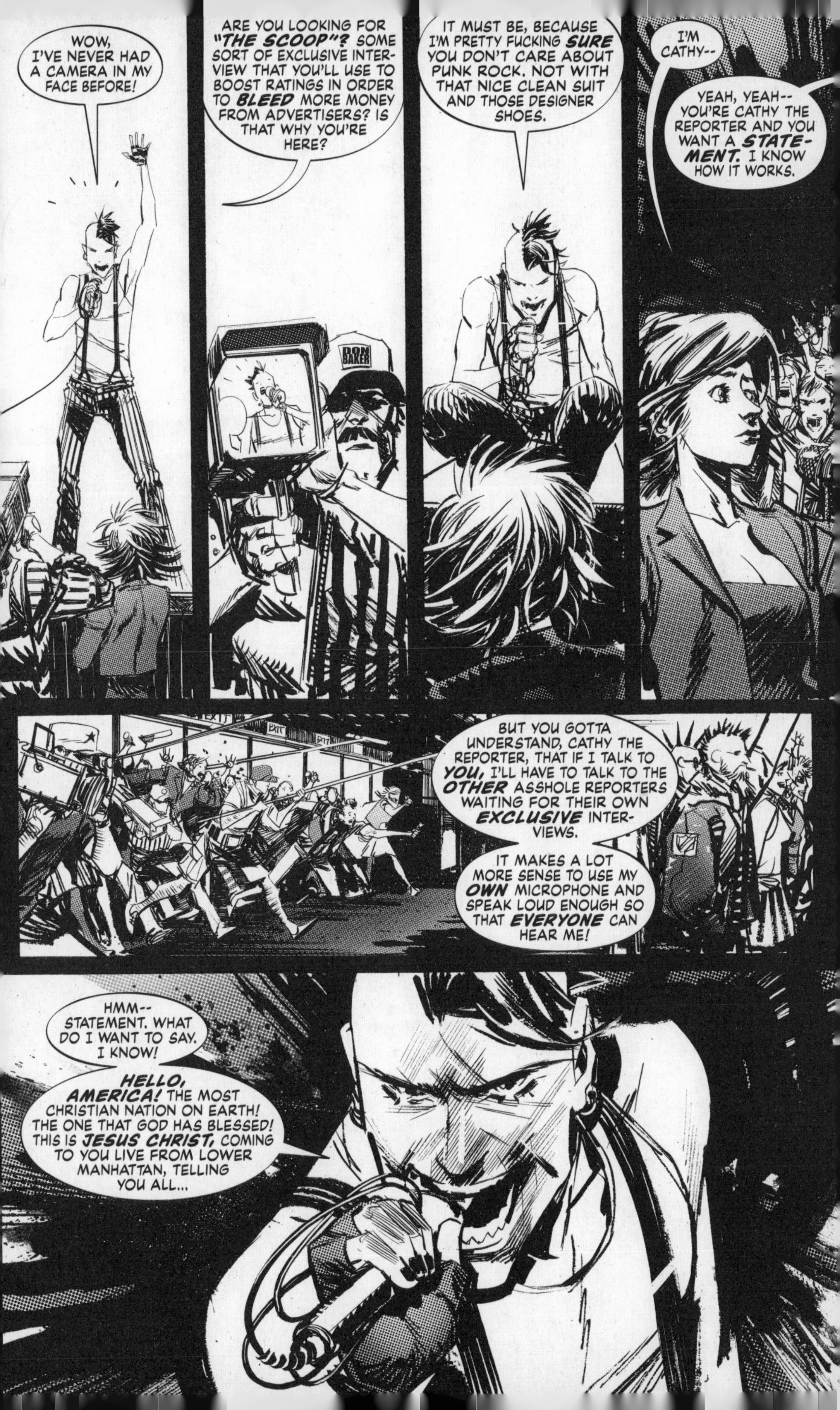
WOW, I'VE NEVER HAD A CAMERA IN MY FACE BEFORE!
ARE YOU LOOKING FOR "THE SCOOP"? SOME SORT OF EXCLUSIVE INTERVIEW THAT YOU'LL USE TO BOOST RATINGS IN ORDER TO BLEED MORE MONEY FROM ADVERTISERS? IS THAT WHY YOU'RE HERE?
DON BAKER
IT MUST BE, BECAUSE I'M PRETTY FUCKING SURE YOU DON'T CARE ABOUT PUNK ROCK. NOT WITH THAT NICE CLEAN SUIT AND THOSE DESIGNER SHOES.
I'M CATHY--
YEAH, YEAH-- YOU'RE CATHY THE REPORTER AND YOU WANT A STATEMENT. I KNOW HOW IT WORKS.
EXIT
BUT YOU GOTTA UNDERSTAND, CATHY THE REPORTER, THAT IF I TALK TO YOU, I'LL HAVE TO TALK TO THE OTHER ASSHOLE REPORTERS WAITING FOR THEIR OWN EXCLUSIVE INTERVIEWS.
IT MAKES A LOT MORE SENSE TO USE MY OWN MICROPHONE AND SPEAK LOUD ENOUGH SO THAT EVERYONE CAN HEAR ME!
HMM-- STATEMENT. WHAT DO I WANT TO SAY. I KNOW!
HELLO, AMERICA! THE MOST CHRISTIAN NATION ON EARTH! THE ONE THAT GOD HAS BLESSED! THIS IS JESUS CHRIST, COMING TO YOU LIVE FROM LOWER MANHATTAN, TELLING YOU ALL...

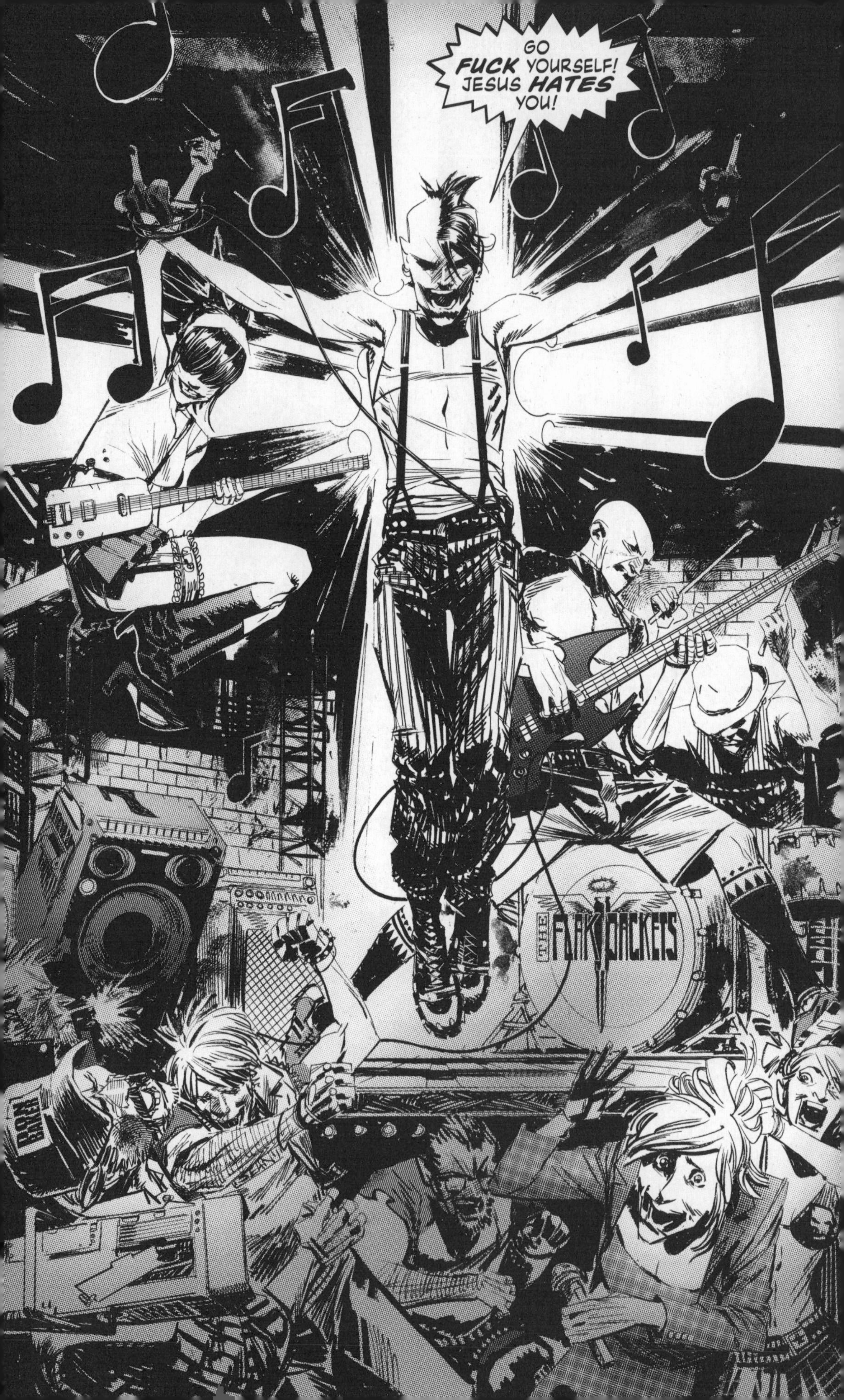
GO FUCK YOURSELF! JESUS HATES YOU!
THE FLAK JACKETS

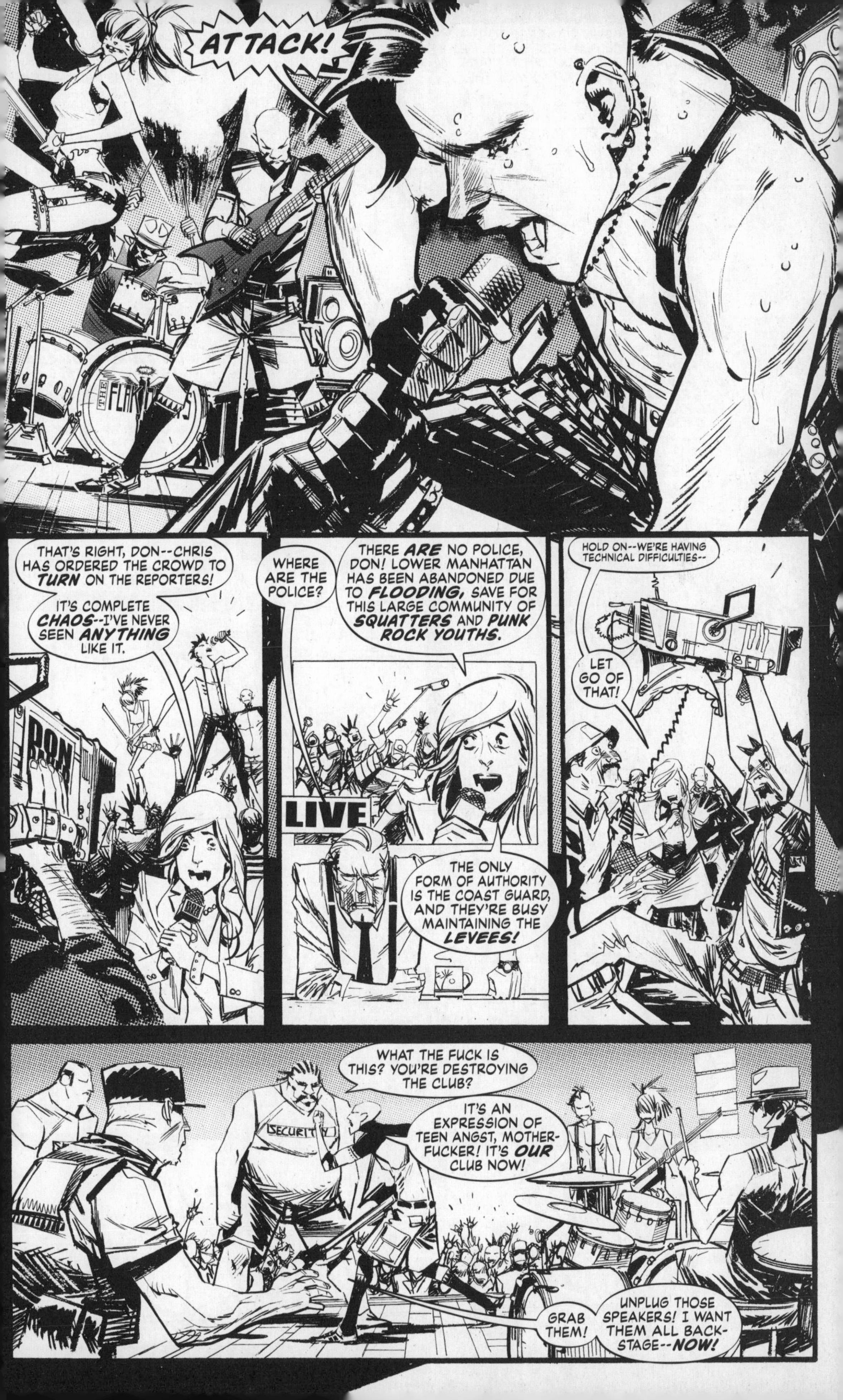
ATTACK!
THAT'S RIGHT, DON--CHRIS HAS ORDERED THE CROWD TO TURN ON THE REPORTERS!
IT'S COMPLETE CHAOS--I'VE NEVER SEEN ANYTHING LIKE IT.
WHERE ARE THE POLICE?
THERE ARE NO POLICE, DON! LOWER MANHATTAN HAS BEEN ABANDONED DUE TO FLOODING, SAVE FOR THIS LARGE COMMUNITY OF SQUATTERS AND PUNK ROCK YOUTHS.
LIVE
THE ONLY FORM OF AUTHORITY IS THE COAST GUARD, AND THEY'RE BUSY MAINTAINING THE LEVEES!
HOLD ON--WE'RE HAVING TECHNICAL DIFFICULTIES--
LET GO OF THAT!
WHAT THE FUCK IS THIS? YOU'RE DESTROYING THE CLUB?
SECURITY
IT'S AN EXPRESSION OF TEEN ANGST, MOTHER-FUCKER! IT'S OUR CLUB NOW!
GRAB THEM!
UNPLUG THOSE SPEAKERS! I WANT THEM ALL BACK-STAGE--NOW!

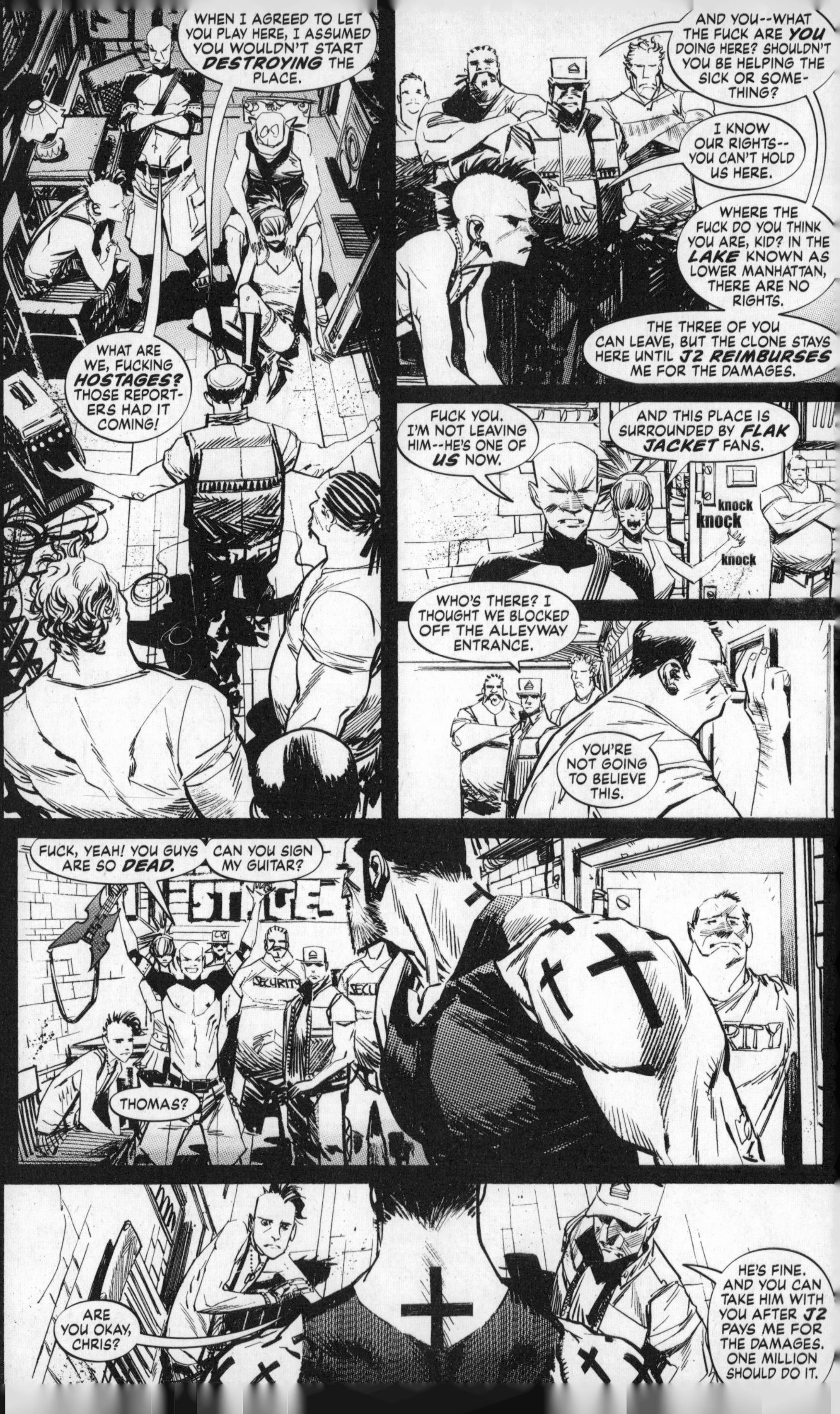
WHEN I AGREED TO LET YOU PLAY HERE, I ASSUMED YOU WOULDN'T START DESTROYING THE PLACE.
WHAT ARE WE, FUCKING HOSTAGES? THOSE REPORTERS HAD IT COMING!
AND YOU--WHAT THE FUCK ARE YOU DOING HERE? SHOULDN'T YOU BE HELPING THE SICK OR SOMETHING?
I KNOW OUR RIGHTS--YOU CAN'T HOLD US HERE.
WHERE THE FUCK DO YOU THINK YOU ARE, KID? IN THE LAKE KNOWN AS LOWER MANHATTAN, THERE ARE NO RIGHTS.
THE THREE OF YOU CAN LEAVE, BUT THE CLONE STAYS HERE UNTIL J2 REIMBURSES ME FOR THE DAMAGES.
FUCK YOU. I'M NOT LEAVING HIM--HE'S ONE OF US NOW.
AND THIS PLACE IS SURROUNDED BY FLAK JACKET FANS.
knock
knock
knock
WHO'S THERE? I THOUGHT WE BLOCKED OFF THE ALLEYWAY ENTRANCE.
YOU'RE NOT GOING TO BELIEVE THIS.
FUCK, YEAH! YOU GUYS ARE SO DEAD.
CAN YOU SIGN MY GUITAR?
THOMAS?
ARE YOU OKAY, CHRIS?
HE'S FINE. AND YOU CAN TAKE HIM WITH YOU AFTER J2 PAYS ME FOR THE DAMAGES. ONE MILLION SHOULD DO IT.

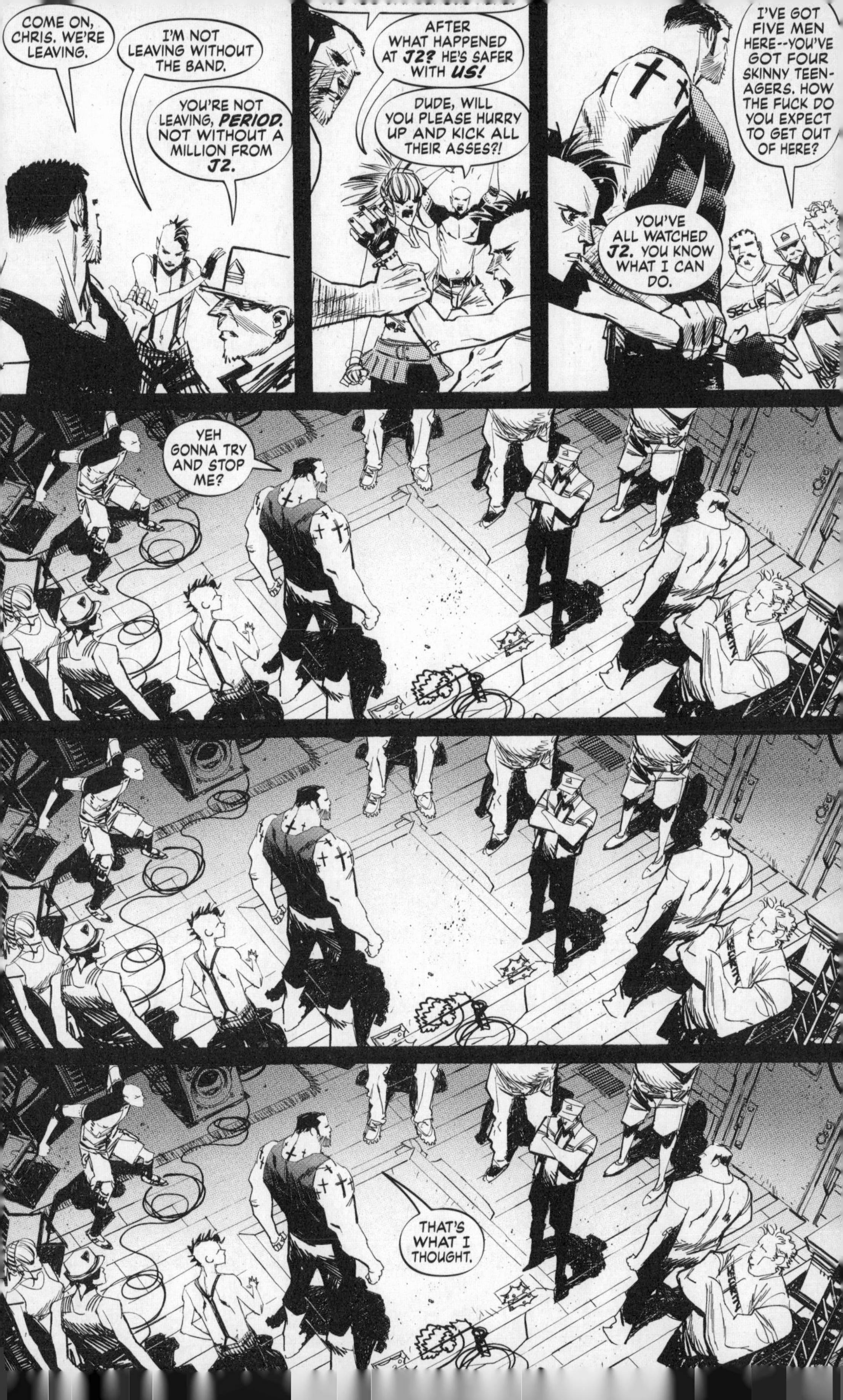
COME ON, CHRIS. WE'RE LEAVING.
I'M NOT LEAVING WITHOUT THE BAND.
YOU'RE NOT LEAVING, PERIOD. NOT WITHOUT A MILLION FROM J2.
AFTER WHAT HAPPENED AT J2? HE'S SAFER WITH US!
DUDE, WILL YOU PLEASE HURRY UP AND KICK ALL THEIR ASSES?!
I'VE GOT FIVE MEN HERE--YOU'VE GOT FOUR SKINNY TEEN-AGERS. HOW THE FUCK DO YOU EXPECT TO GET OUT OF HERE?
YOU'VE ALL WATCHED J2. YOU KNOW WHAT I CAN DO.
YEH GONNA TRY AND STOP ME?
THAT'S WHAT I THOUGHT.

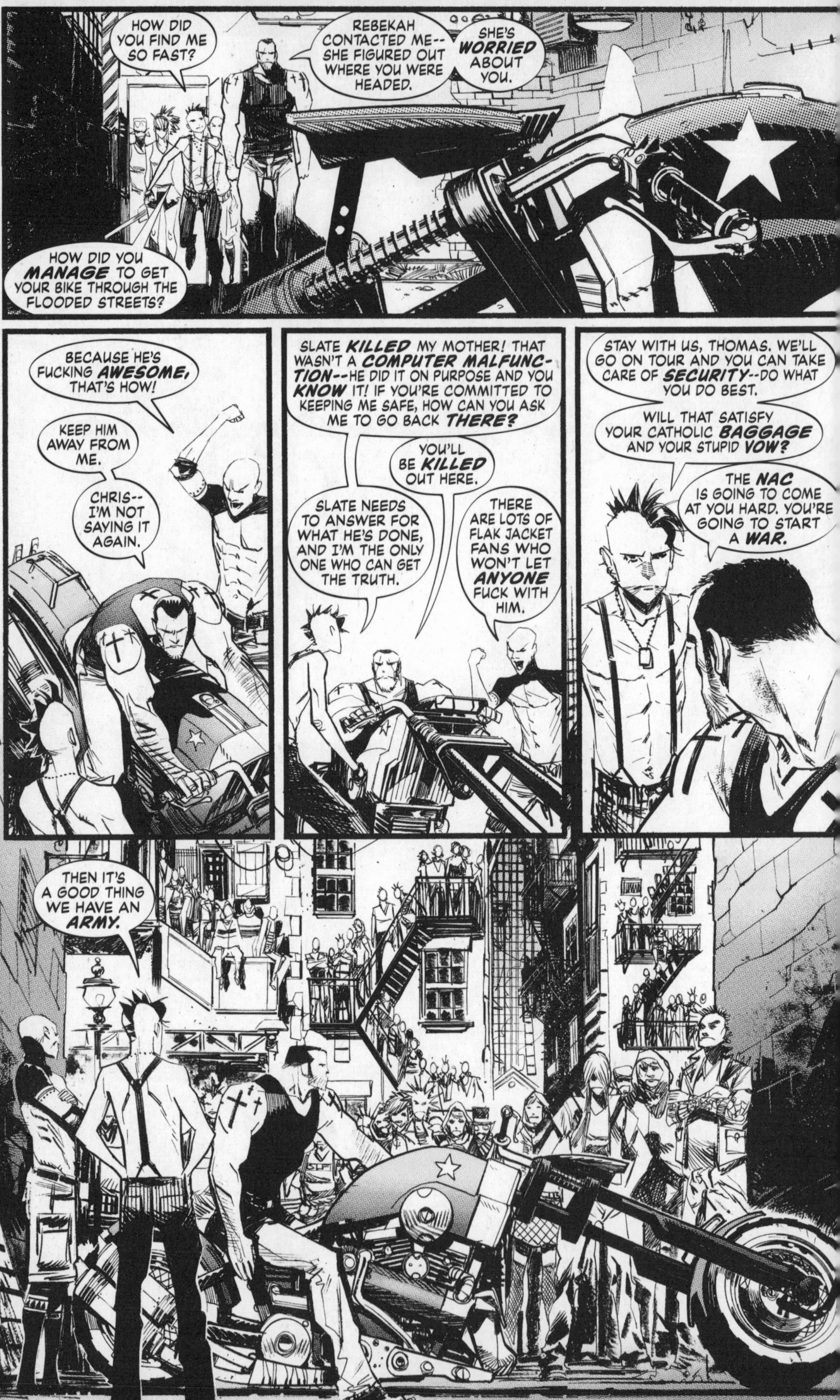
HOW DID YOU FIND ME SO FAST?
REBEKAH CONTACTED ME-- SHE FIGURED OUT WHERE YOU WERE HEADED.
SHE'S WORRIED ABOUT YOU.
HOW DID YOU MANAGE TO GET YOUR BIKE THROUGH THE FLOODED STREETS?
BECAUSE HE'S FUCKING AWESOME, THAT'S HOW!
KEEP HIM AWAY FROM ME.
CHRIS-- I'M NOT SAYING IT AGAIN.
SLATE KILLED MY MOTHER! THAT WASN'T A COMPUTER MALFUNCTION--HE DID IT ON PURPOSE AND YOU KNOW IT! IF YOU'RE COMMITTED TO KEEPING ME SAFE, HOW CAN YOU ASK ME TO GO BACK THERE?
YOU'LL BE KILLED OUT HERE.
SLATE NEEDS TO ANSWER FOR WHAT HE'S DONE, AND I'M THE ONLY ONE WHO CAN GET THE TRUTH.
THERE ARE LOTS OF FLAK JACKET FANS WHO WON'T LET ANYONE FUCK WITH HIM.
STAY WITH US, THOMAS. WE'LL GO ON TOUR AND YOU CAN TAKE CARE OF SECURITY--DO WHAT YOU DO BEST.
WILL THAT SATISFY YOUR CATHOLIC BAGGAGE AND YOUR STUPID VOW?
THE NAC IS GOING TO COME AT YOU HARD. YOU'RE GOING TO START A WAR.
THEN IT'S A GOOD THING WE HAVE AN ARMY.

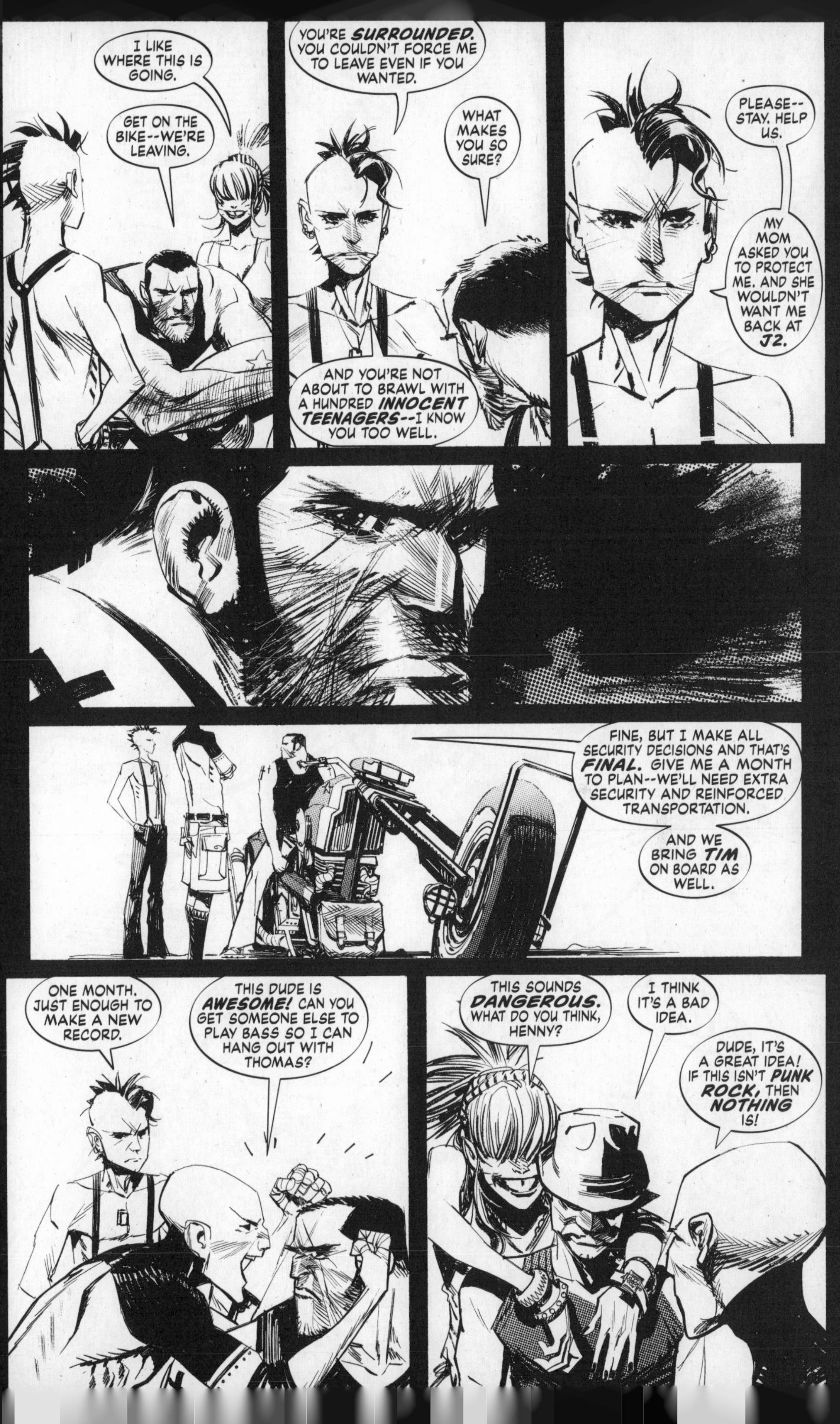
I LIKE WHERE THIS IS GOING.
GET ON THE BIKE--WE'RE LEAVING.
YOU'RE SURROUNDED. YOU COULDN'T FORCE ME TO LEAVE EVEN IF YOU WANTED.
WHAT MAKES YOU SO SURE?
AND YOU'RE NOT ABOUT TO BRAWL WITH A HUNDRED INNOCENT TEENAGERS--I KNOW YOU TOO WELL.
PLEASE--STAY. HELP US.
MY MOM ASKED YOU TO PROTECT ME. AND SHE WOULDN'T WANT ME BACK AT J2.
FINE, BUT I MAKE ALL SECURITY DECISIONS AND THAT'S FINAL. GIVE ME A MONTH TO PLAN--WE'LL NEED EXTRA SECURITY AND REINFORCED TRANSPORTATION.
AND WE BRING TIM ON BOARD AS WELL.
ONE MONTH. JUST ENOUGH TO MAKE A NEW RECORD.
THIS DUDE IS AWESOME! CAN YOU GET SOMEONE ELSE TO PLAY BASS SO I CAN HANG OUT WITH THOMAS?
THIS SOUNDS DANGEROUS. WHAT DO YOU THINK, HENNY?
I THINK IT'S A BAD IDEA.
DUDE, IT'S A GREAT IDEA! IF THIS ISN'T PUNK ROCK, THEN NOTHING IS!

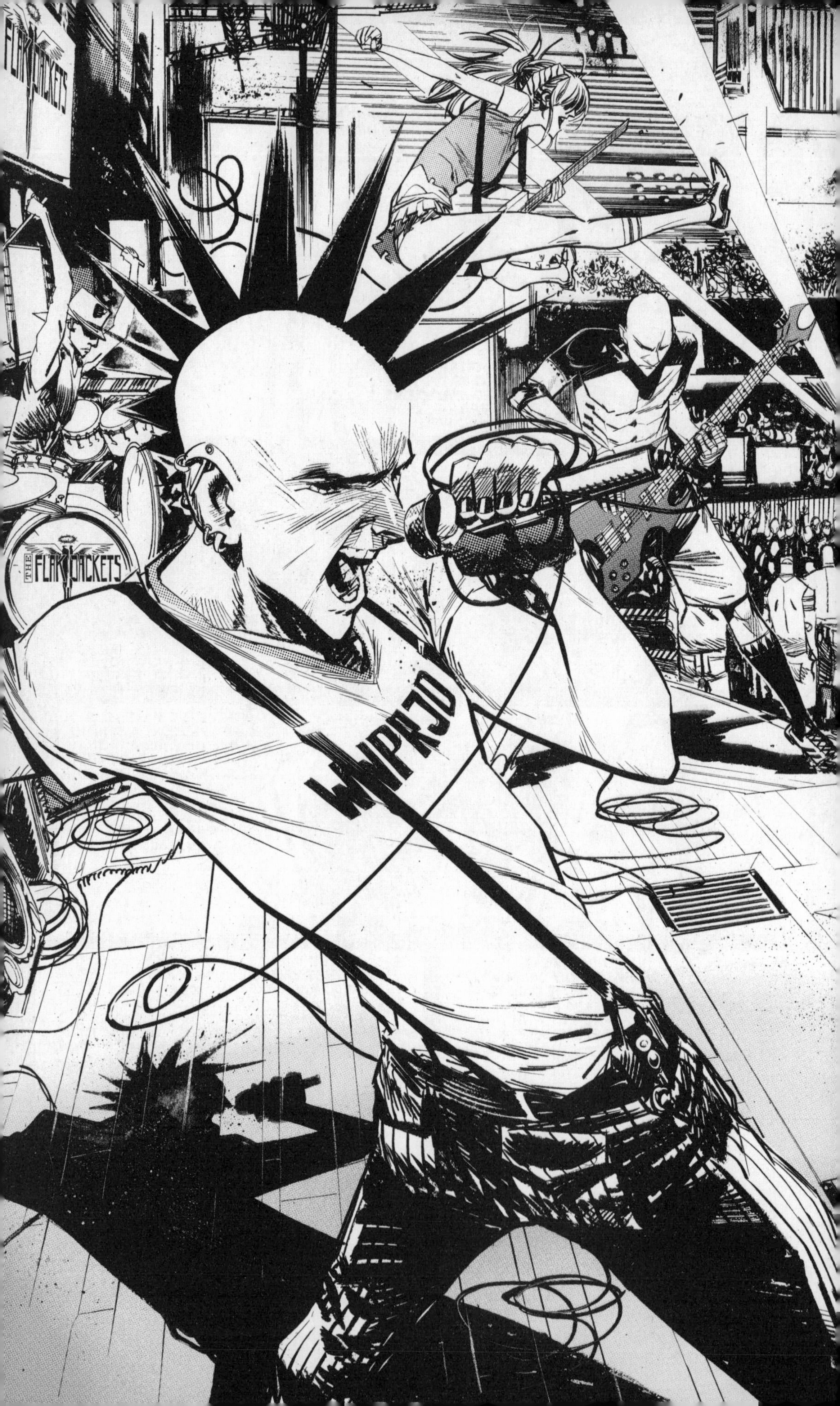
FLAK JACKETS
THE FLAK JACKETS

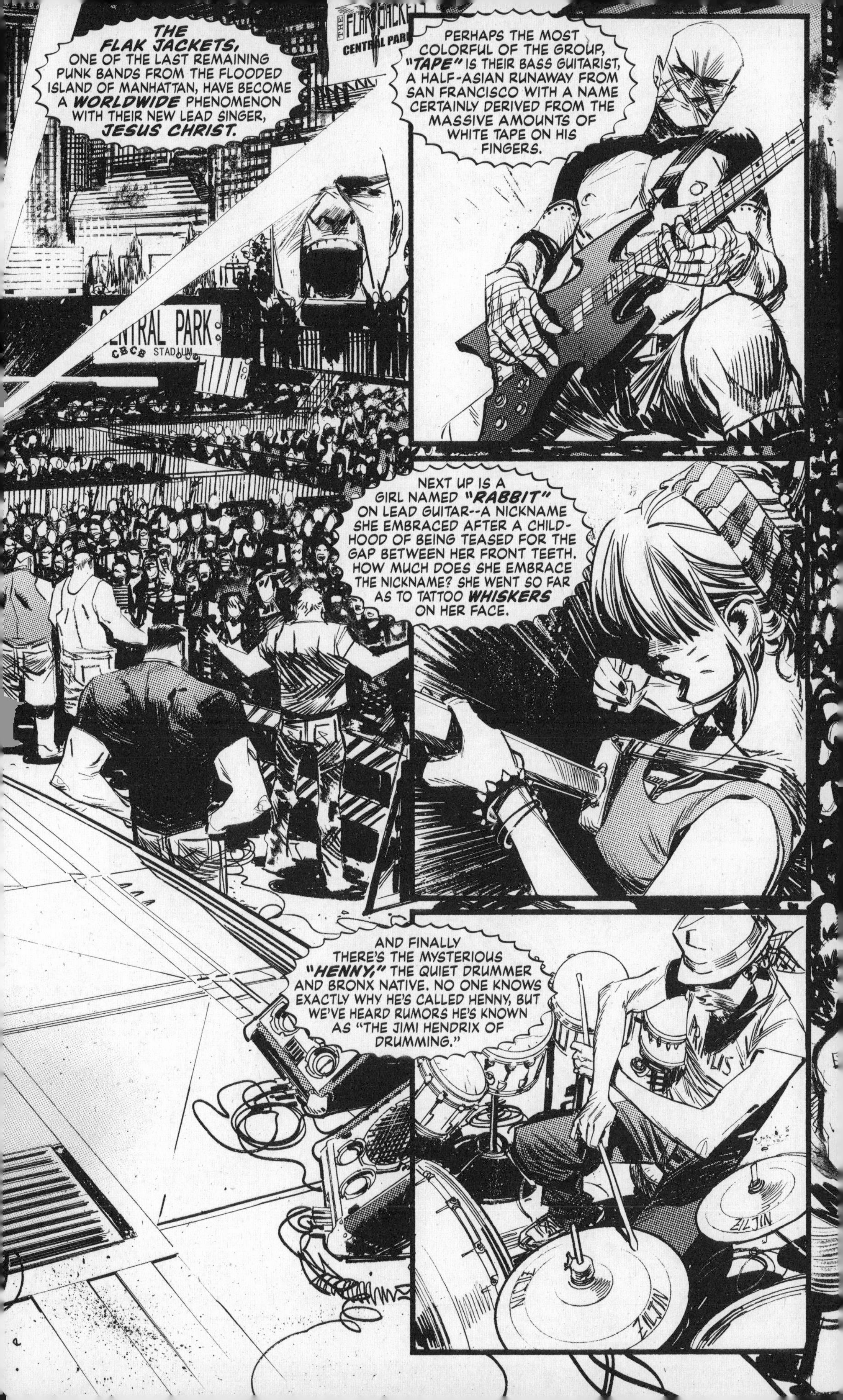
THE FLAK JACKETS, ONE OF THE LAST REMAINING PUNK BANDS FROM THE FLOODED ISLAND OF MANHATTAN, HAVE BECOME A WORLDWIDE PHENOMENON WITH THEIR NEW LEAD SINGER, JESUS CHRIST.
THE FLAK JACKETS CENTRAL PARK
CENTRAL PARK
CBCB STADIUM
PERHAPS THE MOST COLORFUL OF THE GROUP, "TAPE" IS THEIR BASS GUITARIST, A HALF-ASIAN RUNAWAY FROM SAN FRANCISCO WITH A NAME CERTAINLY DERIVED FROM THE MASSIVE AMOUNTS OF WHITE TAPE ON HIS FINGERS.
NEXT UP IS A GIRL NAMED "RABBIT" ON LEAD GUITAR--A NICKNAME SHE EMBRACED AFTER A CHILD-HOOD OF BEING TEASED FOR THE GAP BETWEEN HER FRONT TEETH. HOW MUCH DOES SHE EMBRACE THE NICKNAME? SHE WENT SO FAR AS TO TATTOO WHISKERS ON HER FACE.
AND FINALLY THERE'S THE MYSTERIOUS "HENNY," THE QUIET DRUMMER AND BRONX NATIVE. NO ONE KNOWS EXACTLY WHY HE'S CALLED HENNY, BUT WE'VE HEARD RUMORS HE'S KNOWN AS "THE JIMI HENDRIX OF DRUMMING."
ZILJIN
ZILJIN

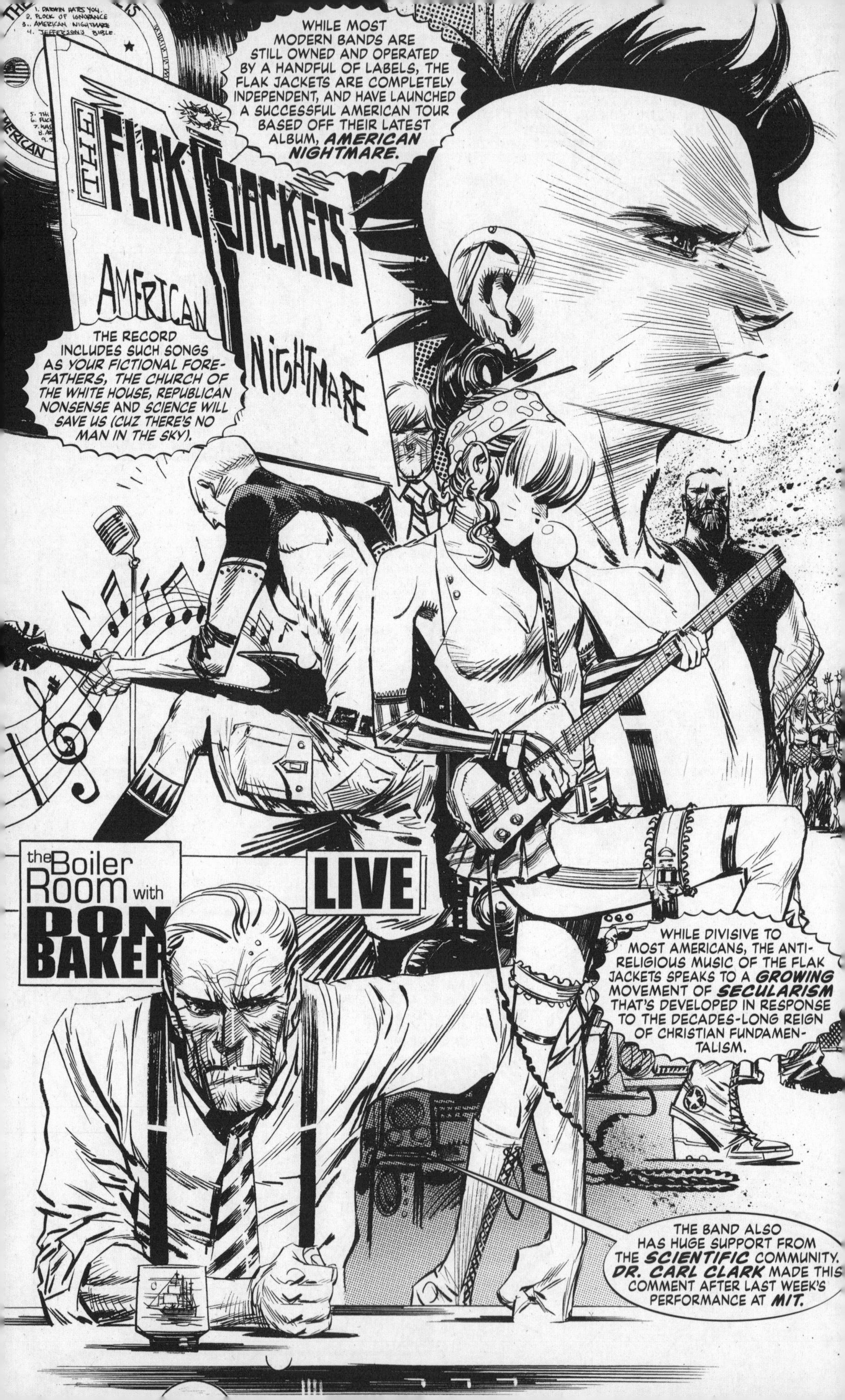

1. DARWIN HATES YOU.
2. FLOCK OF IGNORANCE
3.. AMERICAN NIGHTMARE
4. JEFFERSON'S BIBLE.
WHILE MOST MODERN BANDS ARE STILL OWNED AND OPERATED BY A HANDFUL OF LABELS, THE FLAK JACKETS ARE COMPLETELY INDEPENDENT, AND HAVE LAUNCHED A SUCCESSFUL AMERICAN TOUR BASED OFF THEIR LATEST ALBUM, ***AMERICAN NIGHTMARE.***
THE FLAK JACKETS
AMERICAN NIGHTMARE
THE RECORD INCLUDES SUCH SONGS AS *YOUR FICTIONAL FORE-FATHERS, THE CHURCH OF THE WHITE HOUSE, REPUBLICAN NONSENSE* AND *SCIENCE WILL SAVE US (CUZ THERE'S NO MAN IN THE SKY).*
the Boiler Room with DON BAKER
LIVE
WHILE DIVISIVE TO MOST AMERICANS, THE ANTI-RELIGIOUS MUSIC OF THE FLAK JACKETS SPEAKS TO A ***GROWING*** MOVEMENT OF ***SECULARISM*** THAT'S DEVELOPED IN RESPONSE TO THE DECADES-LONG REIGN OF CHRISTIAN FUNDAMEN-TALISM.
THE BAND ALSO HAS HUGE SUPPORT FROM THE ***SCIENTIFIC*** COMMUNITY. ***DR. CARL CLARK*** MADE THIS COMMENT AFTER LAST WEEK'S PERFORMANCE AT ***MIT.***

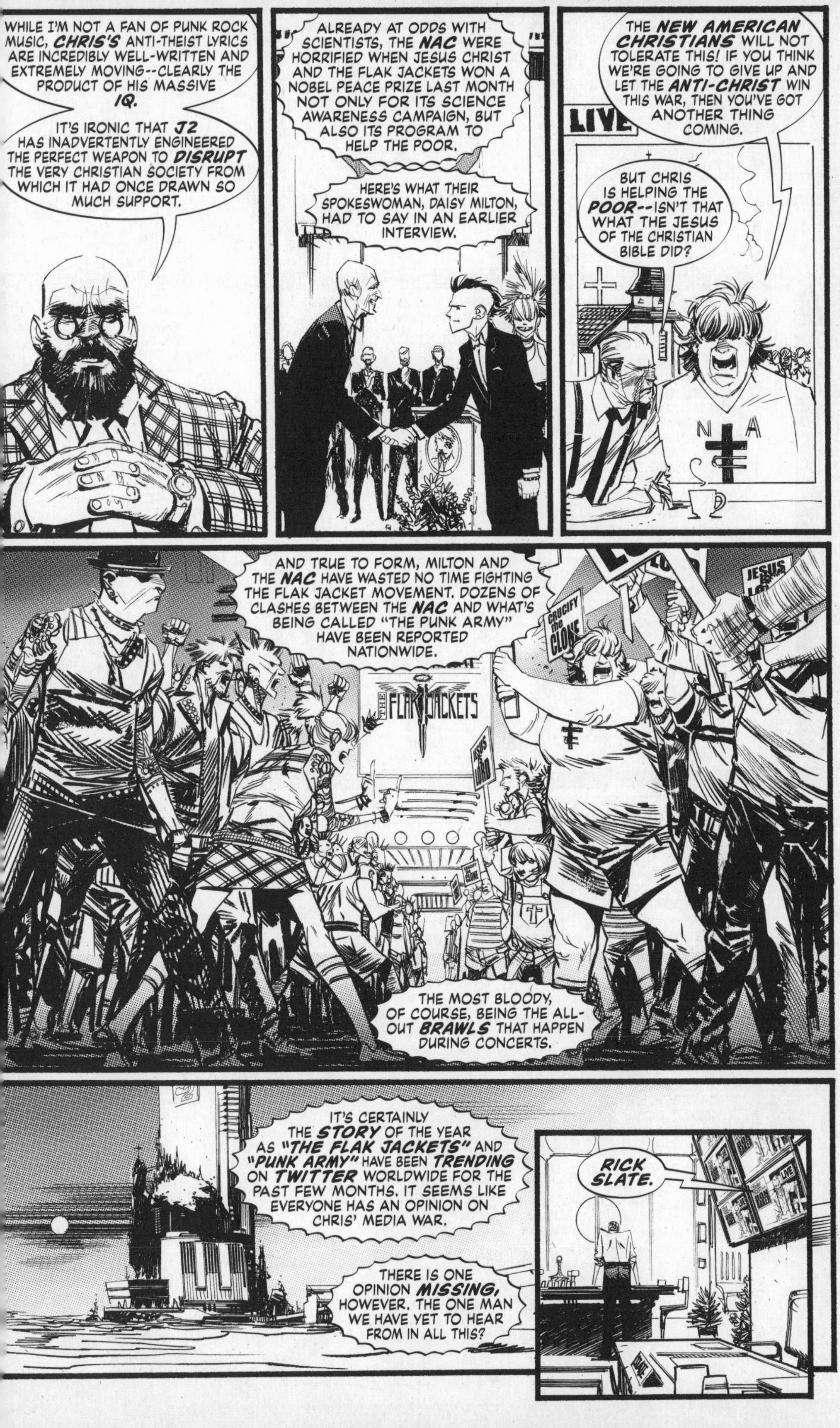
WHILE I'M NOT A FAN OF PUNK ROCK MUSIC, CHRIS'S ANTI-THEIST LYRICS ARE INCREDIBLY WELL-WRITTEN AND EXTREMELY MOVING--CLEARLY THE PRODUCT OF HIS MASSIVE IQ.
IT'S IRONIC THAT J2 HAS INADVERTENTLY ENGINEERED THE PERFECT WEAPON TO DISRUPT THE VERY CHRISTIAN SOCIETY FROM WHICH IT HAD ONCE DRAWN SO MUCH SUPPORT.
ALREADY AT ODDS WITH SCIENTISTS, THE NAC WERE HORRIFIED WHEN JESUS CHRIST AND THE FLAK JACKETS WON A NOBEL PEACE PRIZE LAST MONTH NOT ONLY FOR ITS SCIENCE AWARENESS CAMPAIGN, BUT ALSO ITS PROGRAM TO HELP THE POOR.
HERE'S WHAT THEIR SPOKESWOMAN, DAISY MILTON, HAD TO SAY IN AN EARLIER INTERVIEW.
LIVE
THE NEW AMERICAN CHRISTIANS WILL NOT TOLERATE THIS! IF YOU THINK WE'RE GOING TO GIVE UP AND LET THE ANTI-CHRIST WIN THIS WAR, THEN YOU'VE GOT ANOTHER THING COMING.
BUT CHRIS IS HELPING THE POOR--ISN'T THAT WHAT THE JESUS OF THE CHRISTIAN BIBLE DID?
N A
AND TRUE TO FORM, MILTON AND THE NAC HAVE WASTED NO TIME FIGHTING THE FLAK JACKET MOVEMENT. DOZENS OF CLASHES BETWEEN THE NAC AND WHAT'S BEING CALLED "THE PUNK ARMY" HAVE BEEN REPORTED NATIONWIDE.
CRUCIFY the CLONE
THE FLAK JACKETS
JESUS IS LORD
THE MOST BLOODY, OF COURSE, BEING THE ALL-OUT BRAWLS THAT HAPPEN DURING CONCERTS.
IT'S CERTAINLY THE STORY OF THE YEAR AS "THE FLAK JACKETS" AND "PUNK ARMY" HAVE BEEN TRENDING ON TWITTER WORLDWIDE FOR THE PAST FEW MONTHS. IT SEEMS LIKE EVERYONE HAS AN OPINION ON CHRIS' MEDIA WAR.
THERE IS ONE OPINION MISSING, HOWEVER. THE ONE MAN WE HAVE YET TO HEAR FROM IN ALL THIS?
RICK SLATE.
LIVE

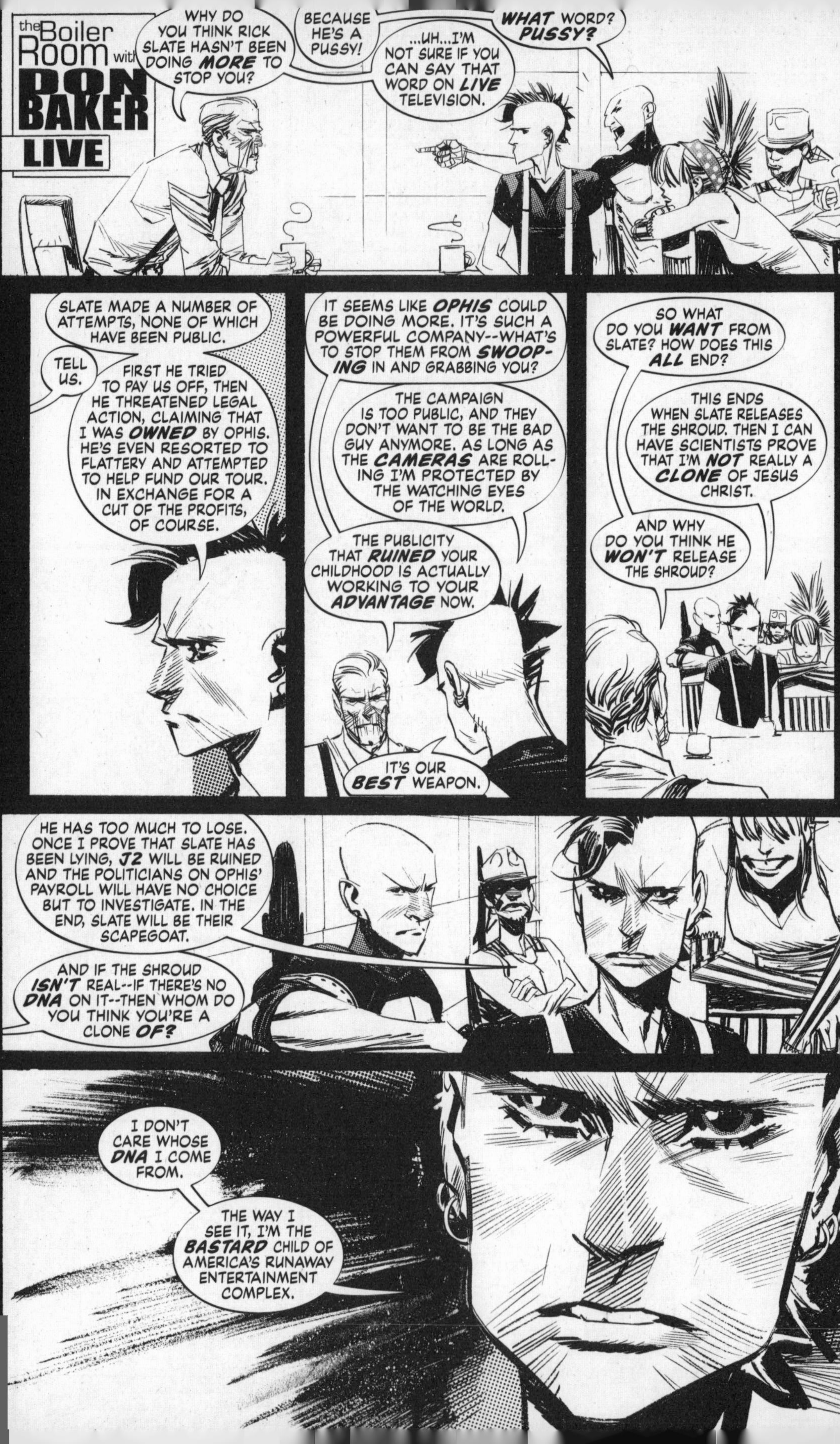
the Boiler Room with DON BAKER LIVE
WHY DO YOU THINK RICK SLATE HASN'T BEEN DOING MORE TO STOP YOU?
BECAUSE HE'S A PUSSY!
...UH...I'M NOT SURE IF YOU CAN SAY THAT WORD ON LIVE TELEVISION.
WHAT WORD? PUSSY?
SLATE MADE A NUMBER OF ATTEMPTS, NONE OF WHICH HAVE BEEN PUBLIC.
TELL US.
FIRST HE TRIED TO PAY US OFF, THEN HE THREATENED LEGAL ACTION, CLAIMING THAT I WAS OWNED BY OPHIS. HE'S EVEN RESORTED TO FLATTERY AND ATTEMPTED TO HELP FUND OUR TOUR. IN EXCHANGE FOR A CUT OF THE PROFITS, OF COURSE.
IT SEEMS LIKE OPHIS COULD BE DOING MORE. IT'S SUCH A POWERFUL COMPANY--WHAT'S TO STOP THEM FROM SWOOP-ING IN AND GRABBING YOU?
THE CAMPAIGN IS TOO PUBLIC, AND THEY DON'T WANT TO BE THE BAD GUY ANYMORE. AS LONG AS THE CAMERAS ARE ROLL-ING I'M PROTECTED BY THE WATCHING EYES OF THE WORLD.
THE PUBLICITY THAT RUINED YOUR CHILDHOOD IS ACTUALLY WORKING TO YOUR ADVANTAGE NOW.
IT'S OUR BEST WEAPON.
SO WHAT DO YOU WANT FROM SLATE? HOW DOES THIS ALL END?
THIS ENDS WHEN SLATE RELEASES THE SHROUD. THEN I CAN HAVE SCIENTISTS PROVE THAT I'M NOT REALLY A CLONE OF JESUS CHRIST.
AND WHY DO YOU THINK HE WON'T RELEASE THE SHROUD?
HE HAS TOO MUCH TO LOSE. ONCE I PROVE THAT SLATE HAS BEEN LYING, J2 WILL BE RUINED AND THE POLITICIANS ON OPHIS' PAYROLL WILL HAVE NO CHOICE BUT TO INVESTIGATE. IN THE END, SLATE WILL BE THEIR SCAPEGOAT.
AND IF THE SHROUD ISN'T REAL--IF THERE'S NO DNA ON IT--THEN WHOM DO YOU THINK YOU'RE A CLONE OF?
I DON'T CARE WHOSE DNA I COME FROM.
THE WAY I SEE IT, I'M THE BASTARD CHILD OF AMERICA'S RUNAWAY ENTERTAINMENT COMPLEX.

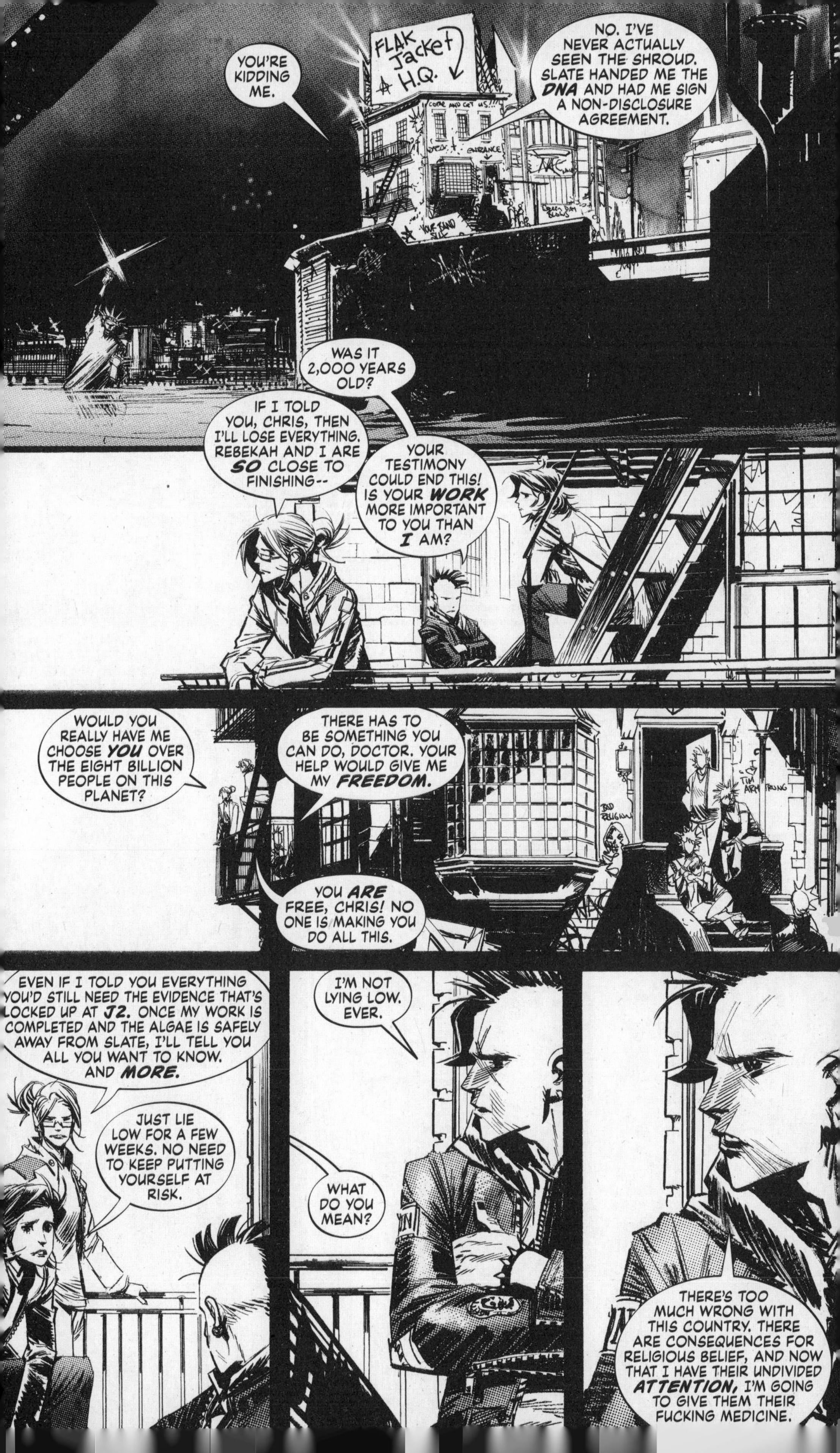
FLAK Jacket H.Q.
YOU'RE KIDDING ME.
NO. I'VE NEVER ACTUALLY SEEN THE SHROUD. SLATE HANDED ME THE DNA AND HAD ME SIGN A NON-DISCLOSURE AGREEMENT.
WAS IT 2,000 YEARS OLD?
IF I TOLD YOU, CHRIS, THEN I'LL LOSE EVERYTHING. REBEKAH AND I ARE SO CLOSE TO FINISHING--
YOUR TESTIMONY COULD END THIS! IS YOUR WORK MORE IMPORTANT TO YOU THAN I AM?
WOULD YOU REALLY HAVE ME CHOOSE YOU OVER THE EIGHT BILLION PEOPLE ON THIS PLANET?
THERE HAS TO BE SOMETHING YOU CAN DO, DOCTOR. YOUR HELP WOULD GIVE ME MY FREEDOM.
YOU ARE FREE, CHRIS! NO ONE IS MAKING YOU DO ALL THIS.
EVEN IF I TOLD YOU EVERYTHING YOU'D STILL NEED THE EVIDENCE THAT'S LOCKED UP AT J2. ONCE MY WORK IS COMPLETED AND THE ALGAE IS SAFELY AWAY FROM SLATE, I'LL TELL YOU ALL YOU WANT TO KNOW. AND MORE.
JUST LIE LOW FOR A FEW WEEKS. NO NEED TO KEEP PUTTING YOURSELF AT RISK.
WHAT DO YOU MEAN?
I'M NOT LYING LOW. EVER.
THERE'S TOO MUCH WRONG WITH THIS COUNTRY. THERE ARE CONSEQUENCES FOR RELIGIOUS BELIEF, AND NOW THAT I HAVE THEIR UNDIVIDED ATTENTION, I'M GOING TO GIVE THEM THEIR FUCKING MEDICINE.

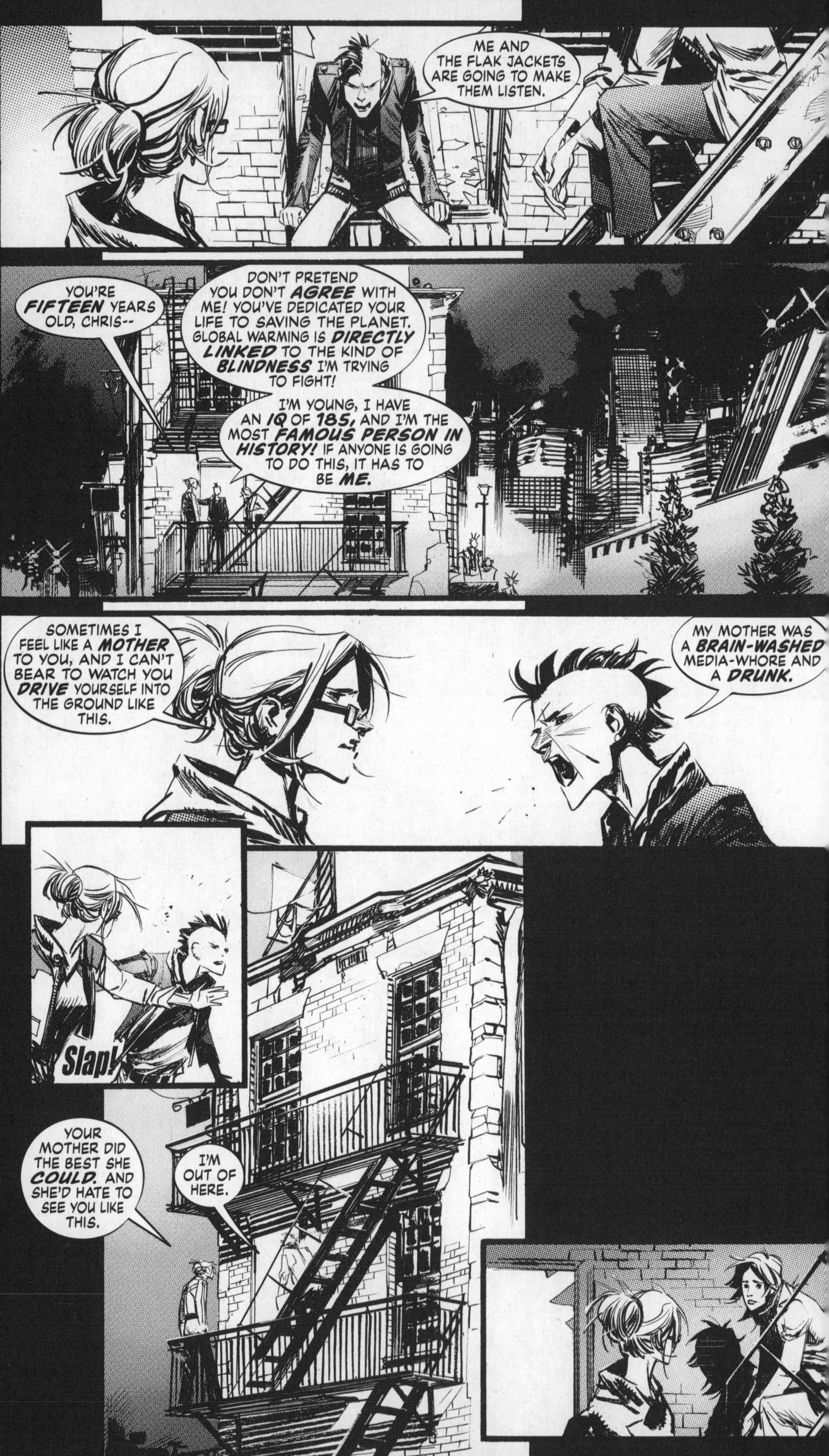
ME AND THE FLAK JACKETS ARE GOING TO MAKE THEM LISTEN.
YOU'RE FIFTEEN YEARS OLD, CHRIS--
DON'T PRETEND YOU DON'T AGREE WITH ME! YOU'VE DEDICATED YOUR LIFE TO SAVING THE PLANET. GLOBAL WARMING IS DIRECTLY LINKED TO THE KIND OF BLINDNESS I'M TRYING TO FIGHT!
I'M YOUNG, I HAVE AN IQ OF 185, AND I'M THE MOST FAMOUS PERSON IN HISTORY! IF ANYONE IS GOING TO DO THIS, IT HAS TO BE ME.
SOMETIMES I FEEL LIKE A MOTHER TO YOU, AND I CAN'T BEAR TO WATCH YOU DRIVE YOURSELF INTO THE GROUND LIKE THIS.
MY MOTHER WAS A BRAIN-WASHED MEDIA-WHORE AND A DRUNK.
Slap!
YOUR MOTHER DID THE BEST SHE COULD. AND SHE'D HATE TO SEE YOU LIKE THIS.
I'M OUT OF HERE.

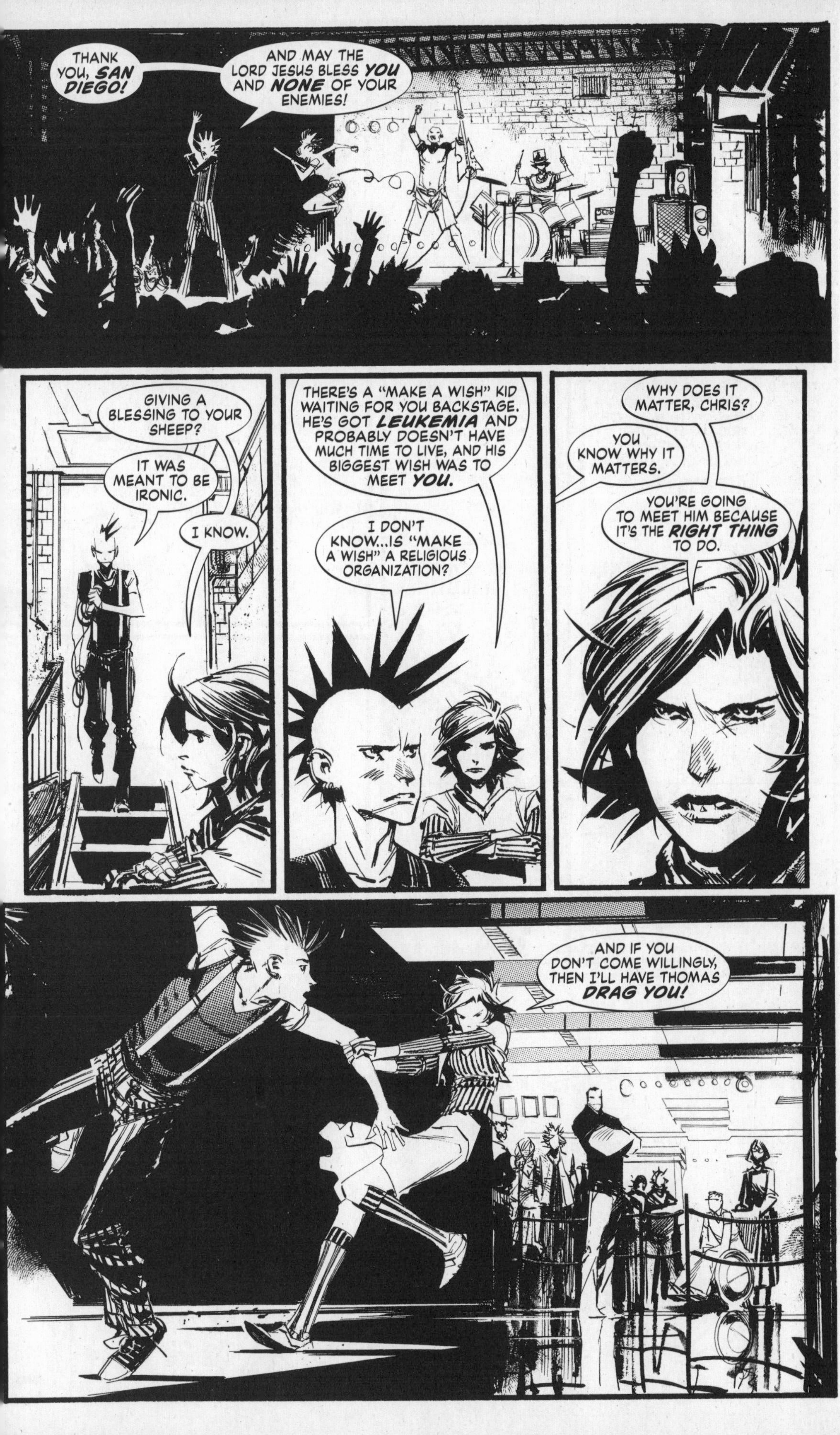
THANK YOU, SAN DIEGO!
AND MAY THE LORD JESUS BLESS YOU AND NONE OF YOUR ENEMIES!
GIVING A BLESSING TO YOUR SHEEP?
IT WAS MEANT TO BE IRONIC.
I KNOW.
THERE'S A "MAKE A WISH" KID WAITING FOR YOU BACKSTAGE. HE'S GOT LEUKEMIA AND PROBABLY DOESN'T HAVE MUCH TIME TO LIVE, AND HIS BIGGEST WISH WAS TO MEET YOU.
I DON'T KNOW...IS "MAKE A WISH" A RELIGIOUS ORGANIZATION?
WHY DOES IT MATTER, CHRIS?
YOU KNOW WHY IT MATTERS.
YOU'RE GOING TO MEET HIM BECAUSE IT'S THE RIGHT THING TO DO.
AND IF YOU DON'T COME WILLINGLY, THEN I'LL HAVE THOMAS DRAG YOU!

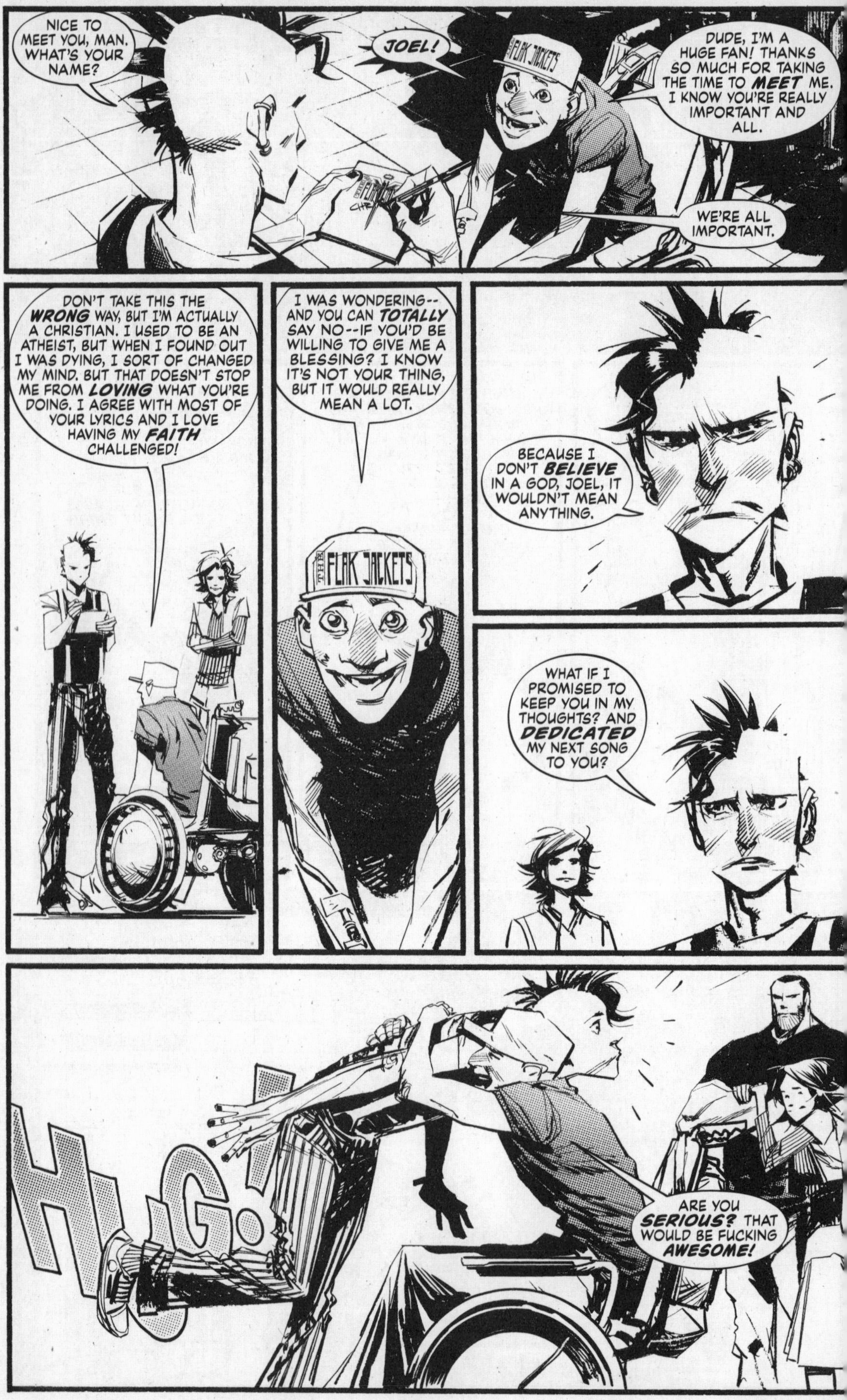
NICE TO MEET YOU, MAN. WHAT'S YOUR NAME?
JOEL!
DUDE, I'M A HUGE FAN! THANKS SO MUCH FOR TAKING THE TIME TO MEET ME. I KNOW YOU'RE REALLY IMPORTANT AND ALL.
WE'RE ALL IMPORTANT.
DON'T TAKE THIS THE WRONG WAY, BUT I'M ACTUALLY A CHRISTIAN. I USED TO BE AN ATHEIST, BUT WHEN I FOUND OUT I WAS DYING, I SORT OF CHANGED MY MIND. BUT THAT DOESN'T STOP ME FROM LOVING WHAT YOU'RE DOING. I AGREE WITH MOST OF YOUR LYRICS AND I LOVE HAVING MY FAITH CHALLENGED!
I WAS WONDERING--AND YOU CAN TOTALLY SAY NO--IF YOU'D BE WILLING TO GIVE ME A BLESSING? I KNOW IT'S NOT YOUR THING, BUT IT WOULD REALLY MEAN A LOT.
THE FLAK JACKETS
BECAUSE I DON'T BELIEVE IN A GOD, JOEL, IT WOULDN'T MEAN ANYTHING.
WHAT IF I PROMISED TO KEEP YOU IN MY THOUGHTS? AND DEDICATED MY NEXT SONG TO YOU?
HUG!
ARE YOU SERIOUS? THAT WOULD BE FUCKING AWESOME!

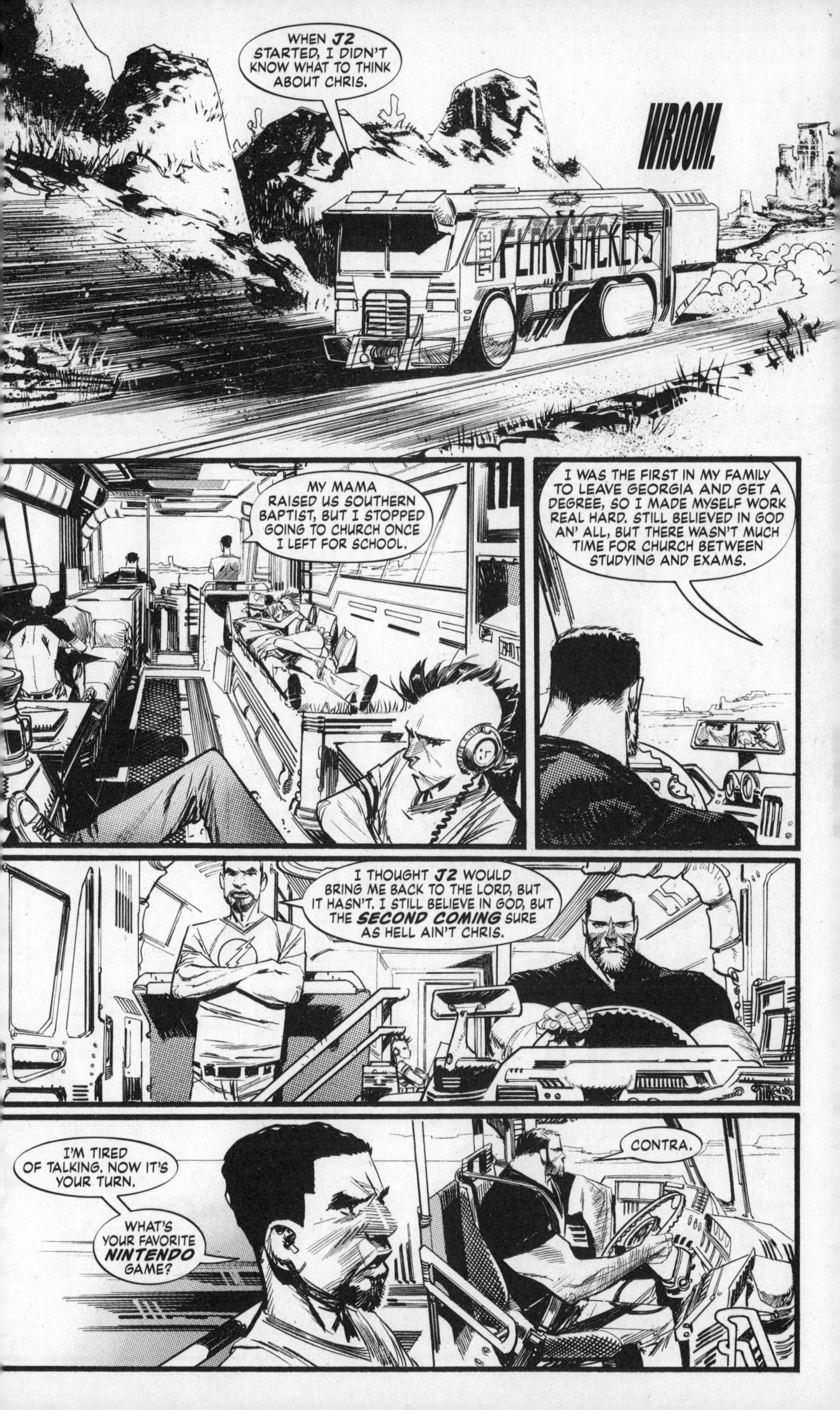
WHEN J2 STARTED, I DIDN'T KNOW WHAT TO THINK ABOUT CHRIS.
WROOM.
THE FLAK JACKETS
MY MAMA RAISED US SOUTHERN BAPTIST, BUT I STOPPED GOING TO CHURCH ONCE I LEFT FOR SCHOOL.
I WAS THE FIRST IN MY FAMILY TO LEAVE GEORGIA AND GET A DEGREE, SO I MADE MYSELF WORK REAL HARD. STILL BELIEVED IN GOD AN' ALL, BUT THERE WASN'T MUCH TIME FOR CHURCH BETWEEN STUDYING AND EXAMS.
I THOUGHT J2 WOULD BRING ME BACK TO THE LORD, BUT IT HASN'T. I STILL BELIEVE IN GOD, BUT THE SECOND COMING SURE AS HELL AIN'T CHRIS.
I'M TIRED OF TALKING. NOW IT'S YOUR TURN.
WHAT'S YOUR FAVORITE NINTENDO GAME?
CONTRA.

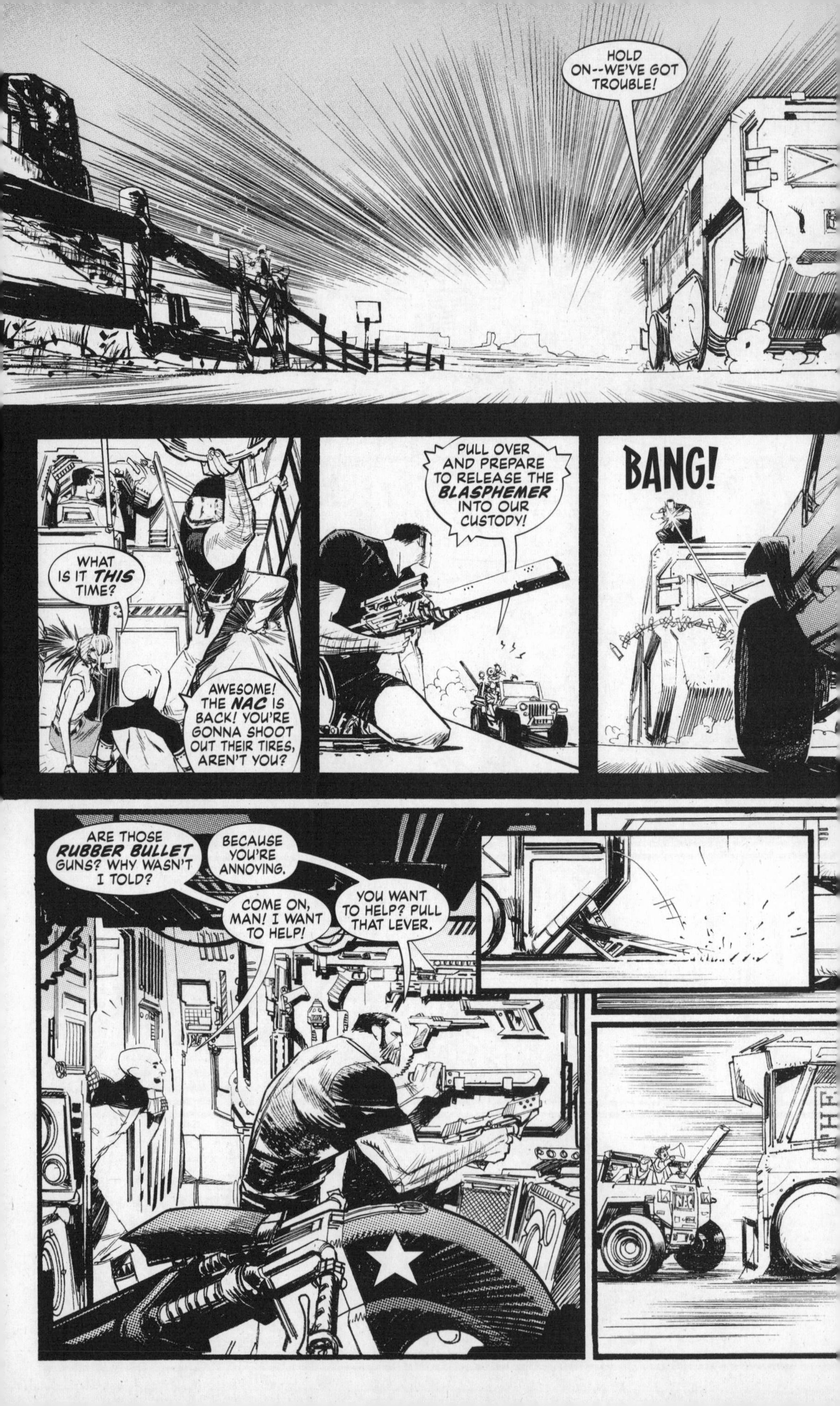
HOLD ON--WE'VE GOT TROUBLE!
WHAT IS IT THIS TIME?
AWESOME! THE NAC IS BACK! YOU'RE GONNA SHOOT OUT THEIR TIRES, AREN'T YOU?
PULL OVER AND PREPARE TO RELEASE THE BLASPHEMER INTO OUR CUSTODY!
BANG!
ARE THOSE RUBBER BULLET GUNS? WHY WASN'T I TOLD?
BECAUSE YOU'RE ANNOYING.
COME ON, MAN! I WANT TO HELP!
YOU WANT TO HELP? PULL THAT LEVER.
NAC

THIS IS DAISY MILTON OF THE NAC! WE HAVE YOU SURROUNDED!
TAKE THE WHEEL.
NAC
KREED
VOTE 4 BUSH
GODMBL
THROW!
THE REIGN OF THE ANTI-CHRIST IS OVER!
KTTSH!!
WAS THAT A MOLOTOV COCKTAIL? SWEET!
GET OUT OF MY WAY.
JUST LIKE KNIGHT RIDER!
VROOM!

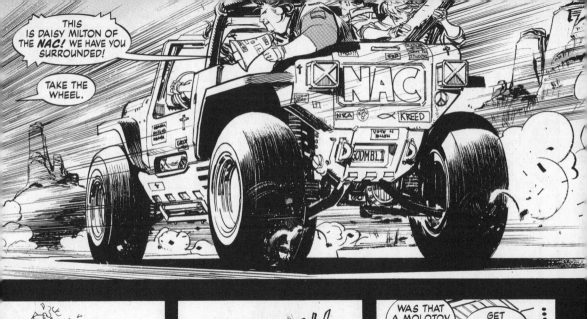

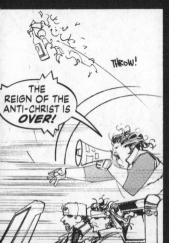

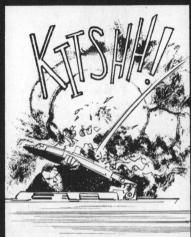

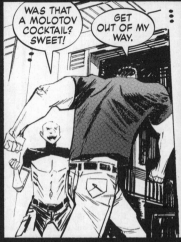

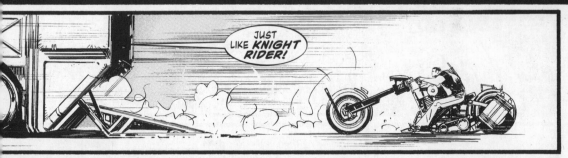

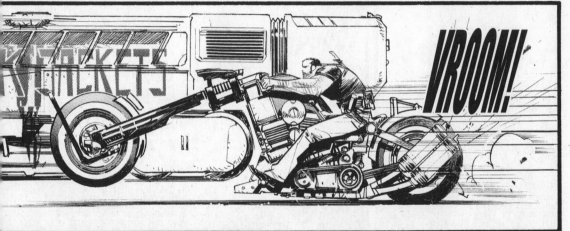

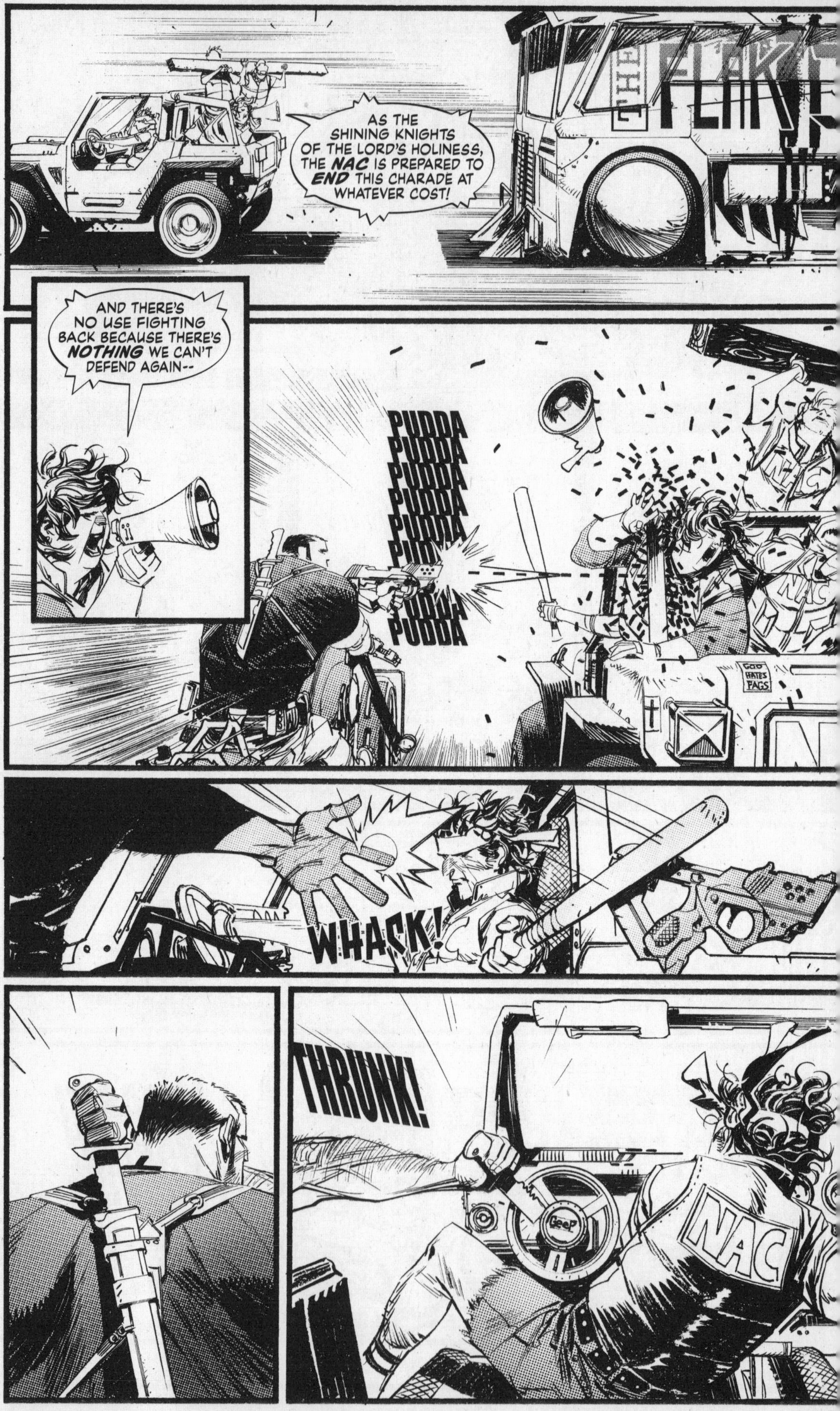

AS THE SHINING KNIGHTS OF THE LORD'S HOLINESS, THE NAC IS PREPARED TO END THIS CHARADE AT WHATEVER COST!
AND THERE'S NO USE FIGHTING BACK BECAUSE THERE'S NOTHING WE CAN'T DEFEND AGAIN--
PUDDA PUDDA PUDDA PUDDA PUDDA PUDDA PUDDA PUDDA
GOD HATES FAGS
NAC
WHACK!
THRUNK!
NAC

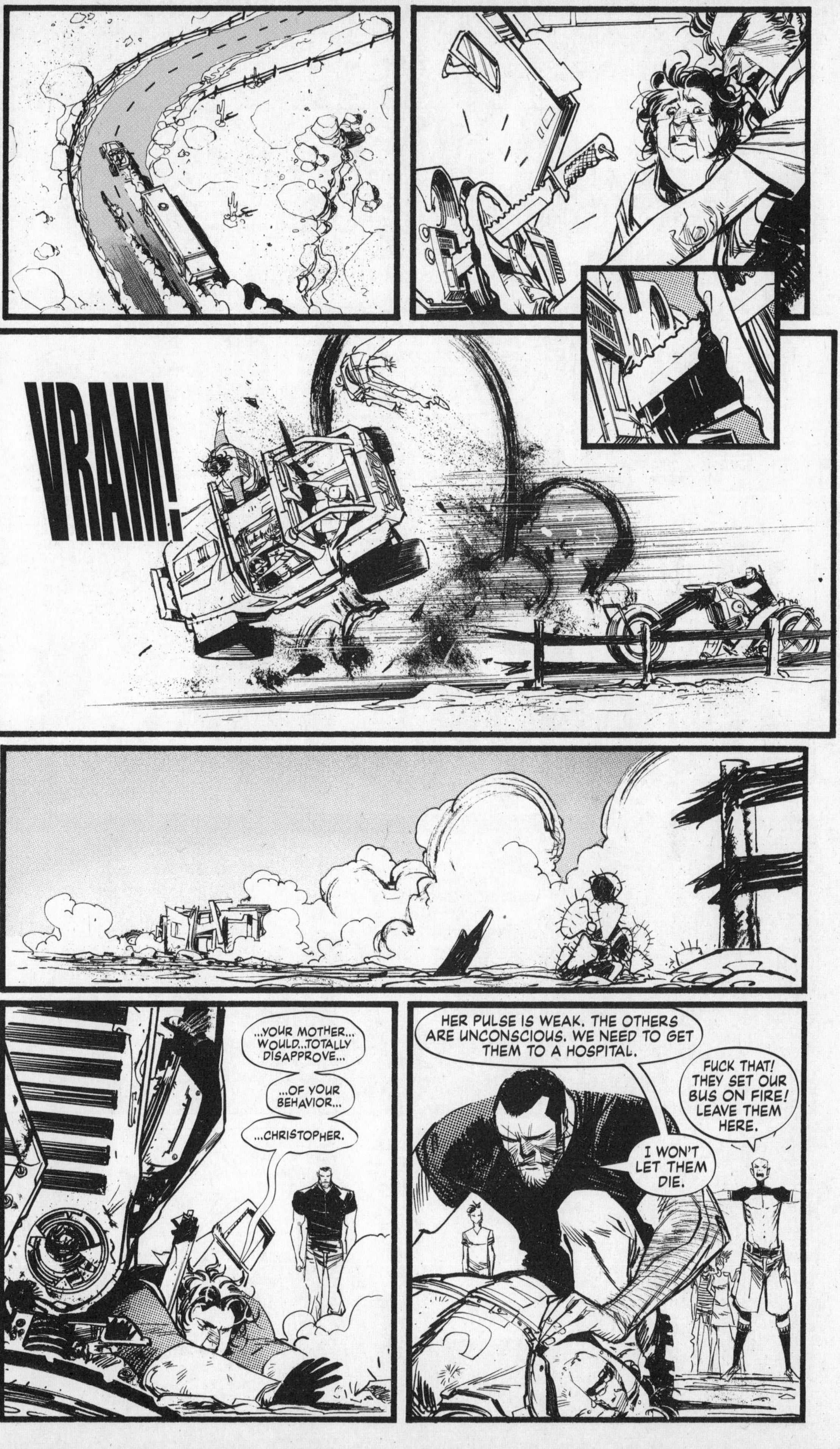
CRUISE CONTROL
VRAM!
...YOUR MOTHER... WOULD...TOTALLY DISAPPROVE...
...OF YOUR BEHAVIOR...
...CHRISTOPHER.
HER PULSE IS WEAK. THE OTHERS ARE UNCONSCIOUS. WE NEED TO GET THEM TO A HOSPITAL.
FUCK THAT! THEY SET OUR BUS ON FIRE! LEAVE THEM HERE.
I WON'T LET THEM DIE.

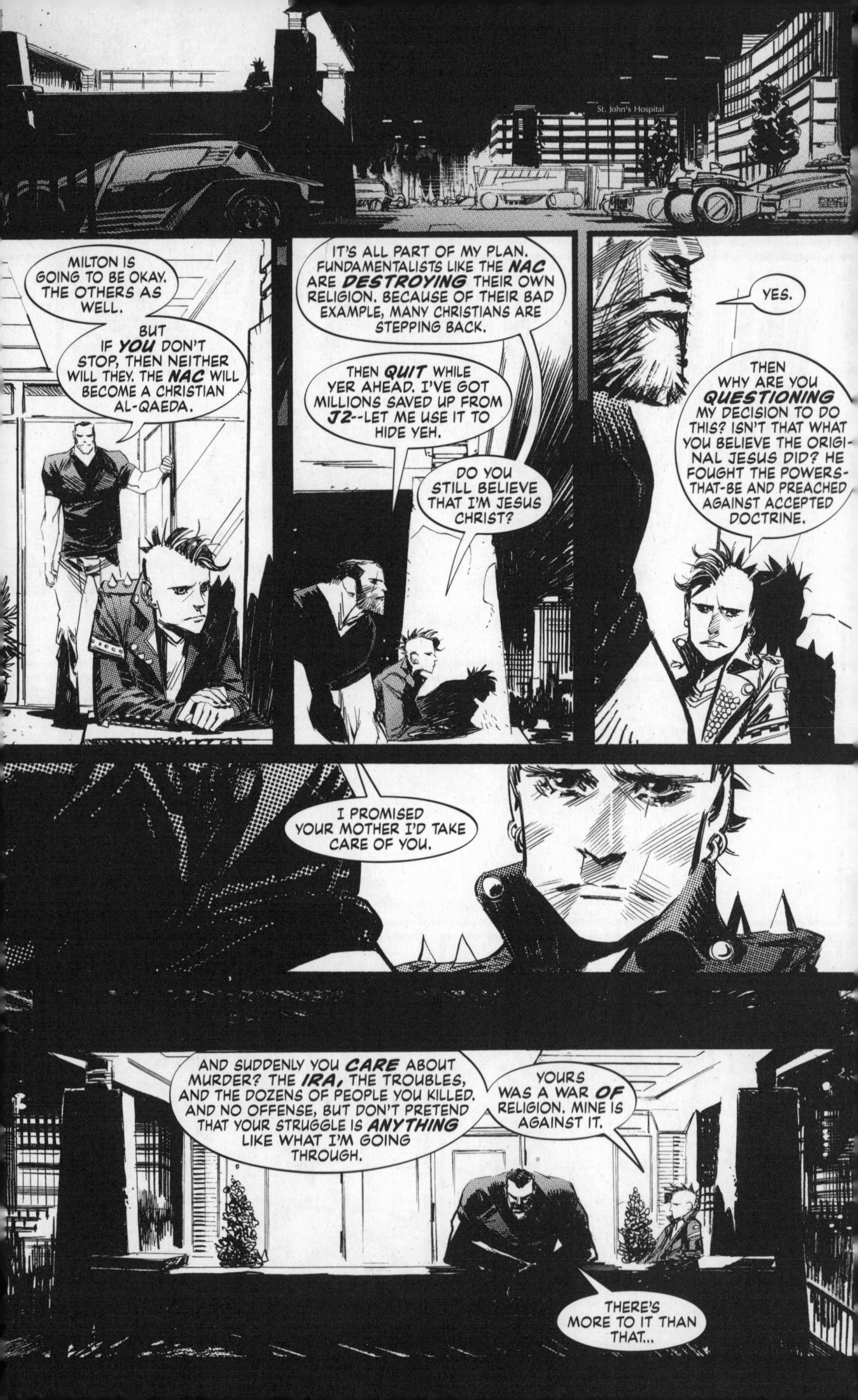
St. John's Hospital
MILTON IS GOING TO BE OKAY. THE OTHERS AS WELL.
BUT IF YOU DON'T STOP, THEN NEITHER WILL THEY. THE NAC WILL BECOME A CHRISTIAN AL-QAEDA.
IT'S ALL PART OF MY PLAN. FUNDAMENTALISTS LIKE THE NAC ARE DESTROYING THEIR OWN RELIGION. BECAUSE OF THEIR BAD EXAMPLE, MANY CHRISTIANS ARE STEPPING BACK.
THEN QUIT WHILE YER AHEAD. I'VE GOT MILLIONS SAVED UP FROM J2--LET ME USE IT TO HIDE YEH.
DO YOU STILL BELIEVE THAT I'M JESUS CHRIST?
YES.
THEN WHY ARE YOU QUESTIONING MY DECISION TO DO THIS? ISN'T THAT WHAT YOU BELIEVE THE ORIGINAL JESUS DID? HE FOUGHT THE POWERS-THAT-BE AND PREACHED AGAINST ACCEPTED DOCTRINE.
I PROMISED YOUR MOTHER I'D TAKE CARE OF YOU.
AND SUDDENLY YOU CARE ABOUT MURDER? THE IRA, THE TROUBLES, AND THE DOZENS OF PEOPLE YOU KILLED. AND NO OFFENSE, BUT DON'T PRETEND THAT YOUR STRUGGLE IS ANYTHING LIKE WHAT I'M GOING THROUGH.
YOURS WAS A WAR OF RELIGION. MINE IS AGAINST IT.
THERE'S MORE TO IT THAN THAT...

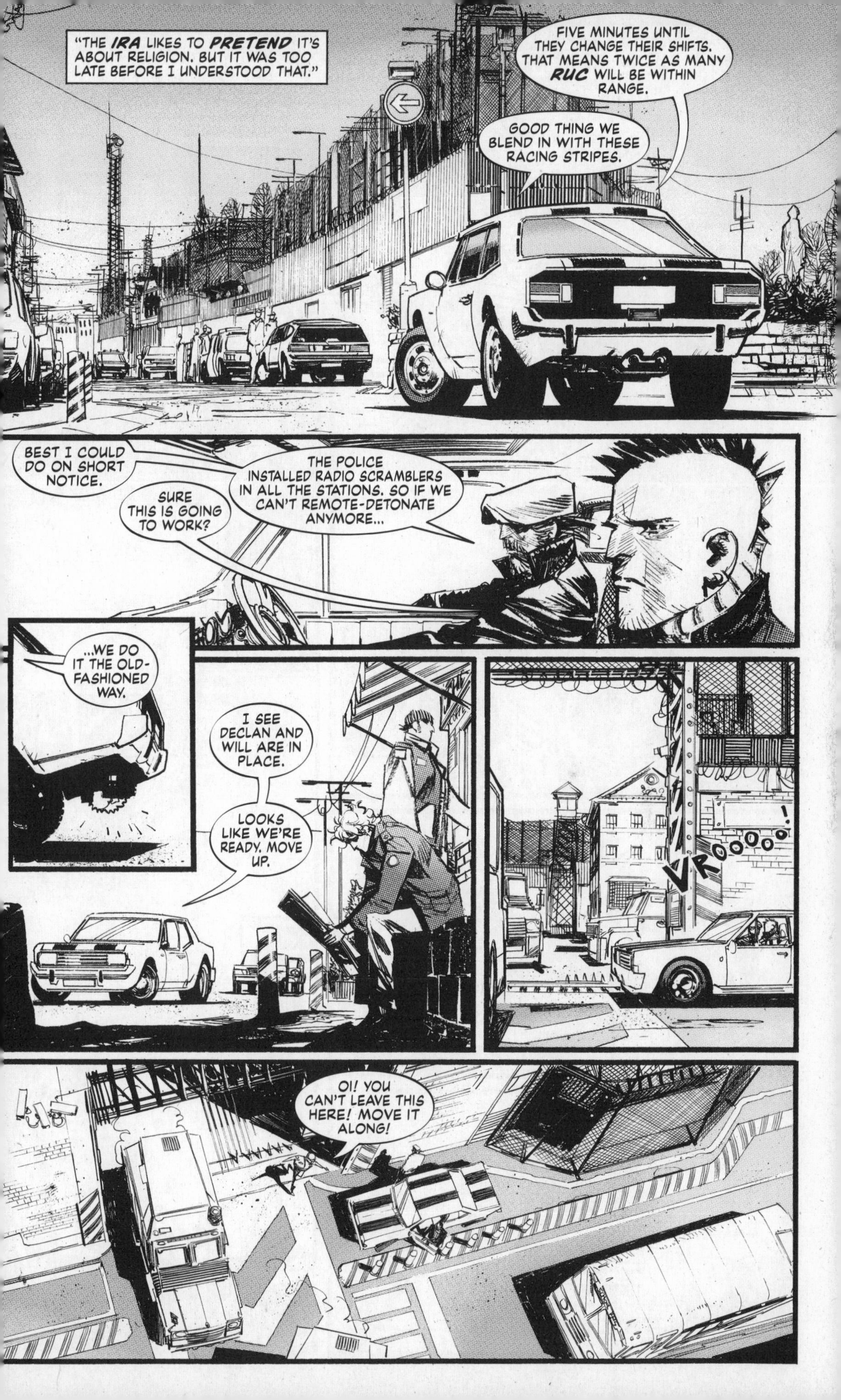

"THE IRA LIKES TO PRETEND IT'S ABOUT RELIGION. BUT IT WAS TOO LATE BEFORE I UNDERSTOOD THAT."
FIVE MINUTES UNTIL THEY CHANGE THEIR SHIFTS. THAT MEANS TWICE AS MANY RUC WILL BE WITHIN RANGE.
GOOD THING WE BLEND IN WITH THESE RACING STRIPES.
BEST I COULD DO ON SHORT NOTICE.
SURE THIS IS GOING TO WORK?
THE POLICE INSTALLED RADIO SCRAMBLERS IN ALL THE STATIONS. SO IF WE CAN'T REMOTE-DETONATE ANYMORE...
...WE DO IT THE OLD-FASHIONED WAY.
I SEE DECLAN AND WILL ARE IN PLACE.
LOOKS LIKE WE'RE READY. MOVE UP.
VROOOOOO!
OI! YOU CAN'T LEAVE THIS HERE! MOVE IT ALONG!

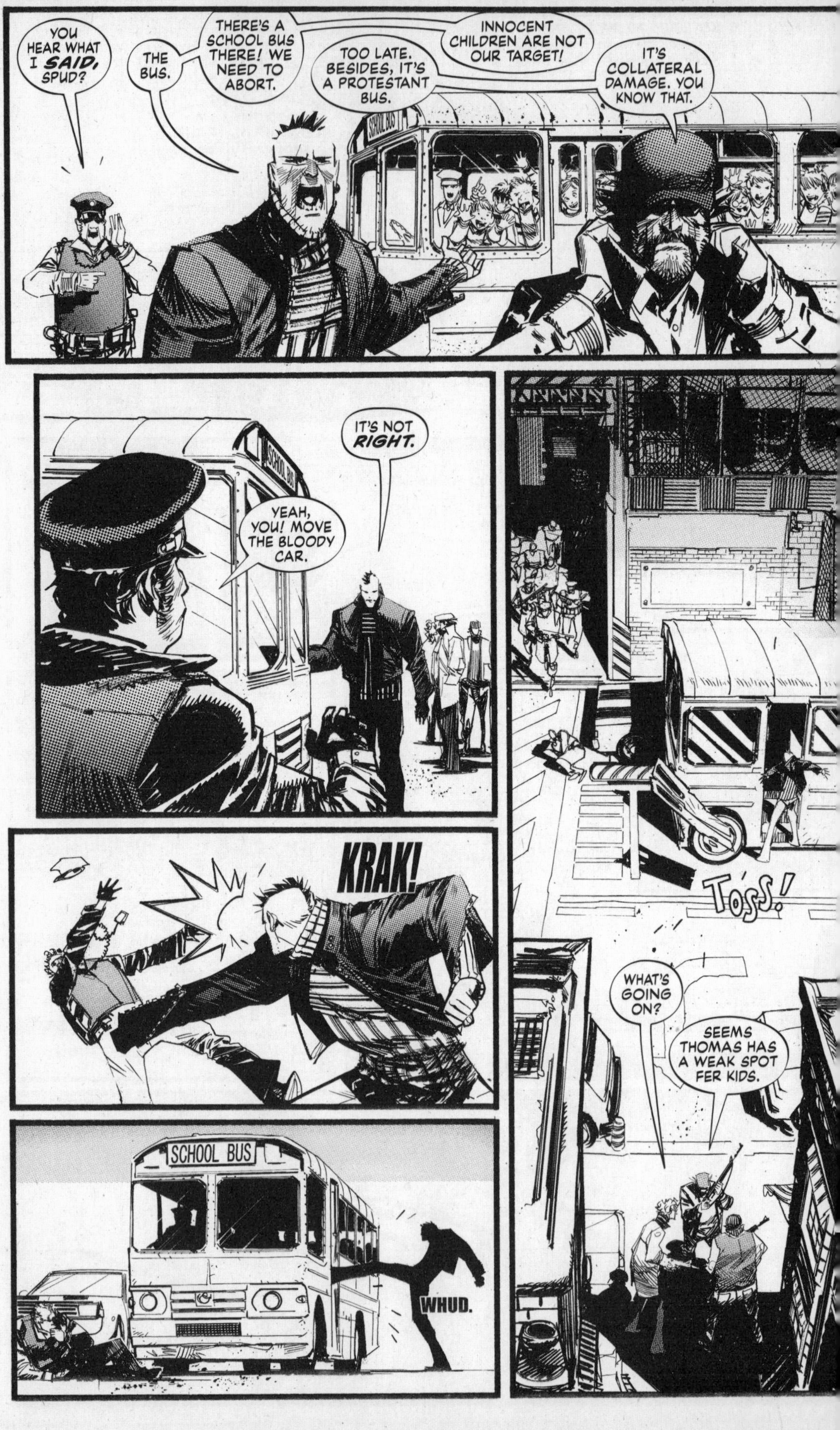

YOU HEAR WHAT I SAID, SPUD?
THE BUS.
THERE'S A SCHOOL BUS THERE! WE NEED TO ABORT.
TOO LATE. BESIDES, IT'S A PROTESTANT BUS.
INNOCENT CHILDREN ARE NOT OUR TARGET!
IT'S COLLATERAL DAMAGE. YOU KNOW THAT.
SCHOOL BUS
IT'S NOT RIGHT.
YEAH, YOU! MOVE THE BLOODY CAR.
KRAK!
TOSS!
WHAT'S GOING ON?
SEEMS THOMAS HAS A WEAK SPOT FER KIDS.
SCHOOL BUS
WHUD.

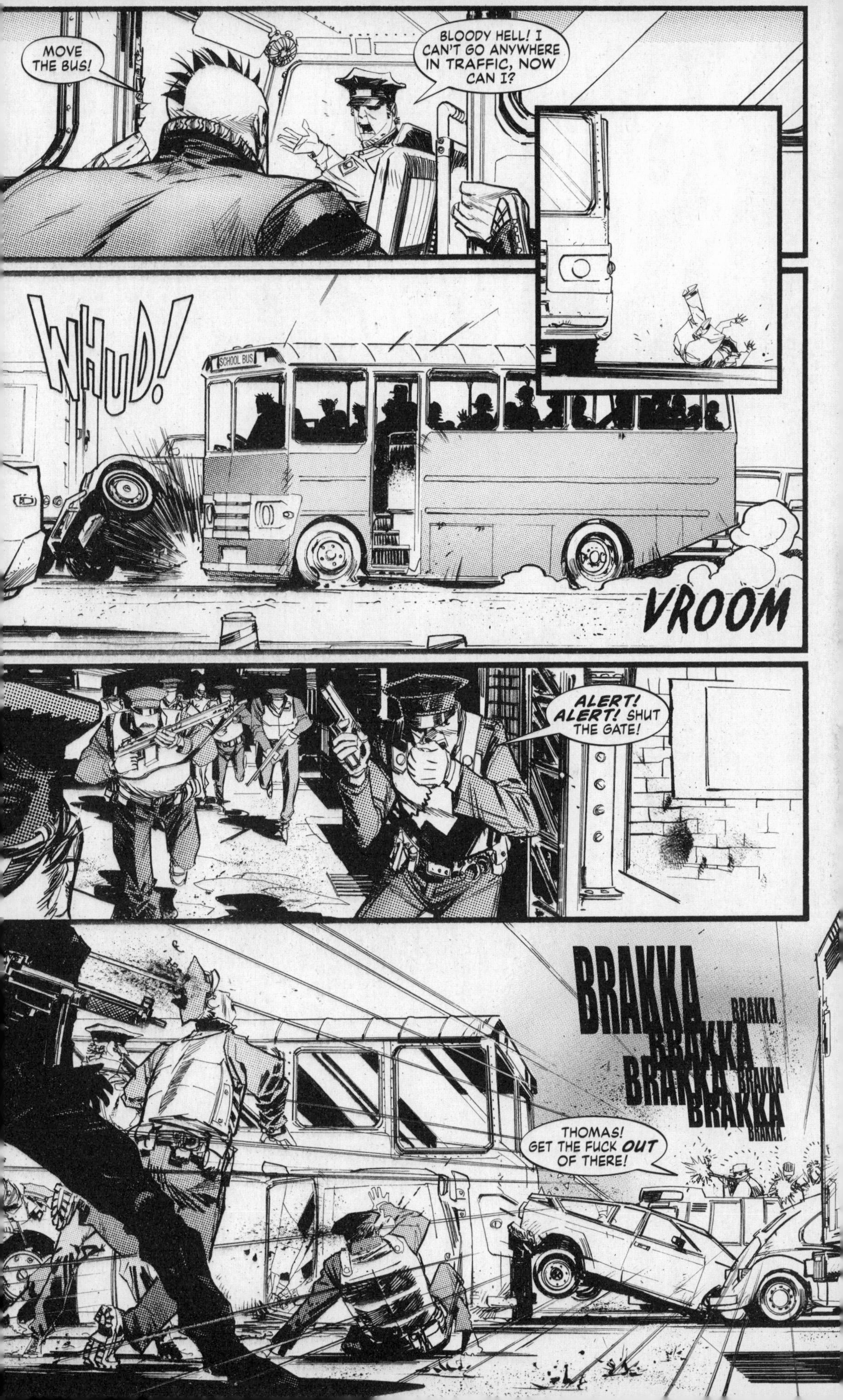

MOVE THE BUS!
BLOODY HELL! I CAN'T GO ANYWHERE IN TRAFFIC, NOW CAN I?
WHUD!
SCHOOL BUS
VROOM
ALERT! ALERT! SHUT THE GATE!
BRAKKA BRAKKA BRAKKA BRAKKA BRAKKA BRAKKA BRAKKA
THOMAS! GET THE FUCK OUT OF THERE!

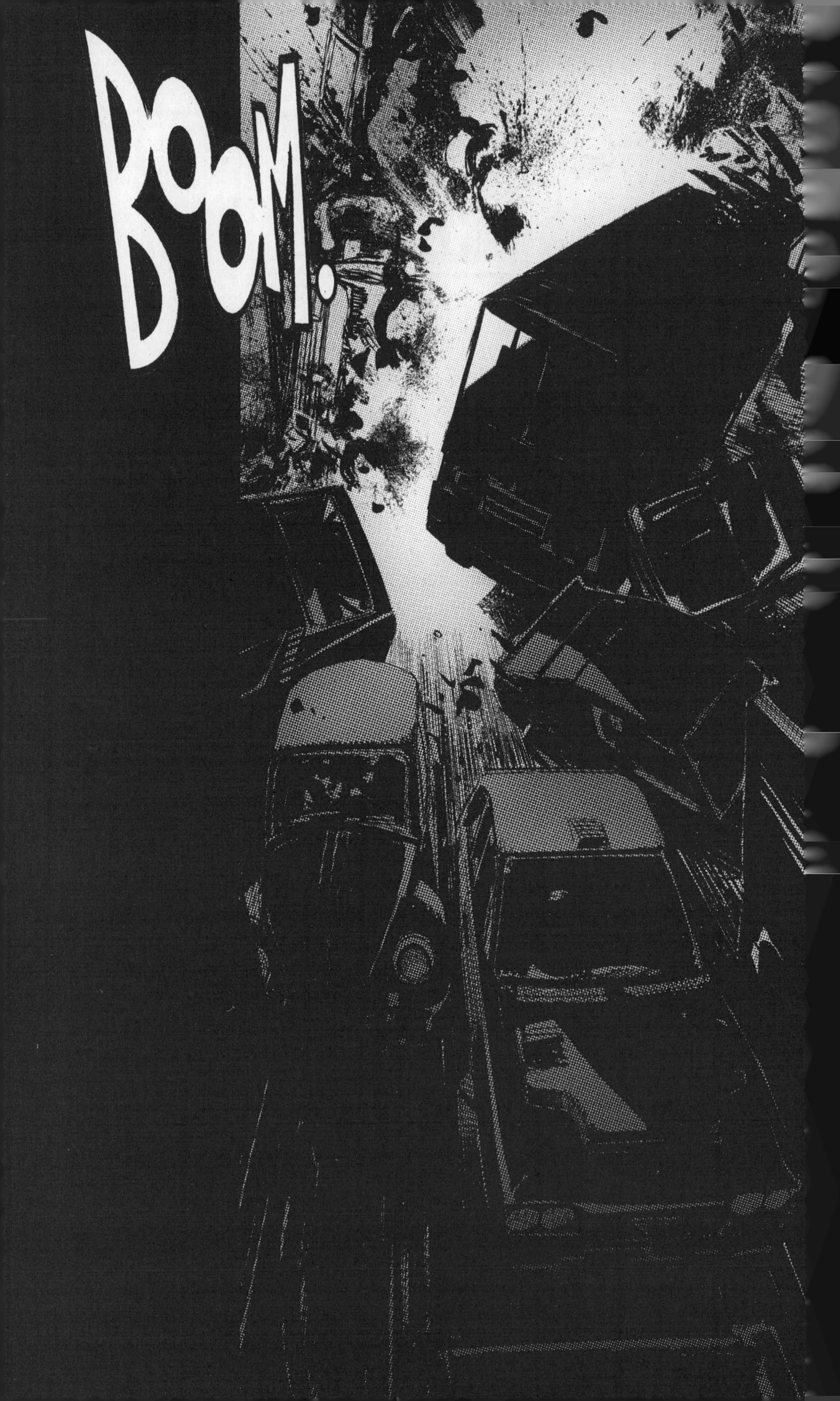
BOOM.

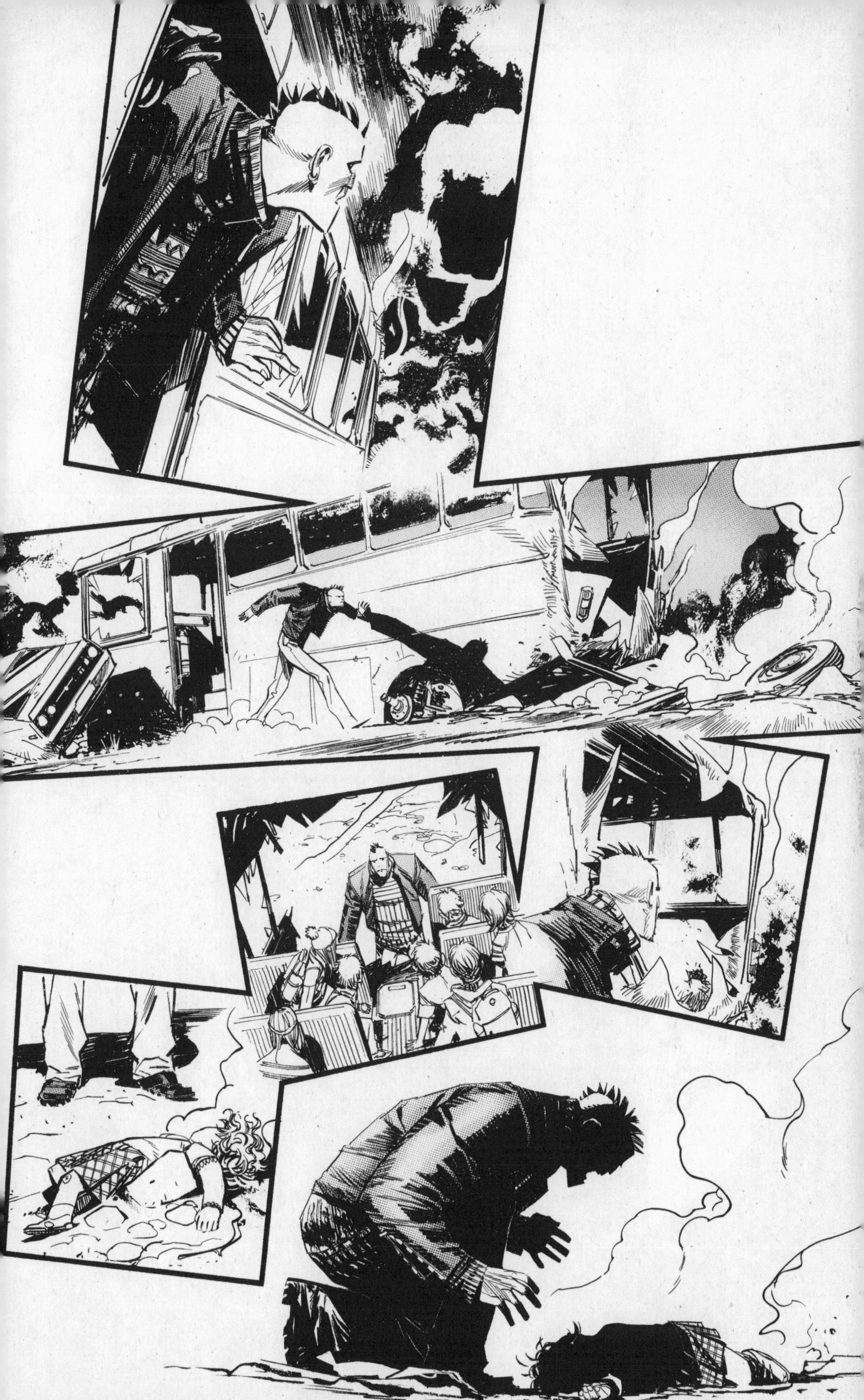

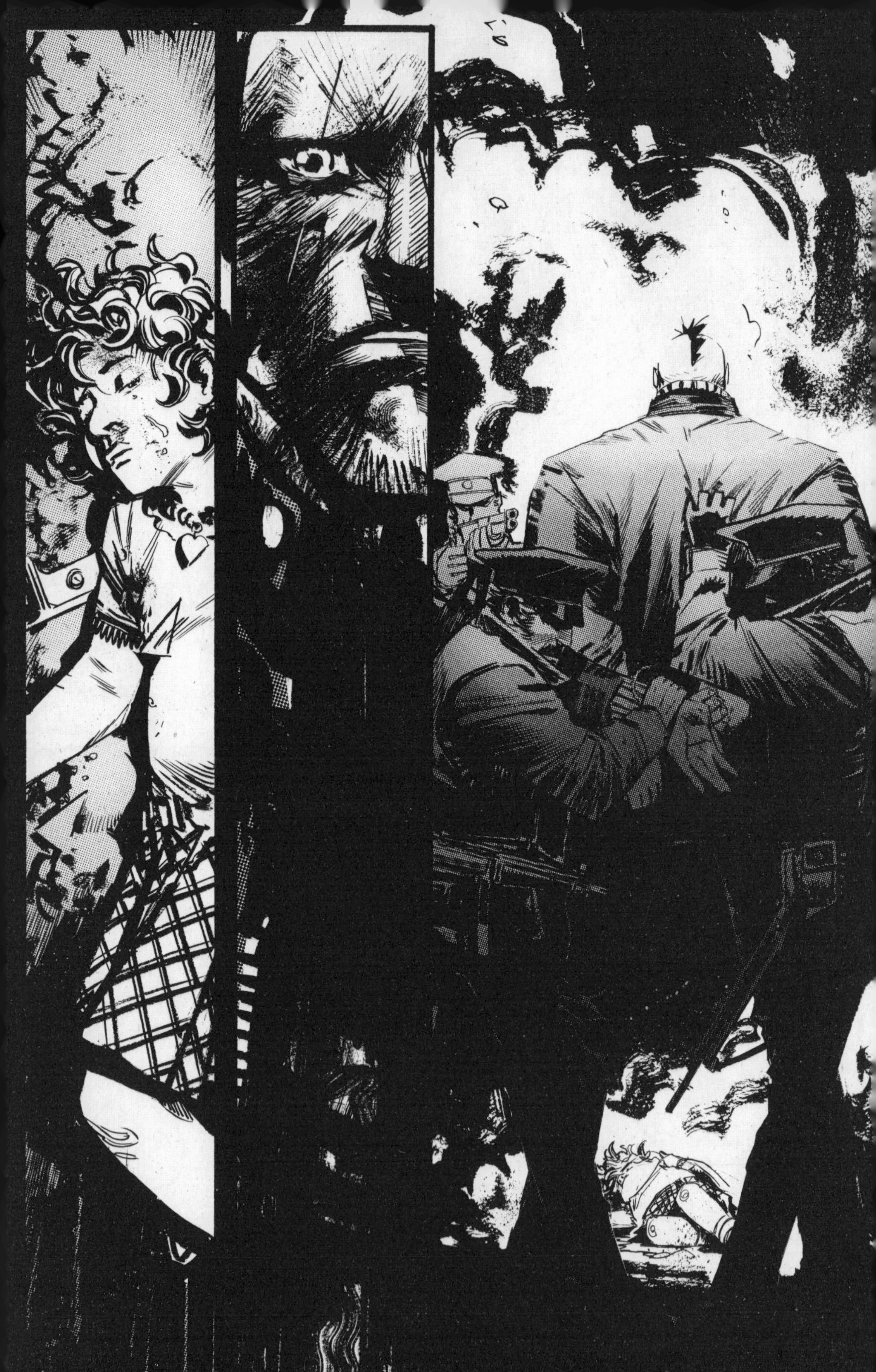

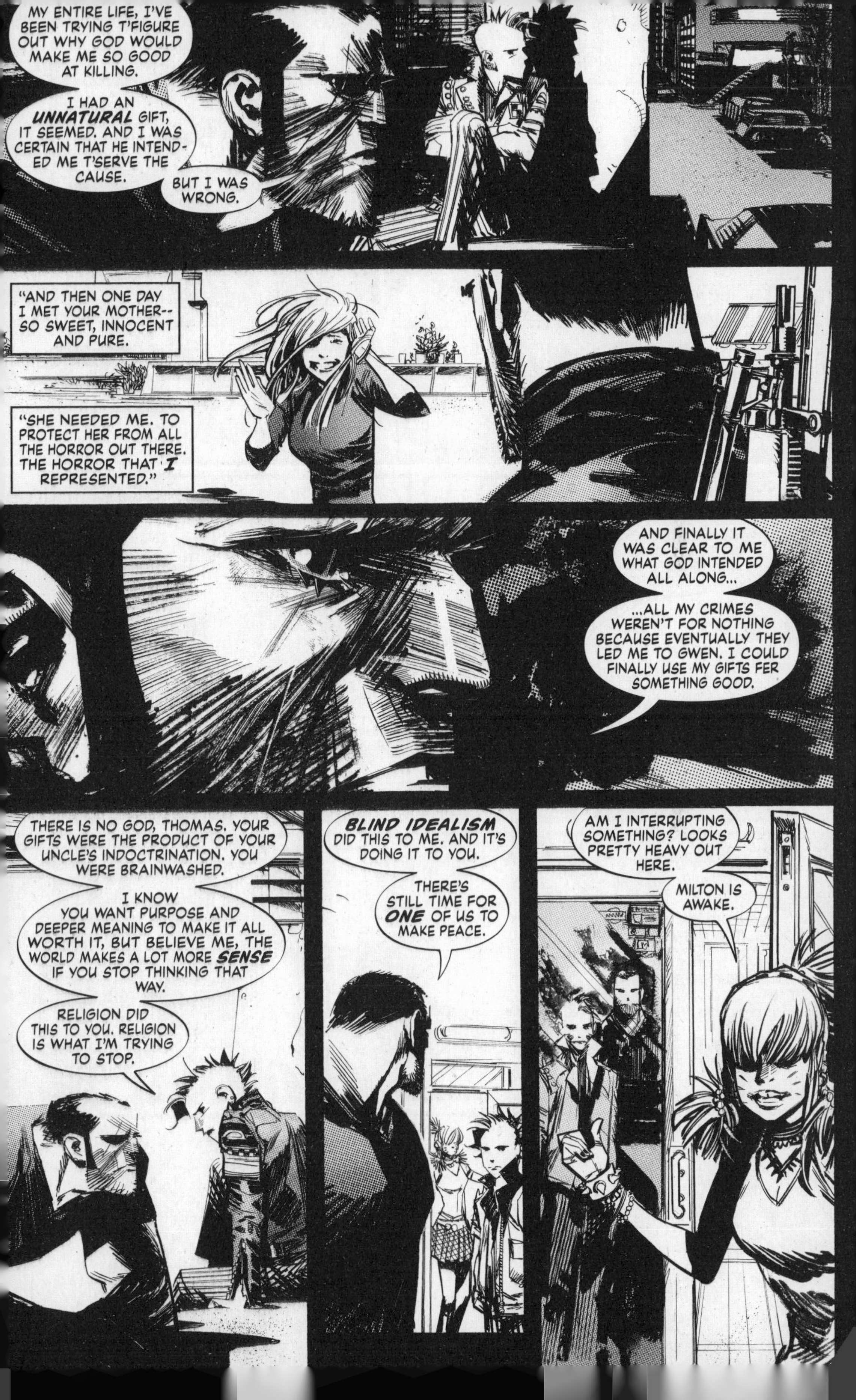

MY ENTIRE LIFE, I'VE BEEN TRYING T'FIGURE OUT WHY GOD WOULD MAKE ME SO GOOD AT KILLING.
I HAD AN UNNATURAL GIFT, IT SEEMED. AND I WAS CERTAIN THAT HE INTENDED ME T'SERVE THE CAUSE.
BUT I WAS WRONG.
"AND THEN ONE DAY I MET YOUR MOTHER-- SO SWEET, INNOCENT AND PURE.
"SHE NEEDED ME. TO PROTECT HER FROM ALL THE HORROR OUT THERE. THE HORROR THAT I REPRESENTED."
AND FINALLY IT WAS CLEAR TO ME WHAT GOD INTENDED ALL ALONG...
...ALL MY CRIMES WEREN'T FOR NOTHING BECAUSE EVENTUALLY THEY LED ME TO GWEN. I COULD FINALLY USE MY GIFTS FER SOMETHING GOOD.
THERE IS NO GOD, THOMAS. YOUR GIFTS WERE THE PRODUCT OF YOUR UNCLE'S INDOCTRINATION. YOU WERE BRAINWASHED.
I KNOW YOU WANT PURPOSE AND DEEPER MEANING TO MAKE IT ALL WORTH IT, BUT BELIEVE ME, THE WORLD MAKES A LOT MORE SENSE IF YOU STOP THINKING THAT WAY.
RELIGION DID THIS TO YOU. RELIGION IS WHAT I'M TRYING TO STOP.
BLIND IDEALISM DID THIS TO ME. AND IT'S DOING IT TO YOU.
THERE'S STILL TIME FOR ONE OF US TO MAKE PEACE.
AM I INTERRUPTING SOMETHING? LOOKS PRETTY HEAVY OUT HERE.
MILTON IS AWAKE.

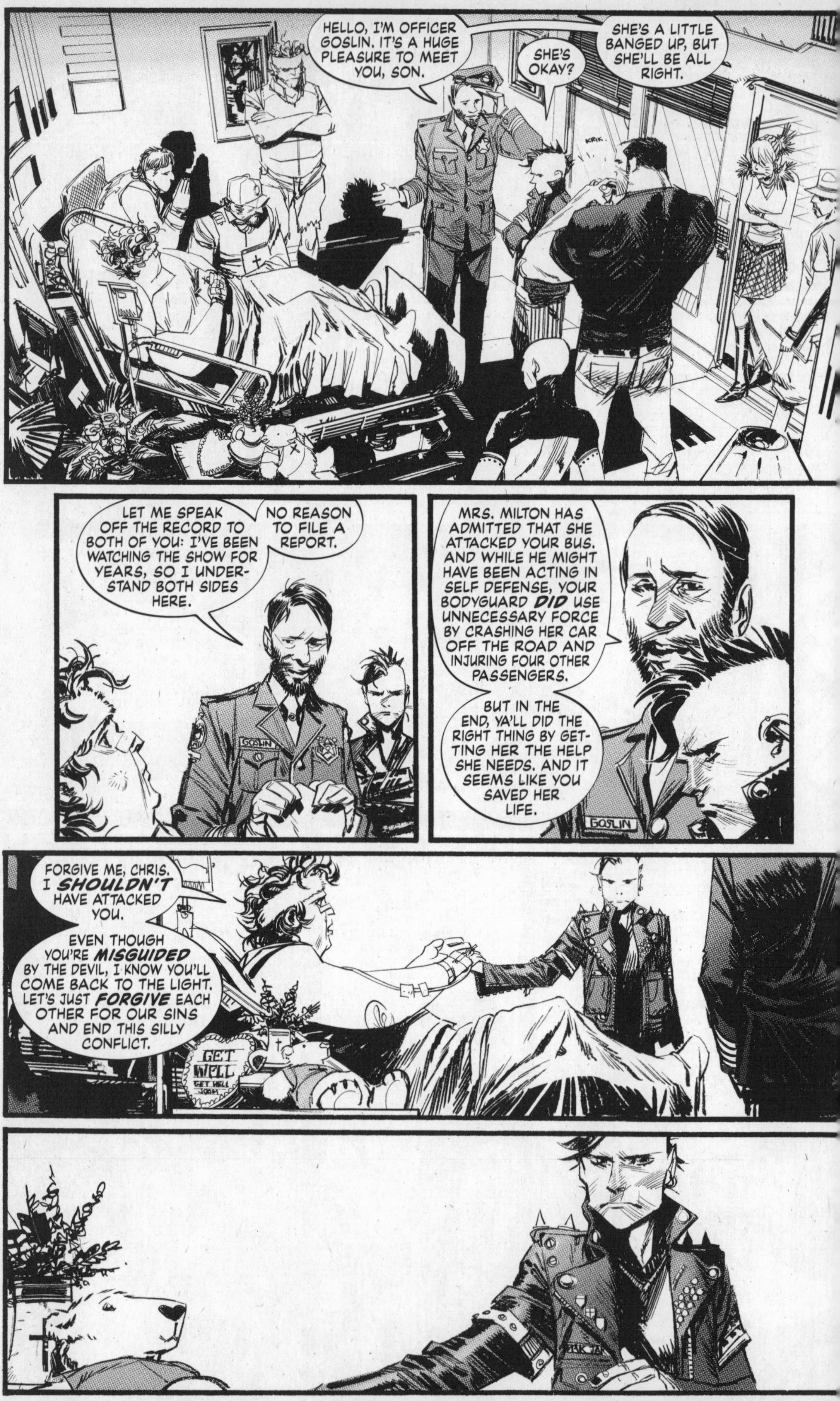
HELLO, I'M OFFICER GOSLIN. IT'S A HUGE PLEASURE TO MEET YOU, SON.
SHE'S OKAY?
SHE'S A LITTLE BANGED UP, BUT SHE'LL BE ALL RIGHT.
KRIK.
LET ME SPEAK OFF THE RECORD TO BOTH OF YOU: I'VE BEEN WATCHING THE SHOW FOR YEARS, SO I UNDERSTAND BOTH SIDES HERE.
NO REASON TO FILE A REPORT.
GOSLIN
MRS. MILTON HAS ADMITTED THAT SHE ATTACKED YOUR BUS. AND WHILE HE MIGHT HAVE BEEN ACTING IN SELF DEFENSE, YOUR BODYGUARD DID USE UNNECESSARY FORCE BY CRASHING HER CAR OFF THE ROAD AND INJURING FOUR OTHER PASSENGERS.
BUT IN THE END, YA'LL DID THE RIGHT THING BY GETTING HER THE HELP SHE NEEDS. AND IT SEEMS LIKE YOU SAVED HER LIFE.
GOSLIN
FORGIVE ME, CHRIS. I SHOULDN'T HAVE ATTACKED YOU.
EVEN THOUGH YOU'RE MISGUIDED BY THE DEVIL, I KNOW YOU'LL COME BACK TO THE LIGHT. LET'S JUST FORGIVE EACH OTHER FOR OUR SINS AND END THIS SILLY CONFLICT.
GET WELL

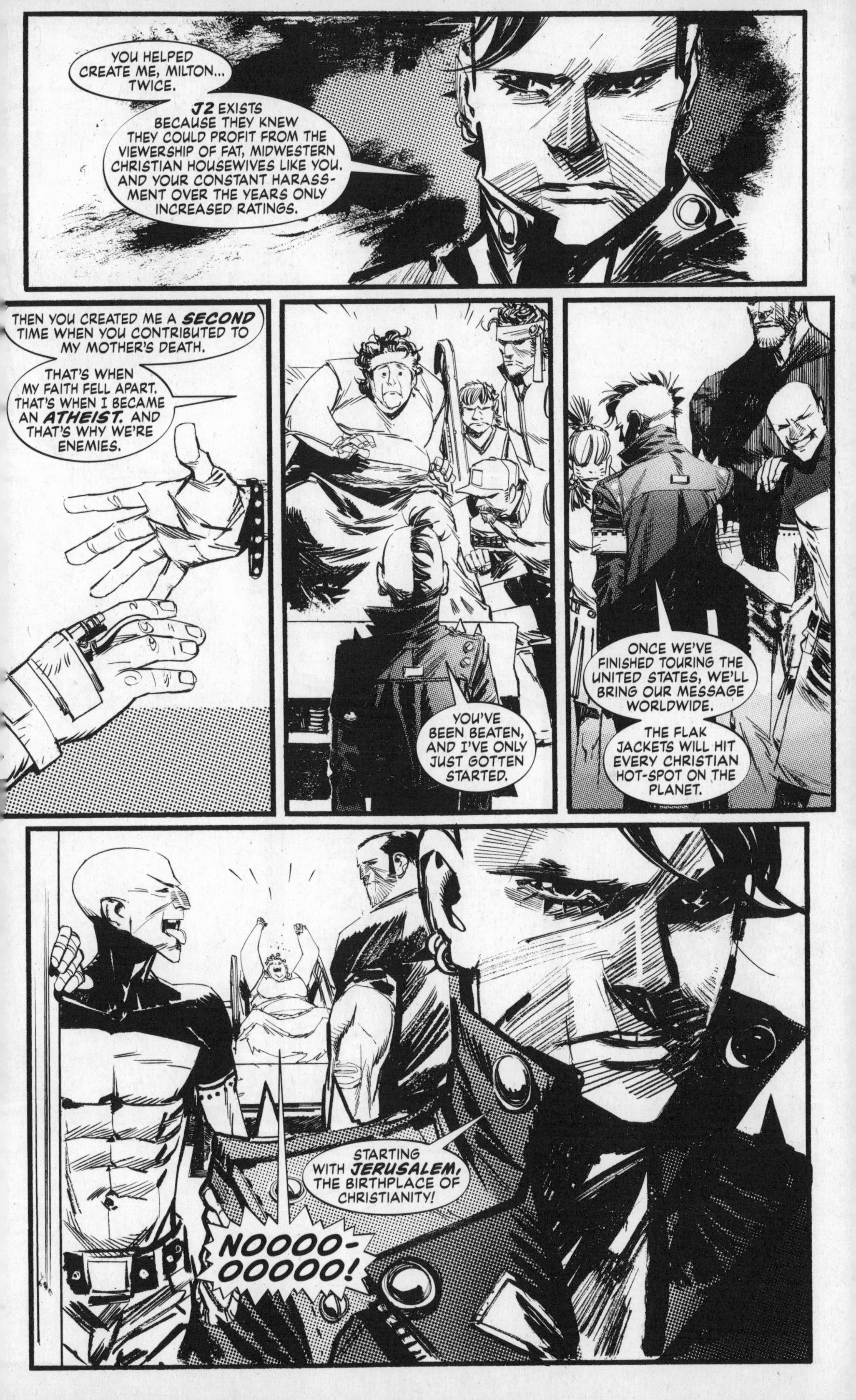
YOU HELPED CREATE ME, MILTON... TWICE.
J2 EXISTS BECAUSE THEY KNEW THEY COULD PROFIT FROM THE VIEWERSHIP OF FAT, MIDWESTERN CHRISTIAN HOUSEWIVES LIKE YOU. AND YOUR CONSTANT HARASS-MENT OVER THE YEARS ONLY INCREASED RATINGS.
THEN YOU CREATED ME A SECOND TIME WHEN YOU CONTRIBUTED TO MY MOTHER'S DEATH.
THAT'S WHEN MY FAITH FELL APART. THAT'S WHEN I BECAME AN ATHEIST. AND THAT'S WHY WE'RE ENEMIES.
YOU'VE BEEN BEATEN, AND I'VE ONLY JUST GOTTEN STARTED.
ONCE WE'VE FINISHED TOURING THE UNITED STATES, WE'LL BRING OUR MESSAGE WORLDWIDE.
THE FLAK JACKETS WILL HIT EVERY CHRISTIAN HOT-SPOT ON THE PLANET.
STARTING WITH JERUSALEM, THE BIRTHPLACE OF CHRISTIANITY!
NOOOO-OOOOO!

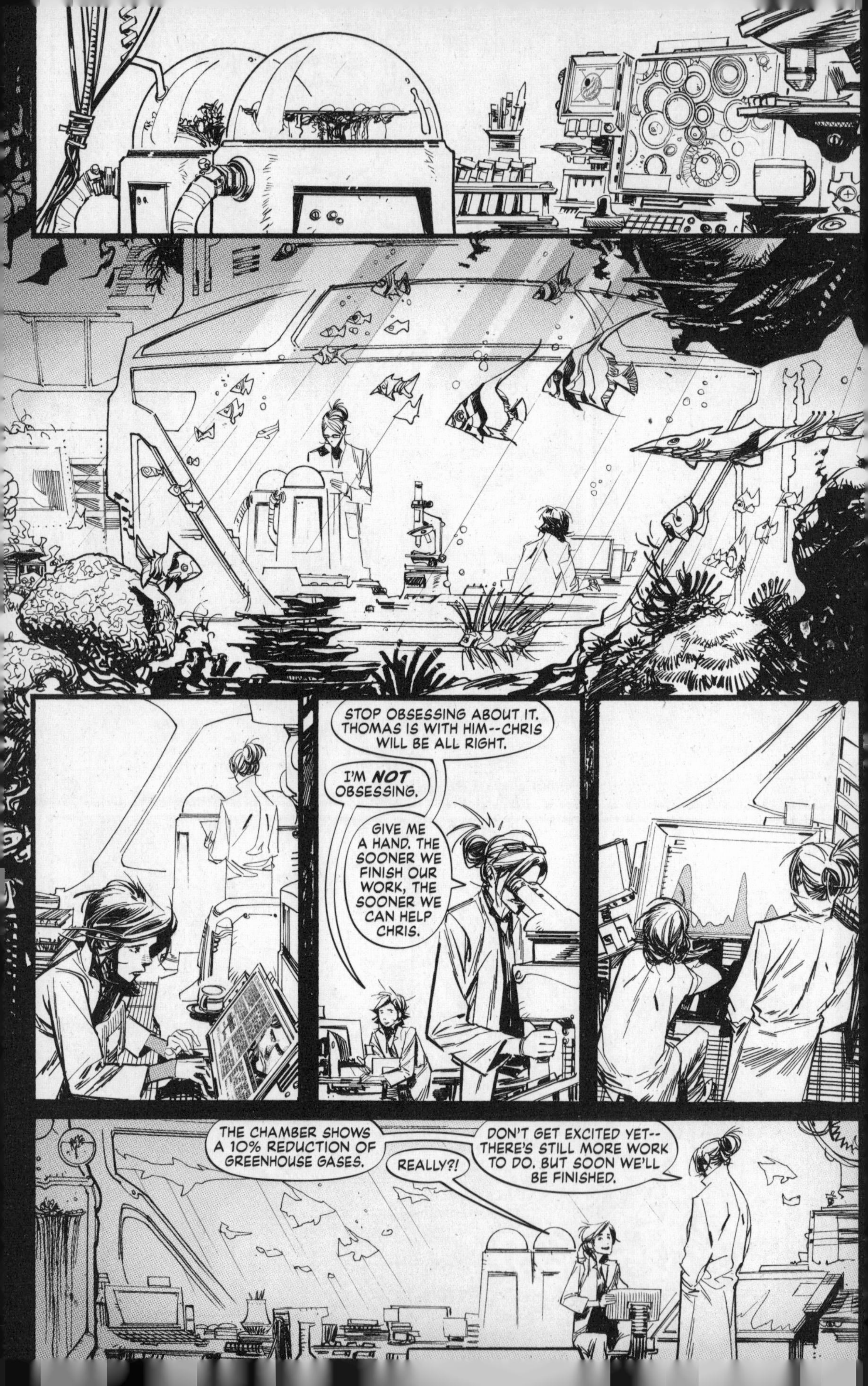
STOP OBSESSING ABOUT IT. THOMAS IS WITH HIM--CHRIS WILL BE ALL RIGHT.
I'M *NOT* OBSESSING.
GIVE ME A HAND. THE SOONER WE FINISH OUR WORK, THE SOONER WE CAN HELP CHRIS.
THE CHAMBER SHOWS A 10% REDUCTION OF GREENHOUSE GASES.
REALLY?!
DON'T GET EXCITED YET--THERE'S STILL MORE WORK TO DO. BUT SOON WE'LL BE FINISHED.

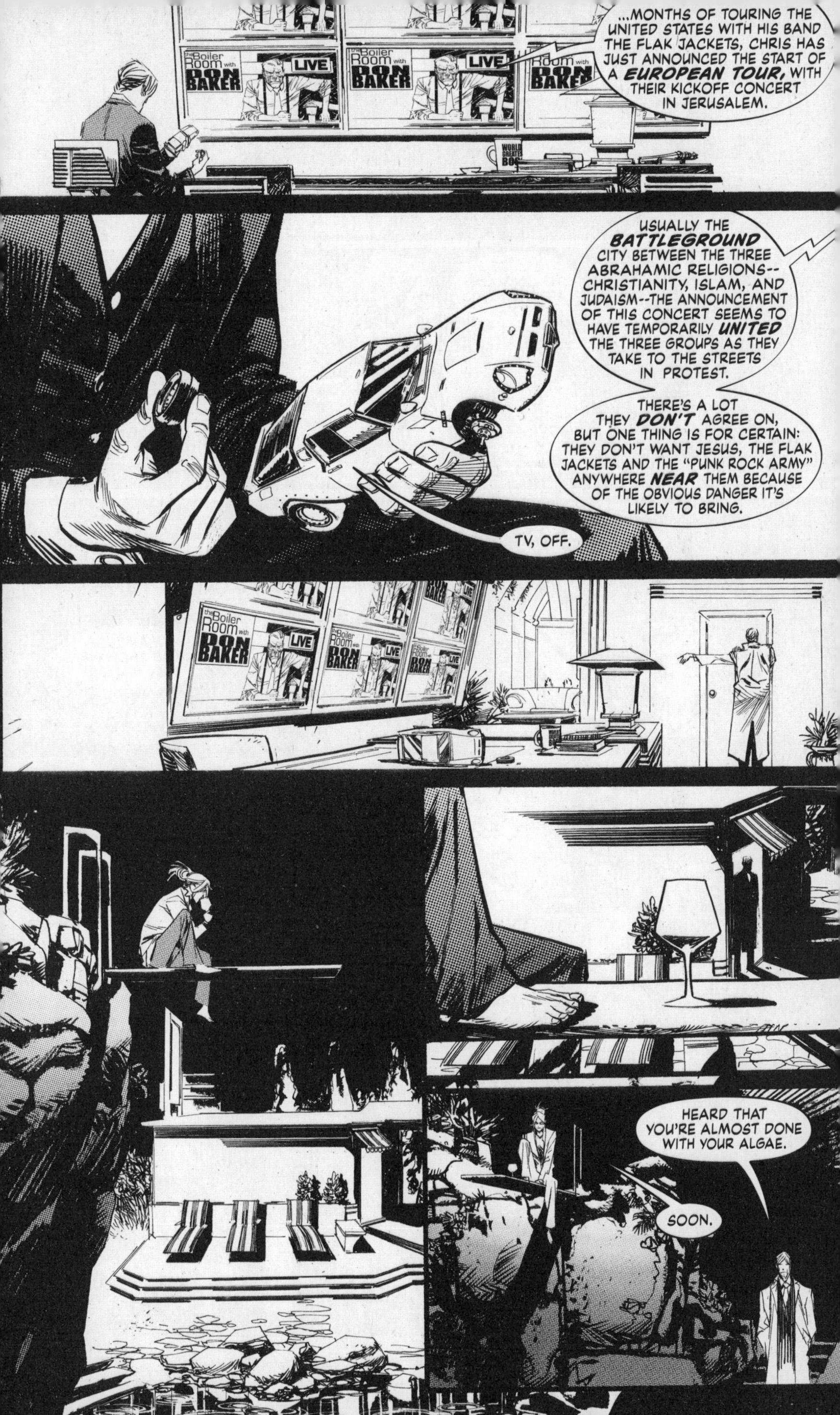

...MONTHS OF TOURING THE UNITED STATES WITH HIS BAND THE FLAK JACKETS, CHRIS HAS JUST ANNOUNCED THE START OF A EUROPEAN TOUR, WITH THEIR KICKOFF CONCERT IN JERUSALEM.
USUALLY THE BATTLEGROUND CITY BETWEEN THE THREE ABRAHAMIC RELIGIONS--CHRISTIANITY, ISLAM, AND JUDAISM--THE ANNOUNCEMENT OF THIS CONCERT SEEMS TO HAVE TEMPORARILY UNITED THE THREE GROUPS AS THEY TAKE TO THE STREETS IN PROTEST.
THERE'S A LOT THEY DON'T AGREE ON, BUT ONE THING IS FOR CERTAIN: THEY DON'T WANT JESUS, THE FLAK JACKETS AND THE "PUNK ROCK ARMY" ANYWHERE NEAR THEM BECAUSE OF THE OBVIOUS DANGER IT'S LIKELY TO BRING.
TV, OFF.
HEARD THAT YOU'RE ALMOST DONE WITH YOUR ALGAE.
SOON.

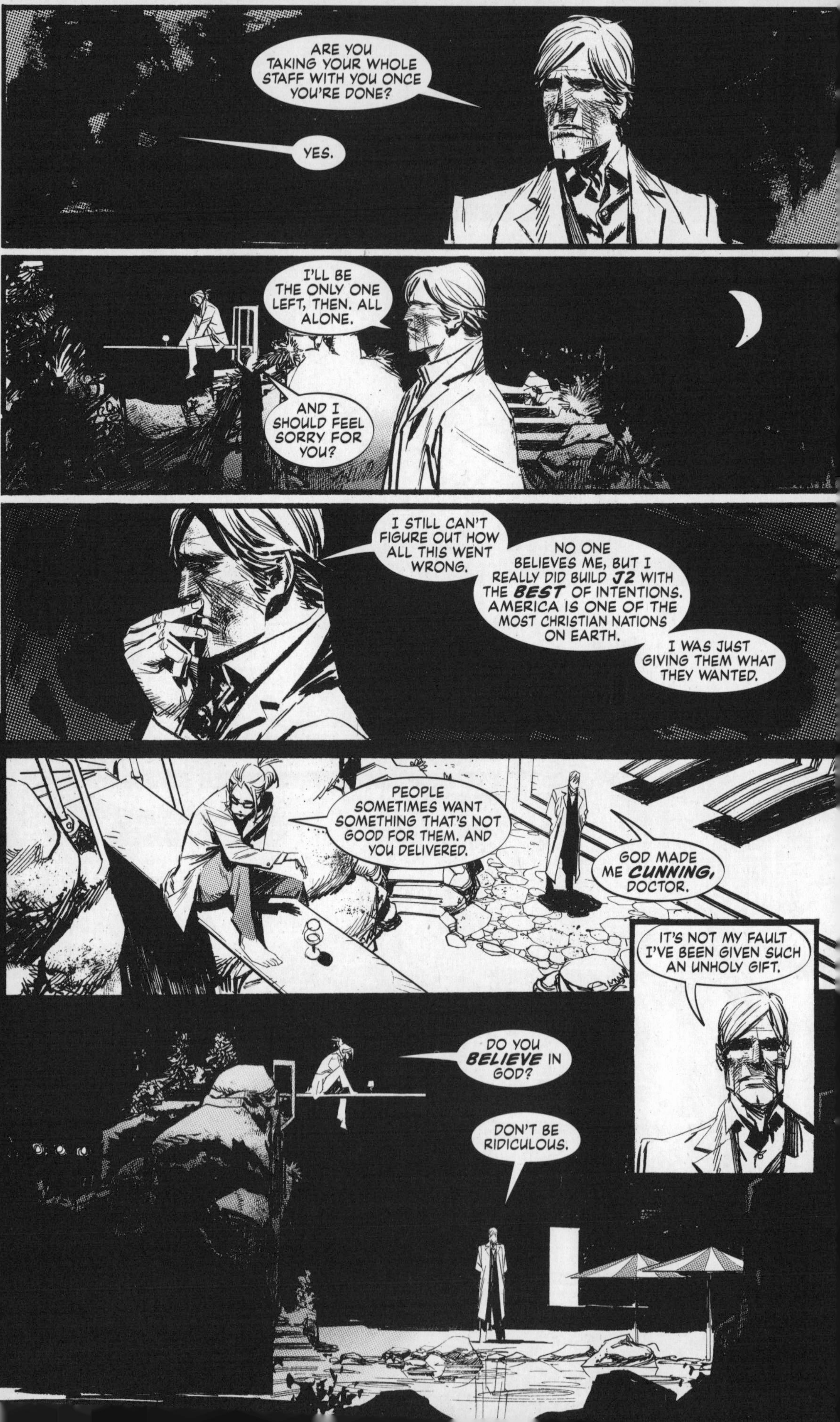
ARE YOU TAKING YOUR WHOLE STAFF WITH YOU ONCE YOU'RE DONE?
YES.
I'LL BE THE ONLY ONE LEFT, THEN. ALL ALONE.
AND I SHOULD FEEL SORRY FOR YOU?
I STILL CAN'T FIGURE OUT HOW ALL THIS WENT WRONG.
NO ONE BELIEVES ME, BUT I REALLY DID BUILD J2 WITH THE BEST OF INTENTIONS. AMERICA IS ONE OF THE MOST CHRISTIAN NATIONS ON EARTH.
I WAS JUST GIVING THEM WHAT THEY WANTED.
PEOPLE SOMETIMES WANT SOMETHING THAT'S NOT GOOD FOR THEM. AND YOU DELIVERED.
GOD MADE ME CUNNING, DOCTOR.
IT'S NOT MY FAULT I'VE BEEN GIVEN SUCH AN UNHOLY GIFT.
DO YOU BELIEVE IN GOD?
DON'T BE RIDICULOUS.

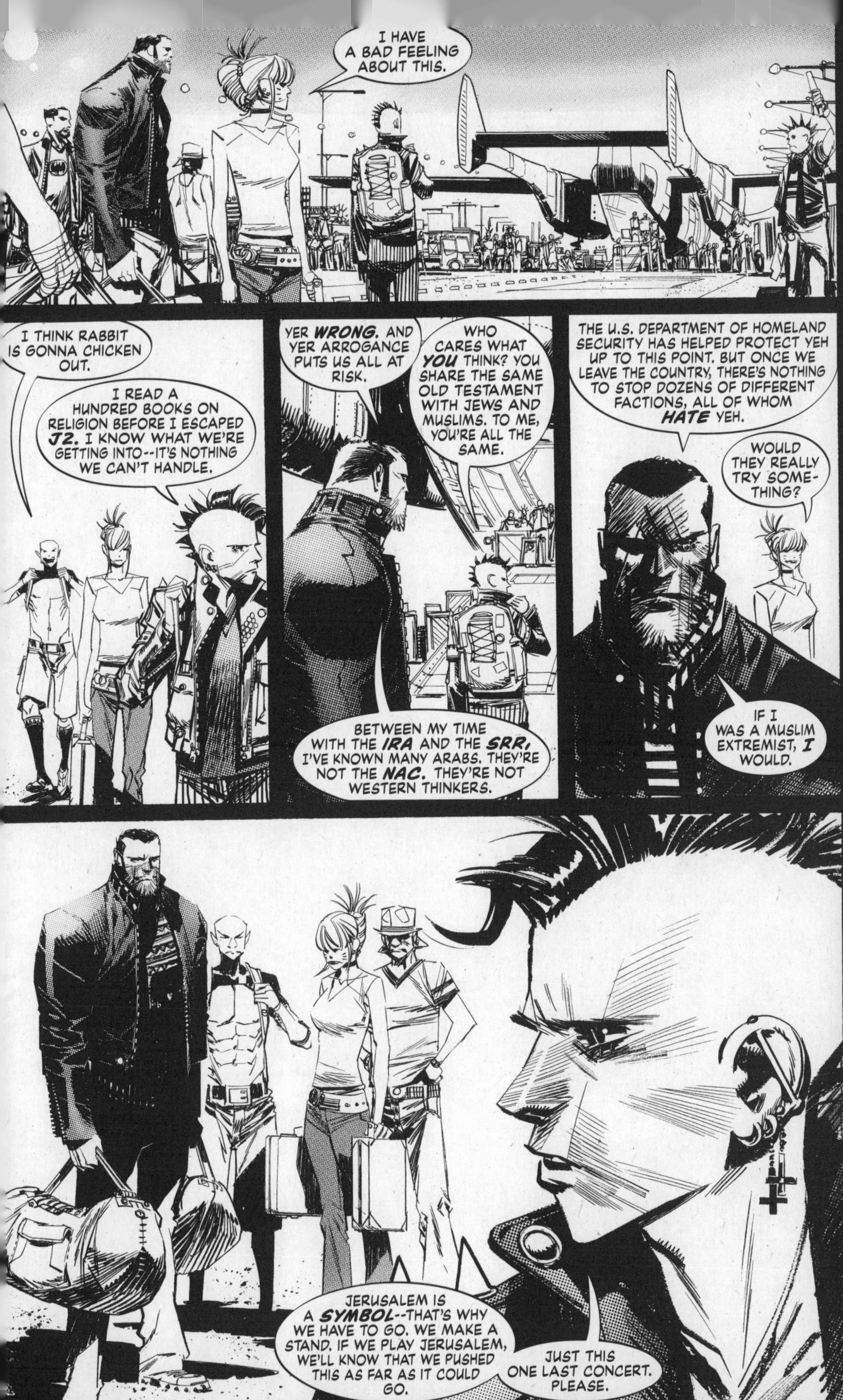
I HAVE A BAD FEELING ABOUT THIS.
I THINK RABBIT IS GONNA CHICKEN OUT.
I READ A HUNDRED BOOKS ON RELIGION BEFORE I ESCAPED J2. I KNOW WHAT WE'RE GETTING INTO--IT'S NOTHING WE CAN'T HANDLE.
YER WRONG. AND YER ARROGANCE PUTS US ALL AT RISK.
WHO CARES WHAT YOU THINK? YOU SHARE THE SAME OLD TESTAMENT WITH JEWS AND MUSLIMS. TO ME, YOU'RE ALL THE SAME.
BETWEEN MY TIME WITH THE IRA AND THE SRR, I'VE KNOWN MANY ARABS. THEY'RE NOT THE NAC. THEY'RE NOT WESTERN THINKERS.
THE U.S. DEPARTMENT OF HOMELAND SECURITY HAS HELPED PROTECT YEH UP TO THIS POINT. BUT ONCE WE LEAVE THE COUNTRY, THERE'S NOTHING TO STOP DOZENS OF DIFFERENT FACTIONS, ALL OF WHOM HATE YEH.
WOULD THEY REALLY TRY SOME-THING?
IF I WAS A MUSLIM EXTREMIST, I WOULD.
JERUSALEM IS A SYMBOL--THAT'S WHY WE HAVE TO GO. WE MAKE A STAND. IF WE PLAY JERUSALEM, WE'LL KNOW THAT WE PUSHED THIS AS FAR AS IT COULD GO.
JUST THIS ONE LAST CONCERT. PLEASE.

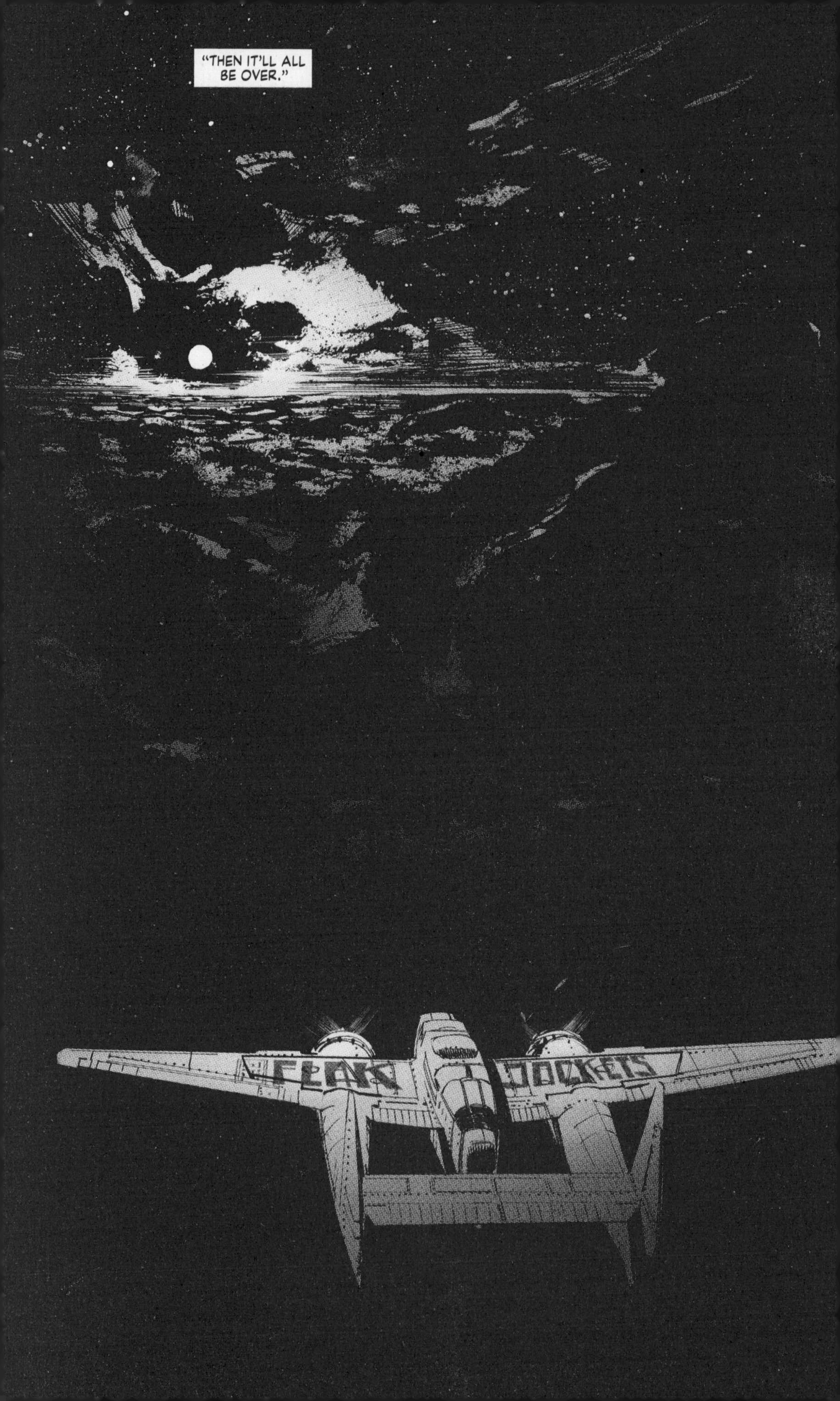
"THEN IT'LL ALL BE OVER."

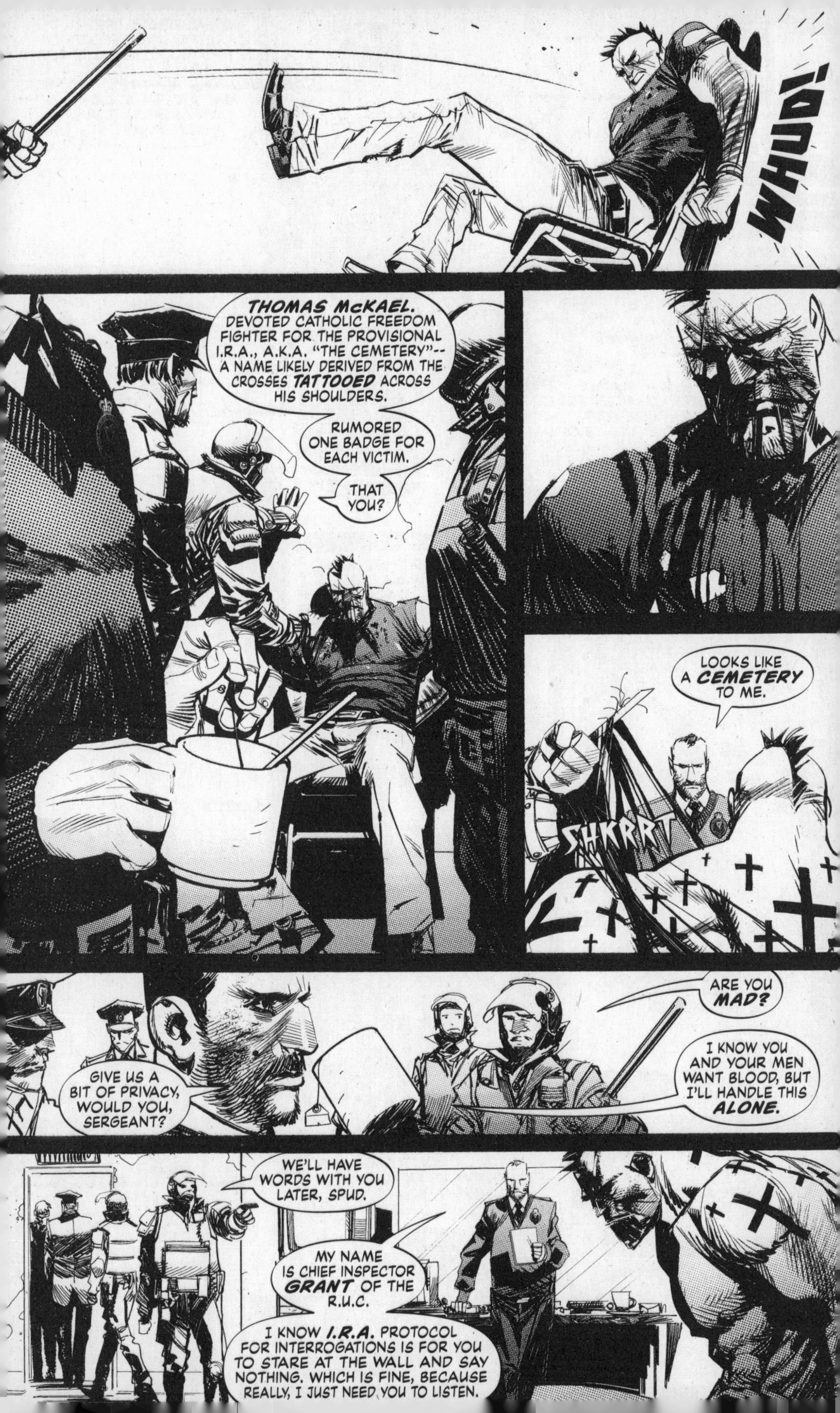
WHUD!
THOMAS McKAEL. DEVOTED CATHOLIC FREEDOM FIGHTER FOR THE PROVISIONAL I.R.A., A.K.A. "THE CEMETERY"-- A NAME LIKELY DERIVED FROM THE CROSSES TATTOOED ACROSS HIS SHOULDERS.
RUMORED ONE BADGE FOR EACH VICTIM.
THAT YOU?
LOOKS LIKE A CEMETERY TO ME.
SHKRRT
GIVE US A BIT OF PRIVACY, WOULD YOU, SERGEANT?
ARE YOU MAD?
I KNOW YOU AND YOUR MEN WANT BLOOD, BUT I'LL HANDLE THIS ALONE.
WE'LL HAVE WORDS WITH YOU LATER, SPUD.
MY NAME IS CHIEF INSPECTOR GRANT OF THE R.U.C.
I KNOW I.R.A. PROTOCOL FOR INTERROGATIONS IS FOR YOU TO STARE AT THE WALL AND SAY NOTHING. WHICH IS FINE, BECAUSE REALLY, I JUST NEED YOU TO LISTEN.

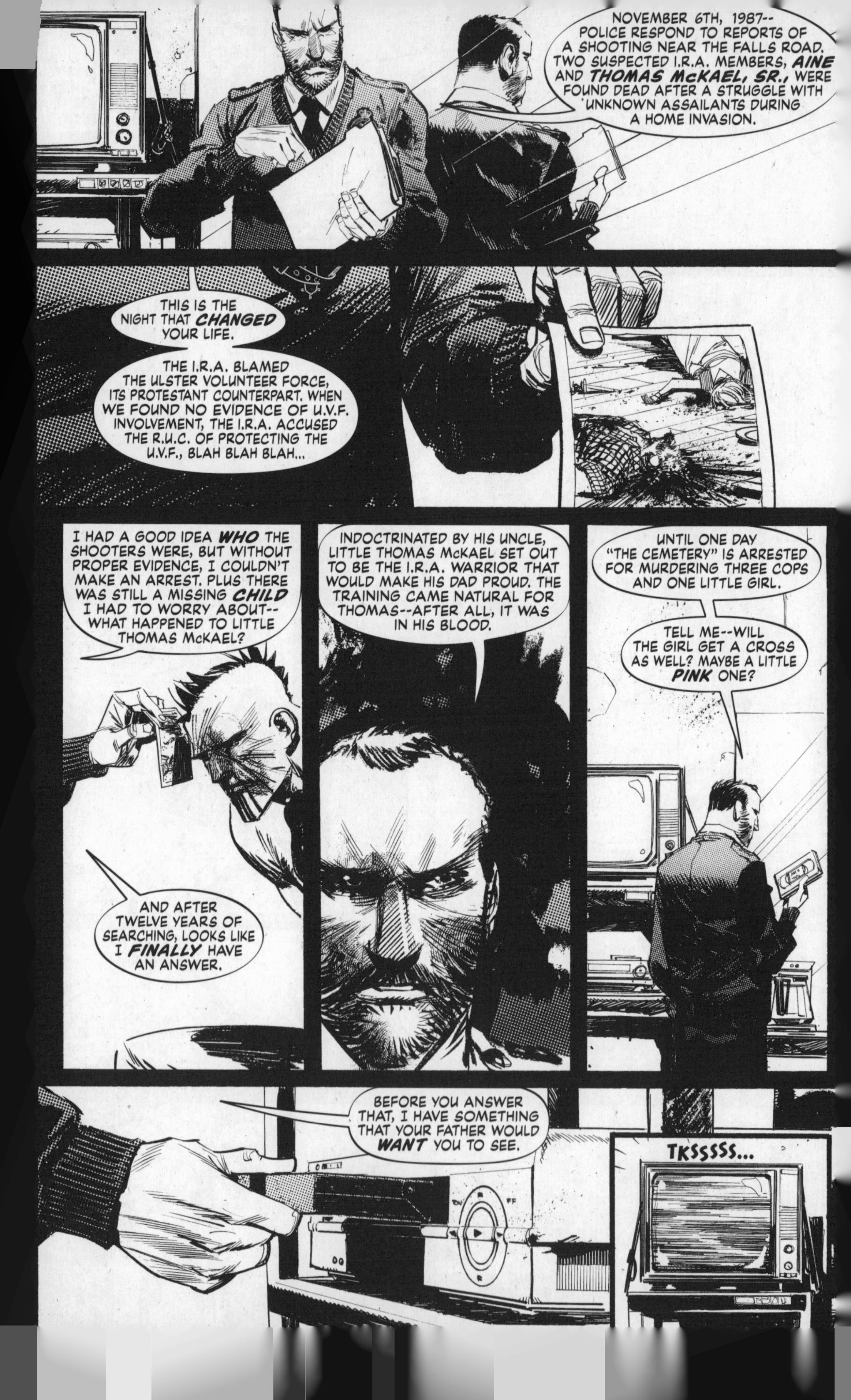
NOVEMBER 6TH, 1987-- POLICE RESPOND TO REPORTS OF A SHOOTING NEAR THE FALLS ROAD. TWO SUSPECTED I.R.A. MEMBERS, AINE AND THOMAS McKAEL, SR., WERE FOUND DEAD AFTER A STRUGGLE WITH UNKNOWN ASSAILANTS DURING A HOME INVASION.
THIS IS THE NIGHT THAT CHANGED YOUR LIFE.
THE I.R.A. BLAMED THE ULSTER VOLUNTEER FORCE, ITS PROTESTANT COUNTERPART. WHEN WE FOUND NO EVIDENCE OF U.V.F. INVOLVEMENT, THE I.R.A. ACCUSED THE R.U.C. OF PROTECTING THE U.V.F., BLAH BLAH BLAH...
I HAD A GOOD IDEA WHO THE SHOOTERS WERE, BUT WITHOUT PROPER EVIDENCE, I COULDN'T MAKE AN ARREST. PLUS THERE WAS STILL A MISSING CHILD I HAD TO WORRY ABOUT-- WHAT HAPPENED TO LITTLE THOMAS McKAEL?
AND AFTER TWELVE YEARS OF SEARCHING, LOOKS LIKE I FINALLY HAVE AN ANSWER.
INDOCTRINATED BY HIS UNCLE, LITTLE THOMAS McKAEL SET OUT TO BE THE I.R.A. WARRIOR THAT WOULD MAKE HIS DAD PROUD. THE TRAINING CAME NATURAL FOR THOMAS--AFTER ALL, IT WAS IN HIS BLOOD.
UNTIL ONE DAY "THE CEMETERY" IS ARRESTED FOR MURDERING THREE COPS AND ONE LITTLE GIRL.
TELL ME--WILL THE GIRL GET A CROSS AS WELL? MAYBE A LITTLE PINK ONE?
BEFORE YOU ANSWER THAT, I HAVE SOMETHING THAT YOUR FATHER WOULD WANT YOU TO SEE.
TKSSSSS...

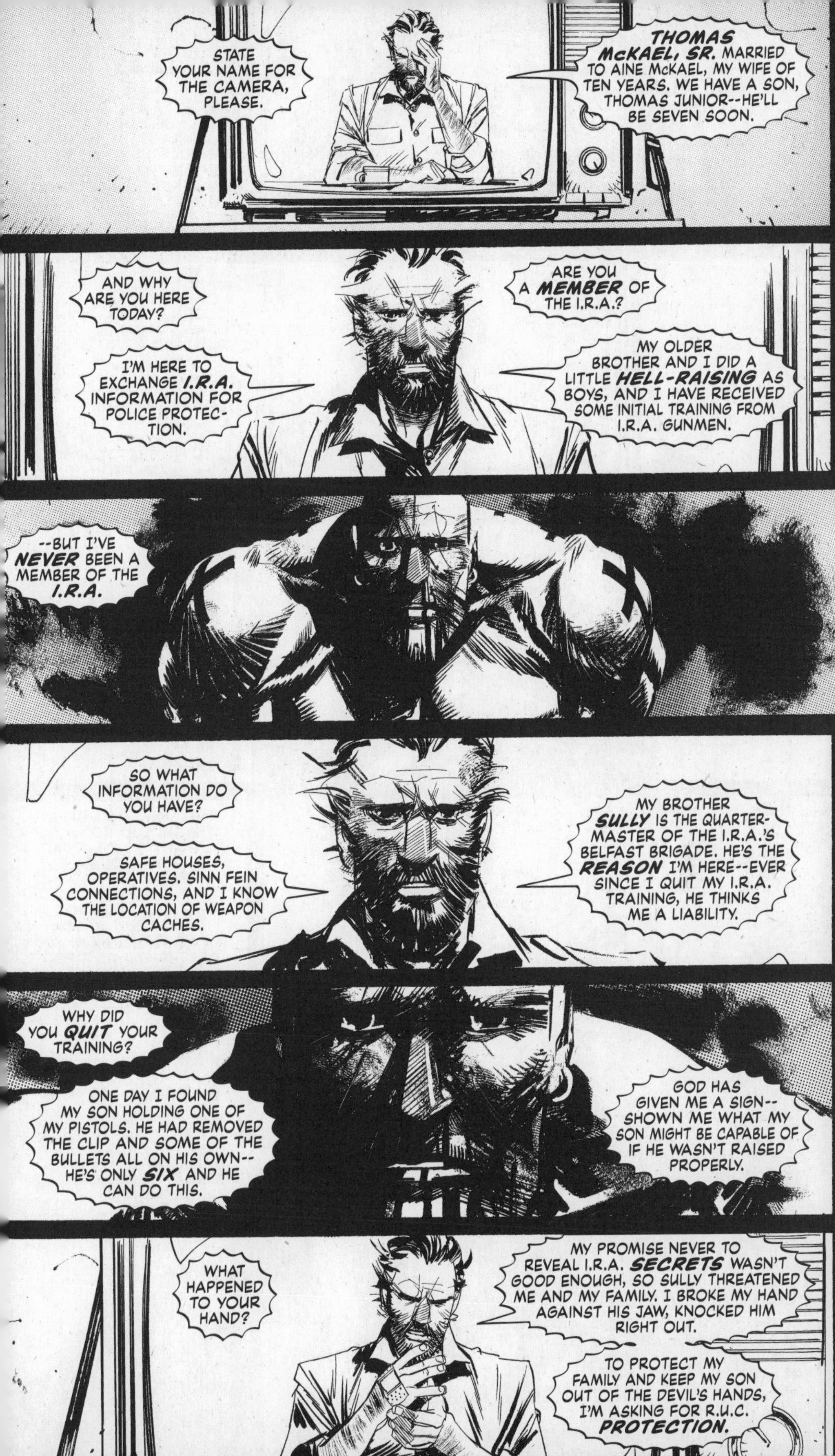
STATE YOUR NAME FOR THE CAMERA, PLEASE.
THOMAS McKAEL, SR. MARRIED TO AINE McKAEL, MY WIFE OF TEN YEARS. WE HAVE A SON, THOMAS JUNIOR--HE'LL BE SEVEN SOON.
AND WHY ARE YOU HERE TODAY?
I'M HERE TO EXCHANGE I.R.A. INFORMATION FOR POLICE PROTECTION.
ARE YOU A MEMBER OF THE I.R.A.?
MY OLDER BROTHER AND I DID A LITTLE HELL-RAISING AS BOYS, AND I HAVE RECEIVED SOME INITIAL TRAINING FROM I.R.A. GUNMEN.
--BUT I'VE NEVER BEEN A MEMBER OF THE I.R.A.
SO WHAT INFORMATION DO YOU HAVE?
SAFE HOUSES, OPERATIVES. SINN FEIN CONNECTIONS, AND I KNOW THE LOCATION OF WEAPON CACHES.
MY BROTHER SULLY IS THE QUARTER-MASTER OF THE I.R.A.'S BELFAST BRIGADE. HE'S THE REASON I'M HERE--EVER SINCE I QUIT MY I.R.A. TRAINING, HE THINKS ME A LIABILITY.
WHY DID YOU QUIT YOUR TRAINING?
ONE DAY I FOUND MY SON HOLDING ONE OF MY PISTOLS. HE HAD REMOVED THE CLIP AND SOME OF THE BULLETS ALL ON HIS OWN--HE'S ONLY SIX AND HE CAN DO THIS.
GOD HAS GIVEN ME A SIGN--SHOWN ME WHAT MY SON MIGHT BE CAPABLE OF IF HE WASN'T RAISED PROPERLY.
WHAT HAPPENED TO YOUR HAND?
MY PROMISE NEVER TO REVEAL I.R.A. SECRETS WASN'T GOOD ENOUGH, SO SULLY THREATENED ME AND MY FAMILY. I BROKE MY HAND AGAINST HIS JAW, KNOCKED HIM RIGHT OUT.
TO PROTECT MY FAMILY AND KEEP MY SON OUT OF THE DEVIL'S HANDS, I'M ASKING FOR R.U.C. PROTECTION.

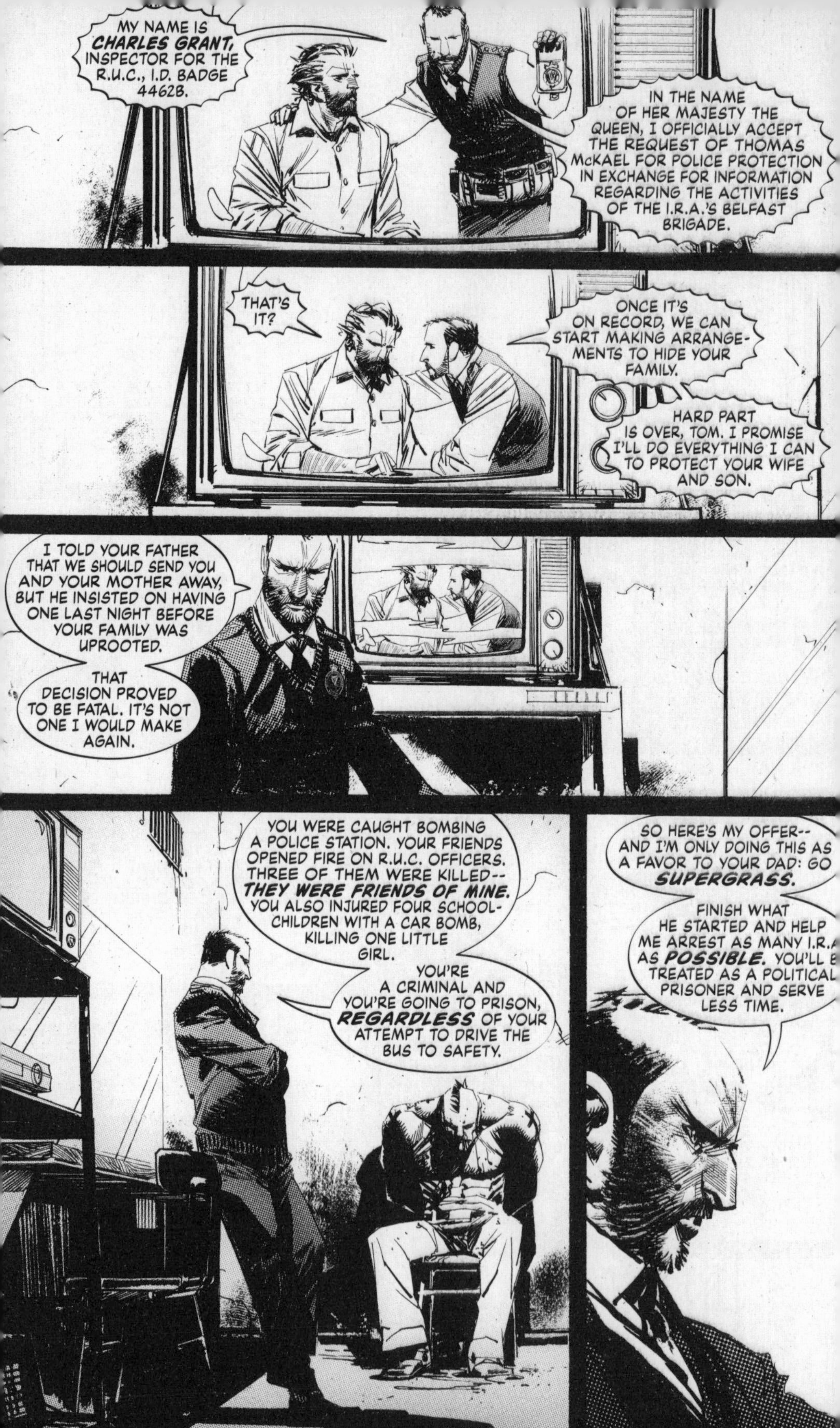
MY NAME IS **CHARLES GRANT,** INSPECTOR FOR THE R.U.C., I.D. BADGE 44628.
IN THE NAME OF HER MAJESTY THE QUEEN, I OFFICIALLY ACCEPT THE REQUEST OF THOMAS McKAEL FOR POLICE PROTECTION IN EXCHANGE FOR INFORMATION REGARDING THE ACTIVITIES OF THE I.R.A.'S BELFAST BRIGADE.
THAT'S IT?
ONCE IT'S ON RECORD, WE CAN START MAKING ARRANGE-MENTS TO HIDE YOUR FAMILY.
HARD PART IS OVER, TOM. I PROMISE I'LL DO EVERYTHING I CAN TO PROTECT YOUR WIFE AND SON.
I TOLD YOUR FATHER THAT WE SHOULD SEND YOU AND YOUR MOTHER AWAY, BUT HE INSISTED ON HAVING ONE LAST NIGHT BEFORE YOUR FAMILY WAS UPROOTED.
THAT DECISION PROVED TO BE FATAL. IT'S NOT ONE I WOULD MAKE AGAIN.
YOU WERE CAUGHT BOMBING A POLICE STATION. YOUR FRIENDS OPENED FIRE ON R.U.C. OFFICERS. THREE OF THEM WERE KILLED-- ***THEY WERE FRIENDS OF MINE.*** YOU ALSO INJURED FOUR SCHOOL-CHILDREN WITH A CAR BOMB, KILLING ONE LITTLE GIRL.
YOU'RE A CRIMINAL AND YOU'RE GOING TO PRISON, ***REGARDLESS*** OF YOUR ATTEMPT TO DRIVE THE BUS TO SAFETY.
SO HERE'S MY OFFER-- AND I'M ONLY DOING THIS AS A FAVOR TO YOUR DAD: GO ***SUPERGRASS.***
FINISH WHAT HE STARTED AND HELP ME ARREST AS MANY I.R.A. AS ***POSSIBLE.*** YOU'LL BE TREATED AS A POLITICAL PRISONER AND SERVE LESS TIME.

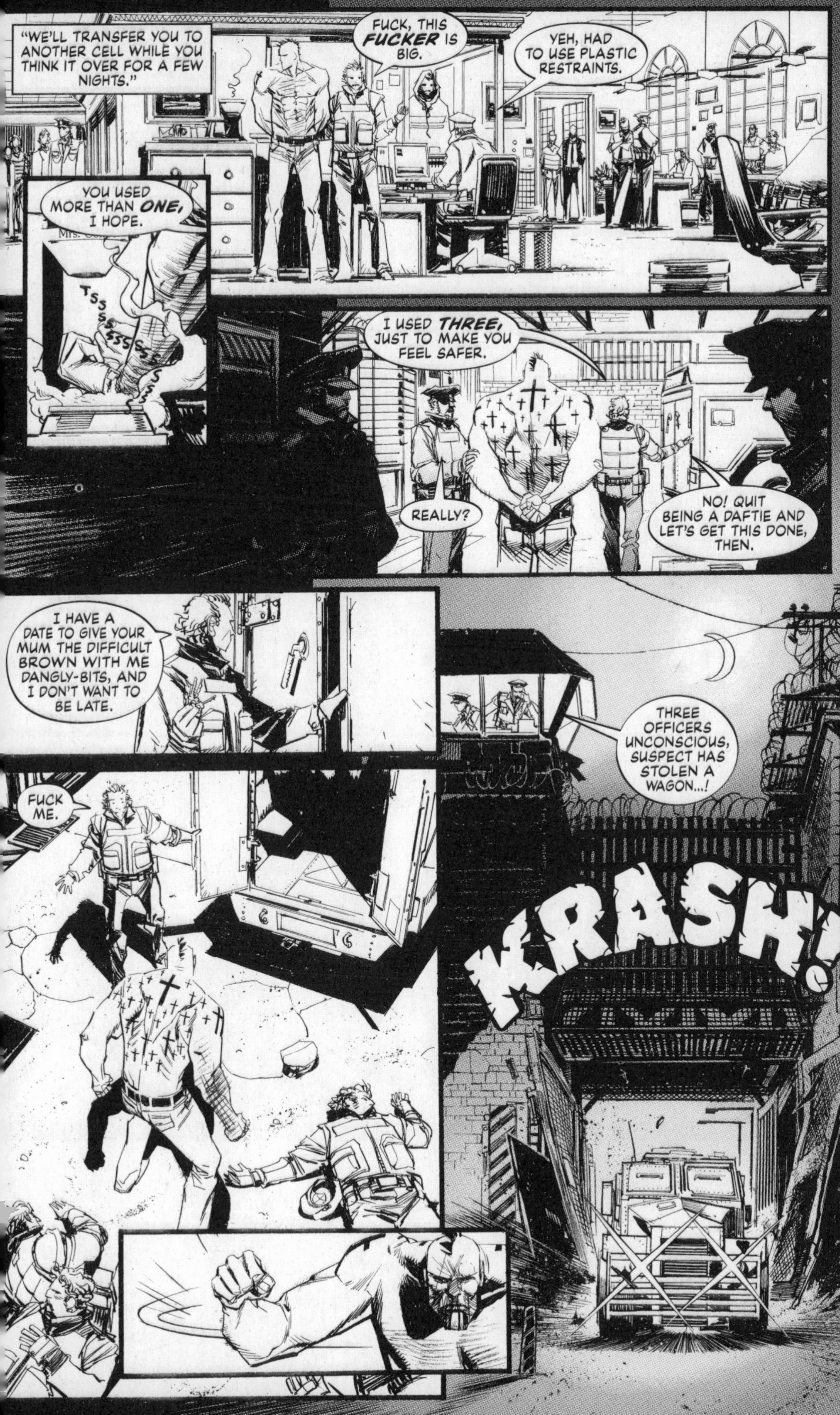
"WE'LL TRANSFER YOU TO ANOTHER CELL WHILE YOU THINK IT OVER FOR A FEW NIGHTS."
FUCK, THIS FUCKER IS BIG.
YEH, HAD TO USE PLASTIC RESTRAINTS.
YOU USED MORE THAN ONE, I HOPE.
TSSSSSSSSS
I USED THREE, JUST TO MAKE YOU FEEL SAFER.
REALLY?
NO! QUIT BEING A DAFTIE AND LET'S GET THIS DONE, THEN.
I HAVE A DATE TO GIVE YOUR MUM THE DIFFICULT BROWN WITH ME DANGLY-BITS, AND I DON'T WANT TO BE LATE.
FUCK ME.
THREE OFFICERS UNCONSCIOUS, SUSPECT HAS STOLEN A WAGON...!
KRASH!

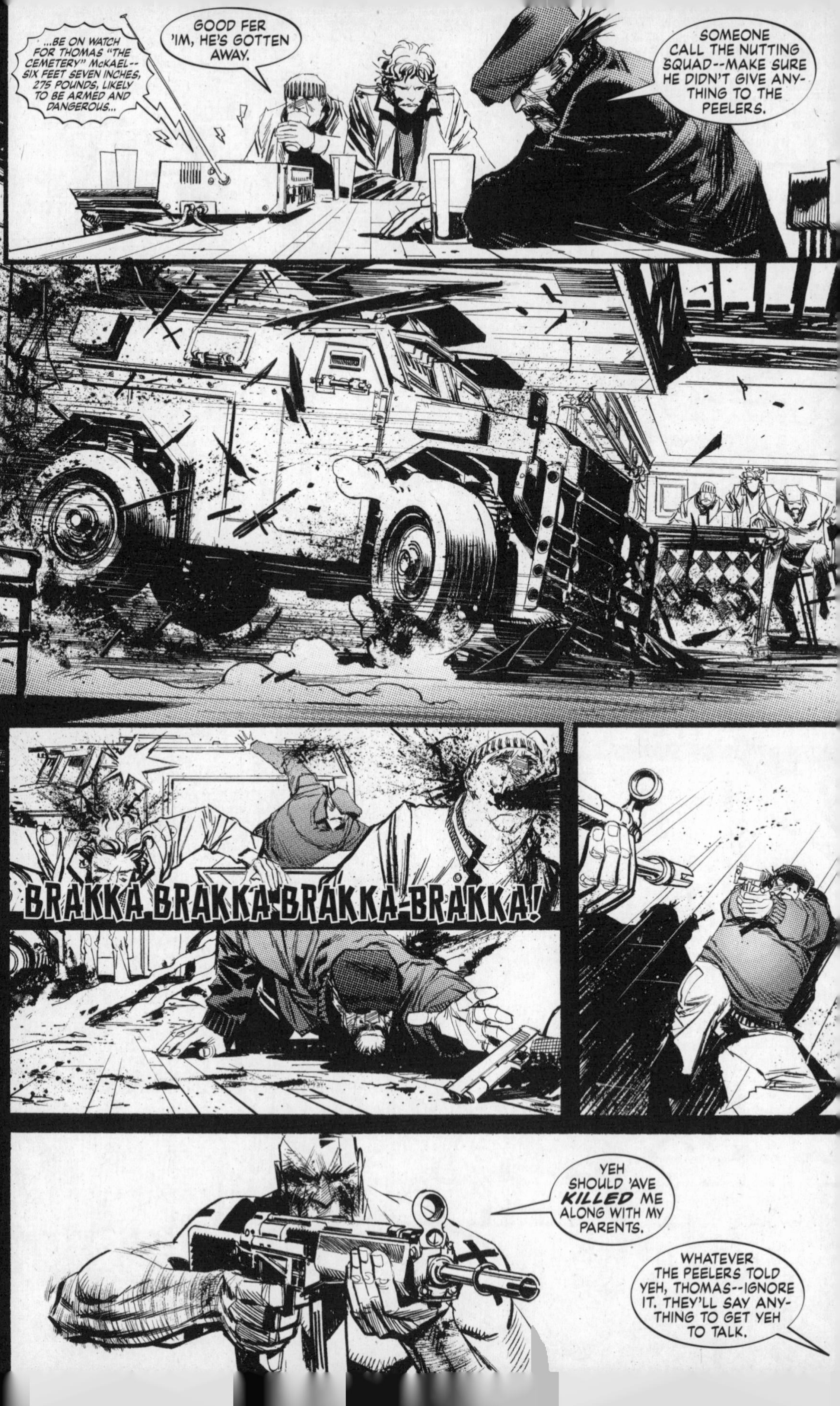
...BE ON WATCH FOR THOMAS "THE CEMETERY" McKAEL--SIX FEET SEVEN INCHES, 275 POUNDS, LIKELY TO BE ARMED AND DANGEROUS...
GOOD FER 'IM, HE'S GOTTEN AWAY.
SOMEONE CALL THE NUTTING SQUAD--MAKE SURE HE DIDN'T GIVE ANYTHING TO THE PEELERS.
BRAKKA BRAKKA BRAKKA-BRAKKA!
YEH SHOULD 'AVE KILLED ME ALONG WITH MY PARENTS.
WHATEVER THE PEELERS TOLD YEH, THOMAS--IGNORE IT. THEY'LL SAY ANYTHING TO GET YEH TO TALK.

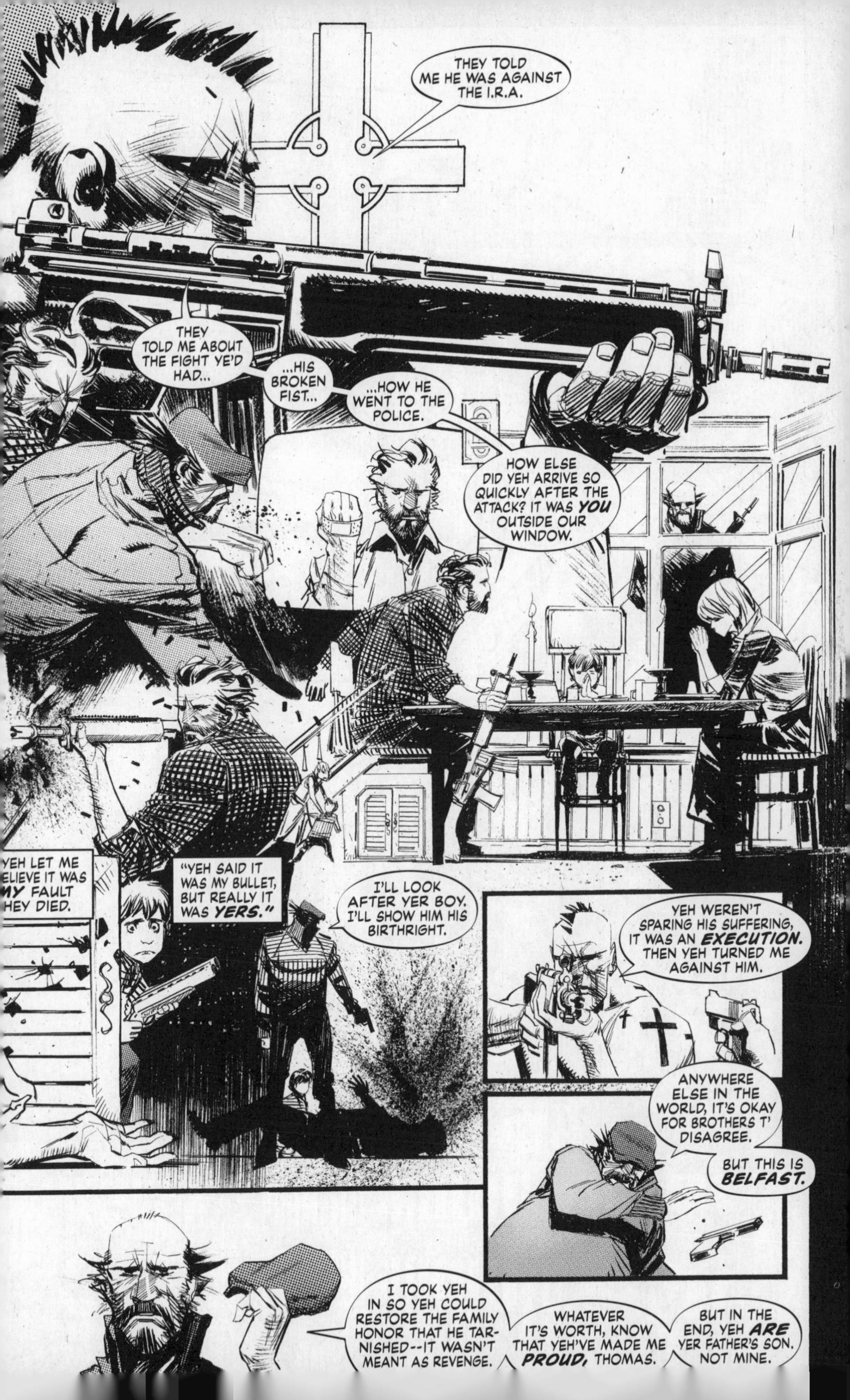
THEY TOLD ME HE WAS AGAINST THE I.R.A.
THEY TOLD ME ABOUT THE FIGHT YE'D HAD...
...HIS BROKEN FIST...
...HOW HE WENT TO THE POLICE.
HOW ELSE DID YEH ARRIVE SO QUICKLY AFTER THE ATTACK? IT WAS YOU OUTSIDE OUR WINDOW.
YEH LET ME ELIEVE IT WAS MY FAULT HEY DIED.
"YEH SAID IT WAS MY BULLET, BUT REALLY IT WAS YERS."
I'LL LOOK AFTER YER BOY. I'LL SHOW HIM HIS BIRTHRIGHT.
YEH WEREN'T SPARING HIS SUFFERING, IT WAS AN EXECUTION. THEN YEH TURNED ME AGAINST HIM.
ANYWHERE ELSE IN THE WORLD, IT'S OKAY FOR BROTHERS T' DISAGREE.
BUT THIS IS BELFAST.
I TOOK YEH IN SO YEH COULD RESTORE THE FAMILY HONOR THAT HE TARNISHED--IT WASN'T MEANT AS REVENGE.
WHATEVER IT'S WORTH, KNOW THAT YEH'VE MADE ME PROUD, THOMAS.
BUT IN THE END, YEH ARE YER FATHER'S SON. NOT MINE.

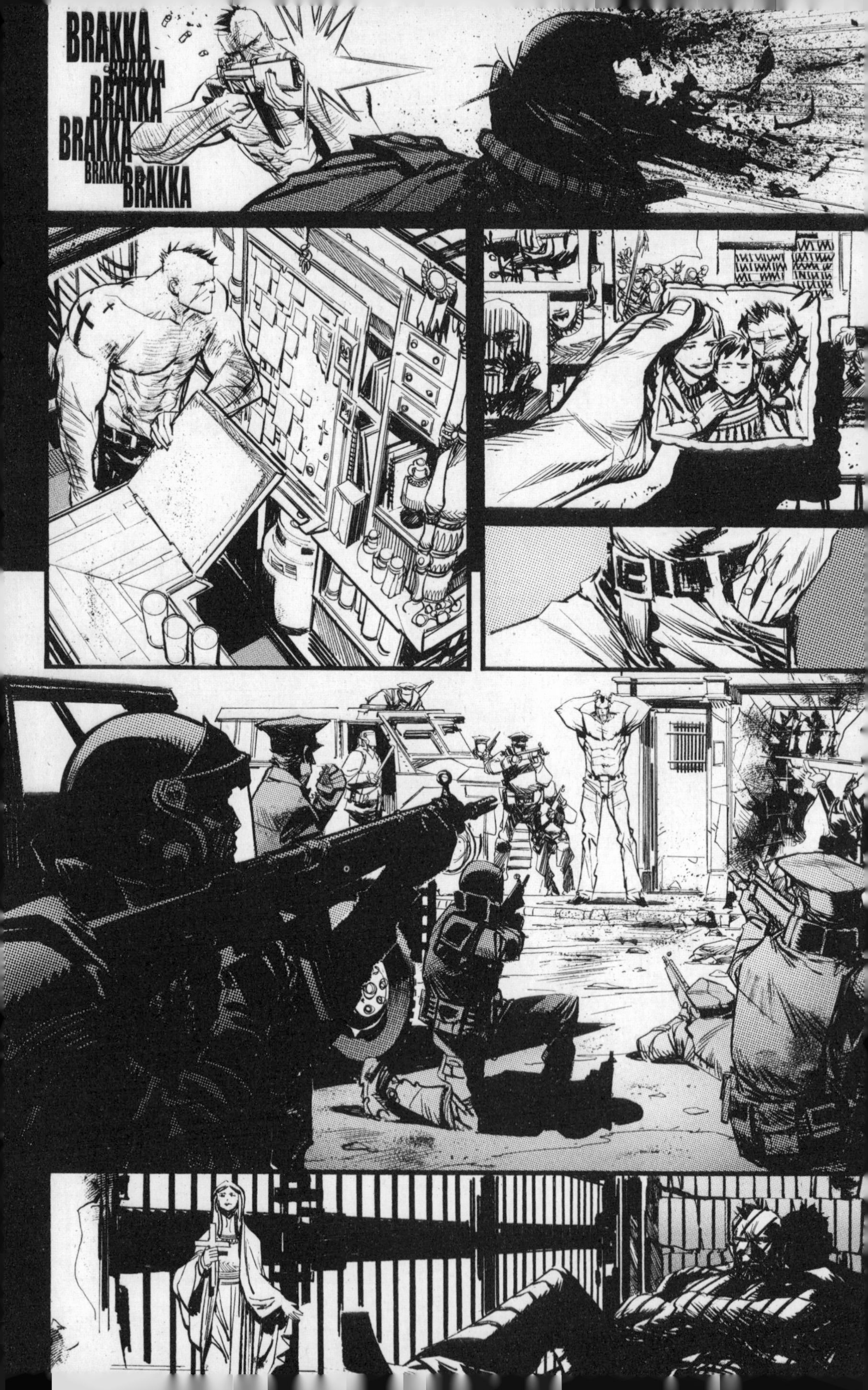
BRAKKA
BRAKKA
BRAKKA
BRAKKA
BRAKKA
BRAKKA

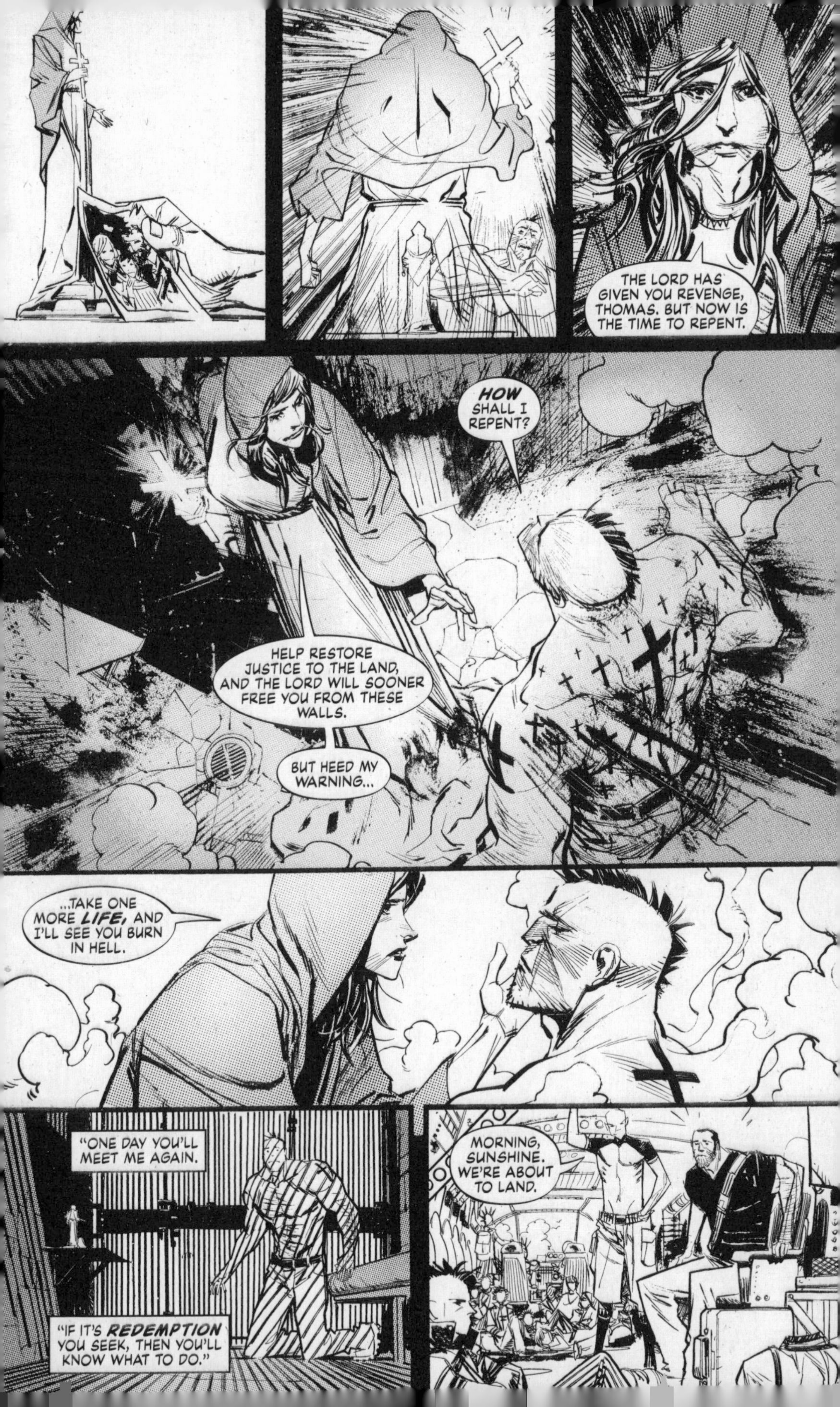
THE LORD HAS GIVEN YOU REVENGE, THOMAS. BUT NOW IS THE TIME TO REPENT.
HOW SHALL I REPENT?
HELP RESTORE JUSTICE TO THE LAND, AND THE LORD WILL SOONER FREE YOU FROM THESE WALLS.
BUT HEED MY WARNING...
...TAKE ONE MORE LIFE, AND I'LL SEE YOU BURN IN HELL.
"ONE DAY YOU'LL MEET ME AGAIN.
"IF IT'S REDEMPTION YOU SEEK, THEN YOU'LL KNOW WHAT TO DO."
MORNING, SUNSHINE. WE'RE ABOUT TO LAND.

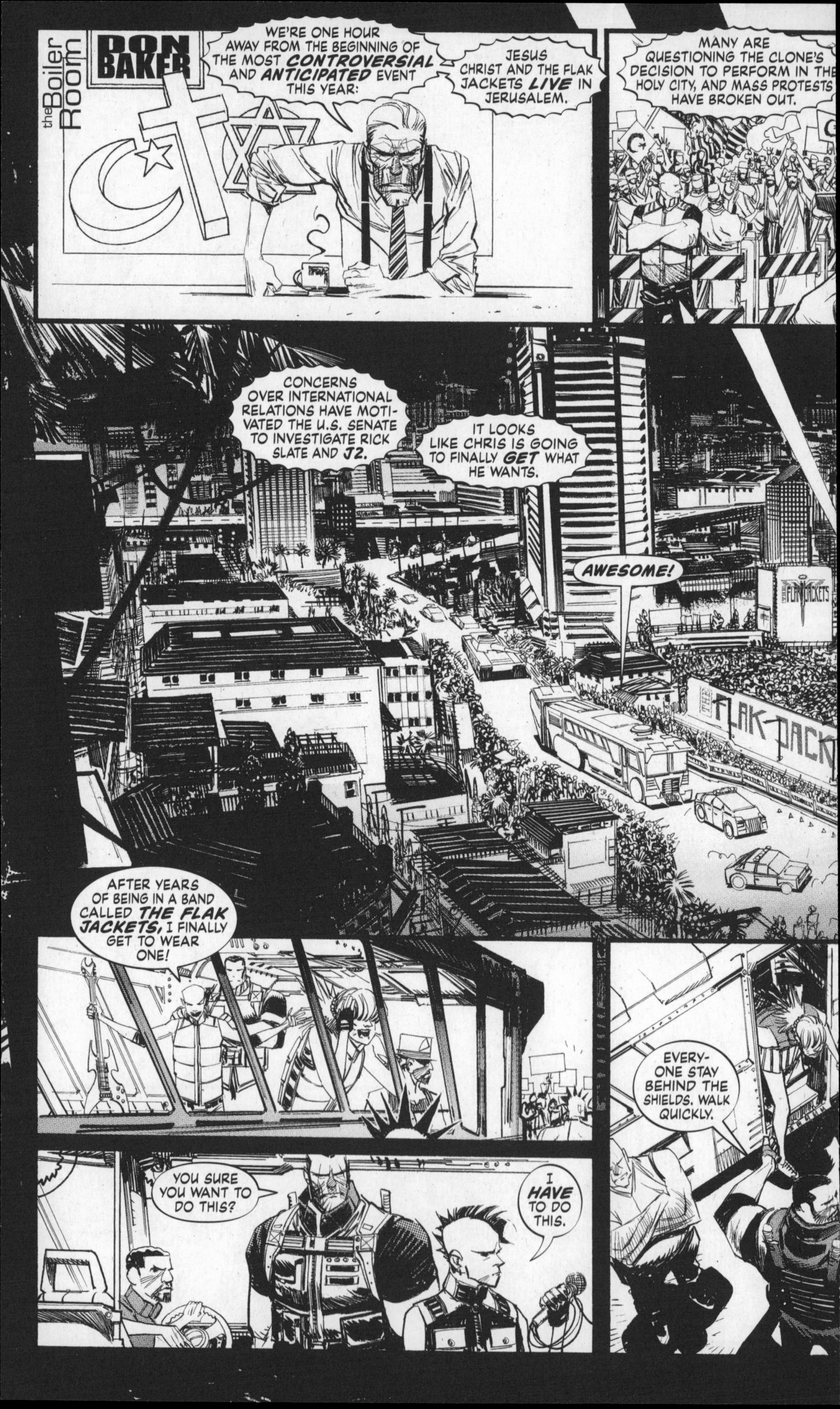

the Boiler Room
DON BAKER
WE'RE ONE HOUR AWAY FROM THE BEGINNING OF THE MOST *CONTROVERSIAL* AND *ANTICIPATED* EVENT THIS YEAR:
JESUS CHRIST AND THE FLAK JACKETS *LIVE* IN JERUSALEM.
MANY ARE QUESTIONING THE CLONE'S DECISION TO PERFORM IN THE HOLY CITY, AND MASS PROTESTS HAVE BROKEN OUT.
CONCERNS OVER INTERNATIONAL RELATIONS HAVE MOTIVATED THE U.S. SENATE TO INVESTIGATE RICK SLATE AND *J2*.
IT LOOKS LIKE CHRIS IS GOING TO FINALLY *GET* WHAT HE WANTS.
AWESOME!
AFTER YEARS OF BEING IN A BAND CALLED *THE FLAK JACKETS*, I FINALLY GET TO WEAR ONE!
EVERY-ONE STAY BEHIND THE SHIELDS. WALK QUICKLY.
YOU SURE YOU WANT TO DO THIS?
I *HAVE* TO DO THIS.

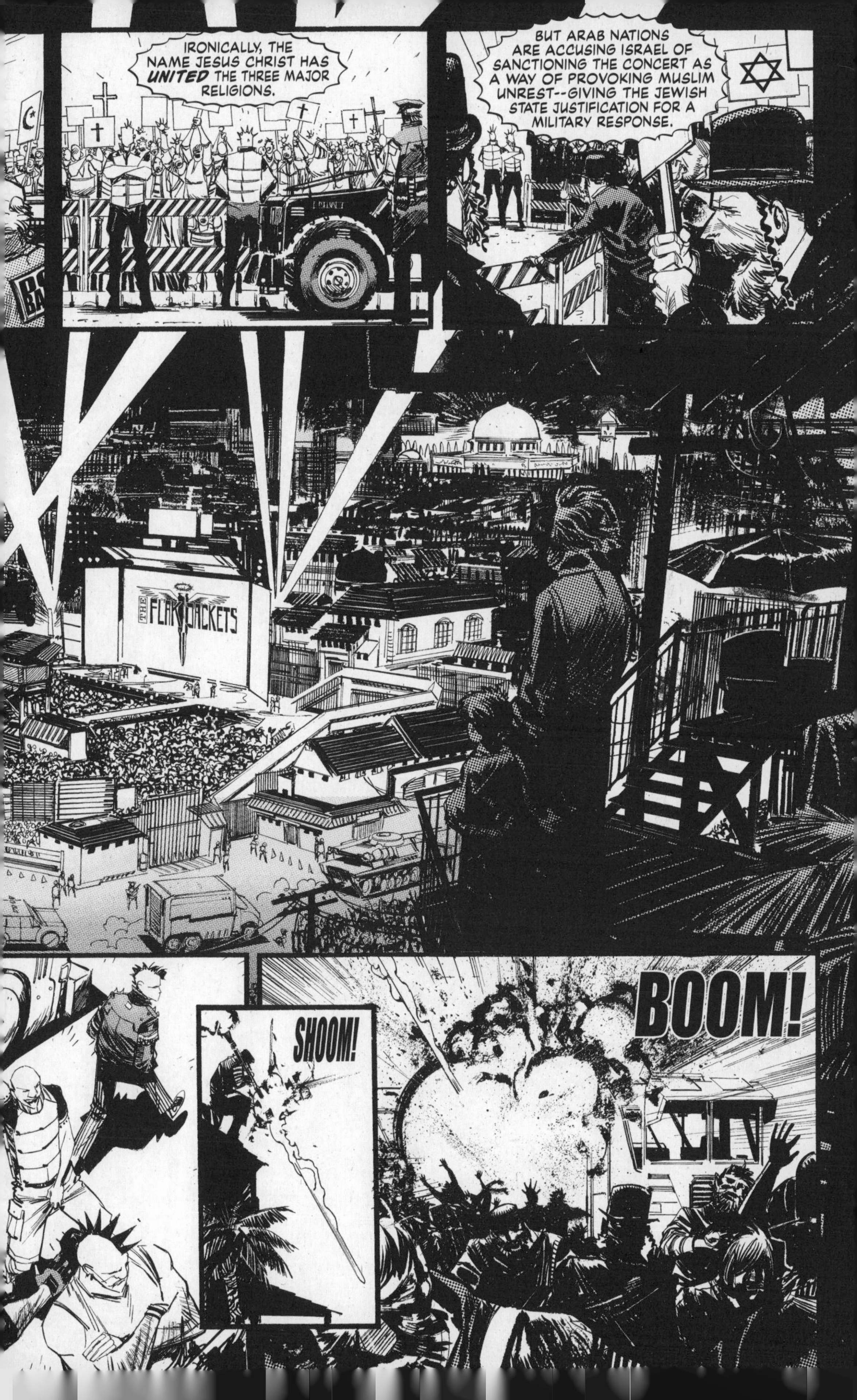
IRONICALLY, THE NAME JESUS CHRIST HAS *UNITED* THE THREE MAJOR RELIGIONS.
BUT ARAB NATIONS ARE ACCUSING ISRAEL OF SANCTIONING THE CONCERT AS A WAY OF PROVOKING MUSLIM UNREST--GIVING THE JEWISH STATE JUSTIFICATION FOR A MILITARY RESPONSE.
THE FLAK JACKETS
SHOOM!
BOOM!

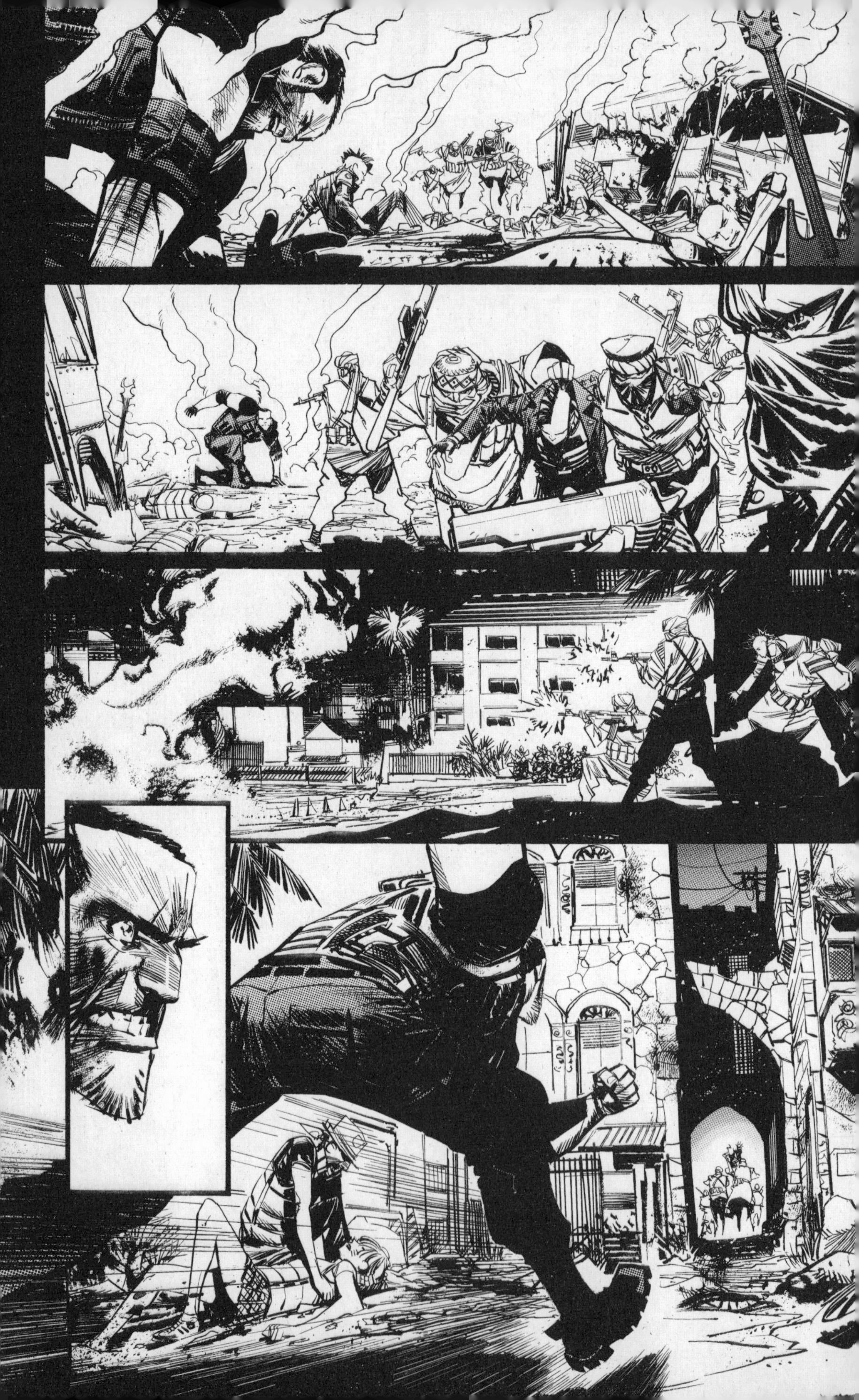

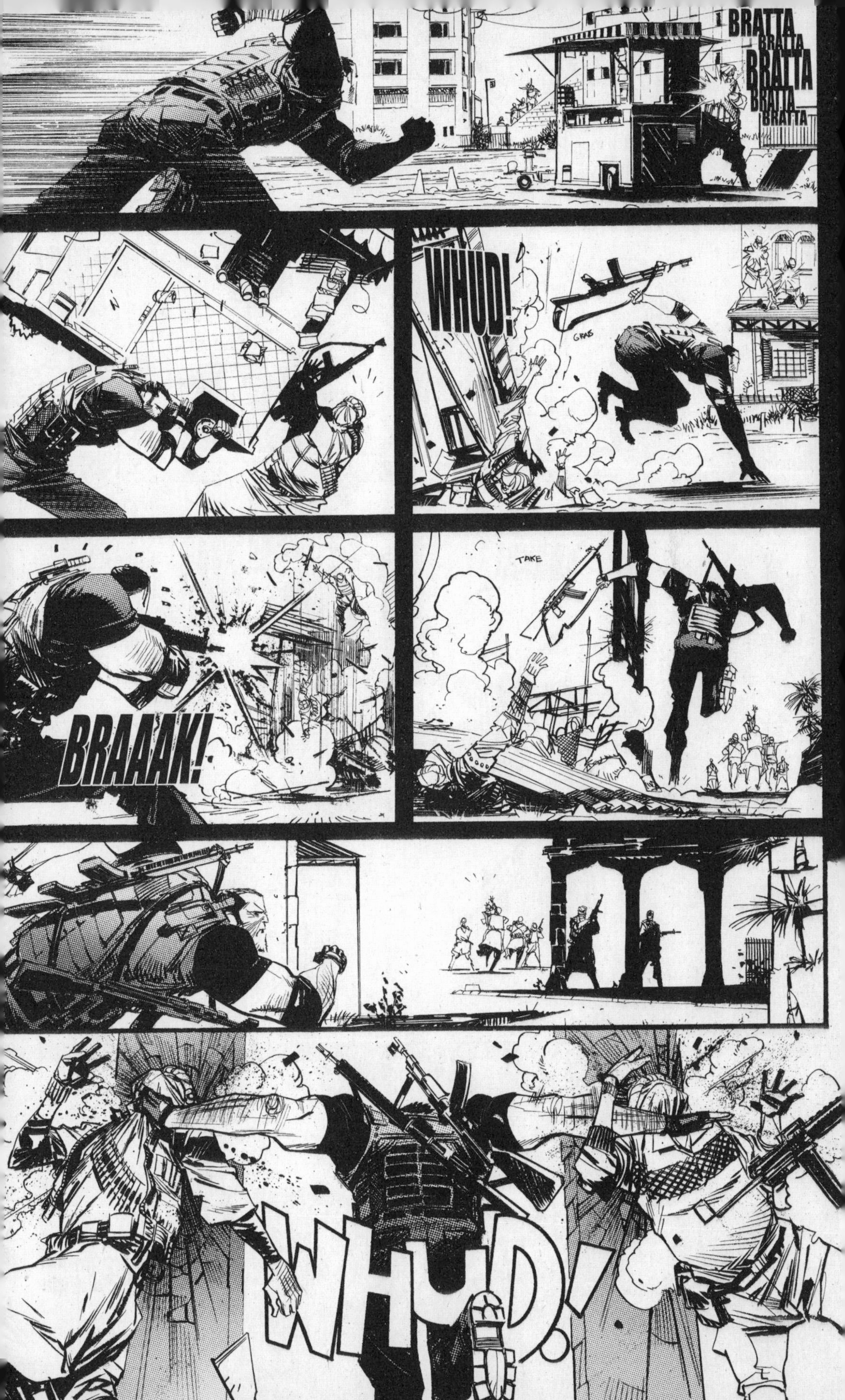
BRATTA
BRATTA
BRATTA
BRATTA
BRATTA
WHUD!
GRAB
BRAAAK!
TAKE
WHUD!

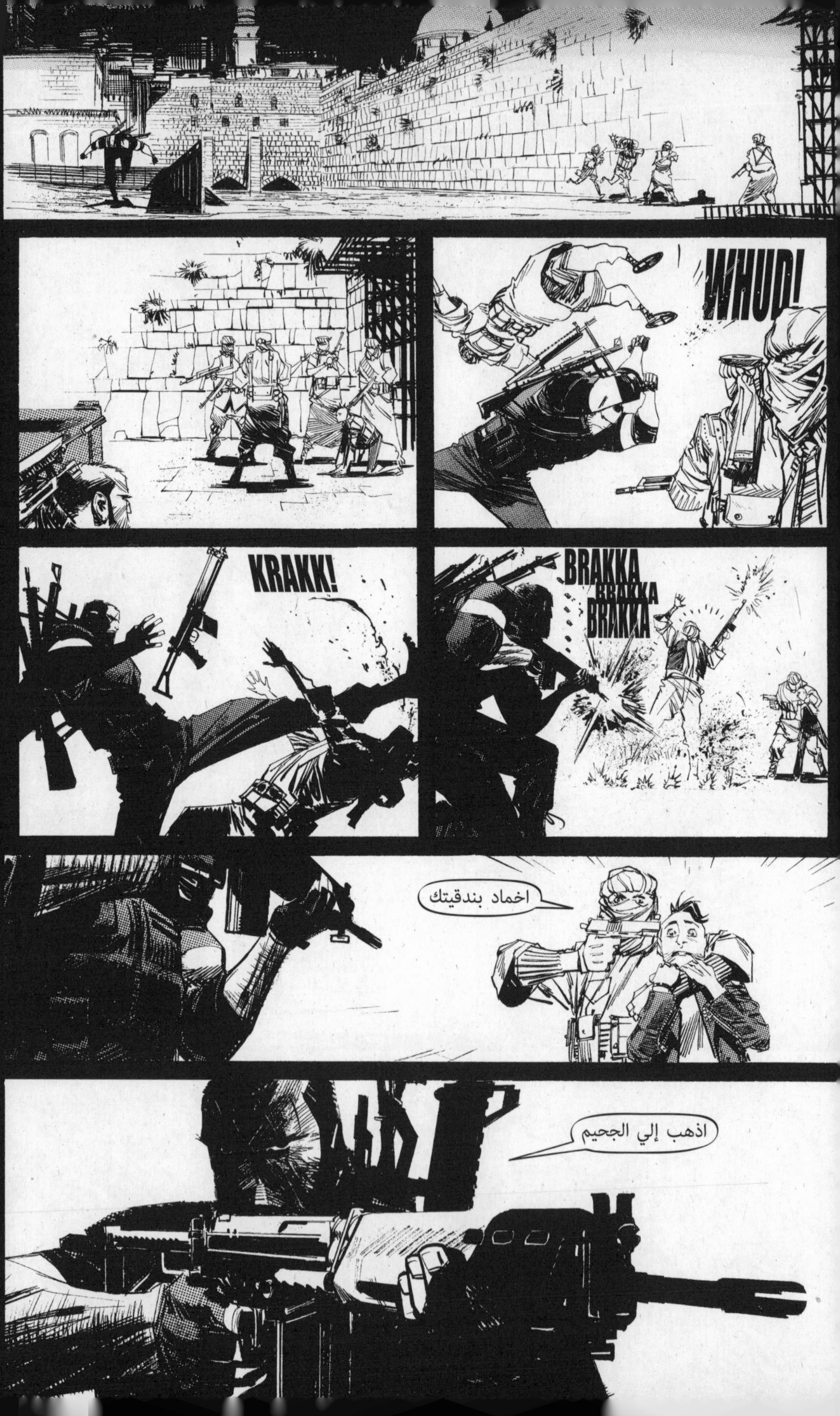

WHUD!
KRAKK!
BRAKKA BRAKKA BRAKKA
اخماد بندقيتك
اذهب إلي الجحيم

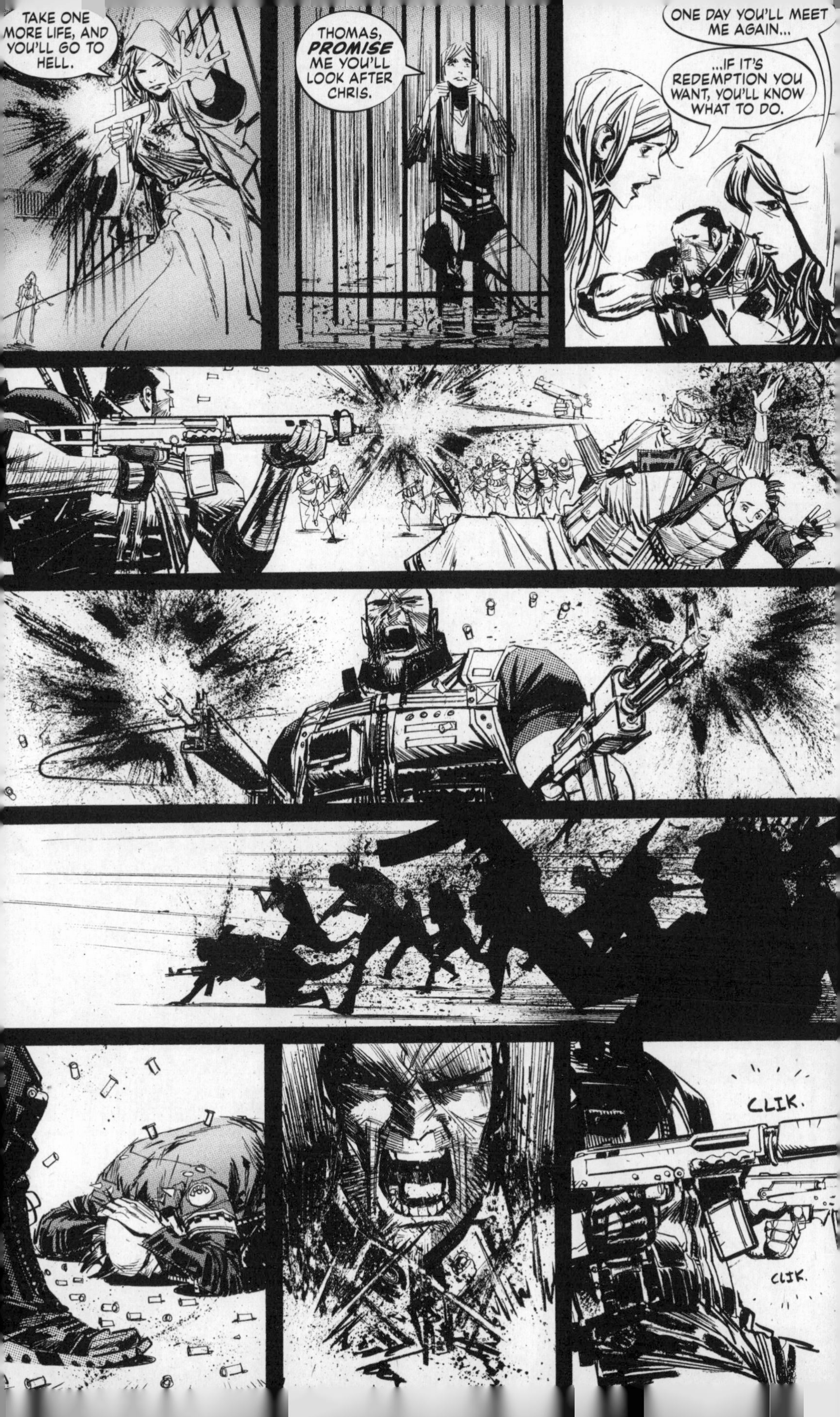
TAKE ONE MORE LIFE, AND YOU'LL GO TO HELL.
THOMAS, PROMISE ME YOU'LL LOOK AFTER CHRIS.
ONE DAY YOU'LL MEET ME AGAIN...
...IF IT'S REDEMPTION YOU WANT, YOU'LL KNOW WHAT TO DO.
CLIK.
CLIK.

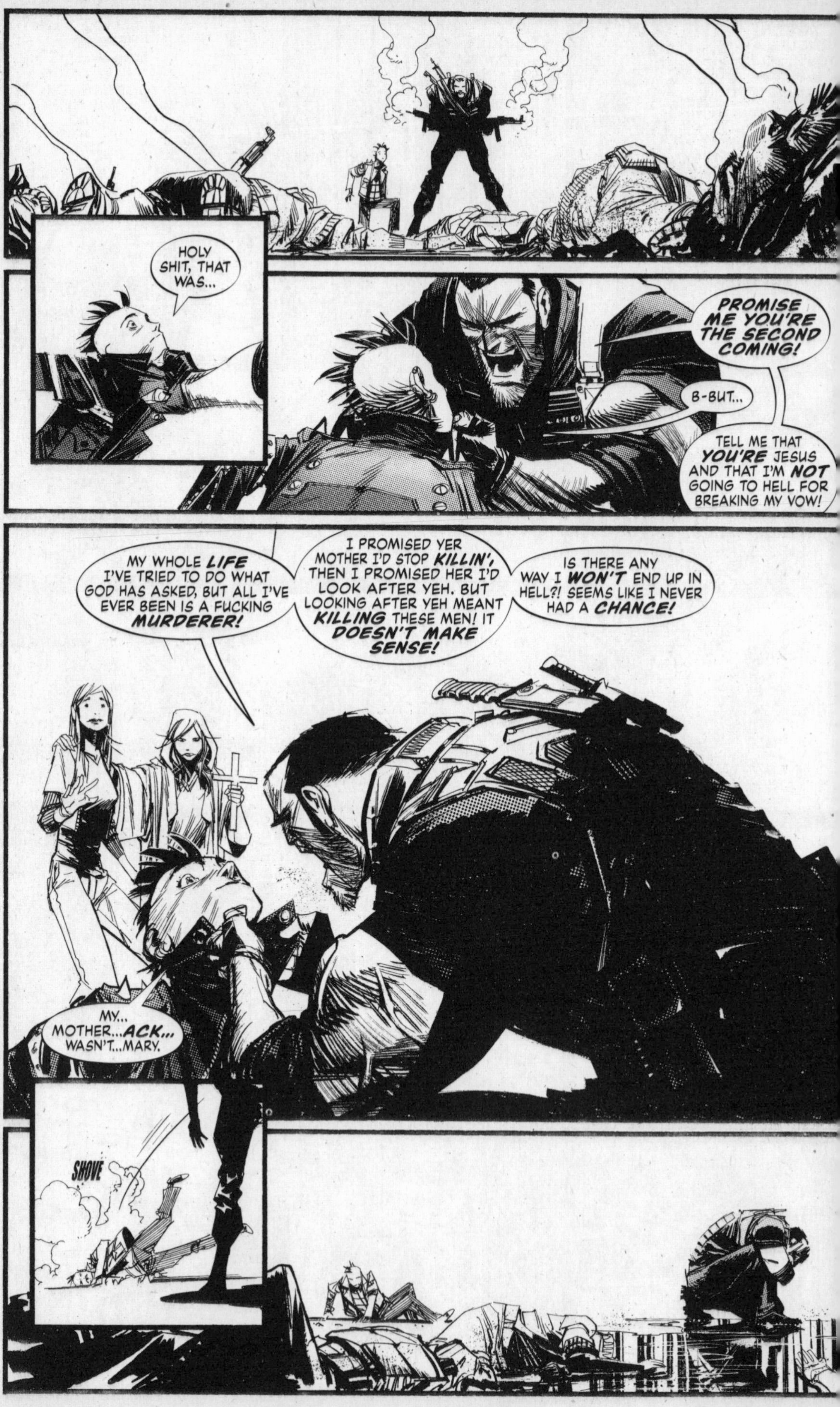
HOLY SHIT, THAT WAS...
PROMISE ME YOU'RE THE SECOND COMING!
B-BUT...
TELL ME THAT YOU'RE JESUS AND THAT I'M NOT GOING TO HELL FOR BREAKING MY VOW!
MY WHOLE LIFE I'VE TRIED TO DO WHAT GOD HAS ASKED, BUT ALL I'VE EVER BEEN IS A FUCKING MURDERER!
I PROMISED YER MOTHER I'D STOP KILLIN', THEN I PROMISED HER I'D LOOK AFTER YEH. BUT LOOKING AFTER YEH MEANT KILLING THESE MEN! IT DOESN'T MAKE SENSE!
IS THERE ANY WAY I WON'T END UP IN HELL?! SEEMS LIKE I NEVER HAD A CHANCE!
MY... MOTHER...ACK... WASN'T...MARY.
SHOVE

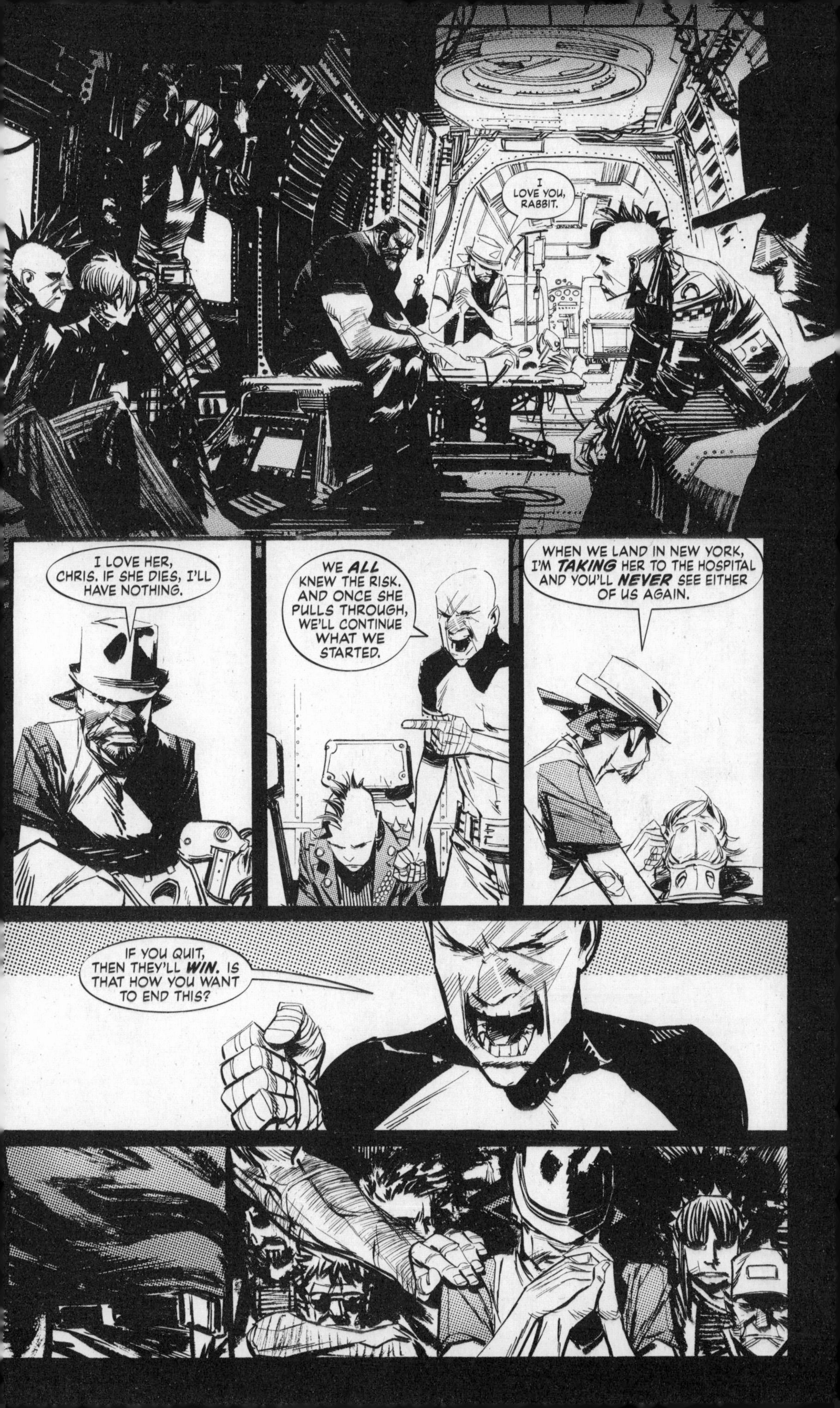
I LOVE YOU, RABBIT.
I LOVE HER, CHRIS. IF SHE DIES, I'LL HAVE NOTHING.
WE ALL KNEW THE RISK. AND ONCE SHE PULLS THROUGH, WE'LL CONTINUE WHAT WE STARTED.
WHEN WE LAND IN NEW YORK, I'M TAKING HER TO THE HOSPITAL AND YOU'LL NEVER SEE EITHER OF US AGAIN.
IF YOU QUIT, THEN THEY'LL WIN. IS THAT HOW YOU WANT TO END THIS?

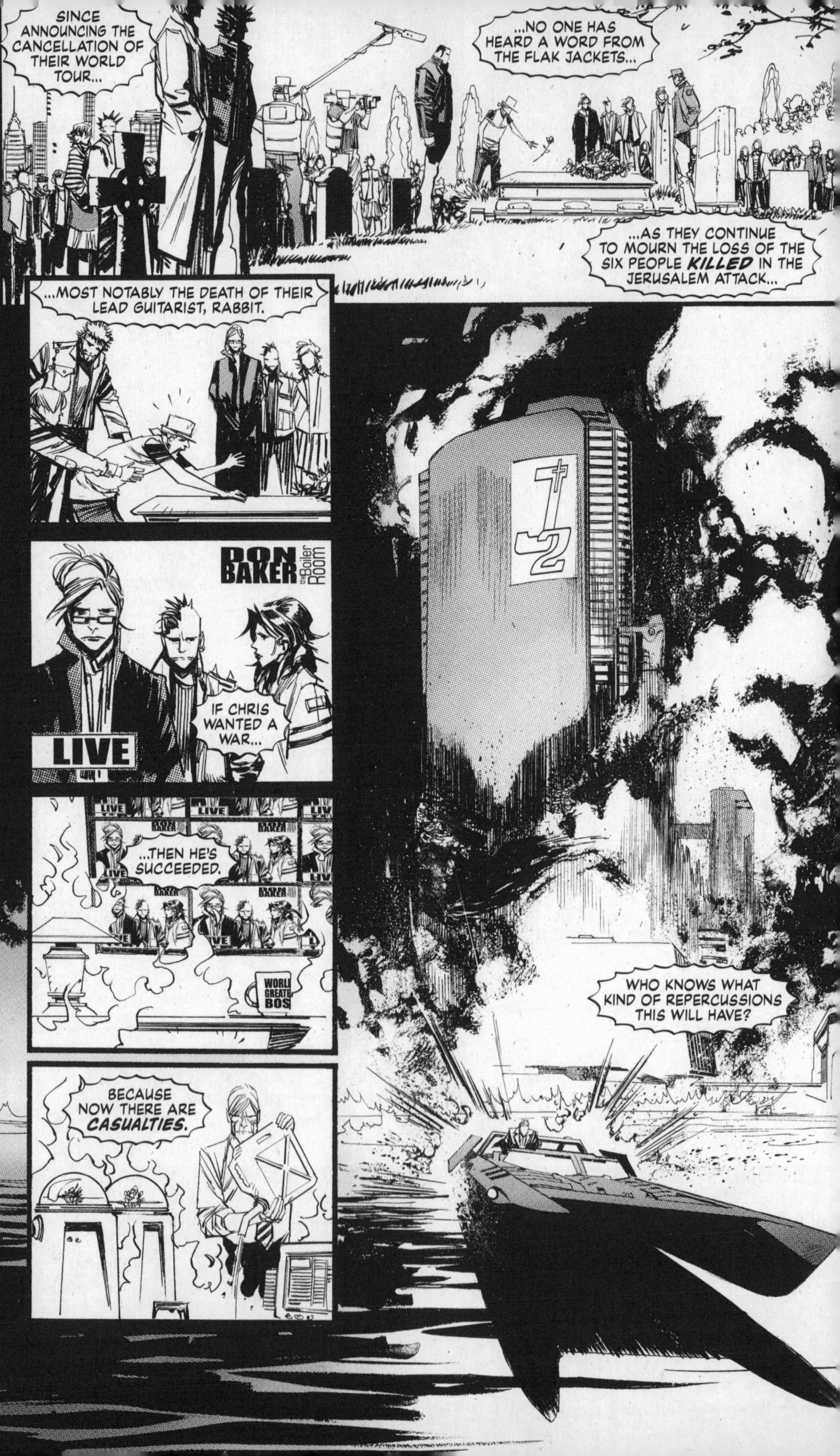
SINCE ANNOUNCING THE CANCELLATION OF THEIR WORLD TOUR...
...NO ONE HAS HEARD A WORD FROM THE FLAK JACKETS...
...AS THEY CONTINUE TO MOURN THE LOSS OF THE SIX PEOPLE KILLED IN THE JERUSALEM ATTACK...
...MOST NOTABLY THE DEATH OF THEIR LEAD GUITARIST, RABBIT.
DON BAKER the Boiler Room
LIVE
IF CHRIS WANTED A WAR...
...THEN HE'S SUCCEEDED.
BECAUSE NOW THERE ARE CASUALTIES.
WHO KNOWS WHAT KIND OF REPERCUSSIONS THIS WILL HAVE?

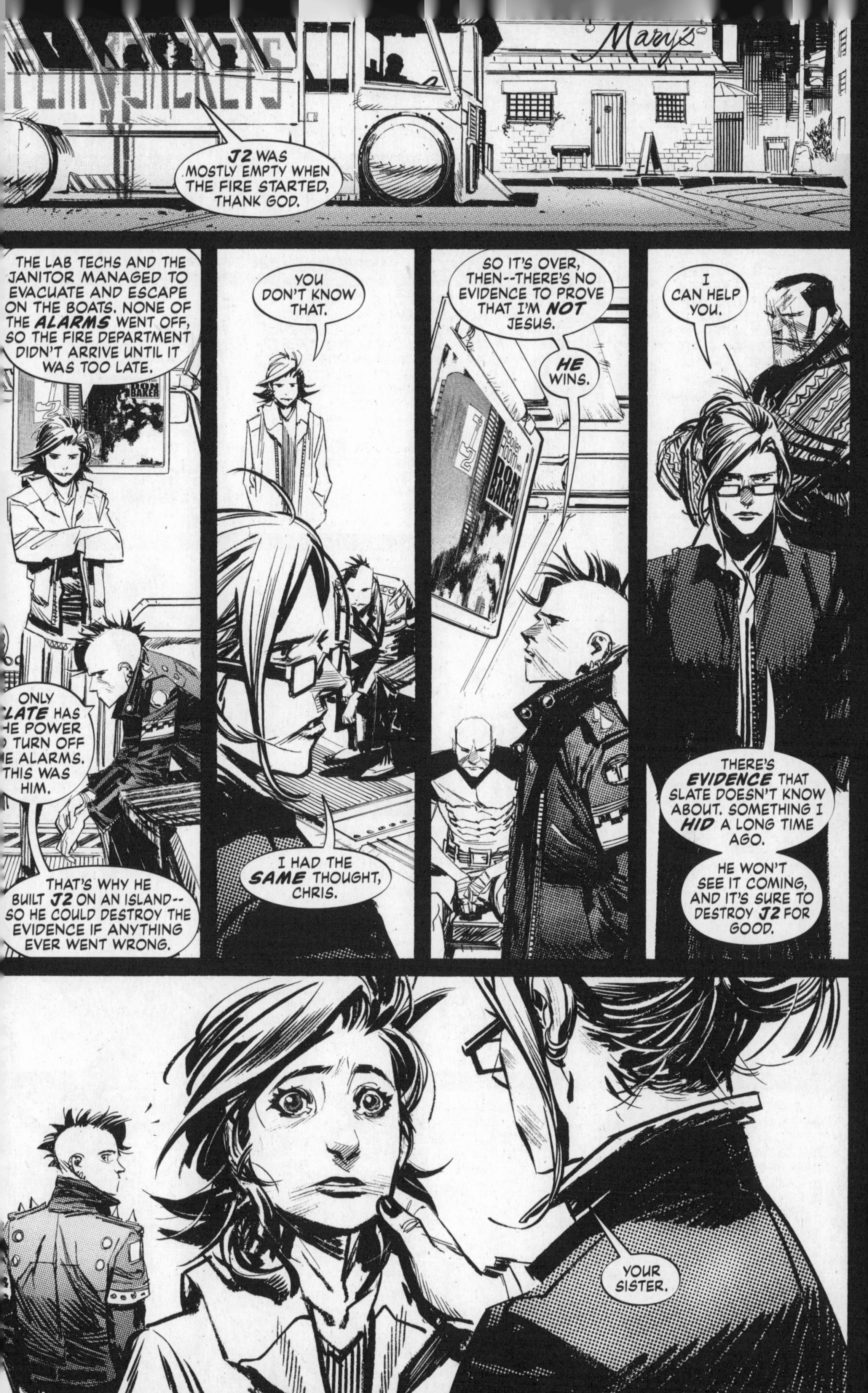

Mary's
J2 WAS MOSTLY EMPTY WHEN THE FIRE STARTED, THANK GOD.
THE LAB TECHS AND THE JANITOR MANAGED TO EVACUATE AND ESCAPE ON THE BOATS. NONE OF THE ALARMS WENT OFF, SO THE FIRE DEPARTMENT DIDN'T ARRIVE UNTIL IT WAS TOO LATE.
ONLY LATE HAS HE POWER TURN OFF E ALARMS. THIS WAS HIM.
THAT'S WHY HE BUILT J2 ON AN ISLAND--SO HE COULD DESTROY THE EVIDENCE IF ANYTHING EVER WENT WRONG.
YOU DON'T KNOW THAT.
I HAD THE SAME THOUGHT, CHRIS.
SO IT'S OVER, THEN--THERE'S NO EVIDENCE TO PROVE THAT I'M NOT JESUS.
HE WINS.
I CAN HELP YOU.
THERE'S EVIDENCE THAT SLATE DOESN'T KNOW ABOUT. SOMETHING I HID A LONG TIME AGO.
HE WON'T SEE IT COMING, AND IT'S SURE TO DESTROY J2 FOR GOOD.
YOUR SISTER.

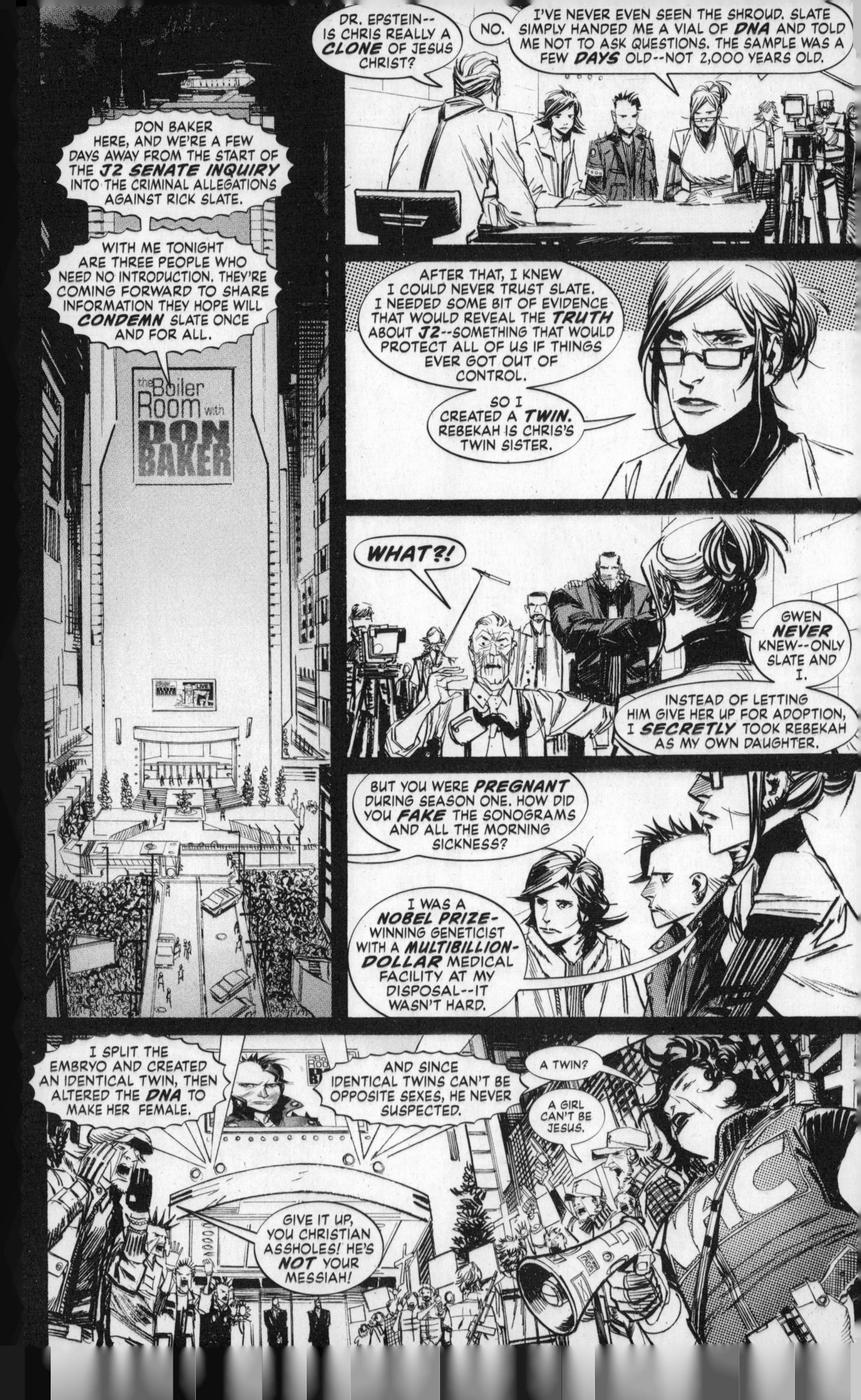

DON BAKER HERE, AND WE'RE A FEW DAYS AWAY FROM THE START OF THE J2 SENATE INQUIRY INTO THE CRIMINAL ALLEGATIONS AGAINST RICK SLATE.
WITH ME TONIGHT ARE THREE PEOPLE WHO NEED NO INTRODUCTION. THEY'RE COMING FORWARD TO SHARE INFORMATION THEY HOPE WILL CONDEMN SLATE ONCE AND FOR ALL.
the Boiler Room with DON BAKER
DR. EPSTEIN-- IS CHRIS REALLY A CLONE OF JESUS CHRIST?
NO.
I'VE NEVER EVEN SEEN THE SHROUD. SLATE SIMPLY HANDED ME A VIAL OF DNA AND TOLD ME NOT TO ASK QUESTIONS. THE SAMPLE WAS A FEW DAYS OLD--NOT 2,000 YEARS OLD.
AFTER THAT, I KNEW I COULD NEVER TRUST SLATE. I NEEDED SOME BIT OF EVIDENCE THAT WOULD REVEAL THE TRUTH ABOUT J2--SOMETHING THAT WOULD PROTECT ALL OF US IF THINGS EVER GOT OUT OF CONTROL.
SO I CREATED A TWIN. REBEKAH IS CHRIS'S TWIN SISTER.
WHAT?!
GWEN NEVER KNEW--ONLY SLATE AND I.
INSTEAD OF LETTING HIM GIVE HER UP FOR ADOPTION, I SECRETLY TOOK REBEKAH AS MY OWN DAUGHTER.
BUT YOU WERE PREGNANT DURING SEASON ONE. HOW DID YOU FAKE THE SONOGRAMS AND ALL THE MORNING SICKNESS?
I WAS A NOBEL PRIZE-WINNING GENETICIST WITH A MULTIBILLION-DOLLAR MEDICAL FACILITY AT MY DISPOSAL--IT WASN'T HARD.
I SPLIT THE EMBRYO AND CREATED AN IDENTICAL TWIN, THEN ALTERED THE DNA TO MAKE HER FEMALE.
AND SINCE IDENTICAL TWINS CAN'T BE OPPOSITE SEXES, HE NEVER SUSPECTED.
A TWIN?
A GIRL CAN'T BE JESUS.
GIVE IT UP, YOU CHRISTIAN ASSHOLES! HE'S NOT YOUR MESSIAH!

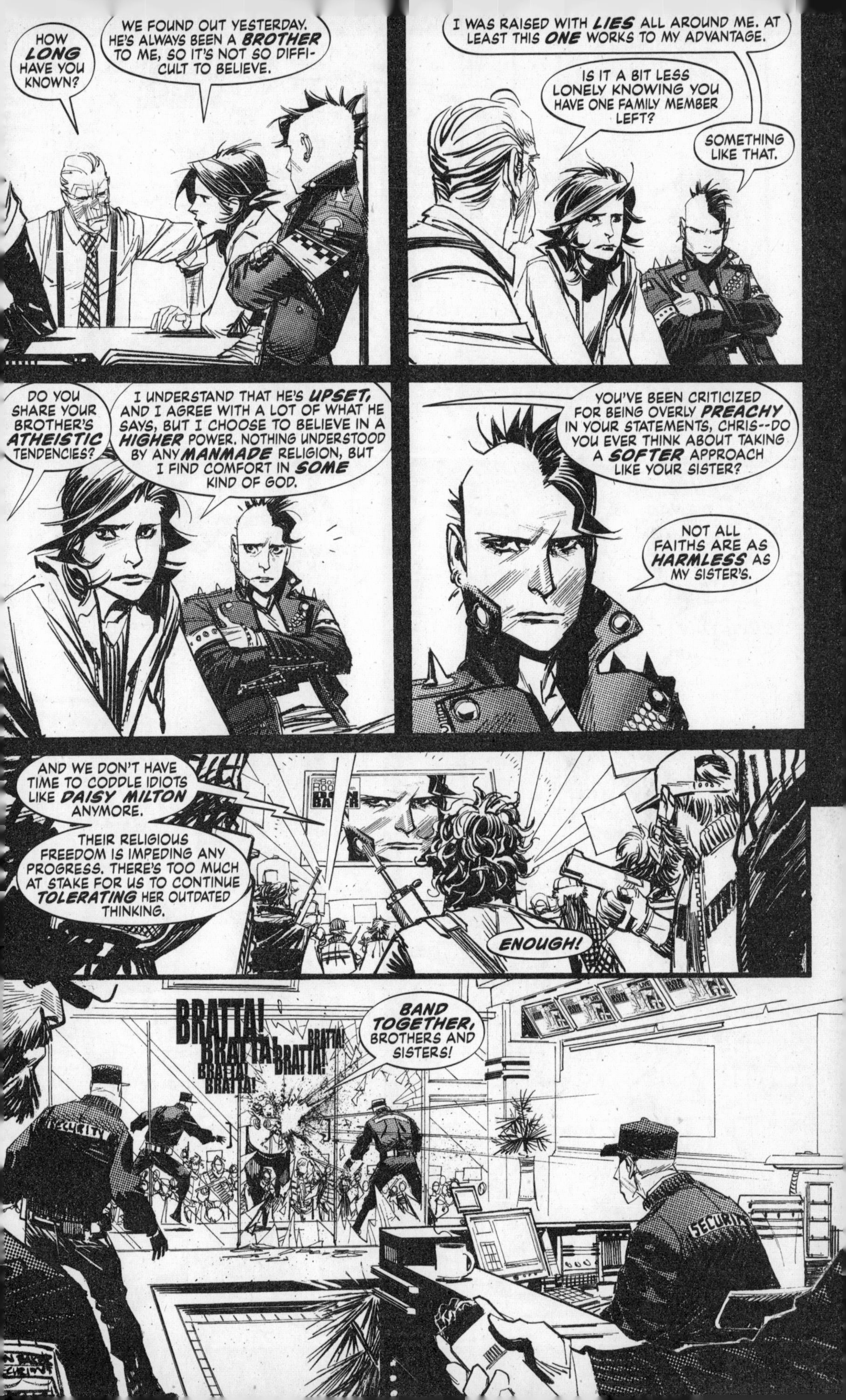

HOW LONG HAVE YOU KNOWN?
WE FOUND OUT YESTERDAY. HE'S ALWAYS BEEN A BROTHER TO ME, SO IT'S NOT SO DIFFICULT TO BELIEVE.
I WAS RAISED WITH LIES ALL AROUND ME. AT LEAST THIS ONE WORKS TO MY ADVANTAGE.
IS IT A BIT LESS LONELY KNOWING YOU HAVE ONE FAMILY MEMBER LEFT?
SOMETHING LIKE THAT.
DO YOU SHARE YOUR BROTHER'S ATHEISTIC TENDENCIES?
I UNDERSTAND THAT HE'S UPSET, AND I AGREE WITH A LOT OF WHAT HE SAYS, BUT I CHOOSE TO BELIEVE IN A HIGHER POWER. NOTHING UNDERSTOOD BY ANY MANMADE RELIGION, BUT I FIND COMFORT IN SOME KIND OF GOD.
YOU'VE BEEN CRITICIZED FOR BEING OVERLY PREACHY IN YOUR STATEMENTS, CHRIS--DO YOU EVER THINK ABOUT TAKING A SOFTER APPROACH LIKE YOUR SISTER?
NOT ALL FAITHS ARE AS HARMLESS AS MY SISTER'S.
AND WE DON'T HAVE TIME TO CODDLE IDIOTS LIKE DAISY MILTON ANYMORE.
THEIR RELIGIOUS FREEDOM IS IMPEDING ANY PROGRESS. THERE'S TOO MUCH AT STAKE FOR US TO CONTINUE TOLERATING HER OUTDATED THINKING.
ENOUGH!
BRATTA! BRATTA! BRATTA! BRATTA! BRATTA! BRATTA!
BAND TOGETHER, BROTHERS AND SISTERS!
SECURITY

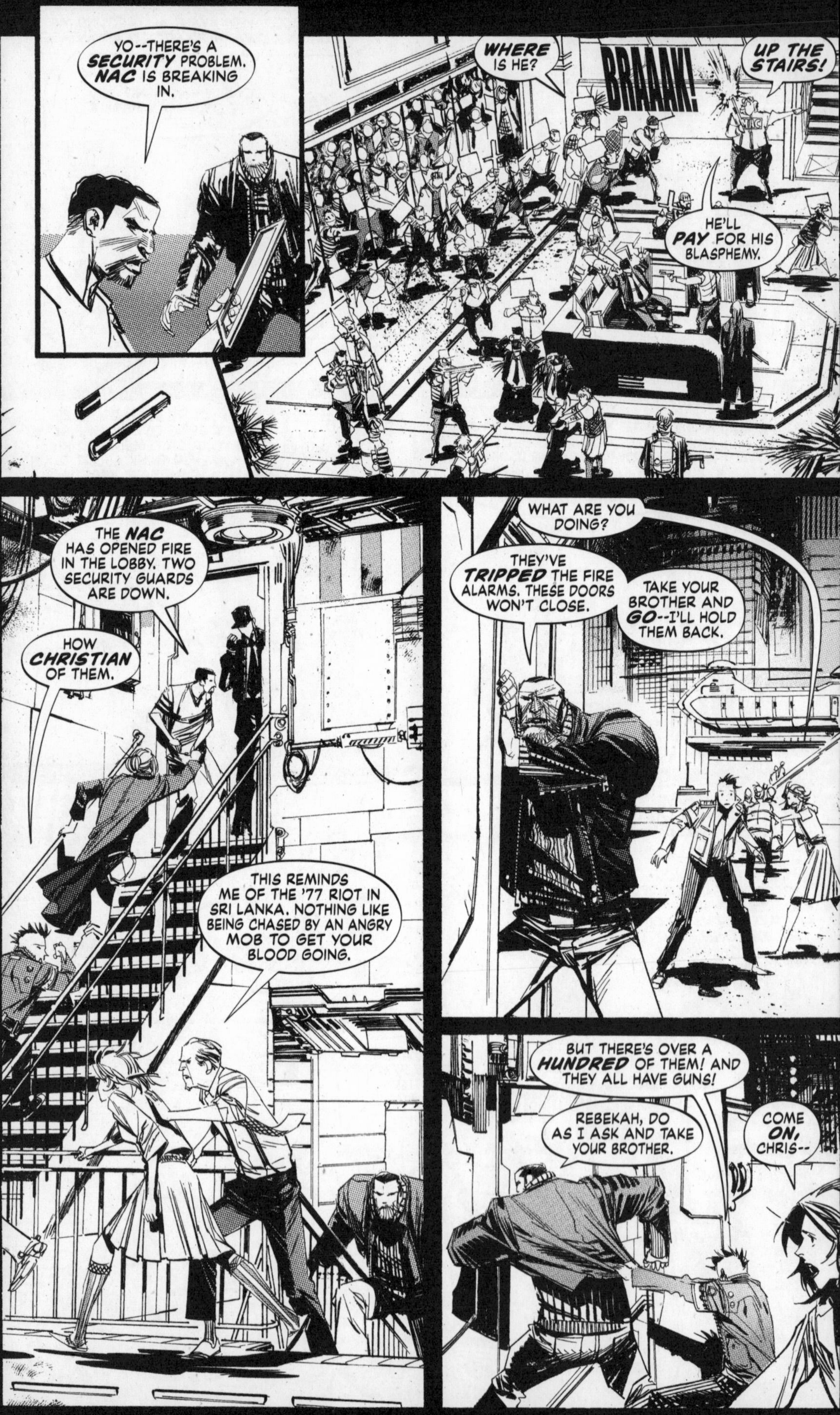
YO--THERE'S A SECURITY PROBLEM. NAC IS BREAKING IN.
WHERE IS HE?
BRAAAK!
UP THE STAIRS!
HE'LL PAY FOR HIS BLASPHEMY.
THE NAC HAS OPENED FIRE IN THE LOBBY. TWO SECURITY GUARDS ARE DOWN.
HOW CHRISTIAN OF THEM.
THIS REMINDS ME OF THE '77 RIOT IN SRI LANKA. NOTHING LIKE BEING CHASED BY AN ANGRY MOB TO GET YOUR BLOOD GOING.
WHAT ARE YOU DOING?
THEY'VE TRIPPED THE FIRE ALARMS. THESE DOORS WON'T CLOSE.
TAKE YOUR BROTHER AND GO--I'LL HOLD THEM BACK.
BUT THERE'S OVER A HUNDRED OF THEM! AND THEY ALL HAVE GUNS!
REBEKAH, DO AS I ASK AND TAKE YOUR BROTHER.
COME ON, CHRIS--

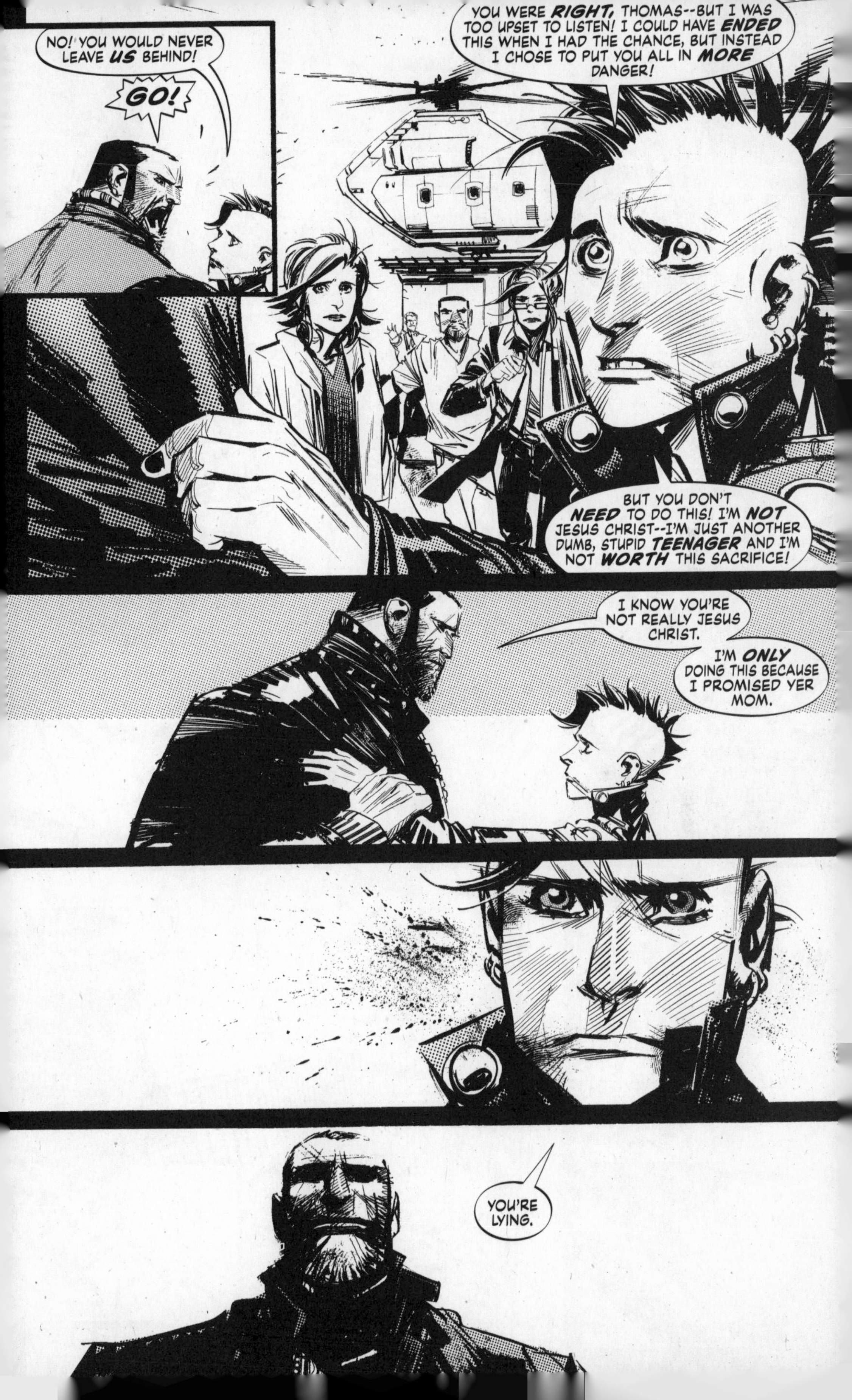
NO! YOU WOULD NEVER LEAVE US BEHIND!
GO!
YOU WERE RIGHT, THOMAS--BUT I WAS TOO UPSET TO LISTEN! I COULD HAVE ENDED THIS WHEN I HAD THE CHANCE, BUT INSTEAD I CHOSE TO PUT YOU ALL IN MORE DANGER!
BUT YOU DON'T NEED TO DO THIS! I'M NOT JESUS CHRIST--I'M JUST ANOTHER DUMB, STUPID TEENAGER AND I'M NOT WORTH THIS SACRIFICE!
I KNOW YOU'RE NOT REALLY JESUS CHRIST.
I'M ONLY DOING THIS BECAUSE I PROMISED YER MOM.
YOU'RE LYING.

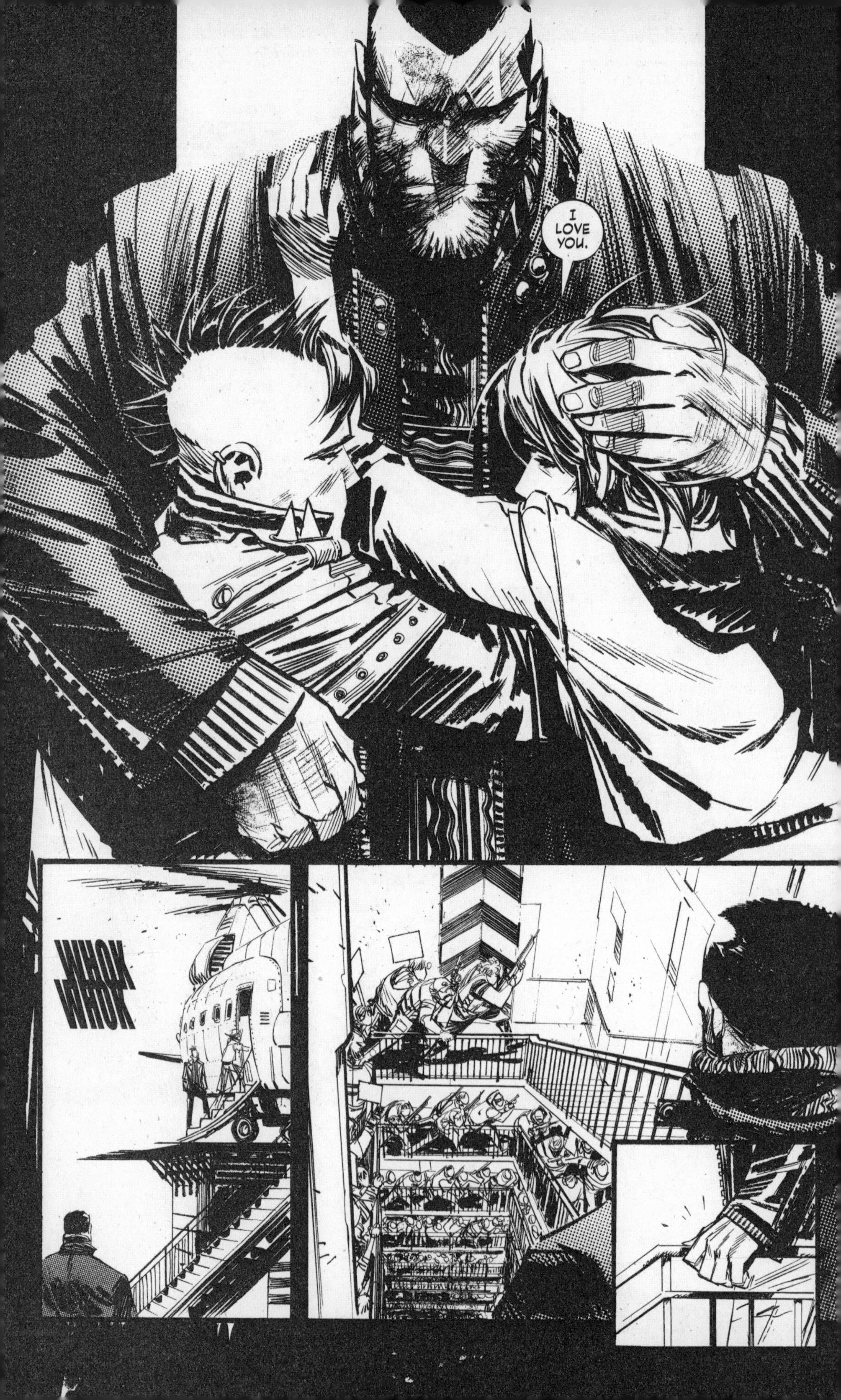
I LOVE YOU.
WHOK WHOK

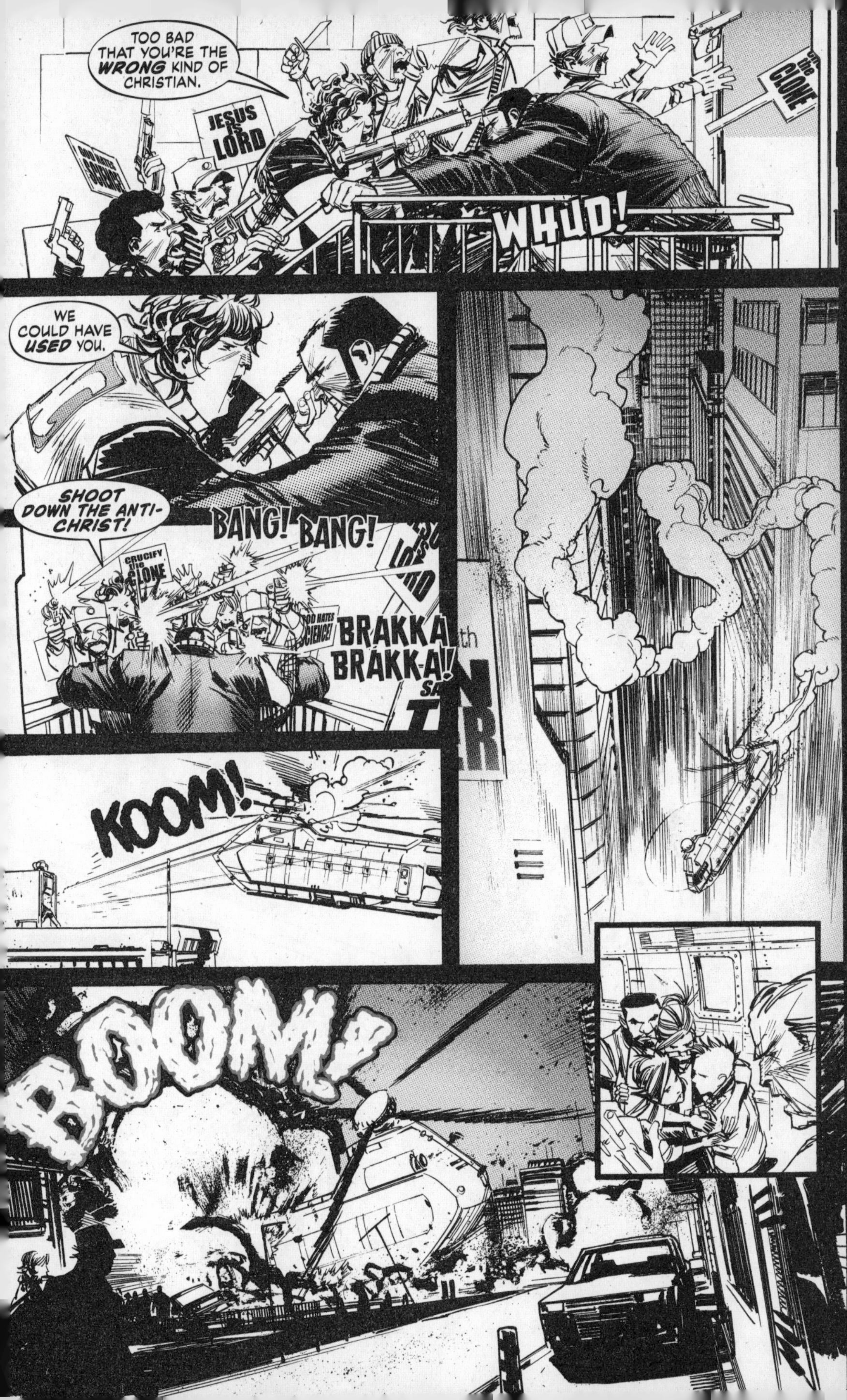
TOO BAD THAT YOU'RE THE WRONG KIND OF CHRISTIAN.
JESUS IS LORD
the CLONE
WHUD!
WE COULD HAVE USED YOU.
SHOOT DOWN THE ANTI-CHRIST!
CRUCIFY the CLONE
BANG! BANG!
GOD HATES SCIENCE!
BRAKKA BRAKKA!
KOOM!
BOOM!

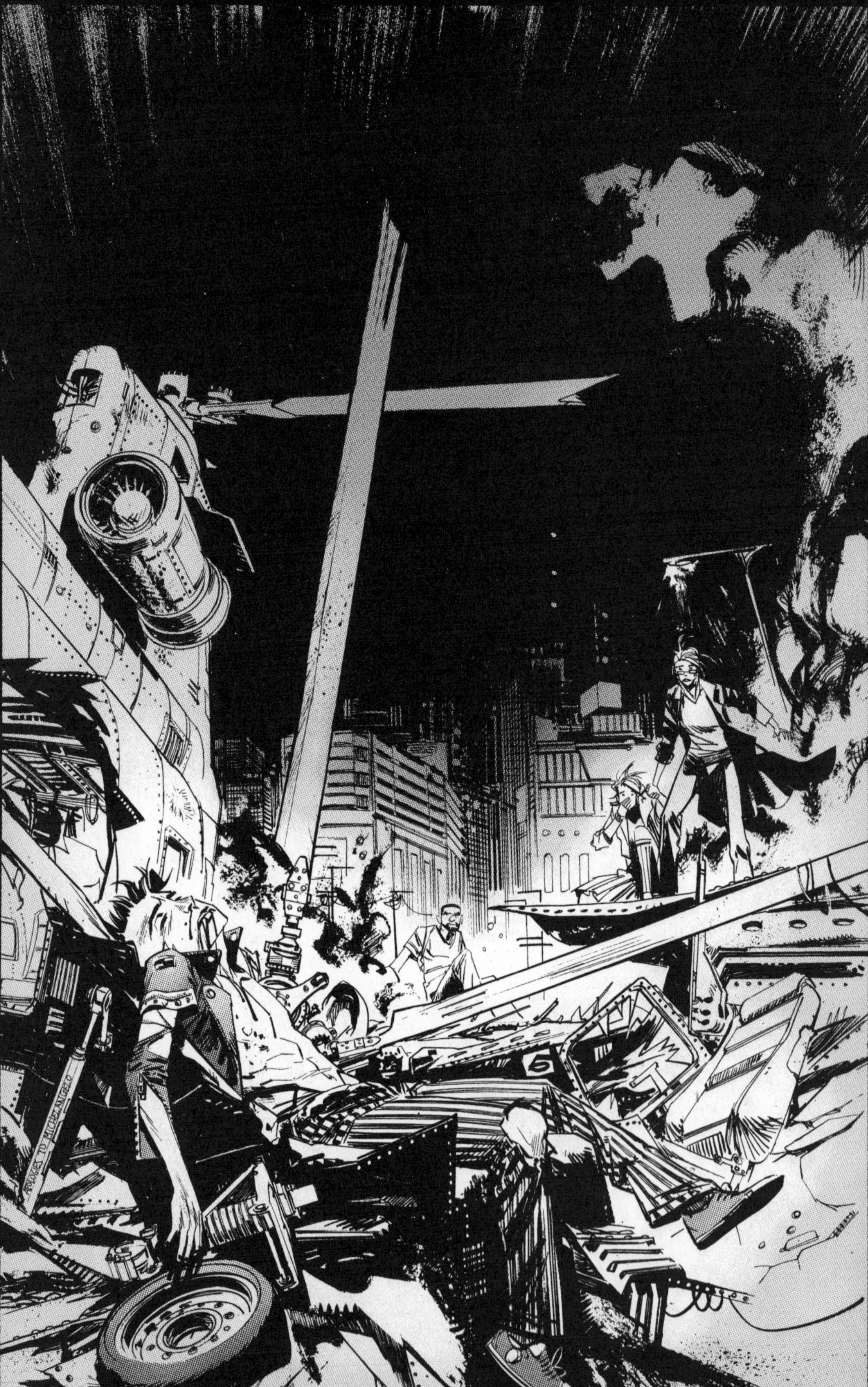
APOLOGIES TO MICHELANGELO
6

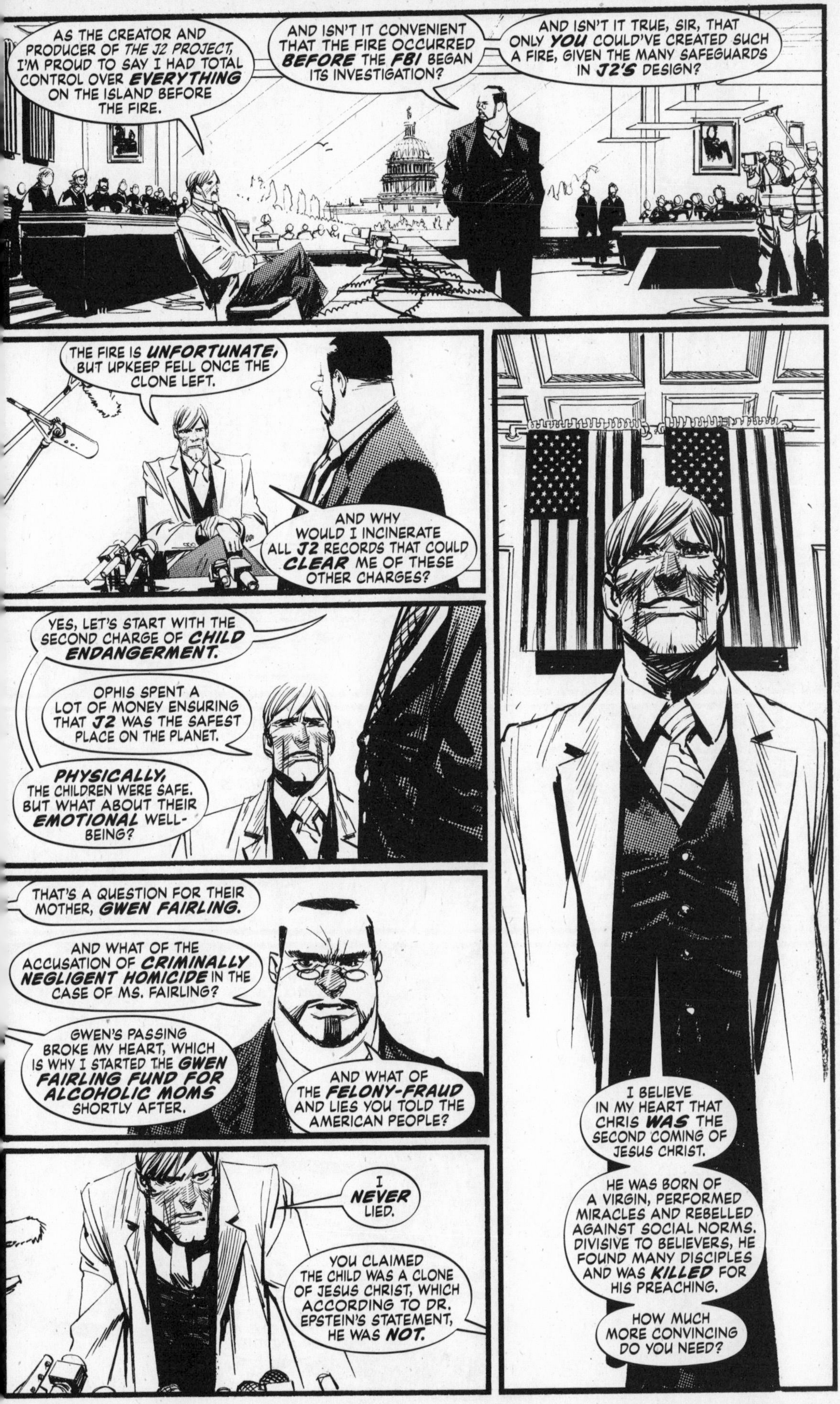

AS THE CREATOR AND PRODUCER OF THE J2 PROJECT, I'M PROUD TO SAY I HAD TOTAL CONTROL OVER EVERYTHING ON THE ISLAND BEFORE THE FIRE.
AND ISN'T IT CONVENIENT THAT THE FIRE OCCURRED BEFORE THE FBI BEGAN ITS INVESTIGATION?
AND ISN'T IT TRUE, SIR, THAT ONLY YOU COULD'VE CREATED SUCH A FIRE, GIVEN THE MANY SAFEGUARDS IN J2'S DESIGN?
THE FIRE IS UNFORTUNATE, BUT UPKEEP FELL ONCE THE CLONE LEFT.
AND WHY WOULD I INCINERATE ALL J2 RECORDS THAT COULD CLEAR ME OF THESE OTHER CHARGES?
YES, LET'S START WITH THE SECOND CHARGE OF CHILD ENDANGERMENT.
OPHIS SPENT A LOT OF MONEY ENSURING THAT J2 WAS THE SAFEST PLACE ON THE PLANET.
PHYSICALLY, THE CHILDREN WERE SAFE. BUT WHAT ABOUT THEIR EMOTIONAL WELL-BEING?
THAT'S A QUESTION FOR THEIR MOTHER, GWEN FAIRLING.
AND WHAT OF THE ACCUSATION OF CRIMINALLY NEGLIGENT HOMICIDE IN THE CASE OF MS. FAIRLING?
GWEN'S PASSING BROKE MY HEART, WHICH IS WHY I STARTED THE GWEN FAIRLING FUND FOR ALCOHOLIC MOMS SHORTLY AFTER.
AND WHAT OF THE FELONY-FRAUD AND LIES YOU TOLD THE AMERICAN PEOPLE?
I NEVER LIED.
YOU CLAIMED THE CHILD WAS A CLONE OF JESUS CHRIST, WHICH ACCORDING TO DR. EPSTEIN'S STATEMENT, HE WAS NOT.
I BELIEVE IN MY HEART THAT CHRIS WAS THE SECOND COMING OF JESUS CHRIST.
HE WAS BORN OF A VIRGIN, PERFORMED MIRACLES AND REBELLED AGAINST SOCIAL NORMS. DIVISIVE TO BELIEVERS, HE FOUND MANY DISCIPLES AND WAS KILLED FOR HIS PREACHING.
HOW MUCH MORE CONVINCING DO YOU NEED?

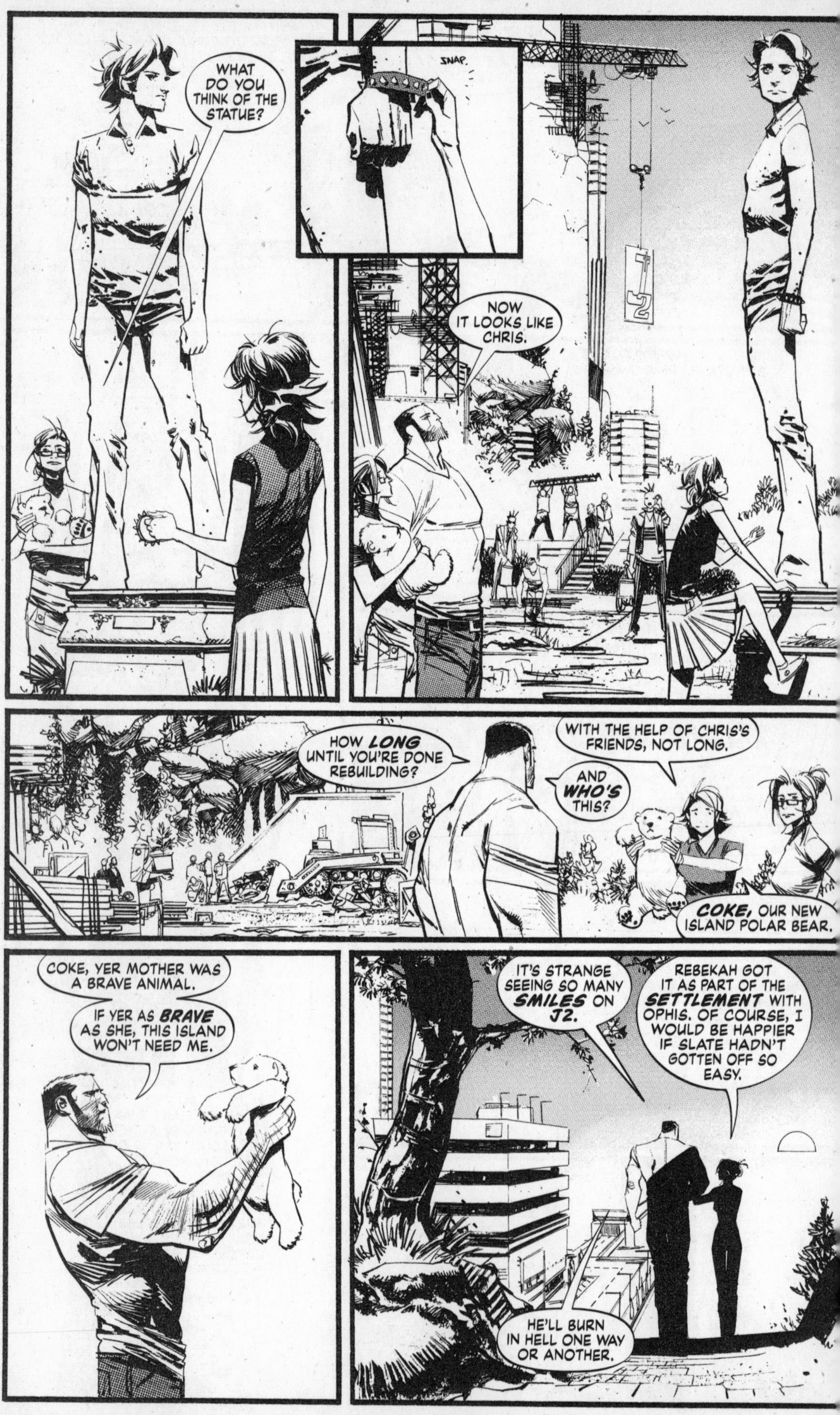
WHAT DO YOU THINK OF THE STATUE?
SNAP.
NOW IT LOOKS LIKE CHRIS.
HOW LONG UNTIL YOU'RE DONE REBUILDING?
WITH THE HELP OF CHRIS'S FRIENDS, NOT LONG.
AND WHO'S THIS?
COKE, OUR NEW ISLAND POLAR BEAR.
COKE, YER MOTHER WAS A BRAVE ANIMAL.
IF YER AS BRAVE AS SHE, THIS ISLAND WON'T NEED ME.
IT'S STRANGE SEEING SO MANY SMILES ON J2.
REBEKAH GOT IT AS PART OF THE SETTLEMENT WITH OPHIS. OF COURSE, I WOULD BE HAPPIER IF SLATE HADN'T GOTTEN OFF SO EASY.
HE'LL BURN IN HELL ONE WAY OR ANOTHER.

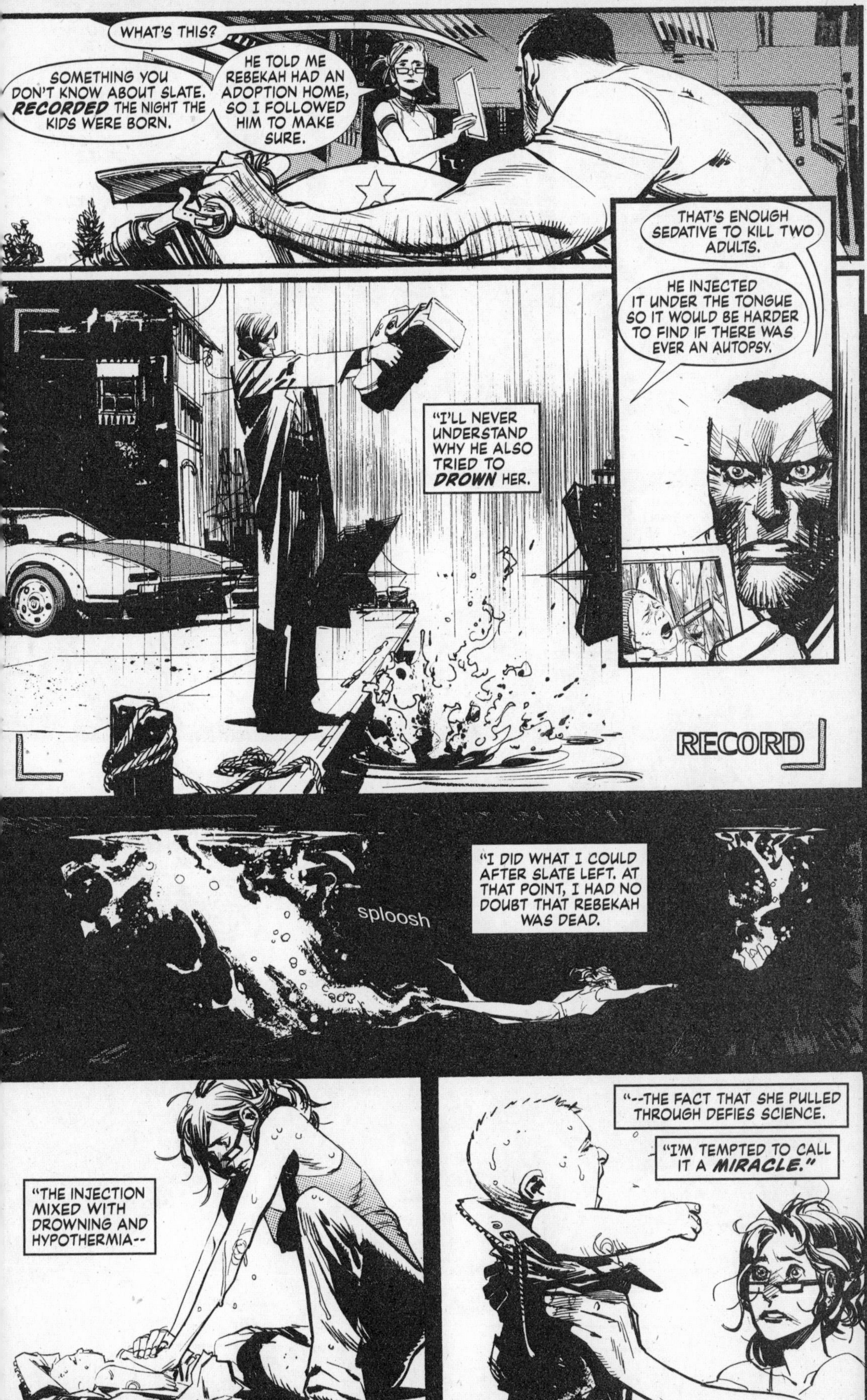
WHAT'S THIS?
SOMETHING YOU DON'T KNOW ABOUT SLATE. RECORDED THE NIGHT THE KIDS WERE BORN.
HE TOLD ME REBEKAH HAD AN ADOPTION HOME, SO I FOLLOWED HIM TO MAKE SURE.
THAT'S ENOUGH SEDATIVE TO KILL TWO ADULTS.
HE INJECTED IT UNDER THE TONGUE SO IT WOULD BE HARDER TO FIND IF THERE WAS EVER AN AUTOPSY.
"I'LL NEVER UNDERSTAND WHY HE ALSO TRIED TO DROWN HER.
RECORD
"I DID WHAT I COULD AFTER SLATE LEFT. AT THAT POINT, I HAD NO DOUBT THAT REBEKAH WAS DEAD.
sploosh
"THE INJECTION MIXED WITH DROWNING AND HYPOTHERMIA--
"--THE FACT THAT SHE PULLED THROUGH DEFIES SCIENCE.
"I'M TEMPTED TO CALL IT A MIRACLE."

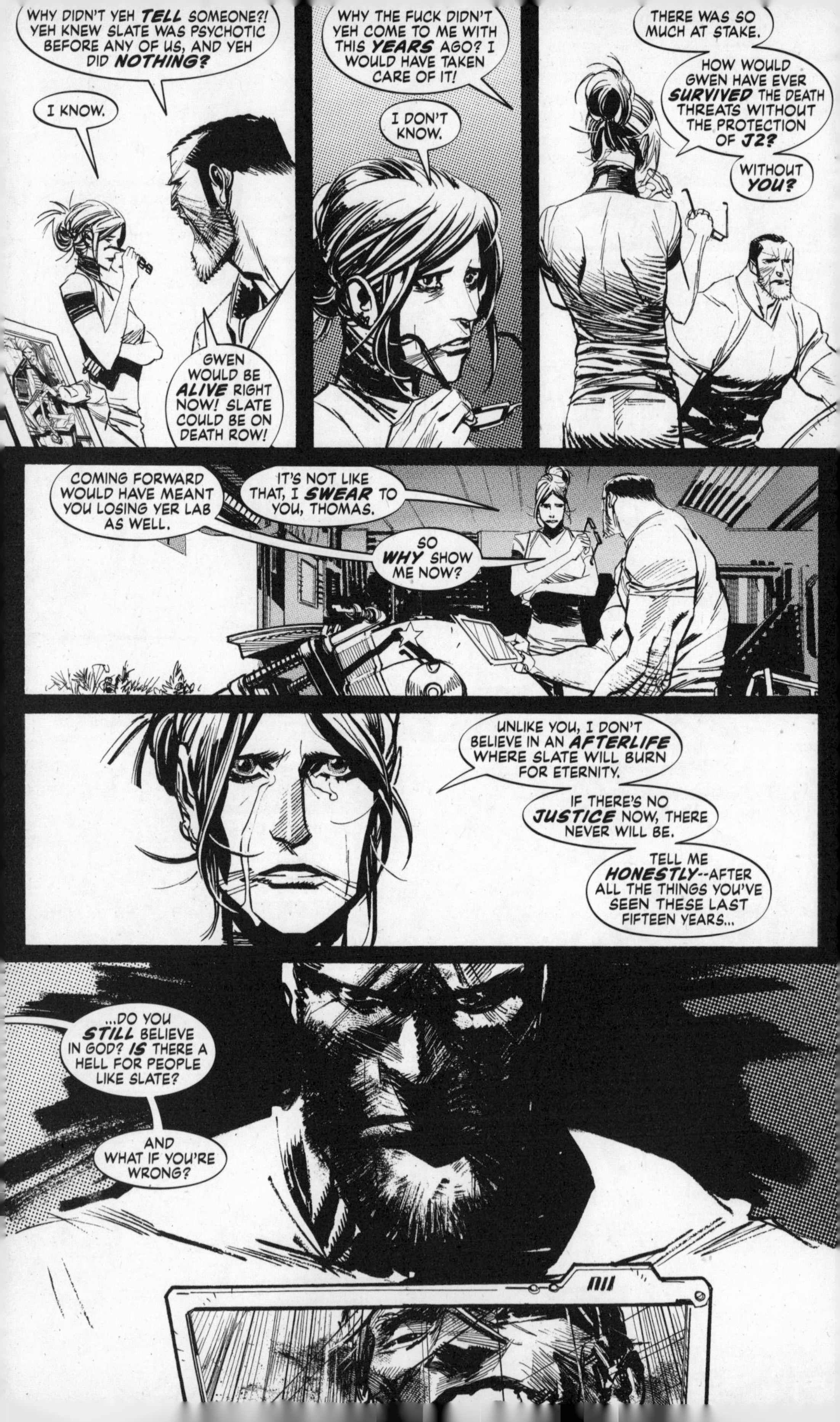
WHY DIDN'T YEH TELL SOMEONE?! YEH KNEW SLATE WAS PSYCHOTIC BEFORE ANY OF US, AND YEH DID NOTHING?
I KNOW.
GWEN WOULD BE ALIVE RIGHT NOW! SLATE COULD BE ON DEATH ROW!
WHY THE FUCK DIDN'T YEH COME TO ME WITH THIS YEARS AGO? I WOULD HAVE TAKEN CARE OF IT!
I DON'T KNOW.
THERE WAS SO MUCH AT STAKE.
HOW WOULD GWEN HAVE EVER SURVIVED THE DEATH THREATS WITHOUT THE PROTECTION OF J2?
WITHOUT YOU?
COMING FORWARD WOULD HAVE MEANT YOU LOSING YER LAB AS WELL.
IT'S NOT LIKE THAT, I SWEAR TO YOU, THOMAS.
SO WHY SHOW ME NOW?
UNLIKE YOU, I DON'T BELIEVE IN AN AFTERLIFE WHERE SLATE WILL BURN FOR ETERNITY.
IF THERE'S NO JUSTICE NOW, THERE NEVER WILL BE.
TELL ME HONESTLY--AFTER ALL THE THINGS YOU'VE SEEN THESE LAST FIFTEEN YEARS...
...DO YOU STILL BELIEVE IN GOD? IS THERE A HELL FOR PEOPLE LIKE SLATE?
AND WHAT IF YOU'RE WRONG?

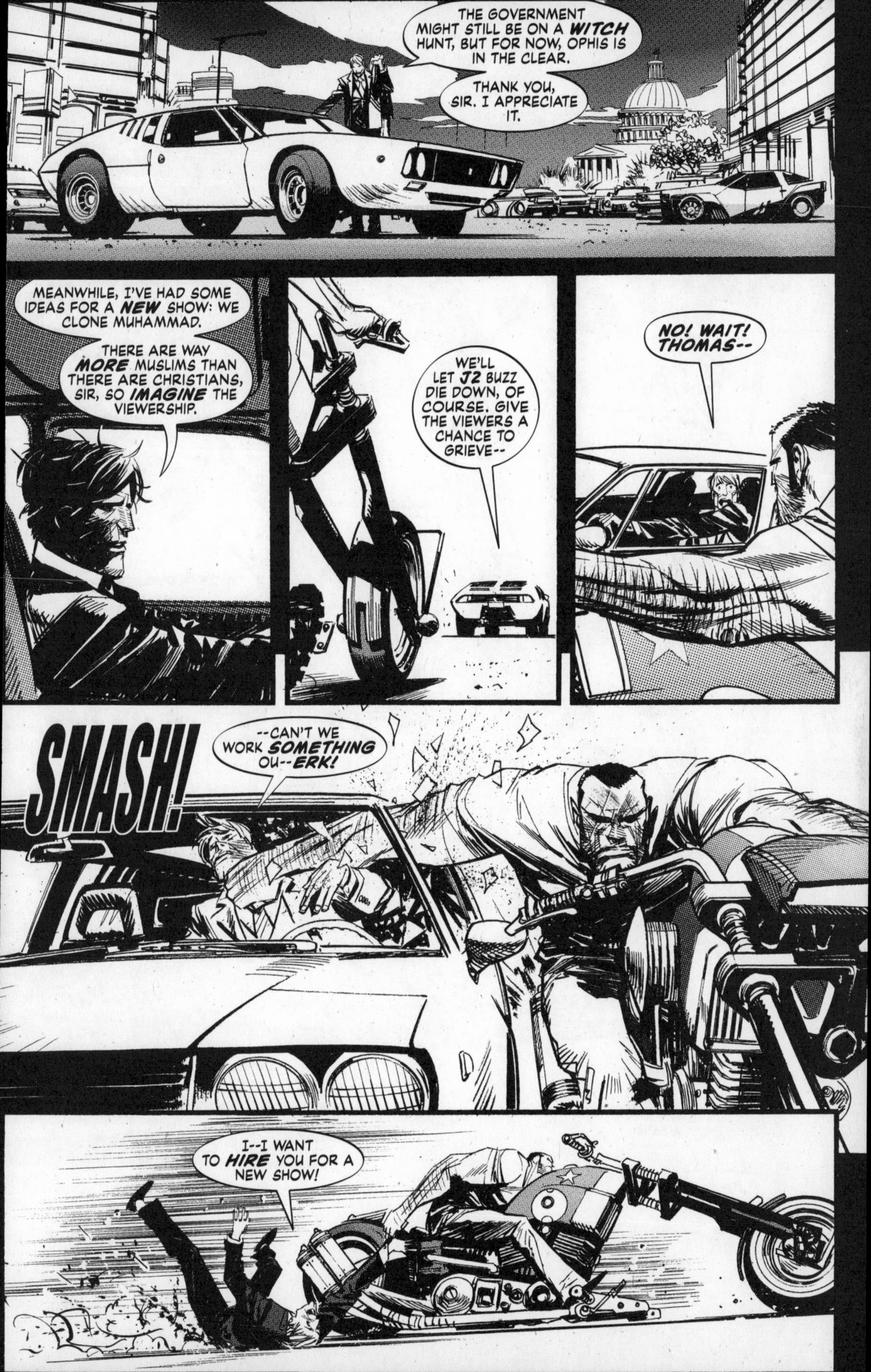

THE GOVERNMENT MIGHT STILL BE ON A WITCH HUNT, BUT FOR NOW, OPHIS IS IN THE CLEAR.
THANK YOU, SIR. I APPRECIATE IT.
MEANWHILE, I'VE HAD SOME IDEAS FOR A NEW SHOW: WE CLONE MUHAMMAD.
THERE ARE WAY MORE MUSLIMS THAN THERE ARE CHRISTIANS, SIR, SO IMAGINE THE VIEWERSHIP.
WE'LL LET J2 BUZZ DIE DOWN, OF COURSE. GIVE THE VIEWERS A CHANCE TO GRIEVE--
NO! WAIT! THOMAS--
SMASH!
--CAN'T WE WORK SOMETHING OU--ERK!
I--I WANT TO HIRE YOU FOR A NEW SHOW!

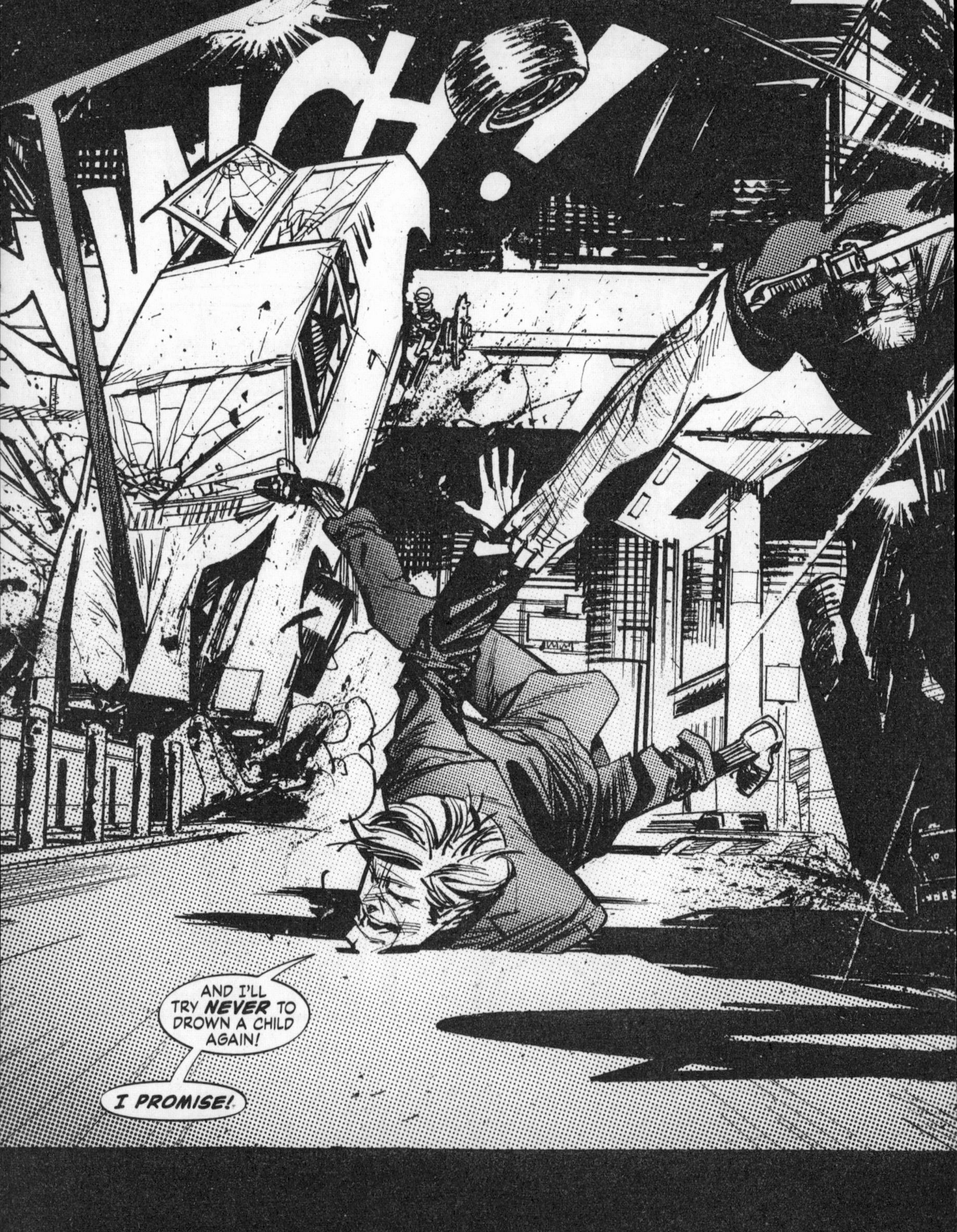
AND I'LL TRY NEVER TO DROWN A CHILD AGAIN!
I PROMISE!

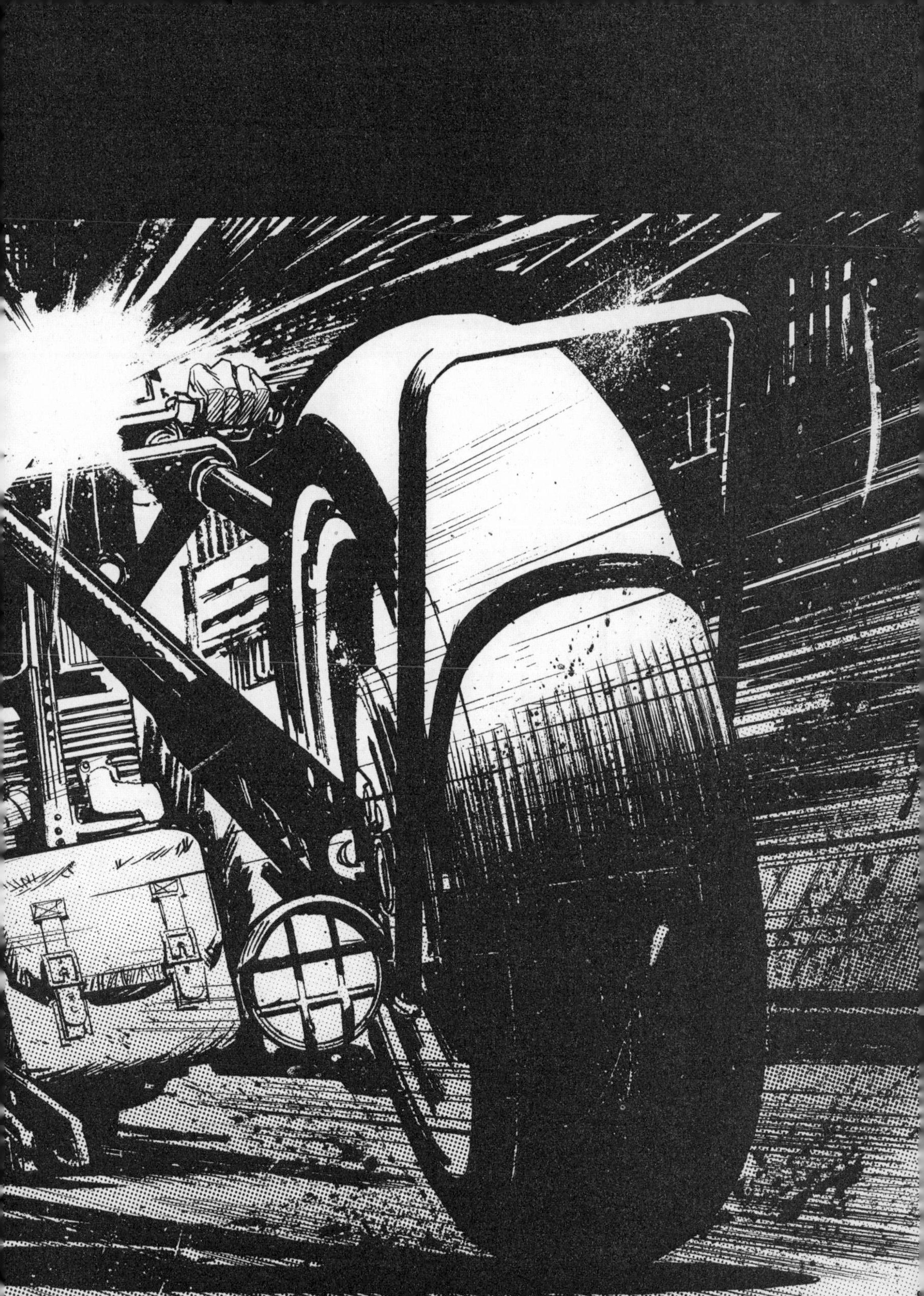

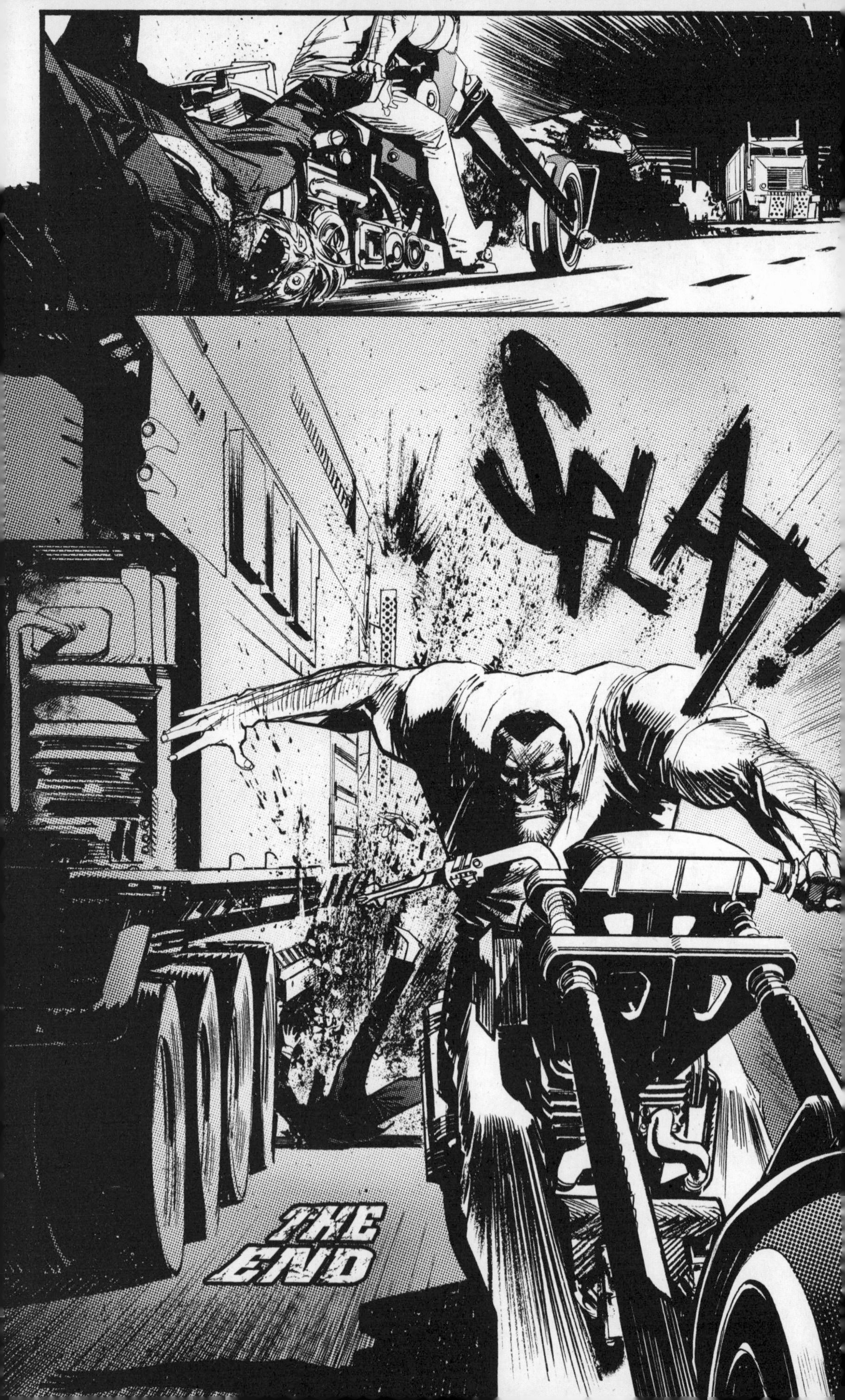
SPLAT!
THE END

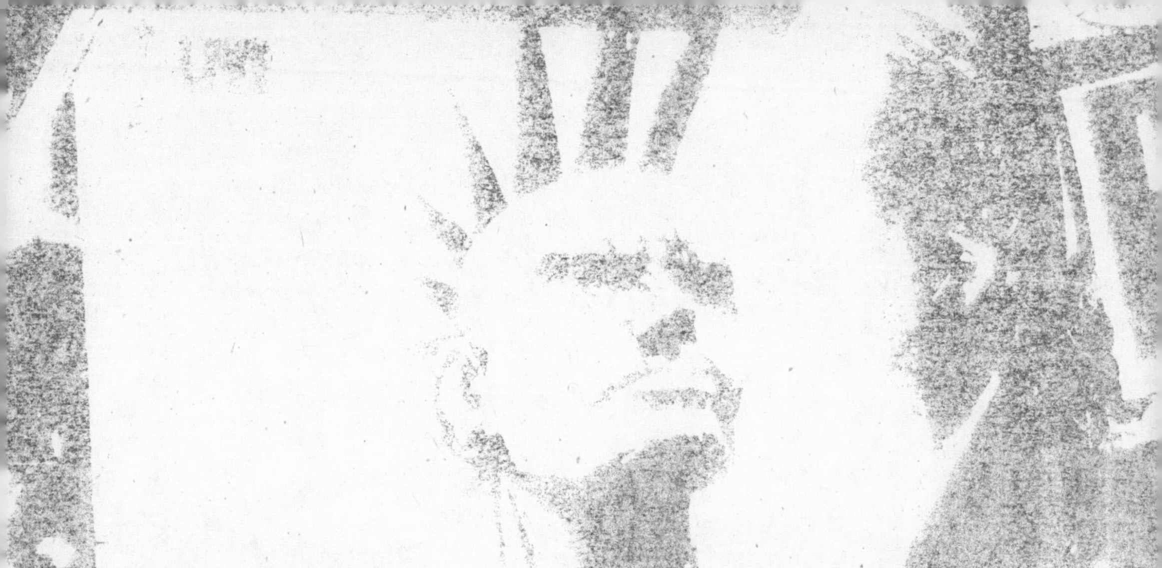

I stopped praying in 2003.

I was living with a friend in Colorado who loved to surf. I loved road trips, so we threw two boards into my pickup and headed to California. It was good to get away--I'd hit a major writer's block with a script I'd been working on called PUNK ROCK JESUS. One of my main characters was (like me) a devoted Catholic. He was also in the IRA, so I ended up doing a lot of research into the history of The Cause. Much of the IRA dogma made no sense to me, and while I began questioning the motivation behind IRA convictions, I also began questioning my own Christianity. I didn't know what to think anymore, so I put both PRJ and my faith on hold.

My friend was an atheist, and soon I found myself very convinced by his beliefs--those based on science and not on dogma. But becoming an atheist overnight was too scary, so instead I decided to try it for a month and see how it fit me.

Indeed, I had a lot to think about while we made our way to California.

My test came once we arrived. I have a fear of the ocean, so naturally I was a terrible surfer. At one point I was knocked down really hard by a roaring wave-- I wasn't even able to take a full breath before being sucked under the black currents. I waited for the wave to pass over before trying to head back to the surface, but once I did, I realized that I didn't know where the surface was. Then I felt another wave pass overhead--this one scraping my head against the surrounding coral. I didn't know which way was up and I was too scared to open my eyes. Panicking, I began doing the thing I'd spent twenty-three years doing whenever I was in trouble: I started praying.

But then I stopped. I promised myself that I wouldn't pray for a month, and it wouldn't be much of an effort if I broke that promise the very same week. So instead of panicking, I managed to use my head.

Just then I felt my leg tug. Luckily the leash to the board hadn't slipped off. Somewhere, floating on the surface, was a surfboard that had my name on it. I quickly followed the leash to the surface and got my head above water. Fresh air.

If I had allowed myself to pray in that instant before finding the leash, I would have been *certain* that a god had saved me. Instead, I'd found the leash on my own. I no longer believed in a god, rather that we're each the master of our own fate.

Back in Colorado, I found that fixing *Punk Rock Jesus* meant starting over, changing the Jesus clone from a Christian into an atheist. As my script began taking form, so did my atheistic convictions. And I would finally be able to publish.

--Sean Murphy

PUNK ROCK JESUS

ENCORE
X-tras

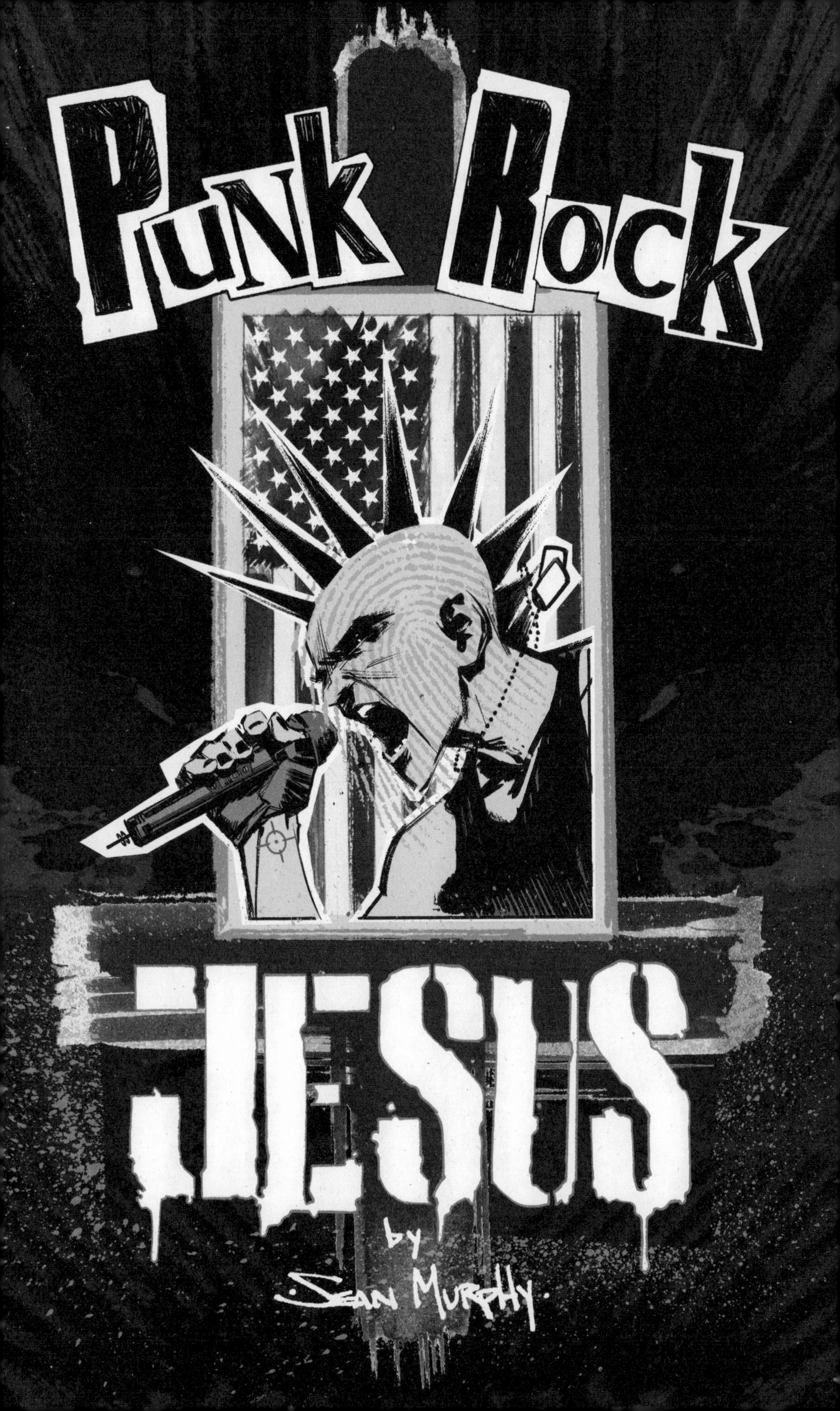
Punk Rock
JESUS
by
Sean Murphy

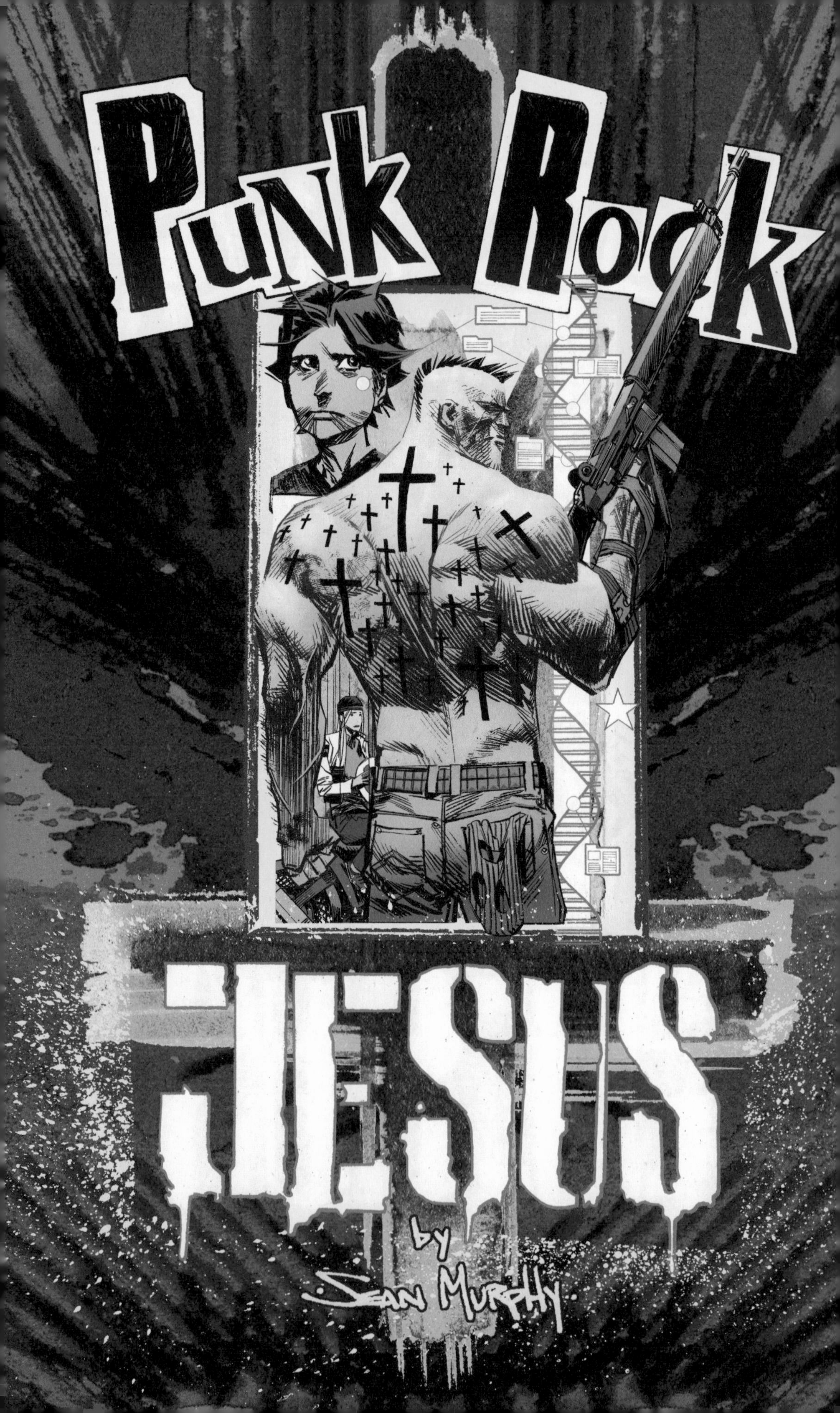
Punk Rock
JESUS
by
Sean Murphy

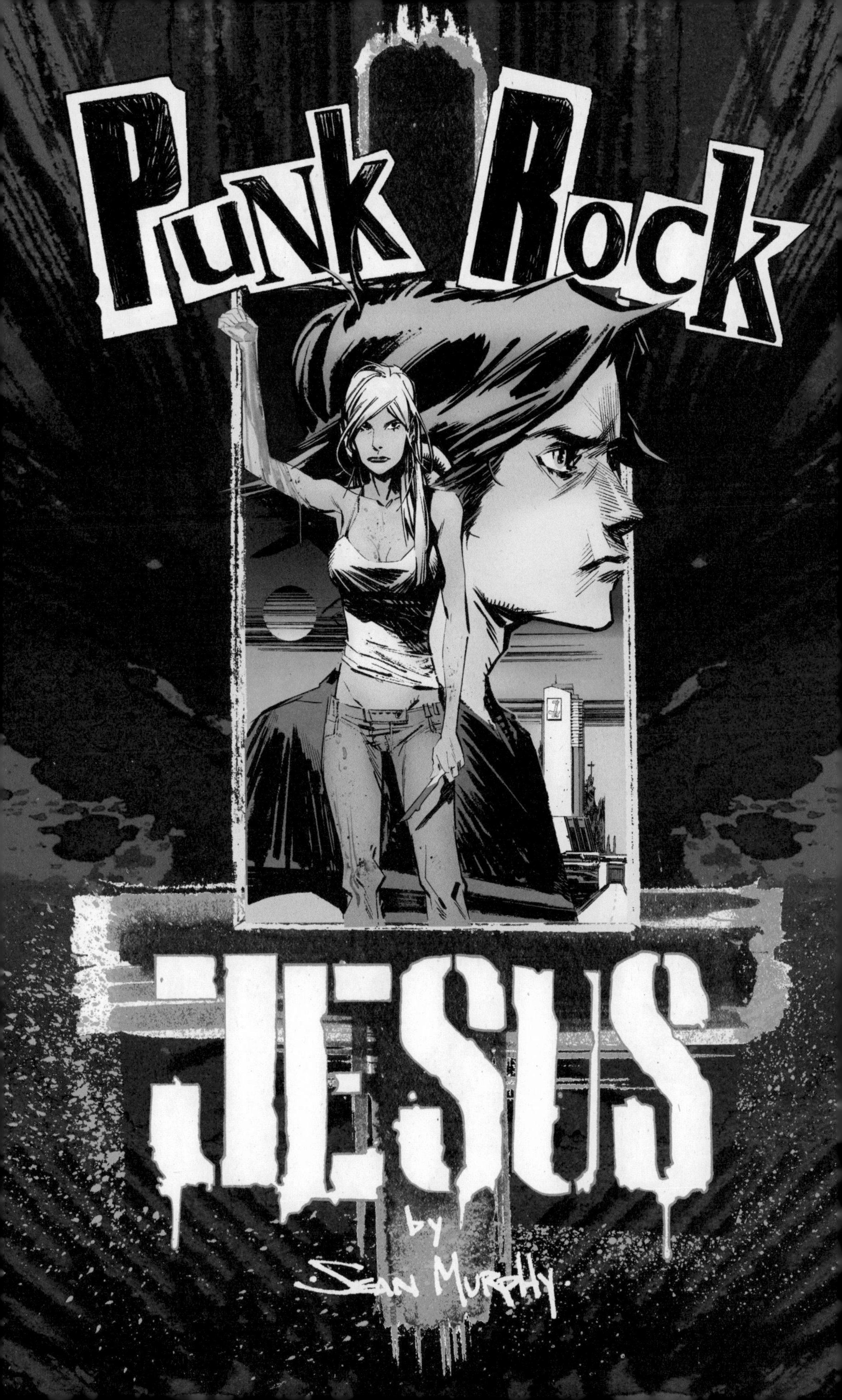
Punk Rock
JESUS
by
Sean Murphy

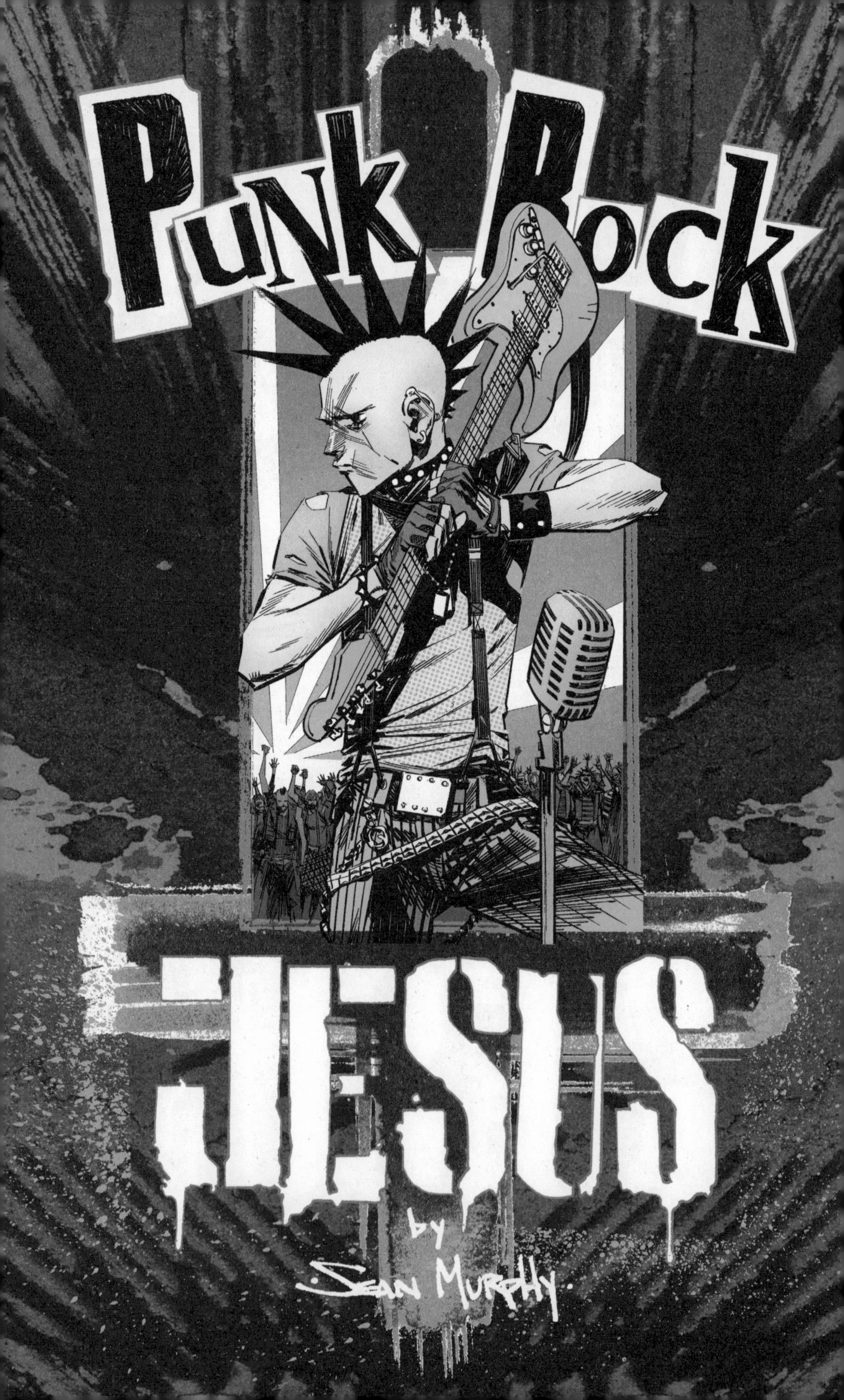
Punk Rock
JESUS
by
Sean Murphy

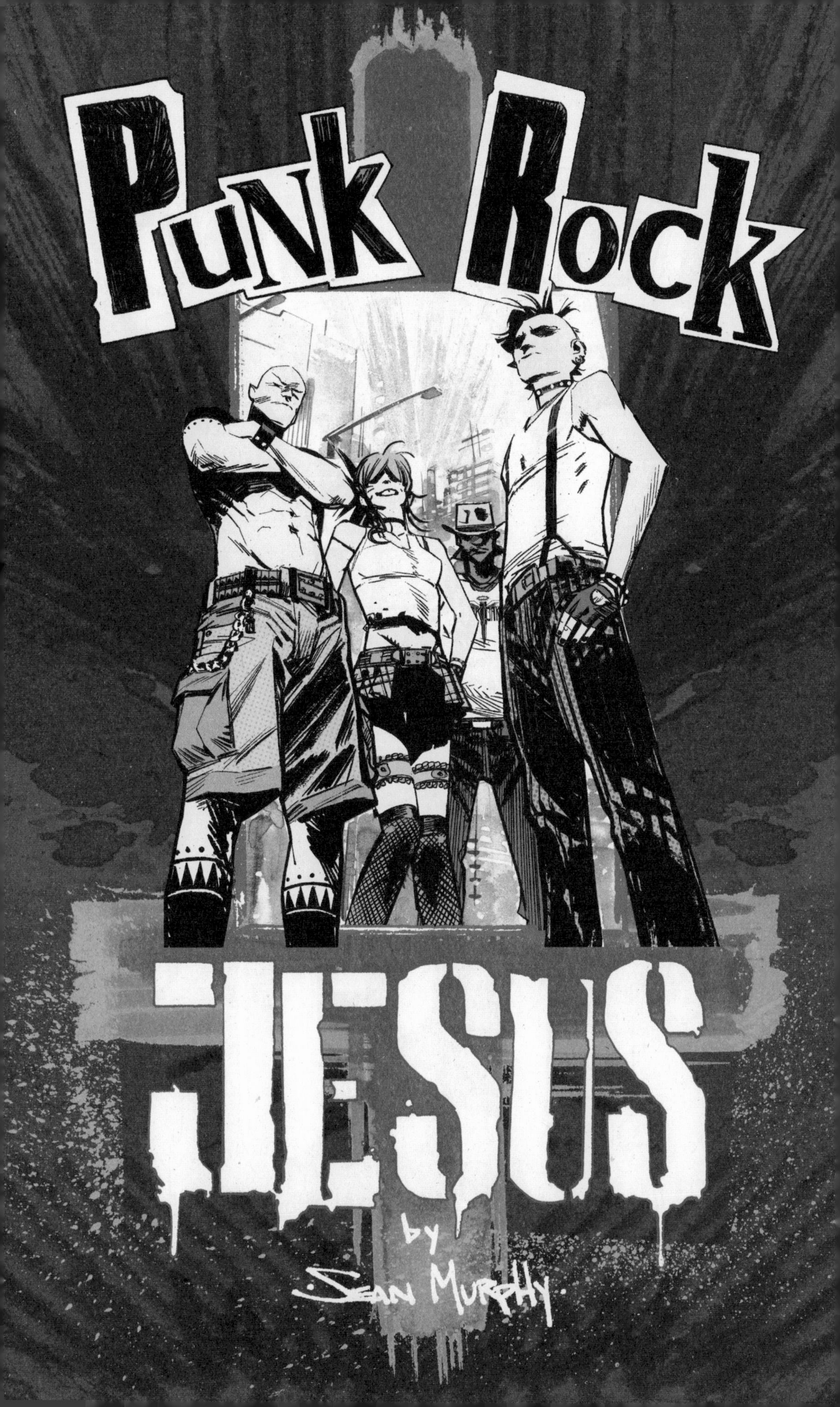

Punk Rock
JESUS
by
Sean Murphy

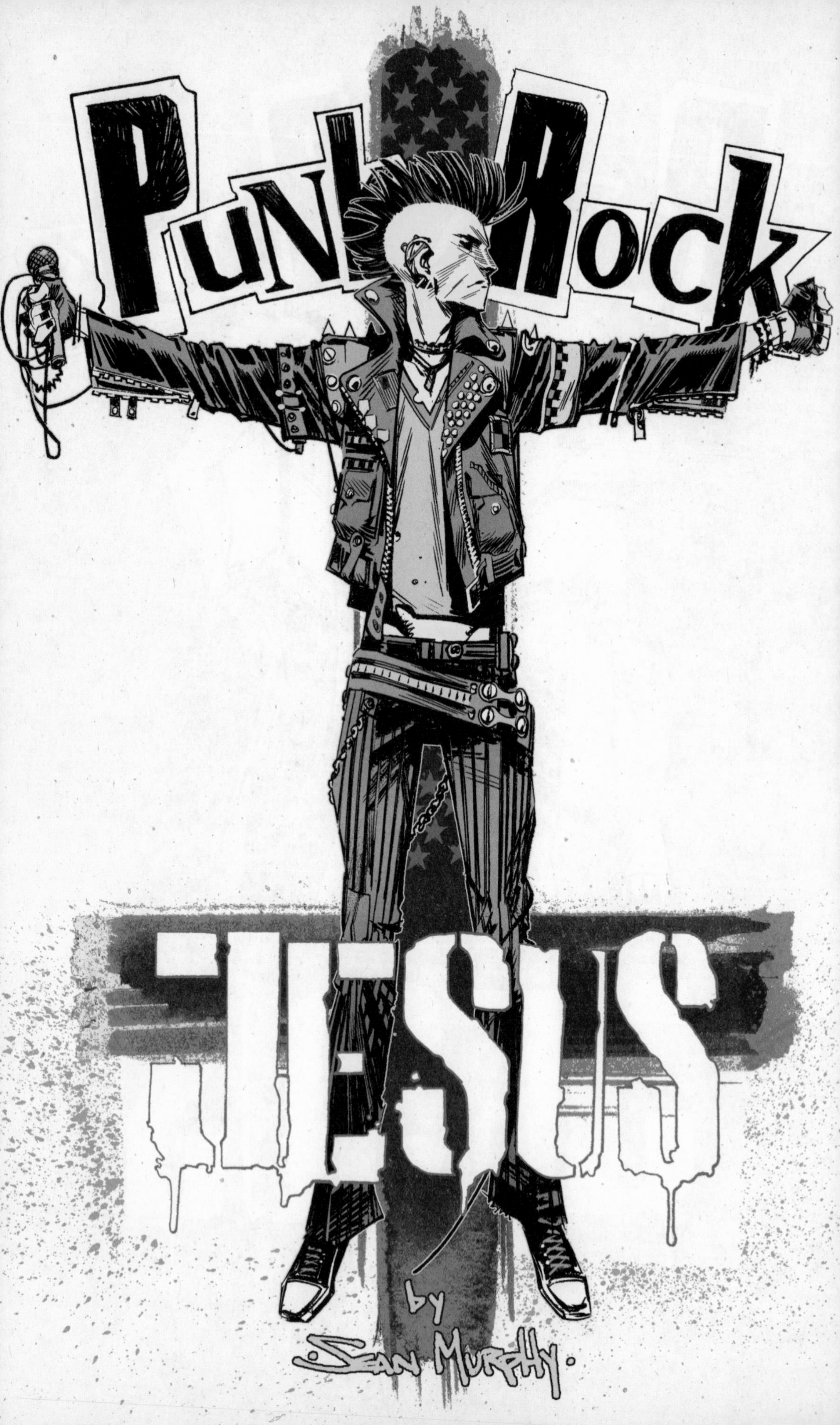

Punk Rock
JESUS
by
Sean Murphy

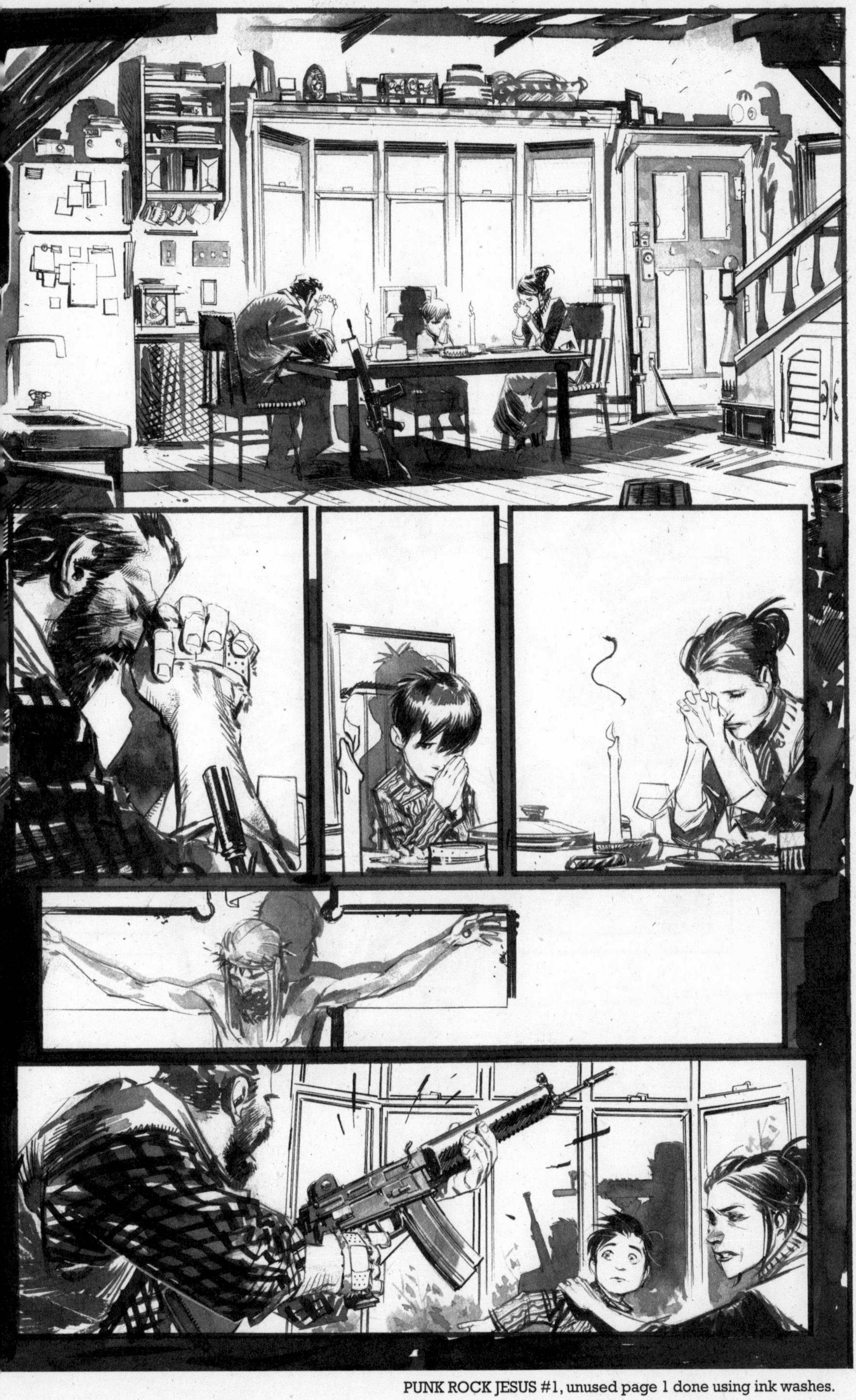

PUNK ROCK JESUS #1, unused page 1 done using ink washes.

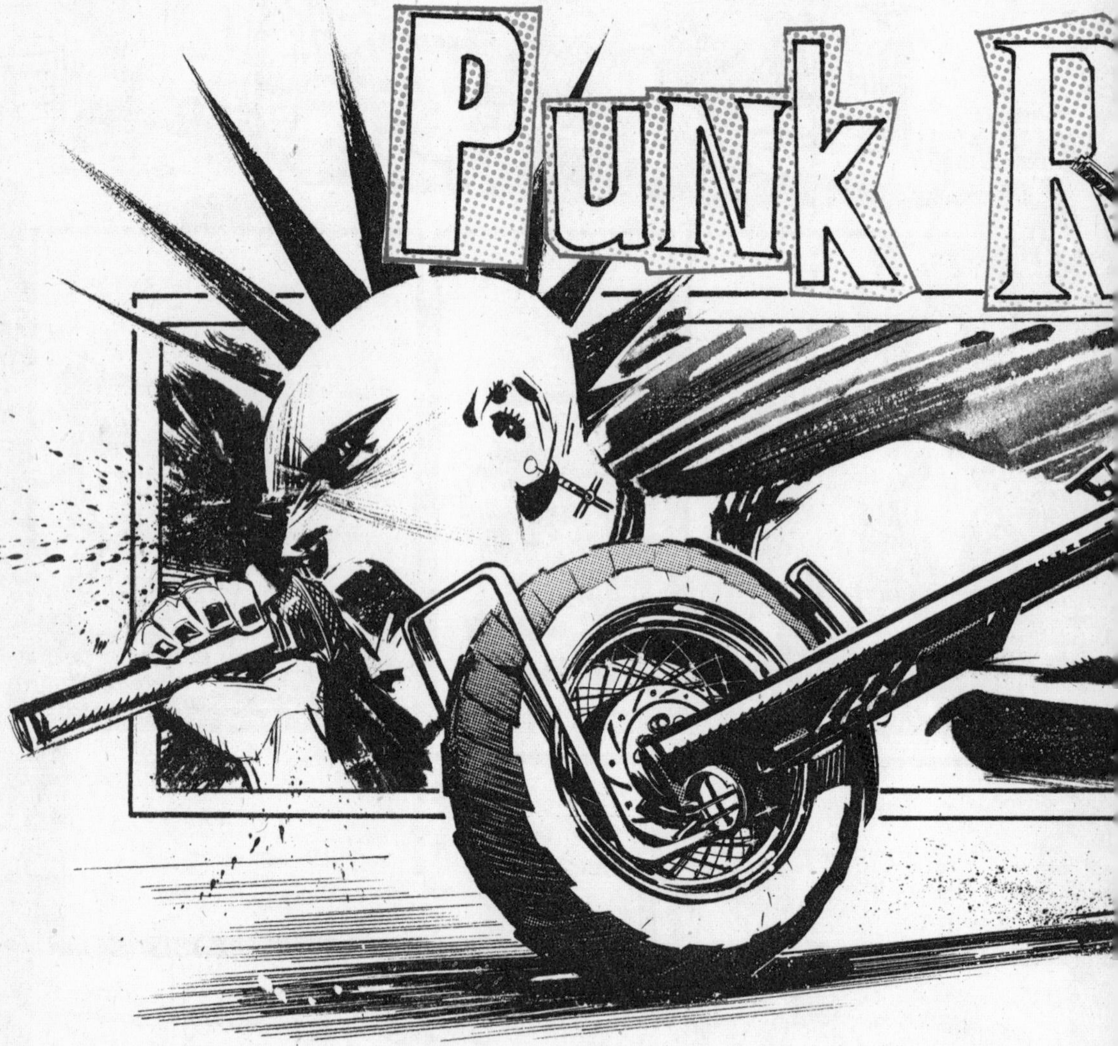
Punk R

ck Jesus
by Sean Murphy

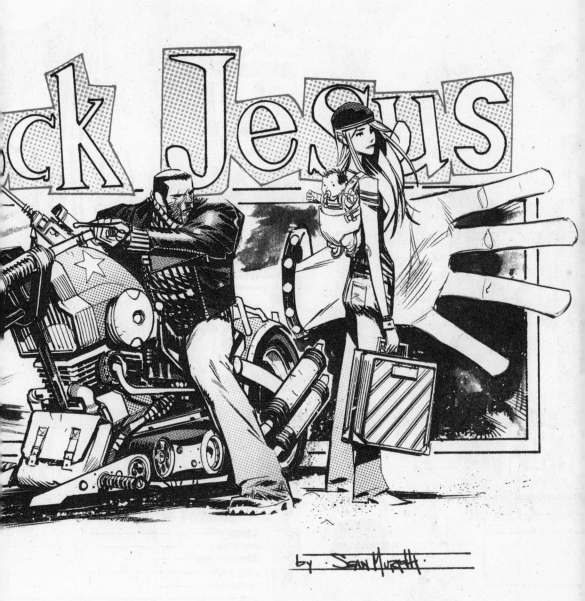

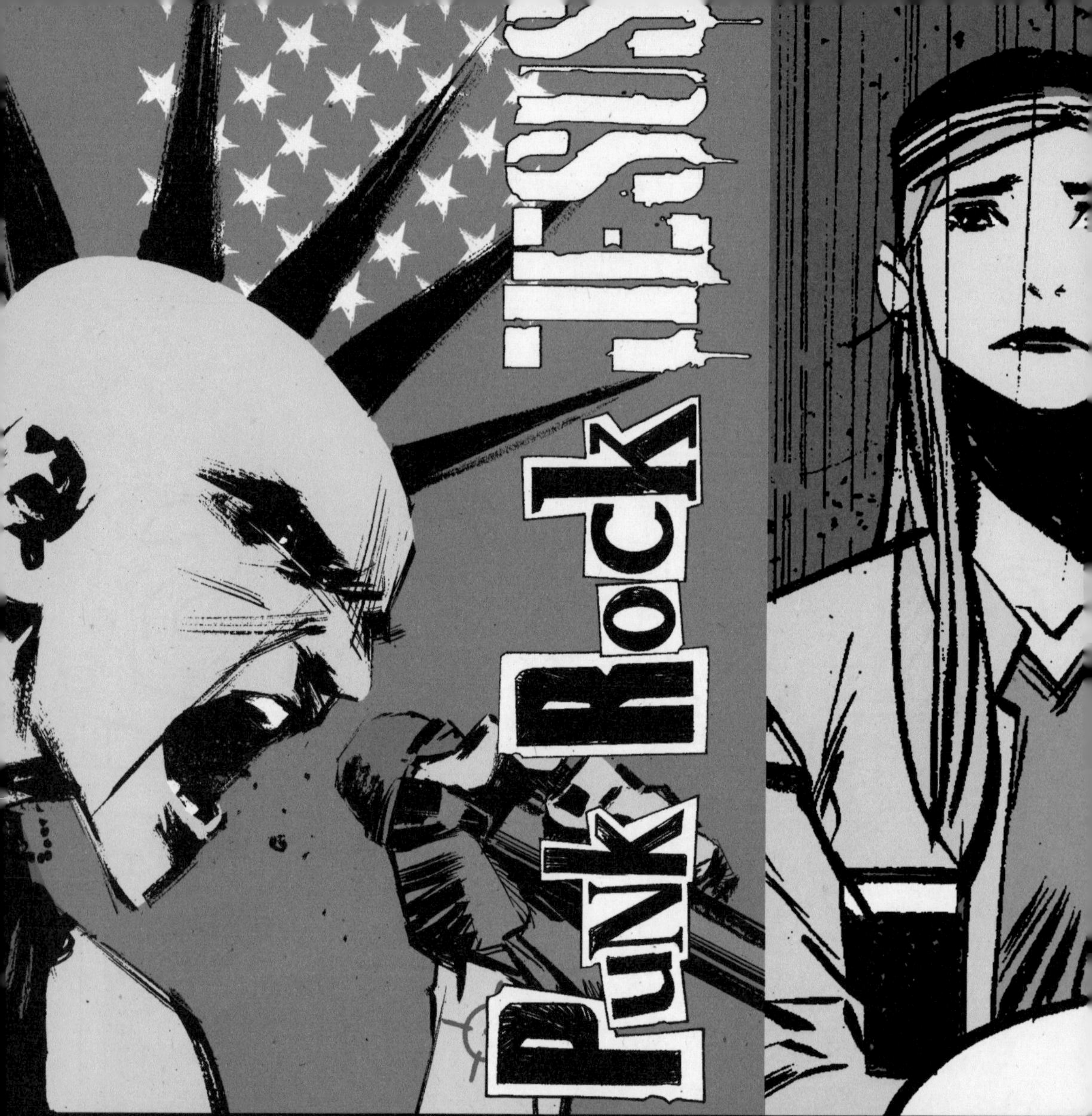
PUNK ROCK JESUS

JESUS
phy.com

AGE | WAY AWESOME

rime with IRA,
n until he
r Constabulary
in Belfast?
homas agreed to
nce Regiment
in classified
his previous
certain parts
a major asset

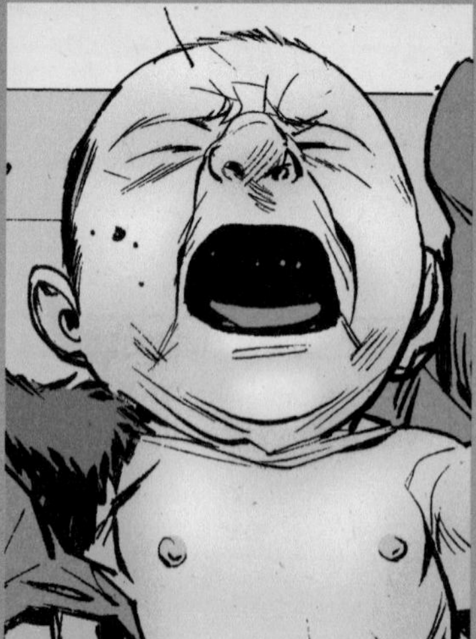

"Waahhhhhhhhhh!"

Real Name: Jesus Christ
Nickname: Chris
Occupation: Savior/celebrity
First Appearance: Punk Rock Jesus #1

Sean Murphy's
Punk Rock JESUS
www.seangordonmurphy.com

POWER RATINGS	NORMAL	ABOVE AVERAGE	WAY AWES
STRENGTH			
INTELLIGENCE			
ENERGY PROJECTION			
MENTAL POWERS			
FIGHTING ABILITY			
SPEED			

DID YOU KNOW that J2 Producer Rick Slate had Jesus' appearance altered via genetic mutation? In order to fit the Caucasian icon on most children's Bibles, Slate ordered J2's head cloning scientist Dr. Sarah Epstein to make the changes. Not wanting to jeopardize her life's work, Dr. Epstein reluctantly made the changes, transforming the Persian fetus into a pale-skinned, blonde-haired, blue-eyed boy. But because mutations are risky, the doctor also boosted the child's immune system in hopes of countering the side affects. Secretly, she also boosted the infant's IQ--something that will eventually give the clone the edge in his media war against OPHIS and Rick Slate.

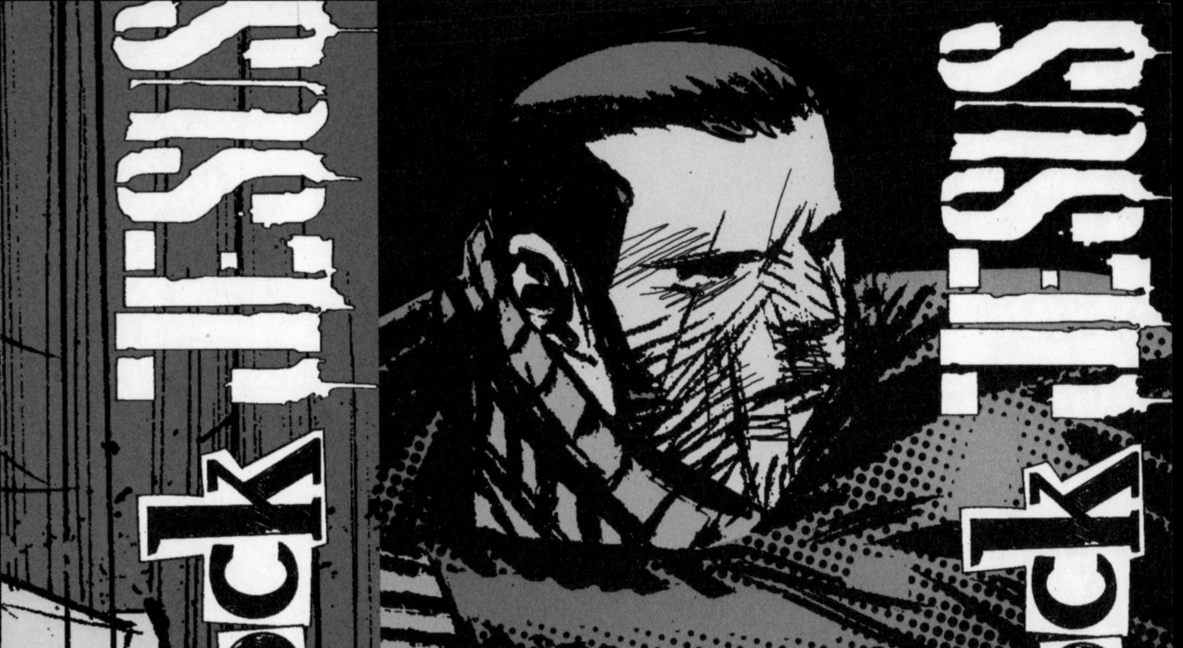
PUNK ROCK JESUS
PUNK ROCK JESUS

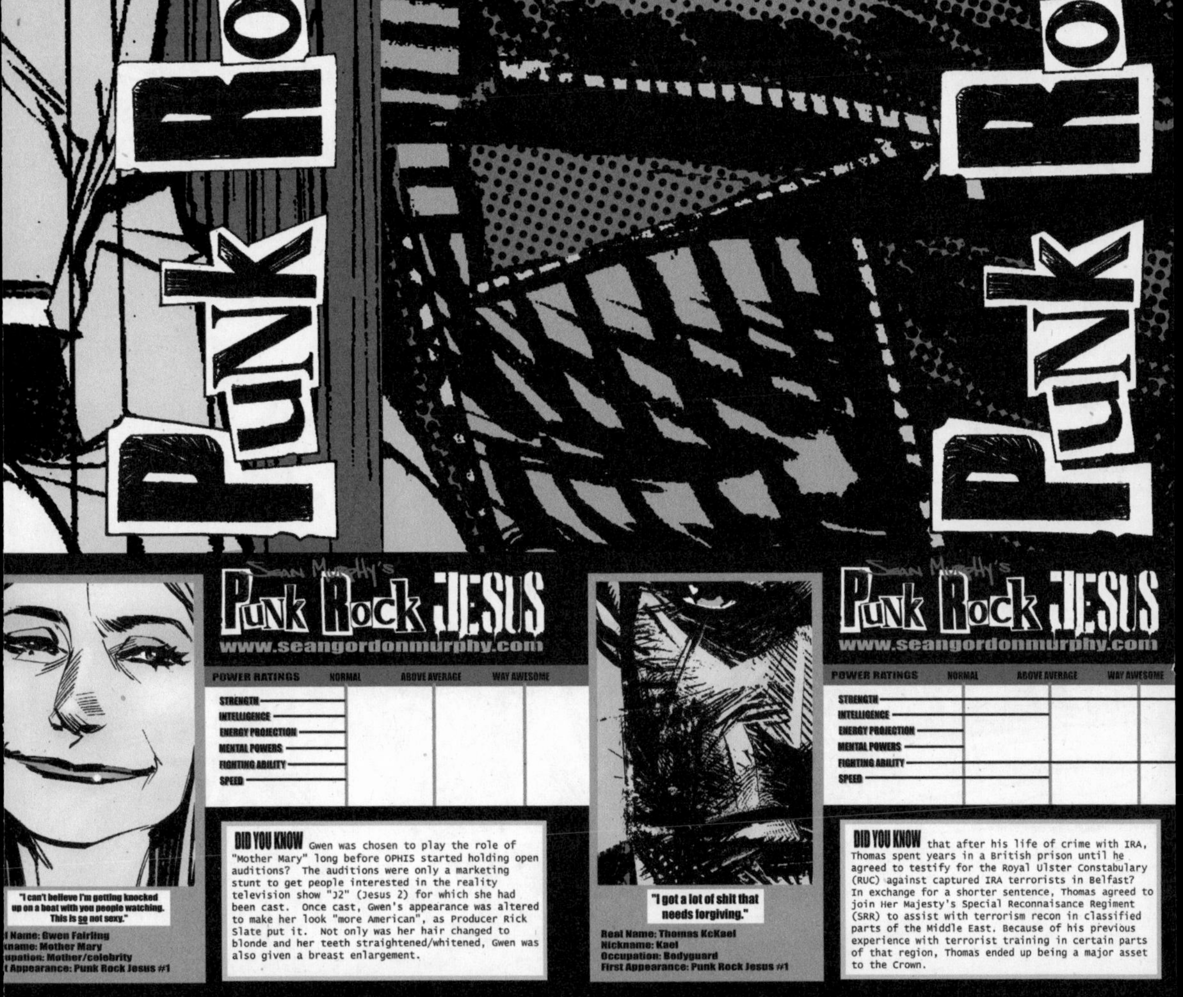
Sean Murphy's
Punk Rock JESUS
www.seangordonmurphy.com
POWER RATINGS
NORMAL
ABOVE AVERAGE
WAY AWESOME
STRENGTH
INTELLIGENCE
ENERGY PROJECTION
MENTAL POWERS
FIGHTING ABILITY
SPEED
"I can't believe I'm getting knocked up on a beat with you people watching. This is so not sexy."
l Name: Gwen Fairling
kname: Mother Mary
upation: Mother/celebrity
t Appearance: Punk Rock Jesus #1
DID YOU KNOW Gwen was chosen to play the role of "Mother Mary" long before OPHIS started holding open auditions? The auditions were only a marketing stunt to get people interested in the reality television show "J2" (Jesus 2) for which she had been cast. Once cast, Gwen's appearance was altered to make her look "more American", as Producer Rick Slate put it. Not only was her hair changed to blonde and her teeth straightened/whitened, Gwen was also given a breast enlargement.
Sean Murphy's
Punk Rock JESUS
www.seangordonmurphy.com
POWER RATINGS
NORMAL
ABOVE AVERAGE
WAY AWESOME
STRENGTH
INTELLIGENCE
ENERGY PROJECTION
MENTAL POWERS
FIGHTING ABILITY
SPEED
"I got a lot of shit that needs forgiving."
Real Name: Thomas KcKael
Nickname: Kael
Occupation: Bodyguard
First Appearance: Punk Rock Jesus #1
DID YOU KNOW that after his life of crime with IRA, Thomas spent years in a British prison until he agreed to testify for the Royal Ulster Constabulary (RUC) against captured IRA terrorists in Belfast? In exchange for a shorter sentence, Thomas agreed to join Her Majesty's Special Reconnaisance Regiment (SRR) to assist with terrorism recon in classified parts of the Middle East. Because of his previous experience with terrorist training in certain parts of that region, Thomas ended up being a major asset to the Crown.

The front and back of Punk Rock Jesus trading cards created by Sean Murphy as promotional items for the series.

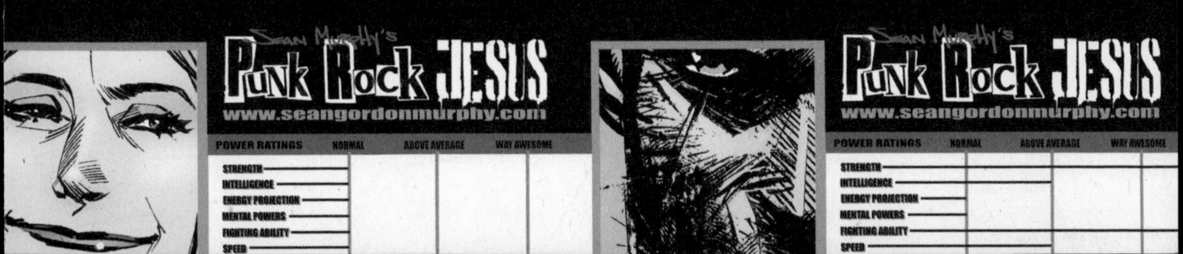
Sean Murphy's
Punk Rock JESUS
www.seangordonmurphy.com
POWER RATINGS
NORMAL
ABOVE AVERAGE
WAY AWESOME
STRENGTH
INTELLIGENCE
ENERGY PROJECTION
MENTAL POWERS
FIGHTING ABILITY
SPEED
Sean Murphy's
Punk Rock JESUS
www.seangordonmurphy.com
POWER RATINGS
NORMAL
ABOVE AVERAGE
WAY AWESOME
STRENGTH
INTELLIGENCE
ENERGY PROJECTION
MENTAL POWERS
FIGHTING ABILITY
SPEED

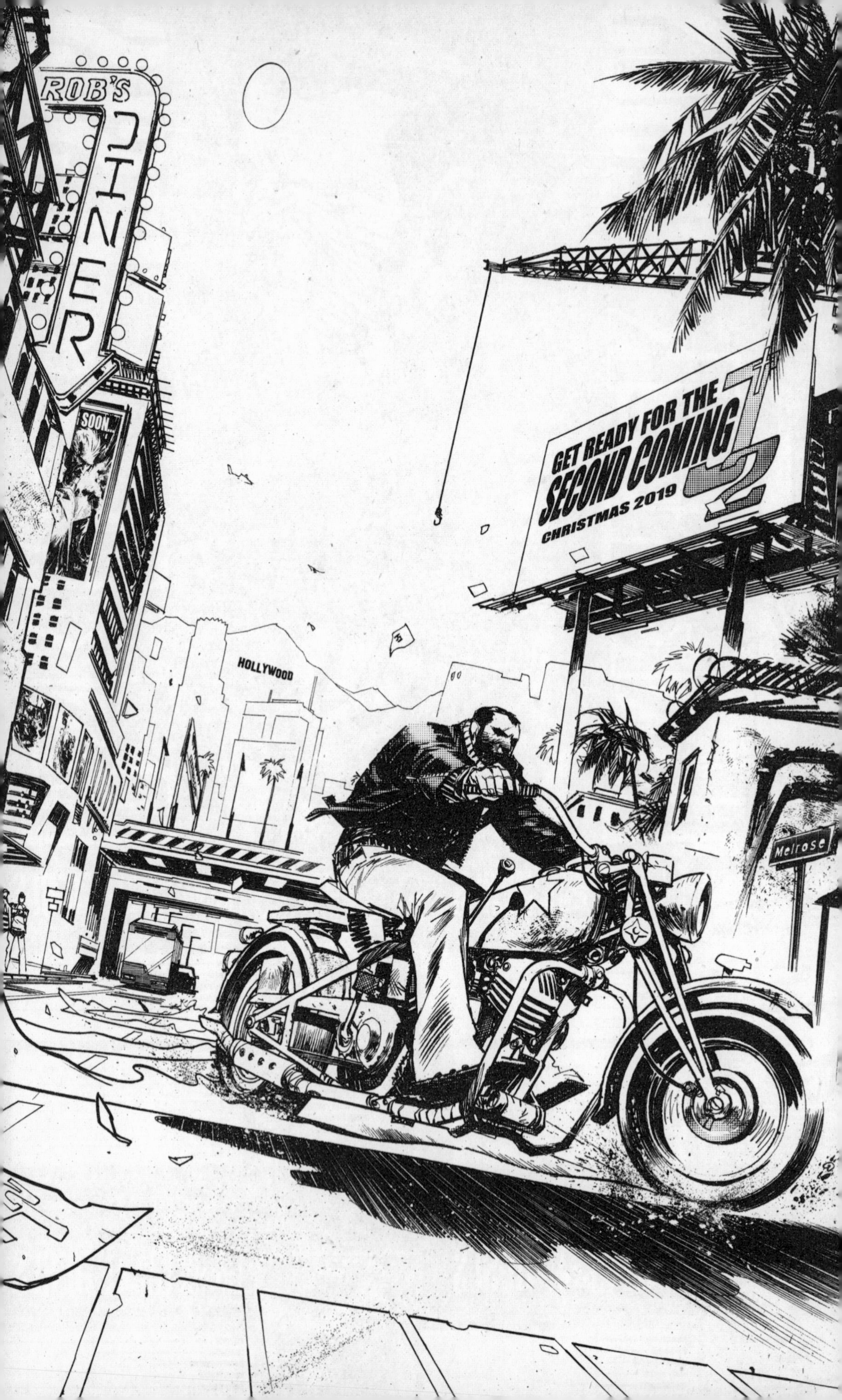

ROB'S
DINER
SOON...
GET READY FOR THE
SECOND COMING
CHRISTMAS 2019
HOLLYWOOD
Melrose

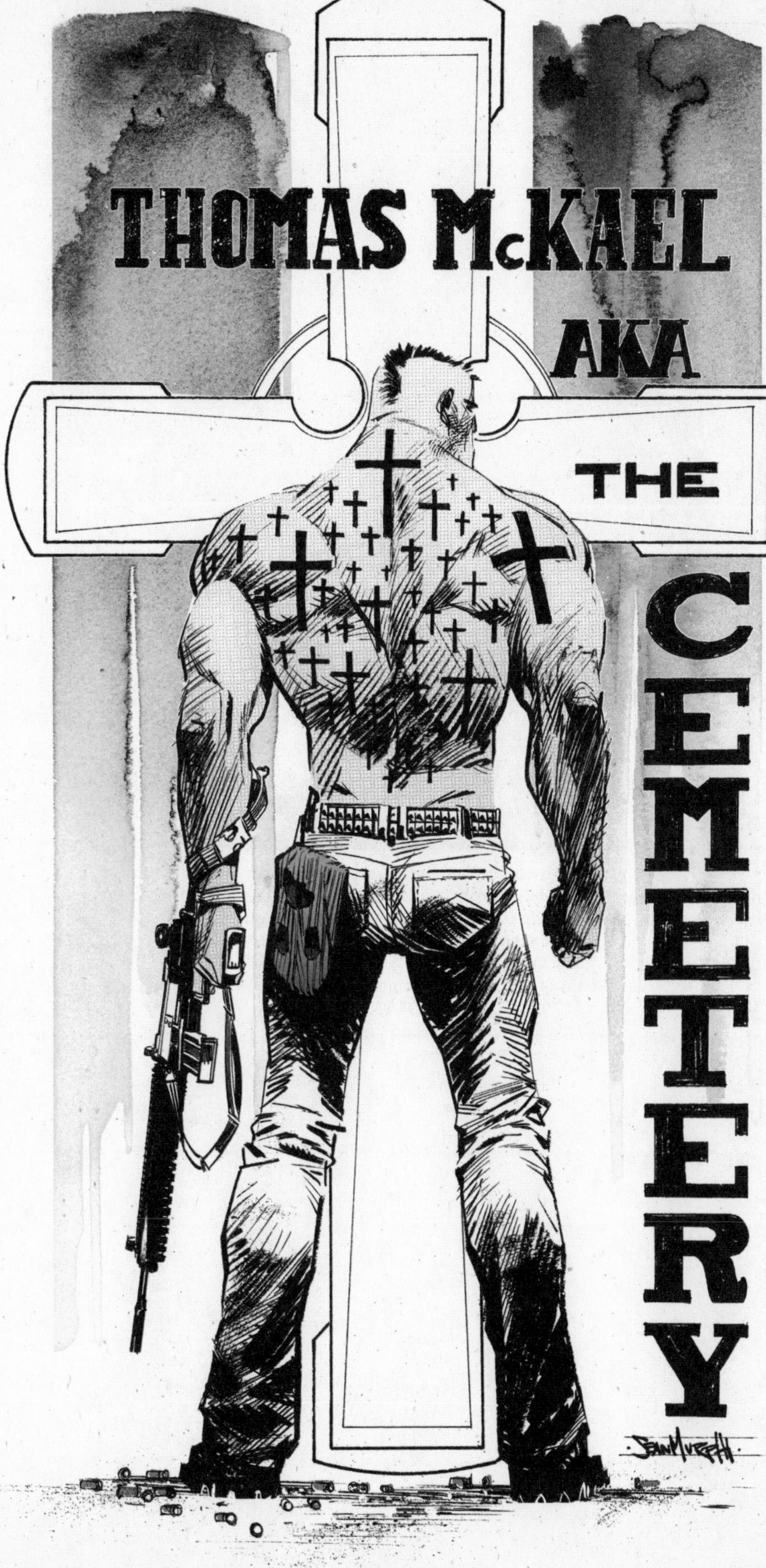
THOMAS McKAEL
AKA
THE
CEMETERY
SEAN MURPHY

Opposite page: Unused page for Punk Rock Jesus #1 page 8.

After breaking into the industry at a young age, Sean Murphy made a name for himself in the world of indie comics before joining up with DC for such titles as BATMAN/SCARECROW: YEAR ONE, TEEN TITANS, JOE THE BARBARIAN, HELLBLAZER and the miniseries AMERICAN VAMPIRE: SURVIVAL OF THE FITTEST. He also wrote and illustrated the original graphic novel *Off Road*.